Get Ahead of the Curve

Save Time. Improve Results!

Use *MyEconLab* to prepare for tests and exams and to go to class ready to learn.

When you use *MyEconLab* you don't just learn more about economics—you learn how to learn.

Since 2002, more than 70 000 students have used *MyEconLab* at more than 600 institutions around the world.

We asked some of these students what they thought about *MyEconLab*. Here are some of the things they had to say:

"MyEconLab allowed me to see where I stood on all the topics so I knew what to study more."

"MyEconLab was a good asset to the course. It almost serves as an online tutor when you don't have an answer."

"I was able to study better and teach myself without costly errors. I could see where I went wrong and go back and understand the concept."

"MyEconLab helped me master economic concepts. Using it put the textbook to work before test day."

90% of students surveyed who used the Study Plan practice questions and feedback felt it helped them to prepare for tests.

87% of students who regularly used *MyEconLab* felt it improved their grades.

84% said they would recommend *MyEconLab* to a friend.

Unlimited Practice!

MyEconLab offers a wide variety of problems that let you practise the theories and models being learned.

Practice Problems

Many Study Plan and instructor-assigned problems contain algorithmically generated values, ensuring you get as much practice as you need.

Learning Resources

Each problem links to the eText page discussing the very concept being applied. You also have access to guided solutions and a suite of other practice tools.

Pearson eText

Included in your MyEconLab is an online version of your textbook. You can navigate your eText by key concept and post notes online.

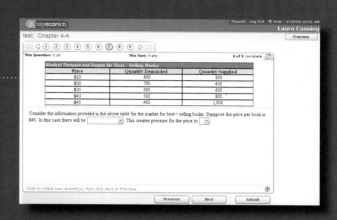

Personalized Learning!

The *MyEconLab* Study Plan is based on your specific learning needs.

Auto-Graded Tests and Assignments

MyEconLab comes with two pre-loaded Sample Tests for each chapter so you can self-assess your understanding of the material.

Personalized Study Plan

A Study Plan is generated based on your results on Sample Tests and instructor assignments. You can clearly see which topics you have mastered and, more importantly, which topics you need to work on!

"I just wanted to let you know how helpful the Study Plan in MyEconLab is. Everything's clicking… so two thumbs up!"
—Student, Ryerson University

Practice Problems

Use the Study Plan exercises to get practice where you need it. To check how you're doing, click Results to get an overview of all your scores.

MACRO   COHEN • HOWE

ECONOMICS FOR LIFE

smart
choices
for
all?

Avi J. Cohen
York University

Ian Howe
**Human Resources and Skills
Development Canada***

*The views expressed are the author's and do not
necessarily represent the views of the Department.

Pearson Canada
Toronto

Library and Archives Canada Cataloguing in Publication

Cohen, Avi J.
     Economics for life: smart choices for all? / Avi J. Cohen, Ian Howe.

Includes index.
ISBN 978-0-321-36448-7

1. Economics — Textbooks.   I. Howe, Ian, 1981–   II. Title.

HB171.5.C74 2010   330   C2010-903288-8

ISBN 978-0-321-36448-7

Vice-President, Editorial Director: Gary Bennett
Acquisitions Editor: Claudine O'Donnell
Sponsoring Editor: Don Thompson
Marketing Manager: Leigh-Anne Graham
Project Developer: Joseph Gladstone
Developmental Editor: Toni Chahley
Project Manager: Cheryl Jackson
Copy Editor: Susan Bindernagel
Proofreader: Caroline Winter
Compositor: Heather Brunton/Miriam Brant/ArtPlus Limited
Photo and Permissions Researcher: Heather L. Jackson
Art Director: Julia Hall
Cover and Interior Designer: Anthony Leung
Cover Image: Jupiter Images

For permission to reproduce copyrighted material, the publisher gratefully acknowledges the copyright holders listed throughout the book in abbreviated form and on pages 515–518, which are considered an extension of this copyright page.

Statistics Canada information is used with the permission of Statistics Canada. Users are forbidden to copy the data and redisseminate them, in an original or modified form, for commercial purposes, without permission from Statistics Canada. Information on the availability of the wide range of data from Statistics Canada can be obtained from Statistics Canada's Regional Offices, its World Wide Web site at **www.statcan.gc.ca**, and its toll-free access number 1-800-263-1136.

1 2 3 4 5   14 13 12 11 10

Printed and bound in the United States of America.

To Susan — for encouraging me to find my voice.

A.J.C.

About the Authors

Showing his interest in technology and teaching, Professor Cohen is holding an actual piece of the first transatlantic telegraph cable, laid in 1856 between Cape Breton and Newfoundland, and on to London, England.

Avi J. Cohen

Avi J. Cohen is Professor of Economics and former Dean's Advisor on Technology Enhanced Learning at York University. He has a PhD from Stanford University; is a Life Fellow of Clare Hall, University of Cambridge; and is past Co-Chair of the Canadian Economics Association Education Committee.

Professor Cohen is a past President of the History of Economics Society, and has research interests in the history of economics, economic history, and economic education. He has published in *Journal of Economic Perspectives*, *Journal of Economic Education*, *History of Political Economy*, *Journal of the History of Economic Thought*, *Journal of Economic History*, and *Explorations in Economic History*, among other journals.

Professor Cohen is co-author of the best-selling *Study Guide* that accompanies Parkin/Bade's *Economics* (seventh edition). He is the winner of numerous teaching awards, including Canada's most prestigious national award for educational leadership, the 3M Teaching Fellowship.

Ian Howe

Ian Howe is a senior policy analyst with the Strategic Policy and Research Branch at Human Resources and Skills Development Canada.* Ian has an MA in Economic Policy from McMaster University and a BCom degree from the University of Toronto.

As the head undergraduate teaching assistant for the Department of Economics and as a workshop facilitator for the Academic Skills Centre at the University of Toronto at Mississauga, Ian provided tutorials and workshops in economics for first- and second-year undergraduates. Ian was awarded the Mississauga Board of Trade Scholarship for Commerce and Management in 2001 for his tutoring involvement in the community.

*The views expressed are the author's and do not necessarily represent the views of the Department.

Brief Contents

Table of Contents

Preface to Students

Economics for Life: Smart Choices for All? is not a typical economics textbook—it has almost no abstract graphs or math. It is not designed to teach you to be an economist but to show you how to use economic ideas to make smart choices in life—as a consumer, a businessperson, an investor, and an informed citizen and voter.

The question in this book's subtitle—Smart Choices for All?—comes from the question, "Do markets coordinate smart individual choices to produce the products and services we want, or do markets produce undesirable outcomes like unemployment, falling living standards, bankruptcies, financial bubbles, and inflation?"

Economists ask this fundamental macroeconomic question this way:

> **If left alone by government, do the price mechanisms of market economies adjust quickly to maintain steady growth in living standards, full employment, and stable prices?**

There is no single right answer. Economists, politicians, and citizens fall into two main camps in answering this question.

The "Yes—Left Alone, Markets Quickly Self-Adjust" camp believes that our market economy generally performs well and that government will only make it worse. They argue government should keep its hands off the economy: the hands-off camp.

▲ Whenever you see this icon, the ideas of the hands-off camp are being discussed.

The "No—Left Alone, Markets Fail to Quickly Self-Adjust" camp has less faith in the market economy's ability to perform consistently well and believes that government must get involved to improve the market's performance. They argue for a hands-on role for government: the hands-on camp.

Your vote helps elect a government whose policy decisions influence our economy's performance—living standards, unemployment, and inflation. Those policies can make the difference between steady growth in living standards or a prolonged recession where jobs are hard to find—in other words, your economic well-being. Do you think policies based on a hands-off or hands-on view of the market economy will make you, and Canada, better off? Learning the core concepts of macroeconomics enables you to make an informed choice about the fundamental macroeconomic question. My goal is to provide you the tools for answering that question in a way that makes most sense *to you*.

▲ Whenever you see this icon, the ideas of the hands-on camp are being discussed.

The only way for me to know how close I've come to achieving my goal is to hear from you. Let me know what works for you in this book—and, more importantly, what doesn't. You can write to me at **avicohen@yorku.ca**. In future editions, I will acknowledge by name all students who help improve *Economics for Life*.

Professor Avi J. Cohen
Department of Economics
York University

P.S. If you have not previously studied microeconomics, before starting *Economics for Life: Smart Choices for All?* read the four appendices, which start on page 392.

Features of This Book

Welcome to *Economics for Life: Smart Choices for All?* This tour of your textbook is designed to help you use this book effectively and complete your course successfully.

Chapter Opener

Every chapter begins with a two-page spread. These two pages set the theme for the chapter. Like a trailer for a movie, this opening spread gives you a preview of what is coming and prepares you for the "feature presentation."

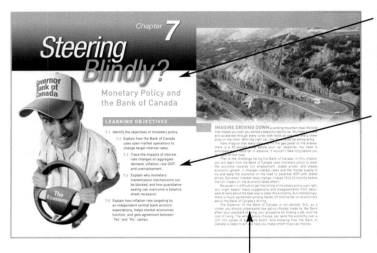

Every chapter has a title and a subtitle. The main title summarizes the content of the chapter in plain language. The subtitle for the chapter is in the language economists use when referring to the concepts.

Every chapter is divided into main sections, and each of these sections is accompanied by a learning objective. The learning objective describes what you will have learned after reading each section. Once you have read the chapter, you can review these learning objectives to test your understanding of the chapter material.

Every chapter begins with an overview that introduces you to the main ideas and themes in the chapter. This introduction connects the economic principles discussed in the chapter to the choices and decisions you make in your everyday life.

Learning Objectives

Learning objectives are repeated at the beginning of each main section of the book and provide an important reminder of what you will learn in each section.

Special Features

FOR YOUR INFORMATION

Say's most important book, *Traité d'économie politique (A Treatise on Political Economy)* was first published in 1803. Say, who spoke fluent English as well as French, was internationally known, and his book, translated into many languages, was a best-selling university economics textbook in Europe and North America.

Ironically, Say never used the words "supply creates its own demand." That paraphrase was created by James Mill in his *Commerce Defended* (1808).

work by Jean-Baptiste Say (1767–1832), a French economist and supporter of Adam Smith's views on free trade and markets. **Say's Law** claimed that "supply creates its own demand."

We can illustrate Say's Law using the circular flow diagram in Figure 1.1 on page 8. Starting at the top, households *supply* inputs to businesses in exchange for money. The only reason households sell their inputs in input markets is because they want the money to *demand* products/services in output markets. When households spend all of the money they have earned in input markets to buy products/services in output markets, supply does create its own demand, and the flow continues smoothly around the circle.

In the middle of the Great Depression, economists who continued to believe in Say's Law started to look pretty silly. Economic events were crying out for a better explanation of the ups and downs of business cycles, especially the "downs" of falling output and living standards, unemployment, and deflation.

For Your Information

These FYI boxes introduce interesting facts and figures related to the economic principle being explored.

Refresh

1. What is the fundamental macroeconomic question?

2. In your own words, list the key arguments for each side of the hands-off versus hands-on debate.

3. Ask your instructor which side of the debate she/he tends to support. From your own current experience and economic understanding, which side do you tend to support? Explain why.

Refresh
1.2

www.myeconlab.com

The Refresh feature provides three questions that require you to review and apply the concepts in the preceding section. These questions give you the opportunity to assess your understanding of the principles developed in the section. Answers to these questions are located on the MyEconLab (**www.myeconlab.com**) that accompanies this book.

Unemployment

In a market economy, to be able to buy products and services in output markets, you usually must earn income by selling something you own in input markets. For most households, that means finding a job—selling your capacity to work in labour markets to a business.

While we have it on the authority of the Beatles that "money can't buy you love," money buys everything else in a market economy, and is necessary for survival. That is why not having a job, and not earning money, is such a serious hardship.

A person is counted as **unemployed** if she is not employed *and* actively seeking work. If you are voluntarily staying at home to look after your kids, or are retired, you are not counted as unemployed. The unemployment rate is calculated as the number of people unemployed as a percentage of the total number of people both employed and unemployed. If 93

unemployed: not employed and actively seeking work

Key Terms

Key terms are bolded in the text where they first appear, and definitions for key terms are provided in the margin. A complete list of all key terms and definitions are in the glossary at the end of the book.

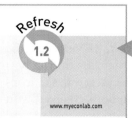

ECONOMICS Out There

End of the Spendthrift Ethos
The serious economic downturn of 2008–2009 is dramatically changing the spending habits of American consumers. Joe Rudyck is a 21-year-old university graduate who recently purchased a new car and laptop, and used to make frequent shopping trips to the mall. While in school, he worked at two part-time jobs, took out student loans, and spent everything he earned.

Now, as the U.S. savings rate has jumped to a 15-year high, he is "living proof" that the spend-spend-spend attitude of American consumers has been squashed. He now thinks before any purchase, and has stepped up his savings in case his car breaks down.

- Mr. Rudyk's new savings behaviour, shared now by millions of U.S. consumers, is what we call the paradox of thrift. Saving more is prudent behaviour in hard times, but has the unintended consequences of reducing demand for products/services, causing businesses to lay off workers, and making it even harder for people to save.

- The change in U.S. savings behaviour is worrisome to Canadians because most Canadian exports are sold in the United States. A senior economist at BMP Capital Markets said, "it's very hard for Canada to dig itself out of the recession unless Americans start spending again."

Source: "End of the Spendthrift Ethos," Joe Friesen, *The Globe and Mail*, March 3, 2009.

Economics Out There

These feature boxes provide real-world examples of the economic principle being discussed. The stories told in Economics Out There help you make connections between the concepts in the chapter and everyday life.

Notes

In the margin, you will see "hand-written" notes. These notes provide a quick explanation of the idea, concept, or principle being discussed in the narrative.

Individuals in households supply labour and other inputs in input markets, and use the income they earn to buy products and services in output markets. For our macroeconomic map, we will focus on the choices households make about spending the money they have earned. Because of this focus on spending, we will rename this group of players as *consumers*.

Consumer Choices   You have two major choices as a consumer. First, you can spend your money or save it. Second, you can buy Canadian-produced products/services, or buy products/services imported from other countries. With our focus on the forest instead of the trees, we will not be concerned about microeconomic choices such as whether you buy a Nokia cell phone or a Motorola, or if you eat out in a restaurant or cook dinner at home.

Consumer choices are: to spend or save; to buy Canadian products/services or imports

The Three MAPS

Like a Global Positioning System (GPS) that helps you find your way through unknown territory, our MAcroeconomic Positioning System (MAPS) will help you find your way through the macroeconomic forest, through media reports on the economy, and through debates on the best economic policies for Canada and the globe. You will see icons in the margin at different places in the book that tell you which of the three MAPS to focus on to best understand the macroeconomic ideas being presented.

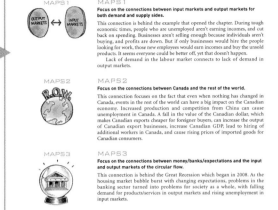

MAPS 1

Focus on the connections between input markets and output markets for both demand and supply sides.

This connection is behind the example that opened the chapter. During tough economic times, people who are unemployed aren't earning incomes, and cut back on spending. Businesses aren't selling enough because individuals aren't buying, and profits are down. But if only businesses would hire the people looking for work, those new employees would earn incomes and buy the unsold products. It seems everyone could be better off, yet that doesn't happen.

Lack of demand in the labour market connects to lack of demand in output markets.

MAPS 2

Focus on the connections between Canada and the rest of the world.

This connection focuses on the fact that even when nothing has changed in Canada, events in the rest of the world can have a big impact on the Canadian economy. Increased production and competition from China can cause unemployment in Canada. A fall in the value of the Canadian dollar, which makes Canadian exports cheaper for foreign buyers, can increase the output of Canadian export businesses, increase Canadian GDP, lead to hiring of additional workers in Canada, and cause rising prices of imported goods for Canadian consumers.

MAPS 3

Focus on the connections between money/banks/expectations and the input and output markets of the circular flow.

This connection is behind the Great Recession which began in 2008. As the housing market bubble burst with changing expectations, problems in the banking sector turned into problems for society as a whole, with falling demand for products/services in output markets and rising unemployment in input markets.

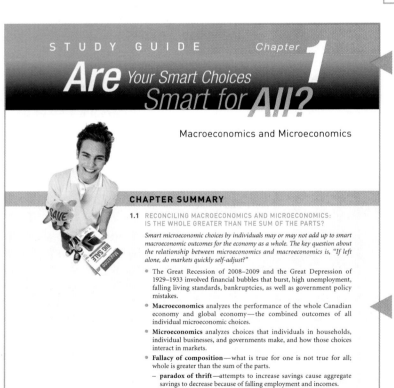

Study Guide

At the end of each chapter you will find a study guide designed to assist you in reviewing and testing your understanding of the material in the chapter. The study guide for each chapter includes:

- Chapter Summary
- True/False Questions
- Multiple Choice Questions
- Short Answer Questions

Chapter Summary

Organized by section, the summary recaps the main ideas in each chapter. The first item (in *italics*) under each section head is the most important point in that section. All key terms are in bold.

Content shown in the Study Guide image:

STUDY GUIDE — **Chapter 1**

Are Your Smart Choices **Smart for All?**

Macroeconomics and Microeconomics

CHAPTER SUMMARY

1.1 RECONCILING MACROECONOMICS AND MICROECONOMICS: IS THE WHOLE GREATER THAN THE SUM OF THE PARTS?

Smart microeconomic choices by individuals may or may not add up to smart macroeconomic outcomes for the economy as a whole. The key question about the relationship between microeconomics and macroeconomics is, "If left alone, do markets quickly self-adjust?"

- The Great Recession of 2008–2009 and the Great Depression of 1929–1933 involved financial bubbles that burst, high unemployment, falling living standards, bankruptcies, as well as government policy mistakes.
- **Macroeconomics** analyzes the performance of the whole Canadian economy and global economy—the combined outcomes of all individual microeconomic choices.
- **Microeconomics** analyzes choices that individuals in households, individual businesses, and governments make, and how those choices interact in markets.
- **Fallacy of composition**—what is true for one is not true for all; whole is greater than the sum of the parts.
  - **paradox of thrift**—attempts to increase savings cause aggregate savings to decrease because of falling employment and incomes.
- The circular flow diagram reduces the complexity of the Canadian economy to three sets of players—households, businesses, and governments.
  - input markets determine incomes; households are sellers and businesses are buyers.
  - output markets determine the value of all products/services sold; households are buyers and businesses are sellers.
- **Business cycles**—ups and downs of overall economic activity.

TRUE/FALSE

Circle the correct answer.

A tall man wearing an expensive suit and tinted sunglasses walks into the coffee shop where you are studying. He notices your macroeconomics textbook and says:

"I have a top secret mission for you. We've detected aliens on the Planet of Plutonomics. Some of these aliens look like Klingons from the Star Trek movies and some look like Yoda from the Star Wars movies. We need you to verify whether our findings about their economy—based on satellite images—are true or false."

Use this scenario to answer questions 1–15.

1.1 RECONCILING MACRO AND MICRO

1. Klingon look-alikes are working in exchange for money, and paying money to purchase products and services. This evidence suggests that there are input and output markets. **True   False**

2. Yoda look-alikes are paying taxes, and some are receiving transfer payments from the government. This evidence suggests that the government is part of the circular flow of economic life. **True   False**

3. Every government worker on the Planet of Plutonomics is a superstar at solving microeconomic problems. Therefore, the government of the Planet of Plutonomics must be a superstar at solving macroeconomic problems. **True   False**

True/False Questions

There are 15 true/false questions, organized by learning objective. The heading next to each learning objective number gives you the topic of the questions that follow. Each question is answered at the end of the book, and questions with "false" answers have explanations why.

MULTIPLE CHOICE

Circle the correct answer.

1.1 RECONCILING MACRO AND MICRO

1. What do the Great Depression and Great Recession have in common?
   A) Both were great for depression.
   B) Both had a stock market crash.
   C) Both experienced a rise in prices.
   D) Both had government programs like employment insurance.

2. Who is to blame for inflating the housing price bubble?
   A) Homeowners
   B) Mortgage lenders
   C) Banks and other financial institutions
   D) All of the above

Multiple Choice Questions

There are 15 multiple choice questions organized by learning objective. The heading next to each learning objective number gives you the topic of the questions that follow. Each question is answered at the end of the book.

SHORT ANSWER

Write a short answer to each question. Your answer may be in point form.

1. The "trees" and the "forest" can be used to distinguish microeconomics from macroeconomics.
   A) Which "economics" looks at the trees? Which looks at the forest?
   B) According to Adam Smith, how do we achieve a healthy forest?

2. Smart choices by people and businesses do not necessarily imply that smart choices are being made for the economy as a whole. Explain how the fallacy of composition applies to each of the following scenarios.
   A) Producers decide to increase the output of their product or service.
   B) Consumers decide to save more of their income.

3. Suppose that you're at a party when the topic of the Great Recession comes up. People are wondering what caused the recession. Luckily a balloon is nearby, which you use as a prop to demonstrate the housing price bubble and burst of the Great Recession.
   A) Why did the housing prices balloon inflate?
   B) Why did the housing prices balloon burst?

Short Answer Questions

There are 10 short answer questions that test your overall understanding of the chapter. These questions help you connect the main ideas in the different sections of the chapter. Answers to these questions are at the end of the book.

Using Your Textbook to Achieve Success in Your Course

This textbook is set up for your success. Each element is designed to help you organize, understand, and learn the material efficiently and easily. Here is a quick guide to being successful in this course.

1: Fully understand the learning objectives

The learning objectives in each chapter are presented in the chapter opener and repeated in the margin at the beginning of each section of the chapter. If you can do what each learning objective asks, you will understand what is most important in each section. These learning objectives are the core of the course. Master these and you have mastered the course. The most important point in each section—a one- to two-sentence summary of what each learning objective asks—appears in italics after each section head in the Study Guide's Chapter Summary.

2: Check your understanding of the learning objectives

At the end of each complete section, there are three questions titled Refresh. When you complete a section, take the 5 to 10 minutes required to answer the Refresh questions. These questions are designed for you to assess how well you have mastered the learning objective. They will help you make sure you understand what is important.

3: Complete the Study Guide material

After finishing the chapter, complete the Study Guide pages—it will save you study time and reinforce what you have mastered. The Study Guide is divided into two main sections, a chapter summary and a set of exam-like questions.

Chapter Summary   The Chapter Summary contains the key points you need to know. It is organized using the same major sections as the chapter. The first item in *italics* under each section head is the most important point in that section. The chapter summary is an excellent study aid for the night before a test. It's a final check of the ideas—the learning objectives—you have studied.

Exam-like Questions   Do the True/False, Multiple-Choice, and Short Answer questions *without looking at the answers*. This is the single most important tip for profitably using the Study Guide. Struggling for the answers to questions you find challenging is one of the most effective ways to learn. The athletic saying of "No pain, no gain" applies equally to studying. You will learn the most from right answers you have had to struggle for and from your wrong answers and mistakes. Look at the answers only *after* you have attempted all the questions. When you finally do check the answers, be sure to understand where you went wrong and why your right answers are right.

4: Know it before you go on

Master each chapter by taking the above three actions before moving on. Feel confident that you understand the chapter's objectives. By following this plan you will be making a smart choice for learning, and you will do well in the course.

Preface to Instructors

When people ask me what I do, I say, "I teach Economics at York University." While I am a full Professor, a productive academic with an active research program (past President of the History of Economics Society) and honourable service commitments to my school, my professional identity is largely tied to my teaching.

As a young assistant professor, the immortality of publishing articles in journals that would forever be in libraries was an important goal. But over time, I came to realize how few people would read those articles, let alone be affected by them. Most of my, and I suspect your, "academic footprint" on this earth will be through our students. Over a career, we teach tens of thousands students.

As economists and teachers, what do we want our lasting "economic footprint" to be? There is a wonderful old *Saturday Night Live* skit by Father Guido Sarducci called "The Five Minute University" (**www.youtube.com/watch?v=kO8x8eoU3L4**). Watch it. His premise is to teach in five minutes what an average college or university graduate remembers five years after graduating. For economics, he states it's the two words "supply and demand." That's it.

The serious question behind the skit, the one that motivates this book—and its microeconomics companion, *Economics for Life: Smart Choices for You*—is "What do we really want our students to remember of what we teach them in an introductory economics class?" I posed this question to college and university instructors at the British Columbia Economics Articulation meeting in May 2008.

I asked instructors the following questions. Five years after your students have gone, what microeconomic concepts would you:

- want students to remember as ***essential***?
  (What would you be upset at hearing they didn't remember.)
- want students to remember as ***nice to have***?
- allow students to ***let go***?
  (It wouldn't bother you if they didn't remember these.)

Their responses coincided with my teaching experience and informed what was included—and excluded—in the microeconomics textbook, *Economics for Life: Smart Choices for You*.

Macroeconomics for Citizens

I then used my teaching experience and many discussions with other economists to decide what should be included—and excluded—from this macroeconomics textbook. We economists disagree far more about macroeconomics than microeconomics. So I have incorporated that disagreement into the core of this book as "the fundamental macroeconomic question."

If left alone by government, do the price mechanisms of market economies adjust quickly to maintain steady growth in living standards, full employment, and stable prices?

Not only do economists disagree over this question, so do the politicians our students will be voting for, not only five years later, but for the rest of their lives. I believe the essential macroeconomic concepts students must know to answer that question for themselves—the macroeconomics they need to know *as citizens*—are included in this textbook.

When students see this icon, they will know we are discussing the ideas of the hands-off camp.

Where disagreements exists, this book divides economists, politicians, and citizens into two camps based on their answers to the fundamental macroeconomic question.

The "Yes—Left Alone, Markets Quickly Self-Adjust" camp believes that markets effectively channel self-interest to promote efficiency and economic growth, and are the most flexible way for the economy to adjust to changes. The "Yes" camp allows for business cycles, but believes they are caused largely by external shocks or government policies. Because they believe government failure is worse than market failure, they advocate, Chicago-style, a "hands-off" role for government.

The "No—Left Alone, Markets Fail to Quickly Self-Adjust" camp believes the self-adjusting mechanisms of markets can be slow and weak, so that business cycles, unemployment, and inflation will recur regularly unless the government steps in. The "No" camp believes business cycles are caused internally as unintended consequences of normally functioning markets—due to volatile expectations, money and banking, and Keynesian-style coordination failures between input and output markets. Because they believe market failure is worse than government failure, they advocate a "hands-on" role for government.

When students see this icon, they will know we are discussing the ideas of the hands-on camp.

I sympathetically present the strongest case for each camp. These camps, of course, are metaphors for extreme positions. No economist—or political party—fits entirely into either one. Think of the camps as the end points of a continuum along which economists and politicians are located. The extreme answers of the "Yes" and "No" camps are intended to sharpen students' thinking about macroeconomic issues. This is what we do in microeconomics in presenting first the extremes of market structure—perfect competition and pure monopoly—to isolate the key issues before moving to the middle—monopolistic competition and oligopoly—where most industries are located.

The core concepts include an aggregate supply and aggregate demand framework, complete with shocks and output gaps, that is developed in Chapter 4. But the heart of the framework is the enlarged circular flow diagram below, which recurs throughout the book.

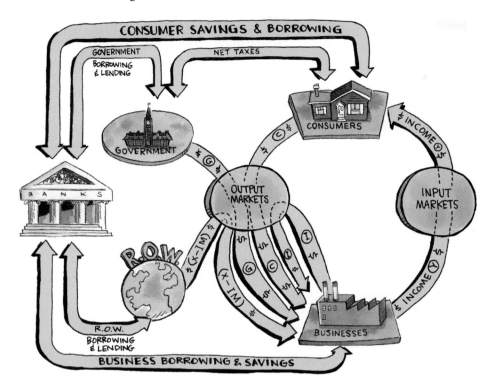

I believe that most essential macroeconomic issues can be presented simply and intelligently using this diagram.

Concepts *not* covered in this textbook (the ones I **let go**) include:

- Detailed measurement concepts like net domestic income at factor cost, chained-dollar real GDP, and differences between the consumer price index, GDP deflator, and chained price index for consumption.
- Aggregate production function models.
- Graphical models of the global loanable funds market.
- Detailed formulas for the money multiplier and for alternative (Taylor, McCallum) monetary policy targeting rules.
- Graphical derivation of the aggregate demand curve from the aggregate expenditure model.
- Algebraic derivations of expenditure, tax, and transfer multipliers.

I consider these exclusions to be a major strength of this textbook. The excluded topics detract from the student's accepting the value of the basic economic analysis that will enhance her decision-making throughout her life. As one strays beyond the core concepts and stories set out in this book, diminishing returns set in rapidly.

It is far more valuable, I believe, for most students to understand and apply the core economic concepts well—using the circular flow diagram to understand the "Yes, so government hands-off" and "No, so government hands-on" answers—than to be exposed to a wide range of concepts they will not master and therefore will likely soon forget.

Economics for Life uses no abstract graphs (many data graphs and charts of data are used for visual clarity) and almost no math. Many of my colleagues exclaim, "How can you teach economics without graphs? No math! Where is the rigour of the discipline?"

Economics for Life has the same rigour as *The Economist,* the *Wall Street Journal, The New York Times,* and *The Globe and Mail.* None of these publications use abstract graphs or equations, yet they present sophisticated economic analysis. The rigour comes from learning to think about and analyze situations like an economist.

If Stephen Hawking can explain theoretical physics in his book *A Brief History of Time* with only one equation, I believe the same can be done for economics.

What I find exciting about this book is the possibility of helping far more students "get" the benefit of thinking like an economist. Since working on *Economics for Life,* I have been using the stories in my introductory university course for economics majors. Instead of lecturing on differences between real business cycle theorists, new Keynesians, and Monetarists, for example, I ask how Progressive Conservatives or the NDP fit into the hands-off and hands-on camps, and evaluate policy proposals in those terms.

There has been a marked improvement in student interest and engagement. Instead of struggling to get them to pay attention to topics most view as irrelevant, I present narratives that come from their everyday experiences to make the concepts both meaningful and useful.

If this book succeeds in doing what it has set out to do—and you and your students will be the judges of that—then your students will be more actively engaged with the material. Students will learn economics in a way that will stay with them—even five years after leaving your classroom.

This brings us back to the question of your "economic footprint." You will cover fewer topics using *Economics for Life* (the nine chapters can easily be covered in a semester, with room for discussion of current events), but your students will retain more. After five years, they will actually be *ahead* of students who were exposed to the full range of topics. Your economic footprint will be larger. You will have produced more students who have better learned the fundamentals of thinking like an economist, and who are making smarter choices in their lives as consumers, businesspeople, investors, and as citizens evaluating macroeconomic policies proposed by politicians.

You will have succeeded in helping your students learn economics.

Avi Cohen
http://dept.econ.yorku.ca/~avicohen
Toronto
April 2010

Organization of This Book

The Table of Contents for this book will most likely look unusual and unfamiliar to you. How it developed reveals why this book is different from other textbooks, and how that difference is an advantage to you and your students.

Many authors, including me, have tried for years to write a textbook that would meet the needs of students in introductory, non-transfer economics courses. These students come from different majors and most take the course only to fulfill their diploma requirements, not because they are particularly interested in economics. They all bring special skill sets and special skill-based needs to your classroom.

The challenge is to get these students to recognize that economic literacy enables them to gain personal benefits and become more intelligent consumers and better-informed citizens. There are gains beyond the classroom for learning economics. At first, we tried stripping down the table of contents for a standard university or college economics text and simplifying the contents of each chapter. We kept hitting brick walls. One day, I had an epiphany—it was the table of contents that was the problem! The standard economics textbook has a table of contents and chapter content that makes sense to economists—aggregate supply and aggregate demand, expenditure multipliers, open-economy macroeconomics, fiscal policy, the foreign sector—but to non-economists, the material is meaningless jargon. I realized that the chapter titles and content must make sense to, and have relevance for, your students—most of whom will not become economists. As the book evolved, it also became clear that this book would be useful and important to a wide range of students, beyond just those in non-transfer courses.

In *Economics for Life,* chapter titles are designed for student understanding. The subtitles reflect the economic content and will be familiar to you, the instructor. The section heads within chapters use the same dual convention—titles for students, subtitles for economic content. This juxtaposition of titles adds more meaning to the economic concepts, provides an initial purpose for the student reading, and more closely ties the content to life outside the classroom.

The following is an overview of what each chapter covers. The **Instructor's Manual** contains a more detailed discussion of what's in each chapter, what's not, and why.

PART 1 Thinking Like A Macroeconomist

Chapter 1
Are Your Smart Choices Smart for All?
Macroeconomics and Microeconomics

Transitions from micro to macro, asking whether combined smart choices of individuals yield the best outcome for the economy as a whole. Using stories of the Great Recession and Great Depression, we introduce reasons why markets may not yield ideal aggregate results: fallacy of composition, connections between labour and output markets, and impact of money, banks, and expectations. The fundamental macroeconomic question is introduced: "If left alone by government, do the price mechanisms of market economies adjust quickly to maintain steady growth in living standards, full employment, and stable prices?" The "Yes" answer is tied to Say's Law, the "No" answer to Keynes. We connect "Yes" answers to a government hands-off position and the political right; "No" to a government hands-on position and the political left. We sketch macroeconomic performance outcomes—GDP, unemployment, inflation—which affect students' lives. We introduce macroeconomic players: consumers, businesses, government, the banking system, and the rest of the world (R.O.W.).

Chapter 2
Up Around the Circular Flow:
GDP, Economic Growth, and Business Cycles

Distinguishes nominal, real, and potential GDP, as well as limitations of GDP as a measure of well-being. In explaining potential GDP, there is an overview of sources of economic growth, emphasizing creative destruction and how increases in the quantity and quality of inputs expand the circular flow and improve productivity. We define phases of business cycles and explain output gaps and connections to unemployment and inflation. The choices of all macroeconomic players are combined to create the circular flow diagram—the analytical core of the book—together with the "mantra"

$$C + I + G + X - IM = Y.$$

Chapter 3
Costs of (Not) Working and Living:
Unemployment and Inflation

Details measurements of unemployment and inflation. We begin with unemployment rates, issues of involuntary part-time and discouraged workers, and differentiate "healthy" unemployment (frictional, structural) from "unhealthy" unemployment (cyclical). We define the natural rate, connecting all forms of unemployment to recessionary and inflationary gaps. We explain inflation rates using the Consumer Price Index and identify limitations of inflation measurements. We differentiate the core inflation rate, nominal, and realized real interest rates and explain inflation problems for fixed income streams, investors, and expectations. We present the quantity theory of money to help explain inflation. After illustrating the Phillips Curve, the final section connects unemployment to inflation and distinguishes demand-pull from cost-push inflations. Long-run Phillips Curve complications are postponed until Chapter 7.

Chapter 4

Skating to Where the Puck is Going:
Aggregate Supply and Aggregate Demand

Develops a framework for thinking about macroeconomics. We start with macroeconomic players' choices that determine aggregate supply; we then develop aggregate demand choices to ask if aggregate supply and aggregate demand match. Matches yield steady growth, full employment, and stable prices; mismatches may yield business cycles, unemployment, and inflation. Without demand and supply curves, we use circular flow diagrams to explain the framework. Paralleling micro distinctions between quantity supplied and supply, aggregate supply choices are divided into supply plans with existing inputs (law of aggregate supply), supply plans to increase inputs (increase in aggregate supply), and supply shocks. The question is: will supply plans create their own demand?

Again using circular flow diagrams, we differentiate the law of aggregate demand, changes in aggregate demand, and demand shocks. We use the fallacy of composition to explain the inverse relation between the price level and aggregate quantity demanded as different from micro explanations, focusing on substitution of foreign for domestic products. Equilibrium matches between aggregate supply and aggregate demand are tied to Say's Law ("Yes—markets quickly self-adjust, so hands-off") both for existing inputs and for growth over time with increasing inputs. We introduce the banking system and loanable funds market to "rescue" Say's Law when saving is possible. Disequilibrium mismatches between aggregate supply and aggregate demand are tied to Keynes ("No—markets fail to quickly adjust, so hands-on") and we explain short-run consequences of positive/negative aggregate supply and demand shocks for output gaps, unemployment, and inflation. The final section differentiates "Yes" and "No" explanations of origins of shocks, role of expectations, price adjustments, and operation of the loanable funds market.

PART 2   The Price of Money

Chapter 5

Money is for Lunatics:
Demanders and Suppliers of Money

Emphasizes acceptability as key feature of money, and explains functions of money as medium of exchange, unit of account, and store of value. Motivated by Keynes's question of why hold assets as money, which pays no interest, we develop the demand for money in the context of the asset choice of holding money (for liquidity) or bonds (for interest). We identify factors changing the demand for money: real GDP and average prices. We differentiate the relative de-emphasis on the store-of-value function of money by the "Yes" camp—when Say's Law holds and loanable funds markets clear, bonds are a relatively safe investment. For the "No" camp, with Keynes's business cycles and fundamental uncertainty, money is more appealing as a store of value. The supply of money story begins with four forms of money, the definition of M1, and roles of the Bank of Canada and chartered banks in creating money through fractional reserve banking. We emphasize banking tradeoffs between profits and prudence and explain bank runs. We explain the interest rate as the price of money in terms of connected money and bond markets. The inverse relation between bond prices and interest rates has centre stage in explaining adjustments to equilibrium. The final section explains monetary transmission mechanisms connecting interest rate changes to real GDP through aggregate demand. We differentiate camps in terms of "how much does money change the economy out of equilibrium?" The "Yes" camp answer is "not much" with loanable funds markets facilitating adjustment to equilibrium, while the "No" camp answer is "a lot" with money as a store of value adding new internal demand shocks slowing adjustment to equilibrium.

Chapter 6
Trading Dollars for Dollars?
Exchange Rates with the Rest of the World

Explains exchange rates as a prerequisite for understanding monetary policy. After explaining the foreign exchange market, we outline derived demands for Canadian dollars to buy Canadian exports, assets, and for speculation. The supply of Canadian dollars is demand for foreign currency derived from Canadians' demand for imports, for R.O.W. assets, and for speculation. We explain how exchange rates adjust to equilibrium and calculate reciprocal and cross exchange rates. We explain exchange rate fluctuations from interest and inflation rate differentials, GDP, and speculators' expectations. We trace international transmission mechanisms from exchange rates to net exports, aggregate demand, and to prices, explaining advantages/disadvantages of higher and lower exchange rates. The final section explains overvalued or undervalued currencies using purchasing power parity examples and the Big Mac index. We use the law of one price to motivate purchasing power parity and rate of return parity, and differentiate floating and fixed exchange rates.

PART 3   Macroeconomic Policy for Citizens— Hands-Off or Hands-On?

Chapter 7
Steering Blindly?
Monetary Policy and the Bank of Canada

Portrays challenges of monetary policy using the metaphor of driving down mountain roads with 30-second delays in pressing the accelerator and brake. After explaining origin and objectives of the Bank of Canada, we explain open bond market operations for changing the overnight rate and other short-term interest rates. We then use domestic and international transmission mechanisms from Chapters 5 and 6 to illustrate the impact of monetary policy on aggregate demand, GDP, employment, and inflation, and explain how the balance sheet recession of 2008–2009 highlighted store-of-value functions of money, blocked transmission mechanisms, and was addressed through quantitative easing. We discuss Bank of Canada independence, how the original Phillips Curve relationships broke down with changing expectations, and the importance of inflation rate targeting in anchoring inflationary expectations. While highlighting the agreement on the need for a central bank, we identify differences between the "Yes" camp's preference for hands-off monetary policy rules and "No" camp's preference for hands-on government policy discretion to correct transmission breakdowns and to allow for government-set targets besides inflation.

Chapter 8

Spending Others' Money:
Fiscal Policy, Deficits, and National Debt

Begins with use of demand-side fiscal policies to correct output gaps, working through expenditure and tax multipliers based on injections and leakages in the circular flow. We then review supply-side policies to promote growth by stimulating savings and capital investment, encouraging R&D and improving education and training. While both camps largely agree on supply-side policies, differences exist on savings policies. The "Yes" camp emphasizes long-run benefits of growth; "No" camp worries about short-run consequences of decreased aggregate demand. We also explain supply-side incentive effects, reviewing supply-sider arguments politicians make that tax cuts increase tax revenues. For government budgets, we document revenues and expenditures and explain deficits and surpluses, distinguishing cyclical from structural. We trace how automatic stabilizers have moderated business cycles and automatically generate cyclical deficits and surpluses, and the destabilizing risk of forcing always-balanced government budgets. We suggest balancing the budget over the cycle to avoid structural deficits. The section on national debt distinguishes flows (deficits) from stocks (debt) and documents Canada's national debt as a percentage of GDP. We explore five common arguments about national debt, distinguishing myths and genuine problems: will Canada go bankrupt?; burden for future generations; debt is always bad; interest payments creating self-perpetuating debt; crowding out and crowding in. The final section differentiates economic and political statements about deficits and debt as positive or normative to help students make informed choices as citizens about hands-off and hands-on roles for government fiscal policy.

Chapter 9

Are Sweatshops All Bad?
Globalization and Trade Policy

Begins with a basic choice—producing for yourself or specializing and trading. A simple example—reproduced from microeconomics Chapter 1—uses tables of numbers that are implicit production possibility frontiers, illustrating gains from trade and comparative advantage. We define terms of trade and emphasize the role of creative destruction in creating winners, losers, and opponents to trade. Winners are consumers and export industries; losers are businesses and workers in import-competing industries. We explain protectionism—tariffs, quotas, domestic subsidies—by the unequal distribution of gains and losses producing political pressure to protect those who lose from trade. We review protectionist arguments—saving Canadian jobs; competing with cheap foreign labour; national security and cultural identity—and risks of trade wars. The section on economic globalization begins with anti-globalization protests against trade, the World Bank and IMF, and explains the "Yes" camp's hands-off "free market" conditions on assistance to developing countries during the 1990s. We explain forces driving globalization and present a history of sweatshops and trade. We propose the opportunity-cost question: are workers' lives better off, or worse off, compared to a situation without globalization, trade, and the factory jobs that follow? We use Stiglitz's views for hands-on arguments, partially supporting protesters, for a limited role for government to maintain a social safety net for those left behind by trade and markets. We present *The Economist's* criticisms of international trade negotiations—

problems for developing countries are not caused by trade, but by protectionist policies in developed countries. A power struggle over tariffs and subsidies between rich and poor countries affects terms of trade and how gains are divided. We outline hands-off and hands-on positions on government in global markets, to enable students—as citizens of Canada and the world—to reach an informed position on globalization.

Adapting This Book to Your Course

As you can see from this detailed overview, the chapters in this book can quite easily be mapped onto your current course. Chapters 1 to 3 introduce the fundamental macroeconomic question and explain GDP, economic growth, business cycles, unemployment, and inflation. These are the key outcomes for judging how well the economy performs. Chapter 4 presents the aggregate supply and aggregate demand framework. Chapters 5 and 6 examine money, bond, and foreign exchange markets. And Chapters 7 to 9 cover monetary policy, fiscal policy, and international trade and trade policy.

If you are teaching a one-semester macro course without micro prerequisites, you will first want to cover the four appendices, which are the opening chapters from *Economics for Life: Smart Choices for You*. The macro chapters are written to flow from the end of those microeconomics chapters, or from any other introductory microeconomics textbook.

The unique nature of this textbook helps you make the course material more relevant to your students and thus provides a solid basis for a more positive classroom experience. In addition, the style of the textbook, its features, and its learning aids are designed to meet the skill levels, interests, and needs of a wide range of students who are not training to be economists but who—as consumers, as businesspeople, and as citizens—will benefit from learning to think like an economist. All these features enable students to learn economics in a way that will stay with them—even five years after leaving your classroom.

Supplements

This textbook is supported by many materials designed to enhance learning and understanding for students and to make the course exciting and rewarding for instructors. The following support materials are available for instructors.

Instructor's Resource CD-ROM

The Instructor's Resource CD-ROM contains the Instructor's Manual, PowerPoint® Presentations, and Pearson TestGen.

Instructor's Manual: The manual includes teaching notes and suggestions for classroom discussion.

PowerPoint Presentations: PowerPoint™ presentations are available for each chapter of the book. The presentations integrate key concepts and visuals from the text and have been designed to reflect and embody the unique philosophy behind and structure of the textbook.

Pearson TestGen: This computerized test item file enables instructors to view and edit existing test questions, add questions, generate tests, and print tests in a variety of formats. Powerful search and sort functions make it easy to locate questions and arrange them in any order. TestGen also enables instructors to administer tests on a local area network, have the tests graded electronically, and have the results prepared in electronic or printed reports. These questions are also available in MyTest, which is available through MyEconLab at www.myeconlab.com.

MyEconLab

Pearson Canada's online resource, MyEconLab, offers instructors and students all of their resources in one place, written and designed to accompany this text. MyEconLab creates a perfect pedagogical loop that provides not only text-specific assessment and practice problems, but also tutorial support to make sure students learn from their mistakes.

MyEconLab is available to instructors by going to www.myeconlab.com and following the instructions. Students access MyEconLab with an access code that is available with the purchase of a new text.

At the core of MyEconLab are the following features:

Auto-Graded Tests and Assignments: MyEconLab comes with two preloaded Sample Tests for each chapter. Students can use these tests for self-assessment and obtain immediate feedback. Instructors can assign the Sample Tests or use them along with Test Bank questions or their own exercises to create tests or quizzes.

Study Plan: A Study Plan is generated from each student's results on Sample Tests and instructor assignments. Students can clearly see which topics they have mastered and, more importantly, which they need to work on.

Unlimited Practice: Many Study Plan and instructor-assigned exercises contain algorithmically generated values to ensure that students get as much practice as they need. Every problem links students to learning resources that further reinforce concepts they need to master.

Learning Resources: Each practice problem contains a link to the eText page that discusses the concept being applied. Students also have access to guided solutions, flashcards, Student PowerPoints and answers to Refresh Questions.

Economics in the News: Each Economics in the News article is accompanied by additional links, discussion questions, and a reference to relevant textbook chapters.

Technology Specialists

Pearson's Technology Specialists work with faculty and campus course designers to ensure that Pearson technology products, assessment tools, and online course materials are tailored to meet your specific needs. This highly qualified team is dedicated to helping schools take full advantage of a wide range of educational resources by assisting in the integration of a variety of instructional materials and media formats. Your local Pearson Education sales representative can provide you with more details about this service program.

CourseSmart

CourseSmart is a new way for instructors and students to access textbooks online anytime from anywhere. With thousands of titles across hundreds of courses, CourseSmart helps instructors choose the best textbook for their class and give their students a new option for buying the assigned textbook as a lower cost eTextbook. For more information, visit www.coursesmart.com.

Acknowledgments

Joseph Gladstone, Project Developer, had the original vision for this book. While we have developed that vision collaboratively, Joseph has been the guiding force and, in all but title, a co-author. Without his counsel, wisdom, and vast experience in teaching and publishing, this book would not have come to life.

Reviewers play a crucial role in the development of any textbook. The better the reviewers, the better the textbook. I hit the reviewer jackpot when Peter Kennedy of Simon Fraser University agreed to read, review, and make detailed suggestions on every chapter of the first draft of this textbook. Peter—a 3M Teaching Fellow, an editor of the *Journal of Economic Education*, and the author of the bestselling *A Guide to Econometrics*, 6th edition (Wiley-Blackwell, 2008) and *Macroeconomic Essentials: Understanding Economics in the News*, 3rd edition (MIT Press, 2010)—is known, both as a teacher and author, for his clarity, economy of expression, intuition, and accessibility to non-technical readers. These strengths and his dedication to student learning made him my perfect reviewer. His comments were insightful, extremely frank, and always constructive. It was an exhilarating experience to productively argue with a teacher and author of Peter's calibre about fundamental differences in how to present macroeconomic topics. I did not always take Peter's advice, and remaining shortcomings in the book are solely my responsibility.

Much of what is good (I think; you judge) in this book also comes from my long association with Robin Bade and Michael Parkin. During almost 20 years as an author to the *Study Guide* accompanying their *Economics: Canada In the Global Environment,* I have learned so much from their skills as teachers, writers, and economists. Their commitment to clarity, conciseness, and helping students learn has made them both an inspiration and role models. Although this textbook is intended for a different audience, I can only hope that it will be judged to be in their league.

Many others contributed to the development of this book. My co-author, Ian Howe, has not only written an excellent and imaginative *Study Guide* for the end of each chapter, but has also improved the content and presentation of the text. Thanks also to Gord Fairfield, George Fallis, Eric Kam, Harvey King, and John Sloane. Jessica Courtney skillfully hunted and gathered data for all graphs and tables. Thanks to all who participated in the 2009 B.C. Economics Articulation meetings at Columbia College, especially to Stephane Deseau for hospitality and Ron Kneebone for sharpening the fundamental macroeconomic question at the core of this book.

The Pearson team—Don Thompson, Claudine O'Donnell, Cheryl Jackson, Toni Chahley, Leigh-Anne Graham, Susan Bindernagel—have taught me how much skill and professionalism go into transforming a manuscript into a book. Thank you.

Gary Bennett and Allan Reynolds at Pearson deserve special thanks. Without their faith (often tested) and support, this book would not be before you.

Avi J. Cohen
Toronto, April 2010

The authors and the publisher thank other reviewers and consultants for their time, ideas, and suggestions that have helped make this textbook better. Their input has been extremely positive and their expertise invaluable in making this new economics book more accessible and useful to both professors and students.

Sarah Arliss, Seneca College
Darren Chapman, Fanshawe College
Mark Loken, Vancouver Island University
Peter MacDonald, Cambrian College
Brian Murray, Holland College
Geoffrey Prince, Centennial College
Dustin Quirk, Red Deer College
Jim Spencer, Cambrian College
Russell Turner, Fleming College
Jonathan Warner, Quest University Canada

MACRO COHEN • HOWE

ECONOMICS FOR LIFE

smart choices for all?

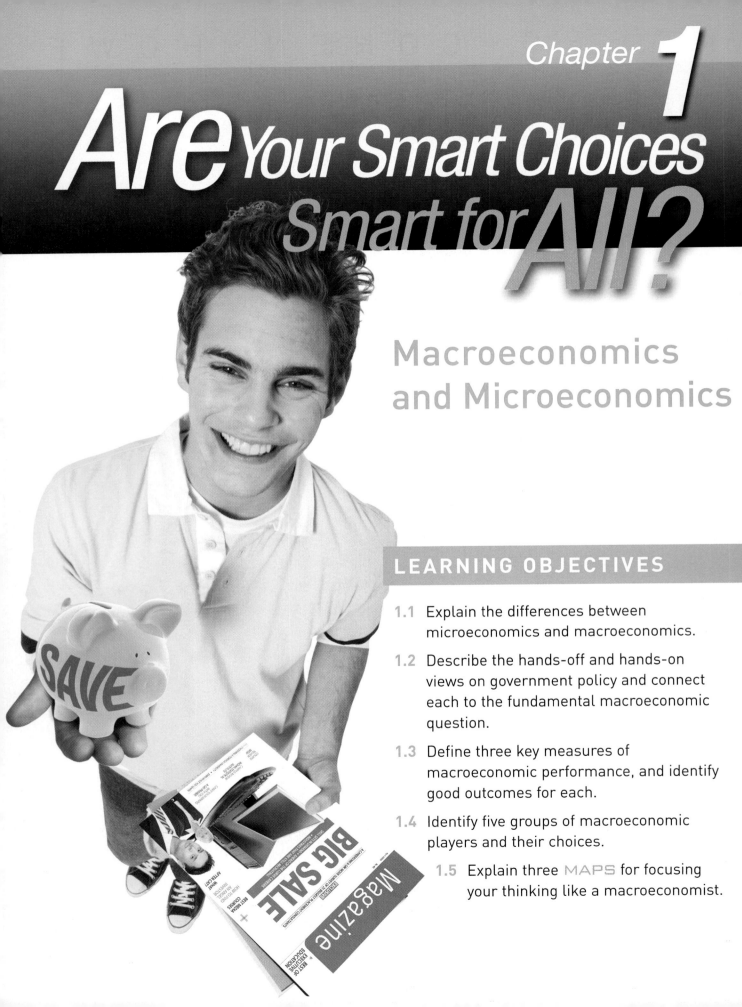

Are Your Smart Choices Smart for All?

Macroeconomics and Microeconomics

LEARNING OBJECTIVES

1.1 Explain the differences between microeconomics and macroeconomics.

1.2 Describe the hands-off and hands-on views on government policy and connect each to the fundamental macroeconomic question.

1.3 Define three key measures of macroeconomic performance, and identify good outcomes for each.

1.4 Identify five groups of macroeconomic players and their choices.

1.5 Explain three MAPS for focusing your thinking like a macroeconomist.

WE ARE SHIFTING OUR GAZE from individual trees to the whole forest. Microeconomics looks at smart choices of individual consumers and individual businesses, while macroeconomics looks at the combined market outcomes of all of those individual choices.

According to Adam Smith's invisible hand, price signals in markets create incentives so that while each individual (a micro focus on each tree) acts only in his self-interest, the unintended consequence is the production of all of the products and services we want (a healthy, growing forest).

Macroeconomics questions how well Smith's invisible hand works in a broader context. When all the smart choices of individuals are combined, is the result the best outcome for the economy as a whole?

Consider this example. During tough economic times, many people are unemployed — they can't find jobs, aren't earning incomes, and cut back on their spending. Businesses aren't selling enough because consumers aren't buying — products sit on shelves and profits are down. But if only businesses would hire the people looking for work, those new employees would earn incomes and buy the unsold products. It seems everyone (workers and businesses) could be better off, yet that doesn't happen. Why?

This is the core question for macroeconomics. Do smart choices by consumers and businesses imply that smart choices are being made for the economy as a whole? What are the implications of this question for government economic policy; for you as a consumer, a businessperson, and an investor; and for your choices as a voter? This chapter examines macroeconomics by questioning whether microeconomic lessons can be extended to the economy as a whole.

1.1 Reconciling Macroeconomics and Microeconomics: Is the Whole Greater Than the Sum of the Parts?

Explain the differences between microeconomics and macroeconomics.

Economics is nicknamed "the dismal science," and 2008 and 2009 were certainly dismal years for the economies of Canada, the United States, and most countries around the globe.

The Great Recession and Great Depression

Ads like this one encouraged people to believe that the price of real estate would go up and up forever. You would be rich tomorrow with no risk by going into debt today. Does this make sense to you?

The story of where we were in 2009 begins with constantly rising, or inflating, housing prices in the U.S. (and Canada) between 1996 and 2006. This housing price bubble (you inflate bubbles with air; you inflate housing prices with demand) led homeowners, real estate investors, mortgage lenders (a mortgage is a loan to buy a house), and financial institutions to take bigger and bigger risks. It seemed that prices could only go up, and there was easy money to be made. Banks issued mortgages with no down payments to borrowers who really couldn't afford them (called "sub-prime" mortgages), assuming that even if a borrower couldn't make his payments, the bank could sell the house at an ever-rising price to recover the loan. Banks and other financial institutions bundled these mortgages together and sold them to others as mortgage-backed securities. (Buyers of the securities received the mortgage payments.) These securities provided more money for mortgages, making it easier for house buyers to demand houses, which further inflated housing prices.

The Great Recession When housing prices began to fall, the bubble burst, and the value of all of those mortgages and securities plummeted. Investors and banks holding now almost worthless assets were forced to sell other assets to meet their obligations, and panicked selling led to the failure of banks, other financial institutions, and broadly falling asset prices. Stock market values plunged 40 percent, housing prices kept falling, and in the U.S. borrowers walked away from houses that were worth less than the mortgages they owed. Businesses went bankrupt, the Canadian auto industry was in danger of collapse, and unemployment kept rising, predicted to exceed ten percent.

The economic downturn of 2008–2009 has been nicknamed the "Great Recession" in comparison with the even more severe downturn between 1929 and 1933 called the "Great Depression." (As you will learn in Chapter 2, a recession is a milder downturn than a depression).

"My bubble burst!"

Source: www.CartoonStock.com.

The Great Depression As bad as things appeared in 2009, they were nowhere near as dismal as the hardships people endured during the Great Depression. Triggered by a stock market crash in 1929, economic activity collapsed. By 1933, 20 percent of the Canadian and U.S. workforce was unemployed, and output of products/services fell by more than 30 percent. That meant there were 30 percent fewer products, including food, to sustain a population that kept increasing. The prices consumers paid for products/services fell by over 20 percent. (Falling prices, called deflation, are the opposite of rising prices, called inflation. We will discuss these topics in Chapter 3). While falling prices sound good to those of us used to rising prices, because of unemployment, wages were falling even faster. And falling prices for businesses are a disaster, as falling revenues mean it is harder to pay off existing debts, so there is less to invest in expanding output or improving productivity. To make things worse, there were no government programs like employment insurance, welfare, health care, or the Canada Pension Plan to cushion the blow. The effects of the Great Depression lasted over a decade. Standards of living returned to 1929 levels only in 1941 with government spending on military production for World War II.

Unemployed men like those shown had to line up at soup kitchens for a meal during the Great Depression. Could this happen today?

Government Blunders Governments tried to counteract the downturn, but they took almost all of the *wrong* policy actions, making the downturn worse, not better. Britain's decision to base the value of its currency on the value of gold (the Gold Standard) raised the value of the British Pound relative to other currencies, making British exports more expensive and slowing their sales, contributing to the downturn in Britain and elsewhere. (We will discuss exchange rates between currencies in Chapter 6.) Central banks, especially the Federal Reserve in the U.S., implemented monetary policy (coming in Chapter 7) that allowed banks to fail, reduced the supply of money, and made it more difficult for consumers and businesses to restore the spending necessary to turn around the economy. Governments, faced with declining tax revenues, tried to balance their budgets and avoid deficits by reducing spending and increasing taxes (fiscal policy, coming in Chapter 8), which pushed economies further into recession. And governments, attempting to protect their domestic industries from foreign competitors during difficult business conditions, put up tariffs (taxes on imports) that caused international trade to break down, reducing the gains from trade. (We will discuss trade policy in Chapter 9.)

Governments around the world made disastrous economic policy decisions, causing the Great Depression to become worse and last longer than it needed to be. Macroeconomics looks at and grows out of those decisions.

Macroeconomics These topics—business cycle bubbles and recessions; unemployment and inflation; money and the financial system; exchange rates between currencies; government fiscal, monetary, and trade policies—are all part of macroeconomics. **Macroeconomics** analyzes the performance of the whole Canadian economy and the global economy—the combined outcomes of all individual microeconomic choices.

macroeconomics: analyzes performance of the whole Canadian economy and global economy—the combined outcomes of all individual microeconomic choices

What Happened to the Miracle of Markets?

Believe it or not, I hope you are feeling a bit puzzled by this discussion of macroeconomics, because it should sound very contradictory to what you learned about microeconomics.

microeconomics: *analyzes choices that individuals in households, individual businesses, and governments make, and how those choices interact in markets*

Microeconomics Microeconomics analyzes the choices made by individuals in households, individual businesses, and governments, and how those choices interact in markets. When we looked at the interaction of those choices in markets, we found (in *Economics for Life: Smart Choices for You*, Appendix D, page 487):

> Markets are adept at reacting to change. Whether there are shortages, surpluses, or changes in . . . demand or supply, markets react quickly because prices create incentives for consumers and businesses to adjust their smart choices. Price signals in markets create incentives so that while each person acts only in her own self-interest, the result (coordinated through Adam Smith's invisible hand of competition) is the miracle of continuous, ever-changing production of the products/services we want.

So how does market coordination of smart choices produce outcomes like mass unemployment, falling living standards, bankruptcies, financial bubbles, and deflation or inflation?

We will spend the rest of this book finding answers to those questions, but let's start with a basic explanation about why smart microeconomic choices by individuals may not add up to smart macroeconomic outcomes.

fallacy of composition: *what is true for one is not true for all; whole is greater than the sum of the parts*

Fallacy of Composition Sometimes a choice made by one person produces a different outcome from the same choice made by many people. Let's look at two examples.

Suppose an individual farmer in Saskatchewan plants more wheat than usual. Prairie weather is perfect for growing, and he harvests a big bumper crop. Because the farmer is a small producer (remember the market structure of extreme competition, where each of the many small businesses are price takers?), his increase in supply has almost no impact on the world price for wheat. The farmer's income goes up with a greater quantity and a constant price of wheat. But if *all* farmers plant more wheat, and weather is good in wheat-growing regions around the world, the great increase in supply drives down the world price of wheat so much that all farmers end up with less income than before.

This is an example of the **fallacy of composition**—what is true for one (micro) is not necessarily true for all (macro). The other phrase that describes the fallacy of composition is "the whole is greater than the sum of the parts."

◀

This farmer is harvesting a bumper crop. He hopes he will make a huge profit on such a good crop, but his profit will depend on world prices.

Paradox of Thrift   The second example is about your decision to save. If you decide to save more from your income, then your savings will increase and your spending will decrease. But if many people decide to save more and spend less, businesses experience falling sales, cut back production, and lay off workers so that incomes fall. Paradoxically, the result may be that people end up saving less, because without employment income, they have to draw down their savings rather than increase savings. Economists call this the **paradox of thrift**. Again, what is true for one is not necessarily true for all.

Another way the whole economy is greater than the sum of the parts comes from connections between input and output markets.

paradox of thrift: attempts to increase savings cause aggregate savings to decrease because of falling employment and incomes

ECONOMICS Out There

End of the Spendthrift Ethos

The serious economic downturn of 2008–2009 is dramatically changing the spending habits of American consumers. Joe Rudyck is a 21-year-old university graduate who recently purchased a new car and laptop, and used to make frequent shopping trips to the mall. While in school, he worked at two part-time jobs, took out student loans, and spent everything he earned.

Now, as the U.S. savings rate has jumped to a 15-year high, he is "living proof" that the spend-spend-spend attitude of American consumers has been squashed. He now thinks before any purchase, and has stepped up his savings in case his car breaks down.

- Mr. Rudyk's new savings behaviour, shared now by millions of U.S. consumers, is what we call the paradox of thrift. Saving more is prudent behaviour in hard times, but has the unintended consequences of reducing demand for products/services, causing businesses to lay off workers, and making it even harder for people to save.

- The change in U.S. savings behaviour is worrisome to Canadians because most Canadian exports are sold in the United States. A senior economist at BMP Capital Markets said, "it's very hard for Canada to dig itself out of the recession unless Americans start spending again."

Source: "End of the Spendthrift Ethos," Joe Friesen, *The Globe and Mail*, March 3, 2009.

Connections Between Input and Output Markets The map of the circular flow of economic life, Figure 1.1, is at the heart of the microeconomic explanation of the miracle of markets. It will play an equally important role in our study of macroeconomics. On this map, the complexity of the Canadian economy is reduced to three sets of players—households, businesses, and governments. Households and businesses interact in two sets of markets— input markets (where businesses buy from households the inputs they need to produce products/services) and output markets (where businesses sell their products/services to households). Government sets the rules of the game and can choose to interact, or not, in almost any aspect of the economy. When markets work well, self-interest and the invisible hand of competition coordinate the smart choices of households and businesses in both sets of markets.

Figure 1.1	Circular Flow of Economic Life

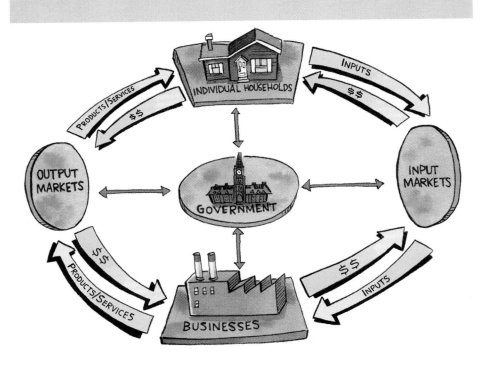

Before we look at the macroeconomic connection between input markets and output markets, let's review the basics of the circular flow.

Input markets determine incomes. Households are sellers and businesses are buyers.

Input Markets Good maps like Figure 1.1 help you find your way by focusing on the most important information. Let's follow the circle, beginning at the top. Individuals in households sell or rent out their labour (ability to work), capital, land, and entrepreneurial abilities to businesses. This is the blue flow on the right side of the circle, from top to bottom. In exchange, businesses pay households wages, interest, rent, and other money rewards. This is the green flow on the right side of the circle, from bottom to top. These exchanges, or trades, happen in input markets, where households are the sellers and businesses are the buyers. When Mr. Sub hires you to work at a Mr. Sub store, that interaction happens in an input market—the labour market. Input markets determine your income.

Output Markets Businesses (at the bottom) use those inputs to produce products/services to sell to households. This is the blue flow on the left side of the circle, from bottom to top. In exchange, households use the income they have earned in input markets to pay businesses for their purchases. This is the green flow on the left side of the circle, from top to bottom. These exchanges, or trades, happen in output markets, where households are the buyers and businesses are the sellers. These are markets where you buy your breakfast from Tim's or Second Cup, or piercings from your neighbourhood piercing parlour. Output markets determine the value of all of products/services sold.

At the end of the trip around the circle, households have the products/services they need to live, and businesses end up with the money. That sets the stage for the next trip around the circle, where businesses again buy inputs from individuals in households in exchange for income, then produce outputs that households buy—and the flow goes on.

Output markets determine the value of all products/services sold. Households are buyers and businesses are sellers.

The Macroeconomic Connection With our microeconomic focus, we looked at the interaction of demand and supply *in input markets alone*, and at the interaction of demand and supply *in output markets alone*.

Suppose wages in the labour market—an input market—are higher than the market-clearing wage. Workers are eager to supply a large quantity of hours. But businesses won't find it as profitable to hire workers at the higher wage, so the quantity of labour supplied is greater than the quantity of labour demanded. There is a surplus of labour. In the labour market alone, wages will fall, decreasing the quantity of labour supplied and increasing quantity demanded. These adjustments to falling wages restore the balance between demand and supply, and coordinate the smart choices of households supplying labour with the smart choices of businesses demanding labour.

Our macroeconomic focus extends this story to connect input and output markets. Falling wages mean falling incomes. If you work 40 hours per week, and your wage falls from $15 per hour to $10 per hour, your weekly income falls from $600 to $400. Ouch. So your demand for products/services decreases in output markets. With decreased demand for their products/services, businesses experience falling prices of outputs and, in turn, will want to hire fewer workers. The *connections* between the forces of demand and supply in input and output markets may impede the coordination of the smart choices of households and businesses.

For a discussion of how price falls to eliminate a surplus, see page 482.

Money, Banks, and Expectations As the stories of the Great Recession and the Great Depression show, money, banks, and expectations played major roles in the speculative bubbles that inflated, burst, and triggered the downturns. We did not focus on any of these factors while studying microeconomics. Money serves the whole economy, as do the banking system and Canada's central bank, the Bank of Canada. They will be part of our macroeconomic focus. Expectations, like believing that housing prices would continue to rise, are judgment-based and depend on the state of the whole economy.

Do Market Economies Quickly Self-Adjust or Not?

So which focus is "right?" Do markets coordinate smart individual choices to produce the miracle of the continuous, ever-changing production of the products/services we want (microeconomic focus), or do markets produce outcomes like unemployment, falling living standards, bankruptcies, financial bubbles, and deflation or inflation (macroeconomic focus)?

As you might guess, there is no single right answer to the question. Sometimes markets work well and quickly in coordinating individual choices, sometimes not. Economists call the periodic ups and downs of overall economic activity **business cycles** (a topic in Chapter 2). A more precise rewording of this question will guide everything we discuss in the rest of the book.

business cycles: ups and downs of overall economic activity

> If left alone by government, do the price mechanisms of market economies adjust quickly to maintain steady growth in living standards, full employment, and stable prices?

> More simply, if left alone, do markets quickly self-adjust?

Say's Law: supply creates its own demand

Say's Law   Some economists today will answer the question "Yes" and others will say "No." Economists in 1929, at the start of the Great Depression, believed only the "Yes" answer: the microeconomic focus on the miracle of markets. The belief that market economies would always quickly self-adjust was based on work by Jean-Baptiste Say (1767–1832), a French economist and supporter of Adam Smith's views on free trade and markets. **Say's Law** claimed that "supply creates its own demand."

We can illustrate Say's Law using the circular flow diagram in Figure 1.1 on page 8. Starting at the top, households *supply* inputs to businesses in exchange for money. The only reason households sell their inputs in input markets is because they want the money to *demand* products/services in output markets. When households spend all of the money they have earned in input markets to buy products/services in output markets, supply does create its own demand, and the flow continues smoothly around the circle.

In the middle of the Great Depression, economists who continued to believe in Say's Law started to look pretty silly. Economic events were crying out for a better explanation of the ups and downs of business cycles, especially the "downs" of falling output and living standards, unemployment, and deflation.

Keynesian Revolution   Economists' reputations were rescued by John Maynard Keynes (1883–1946). Keynes was one of the most brilliant and influential minds of the twentieth century, creating the subject of macroeconomics, representing Britain at the Versailles peace conference at the end of World War I, being a member of the literary Bloomsbury Group, and engineering the creation of the International Monetary Fund (IMF) and the post-World War II international monetary system.

◄

John Maynard Keynes, shown here in his study, was chosen as Man-of-the-Year by *Time* magazine in 1965. He was chosen because his principles helped the country "avoid the violent cycles...to produce a phenomenal economic growth and to achieve remarkably stable prices."

In a famous 1936 book, *The General Theory of Employment, Interest and Money*, Keynes rejected Say's Law as a "special theory" that sometimes holds true but usually does not. Keynes allowed for both answers to the question of the speed of self-adjustment of market economies in his more "general theory." Given enough time, he accepted that self-adjusting mechanisms might bring market economies back to steady growth, full employment, and stable prices. But Keynes believed it could take decades, during which time there would be serious and needless human suffering. He believed proper government policy could correct the problems more quickly in the short run, which was his focus. He famously quipped, "In the long run, we are all dead."

Keynes rejected Say's Law as a general truth, and explained the Great Depression by emphasizing the roles of money, banks, and expectations in connecting input markets and output markets. Households earning incomes in input markets are paid in money. If households save the money rather than spend it, businesses will not find the demand they expect for their products/services in output markets. This is the paradox of thrift, where businesses cut back production, lay off workers, and the economy goes into a downturn.

Expectations can also interfere with the quick self-adjusting mechanisms of market economies. In the stock market bubble of 1929, or the housing price bubble of 1996–2006, people began to *expect* that prices would continue to rise. Expectations can be self-fulfilling, as long as most people share them. If investors expect housing prices to continue rising, they will want to buy (and then sell, or "flip") more houses to make profits, and that demand will cause housing prices to rise. But when rising prices are based only on expectations, not on economic fundamentals, a change in expectations can quickly burst a bubble. If investors start expecting prices to fall, they sell quickly to avoid losses from falling prices. That selling causes housing prices to fall, leading more people to expect prices to fall, leading to more selling, and a rapid collapse in prices. Expectations, which can shift quickly because they are guesses about an uncertain future, help explain the cycles of boom and bust in market economies.

Introducing Macroeconomics Keynes's work created the field of macroeconomics. If you had been studying economics before 1936, there were no macroeconomic textbooks like the one you are reading. Now that macroeconomics exists, let's look in the next section at modern economists' views on whether market economies quickly self-adjust or not, and the implications for government macroeconomic policy.

> *The long run is a misleading guide to current affairs. In the long run we are all dead. Economists set themselves too easy, too useless a task if in tempestuous seasons they can only tell us when the storm is long past, the ocean will be flat again.*
>
> –John Maynard Keynes, 1923

> *"I believe myself to be writing a book on economic theory which will largely revolutionise . . . the way the world thinks about economic problems."*

Keynes wrote the quote above about the General Theory in a 1935 letter to George Bernard Shaw, the playwright whose words inspired the title of this book—Economics for Life.

Refresh 1.1

1. What is a *fallacy of composition*?

2. Use the fundamental macroeconomic question on page 10 to explain conflicts between the predictions of microeconomics and macroeconomics.

3. What media explanations have you seen about the recession of 2008–2009? Where do those explanations fit into the categories of fallacy of composition, connections between input and output markets, and the roles of money/banks/expectations?

www.myeconlab.com

1.2 Should Government Be Hands-Off or Hands-On? Economics and Politics

Describe the hands-off and hands-on views on government policy and connect each to the fundamental macroeconomic question.

Since the time of Keynes, macroeconomics has made great gains in understanding how the economic system functions. Economists have learned from past experiences and have developed more sophisticated mathematical tools for applying and extending Keynes's insights about macroeconomic ups and downs. Economists have also developed sophisticated tools for applying and extending Say's insights, and for understanding the conditions under which markets adjust quickly and well and produce the miracle of the continuous, ever-changing production of the products/services we want. Luckily for you, since you are not trying to become an economist, you don't have to master those tools.

While economists have learned much since the Great Depression, what remains the same are disagreements among economists—as well as among politicians—about the fundamental macroeconomic question. The ideas in the debate between Say and Keynes are very much alive today.

> If left alone by government, do the price mechanisms of market economies adjust quickly to maintain steady growth in living standards, full employment, and stable prices?

> More simply, if left alone, do markets quickly self-adjust?

Because there is no agreement on this question, you will have to decide which answers make most sense to you. The answers are important because they could make the difference between economic prosperity and recession. Your personal economic success will depend on the macroeconomic performance of the economy, and that performance is affected by government policies that will be put in place by politicians you elect. Let me outline the two major camps among economists in terms of "Yes" and "No" answers. In describing the answers, we will extend the concepts of market failure and government failure from microeconomics.

Market Failure versus Government Failure

Since the Great Depression and Great Recession have clearly happened, you might think that the only reasonable answer to the question is, "No—markets fail to quickly self-adjust." Despite these debilitating business cycles, a "Yes—markets quickly self-adjust" answer is also possible because of the importance of the initial, qualifying phrase, "If left alone by government."

Due to economies of scale or externalities, markets can fail to produce outcomes in the public interest. Government policy can improve market outcomes by acting in the public interest. But it is also possible that government may act in the interest of businesses, labour, or other interest groups. When government does not act in the public interest but is "captured" by special interest groups, economists define that as **government failure**.

Even when aiming for the public interest, government failure can occur because policymakers lack adequate and timely information for making good decisions. It is easy to make "honest mistakes" in choosing macroeconomic polices due to the complexity of the economy with its connections to the banking system, changeable expectations, and the global economy.

The macroeconomic consequences of government failure are policies that make economic outcomes like business cycles and unemployment worse. Government failure contributed to the severity of the Great Depression.

It is possible that the problems of business cycles or unemployment may have been caused by government failure—bad policy—not by the market economy. So even when observing the ups and downs of economic activity, the answer to the question, "If left alone, do markets quickly self-adjust?" may still be "Yes" because bad government policies have not left markets alone.

Economists often disagree. There is a joke that if you ask three economists a question, especially about macroeconomics, you will get five opinions. So in sorting economists (and politicians) into only two camps, I will simplify many differences that exist among them. The simplifications focus on the most important differences of this fundamental macroeconomic question. Let's look at the "Yes" and "No" answers, and how they connect to politics.

government failure: government policy fails to serve the public interest

"Yes — Left Alone, Markets Quickly Self-Adjust"

Following in the footsteps of Adam Smith and Jean-Baptiste Say, one camp of economists argues that, if left alone by government, the price mechanisms of market economies adjust quickly to maintain steady growth in living standards, full employment, and stable prices.

The "Yes—Markets Quickly Self-Adjust" camp allows for some ups and downs in economic activity, and occasional unemployment and inflation, but believes those economic problems are caused by events outside the economy or by government policies. The "Yes" camp argues that markets are the most flexible way for the economy to adjust to changes, even if those adjustments take some time. These economists believe that money, banks, and expectations don't significantly affect the exchanges of physical products/services around the circular flow, or impede coordination between input and output markets. Through the invisible hand of competition, markets channel self-interest to promote efficiency and rising living standards.

"Yes—Markets Quickly Self-Adjust" camp supports a hands-off role for government.

Hands-Off With the belief that markets will self-adjust (usually quickly, always in the long run), there is little role for government policy. Furthermore, this group believes that even when markets temporarily fail, government policy will likely make things worse, not better. Government failure is worse than potential market failure for this camp. It also sees government policy as a source of economic problems, not a solution to the problems. Therefore, the "Yes— Markets Quickly Self-Adjust" camp argues for a hands-off role for government.

Politicians on the right of the political spectrum—Conservatives and Libertarians—fit into this camp, supporting a hands-off role for government. They believe that, if left alone, the market economy will produce the miracle of the continuous, ever-changing production of the products/services we want, including rising standards of living, full employment, and stable prices.

"No—Left Alone, Markets Fail to Quickly Self-Adjust"

Following in the footsteps of John Maynard Keynes, the other camp of economists argues that, if left alone by government, the self-adjusting mechanisms of market economies can be slow and weak, so that business cycles, long periods of unemployment that reduce living standards, and rising or falling prices will recur regularly.

The "No—Markets Fail to Quickly Self-Adjust" camp believes that most economic problems are caused internally as unintended by-products of normally functioning markets. This group emphasizes the roles that money, banks, and expectations play in impeding the coordination between input and output markets. While preferring the flexibility of market economies to any other economic system, such as socialism, these economists see self-interest and greed promoting speculative bubbles that inevitably cause cycles of boom and bust.

"No—Markets Fail To Quickly Self-Adjust" camp supports a hands-on role for government.

Hands-On With the belief that markets on their own generate economic problems and fail to quickly self-adjust, there is an important role for government policy. These economists believe government polices generally serve the public interest. Because market failure problems will be serious, market failure is worse than potential government failure for this camp. Therefore, the "No—Markets Fail to Quickly Self-Adjust" economists argue for an essential, hands-on role for government.

Politicians on the left of the political spectrum—Federal Liberals, New Democrats, and the Bloc Québécois—fit into this camp, supporting a hands-on role for government. They believe that if left alone, the market economy will produce inequality in rising living standards, with considerable economic insecurity and hardship for those who do not possess skills that the market values. Government has a responsibility to maintain a social safety net to support the economic welfare of citizens left behind by markets, especially labour markets.

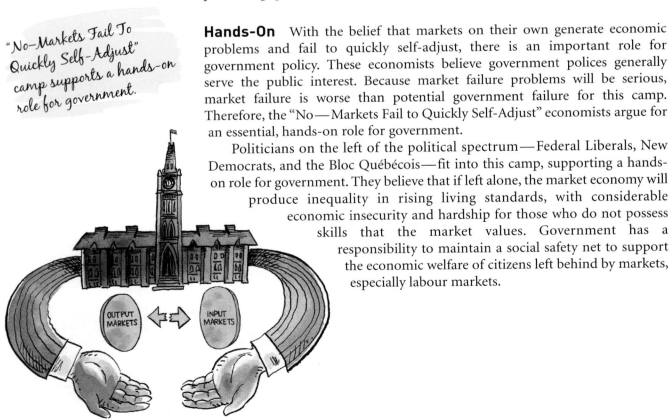

The Fundamental Macroeconomic Question: Comparing Camps

Figure 1.2 is a good study device for reviewing the differences between the two camps. We will be revisiting these differences throughout the following chapters. By the time you finish this course, you should be in a position to decide which camp makes the most sense to how you see the world.

Figure 1.2	The Fundamental Macroeconomic Question	
If left alone by government, do the price mechanisms of market economies adjust quickly to maintain steady growth in living standards, full employment, and stable prices?		
Answer	**Yes — Left Alone, Markets Quickly Self-Adjust**	**No — Left Alone, Markets Fail to Quickly Self-Adjust**
Fallacy of Composition	Macroeconomic and microeconomic outcomes the same	Macroeconomic and microeconomic outcomes different
Origins of Business Cycles	Causes external to markets; government policy	Causes internal to markets; coordination failures between input and output markets; money, banking, expectations
Which Failure is Worse?	Government failure	Market failure
Role for Government	Hands-off	Hands-on
Political Spectrum	Right — Conservative Party of Canada, Libertarian	Left — Liberal Party of Canada, New Democrats, Bloc Québécois, Green

Refresh 1.2

1. What is the fundamental macroeconomic question?

2. In your own words, list the key arguments for each side of the hands-off versus hands-on debate.

3. Ask your instructor which side of the debate she/he tends to support. From your own current experience and economic understanding, which side do you tend to support? Explain why.

www.myeconlab.com

1.3 Does the Economy Measure Up? GDP, Unemployment, and Inflation

Define three key measures of macroeconomic performance, and identify good outcomes for each.

By the time you finish this book, if I have done my job well you will better understand the world around you, see more clearly the connections between your personal choices and outcomes for Canada, and be able to use your knowledge to support politicians and policy proposals that you think best for your future. But right now, I'll bet your brain hurts from reading about abstract, fundamental questions about the speed of the self-adjusting properties of market economies.

So you will be relieved to hear that this section presents more basic and familiar topics—how we define and measure living standards, unemployment, and inflation—topics you see in the media all of the time.

These basic topics are our building blocks. Look again at the definition of macroeconomics, but notice the newly italicized words—macroeconomics analyzes the *performance* of the whole Canadian economy and the global economy, the combined *outcomes* of all individual microeconomic choices.

How do we evaluate the performance of the Canadian economy? You guessed it—by measuring the key outcomes: living standards, unemployment, and inflation.

Gross Domestic Product (GDP)

Gross domestic product (GDP): value of all final products and services produced annually in Canada

The most important concept for understanding your standard of living, and perhaps the most basic macroeconomic concept, is **gross domestic product** or **GDP**. GDP is the value of all final products and services produced annually in a country.

Look again at the circular flow diagram (reproduced in the margin). GDP measures the value of all of the products and services produced and sold in the output markets on the left side of the diagram. The outputs must be produced in Canada—domestically, not in other countries—and we measure the value produced in a calendar year. In Chapter 2 we will examine more details about how GDP is defined (what are "final" products/services, price versus quantity changes) and measured, and explore data about what GDP has been in Canada from the Great Depression to the present.

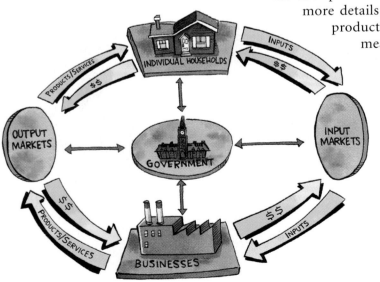

In general, the higher the GDP, the more products and services there are to satisfy our wants. Higher levels of GDP per person mean higher living standards.

Measure In judging the performance of an economy, higher GDP per person is good, and lower GDP per person is bad. It is also better to have "steady growth" in GDP: continuous, yearly increases (good) rather than cyclical ups and then downs in GDP (bad).

Unemployment

In a market economy, to be able to buy products and services in output markets, you usually must earn income by selling something you own in input markets. For most households, that means finding a job—selling your capacity to work in labour markets to a business.

While we have it on the authority of the Beatles that "money can't buy you love," money buys everything else in a market economy, and is necessary for survival. That is why not having a job, and not earning money, is such a serious hardship.

A person is counted as **unemployed** if she is not employed *and* actively seeking work. If you are voluntarily staying at home to look after your kids, or are retired, you are not counted as unemployed. The unemployment rate is calculated as the number of people unemployed as a percentage of the total number of people both employed and unemployed. If 93 people are employed, and 7 people are not employed and seeking work, the unemployment rate is 7 percent $(7 \div (93 + 7))$.

In Chapter 3 we will examine more details about how unemployment is defined and measured, and explore data about unemployment in Canada.

unemployed:
not employed and
actively seeking work

Measure In general, a higher unemployment rate is bad (more people out of work) and a lower unemployment rate is good.

Inflation

In microeconomics, the price of a particular product/service rises or falls with changes in demand and supply. In macroeconomics, **inflation** refers to a rise in the average level of all prices in an economy. When an economy is experiencing inflation, the average price level is rising and the value of money is falling. If, on average, products that used to cost $100 cost $104 a year later, the inflation rate for that year is 4 percent. The flip side of inflation is a falling value of money. If products that used to cost $100 now cost $104, your hundred dollar bill no longer buys as much as it did last year. Money has fallen in value.

In Chapter 3 we will examine more details about how inflation is defined and measured using the Consumer Price Index, and present data about inflation in Canada.

inflation:
rising average prices
and falling value
of money

▶ This worker needs millions of dollars to buy a few groceries in Zimbabwe in 2008. While this level of inflation is not common, it happens when a country's currency loses its value. If money is losing its value at this rate, how can a business price its products/services?

Measure In general, higher and unpredictable inflation rates are bad and lower and predictable inflation rates are good. Mild and steady inflation is not as serious a problem as is unemployment. But if average prices go down, that is defined as deflation—a fall in the average level of prices. This can be a serious problem, which we will discuss in Chapter 3.

These concepts of GDP, unemployment, and inflation are important performance indicators for almost every aspect of macroeconomics. As a bonus, once we can measure these key outcomes, the results will help you evaluate the fundamental claims of the two camps of economists—whether or not market economies maintain steady growth in living standards, full employment, and stable prices.

Refresh

1.3

www.myeconlab.com

1. In your own words, define GDP, the unemployment rate, inflation, and deflation.

2. Explain how the value of your money is connected to inflation.

3. Use the three measures in this section to describe what a healthy economy would look like.

1.4 Can't Tell the Players without a Scorecard: Macroeconomic Players

Identify five groups of macroeconomic players and their choices.

How do we connect smart individual choices from microeconomics to macroeconomic outcomes such as GDP, unemployment, and inflation? One way we will move from a single tree to the whole forest is to organize individuals into groups, based on similar choices among members of the group. We have already begun this collecting with the map of the circular flow of economic life, Figure 1.1, which groups individuals into households, businesses, and government. We used this map constantly in microeconomics (see Appendix A), and will continue to use it in macroeconomics.

But the circular flow of Figure 1.1 needs more information to adequately explain macroeconomic outcomes. The scale of a map is crucial to its usefulness. If you want to drive across Manitoba on the Trans-Canada highway, a detailed map of downtown Winnipeg will not help you much. To get the missing information needed for macroeconomics, we must add two more groups of players—banks and other countries with whom we trade.

Let's look at each of the five groups of players, whose combined choices produce macroeconomic outcomes. For each group, we'll highlight the most important choices to focus on.

Households as Consumers

Individuals in households supply labour and other inputs in input markets, and use the income they earn to buy products and services in output markets. For our macroeconomic map, we will focus on the choices households make about spending the money they have earned. Because of this focus on spending, we will rename this group of players as *consumers*.

Consumer Choices   You have two major choices as a consumer. First, you can spend your money or save it. Second, you can buy Canadian-produced products/services, or buy products/services imported from other countries. With our focus on the forest instead of the trees, we will not be concerned about microeconomic choices such as whether you buy a Nokia cell phone or a Motorola, or if you eat out in a restaurant or cook dinner at home.

Consumer choices are: to spend or save; to buy Canadian products/services or imports.

Businesses

Businesses hire labour and other inputs from consumers in input markets, and sell the products/services produced with those inputs in output markets. Businesses also make decisions about expanding their output by building new factories and buying new machinery. Economists call business purchases of new factories and equipment **investment spending**.

We will not be concerned about microeconomic business choices such as whether a dairy produces more milk or more cream, or whether Ford produces more cars or more trucks.

investment spending: business purchases of new factories and equipment

Business Choices   Business input choices are similar to those made by consumers. They include hiring labour or not, and buying inputs domestically or importing inputs from other countries. In selling their output, businesses can choose to sell domestically or to export products/services to other countries—wherever profits are highest. And growing businesses make investment spending choices, purchasing new equipment or not—and again from domestic or foreign suppliers.

Government

Government, besides setting the legal rules of the game for all economic activity, can choose to interact, or not, in almost any aspect of the economy. We will use *government* to represent all levels of government—federal, provincial, and municipal. But our explanation of government choices will focus largely on the federal government, the Government of Canada.

Government Choices There are a great many possible government choices. We will focus on just two: government purchases of products/services, and government taxes and transfer payments.

When the government hires guides to work for Parks Canada (called "Visitor Experience Managers!") or contracts private construction companies to build new highways, those are purchases of services and products. Government uses tax revenues, collected from personal and corporate income taxes and from the GST (goods and services tax), to pay for purchases. Government also makes transfer payments to consumers, such as Employment Assistance for the unemployed, Old Age Security payments to seniors, and the Canada Child Tax Benefit to low-income families. Transfers are negative taxes, where the government gives you money instead of taking it away.

Government policy decisions to purposefully leave the economy alone or influence it—hands-off or hands-on—take two forms. **Fiscal policy** involves changes in government purchases and taxes/transfers intended to achieve the macroeconomic outcomes of steady growth, full employment, and stable prices. Monetary policy is the responsibility of the Bank of Canada, which is discussed in the next section.

Bank of Canada and the Banking System

The Bank of Canada, together with the system it oversees of chartered banks, credit unions, caisse populaires (in Québec), and trust and mortgage loan companies, is one new player in macroeconomics. The banking system takes deposits of money from consumers and businesses, and makes loans to consumers and businesses. The Bank of Canada is Canada's central bank, responsible for supervising the banking system, financial markets, and conducting monetary policy.

Bank of Canada and Banking System Choices The key choice for banks is whether to make loans or not. The quantity of loans made by the banking system has a large impact on macroeconomic outcomes.

The Bank of Canada chooses **monetary policy**, which involves changes in interest rates and the supply of money, aimed at achieving the macroeconomic outcomes of steady growth, full employment, and stable prices.

Rest of the World (R.O.W.)

Our main focus is on the Canadian economy. But Canada is a relatively small player in the global economy and has extensive trading relationships with many countries, especially the United States. What goes on in these other countries has a large impact on macroeconomic outcomes here in Canada. Because of those trading relationships, it is said "When the United States sneezes, Canada catches a cold." The Great Recession in the United States meant Americans bought far fewer Canadian exports, which in turn helped push Canada into a recession.

R.O.W. Choices Countries in the rest of the world can choose to buy Canadian products/services (exports from Canada) and sell the products/services they produce to us (imports to Canada). There are similar choices about where to invest money. Canadians can invest money in banks and financial assets in other countries, and the R.O.W. can invest money in Canadian banks. Exchanges of exports, imports, and money all require conversions from Canadian dollars into other currencies, so these choices determine the quantity of Canadian dollars demanded. Those demands affect the value of the Canadian dollar (the topic of Chapter 6).

With this overview of the five groups of macroeconomic players—consumers, businesses, government, the banking system, and the rest of the world—along with their key choices, we can move on to look in more detail at the economic outcomes that their choices combine to create.

R.O.W. choices: buying Canadian exports and selling imports to Canada; investing money in Canada, or accepting Canadian investments; demanding Canadian dollars.

Refresh 1.4

1. List the five key macroeconomic players and the macro-related choices they can make.

2. Can any one of the macroeconomic players be considered more important than the others? Explain your answer.

3. Create a simple cause-and-effect diagram that illustrates how a decision of one macroeconomic player affects you directly.

www.myeconlab.com

1.5 Focusing on Your Future:
Living Standards, Voting, and Macroeconomics

Explain three MAPS for focusing your thinking like a macroeconomist.

If I haven't yet convinced you that your future success in life depends on macroeconomics, this last section should do it. What makes macroeconomics personally important for you, long beyond passing this course? Here are the top three reasons.

Your Economic Future

Reason number one: Your personal economic success will depend on the macroeconomic performance of the economy. The three most important performance measures are GDP, unemployment, and inflation.

GDP Most generally, GDP per person indicates average standards of living. The higher the GDP per person, the more products and services there are to satisfy your wants, and everyone else's, too. A higher GDP per person indicates a better living standard.

Unemployment   Unemployment affects the odds of your finding a well-paying job that you also enjoy. When the unemployment rate is high, jobs are hard to find, and you compete against many others eager to land the same job you are after. Employers have the upper hand in bargaining over wages and working conditions. If you are an employer hiring during periods of high unemployment, you can choose your new hire from a large pool of qualified applicants.

When the unemployment rate is low, jobs are more plentiful, and employers are the ones competing against each other for the relatively scarce workers they need. Workers get their pick among jobs, and gain an advantage in bargaining.

Unemployment tends to be inversely related (when one goes up, the other goes down) to growth in levels of GDP. As GDP goes up, unemployment goes down. When the economy is growing, measured in terms of increases in the total value of products/services produced, unemployment falls.

Inflation   Inflation can affect your standard of living. If your income is not rising as fast as the prices of what you buy, your income will buy less. Similarly, inflation erodes the purchasing power of your savings—those unchanged dollars buy fewer products/services. When prices are rising, the same amount of money has lower purchasing power.

These three key macroeconomic outcomes are closely tied to your material well-being.

Your Vote Matters

Reason number two: As a citizen, you vote for governments that make policy decisions that influence our economy's performance—GDP, unemployment, and inflation. Those policies could make the difference between boom and bust, between steady growth in living standards and prolonged recession—in other words, your economic future. Politicians will ask you to support policies based on either a hands-off or hands-on view of the market economy. You can best make an informed choice by understanding the basics of macroeconomics and using that knowledge to come to your own conclusion on the fundamental macroeconomic question: If left alone by government, do the price mechanisms of market economies adjust quickly to maintain steady growth in living standards, full employment, and stable prices? This course (and this book) provides you with key tools you need to answer that question.

You Too Can Think Like a Macroeconomist

Reason number three: If you learn to think like an economist, you will be better able to understand the world around you and make smarter choices for personal success. Will the rising value of the Canadian dollar eliminate the manufacturing jobs you are training for? Based on the Bank of Canada's monetary policy, will you save money by choosing a fixed or variable interest rate mortgage? Fortunately, you don't need to be fully trained as an economist to answer these questions and think like an economist.

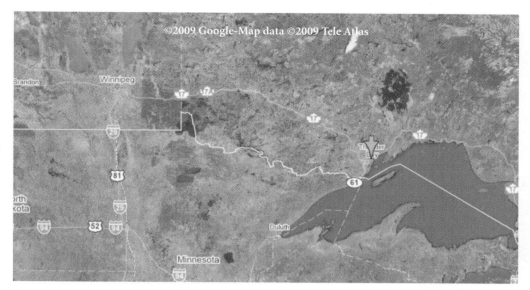

©2009 Google-Map data ©2009 Tele Atlas

Hybrid map of part of Canada along the Trans-Canada Highway—useful for trip planning.

In microeconomics, there are three simple keys to smart individual choices (see FYI on this page and Appendix A). Macroeconomics is not about individual choices, but about the combined outcome of those choices. To think like a macroeconomist, to understand how the economy as a whole works, and how well it performs, the key is to focus on targeted aspects of the economy. The Canadian economy, with all of its complexity and its connections to the banking system, changeable expectations, and to the global economy, may appear overwhelming. My goal is to provide you with maps as guides. They will focus your attention on the most important aspects of the economy, and leave other information in the background. Just as road maps help you find your way in a strange country, the MAPS icons shown on page 24 will guide your journey through the macroeconomics forest. With these MAPS, difficult decisions about which economic policies to support and which personal choices to make, and understanding the complex world around you, will become much simpler.

For a complete explanation of the 3 Keys to Smart Choices, see Appendix A.

MAcroeconomics Positioning System   Today, many of the best maps are digital. Google Earth, the restaurant locator on your iPod touch, or the global positioning system (GPS) in your car all help you find your way. Here is a MAcroeconomics Positioning System (MAPS) to help you find your way through the macroeconomics forest, through media reports on the economy, and through debates on the best economic policies for Canada.

There are three key MAPS.

MAPS 1

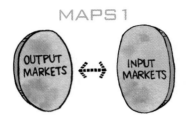

MAPS 1

Focus on the connections between input markets and output markets for both demand and supply sides.

This connection is behind the example that opened the chapter. During tough economic times, people who are unemployed aren't earning incomes, and cut back on spending. Businesses aren't selling enough because individuals aren't buying, and profits are down. But if only businesses would hire the people looking for work, those new employees would earn incomes and buy the unsold products. It seems everyone could be better off, yet that doesn't happen.

Lack of demand in the labour market connects to lack of demand in output markets.

MAPS 2

MAPS 2

Focus on the connections between Canada and the rest of the world.

This connection focuses on the fact that even when nothing has changed in Canada, events in the rest of the world can have a big impact on the Canadian economy. Increased production and competition from China can cause unemployment in Canada. A fall in the value of the Canadian dollar, which makes Canadian exports cheaper for foreigner buyers, can increase the output of Canadian export businesses, increase Canadian GDP, lead to hiring of additional workers in Canada, and cause rising prices of imported goods for Canadian consumers.

MAPS 3

MAPS 3

Focus on the connections between money/banks/expectations and the input and output markets of the circular flow.

This connection is behind the Great Recession which began in 2008. As the housing market bubble burst with changing expectations, problems in the banking sector turned into problems for society as a whole, with falling demand for products/services in output markets and rising unemployment in input markets.

Connections to Key Locations These "connections" between different aspects of the domestic and global economies are usually the key locations determining the success or breakdown of macroeconomic performance. When the economy performs well, as Say's Law predicts, these connections work well in coordinating individuals' decisions and supporting economic growth. When the economy falters, as Keynes predicts it will without government policy assistance, these connections break down and stall economic growth.

Moving On

These MAPS will help you think like a macroeconomist, which in turn will help you achieve personal success, and help you make better, more informed choices as a citizen.

Every time we use a specific MAPS to explain economic events, you will see an icon in the margin. Look for those icons as signposts to guide your macroeconomics journey.

> *Economics does not furnish a body of settled conclusions immediately applicable to policy. It is a method rather than a doctrine, an apparatus of the mind, a technique of thinking which helps its possessor to draw correct conclusions.*
>
> *–John Maynard Keynes*

MAPS 1

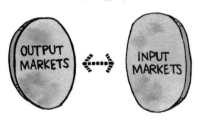

Focus on the connections between input markets and output markets for both demand and supply sides.

MAPS 2

Focus on the connections between Canada and the rest of the world.

MAPS 3

Focus on the connection between money/banks/expectations and the input and output markets of the circular flow.

Refresh 1.5

1. List the three key measures of macroeconomic performance. In a sentence for each, explain how understanding them could help you make better choices for your own future.

2. Review the three MAPS developed in this section. In your own words (point form is fine), explain what each means.

3. Over the next week, make a note each time you see, hear, or read about the three key measures of macroeconomic performance. Include where it occurred and to what it was referring.

www.myeconlab.com

Are Your Smart Choices *Smart for All?*

Macroeconomics and Microeconomics

CHAPTER SUMMARY

1.1 RECONCILING MACROECONOMICS AND MICROECONOMICS: IS THE WHOLE GREATER THAN THE SUM OF THE PARTS?

Smart microeconomic choices by individuals may or may not add up to smart macroeconomic outcomes for the economy as a whole. The key question about the relationship between microeconomics and macroeconomics is, "If left alone, do markets quickly self-adjust?"

- The Great Recession of 2008–2009 and the Great Depression of 1929–1933 involved financial bubbles that burst, high unemployment, falling living standards, bankruptcies, as well as government policy mistakes.

- **Macroeconomics** analyzes the performance of the whole Canadian economy and global economy—the combined outcomes of all individual microeconomic choices.

- **Microeconomics** analyzes choices that individuals in households, individual businesses, and governments make, and how those choices interact in markets.

- **Fallacy of composition**—what is true for one is not true for all; whole is greater than the sum of the parts.
  - **paradox of thrift**—attempts to increase savings cause aggregate savings to decrease because of falling employment and incomes.

- The circular flow diagram reduces the complexity of the Canadian economy to three sets of players—households, businesses, and governments.
  - input markets determine incomes;
    households are sellers and businesses are buyers.
  - output markets determine the value of all products/services sold;
    households are buyers and businesses are sellers.

- **Business cycles**—ups and downs of overall economic activity.

- The fundamental macroeconomic question: "If left alone by government, do the price mechanisms of market economies adjust quickly to maintain steady growth in living standards, full employment, and stable prices?"
  - "Yes" answer based on **Say's Law**—supply creates its own demand.
  - "No" answer from John Maynard Keynes, founder of macroeconomics in 1930s.

1.2 SHOULD GOVERNMENT BE HANDS-OFF OR HANDS-ON? ECONOMICS AND POLITICS

"If left alone, do markets quickly self-adjust?" The "Yes" and "No" camps differ on the fallacy of composition, causes of business cycles, risk of government failure versus market failure, role for government, and the political spectrum.

- Like J.B. Say and J.M. Keynes, economists and politicians today still disagree about the fundamental macroeconomic question, "If left alone by government, do the price mechanisms of market economies adjust quickly to maintain steady growth in living standards, full employment, and stable prices?"
- Market failure—market outcomes fail to serve the public interest.
- **Government failure**—government policy fails to serve the public interest.
- "Yes—Left Alone, Markets Quickly Self-Adjust" camp believes
  - macroeconomic and microeconomic outcomes are the same.
  - external events or government policy cause business cycles.
  - government failure is worse than market failure.
  - government should be hands-off.
- "No—Left Alone, Markets Fail to Quickly Self-Adjust" camp believes
  - fallacy of composition—macroeconomic and microeconomic outcomes different.
  - markets cause business cycles through coordination failures, roles of money, banking, and expectations.
  - market failure is worse than government failure.
  - government should be hands-on.
- Politicians on the right tend to be in "Yes" camp, government as hands-off.
- Politicians on the left tend to be in "No" camp, government as hands-on.

1.3 DOES THE ECONOMY MEASURE UP? GDP, UNEMPLOYMENT, INFLATION

The most important outcome measures of the performance of the Canadian economy are living standards (related to GDP per person), unemployment, and inflation.

- Gross domestic product (GDP)—value of all final products and services produced annually in Canada.
- You are **unemployed** if not employed and actively seeking work.
- **Inflation**—rising average prices and falling value of money.

The five groups of macroeconomic players are consumers, businesses, government, Bank of Canada and the banking system, and the rest of the world. Each group has different choices.

- Consumer choices:
  - spend income or save.
  - buy Canadian products/services or imports.
- Business choices:
  - **investment spending**—business purchases of new factories and equipment—domestically or from foreign suppliers.
  - hiring workers or not.
  - buying inputs domestically or importing.
  - selling outputs domestically or exporting.
- Government choices:
  - purchases of products/services.
  - taxes and transfer payments.
  - **fiscal policy**—changes in government purchases and taxes/transfers to achieve macroeconomic outcomes of steady growth, full employment, and stable prices.
- Bank of Canada and Banking System choices:
  - **monetary policy**—Bank of Canada changes interest rates and the supply of money to achieve macroeconomic outcomes of steady growth, full employment, and stable prices.
  - making loans or not.
- Rest of World (R.O.W.) choices:
  - buying Canadian exports and selling imports to Canada.
  - investing money in Canada or accepting Canadian investments.
  - demanding Canadian dollars.

1.5 FOCUSING ON YOUR FUTURE: LIVING STANDARDS, VOTING, AND MACROECONOMICS

Macroeconomics affects your future—GDP per person affects living standards, unemployment affects the odds of your finding a job, and inflation can reduce your living standards. Macroeconomics also informs your vote for politicians and policies influencing economic performance, and illuminates the important parts of complex economies.

- Your personal economic success depends on
  - GDP—higher GDP per person allows higher living standards.
  - unemployment—affects odds of your finding a job.
  - inflation—can reduce living standards if income not rising as fast as prices of what you buy.

- Your understanding of macroeconomics informs your vote for politicians whose economic policy choices influence economic performance and therefore your economic success.

- Thinking like a macroeconomist means focusing on targeted aspects of the economy. Three key MAPS (MAcroeconomic Positioning Systems) for finding those targets are

    - MAPS 1
    Focus on the connection between input markets and output markets, for both demand and supply sides.

    - MAPS 2
    Focus on connections between Canada and the rest of the world.

    - MAPS 3
    Focus on the connections between money/banks/expectations and the input and output markets of the circular flow.

TRUE/FALSE

Circle the correct answer.

A tall man wearing an expensive suit and tinted sunglasses walks into the coffee shop where you are studying. He notices your macroeconomics textbook and says:

"I have a top secret mission for you. We've detected aliens on the Planet of Plutonomics. Some of these aliens look like Klingons from the Star Trek movies and some look like Yoda from the Star Wars movies. We need you to verify whether our findings about their economy—based on satellite images—are true or false."

Use this scenario to answer questions 1–15.

1.1 RECONCILING MACRO AND MICRO

1. Klingon look-alikes are working in exchange for money, and paying money to purchase products and services. This evidence suggests that there are input and output markets.

    True   **False**

2. Yoda look-alikes are paying taxes, and some are receiving transfer payments from the government. This evidence suggests that the government is part of the circular flow of economic life.

    True   **False**

3. Every government worker on the Planet of Plutonomics is a superstar at solving microeconomic problems. Therefore, the government of the Planet of Plutonomics must be a superstar at solving macroeconomic problems.

    True   **False**

4. Every government worker on the Planet of Plutonomics is a superstar at solving macroeconomic problems. Therefore, the government of the Planet of Plutonomics must be a superstar at solving macroeconomic problems.   **True**   **False**

1.2 HANDS-OFF OR HANDS-ON?

5. A study reveals that government policies on the Planet of Plutonomics were based on the special interests of female Yoda look-alikes rather than on the public interest, resulting in a high level of unemployment for men. This evidence suggests that the high unemployment level for men could have been caused by government failure.   **True**   **False**

6. A political party on the Planet of Plutonomics called the Laissez-Faire-Isn't-Fair Party believes that government policy can improve market outcomes by acting in the public interest. This evidence suggests that this political party prefers a hands-on approach.   **True**   **False**

7. A political party on the Planet of Plutonomics called the Lazy Far Right Party believes that an invisible hand promotes efficiency and raises living standards. This evidence suggests that this political party prefers a hands-on approach.   **True**   **False**

1.3 MEASURING GDP, UNEMPLOYMENT, INFLATION

8. The GDP per person on the Planet of Plutonomics has steadily declined in recent years. This evidence suggests that their standard of living is increasing.   **True**   **False**

9. The level of unemployment on the Planet of Plutonomics has steadily increased in recent years. This evidence suggests that their situation is improving.   **True**   **False**

10. The prices of iPods, Bridgestone tires, slim-fitting jeans, Dippity-Do hair gel, piercings, and tattoos are all rising on the Planet of Plutonomics. This evidence suggests that inflation is occurring in their economy.   **True**   **False**

11. There are lots of hot dogs on the Planet of Plutonomics, but no hot dog buns. This evidence suggests that they could benefit from exporting to and importing from the rest of the universe.　　**True**　　**False**

12. The Planet of Plutonomics does not use Canadian dollars. This evidence suggests that they would never be able to buy Canadian exports.　　**True**　　**False**

13. The Planet of Plutonomics is not using monetary policy in the current recession. This evidence suggests that their central bank will not have a role to play in helping the economy out of a financial crisis.　　**True**　　**False**

1.5 SUCCESS, VOTING, AND MAPS

14. The high level of unemployment on the Planet of Plutonomics suggests that workers have the advantage in bargaining with employers.　　**True**　　**False**

15. If you were thinking of investing in the Planet of Plutonomics, the only MAPS that would be relevant to you would be MAPS2.　　**True**　　**False**

MULTIPLE CHOICE

Circle the correct answer.

1.1 RECONCILING MACRO AND MICRO

1. What do the Great Depression and Great Recession have in common?
   A) Both were great for depression.
   B) Both had a stock market crash.
   C) Both experienced a rise in prices.
   D) Both had government programs like employment insurance.

2. Who is to blame for inflating the housing price bubble?
   A) Homeowners
   B) Mortgage lenders
   C) Banks and other financial institutions
   D) All of the above

3. During the Great Recession, all of the following indicators fell *except*

    A) stock market values.

    B) unemployment.

    C) housing prices.

    D) asset prices.

4. Say's Law claims that

    A) supply is greater than demand.

    B) demand is greater than supply.

    C) supply creates its own demand.

    D) demand creates its own supply.

1.2 HANDS-OFF OR HANDS-ON?

5. Those favouring a government hands-off approach argue that

    A) markets will self-adjust.

    B) markets will quickly self-adjust.

    C) markets will not quickly self-adjust.

    D) markets will quickly-self adjust if left alone by government.

6. Which political party is most likely to support a hands-off approach by government?

    A) Liberal Party of Canada

    B) Conservative Party of Canada

    C) NDP

    D) Bloc Québécois

1.3 MEASURING GDP, UNEMPLOYMENT, INFLATION

7. The performance of the Canadian economy is measured by the key outcome(s) of

    A) GDP.

    B) unemployment.

    C) inflation.

    D) All of the above

8. Which of the following individuals would count as unemployed?

    A) A full-time student

    B) An ex-student who has graduated and is looking for work

    C) An ex-student who has graduated but is not looking for work

    D) An ex-student who has graduated and is working

9. Inflation is a rise in the

    A) average price level in the economy.

    B) value of money.

    C) quantity of products/services in the economy.

    D) standard of living in the economy.

10. Purchases of new factories and equipment by businesses are called

    A) stock investments.

    B) investment spending.

    C) labour costs.

    D) exports.

11. Transfer payments by governments to consumers include

    A) Employment Insurance for the unemployed.

    B) Old Age Security payments to seniors.

    C) Canadian Child Tax Benefit payments to low-income families.

    D) All of the above

12. Monetary policy is the responsibility of the

    A) Bank of Montreal.

    B) Bank of Nova Scotia.

    C) Bank of Canada.

    D) Government of Canada.

1.5 SUCCESS, VOTING, AND MAPS

13. The amount of unemployment in the economy matters to your personal economic success because it affects your ability to

    A) find a job.

    B) bargain for higher wages.

    C) bargain for better working conditions.

    D) All of the above

14. When unemployment increases,

    A) the chance of finding a job decreases.

    B) GDP increases.

    C) the economy is growing.

    D) All of the above

15. Which of the following is *not* part of the MAcroeconomics Positioning System (MAPS)?

    A) Connection between households and consumers

    B) Connection between input and output markets

    C) Connections between Canada and the rest of the world

    D) Connection between money/banks/expectations and input and output markets

SHORT ANSWER

Write a short answer to each question. Your answer may be in point form.

1. The "trees" and the "forest" can be used to distinguish microeconomics from macroeconomics.

   A) Which "economics" looks at the trees? Which looks at the forest?

   B) According to Adam Smith, how do we achieve a healthy forest?

2. Smart choices by people and businesses do not necessarily imply that smart choices are being made for the economy as a whole. Explain how the fallacy of composition applies to each of the following scenarios.

   A) Producers decide to increase the output of their product or service.

   B) Consumers decide to save more of their income.

3. Suppose that you're at a party when the topic of the Great Recession comes up. People are wondering what caused the recession. Luckily a balloon is nearby, which you use as a prop to demonstrate the housing price bubble and burst of the Great Recession.

   A) Why did the housing prices balloon inflate?

   B) Why did the housing prices balloon burst?

4. Economies around the world have been seriously affected by the financial crisis and housing market crash that began in the U.S. in 2007. By October 2008, most economies around the world were in a recession. In March 2009, the International Monetary Fund (IMF) said that global output will probably fall for the first time since the Second World War.

   A) Explain why developments in the rest of the world really matter for Canada.

   B) The World Bank expects the fastest contraction of trade since the Great Depression. Output has shrunk even faster in countries dependent on exports, particularly exports with falling world prices. Explain how this affects income for countries that rely heavily on these exports.

5. In October 2008, employment had reached an all-time high in Canada. Between October 2008 and October 2009, total employment declined by 400 000 jobs, while the unemployment rate rose from 6.3 percent to 8.6 percent.

   A) Using MAPS 1, explain how the job losses could be linked to the decreasing quantities of products and services produced.

   B) Why are government transfers, like Employment Insurance, called "negative taxes"?

   C) Are government transfers an example of fiscal or monetary policy?

6. The Great Recession is reopening one of the most hotly debated questions in macro economics—the choice between government spending (fiscal policy) and interest rate changes (monetary policy) to stimulate demand and get people back to work. Between the 1930s and the 1950s, most macroeconomists agreed that government spending increases and tax cuts were essential for avoiding deep recessions. From the 1960s until now, a more common view was that interest rate cuts by the Central Bank, which made it cheaper for businesses and consumers to borrow money and then spend it, were the best way to fight downturns.

A) Between the 1930s and 1950s, did macroeconomists favour fiscal or monetary policy?

B) From the 1960s until now, did most macroeconomists favour fiscal or monetary policy?

7. Canada's Economic Action Plan will provide about $62 billion in stimulus over 2009 and 2010. According to estimates from the International Monetary Fund, Canada's fiscal stimulus package (as a percentage of GDP) is among the largest in the world.

A) If modern supporters of Say's Law and Keynes were bloggers, which would be more likely to post a support message for these stimulus packages? Why?

B) Should Canadians support stimulus packages by other countries? (Hint: use your MAPS.)

8. In April 2009, the Bank of Canada reduced interest rates to their lowest possible levels. The Bank of Canada believes this is the appropriate policy to move the economy back to full production capacity and to achieve price stability.

A) What key measures would you look at to determine if the performance of the economy improves?

B) In October 2009, the Bank of Canada projected that Canadian GDP (measured in quantities of products/services) will decline by 2.4 percent in 2009 and grow by 3.0 percent in 2010 and by 3.3 percent in 2011. After declines in 2009, inflation is expected to gradually return to 2 percent by the third quarter of 2011. Explain why living standards are expected to be better in 2011 than in 2009.

9. You can categorize macroeconomists based on whether they believe a hands-off or hands-on approach by government is needed to help the economy quickly self-adjust. If there were two Facebook groups—one hands-off and one hands-on—which of these Facebook groups would these economists likely fall in?

A) Milton Friedman has argued that government changes in the money supply explain all of the economy's ups and downs.

B) Robert Lucas Jr. has made the case that large-scale government attempts to stimulate the economy are unlikely to succeed over time.

C) Paul Krugman has argued for the importance of large-scale government spending to avoid a sustained depression.

D) The President of the United States, Barack Obama, has stated that, "There is no disagreement that we need action by our government, a recovery plan that will help to jump-start the economy."

E) Lawrence Summers has argued that monetary policy may be insufficient in the current situation and that further fiscal stimulus may be necessary.

F) The IMF's *World Economic Outlook* (April 2009) states that: "Monetary policy has typically played an important role in ending recessions and strengthening recoveries, although it is less effective during financial crises. Fiscal policy appears to be more reliably helpful in these episodes."

10. Economists in the tradition of Adam Smith and J. B. Say believe that price and wage adjustment quickly leads to full employment in the short run. Keynesians, on the other hand, argue that full employment can only be achieved in the long run, since prices and wages are "sticky" in the short run (meaning they do not quickly adjust to changes in economic conditions).

A) Would price and wage stickiness support a hands-on approach from government in the short run? Why or why not?

B) Why might businesses have difficulty reducing wages in response to unemployment?

C) A business may be willing to hire more workers if wages are lower. However, explain what may happen to employment if all businesses pay lower wages.
(Hint: think about the fallacy of composition.)

---

myeconlab Visit the MyEconLab website at **www.myeconlab.com**. This online homework and tutorial system puts you in control of your own learning with study and practice tools.

Up Around the Circular Flow

GDP, Economic Growth, and Business Cycles

LEARNING OBJECTIVES

2.1 Differentiate nominal GDP, real GDP, and real GDP per person, and how each relates to living standards.

2.2 Explain how economic growth occurs and how it is measured.

2.3 Describe the language of business cycles, including output gaps as a target for hands-on policymakers.

2.4 Explain how value added and the equality of aggregate spending and aggregate income allow us to measure GDP.

2.5 Identify five limitations of real GDP per person as a measure of well-being.

WHY WAS MY GRANDPARENTS' standard of living so different from ours? My grandfather and grandmother were born in the 1890s, "dated" on horseback, and lived through the Great Depression. They took in boarders to make ends meet, and their apartment had few closets since, like many people, they had only a few changes of clothing. Although the prices they paid for products seem unimaginably low (10 cents for a silent movie, 15 cents for a pound of sausages), wages were also low. In 1935, the average wage for a Canadian factory worker, working 44 hours per week, was $870 a year. That's about 38 cents per hour!

What determined my grandparents' standard of living, and our much higher standard of living today? The answer has everything to do with GDP—gross domestic product. In this chapter, we will explore the challenges involved in measuring GDP. You will learn how to compare Canadian GDP over different years. You will come to understand how changes in technology, productivity, quantities, prices, and incomes all affect GDP and our standard of living. Of those changes, you will learn which increase living standards, and which cause fluctuations around a generally upward trend that allows us to enjoy walk-in closets, 3-D movies, and many highly specialized products and services. And what changes in our living standards does GDP totally miss?

While the term *GDP* sounds awfully boring, it is the stuff of the stories you may tell to your grandchildren about what life was like when you were young, during the Great Recession of 2008–2009.

2.1 Higher Prices, More Stuff, or Both? Nominal GDP and Real GDP

Differentiate nominal GDP, real GDP, and real GDP per person, and how each relates to living standards.

The *gross* in *gross domestic product* is not the *gross* you use in conversations with friends. The dictionary definition of *gross* is "total, aggregate, overall, or combined." Those are definitely macroeconomic words, concerned with the *economy as a whole.* When we measure GDP—the value of *all* final products and services produced annually in a country—we measure the total, or combined, output of the economy.

Because GDP measures so much, any of its individual parts can change over time. To sort out the influence of changes in those different parts, economists have developed more precise measures of GDP—nominal GDP, real GDP, and real GDP per person.

Nominal GDP

nominal GDP: value at current prices of all final products/services produced annually in a country

Nominal GDP is the value *at current prices* of all final products/services produced annually in a country. Each word and phrase in this definition is important. Let's examine these key words and phrases.

Value   The worth, in Canadian dollars, of all the products/services.

Current Prices   To add together the value of all automobiles, piercings, movies, and every other final product and service, take the price of each and multiply by the quantity produced. Nominal GDP uses current prices, which means that to calculate nominal GDP for 1935, we use the prices and quantities current in 1935. To calculate nominal GDP for 2008, we use the prices and quantities current in 2008.

We will use abbreviations so we can reduce this huge, macro-size addition problem to a single line. The superscript letters A, B, C, . . . Z, represent the different products/services. For each product/service, P stands for its price, and Q stands for quantity. Each price (P) and quantity (Q) is for a specific year.

In equations, two letters together indicates multiplication. So PQ means P times Q.

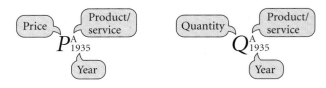

Here's what the calculation of nominal GDP for 1935 looks like.

$$\text{Nominal GDP}_{1935} = P^A_{1935} Q^A_{1935} + P^B_{1935} Q^B_{1935} + P^C_{1935} Q^C_{1935} + \ldots + P^Z_{1935} Q^Z_{1935}$$

The nominal GDP calculation for 2008 is

$$\text{Nominal GDP}_{2008} = P^A_{2008} Q^A_{2008} + P^B_{2008} Q^B_{2008} + P^C_{2008} Q^C_{2008} + \ldots + P^Z_{2008} Q^Z_{2008}$$

This Ford, a fancy car in its time, cost $58 in 1935. A similar car in 2009 cost over $27 000. Price increases contribute to increases in nominal GDP. What other factors contribute to increases in the nominal GDP?

Nominal GDP for Canada in 1935 was $4.3 billion. Nominal GDP for 2008 was $1600 billion. That's 372 times greater! Before you conclude that we are 372 times better off in 2008 than we were in 1935 ($1600 billion divided by $4.3 billion = 372), look again at the two formulas above. In comparing nominal GDPs, notice that the increase from 1935 to 2008 could have been due to changes in prices (for example, if P^A_{2008} is greater than P^A_{1935}—in 1935, gas was 5 cents a litre), or changes in quantities of products/services (if Q^A_{2008} is greater than Q^A_{1935}), or a combination of price and quantity changes.

The source of the increase in nominal GDP makes a big difference. If all of the increase was due to increased prices only, then the higher nominal GDP in 2008 would have the same quantities of products/services as in 1935. We would be no better off. At the other extreme, if all of the increase was due to increased quantities only, then in 2008 we truly would have 372 times as much "stuff" to satisfy our wants compared to 1935. Changes in nominal GDP are due to the combination of many changes including prices and quantities.

Differences in nominal GDP between years are due to either price changes or quantity changes.

Final Products/Services

A final product or service is consumed directly by consumers. A loaf of bread you buy at the supermarket, or your new Honda Civic, are final products. The flour that the bakery purchases as an input to make the bread or the steel Honda purchases to make the car are called intermediate products and are not included in nominal GDP. Why? The value of the intermediate products is already included in the value of the final products, so to add the value of the flour to the value of the bread would be double counting.

Produced Annually

Nominal GDP for any year counts only the products/services produced in that year. Nominal GDP for 2008, for example, would include only those products/services that were actually produced in 2008. Used products, or products produced in previous years but resold later, are not counted as part of nominal GDP. If you resell your 2008 Honda Civic in 2010, its value does not count towards nominal GDP in 2010.

Nominal GDP is measured as a **flow**—an amount per unit of time. Nominal GDP is usually calculated for a period of one year. But economists calculate GDP continuously in order to track and report on how the economy is doing. They provide estimates for each quarter (three months) of a year of economic activity. These quarterly estimates are then added together at the end of the year to yield nominal GDP for the year.

flow: amount per unit of time

In a Country Nominal GDP for Canada includes all final products/services produced within the borders of Canada, no matter what the nationality of the business doing the producing. Honda Civics produced in Alliston, Ontario, are part of Canadian GDP even if the factory is owned and operated by the Japanese head office of Honda. Similarly, Tim Hortons stores in the United States contribute to U.S. GDP, even though the corporation is based in Canada.

Graphing GDP The clearest way to see how nominal GDP changes over time is to put the data into a graph. Figure 2.1 shows nominal GDP (measured in billions of dollars) on the vertical axis, for each year on the horizontal axis. Nominal GDP is the green line, and you can see the dramatic increases over time. (The other line is for real GDP, coming next.)

Figure 2.1 Nominal GDP and Real GDP, 1926–2008

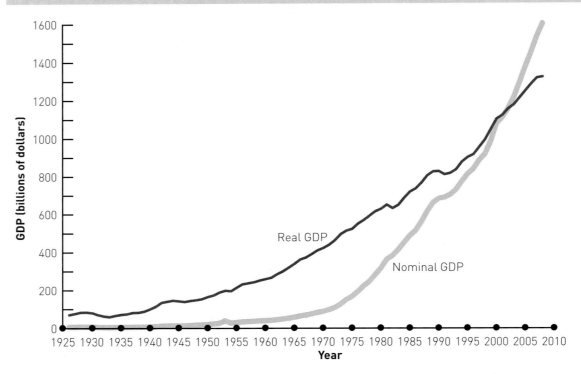

Source: *Historical Statistics of Canada*, 2nd ed., Series F32, F55; Statistics Canada, Table 380-0017.

The words in the definition of nominal GDP are important, as are the calculations and the graph. You will see numbers and graphs of nominal GDP in the media regularly. But we are most interested in how GDP affects us—our standard of living. So how do we sort out how much of the increase in nominal GDP is due to price increases, and how much represents increases in quantities of products/services that make us better off?

Real GDP

Real GDP is the value *at constant prices* of all final products/services produced annually in a country. The only word that is different from the nominal GDP definition is *constant* in place of *current*. By holding prices constant, any differences in real GDP between years must be due to difference in quantities of products/services.

The red line in Figure 2.1 uses 2002 prices to calculate real GDP for every year. If we perform calculations for 1935 and 2008 like those for nominal GDP, but this time for real GDP, we get

$$\text{Real GDP}_{1935} = P^A_{2002} Q^A_{1935} + P^B_{2002} Q^B_{1935} + P^C_{2002} Q^C_{1935} + \ldots + P^Z_{2002} Q^Z_{1935}$$

and

$$\text{Real GDP}_{2008} = P^A_{2002} Q^A_{2008} + P^B_{2002} Q^B_{2008} + P^C_{2002} Q^C_{2008} + \ldots + P^Z_{2002} Q^Z_{2008}$$

By holding prices constant at the 2002 levels, real GDP comparisons eliminate the effects of inflation (or deflation) and isolate the changes in physical quantities of products/services. The red line in Figure 2.1 represents real GDP for each year between 1926 and 2008. Real GDP doesn't rise as steeply as does the green line for nominal GDP. Real GDP in 1935 was $69 billion and in 2008 was $1321 billion. We had about 19 times as much stuff ($1321 billion divided by $69 billion = 19.1) in 2008 as in 1935, which is a much smaller multiple than 372!

To further highlight the difference between nominal GDP and real GDP, Figure 2.2 focuses on just the most recent years, 2002–2008. Because 2002 happens to be the year we use as a standard for constant prices, by definition nominal GDP in 2002 is equal to real GDP in 2002. The increases after 2002 in nominal GDP are greater than the increases in real GDP, because nominal GDP includes both price and quantity increases, while real GDP holds prices constant at the 2002 level and only includes quantity increases.

For answering the fundamental macroeconomic question about how quickly market economies adjust to maintain steady growth in living standards, real GDP provides much more useful information than nominal GDP. For that reason, we will focus on real GDP for the rest of the book, just as economists do.

real GDP: value at constant prices of all final products/services produced annually in a country

Real GDP uses constant prices for a single year to value the quantities of products/services produced in different years. So differences in real GDP between years are due only to changes in quantities.

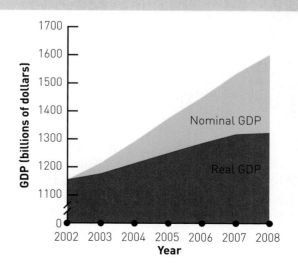

Figure 2.2   Nominal GDP and Real GDP, 2002–2008

Source: Statistics Canada, Table 380-0017.

Real GDP per Person

Real GDP is a better measure than nominal GDP for judging living standards, but there is still a more accurate measurement.

Consider the following question. Measured in constant 2002 U.S. dollars, India's real GDP in 2008 was $427 billion and Israel's was $97 billion. Which country was better off? Israel by far. India has almost a billion people, while Israel has about 6 million. If we calculate GDP per person, it is only $440 in India, but over $16 100 in Israel.

Real GDP per person is equal to real GDP divided by the population of a country. Real GDP per person gives the best measure of a country's ability to meet the material needs of its citizens. Real GDP per person in Canada rose from $7 200 in 1926 to $39 666 in 2008. If we were to graph that trend as a line (coming in Figure 2.3), it rises even more slowly than real GDP because while real GDP was growing, so was the population of Canada, from about 11 million in 1935 to 33 million in 2008.

Each of these measures of GDP gives us some information about what changes—prices or quantities or population—as total economic output has grown over the years. But we have only *measured* the changes. What *causes* the growth of economic output is our next topic.

real GDP per person: real GDP divided by population

Real GDP per person is best measure of country's material standard of living.

Refresh 2.1

1. What is the definition of nominal GDP? What is the one word that is different in the definition of real GDP?

2. In Figure 2.1, explain why the graphs of nominal GDP and real GDP intersect at the year 2002.

3. In your own words, explain why real GDP per person is a more accurate measure of standard of living than nominal GDP.

www.myeconlab.com

2.2 When Macroeconomic Dreams Come True: Potential GDP and Economic Growth

Explain how economic growth occurs and how it is measured.

Have you every been lectured by a parent, teacher, or guidance counsellor about not living up to your potential? Haven't we all? Well, if the economy always lived up to its potential, there would be no lectures from economists or policymakers about how to improve performance. This would be the fairy tale version (where dreams come true) of macroeconomic performance—the ideal hands-off scenario from Chapter 1.

No economists—not those in the hands-off or in the hands-on camps—believe this dream always comes true. But all recognize potential GDP as a key goal that economic performance should strive for in the short run.

A key long-run goal of economic performance is to *increase* the economy's potential for producing products/services. This is the subject of economic growth—how to increase potential GDP over many years in a fast and sustainable way. With more time, economic growth is about how the economy can dream bigger and better dreams.

Potential GDP

Potential GDP is a yearly reference point for a well-functioning market economy, the outcome if Adam Smith's invisible hand works perfectly. Potential GDP is real GDP when all inputs—labour, capital, land (and other resources), and entrepreneurial ability—are fully employed. When real GDP equals potential GDP, the outcome for the economy as a whole is the same as when smart choices of households and smart choices of businesses are coordinated in each separate market. Everyone is getting the most bang per buck for their choices. The whole is equal to the sum of the well-functioning parts.

potential GDP: real GDP when all inputs—labour, capital, land/resources, and entrepreneurial ability—are fully employed

Potential GDP per Person
Just as real GDP per person is a better measure of living standards than is real GDP, potential GDP per person is a better measure of maximum living standards than is potential GDP.

Potential GDP per person is equal to potential GDP divided by the population. Potential GDP per person is the highest material standard of living the economy is normally capable of producing if all existing inputs—labour, capital, land/resources, and entrepreneurship—are fully employed.

potential GDP per person: potential GDP divided by population

Figure 2.3 adds the data for potential GDP per person (the black line) to previous data for real GDP per person.

Figure 2.3 Potential GDP per Person and Real GDP per Person, 1926–2008

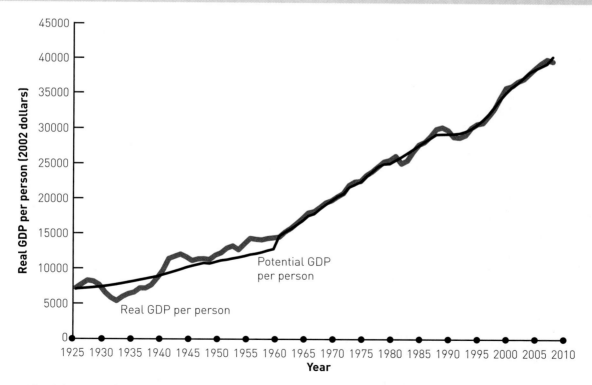

Source: *Historical Statistics of Canada*, 2nd ed., Series F55; Statistics Canada, Table 380-0017, Table 51-001, series v46668, Table 51-0026, series v480567; and author's calculations.

We can examine potential GDP per person more clearly by focusing on a more recent period of time. Figure 2.4 shows potential GDP per person and real GDP per person for the years 1978 to 2008.

Figure 2.4	Potential GDP per Person and Real GDP per Person, 1978–2008

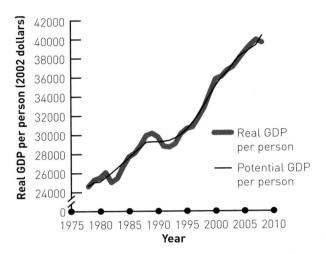

Source: *Historical Statistics of Canada*, 2nd ed., Series F55; Statistics Canada, Table 380-0017, Table 51-0001, series v46668, Table 51-0026, series v480567; and author's calculations.

Notice the similarities between Figures 2.3 and 2.4. First, potential GDP per person increases over time. This is economic growth. Second, real GDP per person fluctuates around potential GDP per person. In some years (1982), real GDP per person is less than potential GDP per person, while in other years (1988), real GDP per person is greater than potential GDP per person. These fluctuations are business cycles. We will next explain economic growth, business cycles, and their relationship.

Sources of Economic Growth

Economic growth is the expansion of the economy's capacity to produce products/services.

Economic growth is caused by increases in the quantity or quality of a country's inputs—its labour, capital, land/resources, and entrepreneurship. These increases enhance the economy's capacity to produce more stuff, increasing potential GDP. Let's look at how changes in quantity and quality for each input contribute to economic growth.

Labour The quantity of labour in a country can increase from growth in the domestic population (caused by more births or a lower death rate due to medical advances) and from immigration. Even for an unchanging population, the quantity of labour inputs supplied to input markets can also increase from an increase in the percentage of the population that works. Economists call this the *labour force participation rate*.

economic growth: expansion of economy's capacity to produce products/services; increase in potential GDP per person

There has been a significant increase in female labour force participation, as you can see from Figure 2.5. Since World War II, more women have been working for many reasons, including having fewer children to raise; labour-saving household appliances like washing machines, clothes dryers, and dishwashers; and changing social attitudes about the role of women.

If you have ever taken care of children or been responsible for cooking and housecleaning, you may be thinking, "what do you mean 'more women working'? It's just working outside the household as opposed to inside!" Then you are anticipating what measurements of GDP miss, which we will discuss in section 2.5.

The quality of labour inputs can increase through training and education. Economists call such quality increases improvements in **human capital**—increased earning potential from work experience, on-the-job training, and education.

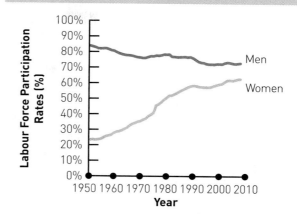

Figure 2.5 Labour Force Participation Rates for Men and Women, 1951–2008

Source: *Historical Statistics of Canada*, 2nd ed., Series D113, D120; Statistics Canada, Table 282-0087.

Capital Capital is the factories and equipment businesses use to produce products/services. When businesses invest in more tools and equipment for their workers to use, they are increasing the quantity of capital. More capital allows workers to produce more. A chef chopping garlic with a food processor can cook more meals than can a chef working only with a knife.

When Paola, the owner of Paola's Piercing and Fingernail Parlour, replaces her old piercing guns with a newly invented piercing gun that allows her employees to double the number of piercings they do in a day, that is an increase in the quality of capital. Economists call improvements in the quality of capital **technological change**.

There are many sources and contributors to technological change. Scientists and engineers, whether they work in universities or corporate research and development laboratories, invent new and better ways of making existing products/services, or new and better products/services. Workers on the assembly line for Toyota who come up with an idea to improve the functioning of the robots they work with are also a source of technological change. Because new technologies are usually embodied in new capital equipment, it is hard to differentiate increases in the quantity of capital from increases in the quality of capital. But both increase potential GDP.

human capital: increased earning potential from work experience, on-the-job training, and education

technological change: improvements in the quality of capital

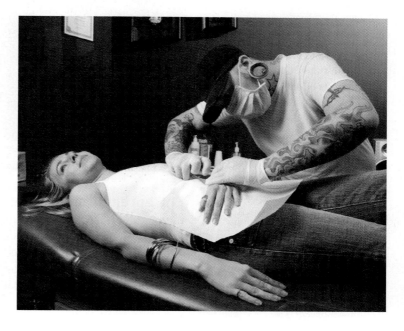

▶ This piercing specialist at Paola's Piercing and Fingernail Parlour is using one of the new piercing guns Paola purchased. This technological change allows him to increase the number of piercings he completes in a day. By investing in better equipment, Paola increases the quality of her capital.

Land and Other Natural Resources

Since the national boundaries of Canada have been set, you may be wondering, "How can you increase the quantity of land?" Good question. The key for increasing potential GDP is to increase the quantity of land *that can contribute to production.* Building the railways in the nineteenth century connected markets in eastern and western Canada with the Prairies. With new markets, it became profitable for prairie farmers to bring previously undeveloped land into production. Just as an increase in labour force participation can increase the quantity of labour even when population is unchanged, the quantity of land can increase even when national boundaries don't change. What is important for increasing potential GDP is *bringing new inputs into the circular flow of markets.*

The discovery of the Hibernia oil fields off the coast of Newfoundland and the discovery of new diamond deposits in Nunavut are also examples of increases in the quantity of land/resources that increase potential GDP. These discoveries don't just happen. They are the result of competitive efforts by businesses and entrepreneurs to find new ways to make profits. Government also plays a role, with the building of the railway and the support for scientific research.

What might appear to be increases in the quality of land/resources is usually due to other factors. When farmers increase the productivity of their land by using fertilizers, the real source of increased output is not better quality land, but better farming techniques using fertilizer as a capital input. Technological change also contributes to increases in the quantity and productivity of land/resources. The invention of new extraction technologies is helping to make Alberta's oil tars sands a profitable "new" resource. Improvements in the "quality" of land and resources are due to these applications of capital or technological change.

▶ Huge trucks and heavy equipment move earth from this open pit mine in the Alberta oil sands. By finding new ways to separate the oil from the sands, such as using super-heated water under extreme pressure, oil companies increase the profitability of their production.

Entrepreneurship

When entrepreneurs come up with improvements in management techniques, corporate organization, or worker/management relations that improve productivity, these also increase potential GDP. Quantity and quality are so interrelated for entrepreneurship that we don't ever try to differentiate them. See Economics Out There for the story of how the CEO of Goldcorp used open source tactics and an online competition to help discover rich new gold deposits.

Expanding the Circular Flow Economic growth happens when increases in the quantity and quality of inputs expand the circular flow. If we choose a moment in time to start the growth story, there is a fixed quantity (and quality) of inputs in an economy. Economists call this a **stock**—an amount at a moment in time. Unlike flows, measurements of stock quantities do not include a time dimension—think of a stock as a snapshot.

The stock of inputs consists of labour (including human capital), capital (including the current state of technology), land/resources, and entrepreneurship. On the basis of this stock of inputs, households, businesses, and government make their best smart choices. Those choices include, for example, going to school (a household choice), investing in new and technologically improved capital equipment (a business choice), or supporting scientific research (a government choice). As a result of those choices, at the end of the flow around the circle, the stock of inputs has changed in quantity and quality, and so has the economy's potential to produce products/services.

The next year starts with that newly expanded stock of inputs. Households, businesses, and government again make their best smart choices. This process where inputs serve as a basis for choices, and choices then transform the stock of inputs, continues in an ever-expanding circle when economic growth progresses smoothly. When Say's Law holds true, market economies maintain steady growth in living standards—as well as full employment and stable prices (coming in Chapter 3).

stock: fixed amount at a moment in time.

Economic growth is caused by increases in the quantity or quality of a country's inputs—its labour, capital, land, and entrepreneurship.

ECONOMICS Out There

Wikinomics

In 1999, a small. struggling Toronto gold-mining firm was headed for bankruptcy. Its fifty-year-old mine in Red Lake, Ontario, seemed to have run dry. Even with a $10-million exploration budget, Goldcorp geologists couldn't locate new gold deposits that they were almost certain were buried on the Red Lake property.

Goldcorp's CEO, Rob McEwan, made a bold and unconventional decision to make public all the secretive and valuable geological data the company had collected going back to 1948. His plan was to use the Internet to "open source" the exploration process.

The "Goldcorp Challenge" offered rewards of over $500 000 to anyone suggesting methods and location estimates for new gold discoveries. Contestants identified 60 targets on the property

that company geologists had missed. More than 80 percent of new targets submitted yielded significant quantities of gold—over 8 million ounces! The untried collaborative process saved 2–3 years of exploration time, dramatically increased productivity, and saved the company. Thanks to Rob McEwan's entrepreneurial decision, the value of Goldcorps' stock increased 300 percent, and he become a wealthy philanthropist.

Source: Don Tapscott and Anthony D. Williams, *Wikinomics: How Mass Collaboration Changes Everything* (New York: Portfolio, 2006).

Measuring Economic Growth Rates

economic growth rate:
annual percentage
change in real GDP
per person

Potential GDP is the dream standard for an economy to achieve. We can measure increases in potential GDP and potential GDP per person. But because dreams don't always come true, macroeconomists judge improvements over time in an economy's actual performance by measuring increases in the real GDP per person the country actually produces.

There is measurable economic growth when real GDP increases over time. The statistic for evaluating economic growth is the **economic growth rate**—the annual percentage change in real GDP per person. The formula is

$$\text{Real GDP per person growth rate (percent)} = \frac{\text{Real GDP per person this year} - \text{Real GDP per person last year}}{\text{Real GDP per person last year}} \times 100$$

For example, if real GDP per person this year is \$42 000, and real GDP per person last year was \$40 000, then

$$\text{Real GDP per person growth rate} = \frac{\$42\ 000 - \$40\ 000}{\$40\ 000} \times 100 = 5 \text{ percent}$$

This means that the total output per person the economy actually produced increased by 5 percent over the year.

Figure 2.6 shows annual growth rates of Canadian real GDP per person since 1926.

Figure 2.6　Annual Growth Rates of Canadian Real GDP per Person, 1926–2008

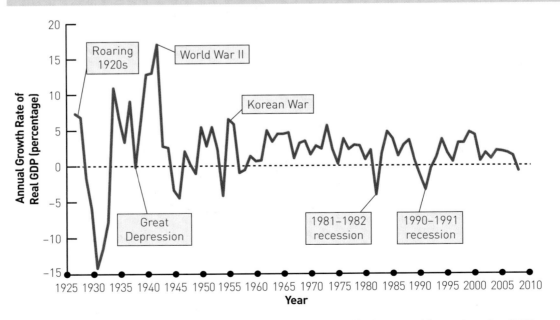

Source: *Historical Statistics of Canada*, 2nd ed., Series F55; Statistics Canada, Table 380-0017, Table 51-0001, series v46668, Table 51-0026, series v480567.

Historical Growth Rates The highest positive rates of annual economic growth occurred in the 1920s (7.4 percent in 1927—one reason they were called the "Roaring '20s"), during World War II wartime production (17.1 percent in 1942), during the U.S. Korean War (5.5 percent in 1952), during the 1960s (4.6 percent from 1964 to 1966), and in the early 1970s (5.7 percent in 1973). Negative growth rates, where real GDP per person actually falls from the previous year, occurred in the Great Depression (−14.1 percent in 1931), in 1982 (−4.0 percent) and 1991 (−3.3 percent) and in the Great Recession of 2008 (−0.7 percent for 2008); the data for 2009 (unavailable at time of writing) are expected to show an even larger downturn.

Over the entire 1926–2008 period, the average annual rate of economic growth of real GDP per person in Canada was 2.1 percent.

Since the purpose of these numbers is to judge economic performance, it is important to understand what the numbers mean. Is 2 percent a "good" number? How much better a number is the 7.4 percent of the Roaring '20s?

What's In a Number? Growth rates for individual years regularly go up and down as a result of business cycles. For long-run changes in living standards, growth rates over longer time spans, like the 2.1 percent over the last 80 years, are more important. Over decades, a market economy whose GDP per person grows at a rate of 2.5 to 3 percent annually is doing very well.

Figure 2.7 shows average annual growth rates in real GDP per person for the industrialized market economies of North America, Europe, Japan, and Australia going back to 1870. Each bar represents a 20-year time span. For most of these 20-year bars, annual growth rates were between 1.2 percent and 2.2 percent. The period of exceptional growth was 1950–1970, with an annual growth rate of almost 4 percent. The average for Canada, of (roughly) the four most recent bars on Figure 2.7 gives the 2.1 percent growth rate.

To take a different historical perspective, the growth rate of real GDP per person in Europe between the years 500 and 1500 was effectively zero! This is one of the reasons this 10-century time span was called the "Dark Ages."

I once thought these small differences in growth rates—1, 2, 4 percent—didn't make much difference. Boy, was I wrong!

Figure 2.7 Growth in Real GDP per Person, Industrialized Countries, 1870–2007

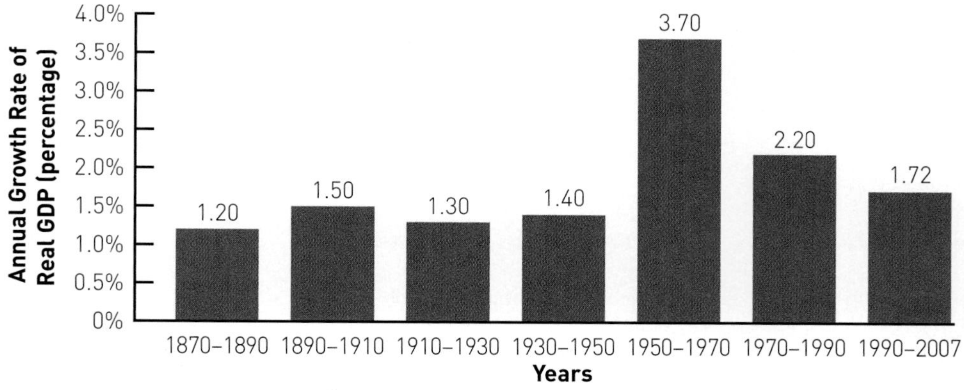

Source: A. Maddison, *Dynamic Forces in Capitalist Development* (1991); World Bank, *World Development Report* (2001–2008).

Compounding and the Rule of 70   What makes small differences so important and powerful is the wonder of compounding.

If you put $100 in a savings account that pays 3 percent interest per year, at the end of the year you have $103. If you leave the money in the account, the second year you earn 3 percent again, but this time on the original $100 and the $3 in interest from the previous year. In year three, you earn 3 percent interest on $106.09 (can you do the calculation for year three?), and the compounding continues as long as you leave your money in the account. How long does it take to double your money?

Don't worry—this is not a dreaded word problem from math class. There is a simple rule that answers the question and illustrates the compounded impact of small differences in growth rates. According to the **Rule of 70**, the number of years it takes for an initial amount to double is roughly 70 divided by the annual percentage growth rate of the amount. For our $100 example, 70 divided by 3 equals 23.3 years to double—to reach $200. Figure 2.8 shows the Rule of 70 for growth rates of 1 to 10 percent.

Rule of 70: number of years it takes for initial amount to double is roughly 70 divided by annual percentage growth rate

Figure 2.8	Rule of 70									
Growth Rate (% per year)	1	2	3	4	5	6	7	8	9	10
Years to Double	70	35	23.3	17.5	14	11.7	10	8.8	7.8	7

The Rule of 70 tells us that, with an average annual growth rate of 2.1 percent (see page 51) between 1926 and 2008, Canadian GDP per person doubles roughly every 35 years (actually, 70 divided by 2.1 equals 33.3 years). That means that over the 80 years, real GDP per person has increased somewhere between 4 times (66.6 years) and 8 times (100 years). The actual number, which requires a bit more calculation, shows Canadian real GDP per person has increased over 6 times (6.1) between 1926 and 2008. We have over 6 times more stuff than my grandparents.

If the growth rate over this entire time span had been 3 percent instead of 2.1 percent, real GDP per person would have increased over 10 times instead of 6.1. In other words, with a 3 percent growth rate, we would be almost twice as well off today as we are currently with our 2.1 percent growth rate. That's almost double the material standard of living for a 0.9 percent difference in annual growth rates! The wonder of compounding comes from the long number of years the compounding is allowed to work. Compounding is the secret to the slogan many banks use, "You work hard for your money; make your money work hard for you."

Productivity, Growth, and Living Standards

Our standard of living has been improving over time because of increases in the quantity and quality of inputs. Just as real GDP per person is the key measure of our standard of living, productivity is the key *source* of our improving standard of living. **Productivity** is usually measured as the quantity of real GDP produced by an hour of labour. Increases in the quantity and quality of inputs increase labour productivity. Not only does that allow an economy to produce more stuff, it also allows us to work fewer hours to be able to afford the same stuff.

productivity: measured as quantity of real GDP produced by an hour of labour

Work Time per Purchase   Let's look at a few examples stretching back to my grandparents' time and up to 1997. These examples come from a U.S. study, but the Canadian numbers would be similar. What the examples allow us to do is to see beyond the simultaneous changes in prices—which seemed absurdly low when compared to the present—and incomes, which were also much lower than today's. This measure of the cost of products/services uses a standard that doesn't change—time at work.

A pair of women's stockings cost just 25 cents in 1897, but workers typically earned about 15 cents per hour. So it took 1 hour and 41 minutes of work to "buy" a pair of stockings. In 1997, a pair of stockings (of far superior quality) cost $4.00, but because of higher wages, the work time required for purchase was only 18 minutes!

A pound of sausages "cost" 70 minutes of work in 1919, but only 12 minutes in 1997. An electric clothes washing machine cost $110 in 1911, which took 553 hours of work to earn. In 1997, a washing machine (again of far superior quality), cost $338 but took only 26 hours of work to buy.

Two more interesting examples are movies and cell phones. In 1926, a silent movie cost 17 cents and took 19 minutes of work to earn. In 1997, a movie cost $4.25, but took the same 19 minutes of work to earn. There was no change in the real cost of going to the movies (although modern movie technology is better). The first cellular phone, the Motorola DynaTAC 8000X, which looked like a brick and weighed just as much, cost $4,195 and took 456 hours of work to earn in 1984. In 1997, a Motorola cell phone cost $120 and only 9 hours of work.

Martin Cooper, a former Motorola researcher, made the first-ever wireless call from a busy New York street corner in April 1973. Cell phones, though, did not become available to the public until 1984. Can you imagine a world without wireless communications?

These two washing machines, one from 1937, and the other from 2008, show how everyday items improve. Changes in technology often decrease the work time per purchase. As well, the newer items are often of much higher quality and capability.

Productivity is Everything   Without gains from trade, there are only two sustainable ways to increase real GDP per person. The first is to put a larger fraction of the population to work—increase the labour force participation rate—as has happened in Canada since World War II. But labour force participation quickly reaches a limit once most people capable of working are working. The second is to increase productivity so that each worker produces more. In other words, sustainable increases in real GDP per person are caused essentially by increases in productivity.

Paul Krugman, a Nobel Prize–winning economist who teaches at Princeton University and writes for *The New York Times*, put it this way:

> Productivity isn't everything, but in the long run it is almost everything. A country's ability to improve its standard of living over time depends almost entirely on its ability to raise its output per worker.

Competition and Creative Destruction   Rising standards of living are caused by increases in the quantity and quality of inputs, which increase productivity and decrease the amount of work it takes to buy products and services. As a result, we are much better off than our grandparents.

There is one more question about the causes of growth. What causes those increases in the quantity and quality of inputs? The answer is competition—the same competitive forces of Adam Smith's invisible hand that channel the restless energy of profit-seeking self-interest into the public good.

Business competition is about figuring out new ways to beat your rival suppliers in the market. In the short run, businesses can earn profits by innovating through cutting costs, developing new technologies of production, inventing new products, exploiting economies of large-scale production, or finding new or cheaper sources of raw materials and resources.

Over longer periods of time, these competitive innovations, which result from the endless quest for profits, make businesses and labour more productive and improve living standards and product choices for consumers. Joseph Schumpeter (1883–1950) was a Harvard economist who saw that competitive actions of business "revolutionize the economic structure from within, incessantly destroying the old one, incessantly creating a new one. This process of **creative destruction** is the essential fact about capitalism." These competitive smart choices of businesses are what expand and transform the stock of inputs as we move around the circular flow from one year to the next.

creative destruction: competitive business innovations generate profits for winners, improving living standards for all, but destroy less productive or less desirable products and production methods

▶

These high school students are in a typing class using—for them—modern electric typewriters. Typewriters and all their related industries were the victims of creative destruction from newer computer technology. What do you use today that you think will be the victim of creative destruction within the next five years.

The increases in the quantity and quality of inputs, which improve productivity and standards of living, also have an opportunity cost—the destruction of less productive and less desirable businesses and products. Computers destroyed typewriters, DVDs destroyed VHS tapes, and robotic assembly lines destroyed the jobs of many workers.

A 2008 report by the Government of Canada, entitled "Compete to Win," concludes that our

> objective [is] to raise Canadians' standard of living by improving our economic performance . . . . [W]e believe that the key will be to encourage more competition at home and more exposure to competition from abroad. Competition drives the productivity that ultimately sustains our incomes, jobs, and quality of life.

We will discuss government policies to promote growth, besides encouraging competition, in Part 3—Macroeconomic Policy for Citizens.

The technological innovations and investments that businesses make for competitive purposes have opportunity costs beyond the obsolete businesses that fail and workers who lose jobs. Economists from both the hands-off and hands-on camps agree that another unintended macroeconomic consequence of these productivity-improving smart choices are the ups and downs of the business cycles.

Refresh
2.2

1. What is potential GDP per person?

2. If real GDP per person was $50 000 last year and increases to $52 000 this year, what is the annual economic growth rate?

3. A country can increase labour force participation, which increases potential GDP, by allowing child labour and reducing vacation time. What do you think about such choices? What questions does it raise about the quests for profits and improved standards of living?

www.myeconlab.com

2.3 Boom and Bust: Business Cycles

Describe the language of business cycles, including output gaps as a target for hands-on policymakers.

When the economy lives up to its potential, real GDP equals potential GDP, and all inputs—labour, capital, land/resources, and entrepreneurship—are fully employed. Since short-run dreams of potential GDP do not always come true, economists and the media have developed a language to describe situations where real GDP is not equal to potential GDP.

How To Speak Business Cycles

In Chapter 1, we defined business cycles as the ups and downs of overall economic activity. But now that you know the more precise terms of real GDP and potential GDP, we can provide a more precise definition. **Business cycles** are fluctuations of real GDP around potential GDP.

business cycles: up and down fluctuations of real GDP around potential GDP

To illustrate the language of business cycles, let's look at the last complete Canadian business cycle. (As I am writing in summer 2009, we are still in the middle of the most recent business cycle, the Great Recession, so there are not yet complete data.) Figure 2.9 is similar to Figure 2.4, but focuses only on the business cycle surrounding the 1990–1991 recession.

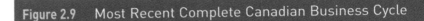

Figure 2.9   Most Recent Complete Canadian Business Cycle

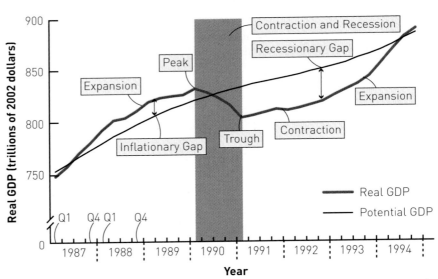

Source: Bank of Canada. (2009). Rates and statistics: Indicators of capacity and inflation pressures for Canada.

Phases of a Business Cycle The "boom and bust" of business cycles usually begins with the "boom." An **expansion** is any period (measured in quarters, or three-month blocks) during which real GDP increases. Real GDP expanded throughout 1987, 1988, and 1989. The expansion reached its peak in the first quarter of 1990. Just as when you reach the peak of a mountain you start down the other side, real GDP started decreasing after the peak. A **contraction** (the "bust") is any period during which real GDP decreases. Real GDP decreased throughout the rest of 1990 and the first quarter of 1991. Because real GDP then started increasing again, the first quarter of 1991 is called the *trough* of the contraction, the lowest point of the cycle.

Notice, in Figure 2.9, the shaded pink area labelled "Contraction and Recession." This 12-month time span (quarters two, three, and four of 1990 and quarter one of 1991) is called a *recession*. The exact definition of **recession** is two or more successive quarters of contraction in real GDP. Notice that a short, one quarter contraction, as occurred in the first quarter of 1992, is a contraction but not a recession.

You might be wondering about the definition of a depression—a word that was much used in discussing the 2008–2009 contraction and comparing it to the Great Depression. There is no agreed-upon, precise definition of a depression. Since macroeconomics was invented after the Great Depression, there has not been any downturn approaching that severity. In plain language, the definition of a depression might be "a really, really bad recession." Economists still have work to do on their language skills.

Output Gaps, Unemployment, and Inflation

These definitions of the language of business cycles have focused on the ups and downs, highs and lows, of fluctuations in real GDP. There are two other important definitions that focus on fluctuations *around* potential GDP—the differences between real GDP and potential GDP.

Look again at Figure 2.9. When real GDP is below potential GDP, as it was between the third quarter of 1990 and the second quarter of 1994, there are unemployed inputs. Labour, capital, land/resources, and/or entrepreneurship are not being fully utilized, which is why actual GDP is less than potential GDP. Workers are unemployed, factories are sitting idle, and land is not being used. Economists call this a **recessionary gap**—when real GDP is below potential GDP. For any time period, we can measure the size of the recessionary gap as the vertical distance between potential GDP and real GDP. Figure 2.9 labels the recessionary gap for the first quarter of 1993, but a recessionary gap exists for every quarter where real GDP is less than potential GDP.

An **inflationary gap** exists when real GDP is above potential GDP. From the expansion of 1987 to the peak in the first quarter of 1991, there was an inflationary gap. This is a scenario when not only are all inputs fully employed, the economy is also working overtime. As you will learn, this overheated economic activity can cause inflation, hence the term *inflationary gap*. (You might be wondering, how can real GDP be above potential GDP when potential GDP is full employment? If so, good for you! The answer will come in the next chapter. But here is a hint—the answer depends on the precise definition of *full employment*.)

expansion: period during which real GDP increases

contraction: period during which real GDP decreases

recession: two or more successive quarters of contraction of real GDP

recessionary gap: real GDP below potential GDP

inflationary gap: real GDP above potential GDP

output gap:
real GDP minus
potential GDP

Both recessionary gaps and inflationary gaps measure the gap between actual output (real GDP) and the full employment output of an economy (potential GDP). Economists refer to both as **output gaps**, which are calculated as real GDP minus potential GDP. For recessionary gaps, the output gap is negative (real GDP less than potential GDP). For inflationary gaps, the output gap is positive (real GDP greater than potential GDP).

Output gaps are important as targets for government policymakers taking a hands-on approach—what can government do to "close the gap?" When there is a recessionary gap, policymakers may take actions to increase real GDP. Where there is an inflationary gap, policymakers may try to decrease real GDP. Remember, the short-run target for economic performance is potential GDP. In Part 3 (Chapters 7, 8, and 9), we will discuss policy options to hit that target and close the output gaps.

Refresh 2.3

www.myeconlab.com

1. Describe the sequence of a typical business cycle, beginning with an expansion and ending with an expansion.

2. In the first quarter of 2009, real GDP (measured in 2002 dollars) was $1292 billion and potential GDP was $1331 billion. What kind of gap existed and what was its size?

3. By the time you read this, there will be data to track the business cycle of the 2008–2009 Great Recession. Go to **www.statcan.gc.ca** to find the quarterly data for real GDP. Identify the quarter when real GDP peaked, and the quarters of contraction. Has the economy hit a trough yet?

2.4 How to Measure GDP: Value Added and the Enlarged Circular Flow

Explain how value added and the equality of aggregate spending and aggregate income allow us to measure GDP.

Real GDP (and nominal GDP) are calculated by adding up the value of all *final* products/services produced annually in a country. Including only final products/services—consumed directly by consumers—and excluding intermediate products/services is necessary to avoid double counting.

There is still, however, another measurement problem. How do GDP statisticians decide which products/services are final, and which are intermediate? When you buy a loaf of bread at the supermarket, that bread is a final product. But when Second Cup buys that same loaf of bread to make sandwiches to sell, that bread is an intermediate product. The same problem applies to the notebook computer you buy for school (final product) and the notebook computers Goldcorp buys for its geologists exploring for new gold deposits (intermediate product). With this problem, statisticians can't calculate GDP by simply adding up all the bread or notebook computers sold.

You are probably not all that interested in the statisticians' problem, but the solution provides the first MAcroeconomic Positioning System— MAPS 1— to help you think like a macroeconomist, achieve personal success, and allow you to make more informed choices as a citizen.

MAPS 1

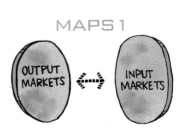

OUTPUT MARKETS ⟷ INPUT MARKETS

Value Added without Double Counting

The solution to the double counting problem is based on the business concept of value added. **Value added** is the value of a business's outputs minus the value of intermediate products/services bought from other businesses.

Let's look at a simple example, with made-up numbers. In Figure 2.10, a farmer grows wheat, which she sells to the miller, who grinds it into flour and sells that to the baker. The baker turns the flour into bread, and sells it to the grocer, who sells the bread to you, the consumer. We will assume the farmer rents her land, but uses her own seeds and doesn't buy any intermediate products/services from anyone else, so that the example doesn't have to go back in time forever.

value added: value output minus value intermediate products/services bought from other businesses

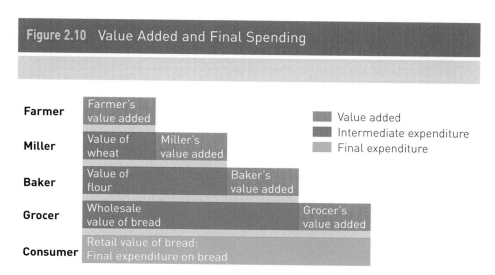

Figure 2.10   Value Added and Final Spending

Farmer	Farmer's value added	
Miller	Value of wheat	Miller's value added
Baker	Value of flour	Baker's value added
Grocer	Wholesale value of bread	Grocer's value added
Consumer	Retail value of bread: Final expenditure on bread	

- ■ Value added
- ■ Intermediate expenditure
- ■ Final expenditure

Here's how the story goes. Because the farmer doesn't buy any intermediate products/services, her value added (in orange) is equal to the value of her wheat output. The miller buys the wheat as an intermediate product (in blue), hires workers who turn the wheat into flour, and sells the flour (at a profit) to the baker. The baker buys the flour (in blue) from the miller, hires workers who bake bread, which he sells (at a profit) to the grocer. The grocer buys the bread and adds value by making it conveniently available to consumers. The consumer finally buys the bread, which is the only final product (in green) in this story.

◄ These consumers are paying the final price for these products. The final price includes all the value added by the various businesses and people who brought the products to market.

Figure 2.11 attaches some simple numbers to this chain of value added.

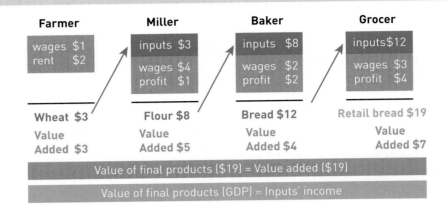

Figure 2.11 Value Added Equals Value of Final Products/Services

The farmer pays herself wages of $1 and pays rent of $2 to the landowner. She sells the wheat for $3 to the miller. The farmer's value added is

$$\$3 = \$3 \text{ (output)} - \$0 \text{ (intermediate products)}$$

The miller pays his workers wages of $4, earns a profit of $1, and sells the flour for $8. The miller's value added is

$$\$5 = \$8 \text{ (output)} - \$3 \text{ (intermediate products)}$$

The baker pays wages of $2, earns a profit of $2, and sells the bread for $12 to the grocer. The baker's value added is

$$\$4 = \$12 \text{ (output)} - \$8 \text{ (intermediate products)}$$

The grocer pays wages of $3, earns a profit of $4, and sells the organic, locally grown, artisanal bread to the final consumer for $19. So the grocer's value added is

$$\$7 = \$19 \text{ (output)} - \$12 \text{ (intermediate products)}$$

The end. (Aren't you glad we didn't go even farther back in time?)

Double Counting There are three payoffs to having slogged through all of these numbers. First, you can see clearly the double-counting problem if we include all intermediate products as well as final products in Figure 2.11. Adding up the value of the wheat, flour, wholesale bread, and retail bread, we get $42 ($3 + $8 + $12 + $19). The problem with the $42 number is that it includes the value of the wheat, flour, and wholesale bread multiple times. This is not a very accurate measure of what this simple economy actually produces. The accurate measure is the sum of the value added: $3 (by the farmer) + $5 (by the miller) + $4 (by the baker) + $7 (by the grocer), for a total of $19.

Value Added Equals Value of Final Products/Services The second payoff to this example comes from looking at the orange value added numbers in the middle of Figure 2.11. If we sum the value added by each of the four businesses ($3 + $5 + $4 + $7), we get $19. That number is exactly the same as the value of the (only) final product/service produced. So to calculate GDP, we don't have to try and sort out intermediate from final products/services. All we have to do is to sum the value added by each business.

Businesses keep good accounting records of their value added in order to make smart business decisions, and because Canada Revenue Agency (the taxman) requires such records.

Value added solves the problems of double-counting and of distinguishing between final and intermediate products/services.

Value Added Equals Inputs' Incomes The third payoff is not just for the statisticians, but gets us to MAPS 1.

Look at the components of value added. Value added is the sum of all wages paid to workers, rent paid to landowners, and profits paid to business entrepreneurs. (The simple example doesn't have interest paid on capital.) In other words, value added is not only equal to the value of final outputs, it is also equal to the value of all incomes earned by owners of inputs ($19), shown at the bottom of Figure 2.11.

Does this equality of the value outputs with the value of inputs remind you of anything? *Hint:* it is round.

Sum of value added equals value of all final products/services, and equals value of all incomes earned by input owners.

Circular Flow of Income and Spending

Travelling clockwise around the circular flow diagram in Figure 2.12, consumers (households) sell inputs to businesses in input markets in exchange for wages, interest, rent, and profits. The value of all transactions in input markets, also equal to value added, equals the aggregate (total) income in the economy as a whole. So the right-hand side of the circle represents aggregate income.

Businesses use the inputs to produce products/services, which are sold in output markets. Consumers use their income to buy those outputs. The value of all final products/services sold in output markets, also equal to GDP, equals the aggregate spending in the economy as a whole.

The equality between the two sides of the circle, between aggregate income and aggregate spending, is a reflection of Say's Law—supply creates its own demand. Consumers supply inputs because they want to spend the income they earn to demand outputs.

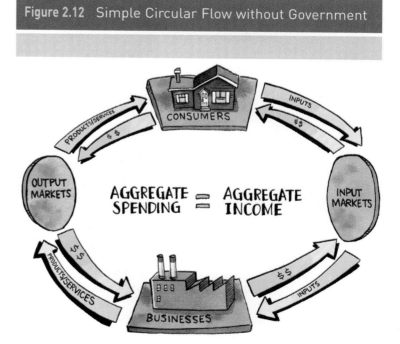

Figure 2.12 Simple Circular Flow without Government

Because of this equality between the two halves of the circular flow, the connection between input markets and output markets, GDP can be calculated using either half of the circular flow. For GDP,

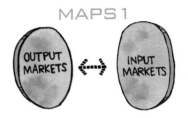

MAPS 1

aggregate spending = aggregate income

spending on final products/services = payments to input owners

This equality between income and spending allows us to expose when output and inputs markets coordinate and Say's Law applies, and to identify when output and input markets don't coordinate and fail to quickly self-adjust.

Enlarging the Circular Flow: Adding R.O.W.

Figure 2.13 Simple GDP Circular Flow of Income and Spending

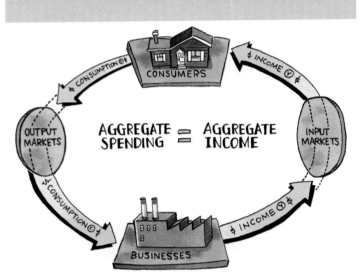

Our final tasks in measuring GDP are to connect aggregate spending to the five groups of macroeconomic players we introduced in Chapter 1—consumers, businesses, government, R.O.W. (the rest of the world), and banks. To do so, we must enlarge the circular flow diagram to include first the rest of the world, and then the Bank of Canada and the banking system.

With an enlarged set of players, the diagram will get more complicated, so to help you follow the flows, we are first going to simplify what is included, and then add the new players one at a time, starting with R.O.W.

Figure 2.13 is a simple circular flow of income and spending. It focuses on consumers and businesses, so government has been removed from the middle. And the only flows shown are the money flows. The key simplification on both sides of the circle is to "follow the money ($)."

Income and Consumer Spending On the right side, consumers earn income by selling inputs to businesses. The flow of physical inputs is omitted, but the dollar flow of income to consumers remains. Economists use the letter Y to represent income. On the left side, consumers use their income to buy products/services from businesses. The flow of physical products/services is omitted, but the dollar flow of consumer spending going to businesses remains. Economists use the letter C to represent *consumption* spending by consumers.

Sticking with the simplified focus on money flows, Figure 2.14

- adds business spending
- moves government out to the side
- adds the rest of the world to the flow of spending on the left side of the circle.

Let's discuss the new flows of spending that appear on this diagram by the macroeconomic players.

Figure 2.14 Enlarged GDP Circular Flow of Income and Spending ($)

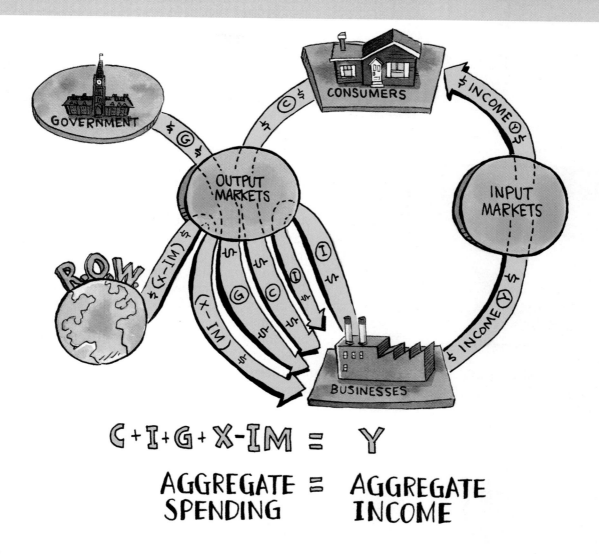

$$C + I + G + X - IM = Y$$

AGGREGATE SPENDING = AGGREGATE INCOME

Business Investment Spending Consumers are not the only ones who spend money buying products/services. When businesses build new factories or buy new machinery, that is called *investment spending*. Economists use the letter *I* to represent business investment spending. Businesses are spending on products/services produced by businesses, which is why the arrow representing investment spending goes from businesses, to output markets, and back to businesses.

Government Spending on Products/Services When governments build highways or hire the services of accounting firms, those are purchases of products/services in output markets. Economists use the letter *G* to represent *government spending on products/services.*

MAPS 2

R.O.W. Exports and Imports
Other countries around the globe spend money on Canadian products/services. When Ontario icewine or Prince Edward Island oysters are sold in the U.S., those are Canadian exports. Other countries also produce products/services that we import into Canada. Your purchase of a Nintendo Wii or a Montreal hockey rink's purchase of a Zamboni machine (made in California) are imports, where spending flows out of Canada to businesses in R.O.W.

Economists use the letter X to represent *exports* and the letters IM to represent *imports* (I was already taken for investment). Combining the flows of exports and imports give us *net exports*, represented as $X - IM$. Net exports takes the spending by R.O.W. on Canadian exports and subtracts Canadian spending on imports from R.O.W. That net flow of spending on Canadian products/services is represented by the arrow from R.O.W. through output markets to Canadian businesses.

This economist is using his own special mantra to gain peace. It's the mantra you should also learn by heart.

Aggregate Spending Equals Aggregate Income
The expanded circular flow in Figure 2.14 still has aggregate spending on the left side, and aggregate income (Y) on the right side. What we have done is provide more detail about the components of spending on the left side by the macroeconomic players. Aggregate spending consists of consumption spending by consumers (C), business investment spending (I), government spending on products/services (G), and net exports ($X - IM$).

This connection between input markets and output markets, between aggregate income and aggregate spending, is so important that economists have what I call a mantra about it. You will need to learn this mantra by heart, and I promise that you will by the end of this book because we use it so often to explain macroeconomic events. The mantra is

$$C + I + G + X - IM = Y$$

Repeat that until you can say it with your eyes closed. It is part of your training to think like a macroeconomist.

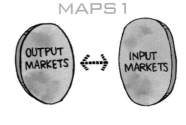

MAPS 1

Only products/services produced in Canada count toward Canadian GDP. Because some consumption and investment spending is on imports, imports must be subtracted to get an accurate measure of GDP.

Why Subtract Imports?
Since our mantra adds up spending, why do we *subtract* imports? Remember, the circular flow shows an alternative way to measure Canadian GDP—the value of all final products/services produced annually in Canada. We can measure Canadian GDP either by aggregate spending on Canadian final products/services or by aggregate income (value added). So of course we would not count imports, which are produced outside of Canada. But then why not just ignore imports? Why do we subtract them?

The answer has to do with how the other spending flows, C, I, and G, are measured. Some consumption spending (C) is on imports, and some business investment spending is on imported machinery. So if we have included imports in those spending measurements, we have to subtract them out at the end to get an accurate measure of Canadian GDP.

Enlarging the Circular Flow: Adding Banks

The last player added is the banking system. Figure 2.15 illustrates all money flows and allows us to describe all choices of the macroeconomic players. A key macroeconomic question is whether individual smart choices add up to smart choices for the economy as a whole. Figure 2.15 is the basis for investigating that.

Figure 2.15 Enlarged GDP Circular Flow of Income and Spending ($) with Banking System

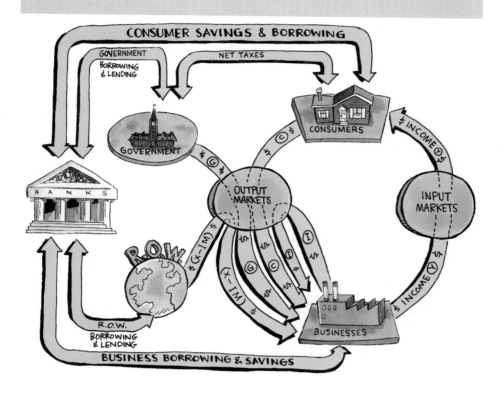

Let's look at the individual choices, including those from the banking system, in the order in which the players appear in our mantra $C + I + G + X - IM = Y$.

Consumer Choices Consumers can choose to spend their income or to save it. The green line at the top, between consumers and banks, is the flow of consumer savings into or loans from the banking system.

The income that consumers can choose to spend or save is called **disposable income**—income after net taxes have been taken away by government. **Net taxes**, represented by the letter T, are equal to taxes paid to government minus transfer payments (Employment Assistance, Old Age Security) consumers receive from government. The green line between consumers and government is the flow of net taxes paid by consumers to government.

disposable income:
aggregate income minus net taxes

net taxes:
taxes minus transfer payments

Business Choices Besides hiring inputs and producing products/services, businesses make investment spending choices. Long before production can begin and before receiving revenues from sales, businesses must invest in building factories and buying the equipment necessary to start production. Because there is a time lag between when businesses build factories and when sales revenues start to flow in, businesses usually need to borrow money for investment spending. In Figure 2.15, the green line between businesses and banks is business borrowing and savings.

Government Choices Government collects taxes, makes transfer payments, and spends to purchase products/services in output markets. Government also borrows money from the banking system, and can deposit, or lend, money to the banking system. In Figure 2.15, the green line between government and banks is government borrowing and lending.

Government policy choices are not yet part of this diagram. We discuss government spending and taxing policies, and government borrowing to finance deficits, in Chapter 8.

R.O.W. Choices The rest of the world can choose to buy Canadian exports (or buy from their own or other countries) and sell their own products/services to us as Canadian imports. R.O.W. can also choose to invest money in Canada or borrow money from Canada. The green line between R.O.W. and banks is R.O.W. borrowing and lending.

MAPS3

Banks Banks take deposits from consumers, businesses, government, and R.O.W., and make loans to all of the players as well. We will discuss the roles of the Bank of Canada in anchoring the banking system and conducting monetary policy in Chapter 7.

Say's Law with Banks Say's Law begins to break down if consumers save their income instead of spending it. But if banks take those savings and lend them to businesses who increase their investment spending, then it is still possible for all income earned in input markets to create equivalent demand for products/services in output markets. This is one reason why the banking system plays a key role in determining whether or not market economies work quickly to maintain steady growth in living standards, full employment, and stable prices.

Refresh
2.4

1. What is value added?

2. Explain how value added solves the double counting problem in calculating GDP.

3. Make a list of the imported products/services you have bought in the last year. Of all of the money you spend in a year, what percentage of it do you think you spend on imported products/services?

2.5 My GDP is Bigger Than Yours: What's Wrong with GDP as a Measure of Well-Being?

Identify five limitations of real GDP per person as a measure of well-being.

Now that we have finished with all of the definitions of GDP, explanations of how it grows and fluctuates over time, and enlargements of the circular flow illustrating how to measure GDP using either aggregate income or aggregate spending, I am hoping you are thinking, "OK, enough with the definitions and measurement problems. Let's move on to more interesting, real-world topics like unemployment, inflation, money, . . ."

I have one last caution about using GDP as a tool for understanding the real world before we do move on in Chapter 3 to unemployment and inflation.

GDP, especially real GDP per person, is the single best measure of economic performance and of material standards of living. Real GDP per person is "the tool" for comparing our standard of living with that of my grandparents or your grandchildren. But that does not mean that the country with the highest real GDP per person has the highest quality of life or is the "best" country in which to live. There are things missing in the measurement of GDP.

What's Missing from Real GDP?

Here are five limitations of real GDP per person as a measure of well-being, or quality of life.

Non-Market Production Productive activities that are counted as part of GDP must be bought and sold in the input or output markets of the circular flow of an economy. Yet many productive activities that contribute to our well-being happen outside of markets. All household activities like cooking, cleaning, and childcare are not counted in GDP statistics. Because women provide the majority of household services, women's contributions to economic well-being are under-represented. In addition, all volunteer services, such as at food banks, in hospitals, and in homeless shelters, are not counted in GDP.

Here's an example of how GDP misses such activities, but with gender role reversal. A high-powered business executive has a chauffeur hired by her corporation. If she falls in love with him, gets married, and he continues to drive for her, but now as a husband rather than a hired chauffeur, real GDP falls. There has been no change in the actual service that contributes to well-being; the service has simply moved from a market transaction to an outside market transaction.

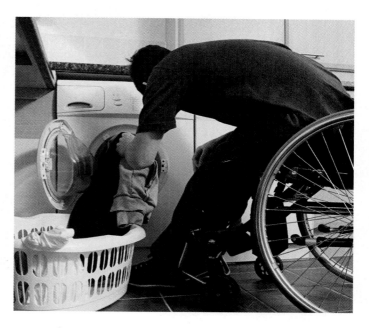

▶

Working in the home for no salary does not get included in the calculation of GDP. This husband, doing the family's laundry, is certainly working and contributing to the well-being of the family and therefore the country. This is just one example of what is missed from real GDP. What do you do that is not counted in real GDP?

Underground economy hides activities that are illegal or legal but avoid taxes.

Underground Economy

Activities in the *underground economy* are purposefully hidden from government, either because they are illegal, or are legal but avoid taxes (which is also illegal). Imagine the response Statistics Canada will get from asking a drug dealer, "Would you please tell me the value of final products/services your business produced in 2009?"

Unreported legal productive activities include cash payments for home renovations or repairs (that avoid income tax for the renovator and GST for the consumer), and unreported tips earned by servers, taxi drivers, and other service workers.

Economists estimate the size of the underground economy in Canada to be between 5 and 15 percent of GDP.

This woman is paying cash for the work she had done. Activities like this are part of the underground economy. Why might this woman and man participate in *illegal* activities?

Environmental Damage

Productive economic activity often produces undesirable negative externalities like pollution, global warming, and resource depletion. The costs of environmental damage are not included in GDP. Higher GDP is often associated with greater environmental damage. Similarly, when economic activity depletes non-renewable resources like oil, GDP goes up, but there is no subtraction for the fewer resources our grandchildren will have as a result.

Real GDP does not subtract costs of environmental damage and resource depletion caused by our consumption.

Leisure

When people work more, real GDP increases. But don't you like your holiday time? The more leisure time people take, the lower real GDP will be.

Most European countries have a lower GDP per person than Canada, but have more vacation time. By law, Canadians get 10 paid vacation days and another 8 paid statutory holidays. But European Union countries like Germany, Italy, and Spain have 20 paid vacation days, and 10–13 paid statutory holidays. Would you sacrifice some material standard of living in exchange for almost three more weeks of vacation a year? Many Europeans look at how hard we work with pity and a sense that they know how to really live better. These are personal choices, but regardless of the choice you or the Europeans might make, GDP per person does not capture the value of leisure.

These women enjoying a coffee in a Parisian outdoor café are not adding to real GDP, beyond the value of the coffees. Should we be worried that leisure time does not increase real GDP?

Political Freedoms and Social Justice There is no necessary connection between higher real GDP per person and the benefits of democracy and political freedom. There are countries, often with rich oil or other natural resources, that have high real GDP per person, but limited political freedom.

In such countries, as well as in democratic countries like Canada with market economies, a high real GDP per person does not guarantee an equitable distribution of income. Real GDP per person is a statistical average for the country as a whole. Even in Canada, the richest 20 percent of households had an average income of $119 300 in 2006 (after taxes and transfer payments) while the poorest 20 percent of households had an average income of $13 100.

Real GDP per person is higher in the United States than in any other country in the world. Yet Americans lack the extensive social welfare programs that are enjoyed in Canada and many European countries. There are 46 million people in the United States, about 15 percent of the population, who do not have health care benefits.

Growth Rates of Real GDP per Person Are Better While these limitations of GDP should give you pause in presuming that higher real GDP per person always means a better quality of life, economists are still comfortable using a country's *growth rate of real GDP per person* to judge economic *progress* over time. As long as there are no significant changes over time in the extent of non-market production, the underground economy, environmental damage, leisure, political freedom, and social justice, most economists believe the growth of real GDP per person is still the best measure of the increase in the standard of living and well-being for a country.

Where Would You Rather Live?

Because of the limitations of real GDP per person as a measure of the quality of life, the United Nations Development Programme developed a broader measure of well-being called the Human Development Index (HDI). The HDI weights equally life expectancy, educational achievement, and income.

In the most recent HDI report, the top five countries are Iceland, Norway, Canada, Australia, and Ireland. The United States ranks fifteenth. The bottom five countries, out of 179 ranked, are Mozambique, Liberia, Congo, Central Africa Republic, and Sierra Leone.

FOR YOUR INFORMATION

According to the United Nations, "Human development is about enlarging people's choices, allowing them to develop their full potential and to lead productive, creative lives in dignity and in accordance with their needs and interests . . . while economic growth is an important measure of development it is nonetheless limited in capturing how expanding income translates also into human development defined more broadly . . . the HDI [combines] indicators of income, education and health into a single index."

Refresh

2.5

1. What is the underground economy?

2. More and more people are eating their meals in restaurants instead of cooking at home. Explain how this social trend affects real GDP. How does it affect your quality of life?

3. Of the five factors not included in real GDP as a measure of well-being, which makes the most difference to your personal quality of life?

www.myeconlab.com

Up *Around the* Circular *Flow*

GDP, Economic Growth, and Business Cycles

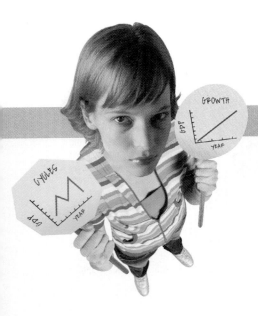

CHAPTER SUMMARY

2.1 HIGHER PRICES, MORE STUFF, OR BOTH? NOMINAL GDP AND REAL GDP

All GDP concepts measure the value of all final products/services produced annually in a country; nominal GDP combines changes in prices and quantities, real GDP measure only changes in quantities, and real GDP per person provides the best measure of material standard of living.

- **Nominal GDP**—value *at current prices* of all final products/services produced annually in a country. This is how you calculate nominal GDP:
  - Nominal GDP$_{1935} = P^A_{1935} Q^A_{1935} + P^B_{1935} Q^B_{1935} + P^C_{1935} Q^C_{1935} + \ldots + P^Z_{1935} Q^Z_{1935}$
  - Nominal GDP$_{2008} = P^A_{2008} Q^A_{2008} + P^B_{2008} Q^B_{2008} + P^C_{2008} Q^C_{2008} + \ldots + P^Z_{2008} Q^Z_{2008}$

- Differences in nominal GDP between years due to either price changes or quantity changes.

- **Flow**—amount per unit of time. GDP usually measured per year.

- GDP includes products/services produced within a country's borders, no matter what the nationality of the business doing the producing.

- **Real GDP**—value *at constant prices* of all final products/services produced annually in a country. This is how you calculate real GDP using 2002 constant prices:
  - Real GDP$_{1935} = P^A_{2002} Q^A_{1935} + P^B_{2002} Q^B_{1935} + P^C_{2002} Q^C_{1935} + \ldots + P^Z_{2002} Q^Z_{1935}$
  - Real GDP$_{2008} = P^A_{2002} Q^A_{2008} + P^B_{2002} Q^B_{2008} + P^C_{2002} Q^C_{2008} + \ldots + P^Z_{2002} Q^Z_{2008}$

  - Real GDP uses constant prices for a single year (2002 in the examples above) to value the quantities of products/services produced in different years. So differences in real GDP between years (1935 and 2008 above) are calculated to show only changes in quantities.

- **Real GDP per person**—real GDP divided by population.
  - Real GDP per person is best measure of material standard of living.

2.2 WHEN MACROECONOMIC DREAMS COME TRUE: POTENTIAL GDP AND ECONOMIC GROWTH

By increasing the quantity and quality of inputs, economic growth increases productivity and potential GDP per person, raising maximum possible living standards.

- **Potential GDP**—real GDP when all inputs are fully employed—labour, capital, land/resources, and entrepreneurship. Short-run goal for ideal economic performance outcome if Adam Smith's invisible hand works perfectly.
- **Potential GDP per person**—potential GDP divided by population. Short-run maximum possible living standards for an economy.
- **Economic growth**—expansion of economy's capacity to produce products/services; increase in potential GDP (per person).
- Economic growth caused by increases in quantity or quality of a country's inputs—labour, capital, land/resources, and entrepreneurship.
- Increases in labour
  - *quantity*—from population growth; immigration; increase in labour force participation rate (percentage of population that works).
  - *quality*—from increases in **human capital**—increased earning potential from work experience, on-the-job training, and education.
- Increases in capital
  - *quantity*—from more factories and equipment.
  - *quality*—from **technological change**—improvements in quality of capital through innovation, research, and development.
- Increases in land/resources
  - *quantity*—by bringing land/resources not connected to markets into the circular flow of markets.
  - *quality*—increases usually due to increases in capital used with land.
- Increases in entrepreneurship
  - *quantity* and *quality* interrelated; improvements from better management techniques, organization, and worker/management relations.
- When economic growth progresses smoothly, stock of inputs serves as a basis for choices, and choices then transform the stock of inputs, continuing in ever-expanding circle.
  - **stock**—fixed amount at a moment in time.
- **Economic growth rate**—annual percentage change in real GDP per person.

$$\text{Real GDP per person growth rate (percent)} = \frac{\text{Real GDP per person this year} - \text{Real GDP per person last year}}{\text{Real GDP per person last year}} \times 100$$

  - Canada's average annual economic growth rate from 1926–2008 was 2.1 percent.

- **Rule of 70**—number of years it takes for initial amount to double is roughly 70 divided by annual percentage growth rate.
  - because of *compounding*, small differences in annual growth rates have large consequences over long time periods.
  - our 2008 real GDP per person would be almost double what it is if average annual growth rate since 1926 had been 3 percent instead of 2.1 percent.
- **Productivity**—measured as quantity of real GDP produced by an hour of labour.
  - increases in productivity increase living standard by allowing more products/services to be produced, and by reducing amount of work time required to buy products/services.
- **Creative destruction**—competitive business innovations generate profits for winners, improving living standards for all, but destroy less productive or less desirable products and production methods.

2.3 BOOM AND BUST: BUSINESS CYCLES

Business cycles—fluctuations of real GDP around potential GDP—track periods of real GDP expansion and contraction. Output gaps measure the difference between real GDP and potential GDP, and "closing the gap" is an important target for policymakers.

- **Business cycles**—up and down fluctuations of real GDP around potential GDP.
- Language of business cycles:
  - **expansion**—period during which real GDP increases.
  - *peak*—highest point of an expansion; turning point beginning contraction.
  - **contraction**—period during which real GDP decreases.
  - *trough*—lowest point of a contraction; turning point beginning expansion.
  - **recession**—two or more successive quarters of contraction of real GDP.
- **Output gap**—real GDP minus potential GDP.
  - **recessionary gap**—real GDP below potential GDP; gap is negative number.
  - **inflationary gap**—real GDP above potential GDP; gap is positive number.

2.4 HOW TO MEASURE GDP: VALUE ADDED AND THE ENLARGED CIRCULAR FLOW

Value added solves the GDP measurement problems of double counting and distinguishing final and intermediate products/services, and reveals the equality of aggregate spending and aggregate income in circular flow diagrams.

- **Value added**—value output minus value intermediate products/services bought from other businesses.
  - the value a business adds to the intermediate products/services it buys from other businesses.

- Value added solves the problems of double counting and of distinguishing between final and intermediate products/services.
  - value of final products/services = value added
  - value of final products/services (GDP) = input's income
- GDP can be calculated using either half of the circular flow of income and spending.
  - aggregate spending (GDP) = aggregate income (Y)
  - spending on final products/services = payments to income owners
- Flows of spending on the enlarged circular flow:
  - C—consumption spending by consumers.
  - I—business investment spending on factories and machines made by businesses.
  - G—government spending on products/services.
  - X—spending by the rest of the world (R.O.W.) on Canadian exports of products/services.
  - IM—Canadian spending on imports of products/services produced by rest of the world.
- Aggregate Spending equals Aggregate Income (Y)
  - $C + I + G + X - IM = Y$
  - Only products/services produced in Canada count toward Canadian GDP. Because some consumption and investment spending is on imports, imports must be subtracted to get an accurate measure of GDP.
- Figure 2.15—Enlarged GDP Circular Flow of Income and Spending with Banking System—will be key for answering all macroeconomic questions.
- Consumer choices:
  - spend or save.
  - **disposable income**—aggregate income minus net taxes.
  - **net taxes**—taxes minus transfer payments.
- Business choices:
  - hiring inputs and producing products/services.
  - investment spending (often financed by borrowing).
- Government choices:
  - collect taxes, make transfer payments.
  - spending on products/services.
  - note: policy choices will be discussed in Chapter 8.
- R.O.W. choices:
  - buy Canadian exports or products/services from elsewhere.
  - sell imports to Canada or elsewhere.
  - invest and borrow money in Canada or elsewhere.
- Bank choices:
  - take deposits and make loans.

2.5 MY GDP IS BIGGER THAN YOURS: WHAT'S WRONG WITH GDP AS A MEASURE OF WELL-BEING?

Real GDP per person is a limited measure of well-being because it excludes non-market production, underground economy, environmental damage, leisure and political freedoms/social justice.

- Real GDP per person is a limited measure of well-being; does not include
  - non-market production—household production not counted but improves quality of life.
  - *underground economy*—hides activities that are illegal, or legal but avoiding taxes (cash payments for services, unreported tips).
  - environmental damage—real GDP does not subtract costs of environmental damage and resource depletion caused by consumption.
  - leisure—more leisure lowers real GDP, but leisure may be desirable.
  - political freedoms and social justice—countries with high real GDP per person could have limited political freedoms, uneven distributions of income.
- Growth rates of real GDP per person still useful for judging economic progress if no significant changes over time in the limitations.
- United Nations Human Development Index (HDI) measures quality of life by combining life expectancy, educational achievement, and income.
  - Canada ranked fourth in world, U.S. ranked fifteenth.

TRUE/FALSE

Circle the correct answer.

An old man wearing a sweater vest and thick-rimmed glasses walks into the coffee shop that you're relaxing in. He notices that you're reading *The Economist* magazine and says:

> *"Hello, youngster. Back in the year 1935, our economy was going through some tough times. I've lived through the Great Depression, the Great Recession, and other recessions. Let me tell you a few stories."*

Use this scenario to answer questions 1–15.

2.1 NOMINAL GDP AND REAL GDP

1. In 1935, Canada's nominal GDP was $5 billion. In 2008, it was $1600 billion. That means that the average Canadian is about 320 times better off today compared to 1935. **True** **False**

2. In 1935, Canada's real GDP was $80 billion. In 2008, it was $1400 billion. That means that the average Canadian is about 18 times better off today compared to 1935. **True** **False**

3. In 1935, Canada's real GDP per person was $7,000. In 2008, it was $41,000. That means that the average Canadian is about 6 times better off today compared to 1935. **True**   **False**

4. During the 1990s, real GDP rose faster than nominal GDP. **True**   **False**

2.2 POTENTIAL GDP AND ECONOMIC GROWTH

5. Back in 1911, it took more hours of work to earn enough money to buy sausages than it takes today. **True**   **False**

6. Back in the 1970s, the cell phone was invented. This increased the quality of labour. **True**   **False**

7. An old friend of mine, Farmer Fred, started using fertilizer back in 1941. This increased the quality of the land. **True**   **False**

8. My sister put $1000 in a savings account in 1935 with a fixed annual interest rate of 1 percent per year, then left the account alone. The savings account balance reached $2000 in 2005. **True**   **False**

2.3 BUSINESS CYCLES

9. The economy had an expansionary period in the late 1980s, then hit a trough in 1990. **True**   **False**

10. Back in my youth, I remember a three quarter contraction in real GDP. This was a recession. **True**   **False**

2.4 VALUE ADDED AND THE ENLARGED CIRCULAR FLOW

11. Back in 2008, I contributed to nominal GDP by selling my used 2005 Ford Truck to my friend. **True**   **False**

12. My rich neighbour, Pablo, purchased a new Ferrari made in Italy, Canadian GDP increases. **True**   **False**

2.5 WHAT'S WRONG WITH GDP AS A MEASURE OF WELL-BEING?

13. If underground economic activity were included in GDP calculations, measured GDP levels would be higher. **True**   **False**

14. Real GDP per person in the United States is higher than that in Canada. This implies that Americans must enjoy a higher level of overall well-being than Canadians. **True**   **False**

15. If two economies have the same real GDP per person, then the overall well-being must be the same in each economy. **True**   **False**

MULTIPLE CHOICE

Circle the correct answer.

1. Gross Domestic Product (GDP) is the value of all products and services
    A) that are gross-looking.
    B) produced in domestic households.
    C) produced in a country, including gross-looking products and services.
    D) produced in a country, excluding gross-looking products and services.

2. To calculate nominal GDP for 1935, we use the prices in
    A) 1935 and quantities in 1935.
    B) 1935 and quantities in 2002.
    C) 2002 and quantities in 1935.
    D) 2002 and quantities in 2002.

3. You observe that nominal GDP increases between 2009 and 2010, and the population also increases. If the entire increase in nominal GDP was due to rising prices, then
    A) nominal GDP remains unchanged.
    B) real GDP remains unchanged.
    C) real GDP per person remains unchanged.
    D) living standards remain unchanged.

4. When real GDP equals potential GDP,
    A) all inputs are fully employed.
    B) everyone is getting the most bang per buck for their choices.
    C) the whole is equal to the sum of the well-functioning parts.
    D) All of the above

5. If real GDP per person this year is $41 000, and real GDP per person last year was $40 000, then the economic growth rate is
    A) 5.0 percent.
    B) 2.5 percent.
    C) −2.5 percent.
    D) −5.0 percent.

6. Which of the following is *not* a source of economic growth?
    A) More workers
    B) Better educated workers
    C) Higher stock market prices
    D) Growing quantities of capital equipment

7. Our long-run standard of living depends most on increases in
   A) population growth.
   B) employment growth.
   C) productivity.
   D) land.

2.3 BUSINESS CYCLES

8. A recession occurs when real GDP
   A) is negative.
   B) growth is negative.
   C) growth is negative for two quarters in a row.
   D) growth is negative for two years in a row.

9. An output gap is
   A) negative if real GDP is above potential GDP.
   B) negative for an inflationary gap.
   C) positive if real GDP equals potential GDP.
   D) positive for an inflationary gap.

2.4 VALUE ADDED AND THE ENLARGED CIRCULAR FLOW

10. GDP equals the value of
    A) spending on final products/services.
    B) business's outputs minus the value of intermediate products/services bought from other businesses.
    C) incomes earned by owners of inputs.
    D) All of the above

11. In the "mantra" for calculating GDP, imports are subtracted because
    A) some consumption spending is on imports.
    B) some business investment spending is on imports.
    C) some government spending is on imports.
    D) All of the above

12. Which of the following increases investment spending (I) by $200?
    A) You are hired by the government to shuffle paper uselessly for $200.
    B) You are hired by Dunder-Mifflin, the business on the television show "The Office," to shuffle paper uselessly for $200.
    C) You hire your significant other to shuffle paper uselessly for $200.
    D) You lose your job because your employer replaces you with a paper shuffler machine that costs $200.

13. Maud and her three sons, Rod, Todd, and Claude are members of a church in their hometown of Springfield. Their church provides many benefits to the community, such as counselling, youth and social activities, worship services, and distributions of food and clothing to the poor. Suppose that Maud's New Year's resolution for 2011 is to give up her $50 000 a year job to devote 100 percent of her time to fundraising for the church. As a result, GDP in 2011

    A) increases by $150 000.

    B) increases by $200 000.

    C) decreases by $50 000.

    D) decreases by $150 000.

14. Economists estimate the size of the underground economy in Canada to be between 5 and 15 percent of GDP. Which of the following activities are considered to be part of the underground economy?

    A) Marijauna sales

    B) Bartender tips

    C) Taxi driver tips

    D) All of the above

15. Suppose that Moby went from a stay-at-home father to a paid worker. He now earns $200 a week but pays $100 a week for day care and $100 a week for a housekeeper. Moby is better off by

    A) $0 and GDP increases by $0.

    B) $0 and GDP increases by $400.

    C) $200 and GDP increases by $0.

    D) $200 and GDP increases by $400.

SHORT ANSWER

Write a short answer to each question. Your answer may be in point form.

1. In Figure 2.14—Enlarged GDP Circular Flow of Income and Spending— the components of spending are consumption, business investment spending, government spending on products/services, exports, and imports.

    A) Provide an example for each spending component.

    B) Provide an example for each spending component of GDP that reduces the quality of life for others.

2. Canada's Wonderland (an amusement park in Ontario) wants to build a new roller coaster ride called the "Boom-and-Buster." Canada's Wonderland wants you to design the roller coaster so that it reflects Canada's business cycle from 1920 to 2010. Pretend that one second on the ride represents one year in history (so the rider will arrive at 1925 five seconds into the ride, and the ride is 90 seconds in total).

A) Should the rollercoaster start with an incline or decline?

B) When will the rollercoaster sharply decline?

C) When will the next major decline occur?

D) How many major dips should there be on the ride?

E) When should be the biggest drop occur?

F) When should the steepest incline (increase) occur?

G) If someone is afraid of big dips in roller coaster rides, will they enjoy the last 10 seconds?

H) Illustrate the Boom-and-Buster roller coaster in a diagram.

3. Suppose you are working on an assignment with your classmate on a cross-country comparison of GDP and its components. He hands you his half of the work, and it is your responsibility to type it up on the computer. Unfortunately, his writing looks like chicken-scratch, and you can't contact him because he went on vacation.

A) Use your math skills to complete the following table.

Spending (in $ billions)	Paradise Island	Lost Island
Gross Domestic Product	100	7
Consumption	60	4
Investment	25	2
Government	?	2
Net Exports	5	?

B) What is the largest component of GDP on Paradise Island?

C) What is larger on Lost Island: exports or imports?

4. Pop City produces two products: pop and popcorn. In 2010, it produced 5 million cans of pop and 6 million bags of popcorn. In 2011, pop production increased to 10 million cans and popcorn production increased to 10 million bags. Over the same time, the price of pop increased from $2/can to $3/can, and the price of popcorn increased from $1/bag to $2/bag.

A) Calculate Pop City's nominal GDP in 2010.

B) Calculate Pop City's nominal GDP in 2011.

C) Calculate Pop City's real GDP in 2010 (using 2010 prices).

D) Calculate Pop City's real GDP in 2011 (using 2010 prices).

E) Calculate Pop City's real GDP per person in 2010 and 2011 (using 2010 prices) if the population was 1 million people in both years.

F) Calculate the rate of economic growth between 2010 and 2011.

5. Barry loves drinking beer. Every week, Barry goes to The Beer Store to buy a 6-pack for $10. He has this conversation with the cashier at The Beer Store:

Barry: "So, you come here often?"

Cashier: "Obviously—I work here."

Barry: "So what inspired you to work at The Beer Store?"

Cashier: "My father has a brewing business, and my grandfather is a barley farmer. Brewers use barley to make beer, which they then sell to The Beer Store. Hey, aren't you in my macroeconomics class?"

Barry: "Yes I am. What are you doing tonight? Would you like to use your knowledge of wages, profits, and sales prices in the beer industry to work out the macroeconomics assignment we got in class today?"

Cashier: "I would love to—that's so romantic."

A) If The Beer Store gets beer from the brewery, and the brewery gets its barley from the barley farmer, determine the value added at each stage using the following information:

   i) The farmer pays herself $1, pays rent of $2 to the landowner, and sells the barley to the brewery for $3.

   ii) The brewer buys the farmer's barley for $3, pays his workers wages of $2, sells the beer to The Beer Store for $6, and earns a profit of $1.

   iii) The Beer Store buys the brewer's beer for $6, pays wages of $3, sells the beer to the final consumer for $10, and earns a profit of $1.

B) If the economy consists only of the farmer, the brewer, and The Beer Store, calculate GDP using the value added approach.

C) Calculate GDP using expenditure on final products/services.

D) Does Say's Law holds true in this example? (Hint: calculate aggregate wages, profits, and rent and compare it to aggregate spending.)

6. A 2009 OECD study, the *OECD Economic Outlook* No. 85, compares the real GDP growth rates of advanced economies ("G7 nations") between 2005 and 2010. See the figures in the table below. Note: figures for 2009 and 2010 are forecasts.

Real GDP Growth Rate (%)	2005	2006	2007	2008	2009	2010
Canada	3.0	2.9	2.5	0.4	−2.6	0.7
United States	2.9	2.8	2.0	1.1	−2.8	0.9
United Kingdom	2.1	2.8	3.0	0.7	−4.3	0.0
Japan	1.9	2.0	2.3	−0.7	−6.8	0.7
France	1.9	2.4	2.3	0.3	−3.0	0.2
Germany	0.9	3.2	2.6	1.0	−6.1	0.2
Italy	0.8	2.1	1.5	−1.0	−5.5	0.4

Source: *OECD Economic Outlook* No. 85 (2009) Database

A) How did Canada's growth rate compare to the other advanced economies in 2005, 2006, and 2007?

B) Are any of these countries expected to have positive growth in real GDP in 2009 or 2010?

C) In the late 1990s, Ireland experienced an "Irish Miracle." Real GDP per person grew at an average annual rate of 8.9 percent between 1995 and 2000. To put that into perspective, that's roughly 3 times the annual rate of growth of Canada over the same period. If Ireland experienced an average annual rate of growth of 9 percent starting in 1995, how long would it take real GDP to double?

7. In June 2009, Statistics Canada released data on GDP and personal disposable income for the last two quarters of 2008 and the first quarter of 2009. Use the table below to answer questions 7A to 7G.

	Third quarter of 2008	Fourth quarter of 2008	First quarter of 2009
Change in real GDP (%), compared to previous quarter	0.1%	−0.9%	−1.4%
Consumption	$813 469	$807 018	$803 863
Government spending	$264 462	$266 084	$266 884
Business investment spending	$318 616	$305 999	$288 780
Exports	$488 152	$464 964	$424 655
Imports	$584 824	$547 196	$485 937
Personal disposable income (millions of dollars, current prices)	$955 512	$960 852	$955 260

Source: Statistics Canada, *Canadian Economic Accounts Quarterly Review*, catalogue number 13-010-X, June 1, 2009.

A) When did the Canadian economy enter a recession?

B) What is the largest spending component of GDP?

C) Have any of the spending components of GDP increased since the third quarter of 2008?

D) What spending component of GDP decreased the most since the third quarter of 2008?

E) Did net exports increase or decrease between third quarter of 2008 and the first quarter of 2009?

F) Compare the fourth quarter of 2008 with the first quarter of 2009. Did disposable income increase over this period?

G) Did real disposable income increase over this period?
(*Hint:* prices decreased over this period.)

8. Consider the sources of economic growth when answering the following questions.

A) Real GDP per person in the U.S. in 2000 was higher than in Europe, partly because a larger proportion of Americans are employed and Americans work longer hours. Explain why high employment rates and high hours of work are important for determining a country's GDP.

B) In 2007, the Government of Ontario introduced Family Day, which provided a new holiday from work and school in February. How will the additional public holiday affect the economy? What if the extra day off increased productivity in the rest of the year?

C) Declining birth rates, increased life expectancy, and an aging population are leading to slower population and labour force growth. Explain why these demographic challenges will limit the pace of economic growth in the future.

D) In 2008, labour productivity in the Canadian business sector declined by 1.1 percent. It was the first annual decline since 1996. The production of products/services by Canadian businesses declined by 0.3 percent and hours worked increased. Explain why productivity would decrease if output declines and hours worked increases.

E) While the entrepreneurial spirit exists in companies in Canada, the Competition Policy Review Panel concluded in their study, entitled "Compete to Win," that Canada lacks sufficient entrepreneurial culture and ambition. Explain why entrepreneurship is a source of economic growth.

9. Alberta is one of the wealthiest provinces in Canada. Alberta's real GDP grew at an annual rate of 2.2 percent between 1961 and 2003. Ecological economists Mark Anielski and Amy Taylor use a broader measure of well-being to determine if Alberta's higher economic growth has led to a better quality of life.

A) Which of the following trends would suggest that the well-being of Albertans has declined since 1961: obesity rates increased, life expectancy increased, unemployment rates decreased, weekly wages increased, household debt increased, the gap between the rich and the poor increased, and greenhouse gas emissions increased.

B) Based on the above trends, would you conclude that the overall well-being of Albertans has increased or decreased?

C) The study uses a Genuine Progress Indicator (GPI) that takes into consideration these trends and other economic, social, and environmental factors (51 in total). The study estimates that GPI declined by 19 percent between 1961 and 2003. Expressed differently, Alberta's GPI indicator declined from a score of 76 to 61 at the same time that the GDP index increased from a score of 17 to 100. Does that suggest that growth is coming at the expense of other social, environmental, or economic factors?

10. As an alternative to the United Nations Human Development Index (HDI), the Canadian Centre for the Study of Living Standards developed the Index of Economic Well-Being (IEWB). It has four components:

- consumption per person
- wealth of human capital, R&D investment, natural resources, and environmental costs
- income distribution and poverty rates
- economic security from job loss and unemployment, illness, family breakup, and poverty in old age

To combine these four dimensions into a single index, it is necessary to specify relative weights for each component. However, people may weight the importance of the components differently because they have different personal values.

A) According to the chart below, is the IEWB closer to real GDP per person when consumption is weighted more, or when all components are equally weighted?

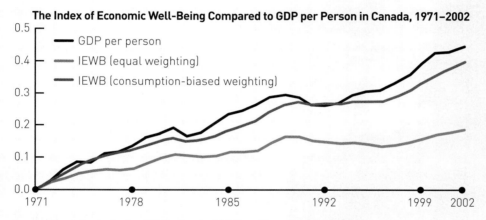

The Index of Economic Well-Being Compared to GDP per Person in Canada, 1971–2002

Source: Centre for the Study of Living Standards' Index of Economic Well-Being. http://www.csls.ca/iwb/weights.xls. Values represent the absolute change in the scaled indexes relative to the 1971 base. Consumption-biased means that consumption flows receive a weight of 70% while the three remaining components each receive a weight of 10%.

B) If you are interested, download the Excel file at http://www.csls.ca/iwb/weights-oecd.xls. What country has the highest index score in 2001 if you put 100 percent of the weight on consumption (and 0 for the others)? What country has the highest score in 2001 if you put 10 percent weight on consumption and 30 percent each for the others?

C) Choose your own weights for the components. What is Canada's ranking in 2001? Has Canada improved over time?

Costs of *(Not)* Working and *Living*

Unemployment and Inflation

LEARNING OBJECTIVES

3.1 Explain what the unemployment rate measures and misses, and identify four types of unemployment.

3.2 Define the natural rate of unemployment and explain its connection to recessionary and inflationary output gaps.

3.3 Explain how the inflation rate is calculated and what it misses, and describe three problems inflation creates.

3.4 Use the quantity theory of money to explain where inflation comes from.

3.5 Describe the Phillips Curve and its connections to demand-pull and cost-push inflations.

IF YOU WERE LOOKING for a summer job in 2009, then you know how hard they were to find. In May of that year, Canada's unemployment rate hit 8.4 percent. The news was worst in the province of Ontario, where the rate reached 9.4 percent — well above the national average. At the same time, Saskatchewan's and Manitoba's fell to 4.9 percent — the lowest in the country.

While the unemployment rate in Canada has been increasing, the inflation rate has been falling. The May 2009 inflation rate in Canada — the average increase in all prices over a year — was almost zero, just 0.1 percent, down from the 3.5 percent inflation rate less than a year earlier (August 2008).

But what do these numbers really mean? In judging the performance of the economy, what are "good" numbers for unemployment and inflation, what are "bad" numbers, and why are the numbers different in different parts of the country? And what do these numbers mean for you personally? Your job prospects? Your standard of living? Your smart investment choices?

In this chapter you will gain an understanding of how unemployment and inflation are measured and compared, how they are connected to each other and to GDP, and how you can find useful information to aid you in your job searches. As a bonus, you will learn how to calculate how much higher the cost of living is now compared to the prices your grandparents or parents paid.

3.1 Who Is Unemployed?
Healthy and Unhealthy Types of Unemployment

Explain what the unemployment rate measures and misses, and identify four types of unemployment.

Unemployment is something everyone worries about. In a market economy, money buys almost everything. Not having a paying job, and not earning money in input markets, creates serious personal hardship—you can't afford to buy the necessities of life in output markets. Unemployment is not good for society as a whole either, because when people are not working, there are fewer products/services available in output markets to meet everyone's needs.

Out of Work Is Not Enough

Government pays close attention to the number of unemployed. Each month, Statistics Canada surveys 54 000 households concerning their employment status, placing everyone in the working-age population (age 15 and over) into one of three categories:

- employed
- unemployed
- not in the labour force.

Calculating the Unemployment Rate   You are counted as employed if you are working either full-time or part-time at a paid job. You are counted as unemployed if you are not doing paid work and are actively searching for a job, as well as if you are on temporary layoff or about to start a new job.

If you do not fit into the employed or unemployed categories—if you are, for example, a full-time student, homemaker, or retiree—you are counted as not in the labour force. Simply not working does not mean you are unemployed.

Figure 3.1 shows the number of Canadians in each category for May 2009.

Figure 3.1	Labour Force Categories for Working-Age Population, May 2009

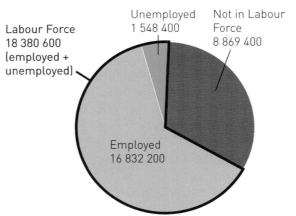

Source: Statistics Canada, Table 282-0087.

In order to calculate the unemployment rate, Statistics Canada first calculates the labour force. The **labour force** is the sum of the employed and the unemployed.

$$\text{Labour force} = \text{employed} + \text{unemployed}$$

The **unemployment rate** is the percentage of the people in the labour force who are unemployed—without work and actively seeking a job.

$$\text{Unemployment rate} = \frac{\text{Unemployed}}{\text{Labour force}} \times 100$$

Plugging in the (rounded) numbers from Figure 3.1 shows how the 8.4 percent unemployment rate for May 2009 was calculated.

$$8.4 \text{ percent} = \frac{1\ 548\ 000}{18\ 381\ 000} \times 100$$

The size of the labour force is also used to calculate the **labour force participation rate**—the percentage of the working-age population who are in the labour force (employed or unemployed):

$$\frac{\text{Labour force}}{\text{participation rate}} = \frac{\text{Labour force}}{\text{Working-age population}} \times 100$$

In May 2009, the working-age population was 27 250 000, so the labour force participation rate was

$$67.5 \text{ percent} = \frac{18\ 381\ 000}{27\ 250\ 000} \times 100$$

Chapter 2 showed that female labour force participation rates have been increasing over time and approaching those for men. In May 2009, the female labour force participation rate was 62.2 percent while the rate for males was 73.5 percent.

labour force:
employed + unemployed

unemployment rate:
percentage of people
in labour force who
are unemployed

labour force
participation rate:
percentage of
working-age population
in the labour force
(employed or
unemployed)

Unemployment in Canada Figure 3.2 shows the unemployment rate, based on the formulas above, in Canada from 1926 to 2009.

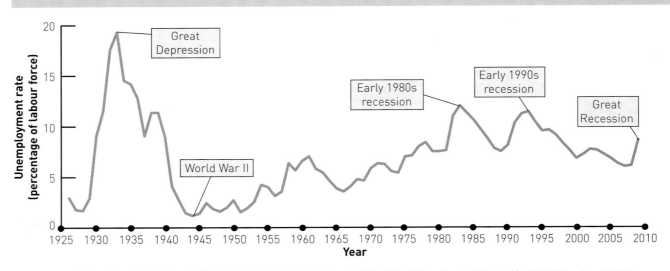

Figure 3.2 Unemployment Rates in Canada, 1926–2009

Source: *Historical Statistics of Canada* (2nd ed.) Series D124-145; Statistics Canada Table 282-0002, series v2461224, Table 282-0087, series v2062815.

The Great Depression began in 1929 and continued until the onset of World War II in 1939.

What stands out most is the spike in unemployment during the Great Depression. The unemployment rate peaked close to 20 percent in 1933. Also notice the lowest unemployment rate, 1.2 percent, which occurred with government organization of production during World War II.

The highest post-war unemployment rate—11.9 percent in 1983—occurred during the recession of the early 1980s. The unemployment rate during the early 1990s' recession reached 11.4 percent in 1993. And most recently, you can see the 2009 upturn in unemployment associated with the Great Recession.

What the Unemployment Rate Misses

Just as the different measurements of GDP have limitations, so too does the measurement of unemployment. The three categories Statistics Canada uses—employed, unemployed, and not in the labour force—each miss some part of the complete unemployment story.

Involuntary Part-time Workers Some workers who are employed part-time would rather have a full-time job, but can't find one. Statistics Canada calls these *involuntary part-time workers*, and keeps track of them, but they don't show up in the official unemployment rate. As the Economics Out There story on page 89 explains, during recessions, businesses often try to hold on to experienced workers but cut back their hours, increasing involuntary part-time unemployment. And during expansions, involuntary part-time unemployment falls as businesses restore full-time work before hiring new workers. These shifts between part-time and full-time work are not picked up in the unemployment rate—they are missed.

Discouraged Workers   Most workers who are unemployed hope to find a job. But more than half of workers who are unemployed end up dropping out of the labour force. Workers may drop out for many reasons, including returning to school or because they have given up on finding a job.

Discouraged workers are those who want to work, but have given up actively searching for jobs. They do not show up in the unemployment rate—they are missed.

Instead, discouraged workers cause changes in the labour force participation rate. During recessions, when it gets harder to find jobs, there are more discouraged workers who drop out of the labour force. Ironically, this causes the official unemployment rate to *fall* when more people are actually out of work.

Consider this simple example from Chapter 1. If 93 people are employed, and 7 people are not employed and seeking work, the official unemployment rate is 7 percent $(7 \div (93 + 7) \times 100)$. But if one of those unemployed people gets discouraged and leaves the labour force, the official unemployment rate falls to 6 percent $(6 \div (93 + 6) \times 100)$.

The number of discouraged workers tends to increase in recessions and decrease in expansions. Once the economy gets past the trough of a recession and begins expanding, the unemployment rate often increases even as the economy is creating more jobs, because previously discouraged workers get encouraged and re-enter the labour force actively seeking work. The recession of the early 1990s ended in 1991, but the unemployment rate kept rising for this reason until its peak in 1993 of 11.4 percent.

Figure 3.3, on page 90 shows how the unemployment rate would be higher if these involuntary part-time workers and discouraged workers were counted as unemployed. Statistics Canada calls this larger percentage the measure of labour underutilization. For May 2009, the *labour underutilization rate* was 11.5 percent, more than the official unemployment rate of 8.7 percent.

discouraged workers: want to work but have given up actively searching for jobs

Jobless Picture May Be Even Worse

When the Art Gallery of Ontario (AGO) reduced its work force, it didn't simply lay off workers. Instead, the gallery eliminated full-time jobs and created part-time jobs.

Previously full-time employees faced a tough choice: Should they apply for the new part-time jobs, with lower pay and responsibilities, or leave the AGO and enter the deteriorating labour market to search for a full-time job?

"They're really put into a corner," said union steward Paula Whitmore, who witnessed her AGO colleagues struggle to make the best decision.

The choices the AGO employees make affect not only their income, but also the unemployment rate. Those full-time employees who accept the new part-time jobs will still be officially counted as employed. Those who instead start searching for full-time work will be officially unemployed.

Source: Heather Schofield, *The Globe and Mail*, April 22, 2009.

Figure 3.3	Unemployment and Underutilization of Labour, May 2009
	Percentage of Labour Force
Official unemployment rate	8.7
Involuntary part-time workers	2.6
Discouraged workers	0.2
Total Underutilization Rate	**11.5**

Source: Statistics Canada, Table 282-0085.

FOR YOUR INFORMATION

You can find detailed information about unemployment rates for Canada, the provinces, and individual cities by going to the Statistics Canada homepage at www. statcan.gc.ca/.

On the opening page, right side, you will see the Latest Indicators. Click on Unemployment Rate. This is also where to find information about GDP and the inflation rates (Consumer Price Index) we will be covering shortly.

Regional Differences The national unemployment rate is calculated by aggregating (there is that macroeconomic word again meaning the whole) the statistics for all of the provinces. That average hides regional differences in unemployment rates across Canada. Figure 3.4 shows the unemployment rates for May 2009 by province.

Figure 3.4	Provincial Unemployment Rates, May 2009
Province	**Unemployment Rate**
Newfoundland/Labrador	15.1
Prince Edward Island	13.1
Nova Scotia	8.9
New Brunswick	8.8
Québec	8.7
Ontario	9.4
Manitoba	4.9
Saskatchewan	4.9
Alberta	6.6
British Columbia	7.6

Source: Statistics Canada, Table 282-0087.

The pattern in these unemployment rates is typical of most years in Canada. Rates in Atlantic Canada are historically higher than the average unemployment rate for all of Canada. Rates in Western Canada are historically lower than average. Central Canada, with more than 60 percent of the Canadian labour force, tends to have rates close to the national unemployment rate.

The Statistics Canada homepage at www.statcan.gc.ca always has the *Latest Indicators* on the right side, including population, inflation rate, unemployment rate and growth rate of GDP. You can check the current unemployment rate any time at this site.

Healthy and Unhealthy Unemployment

What do unemployment and cholesterol have in common? Doctors tell us that there are good and bad forms of cholesterol. Good cholesterol—found in foods like olive oil—contributes to the health of your heart. Bad cholesterol—found in fried fast foods—is unhealthy and increases your risk of heart attacks. Similarly, there are healthy forms of employment—those that help create a more dynamic economy—and unhealthy forms of unemployment—those that hurt economic production.

Economists distinguish four main types of unemployment—frictional, structural, seasonal, and cyclical. Let's look at each and whether each is healthy or unhealthy for the economy.

Frictional Unemployment   Market economies excel at reacting quickly to change. When there are surpluses or shortages, prices change and create incentives for consumers and businesses to adjust their smart choices. Those adjustments mean some businesses shrink and reduce employment, while others grow and hire additional workers. Those same changing prices and wages lead workers to move out of jobs that are disappearing (automobile sales) and into jobs that are expanding (collection agencies). These adjustments, which involve workers moving between jobs, or from school to a job, are part of the normal, healthy functioning of a market economy, with its constant process of creative destruction.

Because of these continuous adjustments, at any moment in time there will be workers between jobs and workers searching for jobs. This unemployment—workers between or searching for jobs—is called **frictional unemployment**.

Frictional unemployment is "healthy" unemployment, and is not a problem that policymakers need to address.

frictional unemployment: due to normal labour turnover and job search; healthy part of changing economy

Structural Unemployment   Businesses and individuals in market economies do not just react to change—they also cause change. Competitive business innovations earn profits for the winners but destroy less productive or less desirable products and production methods. This competition can come from domestic businesses or from business abroad in countries like India or China. Unemployment that arises because changes in technology or international competition makes workers' skills obsolete in Canada is called **structural unemployment**. Robots destroyed the jobs of tool-and-die makers who used to build simpler machines for automobile production. Digital recorders have made the jobs of stenographers, who used to take notes in shorthand, obsolete.

Workers who are structurally unemployed need to retrain to find new and different jobs. Like frictional unemployment, structural unemployment is "healthy" unemployment. It results from the healthy functioning of market economies, part of the process of economic growth that yields rising living standards. But unlike frictional unemployment, structural unemployment is a problem that must be addressed through retraining.

structural unemployment: due to technological change or international competition that makes workers' skills obsolete in Canada

Seasonal Unemployment Jobs like fruit picking or snow shovelling are only available at certain times of the year. Seasonal unemployment arises because of seasonal changes in the weather.

Seasonal unemployment is neither healthy nor unhealthy. It is a function of nature. Those of us who do not live on the west coast might wish for a more California-like climate, but other than wishing, nothing else needs to be done. It is not a problem requiring a policy solution.

seasonal unemployment: due to seasonal changes in weather

Cyclical Unemployment Workers who lose their jobs because of contractions in economic activity suffer from cyclical unemployment. **Cyclical unemployment** arises from fluctuations over the business cycle—increasing during economic contractions and recessions and decreasing during economic expansions.

Cyclical unemployment is the one "unhealthy" unemployment—the bad, deep-fried version. Cyclical unemployment is the barrier to full employment that is part of the fundamental macroeconomic question: "If left alone by government, do the price mechanisms of market economies adjust quickly to maintain steady growth in living standards, full employment, and stable prices?" Cyclical unemployment is a problem that needs addressing, especially according to the hands-on view of market economies.

Figure 3.5 summarizes the different varieties of unemployment. In the next section, we will explain exactly what economists mean by "full employment."

cyclical unemployment: due to fluctuations in economic activity over the business cycle.

Figure 3.5	Varieties of Unemployment		
Type of Unemployment	**Healthy/ Unhealthy**	**Problem that Needs Addressing?**	**Cause**
Frictional	Healthy	No	Normal, healthy market adjustments of demand and supply
Structural	Healthy	Yes (worker retraining)	Technological change, international competition, resource depletion
Seasonal	Neutral	No	Weather and seasons
Cyclical	Unhealthy	Yes (fiscal or monetary policy)	Business cycles

Refresh 3.1

1. State the formula for calculating the unemployment rate, and explain what each word in the formula means.

2. Since the official unemployment rate misses several types of out-of-work people, is the measurement of any use to policymakers? Explain your reasons.

3. How might knowing the regional differences in unemployment rates give you new ideas for looking for work?

www.myeconlab.com

3.2 How Full is "Full Employment?" The Natural Rate of Unemployment

Define the natural rate of unemployment and explain its connection to recessionary and inflationary output gaps.

Most people would say that "full employment" means everyone is employed, that the unemployment rate is zero percent. But economists define it differently.

The Natural Rate of Unemployment

Full employment for economists is the unemployment rate that exists when all markets, including labour input markets, are working well. When markets work well, there still will be frictional unemployment (people between jobs) and structural unemployment (people needing retraining). And then there's also seasonal unemployment—people out of work because of nature. These varieties of unemployment are a normal part of the healthy functioning of market economies. The term "full employment" that is used by Statistics Canada, and that you see in the media, means that there is still unemployment, but it is frictional, structural, and seasonal. Full employment includes these types of unemployment.

The unemployment rate associated with full employment is called the **natural rate of unemployment**—the rate when there is only frictional, structural, and seasonal unemployment.

Notice that the natural rate of employment excludes the one "unhealthy" variety of unemployment—cyclical unemployment that comes from business cycles.

So full employment to economists—the natural rate of unemployment—can also be defined as *zero percent cyclical unemployment.*

Natural Rate of Unemployment and Potential GDP

There is an important connection between the natural rate of unemployment—at full employment—and the discussion of potential GDP and output gaps in Chapter 2.

If the economy is in a position of full employment, that is with no cyclical unemployment, then real GDP is equal to potential GDP. The unemployment rate is equal to the natural rate and there is only frictional, structural, or seasonal unemployment.

Recessionary Gap   When the economy goes into a contraction, real GDP falls below potential GDP—there is a recessionary output gap. In a recessionary gap, there are unemployed inputs—including labour—making real GDP less than potential GDP. That additional unemployment caused by the contraction is cyclical unemployment. Therefore, in a recessionary gap there is no full employment. The unemployment rate rises above the natural rate due to cyclical unemployment.

natural rate of unemployment: unemployment rate at full employment, when there is only frictional, structural, and seasonal unemployment

"Full employment" is not zero percent unemployment, but zero percent cyclical unemployment.

In recessionary gap, unemployment rate above natural rate due to cyclical unemployment.

Inflationary Gap   When the economy is expanding, real GDP can temporarily rise above potential GDP, and there is an inflationary output gap. In an inflationary gap, not only are all inputs fully employed, the economy is working overtime. For the labour market, this means the unemployment rate is driven *below* the natural rate of employment. More workers than normal are being employed, so levels of frictional, structural, or seasonal unemployment fall below normal levels. The demand for labour is so great that jobs are easier to find and search times for jobs are reduced. A strong labour market may also draw people into the labour force who had been out of the labour force, also increasing the ability of the economy to produce more products/services.

The reason it is possible, at least for short periods of time, for real GDP to rise above potential GDP is that the natural rate of unemployment at full employment is not zero percent, but *zero percent cyclical unemployment*. Full employment at potential GDP still allows for frictional, structural, and seasonal unemployment. These types of unemployment, especially frictional unemployment, can fall below normal full employment levels. People who had been unemployed at potential GDP because of frictional, structural, or seasonal reasons are now employed. This explains the question, from Chapter 2, of how real GDP can be above potential GDP.

Figure 3.6 summarizes the connections between output gaps and unemployment rates.

Figure 3.6   Output Gaps and Unemployment

Real GDP and Potential GDP	Output Gap	Unemployment Rate
Real GDP equals potential GDP	None	Natural rate of unemployment — full employment (only frictional, structural, seasonal unemployment)
Real GDP below potential GDP	Recessionary gap	Unemployment rate above natural rate (cyclical unemployment)
Real GDP above potential GDP	Inflationary gap	Unemployment rate below natural rate (less than normal frictional, structural, seasonal unemployment)

What Is The Natural Rate of Unemployment?

You might be wondering, OK, so what is the natural rate of unemployment? What is the "target" rate of unemployment that a hands-off believer in Say's Law could use to show that the economy is doing fine on its own? No government involvement needed, thank you. And for a hands-on believer? What rate would serve as a signal to government that a policy is needed to reduce unemployment? These are reasonable and important questions.

It turns out, however, that economists disagree about what the number is for the natural rate of unemployment. Most would say the natural rate is somewhere between 4 percent and 9 percent unemployment. Others would disagree and argue that whatever unemployment exists is always at the natural rate, so there is never a need for government involvement. There is also some disagreement about whether the natural rate stays relatively constant over time, or whether the natural rate fluctuates frequently with the changes in the economy that affect frictional and structural unemployment.

We will explore these disagreements in Part 3 (Chapters 7, 8, and 9) on Macroeconomic Policy for Citizens.

Refresh

3.2

www.myeconlab.com

1. Define the natural rate of unemployment.

2. Explain the connection between GDP output gaps and the unemployment rate.

3. Find a business story in the media that uses the term *unemployment*. Decide if they are using unemployment the same way an economist would. Explain any differences you discover.

3.3 Lightening Up Your Wallet: What is Inflation?

Inflation is a persistent rise in the average level of all prices. You will often see a headline stating, for example: "Statistics Canada today reported that consumer prices rose 0.1 percent in the 12 months to May 2009." The 0.1 percent is the annual inflation rate in Canada. It means that the same products/services that cost $100 in May 2008 cost $100.10 a year later.

The flip side of prices rising is the value of money falling. If products that used to cost $100 now cost $100.10, your hundred dollar bill no longer buys quite as much as it did last year. Your money has fallen in value.

Where does that number of 0.1 come from, and what does it mean? Is it a "good" number or a "bad" number in evaluating the performance of the economy? And why do people and policymakers worry about inflation?

The question about worry is not as silly as it sounds. Remember from the circular flow that the income you earn depends on prices in input markets—the wage rate is the price of an hour of labour. If *all* prices have risen 0.1 percent, that means your wage rate has also risen 0.1 percent. Yes, products/services in output markets cost more than last year, but your income has gone up by the same percentage, so you are earning more. Your ability to afford those purchases is unchanged. So what's the worry?

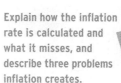

Explain how the inflation rate is calculated and what it misses, and describe three problems inflation creates.

Inflation is both a persistent rise in average prices and a fall in the value of money. When inflation occurs, you must spend more just to get the same products/services as before. Your money is worth less.

Consumer Price Index

Every month Statistics Canada tracks the average prices urban consumers pay for a representative shopping basket of about 600 products and services. Their shopping basket includes such categories as housing, transportation, food, recreation, furniture, and clothing. Those prices are used to construct the **Consumer Price Index (CPI),** which is the most widely used measure of average prices.

Consumer Price Index (CPI): measure of average prices of fixed shopping basket of products and services

Figure 3.7   Consumer Price Index Basket

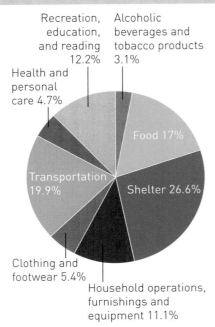

Recreation, education, and reading 12.2%

Alcoholic beverages and tobacco products 3.1%

Health and personal care 4.7%

Food 17%

Transportation 19.9%

Shelter 26.6%

Clothing and footwear 5.4%

Household operations, furnishings and equipment 11.1%

Source: Statistics Canada, *Consumer Price Index Reference Paper*, 62-553-X, Table 1.

inflation rate: annual percentage change in the consumer price index

The CPI Shopping Basket   Figure 3.7 shows the proportion of each category of spending in the CPI shopping basket. A category's proportion in the basket reflects its proportion in a typical consumer's budget. For example, housing is about 27 percent of the basket, reflecting that 27 percent of an urban consumer's spending is on housing (renting or owning). Transportation is 20 percent of spending, food is 17 percent, recreation, education and reading are 12 percent. The smallest category, at 3 percent, is for alcoholic drinks and tobacco products.

Because consumers spend more of their budget on food than on alcohol, a change in the price of food will have a bigger impact on the CPI—the average level of all prices—than a change in the price of alcohol will.

Calculating the CPI   To calculate the CPI, prices for each of the 600 products and services are averaged and weighted by the category for each. That weighted average of prices is the consumer price index.

To make it easier to compare years, prices are measured against a base year. The *base year* is currently 2002, and the cost of the basket for that year is given the value of 100. The CPI for 2008, which takes the same 2002 basket of products/services but priced at 2008 prices, has a value of 114.1. That means that the same products/services that cost $100 in 2002 cost $114.10 in 2008. You can see why the CPI is also called the cost of living index.

Measuring the Inflation Rate   Once we have numbers for the consumer price index, we can calculate the **inflation rate**. The inflation rate is the annual percentage change in the consumer price index (CPI). The general formula for the inflation rate between two years is

$$\text{Inflation rate} = \frac{\text{CPI for current year} - \text{CPI for previous year}}{\text{CPI for previous year}} \times 100$$

Looking back to our original example, the CPI in April 2009 was 114.7 and the CPI a year earlier in April 2008 was 114.6. Plugging that data into the inflation rate formula, we get

$$\text{Inflation rate} = \frac{114.7 - 114.6}{114.6} \times 100 = 0.1 \text{ percent}$$

Statistics Canada selects a basket of products/services to track the inflation rate. In 2002, you would have paid $100 for this basket of products/services, but in 2008 the same basket cost $114.10.

Inflation in Canada Figure 3.8 shows the annual inflation rate, based on the formula on page 96, in Canada from 1960 to 2009.

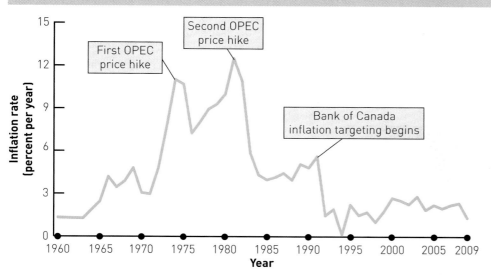

Figure 3.8   Inflation Rates in Canada, 1960–2009

Source: Statistics Canada, Table 3260021.

The inflation rate was under 2 percent during the early 1960s, but then increased during the Vietnam War. The dramatic increases in inflation rates that you can see in 1975 (to 10.9 percent) and 1981 (to 12.4 percent) were triggered by massive increases in the price of oil by the Organization of Petroleum Exporting Countries (OPEC). Inflation rates began dropping during the recession of the early 1980s, due in part to deliberate actions by the Bank of Canada. They fell again during the recession of the early 1990s. Since then, the Bank of Canada, as part of its monetary policy (we will discuss this in Chapter 7) aims to keep the inflation rate between 1 and 3 percent. The most recent May 2009 inflation rate of 0.1 percent is well below the target range of the Bank of Canada.

The Bank of Canada's Inflation Calculator

Source: www.bankofcanada.ca/en/rates/inflation_calc.html.

The inflation calculator allows you to see changes in the cost of living and inflation rates for any years between 1914 and today.

For example, products that cost $100 in 1980 would cost $267.61 in 2009. That is a 168 percent increase over 29 years, which is a 3.45 percent average annual rate of inflation.

Core Inflation Rate Because energy prices are so volatile, as are prices of fresh foods, the inflation rate can change quickly from month to month when energy and food prices change. For example, due largely to changes in energy prices, the inflation rate more than doubled from 1.4 percent in March 2008 to 3.5 percent just five months later in August 2008. When oil and gasoline prices then collapsed, the inflation rate fell in just nine months almost to zero—to 0.1 percent in May 2009.

To get around these large, short-run fluctuations and still provide meaningful data about inflation, the Bank of Canada calculates another measure of inflation. The **core inflation rate** excludes the most volatile categories from the consumer price index basket—fruit, vegetables, gasoline, fuel oil, natural gas, mortgage interest, intercity transportation, and tobacco products. These products are subject to large swings in price from month to month. By ignoring products/services that often experience large price fluctuations, the core inflation rate allows the Bank of Canada to provide key data to the market in a meaningful long-run form. The core inflation rate is the percentage change in the consumer price index excluding those volatile categories.

Figure 3.9 reproduces the inflation rates from 1960–2009, but adds a tan line showing the core inflation rates over the same period. Over the March 2008 to May 2009 period above, the core inflation rate, which removes the effects of energy prices, showed much less fluctuation, rising from 1.3 percent to a high of 2.4 percent, and back down to 2 percent. In monthly media reports of the inflation rate, you will usually hear about the core inflation rate as well as the comprehensive inflation rate.

core inflation rate: inflation rate excluding volatile categories

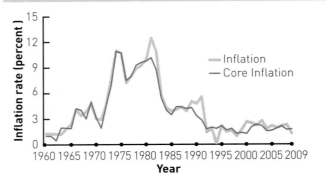

Figure 3.9 Inflation Rates and Core Inflation Rates in Canada, 1960–2009

Source: Statistics Canada, Tables 3260021, 3260022.

Why Worry About Inflation?

Is inflation really a problem you should worry about? If, *on average*, all prices rise by the same percentage, including input prices that determine incomes as well as output prices, then people can afford to buy the same products/services before and after the inflation. So where's the problem? Why worry?

People and policymakers worry about inflation for three good reasons.

Falling Value of Money A four percent inflation rate, for example, means that *on average*, all prices (and incomes) rise by four percent. But four percent is an *average*: some prices and incomes will rise more than four percent, some less, and some will not change at all. So for those whose income rises at or faster than the inflation rate, inflation is not a problem—no worries.

But for people living on fixed incomes, like seniors with a pension that pays a fixed, unchanged dollar amount each month, inflation is a definite worry. For those with fixed incomes, inflation reduces the purchasing power of their unchanged dollar incomes—a serious worry.

Similarly, inflation reduces the purchasing power of any savings you have. Savings account dollars do not change with the inflation rate. As prices rise, those savings account dollars lose their purchasing power. After inflation, your savings buy less than before. Now that's a worry.

Inflation causes the value of money to fall. If the quantity of money you have does not change—as with fixed incomes or savings—inflation reduces your purchasing power and your standard of living. Even if your income is rising, but rising more slowly than the inflation rate, your purchasing power will fall. Definitely something to worry about.

Connecting the Falling Value of Money to Interest Rates The falling value of money also affects interest rates. Whether you are a lender earning interest from savings accounts or loans made to others, or a borrower paying interest on a car loan, a mortgage, or credit card balances—inflation affects the purchasing power of your loan and interest received or paid.

That interest can be measured in two ways. The **nominal interest rate** is the interest rate observed in the markets, paid on mortgages, and earned on savings accounts. If your savings account pays 10 percent interest per year, that is a nominal interest rate. If you kept $1000 in the account for a year, at the end of the year you would earn $100 in interest (0.10 × $1000 = $100) added to the $1000, for a total of $1100.

But what can you buy with those $1100? If the inflation rate over the year has been zero, then the extra $100 on your original $1000 increases your purchasing power by 10 percent. But if average prices rose over the year by 4 percent—an inflation rate of 4 percent—each of those $100 now buys 4 percent fewer products/services than before. Your purchasing power from the earned interest has only increased by 6 per cent.

The realized **real interest rate** adjusts the nominal interest rate to remove the effects of inflation.

$$\text{Real interest rate} = \text{nominal interest rate} - \text{inflation rate}$$

If the inflation rate over the year was 4 percent, then the real interest rate you received, or realized, on your saving account was

$$\text{Real interest rate} = 10 \text{ percent} - 4 \text{ percent}$$

$$\text{Real interest rate} = 6 \text{ percent}$$

nominal interest rate: observed interest rate; equal to number of dollars received per year in interest as percentage of number of dollars saved

real interest rate: nominal interest rate adjusted for effects of inflation

MAPS 1

Unpredictable prices create risk and discourage business investment in future production.

"HOW DO YOU WANT IT—THE CRYSTAL MUMBO-JUMBO OR STATISTICAL PROBABILITY?"

At the end of the year you had 10 percent more dollars, but only 6 percent more purchasing power. The nominal interest rate calculates how many extra dollars you receive or pay at the end of a loan. The realized real interest rate calculates the extra purchasing power you have gained or lost at the end of a loan. Real interest rates are more important than nominal interest rates for making smart saving and investing decisions.

The falling value of money not only affects the purchasing power of your savings; it also affects the purchasing power of any interest earned on that savings. What if the inflation rate turns out to be greater than the nominal interest rate? If the nominal interest rate you earn on your savings is 10 percent—which sounds attractive—but the inflation rate is 12 percent, the realized real rate of interest on your savings account is −2 percent (10% − 12% = −2%). That means, even though you earned $100 in interest, at the end of the year you had lost 2 percent of your previous purchasing power. It would have been smarter to spend the money on products/services at the beginning of the year rather than saving and earning 10 percent nominal interest. Inflation is definitely something to worry about when making a decision to save.

Unpredictable Prices Impede Planning and Investment Unpredictable prices are a serious problem for businesses. Producing for output markets takes time. Business must first buy the labour, capital, land, and resources they need in input markets, produce their products, and then transport them to output markets for sale. All of these steps, connecting input markets and output markets (MAPS 1), take time.

Businesses must make commitments today for production that will only come to market in the future. If your business is not sure of a steady supply of inputs at predictable prices, your costs become unpredictable, and your profits unstable. And if prices and the inflation rate are changing unpredictably, it is hard to set your own output price, and to know what demand will be like if your customers are paying more for all other products/services. Unpredictability creates risk, and risk discourages business investment in future production.

Business planning for the future works best when prices are stable, or when inflation is running at a steady, predictable rate.

Danger of Self-Fulfilling Expectations Imagine this scenario: You have been working for a year on a contract that pays $3000 a month. The contract is up for renegotiation. While the inflation rate this year has been zero, you expect energy prices to rise next year. Because of that, you fear the inflation rate—the cost of living—will rise by 4 percent. In your negotiations for a new contract, what monthly pay rate will you ask for?

If you are like most people, you will be thinking, "The cost of living next year will be four percent higher. Unless I get at least a four percent raise, my income won't keep pace with the rising cost of living. My standard of living will go down. I'd better ask for at least $3120 a month (4 percent of $3000 is $120)."

Source: www.ScienceCartoonsPlus.com.

Once expectations of inflation begin, many people start thinking the same way. Businesses, expecting higher prices for inputs, set output prices higher to protect their profits. Banks, expecting inflation, will increase nominal interest rates on loans to protect the real rate of interest they will receive. When workers, businesses, and banks expect inflation, they reasonably try and protect themselves by pushing up wages, prices of output, and interest rates. This can create self-fulfilling expectations—by reacting to the expectation of inflation we may help cause inflation.

Once inflation takes hold, expectations of higher and higher inflation rates keep rising, creating a vicious cycle that, if not broken, runs the risk of spiraling out of control. Expectations of inflation were one of the causes of the sharp rise in inflation rates and nominal interest rates in the early 1980s. Can this cycle be broken? What can be done? We will discuss the importance of expectations for interest rates and for monetary policy in Chapter 7.

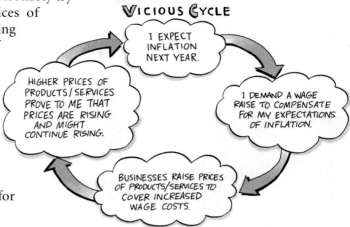

VICIOUS CYCLE

I EXPECT INFLATION NEXT YEAR.

I DEMAND A WAGE RAISE TO COMPENSATE FOR MY EXPECTATIONS OF INFLATION.

BUSINESSES RAISE PRICES OF PRODUCTS/SERVICES TO COVER INCREASED WAGE COSTS.

HIGHER PRICES OF PRODUCTS/SERVICES PROVE TO ME THAT PRICES ARE RISING AND MIGHT CONTINUE RISING.

Acceptable Inflation   Most economists view a low inflation rate, of under three percent per year, as not a serious problem, as long as the inflation rate is also predictable. That is, as long as the inflation rate remains steady from year to year. The Bank of Canada's announced target range for the inflation rate of one to three percent is based on this view.

Since even a low inflation rate hurts people on fixed incomes, you may be wondering why economists don't push for a zero percent inflation rate. That's a good question, and the answer will come in the last section of this chapter on tradeoffs between inflation and unemployment. Every choice, including the policy choice to aim for zero inflation, has an opportunity cost.

Dangerous Downward Spirals: If Low Inflation is OK, Is Deflation Better?

What goes up can also go down. Prices can rise *and* fall. **Deflation** is the opposite of inflation—a persistent fall in average prices and a rise in the value of money. At first, deflation sounds attractive. As consumers, we all like lower prices, and even those on fixed incomes would seem to benefit. But a persistent fall in average prices sets up a dangerous downward spiral.

Once average prices begin falling, a new attitude emerges in the marketplace. Consumers, believing that prices will go even lower very soon, hold off on buying products/services, since they will get a lower price by waiting. Sales collapse and businesses cut back production and employment. Wages, which also fall with falling average prices, will fall further as the economy contracts and unemployment increases. This deflationary spiral becomes the reverse image of the inflationary spiral.

deflation: persistent fall in average prices and rise in the value of money

Savers and Borrowers   A rise in the value of money sounds attractive. If you have savings, deflation increases their value. Deflation increases the purchasing power of money you have in the bank. Deflation benefits savers—the opposite of inflation, which hurts them.

But deflation hurts borrowers. When consumers or businesses pay back loans, they are paying back more valuable dollars—in purchasing power—than the dollars they borrowed. Deflation also means both consumers' incomes and business revenues are falling. Consumers and businesses have less ability to pay back loans, whose dollar amounts do not change.

Deflation benefits savers but hurts borrowers.

Source: © 2008 Ted Rall. Used by permission of Universal Uclick. All rights reserved.

Falling Asset Values   During persistent deflation, the value of assets—like houses and equities—also falls. Imagine you bought a house for $300 000 with a $200 000 mortgage. Deflation sets in, and every month you see your house fall in value, but your mortgage payments stay the same. Soon, your mortgage could be higher than your house's value—you actually owe more on your house than it is worth. Unfortunately, that is the reality many homeowners in the United States faced during the Great Recession.

The falling price of one product/service is not deflation. Falling real estate values alone are not a deflation. A deflation requires a persistent fall in the average of *all* prices, not just prices in one sector of the economy. But the experience of deflation in the U.S. real estate markets gives a good picture of the destructive forces at work in a general deflation.

The Lesson of Japanese Deflation   Japan suffered from a decade of deflation after its real estate bubble burst in 1991. Partly as a result of the destructive downward spiral of deflation, the Japanese economy suffered a decade of economic stagnation, almost no growth, and significant unemployment.

The Japanese experience is one reason policymakers took strong action to try to avoid deflation as a possible outcome of the Great Recession. Deflation is much worse than low inflation.

What the Inflation Rate Misses

There are challenges in using the consumer price index to measure inflation (or deflation), just as there are challenges in measuring GDP or the unemployment rate.

Standard of Living versus Cost of Living   In Chapter 2 you learned that changes in nominal GDP between two years can be due either to changes in the quantities of products/services the economy has produced, or to changes in their prices. Real GDP comparisons keep prices constant, isolating changes in quantities only. Quantities are important for measuring our standard of living.

Quantities are important for measuring standard of living. Prices are important for measuring cost of living.

Changes in consumer spending between two years can involve either changes in the quantities of products/services consumers buy, or changes in their prices. To isolate the impact of changing prices only, the CPI keeps the quantities of products/services in the shopping basket constant from year to year. With quantities constant, all changes in the value of the basket are due to changes in prices only. Prices are important for measuring our cost of living.

To isolate changes in prices only, the consumer price index keeps the quantities constant. But in the real world, as prices change, consumers change the quantities of products/services they buy. Also, consumers eagerly buy new and improved versions of products/services. As a result, the inflation rate, based on the unchanged quantities of the consumer price index, misses two important trends.

Switch to Cheaper Substitutes

When the price of gasoline rises, people drive less and switch to public transit. That is the law of demand as explained in Appendix B. When the price of a product rises, we tend to buy less of it, and switch to cheaper substitutes.

We all save money, and reduce our cost of living, by switching to cheaper substitutes. Because the unchanged products/services included in the basket of the consumer price index do not take the switch to cheaper substitutes into account, the CPI tends to overstate increases in the cost of living.

New and Better Products

The unchanged basket of the consumer price index also misses the introduction of new products, and changes in quality of existing products.

There is no easy way to compare the cost of living in a year when new products/services like the iPhone and BlackBerry Curve are introduced to an earlier year when they didn't exist.

Many businesses upgrade the quality of their products/services while keeping the price constant. But, the CPI basket doesn't change. Even if a product in the CPI basket is improved to give more value and quality, the basket remains the same. For example, Apple has a very specific pricing strategy. Once they introduce a model like the MacBook Pro, they keep the price constant. But every three months or so, Apple upgrades the quality of the model with a faster processor, a bigger hard drive, or more RAM, all for the same price. Because the CPI doesn't capture these improvements in product quality, it again tends to overstate increases in the cost of living.

Statistics Canada is aware of these unavoidable shortcomings of all price indexes, and updates the contents of the CPI shopping basket from time to time to reflect changes in consumer spending habits and changes in products. Nonetheless, the Bank of Canada estimates that the official inflation rate, based on the consumer price index, overstates increases in the cost of living by about 0.5 percent. So an official inflation rate, for example, of 4 percent, translates into an actual increase in cost of living of 3.5 percent, but that is still just an estimate.

Because the CPI misses switches to cheaper substitutes and new and improved products, the official inflation rate based on the CPI overstates the increase in the cost of living.

Refresh 3.3

1. What is the formula for calculating the annual inflation rate?

2. Deflation lowers the cost of living. Why, then, do economists consider it worse than low inflation for the economy in general and for you in particular?

3. If you operate a small business, what problems would unpredictable inflation cause for you?

www.myeconlab.com

3.4 Inflation Starts with "*M*" the Quantity Theory of Money

Use the quantity theory of money to explain where inflation comes from.

Where does inflation come from?

That is a macroeconomic question—dealing with the whole economy—because inflation is a persistent rise in the average of all prices in the aggregate economy.

In microeconomics—dealing with individual choices, individual businesses, and markets for particular products/services—the related question is, Where do prices come from? (see Appendix D)

The answer to the microeconomic question is (p. 480): "Prices come from the interaction of demand and supply, in markets with appropriate property rights." Microeconomics, and the market forces of competing bids (demand) and offers (supply), explains why the price of iPods or piercings rise or fall.

But the explanation of why *all* prices tend to move up together (inflation) or down together (deflation), has a different origin—money. And money is a topic in macroeconomics. Microeconomics explains prices—measured in dollars (units of money). Macroeconomics explains the influence of money itself.

The answer to the macroeconomic question—where does inflation come from—has less to do with demand and supply in each industry, and more to do with the quantity of money in the economy as a whole.

Money and the Circular Flow

The story of where inflation comes from begins with money.

M represents the quantity of money in an economy.

M Is for Money   Economists use the letter *M* to represent the quantity of money in the economy. In the actual Canadian economy, money takes many sophisticated and digital forms, as we will see in Chapter 5. But let's start with a simple story, where the only money consists of loonies, exactly 1000 of them.

The simple economy in our story produces $5000 worth of final products/services in a year—nominal GDP is $5000. Even though our economy is simple, is has the same circular flow of spending and income (Figure 3.10) as sophisticated economies. Businesses buy inputs from consumer households in input markets, paying with loonies. Businesses use the inputs to produce products/services, which they sell to consumers in output markets. Consumers use the loonie income earned in input markets to buy the products/services they want. Cash only—no Visa, no debit cards accepted. The $ signs on the green arrows represent loonies only.

Figure 3.10   Simple Circular Flow

AGGREGATE SPENDING = AGGREGATE INCOME

As we explained in Chapter 2, the value of nominal GDP ($5000 in our story) is equal to both the value of final products/services sold in output markets (left side), and the value-added income earned in input markets (right side). The two sides of the circle are equal by definition. Aggregate spending equals aggregate income.

All purchases and sales, both in output markets and input markets, have to be made with loonies. Do you see a problem? I'm hoping you are wondering if I've made a mistake in my story. How can this simple economy have $5000 worth of sales with only 1000 loonies?

V Is for Velocity

There is no mistake. The problem is fixed if each loonie changes hands more than once in a year. If each loonie was only spent (and received) once in a year, then the limit of aggregate sales in the economy would be $1000. But if each loonie changes hands five times in a year, there could be $5000 worth of purchases/sales. The number of times a unit of money changes hands during a year is called the **velocity of money**. Economists use the letter *V* to represent the velocity of money.

velocity of money (V): number of times a unit of money changes hands during a year

P × *Q* Is for Nominal GDP

The quantity of money and its velocity have a simple relationship to nominal GDP.

Nominal GDP can be represented as $P \times Q$ (P times Q). When we calculated nominal GDP in Chapter 2, we added together price times quantity for every final product/service. $P \times Q$ is a shorthand version of that calculation.

P represents average prices — the consumer price index. (In order to explain where inflation comes from, we will have to explain what causes P to rise. But we are not quite there yet.)

Q represents the aggregate quantity of real output, the sum of all of the physical final products/services produced.

So $P \times Q$ equals nominal GDP, which also equals aggregate income. In our simple story, $P \times Q$ equals $5000.

The relationship between these four variables, M, V, P, and Q is

Nominal GDP is P × Q. P represents average prices (CPI) and Q represents quantity of real output.

$$\underset{\text{of Money}}{\overset{\text{Quantity}}{M}} \times \underset{\substack{\text{Velocity of} \\ \text{Money}}}{V} = \underset{\substack{\text{Average} \\ \text{Prices}}}{P} \times \underset{\substack{\text{Quantity of} \\ \text{Real Output}}}{Q}$$

Reading from left to right, the quantity of money, multiplied by the velocity of money, equals average prices multiplied by the quantity of real output. This simple relationship — between, on the left side, the quantity of money and its velocity, and, on the right side, nominal GDP — is always true. If $5000 worth of final products/services were sold in an economy (nominal GDP is $5000 on the right side), then there had to be enough money, multiplied by the velocity of money, to allow those sales to happen (on the left side).

Fixing the Quantity Theory of Money

The payoff to using this simple relationship to explain inflation finally comes when we fix two of the variables, V and Q; that is, we assume that they do not change. Fixing V, the velocity of money, means that the number of times money changes hands stays constant from year to year. Fixing Q, the quantity of real output, means that the level of real GDP stays constant from year to year. Let's suppose that real GDP stays constant at potential GDP.

$$\underset{\substack{\text{Quantity}\\\text{of Money}}}{M} \times \underset{\substack{\text{Fixed}\\\\\text{Velocity of}\\\text{Money}}}{V} = \underset{\substack{\text{Average}\\\text{Prices}}}{P} \times \underset{\substack{\text{Fixed}\\\\\text{Quantity of}\\\text{Real Output}}}{Q}$$

Now, let's plug in the numbers from our simple story—the quantity of money ($M = \$1000$) and the velocity of money ($V = 5$). For average prices—the consumer price index—let's pick the number 100 ($P = 100$). Since we know that $P \times Q = 5000$, that means the number for real GDP must be 50 ($Q = 50$ since $5000 \div 100 = 50$).

Plugging in those numbers, we get

$$
\begin{array}{ccccccc}
M & \times & V & = & P & \times & Q \\
1000 & \times & 5 & = & 100 & \times & 50 \\
& & 5\,000 & = & 5\,000 & &
\end{array}
$$

The two sides of this equation, just like the two halves of the circular flow, have to be equal. There must be enough money, multiplied by the number of times each loonie changes hands (left side in this equation), to allow for the purchase/sale of nominal GDP (right side in this equation).

More Money Causes Inflation   This relationship is called the **quantity theory of money**. The quantity theory states that an increase in the quantity of money causes an equal percentage increase in average prices—the inflation rate. If someone says that "printing money causes inflation," then they have stated the quantity theory of money.

Here's an example of what happens when the quantity of money increases by 100 percent, doubling from 1000 loonies to 2000 loonies. Since we have fixed the velocity of money to be constant at 5 and real GDP to be constant at 50, if the two sides of the equation are to continue to be equal, then average prices (P)—the CPI—must also double, from 100 to 200.

FOR YOUR INFORMATION

What happens if we leave the simple version of the quantity theory and instead allow real GDP to grow over time, as happens in a real economy?

With velocity still fixed, the results are similar to the simple quantity theory of money. But now the percentage increase in the quantity of money (left side) will be equal to a *combination* of the percentage increase of average prices *and* percentage increase in real GDP (right side).

quantity theory of money: increase in the quantity of money causes an equal percentage increase in the inflation rate

M	$\times$	V	$=$	P	$\times$	Q
2000	$\times$	5	$=$	200	$\times$	50
		10 000	$=$	10 000		

The two sides of the equation must be equal. The increase in the quantity of money from 1000 loonies to 2000 loonies is an increase of 100 percent. The increase in the CPI, from 100 to 200, is also a 100 percent increase in the inflation rate ($(200 - 100) \div 100 \times 100 = 100$ percent).

The quantity theory of money is more than just numbers in a formula. There is an explanation for the inflation rate numbers. The explanation begins with the increase in the quantity of money—in our story, the number of loonies in the economy rises from 1000 to 2000. Chapter 7 explains how the Bank of Canada actually increases the quantity of money. But for now, let's say a Bank of Canada employee in a helicopter carrying loonies decides to play Santa Claus, and throws 1000 loonies into the air. The loonies fall to the ground, where they are quickly scooped up by lucky consumers.

Before the loonies came falling from the sky, consumers had incomes of $1000. After, consumers have incomes of $2000 and are feeling richer. Consumers try to buy more stuff, but—and this is a big but—remember that the quantity of real GDP is fixed. The quantity of products/services available does not change. As consumers bid against each other trying to get more stuff, the prices of products/services rise. Prices will continue to rise, and consumers will continue to offer more money in an attempt to get the products and not be left empty-handed—until the rise in prices matches the rise in the quantity of money.

Even when the velocity of money (V) and real GDP (Q) actually do change in the real world, the basic logic of the quantity theory of money still applies. There is too much money chasing too few products/services. In the long run, there is a connection between the quantity of money and the inflation rate in an economy.

Not all inflation is directly caused by an increase in the quantity of money. The inflation-starting trigger may begin somewhere else, such as with a rise in the price of single product like oil. Those triggers starting inflation are our next topic. But we cannot get inflation in the economy as a whole unless there is an accompanying increase in the quantity of money.

Not all inflation is directly caused by increases in the quantity of money. But when there is inflation, there must be an accompanying increase in the quantity of money.

Refresh 3.4

1. In your own words, explain the quantity theory of money.

2. Based on your explanation in question 1, explain how increasing the amount of money everyone has to spend eventually causes prices to rise.

3. The quantity theory of money assumes that real GDP is at potential GDP and does not change. If instead, real GDP were below potential GDP and could change, what do you think would happen when the quantity of money increased?

www.myeconlab.com

3.5 When Tim Hortons Pays $18 per Hour: Unemployment and Inflation Tradeoffs

Describe the Phillips Curve and its connections to demand-pull and cost-push inflations.

Ever since 2006, Alberta has had among the lowest unemployment rates in Canada and the highest inflation rates. During the peak of the oil-driven boom in 2006, unemployment dipped to 3.4 percent, below Alberta's natural rate of unemployment (or equivalently, employment above full employment levels). The Alberta economy was growing quickly, and demand for labour was far greater than the supply of labour. Businesses faced labour shortages in most occupations. Even entry-level positions at Tim Hortons were offering $18 an hour in an attempt to attract scarce workers.

Demand was so great, and wages so high, that workers from as far away as the Maritimes moved to Alberta to take the higher-paying jobs. No problem of unemployment that needed addressing.

But there was a tradeoff. While unemployment was low, prices were rising. The cost of living index that Statistics Canada calculates for each province showed an inflation rate for Alberta in 2006 of 3.9 percent, far above the national inflation rate of 2 percent.

The Alberta experience is not unique. There is often a tradeoff between unemployment and inflation. In countries around the world, situations with low unemployment often trigger high inflation, and situations with high unemployment are often associated with low inflation.

You can only enjoy the benefits of very low unemployment rates—making it easier to find jobs—for a short time. Inflation soon kicks in.

The Phillips Curve

The tradeoff between unemployment and inflation was made famous by a New Zealand-born economist named A.W. Phillips. He examined data for the United Kingdom from 1861 to 1957 that showed an inverse relation (when one goes up, the other goes down) between unemployment and inflation. In years when the unemployment rate was lower, the inflation rate was higher. In years when the unemployment rate was higher, the inflation rate was lower. The visual representation of that data took the form of a curve, which became known as the **Phillips Curve**. Most countries, including Canada, showed the same inverse relation, as you can see from the Phillips Curve in Figure 3.11.

Phillips Curve: graph showing inverse relation between unemployment and inflation

The horizontal axis measures the unemployment rate. The vertical axis measures the inflation rate. Each dot or point on the graph represents a year between 1946 and 1969. The coordinate of a point on the horizontal axis is the unemployment rate for that year. The coordinate of a point on the vertical axis is the inflation rate that year. For example, in 1962, the unemployment rate in Canada was 5.5 percent (from the point read down to the horizontal axis), and the inflation rate was 1.3 percent (from the point read over to the vertical axis). The brown curve drawn through the points is like the one Phillips sketched to "fit" the data points.

Notice that at the top left of the Phillips Curve, there are points with lower unemployment and higher inflation. At the bottom right of the curve are points with higher unemployment and lower inflation.

Figure 3.11 Phillips Curve in Canada, 1946–1969

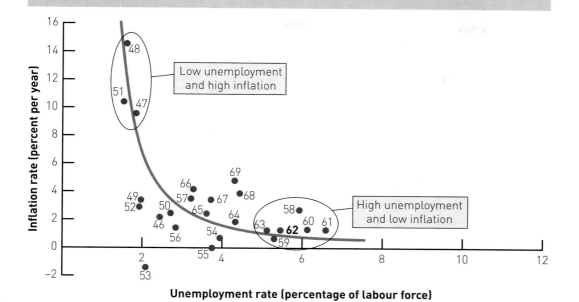

Source: *Historical Statistics of Canada* (2nd ed.) Series D124-145; Statistics Canada Table 282-0002, series v2461224, Table 282-0087, series v2062815; Statistics Canada Table 3260021.

Demand-Pull Inflation   The story behind the Phillips Curve's inverse relation between unemployment and inflation is basically the Alberta 2006 story.

For years corresponding to points on the top left of the Phillips Curve, the economy was booming, with rapid growth and low unemployment. During expansion years, the economy often produces output at levels near potential real GDP, or even slightly above potential GDP. All inputs, including labour, are fully employed. There is no cyclical unemployment, and frictional, structural, and seasonal unemployment rates may fall below normal. Demand is greater than supply in input markets—there are shortages—putting upward pressure on businesses costs, including wages. Since incomes are also expanding with higher wages, demand for outputs is strong—people have more money and are buying more things—which makes it easier for businesses to raise their output prices to match their rising costs.

Demand plays the leading role in this story, and the overall price rises that result are called **demand-pull inflation**. Demand is the key force causing shortages and pulling up prices. There must also be an accompanying increase in the quantity of money.

The story about the quantity theory of money, where the helicopter showers loonies to increase consumers' incomes, was also a demand-pull inflation story. With increased incomes, consumers demanded more products/services. But because the supply was fixed at potential GDP, the increased demand created shortages, and competing consumers bid up prices, just as employers in Alberta bid up entry-level wages to $18 an hour.

demand-pull inflation: rising average prices caused by increases in demand

Downward Demand-Pull Deflation For years corresponding to points on the bottom right of the Phillips Curve, the demand-pull story works in reverse, where decreases in demand pull prices down. During contractions, if demand for output decreases relative to supply, business find themselves with unsold products/services. Businesses may cut their prices in an attempt to sell the inventory that is piling up in warehouses. Businesses will also cut back production, laying off workers. Real GDP falls, and unemployment increases. There is a recessionary gap.

It is difficult to get a raise when people all around you are out of work and eager to find a job or take yours. Increased unemployment puts downward pressure on wages, which allows businesses to either cut output prices or have smaller price increases. High unemployment also means consumers have less income to spend, which puts more downward pressure on output prices. Decreased demand causes surpluses of products/services, leading businesses to cut prices, or at least not raise them as quickly. The end result is a bust instead of a boom, with higher unemployment and lower inflation.

The demand-pull inflation story explains the Phillips curve, with its tradeoff between unemployment and inflation. In years with lower unemployment (strong demand), inflation is higher. In years with higher unemployment (weak demand), inflation is lower.

Economists were very confident about this idea of a tradeoff between unemployment and inflation. Then the 1970s happened.

OPEC Ends the Original Phillips Curve

In 1973, the 12 members of the Organization of Petroleum Exporting Countries, OPEC, successfully agreed to restrict their combined outputs, and reduced the supply of oil. The world price of oil skyrocketed, from US $3 per barrel to $12 per barrel—a 400 percent increase!

Because energy costs are a significant part of the cost of supplying most products/services, businesses around the world were faced with dramatically higher costs. The equivalent of a 400 percent increase for labour costs would see wages rise from $10 per hour to $40 per hour. Imagine the damage that would do to a business's profitability!

While businesses raised prices to try and cover their rising energy costs, consumers had far less income to spend once they paid their dramatically higher fuel bills for driving and home heating. Prices were rising, which means there was an accompanying increase in the quantity of money. But demand and output fell. While the Canadian economy didn't technically fall into a recession—two consecutive quarters of declining real GDP—the pace of economic growth slowed and unemployment increased.

This chain of events repeated with a second OPEC price hike in 1979. If we extend Figure 3.11 to also include the years from 1970 to 2008, years that include the impact of the OPEC price hikes, this is what we see:

◀

OPEC production cutbacks in the 1970s created shortages of gasoline, causing prices to rise and triggering cost-push inflation.

Figure 3.12   Phillips Curve in Canada, 1946–2009

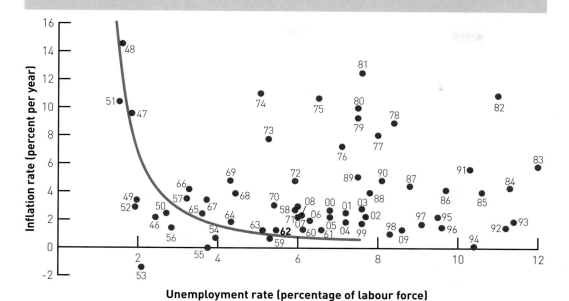

Source: *Historical Statistics of Canada* (2nd ed.) Series D124-145; Statistics Canada Table 282-0002, series v2461224, Table 282-0087, series v2062815; Statistics Canada Table 3260021.

The original, obvious tradeoffs between inflation and unemployment—the brown Phillips Curve—disappear. There are now points on the figure, like those for 1973, 1974, and 1982 that have combinations of both higher unemployment and higher inflation. The demand-pull story of inflation failed to explain the simultaneous existence of higher unemployment and higher inflation.

Supply Shocks and Cost-Push Inflation

Supply shocks are events that directly affect businesses' costs, prices, and supply—they are *not* caused by changes in demand. Energy price increases, droughts that reduce the supply of food, and natural disasters that destroy inputs and reduce an economy's ability to produce are all examples of negative supply shocks. Appendix C explains how an increase in input prices (like energy) reduces business profitability and causes a decrease in supply.

Cost-Push Inflation   Supply shocks like the OPEC price hikes did not fit the demand-pull inflation story behind the Phillips Curve's tradeoff between unemployment and inflation. A new story emerged called **cost-push inflation**. In a cost-push inflation, rising average prices are triggered by decreases in supply. Supply, not demand, plays the leading role in this story. A decrease in supply caused by increasing costs is the key force pushing up output prices. There was also an accompanying increase in the quantity of money.

While averages prices are rising, sales of products/services are decreasing. Decreases in output mean real GDP decreases. Since businesses are cutting back production, unemployment increases. So the economy experiences a double-dose of bad news—higher inflation and higher unemployment—also called **stagflation**. The word *stagflation* is a combination of *stagnation*—the economy is standing still or falling into recession, with higher unemployment—and the rising prices of *inflation*.

supply shocks: events directly affecting businesses' costs, prices, and supply

cost-push inflation: rising average prices caused by decreases in supply

stagflation: simultaneous recession (higher unemployment) and inflation (higher average prices)

The Original Phillips Curve and Beyond

When economists who believed in Say's Law could not explain the unemployment of the Great Depression, Keynes created macroeconomics. Similarly, when the demand-pull inflation story, the only inflation story at the time, could not explain the stagflation of the 1970s and 1980s, economists developed more sophisticated explanations, including the cost-push inflation story. Just as macroeconomics did not replace microeconomics, but supplemented it, these additional explanations supplemented, but did not replace, the original Phillips Curve.

Figure 3.13 summarizes the differences between the demand-pull and cost-push inflation stories. Keep in mind that all of the stories include an accompanying increase in the quantity of money.

Figure 3.13 Types of Inflation		
Type of Inflation	**Demand-Pull**	**Cost-Push**
Phase of business cycle	Expansion	Contraction
Unemployment	↓ unemployment	↑ unemployment
Inflation	↑ inflation	↑ inflation
Relation between Unemployment and Inflation	Tradeoff (Phillips Curve)	Simultaneous (Stagflation)

There are still immediate tradeoffs between inflation and unemployment as the demand-pull explanation of the Phillips Curve suggests. But over longer periods of time, when you allow for more years and more types of triggering events—including supply shocks—the tradeoffs and explanations become more complicated. With more time, many more factors are involved, including the role of expectations of inflation. You will read more about that in Chapter 7.

Changes in the Natural Rate of Unemployment Another complication over longer periods of time comes from changes in what numbers count as high unemployment or high inflation. The number that economists count as the natural rate of unemployment, when the economy is at full employment, has changed over time with changes in the economy. Changes in potential GDP, changes in labour force characteristics and participation rates, and changes in technology can all affect what counts as frictional, structural, and seasonal unemployment. For example, the rise of international competition from China and India has increased structural unemployment in Canada. Higher structural unemployment means the natural rate of employment is higher.

Even changes in government policy can affect the natural rate of unemployment. More generous rules for employment insurance—more benefits and, benefits for longer periods of time—allow workers to take more time to search for the right job, which would show up as higher frictional unemployment. Higher frictional unemployment means the natural rate of employment is higher.

These complications make for tougher choices for policymakers trying to address problems of unemployment and inflation. As we will see in Part 3 (Chapters 7, 8, and 9) on Macroeconomic Policy for Citizens, policies to address unemployment often make inflation worse, and policies to address inflation often make unemployment worse. And when there is stagflation— simultaneous problems of unemployment and inflation—the challenges to policymakers are even more difficult.

Over time, the tradeoffs between unemployment and inflation of the original Phillips Curve become complicated due to changes in expectations and the natural rate of unemployment.

Refresh 3.5

1. Explain the tradeoff that the Phillips Curve illustrates.

2. Describe the difference between demand-pull inflation and cost-push inflation.

3. Would you rather have higher inflation or higher unemployment? What are the reasons behind your personal choice?

www.myeconlab.com

Costs of (Not) Working and Living

Unemployment and Inflation

CHAPTER SUMMARY

3.1 WHO IS UNEMPLOYED?
HEALTHY AND UNHEALTHY TYPES OF UNEMPLOYMENT

The unemployment rate measures the percentage of the labour force who are out of work and actively searching for jobs, but misses involuntary part-time workers and discouraged workers. There are four types of unemployment—frictional, structural, seasonal, and cyclical—but only cyclical unemployment is both unhealthy and a problem.

- Statistics Canada places everyone in working-age population (age 15 and over) into one of three categories:
    - Employed—working full-time or part-time at paid job.
    - Unemployed—not doing paid work and actively searching for job, or on temporary layof, or about to start a new job.
    - Not in the labour force—does not fit into employed or unemployed categories (full-time student, homemaker, retiree).
- **Labour force** = employed + unemployed.
- **Unemployment rate**
    - Percentage of people in labour force who are unemployed.
    - Unemployment Rate = $\dfrac{\text{Unemployed}}{\text{Labour Force}} \times 100$
- **Labour force participation rate**
    - Percentage of working-age population in the labour force (employed or unemployed).
    - Labour Force Participation Rate = $\dfrac{\text{Labour Force}}{\text{Working-Age Population}} \times 100$
- Unemployment rate misses
    - *involuntary part-time workers*—employed part time, would rather have full-time job, but can't find one.

- **discouraged workers**—want to work but have given up actively searching for jobs.
- *Labour underutilization rate*—unemployment rate including unemployed, involuntary part-time workers, discouraged workers.
- Large regional differences in unemployment rates in Canada.
- Healthy and unhealthy types of unemployment:
  - **Frictional unemployment**—due to normal labour turnover and job search; healthy part of changing economy; not a problem.
  - **Structural unemployment**—due to technological change or international competition making workers' skills obsolete; healthy part of changing economy; problem requiring retraining.
  - **Seasonal unemployment**—due to seasonal changes in weather; neither healthy nor unhealthy; not a problem.
  - **Cyclical unemployment**—due to business cycle fluctuations in economic activity; unhealthy part of changing economy; problem needs addressing.

3.2 HOW FULL IS "FULL EMPLOYMENT?" THE NATURAL RATE OF UNEMPLOYMENT

The natural rate of unemployment occurs at full employment, where there is only healthy frictional, structural, and seasonal unemployment. Relative to the natural rate, the unemployment rate is higher in a recessionary gap and lower in an inflationary gap.

- **Natural rate of unemployment**—unemployment rate at full employment; includes frictional, structural, seasonal unemployment.
  - **Full employment** is not zero percent unemployment but zero percent cyclical unemployment.
- Relation between natural rate of unemployment and potential GDP:
  - When unemployment = natural rate of unemployment; real GDP = potential GDP; full employment.
  - When unemployment > natural rate of unemployment; real GDP < potential GDP; recessionary output gap; cyclical unemployment.
  - When unemployment < natural rate of unemployment; real GDP > potential GDP; inflationary output gap.
- Economists disagree about natural rate and whether it changes often.

3.3 LIGHTENING UP YOUR WALLET: WHAT IS INFLATION?

Inflation is measured by changes in the Consumer Price Index, hurts those on fixed incomes, creates risk for business investment, and, through expectations, can create a vicious cycle of more inflation. The inflation rate overstates increases in the cost of living by missing switches to cheaper substitutes and new/improved products/services.

- *Inflation* is both a persistent rise in average prices and a fall in the value of money. When inflation occurs,
  - you must spend more to get same products/services as before.
  - your money is worth less.
- **Consumer Price Index (CPI)**—measure of average prices of fixed shopping basket of products and services.
  - CPI = 100 for the base year, currently 2002.
- **Inflation rate**—annual percentage change in consumer price index.
  - Inflation = $\dfrac{\text{CPI for current year} - \text{CPI for previous year}}{\text{CPI for previous year}} \times 100$
  - **Core inflation rate**—inflation rate excluding volatile categories.
- Inflation is a worry because of falling value of money.
  - Inflation reduces purchasing power of people with fixed (unchanged dollar) income or savings.
  - **Nominal interest rate**—observed interest rate; equal to number of dollars received per year in interest as percentage of number of dollars saved.
  - Realized **real interest rate**
    = nominal interest rate adjusted for effects of inflation
    = nominal interest rate − inflation rate.
- Inflation is a worry because unpredictable prices create risk and discourage business investment in future production.
- Inflation is a worry because expectations of inflation can help cause inflation.
- Economists view predictable inflation rates between 1 and 3 percent as acceptable.
- **Deflation**—persistent fall in average prices and rise in value of money.
  - Falling prices can lead consumers to postpone purchases, causing economic contraction and increasing unemployment.
  - Deflation benefits savers but hurts borrowers.
  - Deflation is worse than low inflation.
- CPI fixes quantities in shopping basket to isolate impact of changing prices only on cost of living.
  - With fixed quantities, when prices rise CPI misses quantity switches to cheaper substitutes and new/improved products. Inflation rate based on CPI *overstates* increases in cost of living.

3.4 INFLATION STARTS WITH "*M*"
THE QUANTITY THEORY OF MONEY

The quantity theory of money explains inflation from an increase in the quantity of money in an economy, holding constant the velocity of money and the quantity of real output.

- For any economy with money, $M \times V = P \times Q$, where
  - *M* represents the quantity of money.

- *V* represents the **velocity of money** — number of times a unit of money changes hands during a year.
- *P* represents average prices—the consumer price index.
- *Q* represents the aggregate quantity of real output.
- $P \times Q$ represents nominal GDP.

- There must be enough money, multiplied by the velocity of money, to allow sales of all final products/services produced (nominal GDP).
- **Quantity Theory of Money** states that an increase in the quantity of money causes an equal percentage increase in the inflation rate.
  - Quantity theory of money takes equation $M \times V = P \times Q$, fixes *V* and fixes *Q* at potential GDP.
  - Quantity theory of money is behind "printing money causes inflation."
- Not all inflation directly caused by increases in quantity of money. But inflation always accompanied by increase in quantity of money.

3.5 WHEN TIM HORTONS PAYS $18 PER HOUR: UNEMPLOYMENT AND INFLATION TRADEOFFS

The Phillips Curve shows an immediate tradeoff between unemployment and inflation consistent with demand-pull stories of inflation. Cost-push inflation—with simultaneous unemployment and inflation—and changes over time in expectations and the natural rate of unemployment all complicate the original Phillips Curve.

- **Phillips Curve**—graph showing inverse relation between unemployment and inflation.
- **Demand-pull inflation**—rising average prices caused by increases in demand—explains Phillips Curve's tradeoff between unemployment and inflation.
  - During expansions, demand is key force causing shortages and pulling up prices for inputs (like wages) and for outputs.
- **Cost-push inflation**—rising average prices caused by decreases in supply— does *not* fit Phillips Curve.
  - Cost-push inflation caused by **supply shocks**—events directly affecting business's costs, prices, and supply. Decrease in supply key force pushing up output prices, while pushing economy into contraction, increasing unemployment.
  - Cost-push inflation can cause **stagflation**—simultaneous recession (higher unemployment) and inflation (higher average prices).
- Both demand-pull and cost-push inflation require accompanying increase in quantity of money.
- Over time, tradeoffs between unemployment and inflation of original Phillips Curve become complicated due to changes in
  - expectations.
  - natural rate of unemployment.

TRUE/FALSE

Circle the correct answer.

Suppose that a group on Facebook has five people: A. J., B. J., C. J., D. J., and V. J. The group members post the following information regarding their job status:

A. J.: *"I worked for BlueBerry Wireless this month and last month."*

B. J.: *"Last month I worked for Canwell Soup. This month I am on temporary layoff because of a temporary slowdown in the economy."*

C. J.: *"Last month I was not working, but I was looking for work. This month I accepted a part-time job at Burger Fling but was hoping for a full-time job."*

D. J.: *"I have never worked and I have never looked for work (I like to party and spin records)."*

V .J.: *"I was not working and looking for work last month. This month I gave up my search for work because I was discouraged."*

Think of this group as a mini-economy. Use this scenario to answer questions 1–11.

3.1 UNEMPLOYMENT

1. B. J. would be counted as unemployed this month.　　**True　False**

2. V. J. was unemployed in both months.　　**True　False**

3. Between last month and this month, the number of employed persons stayed the same, but the number of unemployed decreased.　　**True　False**

4. Between last month and this month, the unemployment rate increased.　　**True　False**

5. If discouraged workers and involuntary part-time workers were counted in the official definition of unemployed, unemployment would have increased between last month and this month.　　**True　False**

3.2 NATURAL RATE OF UNEMPLOYMENT

6. B. J. is cyclically unemployed this month.　　**True　False**

7. There is full employment this month.　　**True　False**

8. If C. J. and V. J. were both structurally unemployed last month, then this economy had a recessionary gap last month.　　**True　False**

9. V. J. is in charge of planning C. J.'s stag party (a party held for a bachelor shortly before he enters marriage). V. J. knows C. J. loves economics and wants to make up T-shirts for the stag that accurately describe the current state of the economy. If average prices are rising and output is decreasing, then the shirts should say *stagnation*.　　**True　False**

3.3 INFLATION

10. A. J. is a nonsmoking vegetarian who walks to work and lives with his parents. If increases in A. J.'s wage were linked to increases in the CPI—and prices of gasoline fuel, housing, meat, and tobacco were on the rise—then the wage increase would underestimate A. J.'s true cost of living increase.   **True   False**

11. V. J. wants to invest his savings with a bank. Suppose that the interest rate he is informed about is 2 percent and the inflation rate is 2 percent. Therefore, the real interest rate is 4 percent.   **True   False**

3.4 QUANTITY THEORY OF MONEY

12. According to the quantity theory, if 20 percent more money were printed, average prices would increase by 20 percent.   **True   False**

13. If the quantity of money is $50 and nominal GDP is $100, the velocity of circulation is 0.5.   **True   False**

3.5 UNEMPLOYMENT–INFLATION TRADEOFFS

14. If the unemployment rate were lower when inflation were higher, this evidence would support the Phillips curve.   **True   False**

15. If the unemployment rate were lower when inflation were higher, this would be evidence of cost-push inflation.   **True   False**

MULTIPLE CHOICE

Circle the correct answer.

3.1 UNEMPLOYMENT

1. Who would be counted as unemployed?
   A) Sirena is a college student with no job.
   B) Miguel starts a new job in a week.
   C) Reetu stopped looking for work because she was unable to find a job.
   D) Rajinder is working part time but wishes he was working full time.

2. If Salma loses her job and starts looking for work, the
   A) number of employed increases.
   B) labour force increases.
   C) labour force decreases.
   D) labour force participation rate remains unchanged.

3. Suppose that there are 19 million people employed, 1 million unemployed, and 25 million people 15 years of age or older. Which of the following statements is *true*?

   A) The size of the labour force is 19 million.

   B) The labour force participation rate is 80 percent.

   C) The unemployment rate is 4 percent.

   D) The unemployment rate is 1 percent.

4. The summer job market for post-secondary students starts in May. In May 2009, 59 000 fewer students were employed compared to a year earlier. These students' labour force participation rate also fell over the year, from 75.2 percent to 68.6 percent. What is the correct interpretation of these results?

   A) More students are working.

   B) More students are in the labour force.

   C) Fewer students are looking for work.

   D) Fewer students are in the labour force.

3.2 NATURAL RATE OF UNEMPLOYMENT

5. Alberta's 2.9 percent unemployment rate in June 2007 was the lowest of any province. High labour demand and wages in Alberta encouraged unemployed workers from Newfoundland and Labrador to move to Alberta, where they found jobs. This increased the

   A) unemployment rate in Newfoundland and Labrador.

   B) labour force in Newfoundland and Labrador.

   C) unemployment rate in Alberta.

   D) labour force in Alberta.

6. Based on the article in Economics Out There (section 3.1) we know that close to 567 000 additional people became officially unemployed between October 2008 and March 2009, and that another 236 000 either gave up looking because they were discouraged, expected to be called back, or were involuntary part-timers. If the 236 000 individuals were counted as unemployed, then the number of people

   A) employed would decrease.

   B) unemployed would decrease.

   C) unemployed would increase.

   D) not in the labour force would increase.

7. In the year grade 13 was eliminated in Ontario, grade twelve students and grade thirteen students graduated at the same time. This resulted in an increase in the number of people leaving school to find jobs. What form of unemployment was likely to be unusually high in that year?

   A) Seasonal unemployment

   B) Frictional unemployment

   C) Structural unemployment

   D) Cyclical unemployment

8. There is a recessionary gap when the unemployment rate is
   A) below the natural rate.
   B) above the natural rate.
   C) at full employment.
   D) at the natural rate.

3.3 INFLATION

9. If the CPI was 120 in 2020 and 126 in 2021, then the inflation rate was
   A) 5 percent, which is above the Bank of Canada's target range for inflation.
   B) 5 percent, which is within the Bank of Canada's target range for inflation.
   C) 20 percent, which is above the Bank of Canada's target range for inflation.
   D) 20 percent, which is within the Bank of Canada's target range for inflation.

10. What does the inflation rate miss?
    A) New products
    B) Better products
    C) Switches to cheaper substitutes
    D) All of the above

11. Inflation can harm those who
    A) are living on fixed incomes.
    B) keep money under their bed.
    C) save money in the bank.
    D) All of the above

3.4 QUANTITY THEORY OF MONEY

12. The number of times a unit of money changes hands during a year is called
    A) money supply.
    B) velocity.
    C) price.
    D) real GDP.

13. Which factors are fixed in the quantity theory of money?
    A) Money and velocity
    B) Velocity and real GDP
    C) Velocity and price
    D) Price and real GDP

3.5 UNEMPLOYMENT–INFLATION TRADEOFFS

14. If the Phillips Curve is true, which of the following could never happen?
    A) Invention of the Phillips screwdriver
    B) Stagflation
    C) Stagnation
    D) Inflation

15. Economists believed there was a clear tradeoff between unemployment and inflation until the

A) 1950s.

B) 1970s.

C) 1990s.

D) 2000s.

SHORT ANSWER

Write a short answer to each question. Your answer may be in point form.

1. For each of the following labour market experiences of Ana Maria, determine if she was employed, unemployed, or not in the labour force during that year.

   A) At age 17, she graduates and starts looking for a job.

   B) At age 18, she finds a part-time job but was hoping for a full-time job.

   C) At age 20, she is laid off but switches to a new job two weeks later.

   D) At age 21, she is not working but is looking for work.

   E) At age 22, she goes to college (but is not working and is not looking for work).

2. Suppose that a labour force of 100 people has 8 unemployed persons.

   A) What is the unemployment rate?

   B) If one of the eight unemployed persons stops looking for work because he found a new job, what is the new unemployment rate?

   C) If one of the eight unemployed persons does not find a job and stops looking for work because she becomes discouraged, what is the new unemployment rate?

3. The unemployment rate is closely connected to economic conditions in output markets. The unemployment rate rose above 10 percent in the 1981–1982 recession and 1990–1991 recession.

   A) Explain how the changes in the unemployment rate are connected to changes in GDP over the business cycle.

   B) What is the cost of not working?

   C) Can a drop in the unemployment rate ever mean that economic conditions are getting worse?

4. The number of full-time jobs in Canada declined by over 400 000 between October 2008 and May 2009.

   A) Over the same period, part-time employment increased by 44 000. If some of those who lost full-time jobs involuntarily took part-time jobs, how would this impact the size of the employed population and the amount of labour underutilization in Canada?

   B) Even though there was no recession between 2002 and 2007, manufacturing employment declined by 241 000 over this period. What type of unemployment would describe those individuals who lost their manufacturing jobs between 2002 and 2007?

C) Construction employment increased between 2002 and 2007, with the largest increase of any industry in 2007. However, between October 2008 and May 2009, the number of workers in construction decreased by 9 percent, resulting in unemployment. What type of unemployment would describe those individuals who lost their construction jobs in the 2008–2009 recession?

D) Manitoba and Saskatchewan had an unemployment rate of 4.9 percent in May 2009, the lowest in the country, and were the only two provinces with an increase in employment since October 2009. If both provinces were relatively unaffected by the cyclical downturn in the economy, what does that say about their natural rate of unemployment?

5. Suppose that the government asks your advice about reducing unemployment in Canada during the 2008–2009 recession.

A) Which form(s) of unemployment should be reduced to zero?

B) Are all of forms of unemployment equally healthy (or equally unhealthy)? Which forms of unemployment would you focus on reducing, and why?

C) Is frictional unemployment all that bad? Explain why waiting to find the right job in some ways is like waiting to find the right person to date in a relationship.

D) Provide an example of how you would reduce each form of unemployment.

E) How can cyclical unemployment be reduced? How can structural unemployment be reduced?

6. Anya lives on the college campus and goes to Loblaws to get groceries. In her first year of college her grocery bill was $100. In her second year of college her grocery bill for the same food climbed to $110.

A) What grocery inflation rate does Anya face? Will this be the inflation rate for the economy as a whole?

B) If some of the products on Anya's grocery list in her second year are new and better products, would your answer in part a) be an underestimate or overestimate of her cost of living?

C) If Anya's income instead increased by 5 percent over this period, what has happened to her grocery purchasing power?

D) If Anya had money in her savings account earning 10 percent interest over the period, what will happen to the value of her money for buying groceries?

7. A Bank of Canada employee disguised as Santa Claus drops 2000 loonies from a helicopter to a small community The loonies fall to the ground, where they are quickly scooped up by lucky consumers.

A) Before the helicopter gifts, consumers had total incomes of $1000. After the gifts, what is the total income of consumers?

B) Consumers try to buy more stuff with their loonies, but the quantity of products/services available does not change. What happens to prices?

C) What will be the inflation rate in the economy if there were already 1000 loonies in the economy (loonies are the only form of money in this simple economy)?

D) What type of inflation occurred in this economy?

8. Consider the relationship between unemployment and inflation.

   A) Why did OPEC end the original Phillips curve?

   B) Does the OPEC example demonstrate demand pull-inflation or cost-push inflation? Why?

   C) Between 2002 and 2007, the inflation rate ranged between 1.8 and 2.8 percent. Did the inflation rate fall within Bank of Canada's target range for stable inflation over this period? Why?

   D) Between 2002 and 2007 there were strong gains in employment and large reductions in the unemployment rate. Labour force participation rates in Canada were at record highs in 2007 and Canada's unemployment rate sank to a 33-year low of 5.8 percent in 2007. Are the 2002 to 2007 trends in the inflation rate and unemployment rate consistent with the Phillips curve?

9. Alvero has been running his own computer business since 2002. Between 2002 and 2007, inflation was running at a steady, predictable rate. When the Great Recession hit in 2008, the inflation rate became less predictable.

   A) In an environment of stable inflation, will Alvero be more likely to raise wages and maintain his workforce without frequent strikes?

   B) Explain how wage changes in input markets contribute to inflation in output markets, and the role of self-fulfilling expectations.

   C) Explain why business planning and investment are more difficult in an environment of price uncertainty.

   D) The falling value of money also affects wage rates. The nominal wage is the wage mentioned in your job interview and recorded on your pay stub. If you agree to a wage that increases by 5 percent per year, then 5 percent is the increase in your nominal wage rate. If Alvero needs to reduce the rate of increase in the wages paid to his workers, is it easier to do this when there is inflation or deflation? Explain.

10. Consider the data in the table below.

Consumer Price Index by Province (2002 = 100)

	May 2008	May 2009	May 2008 to May 2009
			% change
Canada	**114.6**	**114.7**	**0.1**
Newfoundland and Labrador	114.5	115.2	0.6
Prince Edward Island	118.9	117.6	−1.1
Nova Scotia	117.1	115.8	−1.1
New Brunswick	113.9	113.7	−0.2
Québec	113.6	113.7	0.1
Ontario	113.6	114.0	0.4
Manitoba	113.5	114.4	0.8
Saskatchewan	116.2	117.0	0.7
Alberta	122.2	121.4	−0.7
British Columbia	112.8	112.9	0.1

Source: Statistics Canada, Release from the Consumer Price Index, July 18, 2009,
http://www.statcan.gc.ca/subjects-sujets/cpi-ipc/cpi-ipc-eng.htm.

A) Did Canada experience inflation between May 2008 and May 2009?

B) Which provinces experienced deflation between May 2008 and May 2009?

C) The small rise in the CPI (May 2008 to May 2009) was primarily the result of a 18.3 percent year-over-year price drop for energy products. Excluding energy, the CPI rose 2.3 percent. Would the core rate of inflation be lower or higher than the inflation rate based on the CPI?

myeconlab Visit the MyEconLab website at **www.myeconlab.com**. This online homework and tutorial system puts you in control of your own learning with study and practice tools.

Chapter 4

Skating *to Where the Puck Is Going*

Aggregate Supply and Aggregate Demand

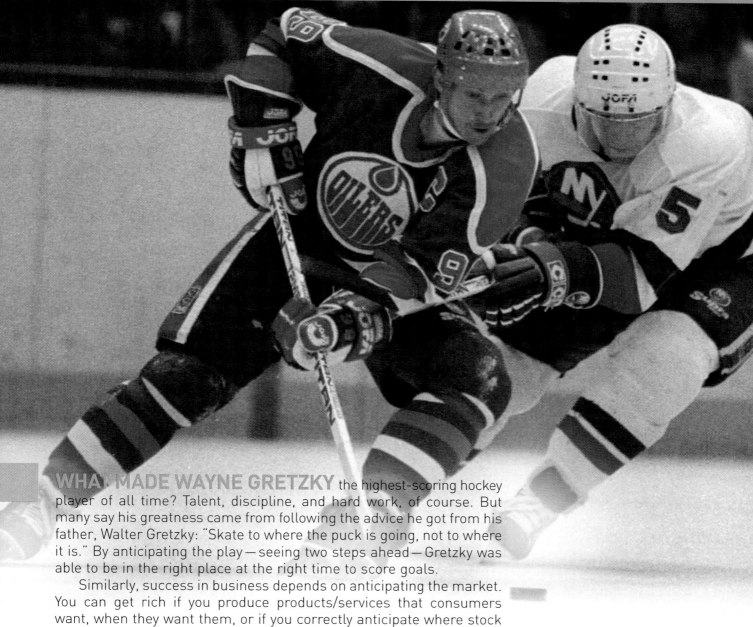

WHAT MADE WAYNE GRETZKY the highest-scoring hockey player of all time? Talent, discipline, and hard work, of course. But many say his greatness came from following the advice he got from his father, Walter Gretzky: "Skate to where the puck is going, not to where it is." By anticipating the play—seeing two steps ahead—Gretzky was able to be in the right place at the right time to score goals.

Similarly, success in business depends on anticipating the market. You can get rich if you produce products/services that consumers want, when they want them, or if you correctly anticipate where stock prices or real estate values are going.

In this chapter, we examine the choices not behind the hockey outcomes of goals and assists, but behind the macroeconomic outcomes of GDP, economic growth, unemployment, and inflation. These outcomes begin two steps earlier, with choices made by consumers, businesses, and governments. We start with the choices these macroeconomic players make, and look at how the players' separate smart choices add up to aggregate (total) supply and aggregate (total) demand. The tools of aggregate supply and aggregate demand allow us to look more carefully at the fundamental macroeconomic question—if left alone, do markets quickly self-adjust? When aggregate supply and aggregate demand match, the economy grows steadily with full employment and stable prices. Where there is a mismatch, the economy fails to operate at it's potential, and business cycles, unemployment, and inflation may result.

4.1 If You Plan and Build It . . . Aggregate Supply

Identify how macroeconomic players choose aggregate quantity supplied and differentiate the choices and supply shocks that change aggregate supply.

The miracle of markets, when they work well, is that businesses produce the products and services that consumers demand, at the right quantities, locations, and times. But production takes time, so businesses have to *anticipate*—plan ahead for—what consumers will be demanding when the product/service finally gets to market—like anticipating where the puck will be. Supply plans and decisions, based on expectations of demand, come before demand.

Supply Plans and the Circular Flow

Let's look again at the circular flow diagram, but this time focusing on the *plans* that businesses, consumers, and governments make, rather than the GDP outcomes of choices. Figure 4.1 is the same as Figure 2.13.

There are many similarities between aggregate supply and supply, and between aggregate demand and demand. This chapter will be easier to understand if you first review microeconomic supply and demand in Appendices B, C, and D.

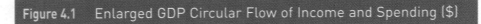

| Figure 4.1 | Enlarged GDP Circular Flow of Income and Spending ($) |

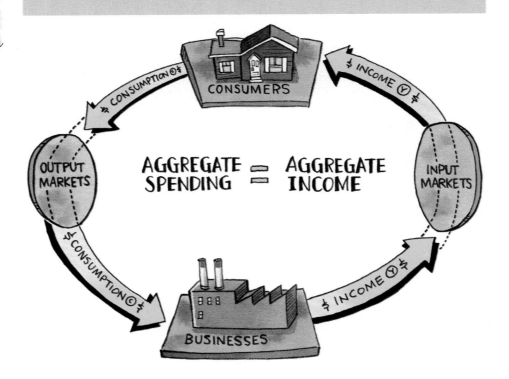

For simplicity, Figure 4.1 shows only the flow of dollars. It omits the reverse flows of physical inputs and outputs.

Everyone in a market economy like Canada's participates in both sets of markets in the circular flow—input markets on the right and output markets on the left.

In input markets, consumer households are the suppliers and businesses are the demanders. Consumer households supply inputs of labour, capital, land/resources, and entrepreneurial ability to businesses. In exchange, they get income—the green arrow of dollars flowing from businesses to consumer households.

In output markets, consumer households are the most important demanders and businesses are the suppliers. Using the income earned in input markets, consumer households (as well as government, the rest of the world, and businesses purchasing investment equipment) buy products/services from businesses in exchange for money—the green arrow of dollars flowing from consumer households to businesses.

To begin, our focus is on the supply plans that consumers, businesses, and governments make first. Because we are focusing on supply, the rest of the world (R.O.W.) is not a player. It does not *supply* any part of Canadian GDP.

There are two types of supply plans: plans based on existing inputs in the economy and plans to increase the inputs.

Businesses such as the one operating this giant digger in the Alberta oil sands must plan far ahead in order to have the right machines in the right place at the right time.

Supply Plans for Existing Inputs

Supply plans for existing inputs are similar to microeconomic choices about *quantity supplied* (Appendix C). Whether you are a consumer deciding on how many hours of labour to supply to your boss in input markets, or a business deciding on how many of your products/services to supply in output markets, your decision connects the price you expect to receive with the quantity you plan to supply.

Microeconomic's *law of supply* states that as the price of a product/service rises, the quantity supplied increases. Higher prices create incentives for increased production through higher profits and by covering higher marginal opportunity costs of production.

The difference in macroeconomics is that the supply plans connecting price and quantity supplied for all of the macroeconomic players must be added together. Economists do have methods for measuring both prices and quantities for the economy as a whole. For prices, we use the average level of prices in the economy, as measured by the consumer price index. For quantities, we use real GDP, which adds together the quantities of all of the different products/services produced in an economy, valued at constant prices.

Aggregate quantity supplied is the quantity of real GDP that macroeconomic players plan to supply at different average levels of prices.

The **law of aggregate supply** states that as the average level of prices rises, the aggregate quantity supplied increases. Higher prices create incentives for increased production through higher profits and by covering higher marginal opportunity costs of production.

These macroeconomic plans to supply different quantities of real output are based on existing inputs, which limit the quantity of real GDP that can be supplied. *Potential GDP* is the quantity of real GDP when all inputs—labour, capital, land/resources, and entrepreneurial ability—are fully employed. With existing inputs, the maximum aggregate quantity supplied for an economy is its potential GDP.

aggregate quantity supplied: quantity of real GDP macroeconomic players plan to supply at different average price levels

law of aggregate supply: as average level of prices rises, aggregate quantity supplied increases

Supply Plans to Increase Inputs Besides decisions about how many/much of their existing inputs they plan to supply, macroeconomic players also make decisions that change the quantities and quality of those inputs available in the future. If you complete your college education, that adds to your human capital and will make you, and the economy, more productive in the future. If a mining company develops a technologically advanced drilling machine that increases the productivity of its workers, that will increase productivity in the future. And if the government builds new transit lines that make it faster and cheaper to transport people and products, that increases the future productivity of the economy. Any decision that increases the quantity or quality of inputs in an economy increases potential GDP. In the language of this chapter, supply plans that increase input quantity or quality cause an **increase in aggregate supply**.

An increase in aggregate supply, in the language of Chapter 2, is economic growth—the expansion of the economy's capacity to produce products/services. We will look at decreases in aggregate supply—which take the form of negative supply shocks—at the end of this section.

I am hoping you notice the parallels to the microeconomic language of supply. In microeconomics, we distinguished between a change in quantity supplied (caused by a change in the price of the product/service) and a change in supply (caused by a change in any other factor). In macroeconomics, given existing inputs, a change in aggregate quantity supplied is caused by a change in the average price level. A change in aggregate supply is caused by other changes in the quantity or quality of inputs.

Let's look at the supply plans for each of the macroeconomic players individually—their plans based on existing inputs and their plans based on increasing inputs. Supply decisions often affect demand as well, but we will postpone the demand implications to the next section.

Business Supply Choices

Businesses are the most important players for aggregate supply plans.

Business Supply Plans with Existing Inputs Once a business looks, Gretzky-like, two steps ahead and anticipates what consumers will be demanding, it starts planning its supply choices. Based on the existing inputs it owns—factories, capital equipment, and land/resources—the first choice is what products/services to produce and in what quantities. Those output choices, in turn, determine choices about how intensively to use inputs. A business might run a single eight-hour shift, a double shift, or even a triple shift operating 24 hours a day.

Another business choice is whether to sell to the Canadian market, or to export products/services. This choice does not affect aggregate quantity supplied, since real GDP counts all output produced in Canada, no matter where it is sold.

The more businesses plan to produce, the greater the aggregate quantity supplied, up to a maximum of potential GDP. The less businesses plan to produce, the lower the aggregate quantity supplied.

increase in aggregate supply: increase in economy's capacity to produce real GDP caused by increases in quantity or quality of inputs

As average prices rise, aggregate quantity supplied increases, up to a maximum of potential GDP.

Business Supply Plans to Increase Inputs   Businesses also look many more steps and years ahead, planning to grow their capacity to produce or to improve their competitiveness. Business choices for growth increase the quantity or quality of inputs. Quantity increases include investing in new factories and capital equipment, and searching for new resources like new oil or gold deposits. Quality increases include creating new products/services, research and development to improve technology, and improving the quality of capital inputs and their productivity. Businesses may also invest in training their workforce, improving the quality of employees' human capital.

Business supply plans to increase inputs increase aggregate supply (as opposed to increasing aggregate quantity supplied), and increase potential GDP.

Business plans to increase inputs increase aggregate supply (not aggregate quantity supplied) and increase potential GDP.

Consumer Supply Choices

The word "consumer" may make you think about households only as shoppers, or demanders. But there are many other consumer supply choices to be made.

Consumer Supply Plans with Existing Inputs   While most adults have the capacity and need to work, it is still a choice whether or not to participate in the labour force. Remember that real GDP counts only paid market activities. So a choice to take a paying job instead of taking care of the kids at home will increase the aggregate quantity supplied of output. Once you or anyone else chooses to participate in the labour force, there is a further choice about how many hours to work. As the law of supply states, the higher the wage, the greater the quantity supplied of labour.

Consumer households also make choices about supplying other inputs they own besides their labour. If you own a house with a finished basement, you can choose to rent it out or not. As rents rise and more such apartments come onto the market, the quantity of housing increases, increasing aggregate quantity supplied.

▲ This young man has decided to re-enter the labour force. His new job will add to GDP.

Consumer Supply Plans to Increase Inputs   Consumer households also make choices that increase the quantity and quality of inputs. While the choice to have children is very personal, it also affects the potential labour force—the future quantity of labour! Your choice as an individual consumer to get an education or training improves the quality of your human capital. These choices to increase the quantity and quality of labour inputs also increase aggregate supply, increasing potential GDP.

Government Supply Choices

Government choices mostly affect demand, but some choices affect aggregate supply, especially policy choices that can increase the quantity and quality of inputs.

Government Supply Plans with Existing Inputs   The Government of Canada owns many natural resources, including forests and mineral rights on Crown land. If rising prices lead the government to allow logging or mining on previously protected Crown land, aggregate quantity supplied increases. (The impact on the environment is another story.)

Government Supply Plans to Increase Inputs   Government can build infrastructure—such as roads, bridges, and sewers—which increases the productivity for everyone else in the economy.

Government also sets the rules of the game for market exchanges. Changes in policy that change those rules can have a large effect on choices that increase the quantity and quality of inputs. For example government can choose to increase the future size of the labour force by allowing more immigration. In 1988, the Government of Québec introduced the Allowance for Newborn Children, which paid up to $8000 to a family after the birth of a child. This baby bonus policy was designed to increase Québec's population and labour force.

Government also can use tax policy as an incentive to increase aggregate supply. Reducing taxes on wages and on business investment allows individuals, businesses, and investors to keep more of what they earn. Taking home more dollars increases the incentive to increase aggregate supply. Eliminating policy restrictions on foreign investment can increase the quantity of capital available in the Canadian economy. Government can also offer grants and subsidies for research and development, supporting science and engineering research at post-secondary institutions and elsewhere. When that research leads to technological change and improves the quality of capital, aggregate supply increases.

We will look more closely at these government policies when we discuss fiscal policy in Chapter 8.

◄

When government invests in building or repairing infrastructure, it makes it easier and less expensive for everyone to do business.

Supply Shocks and Aggregate Supply

Aggregate supply for the Canadian economy is largely determined by the plans and choices that these macroeconomic players—Canadian businesses, consumers, and government—make. But events beyond the control of the players can also affect aggregate supply.

These *supply shocks*, which you read about in Chapter 3, are events that directly affect business costs, prices, and supply, and are not caused by changes in demand. There are both negative supply shocks and positive supply shocks. Both cause a change in aggregate supply, not a change in aggregate quantity supplied.

Negative Supply Shocks Decrease Aggregate Supply   Some negative supply shocks are caused by natural disasters, while others are created by rising input prices. Examples include droughts that decrease the supply of agricultural products, natural disasters like earthquakes that destroy inputs, and energy price increases (such as the OPEC crisis in the 1970s). A negative supply shock in macroeconomics is similar to a decrease in supply (not quantity supplied) in microeconomics.

Negative supply shocks directly increase costs or reduce inputs, and decrease aggregate supply.

Positive Supply Shocks Increase Aggregate Supply   Positive supply shocks can come from new ideas and new resources in Canada or other parts of the world. Examples include scientific discoveries that lead to more productive, lower-cost technologies and lower world prices for resource inputs. A positive supply shock in macroeconomics is similar to an increase in supply (not quantity supplied) in microeconomics.

Figure 4.2 is a good study device for reviewing the difference between the law of aggregate supply (focused on aggregate quantity supplied) and the factors that change aggregate supply.

Positive supply shocks directly decrease costs or improve productivity, and increase aggregate supply.

Figure 4.2 Law of Aggregate Supply and Changes in Aggregate Supply	
The Law of Aggregate Supply	
The aggregate quantity supplied of real GDP	
Decreases if:	*Increases if:*
■ average level of prices falls	■ average level of prices rises
Changes in Aggregate Supply	
The aggregate supply of real GDP	
Decreases if:	*Increases if:*
—————	■ businesses plan to increase quantity or quality inputs
■ negative supply shock raises price for resource inputs	■ positive supply shock lowers price for resource inputs
■ negative supply shock destroys inputs	■ positive supply shock improves technologies

Will Supply Create Its Own Demand? Supply shocks, together with the plans made by businesses, consumers, and government, combine to create aggregate supply. Plans are made two Gretzky-like steps ahead, in anticipation of what demand will be. When businesses follow through on those plans, they hire inputs in input markets, providing income for consumer households. And the products/services appear in output markets, waiting for buyers.

Will supply create its own demand, as Say's Law claims? Will these supply choices create enough demand so that the plans of the macroeconomic players are realized? If there are supply shocks that disrupt an economy at potential GDP, will markets quickly adjust to restore full employment, stable prices, and steady growth? To answer these questions, we must first look at aggregate demand.

Refresh

4.1

www.myeconlab.com

1. Explain the difference between a change in aggregate quantity supplied and a change in aggregate supply.

2. Explain which consumer choices determine aggregate quantity supplied, and which choices change aggregate supply.

3. You own a pickle business and currently supply (sell) 1000 jars a month at a price of $5 per jar. Pick a specific supply shock (negative or positive) and explain your willingness to supply pickles at that same $5 price *after the shock*.

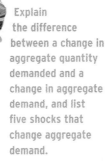

4.2 . . . Will They Come and Buy It? Aggregate Demand

Explain the difference between a change in aggregate quantity demanded and a change in aggregate demand, and list five shocks that change aggregate demand.

How much money are you planning to spend this month? As consumers or businesspeople, we may not have Wayne Gretzky's abilities to see two steps ahead, but we do still plan. As consumers, we set budgets, planning how much of our earned income to spend and how much to save. Every business project has a plan—and its success depends on delivering on time and on budget. Governments also plan. The Finance Minister presents a budget in Parliament outlining the government's taxing and spending plans for the year.

Of course, life happens and plans don't always work out. Things happen. Your car may break down; you could lose your job; you may win the lottery. All of these events will change your actual spending—what you are willing and able to buy—from your planned spending. Before we turn to how plans actually work out, let's look at demand plans.

Demand Plans and the Circular Flow

We'll use the circular flow diagram again, but to explain demand plans we must add the banking system to allow for savings and borrowing, and add government to allow for net taxes. Figure 4.3 is the same as Figure 2.15.

Figure 4.3   Expanded GDP Circular Flow of Income and Spending ($) with Banking System

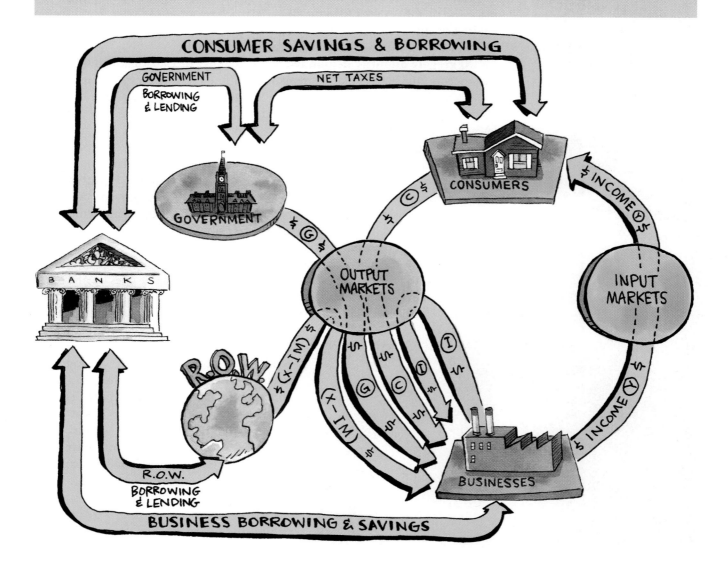

Once aggregate supply decisions have been made, workers' incomes have been earned in input markets, and products/services become available in output markets. Demand plans are mostly about buying products/services in output markets. In output markets, consumers are the most important players, but businesses, government, and the rest of the world (R.O.W.) also play roles in demanding Canadian-produced products/services. Examine Figure 4.3. You can see the spending arrows ($) from all of these players into output markets.

Demand Plans for Spending   Macroeconomic demand plans for spending are similar to microeconomic choices about *quantity demanded* (Appendix B). When you, a consumer, are deciding how many iPods or bottles of Gatorade to buy, the decision about your quantity demanded connects the price you must pay with the quantity you plan to buy.

The microeconomic *law of demand* states that, as the price of a product/service rises, the quantity demanded decreases. Higher prices are incentives for consumers to switch to cheaper substitutes.

For macroeconomics we must add together the demand plans connecting price and quantity demanded for all of the macroeconomic players. For price we again use the average level of prices in the economy, as measured by the consumer price index. For quantities we use real GDP.

Aggregate quantity demanded is the quantity of Canadian real GDP that macroeconomic players plan to demand at different average levels of prices.

According to the **law of aggregate demand**, as the average level of prices rises, the aggregate quantity demanded decreases. While the macroeconomic law of aggregate demand *looks* just like the microeconomic law of demand, there is a surprising difference in the explanations behind them.

In microeconomics we look at the demand for one particular product. For example, when the price of an iPod rises, you switch to cheaper substitutes like other MP3 players, music downloaded to your cell phone, or even your older sister's ancient Discman. In macroeconomics, we look at the aggregate demand for *all* products/services. When the average level of prices rises for *all* products/services produced in Canada, what are the cheaper substitutes to switch to?

Fortunately, the macroeconomic law of aggregate demand still works, so you can continue to rely on the familiar inverse relation (when one goes up, the other goes down) between price and quantity demanded. But the macroeconomic law of demand works for a different reason: Canada's connection to the rest of the world. When the average prices of all Canadian products/services rise, *imported* products/services produced in other countries become relatively cheaper for Canadian consumers. As Canadian *exports* rise in price, the rest of the world buys less of them, switching to cheaper substitutes from other countries. As Canadians buy more imports and R.O.W. buys fewer Canadian exports, the aggregate quantity demanded of Canadian products/services decreases.

This difference in the explanations behind the microeconomic law of demand and the macroeconomic law of aggregate demand is an example of the *fallacy of composition* from Chapter 1—what is true for one is not necessarily true for all.

Let's now look at the demand plans for each of the macroeconomic players that are combined to yield aggregate demand. It is useful to group the players using the letters from the mantra of *C, I, G, X* and *IM*. In Chapter 2, *C, I, G, X* and *IM* measured actual spending on outputs that contributed to real GDP. Here, we will look at the spending *plans* when output has been produced, but not yet sold.

aggregate quantity demanded: quantity of real GDP macroeconomic players plan to demand at different average price levels

law of aggregate demand: as average level of prices rises, aggregate quantity demanded decreases

When the prices of cars made in Canada rise, more consumers shop for imported cars, like this MINI Cooper, and fewer consumers buy Canadian-produced cars.

Consumer Demand Choices: C is for Consumer Spending

Consumer spending plans begin with income earned in input markets. The income that consumers can choose to spend is disposable income—income after net taxes have been paid. Consumers plan to save a certain fraction of their disposable income, and spend the rest. At the top left of Figure 4.3, you can see the flows of consumer savings to banks, and of net taxes to government. Net taxes take about 22 percent of income. Of the disposable income left, Canadian consumers have been saving about 4 percent, and spending the other 96 percent.

For our macroeconomic focus, once consumers plan to spend, the choice between buying burgers from McDonald's or Wendy's makes no difference to Canadian real GDP as long as products/services of both businesses are produced in Canada. Consumers, however, also buy imports. To measure consumers' spending plans for Canadian products/services alone, we need to subtract the planned spending on imports from total consumer spending plans.

Consumer spending accounts for 61 percent of the aggregate quantity demanded of Canadian real GDP. Consumer spending is by far the largest component of aggregate demand. Consumer spending plans are also the most stable, reliable component of aggregate demand from year to year. Whether the economy is booming or busting, consumers still need to eat, have places to live, wear clothes, and use transportation. This constancy in year-to-year spending is not true for business investment spending.

Business Demand Choices: I is for Business Investment Spending

Business's role in aggregate demand is in planned investment spending—building new factories or buying new machinery that adds to inputs and increases the economy's capacity to produce real GDP. These new inputs increase aggregate supply, but because the machinery that businesses buy are outputs produced by other businesses (for example, by industrial robotics companies), the purchases are also part of aggregate demand. That is why the arrow in Figure 4.3 representing planned investment spending goes from businesses to output markets and back to businesses.

Business investment spending accounts for between 15 and 25 percent of the aggregate quantity demanded of real GDP, depending on the year. Those percentages are far smaller than for consumption spending. But what is important about the numbers is how much they can change from one year to the next. Investment spending is the most volatile, unpredictable component of aggregate demand.

There are three reasons why investment spending plans can change so quickly. First, investment spending can be postponed, unlike consumption spending. When a business postpones its plans to build a new factory, it can continue to operate its existing factories. Business investment is a marginal choice about adding to existing inputs. Consumers can't really postpone their plans to eat.

> *The outstanding fact is the extreme precariousness of the basis of knowledge on which our estimates of the prospective yield [of any investment] have to be made. Our knowledge of the factors that will govern the yield of an investment some years hence is usually very slight and often negligible. If we speak frankly, we have to admit that our basis of knowledge for estimating the yield ten years hence of a railway, a copper mine, a textile factory, . . . a building in the City of London amounts to little and sometimes nothing.*
>
> *–John Maynard Keynes*

Second, investment plans are based on expectations that extend far into an uncertain future. When an entrepreneur is deciding about the profitability of investing in a factory that will produce a stream of output and revenues lasting for 10 years, she must make estimates about costs and prices 10 years into the future. Even if she hires the best accountant in the world to make those estimates and calculate whether or not it will be profitable to build the factory, those estimates are ultimately guesses, based on expectations. The expectations may be informed by the best facts available today, but no facts are available about an uncertain future.

Because investment plans are based on expectations, and expectations are based on little beyond informed guesses, expectations can shift quickly and dramatically. That's what happened in the Great Recession, when expectations inflated about ever-rising real estate values and then all of a sudden burst—investors all began expecting values to fall. Business investment then dropped like a lead balloon. See Economics Out There for another example from the Great Recession.

The third reason investment spending plans can change quickly is because they depend on borrowed money. In Figure 4.3, notice the "Business Borrowing and Savings" connection at the bottom left between businesses and banks. Factories and machinery must be paid for before they will produce a stream of revenue for a business long into the future. Most businesses have to borrow the money to finance long-term investments, just as most consumers must borrow mortgage money to finance their buying a house that yields a stream of housing services for many years into the future.

The interest rate that banks charge on loans is the price of the borrowing. The fall or rise of interest rates dramatically changes the cost of borrowing, and affects the profitability of investment plans. When interest rates fall, borrowing to finance investment projects becomes cheaper and more investment projects become profitable. When interest rates rise, borrowing becomes more expensive and the number of profitable investment projects decreases.

ECONOMICS Out There

Putting Off Business Investment

Expenditures on machinery and equipment dropped from $254 billion in 2008 to revised intentions of $228 billion, a drop of $26 billion or 10.4 percent.

This is evidence of "how quickly the views and expectations changed for the worst during a period of unprecedented uncertainty," said Aron Gampel, deputy chief economist with Bank of Nova Scotia.

Yet companies have not said they are actually cancelling big projects, only shelving them for better days, said Yves Gauthier, the Statistics Canada official responsible for the survey.

"We don't want to get to the point that we are cutting off good investments, and of course there is program capital that is required to be spent, but we are cutting or delaying discretionary capital," said Vince Galifi, chief financial officer of Magna International.

From "Private sector spending suffers deep cutbacks," *The Globe and Mail*, Aug 2, 2009, and Statistics Canada, "Private and public investment," July 28, 2009.

Government Demand Choices:
G is for Government Spending on Products/Services

Government spending plans are set by parliament when it passes a budget at the beginning of each year. The type of government spending that contributes to aggregate demand under the category of *G* are plans for buying products/services in output markets. On Figure 4.3, that is the flow on the left side from government, through output markets, to businesses.

Government transfer payments (like the Canada Pension Plan and Employment Insurance) go to consumers, and show up in aggregate demand as part of planned consumer spending from that transfer payment income. Transfer payments are *not* part of the spending category *G*.

Government spending on products/services accounts for about 20 percent of the quantity of real GDP demanded. That percentage has remained relatively stable in Canada since the 1990s.

R.O.W. Demand Choices:
X is for R.O.W. Spending on Canadian Exports

MAPS 2

Canadian exports are products/services produced here, but sold to the rest of the world. When Italians plan to buy Molson Export beer, that spending falls under the category *X*. R.O.W. is the macroeconomic player (Italian or other nationalities) planning to demand our exports. On Figure 4.3, that planned spending is the flow on the bottom left side from R.O.W. through output markets to businesses.

Canada is a trading nation, and trade with the rest of the world is very important for aggregate demand. Spending by R.O.W for Canadian exports accounts for about 36 percent of the quantity of real GDP demanded.

R.O.W. plans to demand Canadian exports can change with changes in real GDP in other countries. If China's economy is booming, that increases demand for Canadian oil, potash, Bombardier trains, and other exports. The Great Recession in the United States caused a decrease in demand for Canadian manufactured products, especially automobiles.

Exchange rates between currencies can also change R.O.W. planned demand for Canadian exports. When the Canadian dollar falls in value relative to the U.S. dollar, Canadian exports become cheaper to Americans, who will then buy more of them. When the Canadian dollar rises in value, our exports become more expensive and R.O.W. will demand fewer of them.

Imports:
IM Eliminates Canadian Choices from R.O.W. Spending

Imports—products/services produced in the rest of world and bought in Canada—do not contribute to Canadian planned aggregate demand or real GDP. However, imports are included in the planned spending categories of consumption, investment, and government purchases of products/services. To eliminate import purchases in output markets from aggregate demand, we must subtract imports. Rather than subtracting imports from the separate categories of *C*, *I*, and *G*, it is easier to subtract them in the single flow in Figure 4.3 from R.O.W. through output markets to businesses.

The flow from R.O.W. through output markets to businesses is labelled $X - IM$ to represent the *net* flow between R.O.W. and Canada. Spending on exports flows from R.O.W. to Canada and is part of aggregate demand for Canadian real GDP. Spending on imports flows from Canada to R.O.W. and must be subtracted to calculate the net impact of the rest of the world on aggregate demand for Canadian products/services.

The net flow between the rest of the world (R.O.W.) and Canada is the difference between what Canada exports and what it imports.

Repeat Your Mantra: $C + I + G + X - IM = Y$

Planned spending on aggregate demand is the sum of planned consumer spending, planned business investment spending, planned government purchases of products/services, and planned net exports. For any average level of prices, there is a planned aggregate quantity demanded. As the average level of prices rises, the aggregate quantity demanded of Canadian real GDP decreases.

Demand Shocks and Aggregate Demand

Holding other factors constant, a change in the average level of prices causes a change in the aggregate *quantity demanded* of Canadian products/services. **Demand shocks** are changes in any factor other than average prices that cause changes in aggregate demand.

Just as we separated out the factors that cause changes in aggregate supply—changes in the quantity or quality of inputs, negative and positive supply shocks—from how the average level of prices causes a change in aggregate *quantity supplied*, we will do the same for aggregate demand. Factors that increase aggregate demand are positive demand shocks. Factors that decrease aggregate demand are negative demand shocks.

The most important factors that change aggregate demand are expectations, interest rates, changes in government policy, GDP in R.O.W., and exchange rates between the Canadian dollar and other currencies. We have mentioned these factors above, but it is useful to group them together.

demand shocks: factors other than average prices changing aggregate demand

changes in aggregate demand: aggregate demand will change with changes in expectations, interest rates, government policy, GDP in R.O.W., and exchange rates

Expectations Expectations affect aggregate demand largely through their impact on business investment spending. When investors become more pessimistic about future economic conditions, investment spending decreases and aggregate demand decreases. When investors become optimistic about the future, investment spending increases and so does aggregate demand.

Expectations can also affect consumer spending. When consumers become more pessimistic about their economic future—expecting to lose their jobs—they may decrease spending and increase savings. When consumers become more optimistic, they increase spending and decrease savings.

Interest Rates Interest rates also affect aggregate demand largely through their impact on business investment spending. When interest rates rise, borrowing to finance investment projects becomes more expensive and fewer investment projects are profitable. Aggregate demand decreases. When interest rates fall, borrowing becomes cheaper and more investment projects become profitable. Aggregate demand increases.

Interest rates affect consumer spending plans for similar reasons. When interest rates on borrowed money (on your Visa bill, student loan, car loan, or mortgage) rise, you will borrow less and spend less. Aggregate demand decreases. When interest rates fall, you borrow more and spend more. Aggregate demand increases.

Government Policy Government policy changes affect aggregate demand. Fiscal policies involve tax and spending changes. When government raises taxes, consumers and businesses have less money to spend, decreasing aggregate demand. Decreases in aggregate demand also occur when government directly decreases its spending on products/services. Tax cuts and more government spending increase aggregate demand.

Monetary policy by the Bank of Canada affects interest rates and exchange rates, and affects aggregate demand through those causes.

Negative demand shocks decrease aggregate demand. Positive demand shocks increase aggregate demand.

GDP in R.O.W. Decreases in GDP in R.O.W. decrease Canadian aggregate demand. Increases in GDP in R.O.W. increase the demand for Canadian exports and increase Canadian aggregate demand.

Exchange Rates When the Canadian dollar rises in value relative to the U.S. dollar or other currencies, Canadian exports become more expensive. Americans and R.O.W. will then buy fewer of them. When the Canadian dollar falls in value, our exports become cheaper and R.O.W. will demand more of them.

Aggregate Demand Summary

You are probably feeling overwhelmed by the choices behind aggregate supply and aggregate demand, and the lists of factors that change or "shock" aggregate supply and aggregate demand. But as we move on, I will do my best to help you absorb this information, which will be amazingly helpful for thinking about the fundamental macroeconomic question—if left alone, do markets quickly self-adjust? The tools of aggregate supply and aggregate demand will help you understand business cycles and government policy options—hands-off or hands-on—for responding to them.

Figure 4.4 is a good study device for reviewing the difference between the law of aggregate demand (focused on aggregate quantity demanded) and the factors that change aggregate demand—negative and positive demand shocks.

Figure 4.4	Law of Aggregate Demand and Changes in Aggregate Demand
The Law of Aggregate Demand	
The aggregate quantity demanded of real GDP	
Decreases if:	*Increases if:*
■ average level of prices rises	■ average level of prices falls
Changes in Aggregate Demand	
The aggregate demand for real GDP	
Decreases if negative demand shock of:	*Increases if positive demand shock of:*
■ expectations more pessimistic	■ expectations more optimistic
■ interest rates rise	■ interest rates fall
■ government spending on products/ services decreases or taxes increase	■ government spending on products/ services increases or taxes decrease
■ GDP in R.O.W. decreases	■ GDP in R.O.W. increases
■ value of Canadian dollar rises	■ value of Canadian dollar falls

Refresh
4.2

1. Explain the difference between a change in aggregate quantity demanded and a change in aggregate demand. Identify five positive demand shocks that increase aggregate demand.

2. Use the fallacy of composition to explain the difference between the two laws of demand (microeconomic) and aggregate demand (macroeconomic).

3. How might a rise in the value of the Canadian dollar relative to the U.S. dollar change your personal consumption plans? What might you buy more of? Less of?

www.myeconlab.com

4.3 Match or Mismatch? Aggregate Supply and Aggregate Demand

Macroeconomic news is always around you. The Great Recession, unemployment rates, and inflation rates are not only news stories, they are real outcomes that will affect your future—your personal economic success. Your own answer to the fundamental macroeconomic question will inform your votes for political parties whose economic policies will influence those outcomes and your future success. Macroeconomics is personal.

In comparison, the tools of aggregate supply and aggregate demand might seem abstract and boring. But this section will connect the stories in earlier chapters about real macroeconomic events like the Great Recession, Great Depression, and 1970s inflation with the categories of aggregate supply and aggregate demand. That connection will help you think like a macroeconomist, enabling you to better understand the news and the world around you and to make smarter choices for personal success.

Let's start with the fundamental macroeconomic question—if left alone by government, do the price mechanisms of market economies adjust quickly to maintain steady growth in living standards, full employment, and stable prices?

The "Yes" answer, following Say's Law, claims supply creates its own demand. Will aggregate supply choices create enough aggregate demand (a match) so that the plans of the macroeconomic players are realized, or disappointed (mismatch)? And if aggregate demand and supply shocks disrupt an economy currently at potential GDP, will markets adjust quickly to restore steady growth in living standards, full employment, and stable prices? Or will markets fail to adjust quickly, resulting in long cycles of boom and bust, with inflation and unemployment?

Match is the World of Say's Law

When aggregate demand matches the aggregate supply choices made two Gretzky-like steps earlier, economists describe that outcome as a *macroeconomic equilibrium*. Equilibrium means balance. My favourite definition of equilibrium is by Joan Robinson: "In a situation which is in equilibrium, no one is kicking himself."

Equilibrium with Existing Inputs Macroeconomic players make aggregate supply choices based on expectations of what the price level and aggregate demand will be when the products/services get to market. In macroeconomic equilibrium, the price level and aggregate demand turn out to be exactly what suppliers expected. Suppliers are happy because all of their products/services get sold at expected prices, and demanders are happy because their spending plans are all realized. Consumers have earned enough income in input markets to buy the products/services they planned for in output markets.

Use matches and mismatches between aggregate supply and aggregate demand to explain the "Yes" and "No" answers to the fundamental macroeconomic question.

GREAT THINKERS IN ECONOMICS
Series Editor: A.P. Thirlwall

JOAN ROBINSON

G. C. Harcourt and Prue Kerr

▲
Joan Robinson (1903–1983) was a University of Cambridge economist and colleague of Keynes. Many believe she should have been the first woman to win the Nobel Prize in Economics but was unfairly denied.

In equilibrium, the aggregate quantity supplied and aggregate quantity demanded of real GPD are equal to potential GDP. All inputs—labour, capital, land/resources, and entrepreneurial ability—are fully employed. The price level is stable. This equilibrium with existing inputs is the world of Say's Law.

Equilibrium Over Time with Increasing Inputs

To fully explain the "Yes" answer to the fundamental macroeconomic question—if left alone by government, do the price mechanisms of market economics quickly adjust to maintain steady growth in living standards, full employment, and stable prices?—we also have to look at *changes over time in this macroeconomic equilibrium*. What happens to economic outcomes over time?

The best measure of living standards is real GDP per person. So "steady growth in living standards" requires real GDP per person to be increasing *over time*, which in turn requires real GDP to be growing faster than the population is growing. An increase in real GDP per person is also economic growth—an increase in potential GDP.

Real GDP per person is a fraction, with real GDP on top as the numerator and population (number of persons) on the bottom as the denominator.

For this fraction to grow larger, the numerator (real GDP) must grow faster than the denominator (number of persons).

The best measure of average prices is the consumer price index. So "stable prices" requires that from one year to the next the CPI—the average price level—is either constant, or increasing at a low, predictable rate of inflation (*one* to *three* percent per year).

Say's Law can still apply to an equilibrium over time with increasing inputs, but we have to add savings and investment to our explanation. Look at the flows in and out of banks in Figure 4.3, on page 135.

The banking system can also be described as the **market for loanable funds**. Banks take in money (funds) in the form of savings from the macroeconomic players—consumer households, businesses, government, and R.O.W. Banks then loan out money (funds) to borrowers, to the same five players. These flows of loanable funds are the straight lines with two-way arrows between banks and the five macroeconomic players. The interest rate is the price in the loanable funds market, determined by the interaction between the demand for loanable funds (by borrowers) and the supply of loanable funds (from savers). As in other markets, an increase in supply will cause the price—the interest rate—to fall. An increase in demand will cause the interest rate to rise.

market for loanable funds: banks coordinate the supply of loanable funds (savings) with the demand for loanable funds (borrowing). The interest rate is the price of loanable funds.

Once macroeconomic players, especially consumers, can save their income instead of spend it, Say's Law appears to be in trouble. If the income earned by supplying inputs in input markets is not all spent in output markets on the products/services produced with those inputs, how does supply create its own demand?

Rescuing Say's Law Over Time

This is where banks can save the day (pun intended). Suppose the banks loan out the saved funds to business borrowers who use the money to finance investment in new factories and equipment. That additional business investment spending, beyond what consumers spend, offsets consumer savings. Then aggregate incomes earned in input markets are once again equal to aggregate spending in output markets. In the language of this chapter, aggregate supply equals aggregate demand.

Business investment based on borrowed funds can not only rescue Say's Law, but it also can explain "steady growth in living standards." As business investment increases the quantity and quality of inputs over time, potential GDP increases.

The match between aggregate supply and aggregate demand can happen with existing inputs, and can continue to match, over time, with increasing inputs that produce economic growth and rising living standards.

With population growth and growing incomes, aggregate supply and aggregate demand both increase, so employment remains at the natural rate of (full) employment, and the average level of prices stays stable. There is no excess demand pulling up average prices; no excess supply pulling down average prices. When Say's Law holds, the circular flow expands smoothly in size from year to year, producing economic growth, rising living standards, full employment, and stable prices. This equilibrium over time with expanding inputs is the world described in Chapter 2 where bigger and better macroeconomic dreams keep coming true.

Figure 4.5 shows the match between aggregate supply and aggregate demand according to the "Yes" camp, and the two equilibrium outcomes.

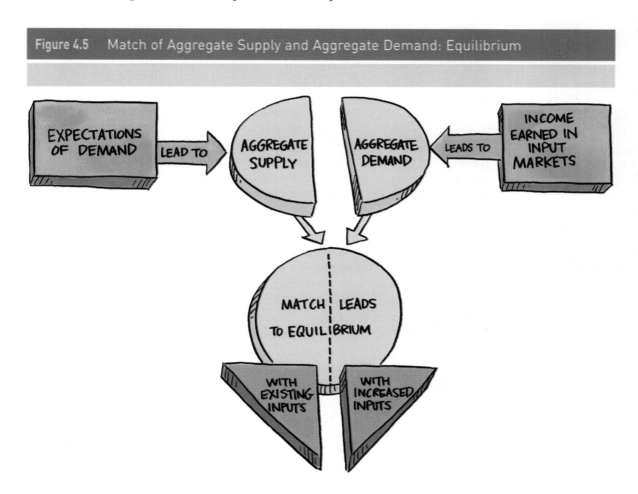

Figure 4.5   Match of Aggregate Supply and Aggregate Demand: Equilibrium

Mismatch is the World of Keynes's Business Cycles

When aggregate demand does *not* match the aggregate supply choices made two steps earlier, businesses and consumer households are kicking themselves. Aggregate supply choices are based on expectations of what the price level and aggregate demand will be when the products/services get to market. If aggregate demand turns out to be *different* from what suppliers expected, there is disappointment all around. Expectations are not realized.

With a mismatch between aggregate supply and aggregate demand, business suppliers will be kicking themselves either because they produced too many products/services that are piling up unsold on shelves (aggregate demand less than aggregate supply), or not enough products/services to satisfy unexpected consumer demand (aggregate supply less than aggregate demand). The price level will either fall below expectations (aggregate demand less than aggregate supply) or rise above expectations (aggregate supply less than aggregate demand).

With a mismatch between aggregate supply and aggregate demand, consumer household demanders will also be kicking themselves. Either businesses begin laying off workers and reducing consumer households' income (aggregate demand less than aggregate supply) or consumers will be disappointed at not finding enough of the products/services they planned to buy (aggregate supply less than aggregate demand).

When expectations are disappointed, macroeconomic outcomes do not work out as planned. What the macroeconomic players thought were smart choices turn out to be not-smart choices. Adjustments are necessary to get back to smart choices, and these adjustments are the stuff business cycles are made of. Recessions and expansions—the world of Keynes's business cycles—are the result of mismatches between aggregate supply and aggregate demand.

There are basically four mismatch scenarios that move an economy away from the equilibrium outcome: a negative demand shock, a positive demand shock, a negative supply shock, and a positive supply shock.

The four mismatch scenarios of negative and positive demand and supply shocks are similar to the microeconomics decreases and increases in demand and supply in Appendix D.4.

Negative Demand Shocks Between the time that aggregate supply decisions have been made in input markets and the time when products/services arrive for sale in output markets, what happens if there is a negative aggregate demand shock—a decrease in aggregate demand?

Aggregate quantity demanded will be less than the aggregate quantity supplied. There is a surplus of products/services in output markets. Facing unsold products sitting on shelves, or rising inventories in warehouses, businesses make both price and quantity adjustments. In an attempt to get rid of unsold products, businesses will cut prices. Surpluses create pressure for average prices to fall. Businesses cut back the quantity supplied of real GDP, and reduce their hiring of labour and other inputs.

Negative demand shocks cause a recessionary gap: falling average prices, decreased real GDP, and increased unemployment.

The net result is a fall in the average price level, a decrease in aggregate quantity supplied, and increased unemployment. Since real GDP falls below potential GDP, there is a recessionary gap.

This was the Great Recession scenario described in Chapter 1. The bursting U.S. housing price bubble caused expectations to plummet. Because of deeply pessimistic expectations, business investment spending fell dramatically. Expectations of hard times ahead, coupled with plummeting values of consumers' savings invested in their houses or the stock market, caused consumers to cut back on their spending and increase savings. These new choices decreased aggregated demand. With lower aggregate demand, there was downward pressure on average prices. Aggregate quantity supplied decreased, businesses laid off workers, and the economy fell into a recessionary gap.

Positive Demand Shocks   Between the time that aggregate supply decisions have been made in input markets, and the time when products/services arrive for sale in output markets, what happens if there is a positive aggregate demand shock—an increase in aggregate demand?

Aggregate quantity demanded will be greater than the aggregate quantity supplied. There will be a shortage of products/services in output markets. Businesses will experience products flying off the shelves and any inventories will quickly dwindle to zero. Consumers will experience long lineups and out-of-stock items at stores. In an attempt to be the one who gets the scarce products, consumers will compete against each other and bid up prices. Businesses will find that they can raise prices and still sell everything they have produced. In response to rising prices, businesses will increase the quantity supplied of real GDP, and will increase their hiring of labour and other inputs.

The net result will be a rise in the average price level, an increase in aggregate quantity supplied, and decreased unemployment. The unemployment rate will fall temporarily below the natural rate of unemployment. Since real GDP will rise above potential GDP, there will be an inflationary gap.

The early 1960s was a classic scenario of positive demand shocks. The U.S. economy was growing quickly, stimulated partly by the positive demand shock of additional U.S. government spending on the Vietnam War. For Canada, this also translated into a positive aggregate demand shock. Increasing GDP in the U.S. (part of R.O.W.) increased demand for Canadian exports. Increasing aggregate demand caused rising prices and increases in aggregate quantity supplied of real GDP. In producing more products/services, businesses hired more workers and unemployment decreased. The Canadian economy was in an inflationary gap.

When there are demand shocks, negative or positive, unemployment and inflation move in opposite directions, as the Phillips Curve suggests. Higher unemployment is associated with lower inflation, and lower unemployment is associated with higher inflation.

Positive demand shocks causs an inflationary gap: rising average prices, increased real GDP, and decreased unemployment.

Demand shocks cause unemployment and inflation to move in opposite directions, as the Phillips Curve suggests.

Negative Supply Shocks
Between the time that aggregate supply decisions have been made in input markets and the time when products/services arrive for sale in output markets, what happens if there is an unexpected negative aggregate supply shock—such as a decrease in aggregate supply caused by rising resource input prices?

In response to rising input prices, businesses are no longer willing to supply the same quantities of products/services as they were before. Aggregate quantity demanded is now greater than aggregate quantity supplied. There is a shortage of products/services in output markets. Businesses raise their output prices to cover the higher input costs. Those rising prices lead consumers to reduce their quantity demanded of products/services. Output decreases and businesses reduce their hiring of labour and other inputs.

The net result is a rise in the average price level, a decrease in real GDP and in aggregate quantity demanded, and increased unemployment. Real GDP falls below potential GDP. This combination of higher inflation and increased unemployment is the stagflation scenario of Chapter 3—inflation and recession. The language of gaps—recessionary gaps versus inflationary gaps—does not apply to the outcomes of supply side shocks.

The OPEC oil price shocks of the 1970s were the classic scenario of negative supply shocks. In response to rising oil prices, businesses raised prices to cover rising energy costs. But consumers couldn't buy the same quantities of products/services as before, since they were using more of their income to pay dramatically higher gasoline and home energy bills. Quantity demanded decreased. Inflation stayed high, output decreased, and unemployment increased throughout the late 1970s. That era was the origin of the word "stagflation."

Negative supply shocks cause stagflation: rising average prices, decreased real GDP, and increased unemployment.

Positive Supply Shocks
Between the time that aggregate supply decisions have been made in input markets, and the time when products/services arrive for sale in output markets, what happens if there is an unexpected positive aggregate supply shock—such as an increase in aggregate supply caused by technological improvements that dramatically lower costs?

With time to adopt the new technology, businesses are willing to supply even larger quantities of products/services than before. Aggregate quantity demanded is now less than aggregate quantity supplied. There is a surplus of products/services in output markets. In an attempt to get rid of unsold products, businesses cut prices. Surpluses create pressure for average prices to fall. As prices fall, aggregate quantity demanded increases. Output increases and businesses increase their hiring of labour and other inputs.

The net result is a fall in the average price level, an increase in real GDP and in aggregate quantity demanded, and decreased unemployment. The unemployment rate falls temporarily below the natural rate of unemployment. Real GDP rises above potential GDP. Instead of stagflation's combination of two undesirable outcomes (unemployment and inflation), the outcome of a positive supply shock is two desirable outcomes: lower unemployment and lower inflation.

Positive supply shocks cause falling average prices, increased real GDP, and decreased unemployment.

The technology boom in the late 1990s was due, in part, to a positive aggregate supply shock. Technological advances in digital information and computer technologies increased productivity and lowered costs. Although you probably can't imagine life without it, the Internet only began to operate effectively for businesses and consumers in 1995. As a result, businesses were able to lower prices, increase production, and hire more workers. Quantity demanded increased.

When there are supply shocks, negative or positive, unemployment and inflation move in the same directions. Higher unemployment is associated with higher inflation, and lower unemployment is associated with lower inflation.

Figure 4.6 shows the mismatch between aggregate supply and aggregate demand according to the "No" camp, and the possible business cycle outcomes from demand and supply shocks.

Supply shocks cause unemployment and inflation to move in the same direction.

Figure 4.6 Mismatch of Aggregate Supply and Aggregate Demand: Leads to Business Cycles

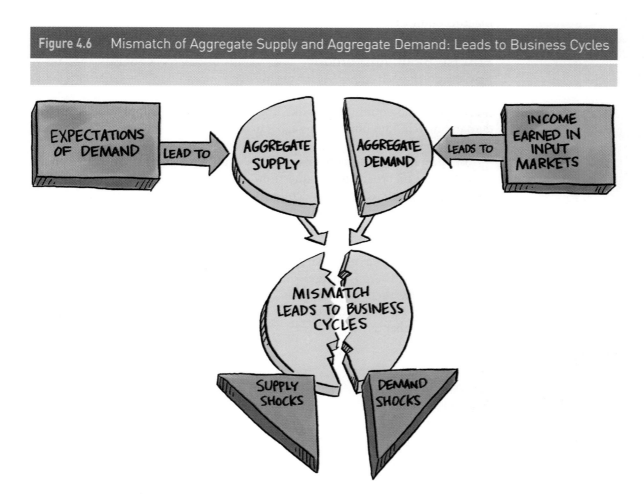

Economic Life is Full of Shocks

In the real world, demand and supply shocks rarely happen one at a time—they usually happen together. For example, in the 1970s, a negative supply shock of rising oil price combined with a negative demand shock of rising interest rates. In late 1990s, the positive supply shock of technology combined with positive demand shock of increased exports. The North American Free Trade Agreement (NAFTA) between Canada, the United States, and Mexico allowed R.O.W. buyers in the United States and Mexico to demand more Canadian exports and increase aggregate demand.

Negative and positive demand shocks can also happen together. For example, there could be a negative demand shock of more pessimistic expectations combined with a positive demand shock of increasing GDP in R.O.W.

Multiple shocks of the same type can also happen together, as seen in the late 1990s when the positive supply shock of digital technology combined with a positive supply shock of falling oil prices.

The impact on the economic outcomes of real GDP, unemployment, and inflation depends on the net effects of the combined shocks. But to be able to think through these more complex scenarios, you still use the tools of aggregate supply and aggregate demand. You break down the real world scenario into the separate effects of demand shocks and supply shocks, and then combine the results. Think of the tools of aggregate supply and aggregate demand as building blocks for more complex explanations, and you will be thinking like a macroeconomist.

Still No Basic Agreement   Both camps of macroeconomists, the "Yes—markets quickly self-adjust" believers in Say's Law and the "No—markets fail to quickly adjust" followers of Keynes, largely agree in describing what a macroeconomic equilibrium looks like when aggregate supply and aggregate demand match. And both camps agree in describing the impact of demand and supply shocks.

But despite those agreements, the "Yes" and "No" camps still disagree on the fundamental macroeconomic question—if left alone by government, do the price mechanisms of market economics quickly adjust to maintain steady growth in living standards, full employment, and stable prices? They disagree over the origins of the shocks triggering business cycles, and over how quickly markets adjust to the shocks. If markets adjust quickly, then the equilibrium stories of matching aggregate supply and aggregate demand are more important, and there is little need for government policy. If markets fail to adjust quickly, then the business cycle stories of mismatching are more important, and government policy is essential. These are the topics of the last section of the chapter.

1. Explain why businesses and consumers are happy when there is an equilibrium with existing inputs.

2. Describe the impact of a positive demand shock on average prices, real GDP, and unemployment.

3. If consumers choose to start saving more, explain how the market for loanable funds can rescue Say's Law.

4.4 Shocking Starts and Finishes: Origins and Responses to Business Cycles

Business cycles are triggered by shocks to aggregate supply and aggregate demand. Both the "Yes—markets quickly self-adjust" camp and the "No—markets fail to quickly adjust" camp agree on that. The differences between the camps, and their differing hands-off and hands-on roles for government policy, have to do with the *origins* of the shocks and the *responses* of markets to the shocks.

Let's look at the positions of the two camps on these topics, beginning with the "Yes" camp and then the "No" camp.

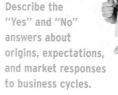

Describe the "Yes" and "No" answers about origins, expectations, and market responses to business cycles.

Yes — Markets Quickly Self-Adjust, So Hands-Off

The "Yes" camp allows for some ups and downs in real GDP, and occasional unemployment and inflation. While believing that Say's Law and matching aggregate supply and aggregate demand prevail most of the time, this camp recognizes that business cycles do happen.

Origins of Shocks and Business Cycles — "Yes" Camp
According to the "Yes" camp, shocks to aggregate supply and aggregate demand that trigger business cycles originate largely outside of the economy. They point to aggregate supply shocks caused by nature or scientific discoveries and aggregate demand shocks caused by mistaken government policies.

Nature-based supply shocks include natural disasters like droughts, floods, and earthquakes that destroy inputs. Scientific discoveries allow for technological change, which can act as both a positive and negative supply shock. For the businesses adopting new technologies, there can be increased productivity from cost-saving machinery, or new technology-based products that open up new markets. These are positive supply shocks. But for businesses based on old competing technologies, the same technology supply shock is negative. Think of what happened to the value of typewriter businesses when computer-based word-processing was invented.

The "Yes" camp also views mistaken government fiscal and monetary policies as demand shocks that can trigger unemployment and inflation. A tax increase that reduces spending is a negative demand shock that can cause a recession. Increased government spending, if the economy is already at potential GDP, is a positive demand shock that will increase inflation. The view is not that government deliberately tries to cause economic problems, but that it is difficult to time policy decisions precisely, and unintentional policy mistakes can cause business cycles. For the "Yes" camp, government is part of the problem, not part of the solution.

For the "Yes" camp, the origins of shocks are external to the economy.

The falling value of old technology businesses is the "destruction" part of the term "creative destruction" discussed in Chapter 1.

Rational Expectations Volatile expectations, which play a major role for the "No" camp about the origin of shocks, are not emphasized by the "Yes" camp. The "Yes" camp sees individuals and businesses as making logical, rational choices, based on the best information available. Like Mr. Spock, the Vulcan of *Star Trek*, even difficult investment spending choices with limited information, according to the "Yes" camp, are made coolly and efficiently. They downplay dramatic mood swings in expectations that shock demand. They de-emphasize the role of overly enthusiastic optimism in creating investment bubbles or of plummeting pessimism in bursting bubbles. Investors, for the "Yes" camp, are clear-thinking, steady calculators of profits and losses.

Spock, a character from the *Star Trek* series, was famous for his ability to make cool, unemotional decisions. The "Yes" camp believes people—business investors and consumers—are able to make Spock-like economic decisions.

For the "Yes" camp, price adjustments in all markets work together to quickly restore a match between aggregate supply and aggregate demand.

Market Price Responses to Business Cycles When external shocks or government policy mistakes trigger contractions or expansions, the "Yes" camp argues that price adjustments in separate markets—input, output, international trade, and loanable funds markets—all work harmoniously to quickly restore the match between aggregate supply and aggregate demand. Consider this recessionary gap example, where a negative demand shock has caused real GDP to decrease below potential GDP, increasing unemployment and putting downward pressure on average prices. It illustrates the arguments about how markets quickly adjust to restore steady growth in living standards, full employment, and stable prices.

The labour market is the most important input market. With increasing unemployment, there is a surplus of labour. The price of labour—the wage rate—will fall, increasing business hiring of workers. As the wage rate falls, the quantity of labour demanded increases and the quantity of labour supplied decreases until the labour market reaches an equilibrium. When the wage rate falls enough, quantity demanded and quantity supplied are equal, and full employment is restored. The same price adjustments occur in all input markets, until all inputs are once again fully utilized and employed.

When aggregate demand is less than aggregate supply, there are also surpluses in output markets, where unsold products/services are sitting on shelves. Businesses cut prices, which increases quantity demanded. As wages and other input costs fall, businesses are willing to supply still more products/services, even at lower prices. The combination of increasing quantity demanded and increasing supply increases sales and restores output to the level of potential GDP.

The international trade market also helps to increase production in output markets back to the level of potential GDP. Falling Canadian prices make our exports more competitive and attractive to R.O.W. Falling Canadian prices also mean consumers will substitute more domestically produced products/services in place of imports. Those additional net export sales increase aggregate quantity demanded and Canadian real GDP.

Finally, price adjustment in the loanable funds market provides a solution to the problem of savings for Say's Law. With a negative demand shock, aggregate planned spending (aggregate demand) is less than aggregate income earned in input markets (aggregate supply). But banks help shift spending and production between the present and the future.

Any additional savings get deposited in banks, increasing the supply of loanable funds. This causes the interest rate—the price of loanable funds—to fall. Falling interest rates induce more consumer and especially business borrowing (increased quantity demanded of loanable funds) to finance investment spending. Business investment spending increases, offsetting the increase in savings and restoring aggregate spending in output markets, making it equal to aggregate income earned in input markets.

Business investment borrowing is based on the coolly logical, Spock-like view of expectations. Although they are currently facing a recession with unsold products/services, businesses observe that consumers are saving more. Business entrepreneurs reason that consumer saving today is a decision to spend more in the future. So to be in a position to meet that future demand, the entrepreneurs start investing today.

In all of these markets, adjustments to smart choices through the price mechanism quickly restore the match between aggregate supply and aggregate demand.

Price mechanisms in markets function like an economic thermostat. If the weather outside gets hotter or colder, a thermostat automatically adjusts the air conditioning or heat to maintain the indoor temperature right where it should be, at the perfect comfortable temperature. Price mechanisms in markets adjust to aggregate supply and demand shocks, bringing the economy back to potential GDP, full employment, and stable prices—right where it should be.

This woman is adjusting the thermostat to keep the temperature inside where she wants it to be, regardless of the weather outside. According to the "Yes" camp, price mechanisms in markets work like a thermostat, keeping the economy where it should be, regardless of external shocks.

No — Markets Fail to Quickly Self-Adjust, So Hands-On

Following Keynes, the "No" camp of economists argues that, if left alone by government, the self-adjusting mechanisms of market economies can be slow and weak, so that business cycles of boom and bust, long periods of unemployment that reduce living standards, and rising or falling prices will occur regularly.

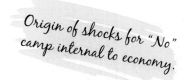

Origin of shocks for "No" camp internal to economy.

Origins of Shocks and Business Cycles — "No" Camp The "No" camp believes that shocks to aggregate supply and aggregate demand that trigger business cycles are largely *internally generated* as unintended byproducts of normal functioning markets. They point to expectations, the role of money, and connections between different market economies in R.O.W. in generating shocks.

Because no one can foretell the future, investment plans are based on expectations, or informed guesses. In contrast to the Spock-like view of purely logical calculation, the "No" camp sees investment decisions as based largely on a gut-level instinct to act, which Keynes called *animal spirits*—"a spontaneous urge to action rather than inaction."

▶

Professors George Akerolf (Nobel Prize Winner) and Robert Shiller (Yale University) returned to Keynes's ideas in this 2009 book explaining business cycles and the Great Recession.

Animal Spirits

HOW HUMAN PSYCHOLOGY DRIVES THE ECONOMY, AND WHY IT MATTERS FOR GLOBAL CAPITALISM

GEORGE A. AKERLOF
AND
ROBERT J. SHILLER

Adjustment problems in all markets fail to restore match between aggregate supply and aggregate demand for "No" camp.

Volatile Expectations   With few solid facts, investors look for guidance to what other investors are doing. This "herd mentality" is at the heart of cycles of boom and bust such as the Great Recession. When housing prices were rising, no one could say with certainty that they would continue to rise. But when you see everyone around you making money in the real estate market, it is easy to jump on the bandwagon and start investing. And without solid facts, when pessimism appears, it can easily spread, causing prices to fall quickly.

Fundamental uncertainty about the future, the reliance on the "herd" of other equally uncertain investors for guidance, and the postponeable nature of investments all combine to make expectations, and investment spending decisions, very volatile. Quickly changeable expectations coming from inside the economy make for aggregate demand shocks, fluctuating between positive and negative.

The "No" camp also emphasizes the role of money, put into savings, in dealing with the fundamental uncertainty about the future. When consumers and businesses become worried about the future, they save more from their incomes and earnings. If you are worried about becoming unemployed or about poor sales, saved money gives you a cushion and flexibility to act in a downturn. Ironically, pessimistic expectations, and higher savings, can become a self-fulfilling prophecy, causing a recession. Decisions to save more can act as a negative aggregate demand shock.

International trade provides the final source of business cycles for the "No" camp. Trade, the exchange of imports and exports, connects the market economies of countries around the world. They become interdependent. But if each of those economies has internally generated business cycles, then a recession in one causes shocks in the others. In the United States, for example, a downturn causes a decreased demand for Canadian exports. That negative demand shock for Canada can trigger a contraction here. Similarly, a boom in another country can cause a positive demand shock for Canada through increased exports.

Market Price Responses to Business Cycles   Besides viewing aggregate demand and aggregate supply shocks as internally generated by market economies, the "No" camp does not have much faith in the ability of markets to quickly adjust to the shocks. To make comparisons with the "Yes" camp easier, let's look at the same recessionary gap example, where a negative demand shock has caused real GDP to decrease below potential GDP, increasing unemployment and putting downward pressure on average prices. The adjustment stories for the "No" camp are very different for the input, output, international trade, and loanable funds markets.

In labour markets, wages don't fall often or easily. Economists describe these as *sticky wages*. Employers will tell you that it is much easier to raise wages than to cut them. There are many reasons for sticky wages. Union and other contracts can't be quickly changed. Workers generally resist having their wages and incomes reduced. Employers also resist wage cuts unless absolutely necessary, because cuts demoralize workers, hurt productivity, and prompt even their best employees to start looking elsewhere for jobs.

In markets, when prices don't adjust, quantities do. Unemployment is a quantity adjustment in labour markets. Workers and employers accept layoffs instead of lower wages in response to a negative demand shock.

When there are surpluses in output markets, both the "No" and "Yes" camps see businesses cutting prices of products/services, which increases quantity demanded. But without lower wages in labour markets, the "No" camp argues that there are no further increases in supply in output markets. And the layoffs in labour markets means less income for workers to spend, which decreases demand for products/services in output markets. The "No" camp focuses on the connections between input and output markets as a barrier to quick market adjustments to a negative demand shock and unemployment. It may take a long time to restore output to the level of potential GDP.

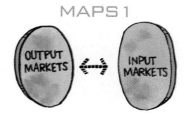

MAPS 1

In international trade markets, both the "No" and "Yes" camps see falling Canadian prices increasing net export sales, aggregate quantity demanded, and Canadian real GDP. But the "No" camp worries about the destabilizing effects of fluctuating Canadian exports due to business cycles in R.O.W. These additional demand shocks from R.O.W. may offset the stabilizing role of price adjustments in export/import markets.

MAPS 2

Finally, the "No" camp argues that increased savings in the loanable funds market does *not* turn into increased investment spending. On its own, an increase in savings—the supply of loanable funds—puts pressure on interest rates to fall. But if the increase in savings is caused by more pessimistic expectations about the future, then business investment spending may decrease, not increase, even if interest rates fall.

The two most important factors determining business investment spending are expectations and interest rates. The "No" camp believes expectations are more important. The "Yes" camp, with its view of rational, stable expectations, believes interest rates are more important.

Expectations and interest rates affect business investment spending. The "No" camp emphasizes expectations. The "Yes" camp emphasizes interest rates.

The "No" camp disagrees with the "Yes" camp argument that business entrepreneurs view consumer savings today as a decision to spend more in the future. The weakness of that argument is that a business does not know *when* in the future consumers will spend, or *on what*. A business must make investment spending plans for a particular product or service. Will the additional consumer savings today be spent next year or in 10 years? Will consumers spend on iPods, automobiles, Caribbean vacations, or your business's product/service? Because businesses can't easily predict when and where consumers will spend, lower interest rates during a recession do not stimulate additional business investment spending. Unsold products today do more to discourage investment spending decisions than lower interest rates do to encourage investing spending. The banking system does not adjust spending to counter the effects of shocks.

MAPS 3

With internally generated shocks regularly causing business cycles, and with weak or slow price adjustment mechanism, the "No" camp sees an obvious role for government in market economies. They see the thermostat as needing an adjustment and that only government is in a position to do it. Government fiscal and monetary policies can be used to counter the shocks that have triggered recessionary or inflationary gaps—they can bring aggregate supply, aggregate demand, and the economy back into balance.

Yes or No: How Do You Decide?

If I have done my job properly, you will find yourself agreeing with some of the arguments of both the "Yes—markets quickly self-adjust" camp and the "No—markets fail to quickly adjust" camp. The positions of both camps contain correct insights about how the Canadian economy works. However, this chapter does not contain enough evidence, especially data about the Canadian and other market economies, to allow you to come to an informed conclusion.

But notice that the disagreements between the "Yes" and "No" camps focus largely on the three MAPS of the MAcroeconomic Positioning Systems.

Figure 4.7	MAPS Icons

MAPS 1   MAPS 2   MAPS 3

The tools of aggregate supply and aggregate demand, together with the MAPS, focus on where the "Yes" and "No" camps disagree and give you a more detailed look at the specific arguments behind each camp's answers to the fundamental macroeconomic question—if left alone by government, do the price mechanisms of market economies adjust quickly to maintain steady growth in living standards, full employment, and stable prices?

As you learn more in coming chapters, and in your own observations of the economy, you will be able to clarify your opinions about the individual arguments within each camp's position. It is easier to make judgments about individual arguments than to pass a single judgment on the whole "Yes–No" macroeconomic question. With those informed opinions, you will better understand how to think like a macroeconomist, make better personal economic choices, and be better able to choose between politicians whose economic policy choices will influence your personal economic success.

Comparing Camps: Origins of Shocks and Business Cycles

Figure 4.8 is a good study device for reviewing the differences between the two camps regarding the origin of shocks and their effect on business cycles. It extends Figure 1.2 comparing the two camps on their answers to the fundamental macroeconomic question.

Figure 4.8 Origins of Shocks and Business Cycles		
Answer to Fundamental Macroeconomic Question	**Yes — Left Alone, Markets Quickly Self-Adjust (Say)**	**No — Left Alone, Markets Fail to Quickly Adjust (Keynes)**
Origin of shocks	External to economy	Internal to economy
Most important shocks	Supply shocks	Demand shocks
Expectations	Rational; steady	Based on animal spirits, herd mentality; volatile
Price adjustments in response to business cycles	Work together to quickly restore equilibrium — match between aggregate supply and demand	Adjustment problems in all markets fail to restore equilibrium
Most important influence changing business investment spending	Interest rates as cost of borrowing	Expectations of future profits
Savings and loanable funds market	Interest rate in loanable funds market adjusts so investment spending offsets savings, maintaining aggregate demand	Savings cause negative demand shock; falling sales and expectations decrease investment spending

Refresh
4.4

1. Identify the origins of shocks causing business cycles for the "Yes" camp.

2. Describe the role of *animal spirits* in the "No" camp explanation of volatile expectations for investors.

3. Based on your current understanding of the "Yes" and "No" camps, which of their individual arguments do you find most convincing? If you had to pick, which camp would you support? Why?

Skating to Where the Puck Is Going

Aggregate Supply and Aggregate Demand

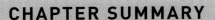

CHAPTER SUMMARY

4.1 IF YOU PLAN AND BUILD IT . . . AGGREGATE SUPPLY

Supply plans for existing inputs determine aggregate quantity supplied. Supply plans to increase the quantity and quality of inputs, together with supply shocks, change aggregate supply.

- Macroeconomic players—consumers, businesses, government— make two kinds of plans for supplying Canadian real GDP:
  - Supply plans for existing inputs.
  - Supply plans to increase inputs.
- Supply plans for existing inputs similar to microeconomic choices about quantity supplied.
  - **Aggregate quantity supplied**—quantity of real GDP macroeconomic players plan to supply at different average price levels.
  - **Law of aggregate supply**—as average level of prices rises, aggregate quantity supplied increases (up to a maximum of potential GDP).
- Supply plans to increase quantity or quality of inputs cause an **increase in aggregate supply**—increase in economy's capacity to produce real GDP.
- Business supply choices:
  - With existing inputs: what to produce, quantities to produce, quantities of inputs to hire.
    Determines aggregate quantity supplied.
  - To increase quantity and quality of inputs: investing in new factories/equipment, searching for new resources, technology improvements.
    Change aggregate supply (not aggregate quantity supplied); increase potential GDP.

- Consumer supply choices:
  - With existing inputs: to participate in labour force, number of hours to work, quantities of owned inputs to supply.
    Determines aggregate quantity supplied.
  - To increase quantity and quality of inputs: having children, education and training.
    Change aggregate supply.
- Government supply choices:
  - With existing inputs: quantities of resources to supply.
    Determines aggregate quantity supplied.
  - To increase quantity and quality of inputs: build infrastructure, change rules of the game, policies affecting inputs.
    Change aggregate supply.
- *Negative supply shocks* directly increase costs or reduce inputs, and decrease aggregate supply.
- *Positive supply shocks* directly decrease costs or improve productivity, and increase aggregate supply.

4.2 . . . WILL THEY COME AND BUY IT?
AGGREGATE DEMAND

Demand plans by macroeconomic players determine aggregate quantity demanded. Demand shocks—from changes in expectations, interest rates, government policy, GDP in R.O.W., exchange rates—change aggregate demand.

- All macroeconomic players—consumers, businesses, government, R.O.W.—make demand plans for spending, similar to microeconomic choices about quantity demanded.
  - **Aggregate quantity demanded**—quantity of real GDP macroeconomic players plan to demand at different average price levels.
  - **Law of aggregate demand**—as average level of prices rises, aggregate quantity demanded decreases.
- *Fallacy of composition* makes macroeconomic law of aggregate demand slightly different from microeconomic law of demand.
  - When average prices rise for all Canadian products/services, only substitutes are imports from R.O.W.
  - Decreased aggregated quantity demanded of Canadian real GDP due to Canadians buying more imports; R.O.W. buying fewer Canadian exports due to higher prices.
- Consumers plans to spend (*C*) fraction of *disposable income*—earned income plus transfer payments less taxes—and save the rest.
  - Consumer spending is largest, most stable component of aggregate demand.
- Businesses plan investment spending (*I*) for new factories and equipment. Investment spending plans volatile because:
  - Can be easily postponed.
  - Based on uncertain expectations that can shift quickly and dramatically.
  - Depend on borrowed money—rise or fall in interest rates makes investment less or more profitable.

- Government spending plans (G) for products/services set by budget.
  - Transfer payments not part of G.
  - G as a percentage of real GDP has been stable since 1990s.
- R.O.W. spending plans (X) for Canadian exports:
  - Exports change with changes in real GDP in other countries.
  - Exports change with exchange rate changes—fall in value of Canadian dollar makes exports cheaper to R.O.W. and increases demand.
  - Must subtract imports (IM) from all other planned spending to get net exports ($X - IM$): net flow between R.O.W. and Canada; difference between what Canada exports and what it imports.
- Planned spending on aggregate demand = planned C + planned I + planned G + planned ($X - IM$).
- **Demand shocks**—factors, other than average prices, changing aggregate demand. **Aggregate demand changes** with changes in expectations, interest rates, government policy, GDP in R.O.W. and exchange rates.
  - Negative demand shocks decrease aggregate demand: more pessimistic expectations, higher interest rates, lower government spending or higher taxes, decreased GDP in R.O.W., higher value Canadian dollar.
  - Positive demand shocks increase aggregate demand: more optimistic expectations, lower interest rates, higher government spending or lower taxes, increased GDP in R.O.W., lower value Canadian dollar.

4.3 MATCH OR MISMATCH? AGGREGATE SUPPLY AND AGGREGATE DEMAND

Matches between aggregate supply and aggregate demand give equilibrium, Say's Law, and the "Yes" answer to the fundamental macroeconomic question; mismatches give Keynes's business cycles, demand and supply shocks, and the "No" answer.

- "Yes" answer: *macroeconomic equilibrium* with existing inputs when aggregate demand *matches* aggregate supply.
  - Aggregate supply choices based on expectations of what price level and aggregate demand will be when products/services get to market.
  - In equilibrium, price level and aggregate demand are what suppliers expected—"no one is kicking himself."
  - Real GDP equals potential GDP; all inputs fully employed.
  - Say's Law—supply creates its own demand.
- "Yes" answer: equilibrium over time with increasing inputs when aggregate demand *matches* aggregate supply.
  - Must add savings and investment to explain growth in living standards over time (increase in real GDP per person).
  - Savings seem to threaten Say's Law, since all income earned in input markets is not spent demanding products/services in output markets.
  - **Market for loanable funds**—banks coordinate the supply of loanable funds (savings) with the demand for loanable funds (borrowing); interest rate is the price of loanable funds.

- If banks loan out savings to businesses who use it for investment spending, that offsets consumer savings, restoring equality between aggregate income and aggregate spending.
- Investment spending also increases quantity and quality of inputs, so potential GDP and real GDP per person increase over time.
- Aggregate supply and aggregate demand both increase, so full employment continues and average prices stay stable.
- "No" answer: *mismatch* between aggregate demand and aggregate supply.
  - Aggregate supply choices based on expectations of what price level and aggregate demand will be when products/services get to market.
  - With mismatch, expectations disappointed, outcomes do not work out as planned.
  - Adjustments, in form of expansions and contractions, necessary to get back to smart choices.
  - Keynes's business cycles.
- Mismatch scenarios from demand shocks:
  - *Negative demand shock* causes a recessionary gap—falling average prices, decreased real GDP, increased unemployment.
  - *Positive demand shock* causes an inflationary gap—rising average prices, increased real GDP, decreased unemployment.
  - Demand shocks cause unemployment and inflation to move in opposite directions, as Philips Curve suggests.
- Mismatch scenarios from supply shocks:
  - *Negative supply shock* causes stagflation—rising average prices, decreased real GDP, increased unemployment.
  - *Positive supply shock* causes falling average prices, increased real GDP, decreased unemployment.
  - Supply shocks cause unemployment and inflation to move in same direction.
- "Yes" and "No" camps agree on descriptions of equilibrium and impact of demand and supply shocks, but disagree on origins of shocks and how quickly markets adjust.

4.4 SHOCKING STARTS AND FINISHES: ORIGINS AND RESPONSES TO BUSINESS CYCLES

The "Yes" and "No" camps disagree about the external/internal origins of shocks, about rational/volatile expectations, and about how quickly price adjustments in all markets restore the match between aggregate supply and aggregate demand.

- "Yes" camp—markets quickly self-adjust, so hands-off.
  - Origins of shocks external to economy—in nature, science, and mistaken government policies.
  - Government part of problem, not part of solution.
  - Emphasizes rational expectations of investors and logical choices.

- For "Yes" camp, when shocks occur, price adjustments in all markets work together to quickly restore match between aggregate supply and aggregate demand—example where negative demand shock causes recessionary gap.
  - In labour market, unemployment causes wage rate to fall, increasing hiring of labour until full employment restored.
  - In output markets, prices fall due to surpluses and falling wage costs, increasing sales of products/services until back to level of potential GDP.
  - In international trade market, falling Canadian prices increase net exports $(X - IM)$, increasing Canadian real GDP and decreasing unemployment.
  - In loanable funds market, additional savings causes interest rates to fall, increasing investment spending (I), increasing Canadian real GDP, and decreasing unemployment.
- "No" camp—markets fail to quickly self-adjust, so hands-on.
  - Origins of shocks internal to economy—from changing expectations, role of money, and connections with R.O.W. market economies.
  - Emphasizes volatile expectations of investors based on fundamental uncertainty about future; reliance on changeable "herd mentality" of other investors and postponeable nature of investments; investment based on *animal spirits*—gut-level instinct to act.
  - Facing uncertainty about the future, consumer decisions to save more money are internal source of negative demand shock.
  - Internally generated business cycles in other market economies affect Canada through international trade markets for exports and imports.
- For "No" camp, when shocks occur—same example where negative demand shock causes recessionary gap—difficult adjustments in all markets.
  - In labour market, wages are *sticky* (don't fall easily) even with unemployment—workers and employers accept layoffs instead of lower wages.
  - In output markets, prices fall due to surpluses, but falling incomes from unemployment in input markets decrease consumption demand (C) for products/services.
  - In international trade market, falling Canadian prices may increase net exports $(X - IM)$, but benefits might be outweighed by destabilizing effects of business cycles in R.O.W.
  - In loanable funds market, even if additional savings cause interest rates to fall, more pessimistic expectations may cause investment spending (I) to decrease, not increase.
  - With weak or slow price adjustment mechanisms, clear role for government to bring aggregate supply and aggregate demand back into balance.
- Disagreement between "Yes" and "No" camps focus largely on
  - MAPS 1—connections between input markets and output markets for both demand and supply sides.
  - MAPS 2—connections between Canada and the rest of the world.
  - MAPS 3—connections between money/banks/expectations and input and output markets.

TRUE/FALSE

Circle the correct answer.

You are skating on an outdoor ice rink when suddenly hockey superstar Sidney Crosby comes by and offers to teach you how to anticipate where the puck is going. After the lesson he notices your economics textbook in your gym bag and says,

I own a small hockey equipment business, and I would like to anticipate where the economy is going in order to make supply plans for my business. If I read an interesting story in the news, I'd like to send you a text message so you can confirm if my statement about the macro economy is true.

Use this scenario to answer questions 1–15.

4.1 AGGREGATE SUPPLY

1. An increase in the CPI means there is economic growth. **True**   **False**

2. An advancement in hockey stick technology increases the aggregate supply of real GDP. **True**   **False**

3. An increase in the supply of hockey skates in the R.O.W. decreases aggregate supply in Canada. **True**   **False**

4. An increase in gas prices increases aggregate supply of real GDP. **True**   **False**

5. A decrease in the hours worked by households decreases aggregate supply of real GDP. **True**   **False**

4.2 AGGREGATE DEMAND

6. An increase in demand for hockey tickets from the R.O.W. increases aggregate demand for Canadian GDP. **True**   **False**

7. An increase in business investment in new hockey equipment increases aggregate demand. **True**   **False**

8. The introduction of a children's fitness tax benefit (a transfer payment) by the government counts as government spending (*G*). **True**   **False**

9. An increase in the value of the Canadian dollar relative to the U.S. dollar increases aggregate demand for Canadian GDP. **True**   **False**

4.3 AGGREGATE SUPPLY AND AGGREGATE DEMAND

10. All economists agree that increases in aggregate supply automatically lead to steady growth in living standards, full employment, and stable prices. **True**   **False**

11. All economists agree on descriptions of equilibrium and on the impact of demand and supply shocks. **True**   **False**

12. All economists agree that government expenditures will quickly lead to steady growth in living standards, full employment, and stable prices.   **True**   **False**

13. In a recession, the "Yes" (hands-off) camp believes that full employment is restored quickly because unemployment will cause wages to fall and employment to increase.   **True**   **False**

14. In a recession, the "No" (hands-on) camp believes that potential GDP is restored quickly because surpluses of products/services will cause prices to fall and sales to increase.   **True**   **False**

15. In a recession, the "Yes" (hands-off) camp believes that potential GDP is restored quickly because additional savings will cause interest rates to rise and investment spending to increase.   **True**   **False**

MULTIPLE CHOICE

Circle the correct answer.

4.1 AGGREGATE SUPPLY

1. Business supply plans to increase inputs increase aggregate
   A) supply.
   B) demand.
   C) quantity supplied.
   D) quantity demanded.

2. Aggregate supply of real GDP increases if
   A) productivity increases.
   B) input prices increase.
   C) output prices increase.
   D) All of the above

3. Suppose that, in the future, businesses will only pay high wages to people with college and university degrees. If people plan ahead and decide to increase their years of schooling, this will result in an increase in aggregate
   A) quantity demanded.
   B) demand.
   C) quantity supplied.
   D) supply.

4.2 AGGREGATE DEMAND

4. If your income is $20 000, your taxes are $6000 and your transfer payments are $3000, then your disposable income is

  A) $11 000.

  B) $14 000.

  C) $17 000.

  D) $20 000.

5. Of all components of aggregate demand, investment spending is the

  A) largest component.

  B) most volatile, unpredictable component.

  C) component that is not postponeable.

  D) least affected by interest rates and expectations.

6. Aggregate demand in Canada increases if

  A) China buys more Canadian oil.

  B) aggregate demand in India decreases.

  C) Canada buys more Porsches from Germany.

  D) the value of the Canadian dollar increases.

7. Aggregate demand decreases if

  A) business investors become more optimistic.

  B) government increases taxes.

  C) transfer payments increase.

  D) the CPI increases.

4.3 AGGREGATE SUPPLY AND AGGREGATE DEMAND

8. ING Direct is known for its slogan "save your money." Suppose a new competitor, BLING Direct, advertises with the slogan "spend your money." If BLING Direct's advertisement encourages households to spend more of their income, this will cause a

  A) positive supply shock.

  B) negative supply shock.

  C) positive demand shock.

  D) negative demand shock.

9. In the Great Recession, changes in unemployment and inflation moved in the opposite directions—unemployment went up and inflation went down. This suggests the Great Recession was mostly a result of a

  A) positive supply shock.

  B) negative supply shock.

  C) positive demand shock.

  D) negative demand shock.

10. Which of the following shocks causes stagflation?
    A) Positive supply shock
    B) Negative supply shock
    C) Positive demand shock
    D) Negative demand shock

11. When consumers save some of their income, what can save Say's Law?
    A) Consumer spending
    B) Consumer saving
    C) Business investment spending based on borrowed funds
    D) Superman

12. Followers of Keynes and of Say's Law disagree on
    A) the impact of demand shocks.
    B) the impact of supply shocks.
    C) what a macroeconomic equilibrium looks like.
    D) the role for government policy.

4.4 ORIGINS AND RESPONSES TO BUSINESS CYCLES

13. Why are wages "sticky"?
    A) Employment contracts can't be quickly changed.
    B) Workers resist having their wages reduced.
    C) Employers resist wage cuts unless absolutely necessary because wage cuts hurt productivity.
    D) All of the above.

14. The "Yes" camp of economists emphasizes
    A) animal spirits.
    B) that individuals and businesses make rational choices based on the best information available.
    C) that expectations are more important than interest rates.
    D) that shocks are generated from inside of the economy.

15. Two businesses, Dunder and Mifflin, need to reduce input costs because of economic conditions. The boss of Dunder announces, "The bad news is that I need to lay off some of you, but the good news is that wages will remain the same for those of you that I don't lay off." The boss of Mifflin announces, "The bad news is that I need to reduce everyone's wages, but the good news is that no one will lose their job."
    A) Dunder's announcement resembles the Keynesian view that wages are sticky and do not fall much during a recession.
    B) Mifflin's announcement resembles the Keynesian view that wages are sticky and do not fall much during a recession.
    C) Dunder's announcement resembles the Keynesian view that jobs are sticky and do not fall much during a recession.
    D) Dunder's announcement resembles the Keynesian view that jobs are sticky and do not fall much during a recession.

SHORT ANSWER

Write a short answer to each question. Your answer may be in point form.

1. Imagine a simple economy where people spend all of their day online. Individuals pay suppliers, such as E-conomics Harmony, for online services. Real GDP consists only of online services.

   A) Describe the equilibrium in this small economy. Is anyone kicking themselves in the equilibrium?

   B) Why would suppliers be kicking themselves if there is a mismatch between demand and supply?

   C) Suppose George Stroumboulopoulos—one of Canada's favourite television and radio personalities—launches a campaign "One Million Acts Not Online," where the goal is to encourage people to spend less time and money online. If his campaign is successful, what kind of shock will this be to the simple online economy?

2. Suppose that Sidney Crosby's son is in your economics class and he asks you to explain why it is important for businesses to anticipate where GDP is going.

   A) Why does success in business depend on anticipating the market?

   B) How are business supply plans similar to hockey player skating plans?

3. Suppose you dream about Chapter 4 the night before the test. You remember parts of five different dreams—and in each dream you are either being initiated by the "Yes" camp or "No" camp. For each of the following five dreams, determine whether it was the "Yes" camp or "No" camp that was involved.

   A) Rollercoaster initiation: you are sent down a rollercoaster that has huge expansions and contractions, which is supposed to represent their understanding of business cycles.

   B) *Star Trek* initiation: they dress you up in their favourite *Star Trek* character—Spock—and remove your blindfold to see if you can determine which camp they are from.

   C) Thermostat initiation: they put you in a room with a really slow thermostat, which represents the speed at which they think the economy automatically adjusts after a shock.

   D) Graffiti initiation: they spray paint your room with an anarchy symbol, which represents "no government intervention."

   E) Saltwater initiation: they take your bed (while you are sleeping) and put it into saltwater. Hint: an excerpt from a *New York Times* article by Paul Krugman published September 6, 2009, (below) explains the difference between "saltwater" economists and "freshwater" economists. "*Macroeconomics has divided into two great factions: "saltwater" economists (mainly in coastal U.S. universities), who have a more or less Keynesian vision of what recessions are all about; and "freshwater" economists (mainly at inland schools), who consider that vision nonsense [and instead have a Say's Law vision].*"

4. The H1N1 flu virus was reported around the world in 2009, and the World Health Organization declared it a pandemic. A Canadian study in 2007 estimated that a 1918–type flu pandemic would likely reduce annual GDP growth by up to 1 percentage point in the pandemic year. For example, if annual GDP growth was expected to be 3 percent in 2010, then a pandemic starting in January 2010 could reduce annual GDP growth to 2 percent in 2010.

A) The availability of workers in a pandemic falls because individuals get sick, die, need to care for someone who is ill, or avoid work in fear of getting the illness. If fewer individuals are available to work, what kind of shock is this?

B) Consumers may reduce face-to-face transactions in fear of getting the illness. What kind of shock is this?

C) Economists may come up with different GDP impacts, depending on how quickly they think markets adjust in each of the four markets— input, output, international trade, and loanable funds. If economists are from the "Yes" camp, how would they think each of the markets quickly restores the match between aggregate supply and aggregate demand after a negative demand shock that causes a recessionary gap?

5. Monique owns a spa business. In answering these questions, remember that a positive supply shock in macroeconomics is similar to an increase in supply (not quantity supplied) in microeconomics.

A) If prices in general increase, including prices for spa services, why should Monique supply more services? What happens to aggregate supply of real GDP?

B) What law is assumed in part a)?

C) If, instead, there is a positive supply shock, what would happened to Monique's willingness to supply services at an unchanged price after the shock?

6. Followers of Keynes and believers in Say's Law disagree about the relative importance of supply and demand.

A) Why do savings seem to cause trouble for Say's Law?

B) What can save the day for Say's Law?

C) Describe the market for loanable funds.

D) How would a decrease in the interest rates affect aggregate demand, potential GDP, and real GDP per person?

E) During the Great Recession, business investors found it difficult to obtain money because lenders did not trust they would be paid back. If people hide money under their mattress or if lenders do not trust they will be paid back, will Say's Law really be saved?

7. Abigail sells shoes, mostly Birkenstocks. She makes her supply decisions based on the level of consumer expectations and confidence in the economy.

   A) Consumer confidence in Canada declined toward the end of 2008, but then started to improve in the spring of 2009. How would these trends in consumer confidence impact aggregate demand in general?

   B) Suppose that Canadian business leaders have optimistic expectations about the economic recovery. How would this impact aggregate demand?

   C) If Abigail anticipates strong demand conditions in the economy, describe her supply plans.

8. Both oil prices and the value of the Canadian dollar fell sharply in 2008.

   A) What kind of shocks are these and how would they have impacted aggregate supply or demand?

   B) If oil prices and the value of the Canadian dollar rose sharply in 2009 and 2010, what type of shocks would they be and what would be the impact of these shocks on unemployment and real GDP?

9. Before the Great Recession, many people made decisions expecting house prices would always rise.

   A) Are these "herd mentality" behaviours characteristic of Spock-types or animal spirit–types?

   B) What camp of economists thinks that overly enthusiastic optimism creates bubbles and that bursting bubbles causes extreme pessimism when the bubble bursts?

   C) John F. "Jack" Welch, CEO of General Electric and one of the world's most successful executives, claims that business decisions are made "from the gut." Would Jack most likely fit into the "Yes" or "No" camp of economists?

10. The first step in an economic recovery from a recession is for real GDP to stop decreasing. Real gross domestic product rose slightly (+0.1 percent) in June 2009, after ten consecutive monthly declines. Economists then wondered whether the path of real GDP from October 2008 to October 2009 would follow a *V* shape or a *W* shape. A *V*-shaped path would imply that real GDP declined and then increased until October 2009. A *W*-shaped path would imply that the economy quickly recovered and then declined again before returning to growth. At the time this chapter was written, it was too soon to know whether the economy followed a *V* shape or a *W* shape.

    A) Which shape do you think the economy took?

    B) Name a supply or demand shock that influenced the economy to take that shape.

---

myeconlab Visit the MyEconLab website at **www.myeconlab.com**. This online homework and tutorial system puts you in control of your own learning with study and practice tools.

Money Is for Lunatics

Demanders and Suppliers of Money

5% BOND **5%**
RICH GOLD COMPANY
$1000
$50 $50 $50 $50
COUPON COUPON COUPON COUPON
$50 $50 $50 $50
COUPON COUPON COUPON COUPON

LEARNING OBJECTIVES

5.1 Explain three functions of money and why people give up interest on bonds to demand money.

5.2 Identify four forms of money and describe how the Bank of Canada and chartered banks create money.

5.3 Relate bond prices and interest rates and explain how money and bond markets determine the interest rate.

5.4 Differentiate the "Yes" and "No" camps' positions on the monetary transmission mechanism and the impact of money on business cycles.

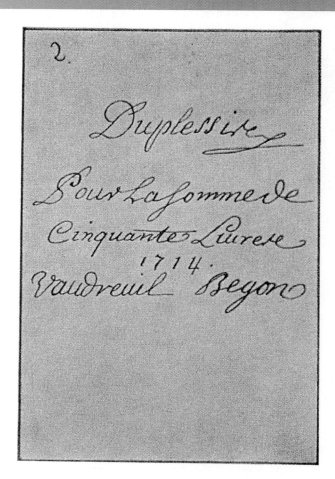

WHO WANTS MORE MONEY? OK, you can all put down your hands. From the title of this chapter, you are probably thinking that I am the lunatic here. Let me explain.

When you want to save money, you can stash it—as cash—under your mattress, which pays no interest. Alternatively, you can invest your money and earn interest on it. So why would you ever choose to hold cash? That's one of the questions this chapter will answer.

"What is money?" is another question with unexpected answers. Historically, precious metals, jewels, beads, stones, and even furs have been used as money. Even the playing cards shown in the photo above once served as paper money as far back as 1685 in Canada. Today, in our world of digital banking, cash is the least common form of money.

In this chapter, we will explain why people demand cash and voluntarily give up the possibility to earn interest. And we answer the question, "Who supplies money?"

The interest rate is the price of money and is the answer to the question, "How much will you pay for money?" But demanders and suppliers of money also have a role to play in setting interest rates. And interest rates, in turn, have an influence on business investment spending, real GDP, and unemployment.

Get ready to enter the world of money, which is not crazy, but is full of surprising answers to many unusual questions.

5.1 Is It Smart to *Not* Want Money? Demand for Money

Explain three functions of money and why people give up interest on bonds to demand money.

There was a good reason why you all raised your hands about wanting more money. In a market economy like Canada's, money buys all of the products/services we want. Any business will accept your cash (or debit card) in exchange for what it is selling. That *acceptability* is the key to what we use as money. **Money** is anything acceptable as a means of paying for products/services.

What makes money acceptable?

money: *anything acceptable as a means of paying for products/services*

What Does Money Do?

Money serves three essential functions: as a medium of exchange, a unit of account, and a store of value.

Medium of Exchange   Markets are based on voluntary exchange. Barter is a simple form of exchange where two people directly trade one product for another, without the use of money. If Samantha has baked bread and Jacqueline has chopped wood, they can trade, or barter, bread for wood.

Suppose these pioneers agree that Samantha will give 1 loaf of bread to Jacqueline in exchange for 10 kilograms of wood. Samantha values the wood she gets more than the loaf of bread she gives up, and Jacqueline values the loaf of bread she gets more than the wood she give up. Both are happy after the trade.

In a barter world, Say's Law is always true. No one supplies—brings a product/service to market—unless she is demanding another product/service in exchange. Supply creates its own demand.

As a medium of exchange, money solves the barter problem of the double coincidence of wants.

The problem with barter exchange is that you must find a trading partner who not only is selling what you want, but who also wants—is willing to accept—what you are selling. Economists call this problem the *double coincidence of wants*. If Samantha is selling bread and wants wood, and Jacqueline is selling wood but wants eggs instead of bread, there is no double coincidence of wants. No trade happens.

If all traders will accept money in exchange for whatever they are selling, this solves the problem of the double coincidence of wants. Samantha only needs to find buyers who want bread, and Jacqueline only needs to find buyers who want wood. Once each exchanges her product for money, she can then buy whatever she wants from whomever she wants.

Money functions as a *medium of exchange*. Its acceptability by all traders as a means of payment overcomes the problem of the double coincidence of wants, and makes exchange or trade much easier for all.

◀

Samantha is trading some of her bread for some of Jacqueline's wood. This form of trade, bartering, can only work when one person is selling what you want and at the same time wants what you're selling. Can you see the limitations in using a barter system for a large economy?

Unit of Account

The second function of money is providing a standard unit for measuring prices. In Canada, the standard unit is the Canadian dollar. All products/services are measured in dollars. A loaf of bread costs $4, a kilo of wood costs $0.40, a dozen eggs costs $2. This convenient and simple system seems so obvious we rarely think about it.

But a comparison with barter again exposes money's usefulness, this time as a unit of account. Prices could be measured in terms of any product instead of money. A loaf of bread could cost 10 kilos of wood, or a dozen eggs could cost half a loaf of bread. It would be difficult to make smart choices in comparing what you must give up to get a product/service when each is priced in terms of a different product/service. Imagine trying to plan your monthly budget if everything you wanted to buy was priced in terms a different product/service.

With money, dollar prices act as a common denominator allowing you to easily see the relative prices of all products/services. For example, a loaf of bread is 10 times as expensive as a kilogram of wood or twice as expensive as a dozen eggs. You can easily figure out what you can afford to buy on your budget. Everything you buy is measured in dollars.

As a unit of account, money functions as a standard unit for measuring prices.

Store of Value

Money allows you to separate supply from demand. With money, Samantha and Jacqueline can supply their bread and wood (products) first—sell them for money—before deciding what to buy, or demand. Once you have sold something of value on the market—usually your ability to work in the labour market in exchange for wages—money allows you to save some of your income for future spending. Income is what you earn, wealth is what you own. Savings become part of your wealth, together with any other assets that you own (property, equities, bonds). Money, as a store of value, functions as a time machine for moving the purchasing power of your wealth from the present to the future—you can earn it now and spend it later.

There are many reasons for storing value for the future. You may be saving for big purchases like a car or tuition. Because the future is uncertain, you may be saving as a precaution, so that you will have money if you become unemployed, or get ill and can't work. As you get older, you will save money for retirement, so that when you are no longer working you can still afford to eat and enjoy your free time!

The store of value function of money is threatened by inflation. If average prices rise while you are saving your money, those saved dollars will not buy as much in the future. Inflation causes the purchasing power of your savings to fall.

As a store of value, money functions as a time machine for moving purchasing power from present to future.

▲

Money's use as a store of value is demonstrated by these very old gold coins, found on a sunken ship dating from 1658. They are still valuable today. What conditions must be met for money to act as a store of value?

Are There Three Functions of Money? Economists since the time of J.B. Say have been aware of these three functions of money. In a world where Say's Law holds true, aggregate supply and aggregate demand match, plans work out as expected, and all savings in the loanable funds market are borrowed by businesses for investment spending. In this world of Say's Law, even without inflation, why would anyone store their wealth in the form of money? In *The General Theory of Employment*, Keynes stated " . . . it is one of the recognised characteristics of money as a store of wealth that it is barren; whereas practically every other form of storing wealth yields some interest or profit. Why should anyone outside a lunatic asylum wish to use money as a store of wealth?"

If all savings can be safely and predictably invested to earn interest, why would anyone want money as a store of value?

Why Hold Money?

There are sane reasons to hold some of your wealth as money, even if it means giving up earned interest. These reasons relate to all three functions of money —medium of exchange, unit of account, and store of value.

Money or Bonds The true cost of any choice is the opportunity cost—the cost of the best alternative given up. The opportunity cost of choosing to hold money is the interest you could have earned by investing the money instead.

Let's take a simple example where there are only two choices for holding wealth: as money, which pays no interest, or as bonds, which do pay interest.

A **bond** is a financial asset where the borrower promises to repay the original value at a specific future date, and to make fixed regular interest payments. For example, the Ford Motor Company may issue a $10 000 bond that promises to pay $10 000 on January 1, 2020, and pay $500 in interest on every January 1st until then. If you invest $10 000 of your savings to buy that bond from Ford, Ford has borrowed $10 000 from you. In exchange, Ford has given you a piece of paper (the bond) which is the promise to repay that amount with interest.

Corporations, governments, public utilities, and even cities issue bonds as a way of borrowing money. There are many other interest-paying assets, but I chose bonds for this example because they are the most important asset in the monetary system worldwide, and are used by the Bank of Canada and other central banks for influencing interest rates.

Liquidity Why would you hold money rather than buy the bond? By holding money you voluntarily give up $500 a year in interest (which is a 5 percent annual rate of interest: $500 per year ÷ $10 000 = 0.05 = 5 percent).

All reasons for wanting to hold money and give up earned interest can be summarized in one word—liquidity. **Liquidity** is the ease with which assets can be converted into the economy's medium of exchange. Money—which is by definition the medium of exchange—is the most liquid of all assets. No conversion is required to use money as a means for paying for products/services. Bonds are much less liquid. If you want to sell a bond, you must use a licensed bond broker, and it may take days to get your money.

bond: financial asset where borrower promises to repay the original value at a specific future date, and to make fixed regular interest payments

liquidity: ease with which assets can be converted into the economy's medium of exchange

What Money Can Buy and Bonds Can't

To illustrate the difference in liquidity, suppose you run out of milk at 10 o'clock at night and walk to the nearest corner store. If you pay with money, the owner readily accepts the $5 bill you offer for the bag of milk. If you try and pay with the bond ("Let me tear off a little corner of the bond for the milk, OK?"), the owner will throw you out and either call the police or the mental health authorities. Bonds are not liquid—not normally acceptable as a means of payment.

In deciding whether to hold your wealth in the form of money or bonds, there is a tradeoff—interest or liquidity. Money pays no interest, but has liquidity. Bonds pay interest, but do not have much liquidity. The liquidity convenience of money has value, both as a medium of exchange (the store owner accepts it) and as unit of account (the price is in dollars, making it easy to compare with other prices also in dollars). Those convenient benefits are worth paying for. The cost of that convenience—the cost of liquidity—is the interest you give up by not holding bonds.

Both J.B. Say and Keynes, and both the "Yes" and "No" camps of macroeconomists today, agree that to gain the liquidity function of money as a medium of exchange and as a unit of account, people are willing to pay the opportunity cost—giving up interest they could have earned.

Money pays no interest, but has liquidity. Bonds pay interest, but do not have liquidity.

Why Hold Money to Store Value?

What about the store of value function of money? While you will hold enough of your wealth as money to be able to make your regular purchases, will you also hold money as a store of value, that is, as savings? Here the "Yes" and "No" camps give different answers.

In a world where Say's Law holds, markets quickly self-adjust and aggregate supply and aggregate demand match (the "Yes" camp), investors have rational expectations, and savings can be relatively safely and predictably invested to earn interest. In this scenario there is not much demand for money as a store of value. People will hold more of their wealth as interest-paying bonds. (Remember, in our simple example, bonds are the only interest-paying asset; think of bonds as representing bonds, savings accounts, equities, and all forms of interest-paying financial assets.) Savings, which reduce aggregate demand, are invested in bonds (loanable funds), which causes the interest rate to fall, increasing business investment spending. Ford buys new robots for its factories with the $10 000 it borrowed from you in exchange for its bond. The additional investment spending increases aggregate demand and offsets the savings, so the economy continues to operate at potential real GDP with full employment. Even with money and savings, supply continues to create its own demand, just as in barter exchanges.

This bond, from the TransCanada Railroad Company, is for $1000.00. Each of the coupons attached to the bond can be redeemed at specific times for the interest payment. At the expiry date, the bond itself can be cashed in for its original value. Why might bonds sometimes be preferred to cash?

DAILY NEWS

MONDAY, SEPTEMBER 15, 2008

LEHMAN BROTHERS BANKRUPT

NEW YORK: Today, Monday, September 15, shock waves hit Wall Street and the world as news of the bankruptcy filing by the once giant Lehman Brothers Investment Bank

In business since 1850, the famous and once all-powerful Lehman Brothers Investment Bank filed for bankruptcy in the

MAPS3

> *Our desire to hold money is a barometer of our distrust of . . . the future. . . . The possession of money lulls our disquietude; and the premium which we require to make us part with money is the measure of the degree of our disquietude.*
>
> *—John Maynard Keynes*

In Keynes's view, where business cycles occur because there is a mismatch between aggregate supply and aggregate demand and markets fail to quickly adjust (the "No" camp), there is fundamental uncertainty about the future and volatile expectations. People will hold more of their wealth as money. With unpredictable recessions, interest-earning bond investments are risky, not safe.

Think of the investors, just before the Great Recession, who invested their wealth in U.S. financial institutions that went bankrupt. The 158-year-old Lehman Brothers investment bank was the most publicized of these bankruptcies. All those with invested assets in Lehman Brothers lost their savings. Similarly, when Chrysler and General Motors went briefly into bankruptcy in 2009, bondholders of those corporations lost much of their invested money.

When investors worry about recessions, they may choose to hold more of their savings and wealth as money, even though money pays no interest. Earning no interest may be better than losing your savings with risky investments. During the Great Recession, most investors wished they had been holding money instead of equities and bonds whose value plunged by 40% during the trough of the business cycle. Similarly, investors (like Joseph Kennedy, father of U.S. President John F. Kennedy) who switched to cash before the stock market crash of 1929 that ushered in the Great Depression, became the wealthy elite of the 1930s.

In Keynes's world, holding money acts like a security blanket, protecting the holder from unpredictable changes in the economy. The more worried investors are, the greater is the interest rate they will demand to let go of the security blanket and move their wealth from money to bonds. Fear about the future may cause interest rates to rise, which will further discourage investment spending by businesses and intensify the recession. Pessimistic expectations can become self-fulfilling expectations—they help create the negative outcome investors are worrying about.

Both the "Yes" and "No" camps agree that people need to be rewarded with interest payments in order to give up the benefits of the liquidity of money. The "No" camp also emphasizes interest as a reward for giving up the security of money as a store of value protecting against the uncertainty of the future.

How Much Money to Hold?
Interest Rates and the Demand for Money

There is a tradeoff in holding your wealth in the form of money or bonds. Money pays no interest, but has liquidity. Bonds pay interest, but do not have much liquidity. How do you make a smart choice about *how much* of your wealth to hold as money, and *how much* as bonds? We each make this choice as individuals, and our combined choices determine the macroeconomic demand for money. That macroeconomic demand for money, together with the supply of money, determines the interest rate.

The story about how the interest rate is determined is like microeconomic stories of how prices are determined. We each make choices about the quantity of a product/service to demand, depending on what the price is. But where does that price come from? It is determined by the interaction of demand and supply in markets. This is the subject of the next section.

Interest Rate as the Price of Money
The **interest rate** is the price of holding money: what you give up by not holding bonds. The interest rate is determined by demand and supply in both the money market and the bond market. You might be surprised about the addition of the bond market in setting the interest rate. But money and bonds are intimately connected, as shown in the definition of the interest rate.

interest rate: price of holding money: what you give up by not holding bonds

To illustrate how interest rates are determined, we will stick with the simple choice between only two assets: money and bonds. First we will look at the demand for money. Then we will look at the supply of money and finally at the interactions of demand and supply in the money and bond markets.

Macroeconomic Demand for Money
According to the microeconomic law of demand (Appendix B), when the price of something rises, the quantity demanded decreases. The law of demand also applies to money. As the price of money—the interest rate—rises, the quantity demanded of money decreases. At higher interest rates people want to hold less money (and hold more of their assets as bonds). The **law of demand for money** works as long as other factors besides the interest rate do not change.

law of demand for money: as the price of money — the interest rate — rises, the quantity demanded of money decreases

Suppose the interest rate on bonds is very low—one percent per year. If you invest $100 of your savings in a bond, at the end of the year you get back $101 (your original $100 plus $1 in interest). It makes almost no difference whether you hold your wealth in the form of money (which pays no interest) or bonds. Since your bond payoff is only $1, you might as well keep most of your wealth in the form of money, to have the convenience of liquidity.

Now imagine that the interest rate on bonds is 100% per year, so each $100 investment yields $200 at the end of the year (your original $100 plus $100 in interest). By choosing bonds you double your assets! Then you might hold the minimum quantity of money you need for purchases and keep as much of your assets as possible as bonds. Comparing these two scenarios, there is an inverse relation between the interest rate and the quantity demanded of money. The higher the interest rate, the lower the quantity demanded of money.

If we sum—aggregate—the demands for money of all individuals, we get the macroeconomic demand for money. Figure 5.1 illustrates the inverse relation between the interest rate and the quantity demanded of money for the economy as a whole. For simplicity, the numbers are made up, but the pattern represents what the actual macroeconomic demand for money looks like.

Figure 5.1	Macroeconomic Demand for Money
Price (interest rate)	**Quantity Demanded (billions of dollars)**
2%	100
4%	90
6%	80
8%	70
10%	60

As your eye goes down the two columns, notice that as the price of money—the interest rate—rises, the quantity demanded of money decreases. Money is similar to other products/services. As the price rises, people look for substitutes. As a form for holding wealth, bonds are a substitute—an alternative—to money. When something, even money, becomes more expensive, people economize on its use.

Factors Changing the Demand for Money In macroeconomics, as in microeconomics, we distinguish between a change in quantity demanded and a change in demand. Only a change in the price of money—the interest rate—changes the *quantity demanded* of money. A change in other factors changes the *demand for money*.

Figure 5.1 assumes that all factors, other than the interest rate, that influence the demand for money remain unchanged. The two factors that can change the macroeconomic demand for money are real GDP and the average level of prices.

Real GDP, in the circular flow diagram (Figure 4.3, p. 135), is always equal to aggregate income. When real GDP increases, the economy has produced more stuff, and income also increases. When income increases, you buy more products/services, which means you need more money to make those purchases. As a student struggling to make ends meet, think about how much cash you carry around in your wallet for your daily purchases. You need to pay transit fares, lunch at Mr. Sub, maybe money for the movies. Now think about what a wealthy entrepreneur carries around in her wallet. Enough cash to fill up the Mercedes with gas, to pay for lunch at expensive restaurants, to tip doormen and parking valets, and maybe for opera tickets. In general, as real GDP and income increase, the demand for money as a medium of exchange also increases.

Changes in real GDP or average prices cause a change in demand for money, not a change in quantity demanded.

Figure 5.2 shows the original demand for money and the new demand for money after real GDP increases. Notice that with more real GDP and real income (column 3), at any interest rate (column 1), the quantity demanded of money is greater than it was originally (column 2). An increase in real GDP causes an increase in the demand for money. And a decrease in real GDP causes a decrease in the demand for money.

An increase in real GDP causes an increase in the demand for money. A decrease in real GDP causes a decrease in the demand for money.

Figure 5.2	Macroeconomic Demand for Money Before and After Real GDP Increases	
Price (interest rate)	Quantity Demanded (billions of dollars)	Quantity Demanded after Real GDP Increases (billions of dollars)
2%	100	200
4%	90	180
6%	80	160
8%	70	140
10%	60	120

Prices are the other factor affecting the demand for money. An increase in the average level of prices—inflation—means you need to carry more dollars in your wallet to be able to purchase the same products and services that you bought before. If the price of milk rises from $5 to $6 a bag, and prices of all other products/services rise similarly, you need to carry more dollars to make the same purchases as before.

An increase in prices affects the demand for money in the same way as an increase in real GDP. The quantity demanded for money *after prices rise* would again look like column 3 in Figure 5.2. An increase in the average level of prices causes an increase in the demand for money. A decrease in the average level of prices—deflation—causes a decrease in the demand for money.

An increase in average prices causes an increase in the demand for money. A decrease in average prices causes a decrease in the demand for money.

So it can be a smart choice to demand to hold your wealth in the form of money, and it can also be a smart choice not to demand money, and instead hold your wealth in the form of interest-earning bonds. Now the question is, where does the supply of money come from?

1. In your own words, what is the law of demand for money?

2. Explain the liquidity advantages of money over bonds.

3. You have just won $5000 in the lottery. You go on a shopping spree with $4000 and save $1000. What benefits or worries will influence your decision to hold the $1000 as cash or to invest it in an interest-earning bond?

Refresh 5.1

www.myeconlab.com

5.2 Legal Counterfeiting?
Supply of Money

Identify four forms of money and describe how the Bank of Canada and chartered banks create money.

Money! We all want it. We all work hard for it. But what is it? And where does it come from?

What's a Money?

Before discussing where money comes from, let's first agree on what money is. Throughout history there have been only four basic forms of money: commodity money, convertible paper money, fiat money, and deposit money.

Commodity Money A commodity is any product that is saleable. Commodity money is exactly what it's name says—a commodity such as fur pelts, beads, cattle, or precious metals serving as money. Commodity money has alternative uses. Gold and silver, for example, can be used for jewellery and industrial purposes, as well as for coins. To be useful as a medium of exchange and as a unit of account, commodity money must be easy to carry, to measure, and to divide into fractions. That's why cattle and fur pelts are inferior forms of commodity money compared to coins (loonies, quarters, dimes, etc.). As a store of value, commodity money must not deteriorate over time. Coins also work well as a store of value. Imagine trying to use sticks of butter as money in a tropical climate. As your savings melted, your money would literally go down the drain.

The earliest known coins made from precious metals date back to 600 BC. They were found by archaeologists in the Temple of Artemis in what is now the county of Turkey. After that, coins quickly became the dominant form of commodity money.

Convertible Paper Money Carrying around large bags of gold coins made you an obvious target for thieves. Merchants began to store, or deposit, their gold with goldsmiths, who had the best safes and security. The goldsmith would issue the depositor a piece of paper—an "I owe you" or IOU—promising to return the gold. Soon these IOUs (one of the first text abbreviations!) began to circulate as money. As long as a seller trusted that the goldsmith would return, or convert, the paper into gold, he would accept as payment the more convenient and easily hidden IOU in place of the actual coins.

Many national paper currencies, including Canadian Dominion Notes introduced after Confederation and U.S. dollar notes, used to be convertible into gold. They were, in effect, IOUs from the government.

This one dollar bill, issued by Canada when it was still a Dominion, is an example of convertible paper money. What is the government promising when it provides you with this form of currency?

Fiat Money The paper dollar bill notes in your wallet are no longer convertible into gold or silver. They have value simply because the government that issued them has decreed that they are valuable. Money that has no alternative uses and is valuable simply by decree, or by fiat, is called fiat money. The paper money and the coins made from non-precious metals that we all use are fiat money. Economists also refer to these government-issued paper bills and coins in circulation as **currency.**

Remember that the key characteristic of money is acceptability. Currency—the paper and coin fiat money we use—is acceptable because we trust the government that issued it. If you look at the paper bills in your wallet, you will see that they are "signed" by the Governor of the Bank of Canada, who decrees that "Ce billet a cours légal—This note is legal tender." Similarly, the playing card money in the opening photograph of the chapter was also fiat money. Its acceptability depended on it being signed by Governor of New France, who was trusted.

currency: government-issued paper bills and coins

Deposit Money Most money today is deposit money. **Demand deposits** are balances in bank accounts that depositors can withdraw on demand by using a debit card or writing a cheque. Currency and demand deposits are today's most widely accepted means of paying for products/services. An exchange of money for products/services is only complete when the buyer has transferred either currency or demand deposits to the seller. Debit cards and cheques are not themselves money. They are just a means of transferring demand deposits, which are money. Credit cards are definitely not money. When you pay using a credit card, Visa or MasterCard is giving you a temporary loan, which they use to pay the merchant. But the transaction is not complete until you have transferred currency or demand deposits to the credit card company to pay off the loan.

demand deposits: balances in bank accounts that depositors can withdraw on demand by using a debit card or writing a cheque

ECONOMICS Out There

Card Money in New France
In 1685, Jacques de Meulles, the Governor of New France, was short of funds to pay his soldiers fighting the English. Typically, the government delayed paying merchants for their products until a fresh supply of gold and silver coins arrived from France. But he could not delay paying his soldiers. De Meulles's ingenious solution was to issue paper money printed on playing cards.

In a letter to France dated September 24, 1685, de Meulles wrote,

"I have found myself this year in great straits with regard to the subsistence of the soldiers. You did not provide for funds, my Lord . . . . Money being extremely scarce . . . for the pay of the soldiers, it occurred to me to issue, instead of money, notes on cards, which I have cut in quarters . . . I have issued an ordinance by which

I have obliged all the inhabitants to receive this money in payments, and to give it circulation, at the same time pledging myself, in my own name, to redeem the said notes."

These cards were widely accepted by merchants, given that they were backed by the government. Even though the cards were redeemable for gold, many were not redeemed and remained in circulation as money.

Playing card money was fiat money. It was valuable by the decree of the government, and functioned as a medium of exchange because of its acceptability by sellers, who trusted the government and obeyed the government decree.

Source: James Powell, *A History of the Canadian Dollar*, Bank of Canada, December 2005, pp 4–6.

Measuring the Money Supply

Where does money come from? In Canada today, money consists of currency issued by the Bank of Canada and deposit money in *chartered banks*, credit unions, and similar financial institutions. Chartered banks—private banks chartered under the *Bank Act* of 1992 to receive deposits and makes loans—are the most important financial institutions for creating the supply of money. Are you surprised? Read on.

M1 and M2 There are many ways to measure the supply of money in Canada. The official measures used by the Bank of Canada are called M1 and M2.

M1 consists of currency in circulation and demand deposits. In August 2009, there was $54 billion in currency and $411 billion in demand deposits. M1 equaled $465 billion.

M2 is a broader measure of the money supply. It includes all of M1 plus all other deposits, like savings accounts and guaranteed investment certificates, (GICs pay higher rates of interest than savings accounts, but lock in your savings for longer periods of time). M2 was $951 billion. These other deposits are not as liquid as demand deposits. They have restrictions or penalties for withdrawal on demand, which is why they are distinguished from M1. But they are relatively easy to convert into money—the medium of exchange—which is why they are included in this broader measure of the money supply.

Notice that currency ($54 billion) is a very small fraction of the money supply—less than 12 percent of M1 and less than 6 percent of M2.

The Bank of Canada: Canada's Central Bank

A **central bank** is a government institution responsible for supervising chartered banks and financial institutions and for regulating the supply of money. Canada's central bank was created in the midst of the Great Depression by the 1935 *Bank of Canada Act*. The Bank of Canada's mandate is to control the quantity of money and interest rates to avoid inflation, business cycles, and unemployment. The U.S. central bank, the Federal Reserve, was created in the midst of an earlier financial crisis in 1907.

The Bank of Canada plays four important roles in the Canadian economy: issuing currency, acting as banker to chartered banks, acting as a banker to government, and conducting monetary policy.

Figure 5.3 The Money Supply

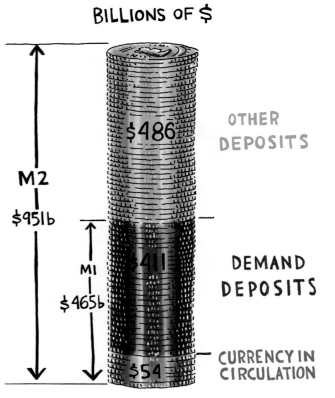

BILLIONS OF $

M2 $951b
M1 $465b
$486 OTHER DEPOSITS
$411 DEMAND DEPOSITS
$54 CURRENCY IN CIRCULATION

Source: Statistics Canada CANSIM Table 176-0020

central bank: government institution responsible for supervising chartered banks and financial institutions and for regulating the supply of money

Issuing Currency   The Bank of Canada is the only legal issuer of bank notes (paper currency) and coins. The Bank of Canada issues instructions to the Royal Mint, which is responsible for actually "making" the bills and coins. Before 1935, private banks could also issue bank notes.

Banker to Chartered Banks   Chartered private banks take deposits from consumer households and businesses and make loans. While you might have demand deposits in a chequing account at Scotiabank, Scotiabank and all other chartered banks have their own demand deposits in accounts at the Bank of Canada. These deposits at the Bank of Canada allow the chartered banks to make payments to each other. When you use your Scotiabank debit card to buy jeans from a merchant who has an account at the Royal Bank of Canada, eventually Scotiabank transfers money to the Royal Bank through accounts at the Bank of Canada.

The Bank of Canada also serves as a **lender of last resort** to the financial system. When chartered banks are short of funds—for example, if borrowers go bankrupt and fail to repay loans owed to the bank—chartered banks can borrow from the Bank of Canada. This role helps maintain stability and liquidity in the financial system. During the Great Recession, the Bank of Canada, the U.S. Federal Reserve, and central banks around the world played crucial roles as lenders of last resort in preventing the breakdown of the financial system, like that which occurred during the Great Depression.

lender of last resort: central bank's role of making loans to banks to preserve the stability of the financial system

Banker to Government   The Government of Canada has a demand deposit account at the Bank of Canada. The Bank of Canada manages the government's accounts, the government's reserves of foreign currency (like U.S. dollars), and the national debt (which we will discuss in Chapter 8).

Conducting Monetary Policy   Monetary policy consists of changes in the supply of money and interest rates, designed to achieve the macroeconomic outcomes of steady growth, full employment, and stable prices. The Bank of Canada is responsible for monetary policy, which we will discuss in detail in Chapter 7.

How Banks Create Money: Profits versus Prudence

The Bank of Canada is the only legal supplier of Canadian currency—paper currency and coins. But currency is only a small fraction of the supply of money. Most money takes the form of demand deposits, and those can be created legally by chartered banks.

Don't you wish you could create money? Me too. But a chartered bank's creation of money comes with risks.

▶

All Canadian currency—paper or coin—is produced by order of the Bank of Canada. The Bank would have placed the order to have these loonies manufactured by the Royal Canadian Mint. The Canadian Bank Note Company and BA International are the only institutions authorized to print Canadian paper money, and they also receive their printing orders from the Bank of Canada. When might the Bank of Canada order the printing or minting of more money?

An Offer You Can't Refuse   To explore how banks create money, let's start with a simple story. Suppose someone gives you $1000 cash to hold. His "offer" is that it will be very unpleasant for you (you might lose a kneecap or other body part) if you don't return the money when he asks for it. He will be back sometime within 10 days. On any given day there is a 1/10 chance he will ask you for the money. You have no choice but to hold the money in a form where you can give it back, in cash.

Now suppose 100 people each give you $1000 on the same terms. Then on any given day, what is the probability—the odds—of your having to give out the whole $100 000? It is $(1/10)^{100}$ which is a very, very, very, very small number. Those tiny odds of being asked for all of the money depends on the probabilities being independent—the likelihood of one person asking for her money is not influenced by whether any of the other people ask for their money. This will be important.

If you want to play it safe, the probability of being asked for more than $20 000 on any given day is still very small. You would be quite safe holding $20 000 in reserve and loaning out $80 000 to other people and collecting interest. By making loans, you can profit from other peoples' money.

This simple story contains all of the main features of banking—deposits ($100 000), loans ($80 000) and reserves ($20 000).

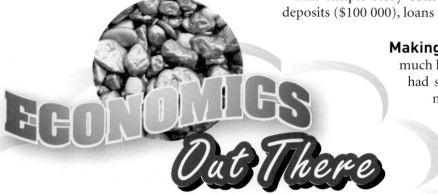

Banking Begins on the Street

The word *bank* comes from the Italian word *banci*, the *benches* that merchants and moneylenders sat at behind tables in the street. The most famous bankers (*banchieri*) in medieval Florence were the Medici family. The original Medici banks' benches were near the Cavalcanti palace, near the main Florentine wool market.

"Perhaps no other family left such an imprint on an age as the Medici left on the Renaissance." They became popes, queens of France, and patrons to Michelangelo and Galileo.

Their wealth came from foreign exchange transactions and from issuing bills of exchange to finance trade. When one merchant owed another an amount that could not be paid in cash until the conclusion of some other business, the seller could have the buyer write an IOU—called a bill of exchange. The seller could use the bill as money to pay for other products or obtain cash for it from a *banchieri* who would "discount the bill" or take a percentage before paying out cash.

Source: Niall Ferguson, *The Ascent of Money*, New York: Penguin, 2008, pp 41–44.

Making Money by Making Money   There is much historical truth to the simple story. Goldsmiths had secure safes that attracted depositors. Goldsmiths not only issued paper IOUs for gold, they also acted like banks. Once the public trusted and accepted paper notes issued by goldsmiths—acceptability is the key to money—goldsmiths could issue notes that were not fully backed by gold.

Goldsmiths made loans, giving the borrower not gold but a paper note convertible into gold. In exchange, the borrower signed a contract to repay the loan plus interest at a future date. The borrower could use the goldsmith's note as money since it was accepted as a means of payment.

The value of the paper notes was greater than the value of gold in the safes. The goldsmiths were relying on (you could say "banking on") the very small probability that all depositors and borrowers would want to withdraw the gold at the same time. By making loans not backed by gold, the goldsmiths created money (acceptable paper notes) and made profits (interest) on the loans. For trust in the paper notes to continue, the goldsmiths had to hold adequate reserves so that when customers did show up with one of their paper notes and ask for the equivalent amount of gold, it was there.

Loans and Money Creation Go Together

This is essentially what chartered banks do today, without the gold. When you or any other depositor put money into a chartered bank, you get a credit on your chequing account balance. If you deposit $1000 cash, you can use your debit card to pay for products/services worth up to $1000. But the bank doesn't keep your cash in their vaults. They keep a very small fraction of your deposit in the form of cash reserves, and loan out the rest at interest. Like the goldsmiths, the banks are banking on the very small probability that depositors and borrowers would all want to withdraw their cash at one. This system of banking is called **fractional-reserve banking**.

Instead of issuing paper notes like goldsmiths, the bank simply creates a digital demand deposit credit in the borrower's chequing account equal to the amount of the loan. Since demand deposits are money—part of M1—the bank has created both a loan and money. When loans are paid off, there is a reduction in the quantity of both loans and money. In the Canadian monetary system, loan creation and money creation are two sides of the same coin. Chartered banks can legally create money, without counterfeiting.

Look Ma, No Reserves!

While the Bank of Canada (and the Office of the Superintendent of Financial Institutions) carefully supervise all banks and financial institutions, you will be surprised to know that chartered banks are not legally required to keep any cash reserves at all! The actual reserves that Canadian banks choose to hold as cash amount to less than one percent of the value of all demand deposits!

Nonetheless, the Canadian banking system is one of the soundest and most admired banking systems in the world. There are many reasons, but we will focus on just a few related to the basics of deposits and loans. First, most bank customers rarely demand cash. Think about the small proportion of bills or purchases that you pay for with currency. Second, in the rare event that customers want to withdraw more demand deposits or currency than the bank has, chartered banks can borrow from each other and from the Bank of Canada (the lender of last resort) to meet their customers' demands and maintain trust.

Probabilities and Bank Runs

Fractional-reserve banking, whether done by individuals, goldsmiths, merchants, or chartered banks, has risks. What happens when probabilities are *not* independent—when the likelihood of one person asking for her money *is* influenced by other people asking for their money? This is what happens when the public loses trust in a goldsmith or a bank. It is called a run on the bank. A **bank run** occurs when many depositors want to get their cash out at the same time. When this happens, banks can fail, or go bankrupt.

Bank runs and bank failures were common during the 1800s, but are rare since the tightening of banking regulation and the *Bank of Canada Act*. The last bank failures in Canada, of four small banks, occurred in the late 1980s and the recession of 1991. While investors in the bank lost money, depositors were largely protected by deposit insurance from the Canadian banking system, administered by the Bank of Canada and the Office of the Superintendent of Financial Institutions.

fractional-reserve banking: banks hold only a fraction of deposits as reserves

bank run: many depositors withdraw cash all at once

Banks create loans and money (demand deposits) together in a fractional-reserve banking system.

If you deposit $1000, what might result is:
* deposit = $1000
* new bank loans = new demand deposits = $800
* bank keeps reserves = $200

The bank has created $800 in new money, new demand deposits!

This is the Northern Rock Bank in Cambridge, U.K., September 15, 2007. Fear of this bank's potential failure caused many depositors to try, all at the same time, to withdraw their savings. The bank closed its doors, received government guarantees, and remains in business still.

Banking Tradeoffs   The everyday risks of fractional-reserve banking and bank loans are that borrowers will default on their loans—not be able to pay back the bank. Banks try and protect against this risk by requiring *collateral* on loans—property pledged as security for repayment of the loan. When a bank loans you money for a car or mortgage on a house, the bank owns the car or the house, as collateral, until you pay off the loan. If you default on the loan, the bank can sell the property to recover the value of the loan. Banks also charge higher interest payments on loans that they consider to be riskier.

With fractional-reserve banking and loans, there is a tradeoff between profits and prudence or safety. Banks make profits by loaning money at interest. The more of their deposits that they turn into loans, the greater their potential profits. And higher risk loans earn the most interest.

But more loans mean more demand deposits created for borrowers' accounts. Banks now have more demand deposits with unchanged reserves, which makes it riskier for banks to be able meet the demands of depositors for withdrawals. Prudence is necessary to maintain the trust of depositors and meet their needs for withdrawals, and more prudence means holding a larger fraction of reserves and earning lower profits. This is a tension in any banking system—between profits and prudence—and why banks are regulated around the world. Without regulation, more banks could be tempted to take risks in pursuit of profits that might lead to the failure of the bank. While bank owners will justifiably lose money they have invested in the bank, innocent, trusting depositors, who did not make the risky loan decisions, also lose their money.

The Supply of Money

In our fractional-reserve banking system, the supply of money is determined by the Bank of Canada and by the chartered banks, through the demand deposits (and matching loans) they create. The Bank of Canada controls the supply of currency, and, as we will see in Chapter 7, also influences the quantity of demand deposits that chartered banks choose to create.

In measuring the supply of money, currency is easy to count. Figure 5.4 gives you a picture of the harder-to-count demand deposits and loans created by the chartered banks. Deposits of $1139.1 billion are part of the money supply. Notice that currency reserves ($6.2 billion) are less than one percent of deposits. Liquid assets ($319.4 billion) consist of the lowest risk Government of Canada Treasury bills (bonds) and commercial bills (bonds) that can instantly be converted into reserves. These earn banks a low interest rate. Securities ($169.8 billion) are slightly riskier bonds, but earn banks higher interest rates. Loans ($1429.9 billion) to businesses and consumers (including credit card balances) are riskiest, and earn banks the highest interest rates.

Figure 5.4	Chartered Banks: Sources and Uses of Funds	
	$ billion (August 2009)	**Percentage of deposits**
Total Funds	1925.3	169.0
Sources		
Deposits	1139.1	100.0
Borrowing and own capital	786.2	69.0
Uses		
Reserves	6.2	0.5
Liquid assets	319.4	28.0
Securities and other assets	169.8	14.9
Loans	1429.9	125.5

Source: Statistics Canada, CANSIM Table 176-0011

The amounts for sources of funds and uses of funds are equal ($1925.3 billion). Having loaned out much of the deposited money, notice that bank currency reserves (0.5 percent) and liquid assets (28 percent) are only a fraction of deposits. That is fractional-reserve banking. Most deposits are not held in banks, but are loaned out to make profits for the banks.

A Fixed Quantity of Money   At any moment in time, the total quantity of money supplied by both the Bank of Canada and the banking system (currency plus demand deposits, measured as M1) is a fixed amount. That supply of money does not depend on the interest rate. If we were to create a table, using simple made-up numbers, relating the interest rate and the quantity of money supplied, it would look like Figure 5.5.

As your eye goes down the table, notice that no matter what the interest rate is, the quantity of money supplied is constant at $80 billion. We will use these simple numbers, together with the simple numbers for the demand for money, in the next section to illustrate how interest rates are determined.

Figure 5.5 Supply of Money	
Price (interest rate)	**Quantity Supplied (billions of dollars)**
2%	80
4%	80
6%	80
8%	80
10%	80

1. Define the two official measures of the money supply in Canada.

2. Explain how a chartered bank can create money.

3. Banks, like other businesses, operate to make profits. Are there reasons why banks should be subject to more government regulations than, for example, shoe stores or dollar stores? Explain your reasons.

www.myeconlab.com

5.3 What Is the Price of Money? Interest Rates, Money, and Bonds

Relate bond prices and interest rates and explain how money and bond markets determine the interest rate.

"How much will you pay for more money?" That question might sound strange, because the price you pay for most products or services is stated in dollars—$1 for a cup of coffee, $12 for a movie. But asking how much will you pay for a dollar is not that crazy. What is the price of money?

The interest rate is the price of money in two ways:

- The interest rate is the price, or opportunity cost, of holding money—what you give up by not holding your wealth as bonds which pay interest. What you get in exchange for giving up interest is liquidity.

- The interest rate is also the price you pay to borrow money. If the interest rate is 5 percent, to borrow $100 for a year you have to pay $105 back at the end of the year—the original $100 plus $5 in interest.

The interest rate is the price of money in two ways: the opportunity cost of holding money and the cost of borrowing money.

To see how the interest rate is determined, we will continue with the simple choice between only two assets: money and bonds. The interest rate is determined by the interaction of the demand for money and the supply of money in both the money and the bond markets.

Before we look at that interaction, we need to explain one other price, the price of bonds.

Opposites by Nature: Bond Prices and Interest Rates

Recall that a *bond* is a financial asset where the borrower promises to repay the original value at a specific future date, and to make fixed regular interest payments. Bonds can be issued for very short (1 month) or long (30 years) time periods. There is a bond market where bonds can be bought and sold after being issued by businesses or governments. The price on the bond market can change from the original value of the bond as economic conditions change, as you are about to see.

Let's take a simple example of a $10 000, bond issued by the Ford Motor Company for one year that promises to repay the $10 000 together with a $500 payment at the end of the year. The original value of the bond is $10 000, and the current price of the bond on the bond market is also $10 000.

If the price of the bond is $10 000, then the $500 payment amounts to 5 percent interest for the year ($500 ÷ $10 000 = 0.05 = 5 percent). It is important to keep in mind that *bonds specify a fixed dollar amount that they will pay* in addition to repaying the original value. Bonds do not specify an interest rate in percent. Why is that specification of the fixed dollar amount so important?

Bonds promise to pay back the original value plus a fixed dollar amount of money. Bonds do not promise a fixed percentage of interest.

When Interest Rates Change, So Do Bond Prices
Suppose you have bought the bond for $10 000. You have loaned Ford $10 000 and Ford has given you a piece of paper—the bond. You are happy to receive the $500 payment at the end of the year (which translates into an interest rate of 5 percent), and Ford is happy to pay you $500 for borrowing $10 000 of your money.

The next day, interest rates around the world rise to 10 percent. You can now get a bond that will pay you $1000 in interest on a $10 000 investment ($1000 ÷ $10 000 = 0.10 = 10 percent). All of a sudden, your Ford bond looks like a bad investment choice. You decide to sell your bond on the bond market, and use the money to buy a new bond that pays 10 percent interest.

Unfortunately, you will not find a buyer for your bond at the price of $10 000. Now that there are other bonds available that yield a $1000 return on $10 000 at the end of a year, why would anyone buy your bond that yields only a $500 return on $10 000 at the end of the year? With no buyers for your bond, the only way to sell it is to lower the price you are willing to accept for the bond. At what new price can you sell your bond—find a buyer—on the bond market?

The market price of your bond will fall to a level where the return it offers at the end of the year ($10 000 + $500 = $10 500) amounts to a 10 percent interest rate—the same rate of return investors can get on other bonds now for sale on the bond market. The price for your Ford bond falls to approximately $9545. If a buyer bought your Ford bond from you for $9545, at the end of the year she receives from Ford $10 500. That difference ($10 500 − $9545) is a gain of $955. In percentage terms, $955 ÷ $9545 = 0.10 = 10 percent.

Don't worry about the precise math involved in the calculations. That's what accountants and calculators and accounting software are for. The only important fact to remember is that *when interest rates rise* (from 5 percent to 10 percent), *the market price of bonds falls* (from $10 000 to $9545). This inverse relation between bond prices and interest rates is the most important feature of all bond markets. Bond prices and interest rates are instantly connected in both directions. If interest rates rise, bond prices fall. If interest rates fall, bond prices rise.

Bond prices and interest rates are inversely related. When interest rates rise, bond prices fall. When bond prices fall, interest rates rise.

Why Bonds are Risky and Less Liquid than Money
This instant and inverse relation between bond prices and interest rates is why bonds are a risky and non-liquid investment. If interest rates change after you buy a bond, the price at which you can sell the bond changes from the original value of the bond. When interest rates rise, the price of the bond falls. If you want to convert your bond back to money by selling it, you will receive less money than you paid for the bond ($9545 instead of $10 000). You take an unexpected loss on your investment. Bonds are inferior to money as store of value for your savings when interest rates rise.

But when interest rates fall, the price of a bond you are holding rises. If you want to convert your bond back to money by selling it, you will receive more money than you paid for the bond. You make an extra, unexpected profit on your investment. Bonds are better than money as store of value for your savings when interest rates fall. If you hold a bond until its time period is up, you receive exactly what you were promised—the original value plus the fixed dollar amount payment. Changes in interest rates do not change the fixed dollar amounts bondholders receive. You receive both the original value and the fixed payments, as promised. The unexpected losses and gains come from selling bonds before their time period is up, something you might need to do for liquidity—because you need the money to pay for products/services or to repay a debt.

Money Markets, Bond Markets, and Interest Rates

In the bond market example, I changed the interest rate from 5 percent to 10 percent without explanation. But what determines the interest rate? Why does the interest rate settle at a specific number, and why do interest rates change?

The economist's short answer to these questions about what determines the interest rate—the price of money—is that "interest rates are determined by the interaction of demand and supply in money markets and bond markets." But that answer, while true, is pretty useless. We can point to anything that happens in an economy and say, in our best educated voice, "It is all determined by the laws of demand and supply." The longer and more useful answer combines the details we have developed about why people choose to demand money and the supply of money decisions by the Bank of Canada and chartered banks.

To answer the question of what determines the interest rate, Figure 5.6 combines the information in Figures 5.1 and 5.5 about the macroeconomic demand for and supply of money. These numbers represent the money market—the demand for and supply of money. But as we will see, these numbers make sense only if we also bring the bond market into the longer explanation.

Figure 5.6	Macroeconomic Demand and Supply for Money	
Price (interest rate)	**Quantity of Money Demanded (billions of dollars)**	**Quantity of Money Supplied (billions of dollars)**
2%	100	80
4%	90	80
6%	**80**	**80**
8%	70	80
10%	60	80

If you scroll down the numbers in Figure 5.6 for columns 1 and 2 together, you see that as the interest rate rises, the quantity of money demanded decreases. This is the macroeconomic law of demand for money. As the price of money—the interest rate—rises, the quantity demanded of money decreases. As the interest rate rises, people look for substitutes for holding wealth, and bonds are a substitute.

If you gaze down columns 1 and 3 together, you see that the supply of money is fixed; the quantity of money supplied remains the same, no matter what the interest rate. The supply of money—M1—consists of currency issued by the Bank of Canada and demand deposits at chartered banks. The decisions to supply currency and demand deposits do not depend on the interest rate.

The interest rate will settle at six percent, the rate where the quantity of money demanded ($80 billion) equals the quantity of money supplied ($80 billion). In this example, six percent is the market-clearing, or equilibrium, interest rate.

As in microeconomics (Appendix D.2), the best way to understand why prices—in this case the interest rate—settle at the particular number of six percent is to look at what happens in markets when prices have not settled.

Excess Demand for Money

What if the interest rate were two percent in the money market? Look at the first row of Figure 5.6. At a two percent interest rate, people want to hold $100 billion worth of money—the quantity of money demanded is $100 billion. But the quantity of money supplied is only $80 billion. There is excess demand—the quantity demanded of money exceeds the quantity supplied of money.

Excess demand for money is a demand for more liquidity. People demand more money (and are willing to give up earned interest on bonds) for the convenience of money's liquidity and its ability to function as a medium of exchange, as a unit of account, and as a store of value. When you are holding assets in either money or bonds, how do you "get more money?" If we rule out counterfeiting or stealing, the solution is to sell some of your bonds to get more money to hold.

The additional supply of bonds for sale on the bond market causes the price of bonds to fall. And as we have just seen, a decrease in the price of bonds instantly causes interest rates to rise.

As long as the interest rate is below six percent, there will continue to be an excess demand for money. People will continue to sell bonds, bond prices will continue to fall, and interest rates will continue to rise. Only when the interest rate rises to six percent does the excess demand for money disappear.

Excess Supply of Money

What if, instead, the interest rate were 10 percent in the money market? Look at the last row of Figure 5.6. At a 10 percent interest rate, people want to hold $60 billion worth of money—the quantity of money demanded is $60 billion. But the quantity of money supplied is $80 billion. There is excess supply—the quantity supplied of money exceeds the quantity demanded of money.

When there is excess demand for money, people sell bonds to get more money. The increased supply of bonds causes bond prices to fall, and interest rates to rise.

When there is excess supply of money, people buy bonds to get rid of money. The increased demand for bonds causes bond prices to rise, and interest rates to fall.

Excess supply of money means there is more liquidity available than people want. Remember, liquidity has an opportunity cost—the earned interest you give up by not holding bonds. If your assets are held in either money or bonds, how do you "get rid of money?" The solution is to use some of your money holdings to buy bonds.

The additional demand for bonds on the bond market causes the price of bonds to rise. An increase in the price of bonds instantly causes interest rates to fall.

As long as the interest rate is above six percent, there will continue to be an excess supply of money. People will continue to buy bonds, bond prices will continue to rise, and interest rates will continue to fall. Only when the interest rate falls to six percent does the excess supply of money disappear.

A Multitude of Interest Rates

I always talk about "the" interest rate, as though there were only one. In fact, there are many interest rates on different financial assets. Interest rates vary depending on the time periods for repaying the original amount (long-term investments like 30-year bonds usually have higher interest rates than short-term investments), the riskiness of the investment, and how liquid the investment is (how easy is it to sell). There are also interest rates on mortgages, on consumer loans, on credit cards, and on savings accounts—there are many interest rates.

While there is a multitude of interest rates, they all tend to move together. Interest rates tend to all rise at the same time, and to fall at the same time. So the stories about how "the" interest rate is determined apply generally to all interest rates.

Refresh 5.3

1. List two ways that the interest rate is the price of money.

2. Explain how interest rates and bond prices are related using an example. What characteristic of bonds causes this relation?

3. If you have bought a bond as an investment, which way do you hope interest rates will move? Explain how you will profit from your investment if interest rates move in the direction you hope.

5.4 J.B. Say and J.M. Keynes as Facebook Friends? Money, Interest Rates, Investment, and Real GDP

We all want more money because our society gives it value. Money does not have inherent value—you can't eat it or wear it or live in it. Money's value comes from its liquidity—sellers will accept money in exchange for the products/services we want. As individuals, money gives us access to stuff that improves our personal standard of living.

But do the demand and supply of money—and the interest rates they determine—affect real GDP, the aggregate amount of stuff the economy produces? Because there is money, are there more products/services produced? Is there any connection between money and the three macroeconomic outcomes that most influence everyone's economic well-being—real GDP per person, unemployment, and inflation?

Chapter 3 examined the answer for the third outcome, inflation. The quantity theory of money states that money can clearly affect inflation. An increase in the supply of money can increase the average level of prices.

But what about the other two outcomes? Does money affect the amount of real GDP the economy produces, and does it affect the unemployment rate and therefore your job prospects? Let me put this last question slightly differently: Once we move from barter exchange to the advantages of a money economy, does money make any difference to the real, or non-price, outcomes of a market exchange economy—real GDP and unemployment? And does money change the operation of markets—how often business cycles occur and how quickly markets adjust?

You might have guessed that big questions like these are answered differently by the two main macroeconomic camps; the "Yes—markets quickly self-adjust" believers in Say's Law and the "No—markets fail to quickly adjust" followers of Keynes. But there are also many areas of agreement between the two camps on the role of money.

Does Money Make the Real World Go Around? Money and Real GDP

Our material standard of living increases only when the economy produces more real GDP per person. Real GDP is the value, at *constant* prices, of all final products/services produced annually in Canada.

For measuring living standards, real GDP per person is superior to nominal GDP per person. Nominal GDP values all final products/services in *current* prices. When the economy produces more nominal GDP from one year to the next, the increase could be due either to increases in prices (which do not improve our standard of living) or increases in the quantities of products/services (which do make us better off). Real GDP per person removes the impact of price changes from nominal GDP per person, leaving only quantities of products/services for consideration.

Real GDP uses constant prices for a single year to value quantities of products/services produced in different years. So differences in real GDP between years are due only to changes in quantities.

We know that the quantity of money—the money supply—affects the average level of prices and therefore affects nominal GDP. But how does money affect real GDP?

As a medium of exchange and unit of account, money overcomes the barter problems of the double coincidence of wants. Money makes exchange or trade much easier for all. With money, it is easier for Samantha and Jacqueline, or for Tim Hortons and Ford Motor Company, to specialize in producing products or services, and to be productive and efficient at what they do. There are gains from having more people and businesses specialize in producing what they are best at, and then trading for other products/services. The resulting mutually beneficial trades (Appendix D) between individuals and businesses increase the production of real GDP beyond what a barter economy would produce.

But once we have a market economy based on money, do *changes* in the demand or supply of money affect real GDP?

Money and Aggregate Supply   There is no direct connection between changes in the money supply and increases in real GDP. Money is not an input into production like labour, capital (equipment), land and other natural resources, or entrepreneurship. And unlike technological change, changes in the money supply do not directly increase the quality of other inputs. Money does not directly increase aggregate supply or directly contribute to economic growth.

Money does not directly increase aggregate supply or directly contribute to economic growth.

Transmission Mechanism Between Money and Real GDP   Changes in the demand or supply of money, however, can indirectly affect real GDP, unemployment, and business cycles—the ups and downs in real GDP. Both the "Yes" and "No" camps agree on that. Economists call the way money changes real GDP, how the impact of money is transmitted to real GDP, the **monetary transmission mechanism**.

The key to the monetary transmission mechanism is the impact of interest rates on spending, both consumer spending and business investment spending. (In the next chapter we will expand the transmission mechanism to include the impact of interest rates on the value of the Canadian dollar and net exports.)

Figure 5.7 illustrates the transmission mechanism from the demand for and supply of money (at the top) to real GDP and inflation (at the bottom). Start at the top of Figure 5.7 and work down. The demand for money and the supply of money interact in money and bond markets to determine the interest rate. The interest rate affects consumer spending (*C*) through the cost of consumer borrowing.

monetary transmission mechanism: how the impact of money is transmitted to real GDP

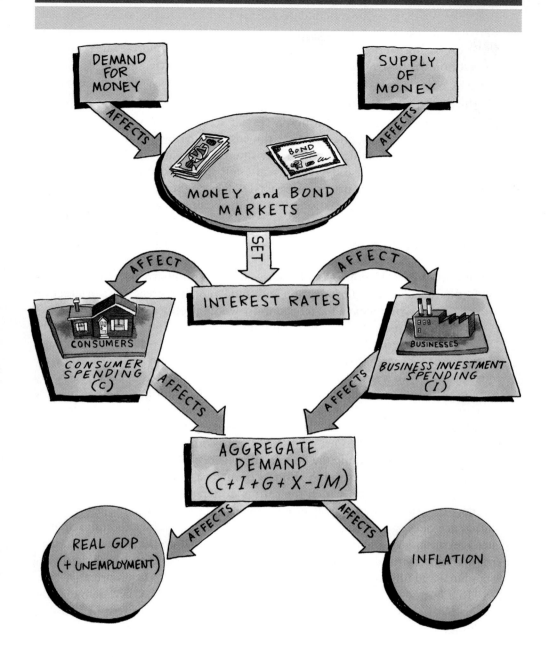

Let's consider what happens when interest rates fall and borrowing becomes cheaper. Spending on expensive consumer purchases that require loans, like houses financed with mortgages, cars with car loans, and major appliances on credit cards, is very interest-sensitive. Lower interest rates reduce the total cost of these interest-sensitive purchases, so consumers buy more of them, thus spending more.

The interest rate also affects the cost of business borrowing. Business investment spending (I) is heavily financed by borrowing and therefore very interest-sensitive. Lower interest rates make investment spending cheaper, and businesses spend more on new factories and equipment.

Lower interest rates are a positive aggregate demand shock, increasing aggregate demand, increasing real GDP, decreasing unemployment, and causing inflation.

Higher interest rates are a negative aggregate demand shock, decreasing aggregate demand, decreasing real GDP, increasing unemployment, and causing deflation.

Lower Interest Rates Are a Positive Aggregate Demand Shock

The net effect of lower interest rates is to increase aggregate demand. Remember your mantra: aggregate demand equals $C + I + G + X - IM$. Increases in C and I both increase aggregate demand. As Chapter 4 explained, a positive aggregate demand shock causes increased real GDP, decreased unemployment, and inflation (rising average prices). As real GDP rises, lower interest rates can push the economy into the expansion phase of the business cycle.

Higher Interest Rates Are a Negative Aggregate Demand Shock

Higher interest rates work through a similar transmission mechanism but in reverse. Higher interest rates increase the cost of borrowing, decrease C and I, and decrease aggregate demand. Higher interest rates are a negative aggregate demand shock and cause decreased real GDP, increased unemployment, and deflation (falling average prices). As real GDP falls, higher interest rates can push the economy into the contraction phase of the business cycle.

How Much Does Money Matter for Business Cycles?

Money overcomes the double-coincidence-of-wants problems of barter exchange. By facilitating specialized production and trade, money increases the production of real GDP beyond what a barter economy would produce.

All economists, including J.B. Say and the "Yes" camp, and J.M. Keynes and the "No" camp, agree on these advantages of money exchange over barter exchange. Both camps also agree that money affects prices and inflation (as explained by the quantity theory of money). And both camps agree that changes in the demand and supply of money can indirectly affect real GDP and other key macroeconomic outcomes through the transmission mechanism between interest rates and aggregate demand. With all of these agreements, it seems like J.B. Say, J.M Keynes, and their followers in the "Yes" and "No" camps could be Facebook friends.

But beyond overcoming the double-coincidence-of-wants problems, beyond causing inflation, and beyond the impact of interest rates on real GDP, there are still money questions on which the camps disagree. With the introduction of money to barter exchange, will supply still create its own demand? How much difference does the existence of money make to the answer to the fundamental macroeconomic question: "If left alone by government, do the price mechanisms of market economies adjust quickly to maintain steady growth in living standards and full employment (leaving out the agreed impact on prices)?"

In a barter exchange economy, supply always creates its own demand, the economy is always in equilibrium, and no one is kicking himself. In a money exchange economy, the two camps disagree about *how much does money change the economy when it is not in equilibrium*, when there are mismatches between aggregate supply and demand, business cycles, and when people are kicking themselves because of disappointed expectations.

The "Yes" and "No" camps disagree about how much difference money makes to two aspects of business cycles:

- how often business cycles happen
- how quickly markets adjust
  (back to equilibrium at potential GDP and full employment).

Let's look at each camp's position on these two ways that money can matter for the fundamental macroeconomic question.

J.B. Say and the Yes Camp Answer, "Not Much"

How much does the move from a barter exchange economy to a money exchange economy affect how often business cycles happen, and how quickly markets adjust? For J.B. Say and the "Yes" camp, the answer is "not much."

Business cycles can be triggered by demand or supply shocks that cause a mismatch between aggregate supply and demand. Say and his followers believe that most shocks to the economy are external, coming from forces outside the economy like scientific discoveries, technological change, and natural disasters. These aggregate supply shocks are the main source of business cycles for the "Yes" camp. Adding money to the "real economy" of inputs, technology, and outputs doesn't affect aggregate supply, and doesn't create a new source of shocks. Money, the "Yes" camp states, does not affect how often business cycles happen.

When there are external supply shocks causing temporary mismatches between aggregate supply and demand, Say and the "Yes" camp believe that price adjustments in separate markets—input, output, international trade, and loanable funds markets—all work harmoniously to quickly restore the match between aggregate supply and aggregate demand.

Money, which creates the possibility of savings, makes the biggest difference for the loanable funds market. After suppliers sell their products/services for money, they may choose to save some of that money instead of demanding products/services. Savings can also cause a temporary mismatch—aggregate demand may be less than aggregate supply. But price adjustments in the loanable funds market quickly restore the match. Any additional saving gets deposited in banks, increasing the supply of loanable funds. This causes the interest rate—the price of loanable funds—to fall. Falling interest rates induce more consumer spending and especially business borrowing to finance more investment spending. Spending increases, which offsets the additional savings and restores aggregate spending in output markets, making it equal to aggregate income earned in input markets.

Money allows savings to flow easily through the loanable funds market to facilitate business borrowing for investment spending. The economy quickly ends up with a match of aggregate supply and aggregate demand—just like the barter outcome—at potential real GDP and full employment. Money, according to the "Yes" camp, helps markets quickly adjust to equilibrium.

Money does not affect external supply shocks that are main source of business cycles for "Yes" camp.

Money allows savings to flow easily through the loanable funds market to facilitate business borrowing for investment spending. For "Yes" camp, money helps markets quickly adjust to equilibrium.

J.M. Keynes and the No Camp Answer, "A Lot"

How much does money affect how often business cycles happen, and how quickly markets adjust? For J.M. Keynes and the "No" camp, the answer is "a lot." Money, especially functioning as a store of value, is a fundamental change to the barter economy match of aggregate supply and aggregate demand.

Business cycles can be triggered by demand or supply shocks. Keynes and his followers believe that most business cycles are caused by demand shocks that are internal to the economy. Volatile (quickly changeable) expectations are an important internal source of demand shocks for the "No" camp, causing investment spending and aggregate demand to fluctuate. When expectations become pessimistic, *money gives people a way not to spend*, causing a negative demand shock. This is a change from barter exchange.

The banking system's tension between profits and prudence is another money-based internal source of demand shocks. With banks creating money through fractional reserve banking, internal crises in the financial sector can affect aggregate demand, real GDP, and employment. Money, the "No" camp states, makes business cycles happen more often.

When there are internal demand shocks causing business cycles, Keynes and the "No" camp believe that adjustment problems in all markets can fail to restore the match between aggregate supply and aggregate demand.

Money, which creates the possibility of savings, makes the biggest difference for the loanable funds market. When worried consumers and businesses stop spending and increase their savings, they may *not* put their savings into loanable funds markets, and businesses may postpone investment spending. Consumers and businesses may hold money instead to calm their unease and reduce risk. The transmission mechanism—where falling interest rates in the loanable funds market increase spending and aggregate demand—gets blocked in the middle by money. Again, the key is *money gives people a way not to spend*.

Money slows the adjustments of markets to equilibrium. It may take years for markets to adjust mismatches between aggregate supply and demand. Without government help, the economy may ultimately fall short of potential real GDP and full employment.

Money gives people a way not to spend, blocking the transmission mechanism so loanable funds market does not match spending to savings.

For "No" camp, money slows markets' adjustments to equilibrium.

ECONOMICS Out There

Canadians Sitting on a $1-Trillion Pile of Idle Cash

Economist Derek Holt of Scotia Capital Inc reports that "risk-averse Canadian households are sitting on up to $1 trillion of cash and near-cash' holdings, earning next to nothing" in interest.

Holt understands why households are so cautious, given the recent "financial shocks" of the Great Recession. But, he argues, households should be holding more of their savings in the form of financial assets like bonds that yield higher returns. Holt is implying that households are acting like lunatics by holding money and giving up earned interest!

As Keynes would predict, households are holding cash to avoid risk and to have the benefits of liquidity. By holding cash, households are betting that earning no interest will be better than losing their savings with higher-interest but risky investments.

Source: "Families sitting on up to $1-trillion," Virginian Galt, found in *Globe and Mail* Update, September 28, 2009.

Money gives people a way not to spend, creating possibility of financial crises with fractional reserve banking, adding new internal sources of demand shocks for "No" camp.

Comparing Camps: How Much Money Matters for Business Cycles

Figure 5.8 is a good study device for reviewing the differences between the two camps regarding money. It extends Figure 1.2's comparison the two camps on their answers to the fundamental macroeconomic question.

Figure 5.8	How Much Does Money Matter for Business Cycles?	
Compared to a barter economy, how does money affect:	**Camp**	
	Yes–Left Alone, Markets Quickly Self-Adjust (Say)	No–Left Alone, Markets Fail to Adjust (Keynes)
How Often Business Cycles Happen	**Money has no effect.** Money does not affect external supply shocks that are main source of business cycles.	**Money creates new shocks.** Money gives people a way not to spend, adding new internal demand shocks.
How Quickly Markets Adjust	**Money helps loanable funds market** quickly adjust to equilibrium.	**Money blocks transmission mechanism,** slowing adjustment to equilibrium.

Back to the Fundamental Question   This discussion of money has probably been full of surprises: why people may not want to hold more money, why currency is the least important form of money, how chartered banks create money and what the price of money is.

But I also hope you now better understand how money helps explain some of the differences between the "Yes" and "No" camps on the fundamental macroeconomic question: "If left alone by government, do the price mechanisms of market economies adjust quickly to maintain steady growth in living standards, full employment (and stable prices)?"

For J.B. Say and the "Yes, markets quickly self-adjust" camp, money does not matter much for business cycles. Money introduces no new supply or demand shocks, and allows savings to flow easily through the loanable funds market to facilitate business borrowing for investment spending. Money helps markets quickly adjust to equilibrium, so government can keeps its hands-off. Aggregate supply and aggregate demand will match at potential real GDP and full employment.

For J.M. Keynes and the "No, markets fail to quickly adjust" camp, money matters a lot for business cycles. Money gives people a way not to spend, adding new internal demand shocks and the possibility of financial crises with fractional reserve banking. Money can also block the transmission mechanism so that the interest rate in the loanable funds market may not adjust spending and aggregate demand to match aggregate supply. Money slows markets' adjustments to equilibrium, so government needs to be hands-on, or the economy may never achieve potential GDP and full employment.

Refresh

5.4

1. What is the connection between money and aggregate supply? Explain your answer.

2. When interest rates rise and borrowing becomes more expensive, use Figure 5.7 to explain the monetary transmission mechanism from money demand and supply to real GDP.

3. Which position seems closer to how you think about how much money matters for business cycles—the "Yes" or "No" camp? Explain why.

www.myeconlab.com

Money Is for Lunatics

Demanders and Suppliers of Money

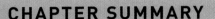

CHAPTER SUMMARY

5.1 IS IT SMART TO *NOT* WANT MONEY? DEMAND FOR MONEY

People demand money for its liquidity as a medium of exchange, unit of account, and store of value, and are often willing to give up interest on bonds in order to hold their wealth as money.

- **Money**—anything *acceptable* as a means of paying for products/services; money has three functions.
  - Medium of exchange—acceptability by all as means of payment solves barter problem of the double coincidence of wants.
  - Unit of account—standard unit for measuring and comparing prices.
  - Store of value—time machine for moving purchasing power from present to future; you can earn now and spend later.

- **Bond**—financial asset where borrower promises to repay the original value at specific future date, and make fixed regular interest payments.

- Why hold wealth (what you own) as money which pays no interest, rather than as bonds which pay interest?
  - Money provides **liquidity**—ease with which assets can be converted into economy's medium of exchange.
  - Money is most liquid of all assets—acceptable by sellers as a means of payment.
  - Money pays no interest, but has liquidity; bonds pay interest, but do not have liquidity.

- Why hold money as a store of value?
  - For "Yes" camp (markets self-adjust, Say's Law holds), people hold more wealth as interest-paying bonds, since savings can be safely invested in loanable funds (bonds).

- For "No" camp (markets fail to quickly adjust, Keynes's business cycles), people hold more wealth as money because fundamental uncertainty about future makes bond investments risky.

- **Interest rate**—price of holding money: what you give up by not holding bonds.
  - Determined by demand and supply in both money and bond markets.

- **Law of demand for money**—as the price of money—the interest rate—rises, quantity demanded of money decreases.
  - Changes in real GDP or average prices cause change in demand for money, *not* a change in quantity demanded.
  - Increase in real GDP increases demand for money; decrease in real GDP decreases demand for money.
  - Increase in average prices increases demand for money; decrease in average prices decreases demand for money.

5.2 LEGAL COUNTERFEITING? SUPPLY OF MONEY

In a fractional-reserve banking system, the supply of money—currency plus demand deposits—is created both by the Bank of Canada and by chartered banks making loans.

- Forms of money:
  - Commodity money—saleable product with alternative uses serving as money.
  - Convertible paper money—paper money that can be converted into gold on demand.
  - Fiat money—**currency** (government-issued paper bills and coins) with no alternative uses, valuable simply by government decree.
  - Deposit money—**demand deposits**—balances in bank accounts that depositors can withdraw on demand by using a debit card or writing a cheque.

- Supply of money in Canada consists of currency and deposit money.
  - M1 = currency in circulation and demand deposits.
  - M2 = M1 plus all other less liquid deposits.

- Bank of Canada is Canada's **central bank**—government institution responsible for supervising chartered banks and financial institutions and for regulating the supply of money; roles include:
  - Issuing currency.
  - Banker to chartered banks—chartered bank deposits at Bank of Canada allow chartered banks to make payments to each other.
  - **Lender of last resort**—making loans to banks to preserve stability of financial system.
  - Banker to government—managing government's accounts, foreign currency reserves, national debt.
  - Conducting monetary policy—changing money supply and interest rates to achieve steady growth, full employment, stable prices.

- Chartered banks can create money (demand deposits) because of **fractional-reserve banking**—banks hold only a fraction of deposits as reserves.
  - Banks create loans and money (demand deposits) together; when bank makes a loan, creates demand deposit credit in borrower's chequing account equal to amount of the loan.
  - With fractional-reserve banking, there is risk of a **bank run**—many depositors withdraw cash all at once, and bank may not have enough cash reserves to pay all depositors.
- Banks face a tradeoff between profits and prudence.
  - Smaller fraction of reserves, more loans, and higher-risk loans may yield more profits.
  - Tradeoff is giving up safety and risking customers' deposits and trust.
- Supply of money determined by Bank of Canada and chartered banks.
  - Quantity of money supplied is a fixed amount at a moment in time.
  - Supply of money does not change when the interest rate changes.

5.3 WHAT IS THE PRICE OF MONEY?
INTEREST RATES, MONEY, AND BONDS

Bond prices and interest rates are inversely related and determined together in the money and bond markets.

- The interest rate is the price of money in two ways:
  - Opportunity cost of holding money.
  - Cost of borrowing money.
- Bonds promise to pay back the original value plus a fixed dollar amount of money.
  - Bonds do *not* promise a fixed percentage of interest.
  - When interest rates rise, market price of a bond falls.
  - When interest rates fall, market price of a bond rises.
  - When holding a bond until its time period is up, you receive, as promised, fixed dollar amount payments plus original value.
- Bonds are riskier and less liquid than money as a store of value, because market price of the bond can change.
- Interest rate determined by the interaction of demand and supply in money and bond markets.
  - At the market-clearing, or equilibrium, interest rate, quantity of money demanded equals quantity of money supplied.
  - When interest rate below market-clearing rate, excess demand for money; people sell bonds to get more money; increased supply of bonds causes bond prices to fall and interest rate to rise.
  - When interest rate above market-clearing rate, excess supply of money; people buy bonds to get rid of money; increased demand for bonds causes bond prices to rise and interest rate to fall.
- There are many different interest rates on different financial assets, but all interest rates tend to rise together and fall together.

5.4 J.B. SAY AND J.M. KEYNES AS FACEBOOK FRIENDS? MONEY, INTEREST RATES, INVESTMENT, AND REAL GDP

"Yes" and "No" camps disagree about money's effect on frequency of business cycles and how quickly markets adjust. For "Yes" camp, money has no effect on business cycles and helps loanable funds markets adjust. For "No" camp, money creates new shocks and blocks transmission mechanism, slowing adjustment.

- Does money affect key macroeconomic outcomes of increasing real GDP per person (economic growth), unemployment, and inflation?
  - Money can affect inflation, according to quantity theory of money.
  - Money does *not* directly increase aggregate supply or economic growth.
- Money indirectly affects real GDP and unemployment through **monetary transmission mechanism**—how impact of money is transmitted to real GDP.
  - Demand and supply of money determine the interest rate.
  - When interest rate falls, interest-sensitive purchases become cheaper so consumer spending (C) and business investment spending (I) increase.
  - Increases in C and I increase aggregate demand.
  - Lower interest rates are positive demand shock, increasing aggregate demand, increasing real GDP, decreasing unemployment, and causing inflation.
  - Higher interest rates are negative demand shock, decreasing aggregate demand, decreasing real GDP, increasing unemployment, and causing deflation.
  - Figure 5.7 of the Monetary Transmission Mechanism is a good review aid.
- Economists disagree on the question "How much does money change the economy when economy is not in equilibrium?"
- J.B. Say and "Yes, markets quickly self-adjust" camp answer "not much."
  - Money does not affect external supply shocks that are main source of business-cycles for "Yes" camp.
  - Money allows savings to flow easily through loanable funds market to facilitate business borrowing for investment spending.
  - Money helps markets quickly adjust to equilibrium.
- J.M. Keynes and "No, markets fail to adjust" camp answer "a lot."
  - Money gives people a way not to spend but to save, creating possibility of financial crises, adding new internal demand shocks for business cycles.
  - Money gives people a way not to spend, blocking transmission mechanism so loanable funds market does not match spending to savings.
  - Money slows markets' adjustments to equilibrium.

TRUE/FALSE

Circle the correct answer.

You sign up for a speed dating event at your campus. It is obvious that your next speed date is obsessed with money for two reasons: (1) your speed date is wearing lots of gold dollar-sign jewellery; and (2) when the speed date announcer asks everyone to make 15 statements about the thing they like most in life, your speed date chooses money as the topic. Use your knowledge of economics to determine whether your speed date's statements are true or false.

Use this scenario to answer questions 1–15.

5.1 DEMAND FOR MONEY

1. If we both desire each other's money, we don't have the double-coincidence-of-wants problem.   **True**   **False**

2. It is always smart to want to hold more money.   **True**   **False**

3. If interest rates increase, it is smarter to want to hold more money.   **True**   **False**

4. If average prices increase, the demand for money increases.   **True**   **False**

5. If I hold more of my wealth as money, this guarantees my purchasing power stays the same.   **True**   **False**

5.2 SUPPLY OF MONEY

6. If you withdraw $50 from your bank account and put it in my wallet, the money supply increases.   **True**   **False**

7. Coins and bills are a large fraction of the money supply.   **True**   **False**

8. Government-issued paper bills and coins are called fiat money.   **True**   **False**

9. The supply of money depends on the interest rate.   **True**   **False**

10. If I shift money from my chequing to savings accounts, M1 decreases and M2 increases.   **True**   **False**

5.3 MONEY AND BONDS

11. Bonds are less risky than money as a store of value.   **True**   **False**

12. Bonds promise to pay back the original value plus a fixed dollar amount of money.   **True**   **False**

13. When the interest rate is above the market-clearing price, people sell bonds to get more money.   **True**   **False**

5.4 MONEY AND BUSINESS CYCLES

14. Economists disagree about whether money helps, or slows, the economy's adjustment to equilibrium.   **True**   **False**

15. Economists all agree that money is a major cause of business cycles.   **True**   **False**

MULTIPLE CHOICE

Circle the correct answer.

5.1 DEMAND FOR MONEY

1. If you sell your bonds in order to hold more of your wealth as money, you
- **A)** get liquidity and give up interest.
- **B)** give up liquidity and earn interest.
- **C)** get liquidity and earn interest.
- **D)** give up liquidity and give up interest.

2. On what function of money do Keynes and Say *disagree*?
- **A)** Medium of exchange
- **B)** Unit of account
- **C)** Store of value
- **D)** Liquidity

3. Double coincidence of wants is
- **A)** buyers wanting the same thing.
- **B)** sellers wanting the same thing.
- **C)** buyers and sellers wanting nothing to do with each other.
- **D)** buyers and sellers wanting what each other has.

4. Money has taken the form of
- **A)** cattle.
- **B)** metal.
- **C)** fur.
- **D)** all of the above.

5.2 SUPPLY OF MONEY

5. When you pay for lunch using your debit card, you are using
- **A)** commodity money.
- **B)** convertible paper money.
- **C)** fiat money.
- **D)** deposit money.

6. When Jean-Luc puts $500 in his chequing account and $500 in his savings account he contributes
- **A)** $500 to M2.
- **B)** $1000 to M1.
- **C)** $1000 to M2.
- **D)** $1000 to M3.

7. In 2009, Lowblaws introduced coinstar machines that turn coins into paper money. This
   A) increases M1.
   B) increases M2.
   C) increases fiat money.
   D) does not change the amount of fiat money or M1 or M2.

8. Which of the following statements about how chartered banks use their funds is *true*?
   A) Loans to businesses and consumers are riskiest and earn banks the highest interest rates.
   B) Loans to businesses and consumers are riskiest and earn banks the lowest interest rates.
   C) Government of Canada Treasury bills are riskiest and earn banks the highest interest rates.
   D) Government of Canada Treasury bills are riskiest and earn banks the lowest interest rates.

9. The Northern Rock Bank in the U.K.
   A) offers commodity money in the form of rocks.
   B) had many depositors withdraw cash all at once in 2007.
   C) is no longer in business.
   D) only plays rock music for its customers.

10. The Bank of Canada does *not*
   A) make currency.
   B) act as lender of last resort to chartered banks.
   C) manage the Government of Canada's demand deposit account.
   D) conduct monetary policy.

5.3 MONEY AND BONDS

11. If interest rates fall, the market price of bonds
   A) falls. If you sell the bond you take an unexpected loss.
   B) falls. If you sell the bond you make an unexpected profit.
   C) rises. If you sell the bond you take an unexpected loss.
   D) rises. If you sell the bond you make an unexpected profit.

12. Excess demand for money
   A) occurs when interest rates are above the market clearing rate.
   B) causes people to sell bonds.
   C) causes people to buy bonds.
   D) causes interest rates to fall.

5.4 MONEY AND BUSINESS CYCLES

13. Both "Yes" and "No" camps agree that
   A) money affects prices and inflation.
   B) money exchange is better than barter exchange.
   C) the monetary transmission mechanism indirectly affects real GDP.
   D) all of the above.

14. Money can directly affect

A) inflation.

B) real GDP.

C) unemployment.

D) all of the above.

15. Money indirectly affects real GDP and unemployment through

A) the monetary transmission mechanism.

B) interest rates.

C) aggregate demand.

D) all of the above.

SHORT ANSWER

Write a short answer to each question. Your answer may be in point form.

1. Products ranging from cigarettes to chocolate have been used as a medium of exchange.

A) What is money?

B) Suppose that the Royal Canadian Mint stops printing money due to a shortage of available metals and instead distributes mint chocolate covered in gold-covered wrappers in the shape of money. How would this meet each of the three functions of money?

C) How did the Governor of New France address a shortage of coins in 1685?

D) Cigarettes once functioned as the currency of Romania. Anything could be bought for cigarettes—for example, food, electronic goods, and alcohol. Explain which functions of money cigarettes can and cannot perform.

2. Consider two individuals: James Bond and Johnny Cash. Suppose James Bond holds most of his wealth in bonds while Johnny Cash holds most of his wealth in cash.

A) Whose wealth is more liquid?

B) What is the price of money? If the price of money falls, will their quantity of money demanded decrease or increase?

3. An article from *The Globe and Mail*, entitled "Why saving too much is scary bad" (September 23, 2009) gives advice for anyone who is waiting for interest rates to rise so they can move out of bank accounts and into bonds.

A) Why would people move money from bank accounts into bonds if interest rates rise?

B) What happens to M1 and M2 if people move their money from bank accounts to bonds?

C) According to the article, CIBC World Markets did not expect interest rates to rise for another six to eight months. Did CIBC think the money market was at the market-clearing interest rate? Why or why not?

D) If you own bonds and want to sell them, is it better to sell them over those next six to eight months (when interest rates are expected to remain the same) or after those six to eight months (when interest rates are expected to rise)? Why?

4. Consider your life 10 years from now. You anticipate a better-paying job, a new car, more expensive clothes, a new house, etc.

   A) What will happen to your demand for money?

   B) Will you hold more fiat money or demand deposits?

   C) Now consider the macroeconomy. If the economy improves and most people get better jobs like you, what happens to the aggregate demand for money?

   D) If there is inflation, will this increase or decrease the demand for money?

5. Suppose your school newspaper is doing an article on the financial crisis that triggered the Great Recession. They interview you and ask the following questions regarding the role of chartered banks in the Canadian economy:

   A) What tradeoffs do banks face?

   B) How do banks protect themselves if lenders are unable to pay back the loan?

   C) Why are banks regulated?

   D) Why are bank runs possible?

   E) Why are bank runs unlikely to happen in Canada?

6. Tanis goes to an African country on a humanitarian mission. She quickly discovers that few stores accept payment by debit or credit card. Fortunately, when she goes to the local store to buy a calling card for her phone, she learns that money can be transferred from one user to another by phone. The process of mobile banking is described in *The Economist* article, "The Power of Mobile Money" (published in September 2009): You give cash to the agent at the store (who credits the money to your mobile-money account) and you can withdraw money or send money to other people (who will be sent a text message containing a special code that can be taken to an agent to withdraw cash).

   A) The Consultative Group to Assist the Poor predicts that about by 2012 1.7 billion people will have a mobile phone but no bank account, and 20 percent of them will be using mobile money. Why would mobile banking be important in regions of the world where there are fewer ATMs and chartered banks?

   B) Based on what you learned in section 5.2, what type of money is mobile money?

   C) Why is mobile banking a safe place for savings?

7. In the 2004 Indian Ocean tsunami, most people who hid their money in their home (for example, under the matress) lost their money due to the tsunami's destruction. Suppose a similar catastrophe is expected to hit the Canadian west coast, where you live.

   A) Thinking like a businessperson, and like goldsmiths, what could you do?

   B) What would you issue to people who deposit money with you?

   C) Why would you not want to loan out all of the money?

   D) If depositors start to get pessimistic about the economy, why might it be a good idea to increase the amount of reserves?

8. According to the Scotia Capital Inc. report in *Economics Out There*, risk-averse Canadian households are sitting on up to $1 trillion of cash and "near-cash" holdings.

   A) What is the opportunity cost of holding nearly $1 trillion of cash and "near-cash" holdings?

   B) According to some economists, there is a tendency to hold money as cash when people have pessimistic expectations. Which camp of economists emphasizes this tendency, and what are the reasons why people who are pessimistic about the economy hold money as cash?

   C) The estimated amount sitting in cash and near-cash holdings includes currency holdings, deposits, and treasury-bills. Are all these parts of M1 and M2?

9. Suppose the transmission mechanism in your car needs repair. You take it to the mechanic and the mechanic explains the "simple" problem and the solution. The mechanic then insults you by asking "What do they teach you in school, anyway?" Use this opportunity to show your smarts and explain the monetary transmission mechanism.

   A) If interest rates are above the market-clearing rate, describe how this could lead to an indirect increase in GDP through the monetary transmission mechanism.

   B) If interest rates are below the market-clearing rate, describe how this could lead to an indirect decrease in GDP through the monetary transmission mechanism.

10. Suppose followers of Say and followers of Keynes became Facebook friends. Some message postings would receive general agreement, and some would result in complete disagreement.

    A) What aspects of money would followers of Say and followers of Keynes agree on?

    B) If someone posted the question "Does money block the monetary transmission mechanism?" how would a follower of Keynes respond?

    C) How would a follower of Say respond to the question "Does money block the money transmission mechanism?"

Trading Dollars *for* Dollars?

Exchange Rates with the Rest of the World

LEARNING OBJECTIVES

6.1 Explain the demand and supply forces that determine the value of the Canadian dollar.

6.2 Identify and explain five forces causing exchange rate fluctuations.

6.3 Trace the impact of high and low exchange rates on real GDP and inflation.

6.4 Describe how purchasing power parity and rate of return parity provide standards for exchange rates.

IF YOU HAVE EVER BEEN to the United States, you know that the shopping experience is much different than in Canada. With a population ten times as large as Canada's, there are more products to choose from and often lower prices, at least in U.S. dollars. In 2007 the Canadian dollar rose to be equal in value to the U.S. dollar for the first time in 30 years. Canadians crossed the border to shop in record numbers. It was like everything in the U.S. was on sale.

What determines the value of the Canadian dollar? Why is it sometimes worth as little as 60 cents U.S. or as much as $1.10 U.S.? In this chapter you will learn what determines exchange rates, the price of one country's money in terms of another country's money. Exchange rates, like interest rates, are another price of money. You will learn why people trade Canadian dollars for U.S. dollars or for euros or Japanese yen.

Interest rates help determine the value of the Canadian dollar. When interest rates in Canada rise, the value of the Canadian dollar usually rises, which affects how much we pay for products imported from the United States or elsewhere. The value of the Canadian dollar also affects how expensive our exports are for foreigners to buy. By affecting the prices and quantities of net exports, the Canadian dollar plays an important role in determining the key macroeconomic outcomes of real GDP, unemployment, and inflation.

While a "high" value for the Canadian dollar is better for cross-border Canadian shoppers, is it better for the economy as a whole than a "low" dollar? And how do we know what counts as "high" or "low?" Our final topic will be understanding the deeper forces, beyond demand and supply, that determine the value of the Canadian dollar. Interest rates appear yet again, but so do Big Macs. Big Macs as a deep force for exchange rates? Read on.

6.1 Shuffling Off to Buffalo: Demand and Supply of Canadian Dollars

Explain the demand and supply forces that determine the value of the Canadian dollar.

Unless you are fabulously wealthy, every purchase you make includes the question, "How much does it cost?" The answer to that question is usually an amount of money per product or service: the Apple iPod touch costs $219, the Ugg boots cost $299, the movie ticket costs $12.

But buying money is different.

How Much Does That Dollar Cost?

The question, "How much does that dollar cost?" is not as silly as it sounds. It's really asking, "What's the exchange rate?" An **exchange rate** is the price at which one currency exchanges for another. When we say the Canadian dollar is worth 95 cents U.S., we are really saying that the exchange rate of the Canadian dollar for the U.S. dollar is US$0.95. You need 95 cents U.S. to buy one Canadian dollar. With exchange rates, think of the Canadian dollar as the product for sale. The exchange rate (US$0.95) is the price for buying one Canadian dollar with U.S. dollars.

Every currency has more than one exchange rate. In 2010, for example, you could also buy a Canadian dollar for 0.63 euros or 85 Japanese yen. These prices, or exchange rates, for the Canadian dollar—and for all other currencies—are determined in the **foreign exchange market**, which is a worldwide market for buying and selling currencies. Money—dollars, euros, yen, Chinese yuan, Mexican pesos—is the only product for sale in the foreign exchange market. Within the foreign exchange market, each currency has its own market with its own demanders and suppliers. But because each currency exchanges for every other currency, the currency markets are tightly integrated.

The foreign exchange market (often abbreviated as *forex*) is the largest financial market in the world, with a trading volume of around 4 trillion U.S. dollars per day. It has multiple locations and trades are made digitally around the world at all hours of the day. About 86 percent of these trades involve the U.S. dollar, about 37 percent involve the euro, 16 percent the yen, 15 percent the British pound, 7 percent the Swiss franc, 7 percent the Australian dollar, and 4 percent the Canadian dollar.

We will focus our attention on the market for Canadian dollars, which determines the exchange rates for Canadian currency. The principles behind the market for Canadian dollars are the same in the markets for U.S. dollars, euros, yen, and all other currencies.

exchange rate: price at which one currency exchanges for another currency

foreign exchange market: worldwide market where all countries' currencies are bought and sold in exchange for each other

Exchange Rates	We Sell
AUSTRALIA	0.8264
BRAZIL	0.5263
CANADA	0.9677
CHINA	0.1417
Costa Rica	0.0023
Euro	1.4093
HONG KONG	0.1412
JAPAN	0.0094
MEXICO	0.1014
NEW ZEALAND	0.7284
S Korea	0.0012
SINGAPORE	0.6922
Sweden	0.1502
Switzerland	0.8837
TAHITI	0.0123
TAIWAN	0.0342
THAILAND	

This electronic board at a U.S. currency exchange booth displays the cost of various currencies in U.S. dollars. The loonie, for example, is selling for over 96 cents U.S. Why isn't the U.S. dollar listed on the board?

Appreciation and Depreciation   Exchange rates fluctuate (go up and down) constantly. Figure 6.1 shows the exchange rate for the Canadian dollar in terms of U.S. dollars since 1970. The exchange rate, the price of a Canadian dollar in U.S. dollars, is on the vertical axis. Notice that the exchange rate fell from 1991 to 2002, and then rose dramatically from 2002 to 2007.

Figure 6.1	Exchange Rate of Canadian Dollar in U.S. Dollars, 1970–2009

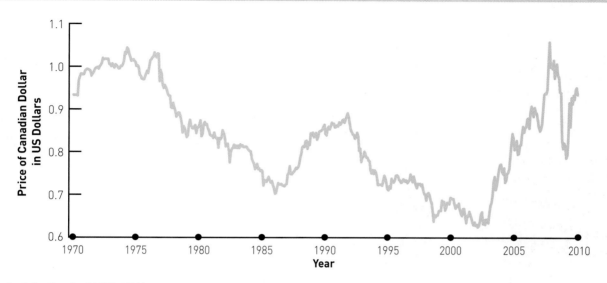

Source: Statistics Canada, CANSIM Table 176-0064.

A fall in the exchange rate is called a **currency depreciation**. The Canadian dollar depreciated against the U.S. dollar between 1991 and 2002. A rise in the exchange rate is called a **currency appreciation**. The Canadian dollar appreciated against the U.S. dollar between 2002 and 2007.

The foreign exchange market has buyers (demanders) and sellers (suppliers), like other markets. But who demands Canadian dollars, and why? And who supplies Canadian dollars, and why? Here is a hint. If you are shuffling off—to Buffalo, New York or to Bellingham, Washington—for a cross-border shopping trip, you are demanding U.S. dollars *and* supplying Canadian dollars.

Identifying demanders and suppliers will help you understand what determines the exchange rate—the price of the Canadian dollar on the foreign exchange market—and why it fluctuates so much.

currency depreciation: fall in exchange rate of one currency for another

currency appreciation: rise in exchange rate of one currency for another

Non-Canadians Demanding Canadian Dollars

Who goes to the worldwide foreign exchange market to demand Canadian dollars? If you live and work in Canada, you are paid in Canadian dollars. You don't need to go to the foreign exchange market to buy money. You can use the Canadian dollars you earn to buy any products/services for sale in Canada. The demanders of Canadian dollars on the foreign exchange market are largely non-Canadians from the rest of the world.

There are two main reasons why non-Canadians demand Canadian dollars on the foreign exchange market. The first—to buy Canadian exports and assets—is discussed below. The second—to speculate on the future value of the Canadian dollar—is discussed in Section 6.2.

Demand for Canadian Exports and Assets A non-Canadian who wants to buy Canadian exports—products/services produced in Canada but sold to the rest of the world—must pay in Canadian dollars. Since non-Canadians do not earn Canadian dollars, they must exchange some of their country's currency for Canadian dollars in order to purchase Canadian exports. Similarly, a non-Canadian investor who wants to buy Canadian assets—bonds, stocks, businesses, or real estate—must pay in Canadian dollars.

Law of Demand for Canadian Dollars The law of demand applies to Canadian dollars, just as it applies to an iPod touch, boots, or any other product/service. The law of demand states that as the price of a product/service rises, the quantity demanded decreases. The exchange rate is the price of a Canadian dollar. So, the **law of demand for Canadian dollars** states that as the exchange rate rises, the quantity demanded of Canadian dollars decreases.

Figure 6.2 illustrates the inverse relation (when one goes up, the other goes down) between the exchange rate and the quantity demanded of Canadian dollars in the foreign exchange market. For simplicity, the numbers are made up, but the pattern is representative of what the actual relationship between the exchange rate and the demand for Canadian dollars looks like.

As you scan down the two columns, notice that as the price of the Canadian dollar—the exchange rate—rises (appreciates), the quantity demanded of Canadian dollars decreases. This inverse relationship is caused by the export effect.

> Demand for Canadian dollars is demand for Canadian exports, assets, and for speculating on the future value of the Canadian dollar.

> law of demand for Canadian dollars: if the exchange rate rises, quantity demanded of Canadian dollars decreases

Figure 6.2	Demand for Canadian Dollars in Foreign Exchange Market
Price of 1 Canadian Dollar (US$ per C$)	**Quantity Demanded (billions of Canadian dollars per month)**
US$0.60	90
US$0.70	80
US$0.80	70
US$0.90	60
US$1.00	50
US$1.10	40

Export Effect Cross-border shopping is a two-way street. When the value of the Canadian dollar—the exchange rate—rises, U.S. products/services become cheaper for Canadians. For example, when the exchange rate is US$0.60 per Canadian dollar, a dress that costs $60 in the United States costs 100 Canadian dollars. But if the exchange rate appreciated to US$1.00 per Canadian dollar, the same US$60 dress would fall in price to only C$60. For U.S. consumers, the price of the dress remains constant at US$60.

The opposite is true for U.S. consumers buying Canadian products/services. Look at Figure 6.3. Suppose a month's supply of Tim Hortons coffee costs C$100. This is the price Canadian consumers will pay (column two), no matter what happens to the exchange rate. But when the exchange rate is US$0.60 per Canadian dollar (row one), the U.S. consumer would pay only US$60 for the coffee. If the exchange rate rose to US$1.00 per Canadian dollar (row two), the same C$100 coffee would now rise in price to US$100. A higher value of the Canadian dollar makes Canadian exports—like Tim Hortons coffee—and Canadian assets—bonds, stocks, businesses, and real estate—more expensive for people in the United States and the rest of the world.

Figure 6.3	Price of Tim Horton's Coffee in Canada and U.S.		
Price of 1 Canadian Dollar (US$ per C$)	Price of Month's Supply of Tim Hortons Coffee in Canada (in C$)	Price of Month's Supply of Tim Hortons Coffee in U.S. (in US$)
US$0.60	C$100	US$60
US$1.00	C$100	US$100

When Canadian exports and assets becomes more expensive, non-Canadians buy less of them. As the exchange rate rises, the prices non-Canadians must pay for Canadian exports and assets in U.S. dollars rises, so they will *not* want to buy as many. With fewer sales to non-Canadians, the quantity demanded of Canadian dollars decreases.

Supplying Canadian Dollars to Non-Canadians

Who supplies Canadian dollars to the worldwide foreign exchange market? Consider this scenario: You are heading south for some cross-border shopping in the United States. That makes you a Canadian who wants U.S. dollars. You must supply Canadian dollars in exchange. Your demand for U.S. dollars is also a supply of Canadian dollars. In the unique world of the foreign exchange market, the demand for one currency is the supply of another.

There are two main reasons why Canadians supply Canadian dollars on the foreign exchange market. The first—to buy imports and assets from the rest of the world—is discussed below. The second—to speculate on the future value of the Canadian dollar—is discussed in Section 6.2.

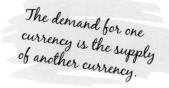

The demand for one currency is the supply of another currency.

Each of these people are buying (demanding) foreign currency and paying for (supplying) it with their own domestic currency. In this way, each demander is also a supplier on the foreign currency market.

Demand for Imports and Foreign Assets

A Canadian who wants to buy imports—products/services produced in the rest of the world—must pay in the currency of the country supplying the imports. The dress in Buffalo that costs US$60 must be paid for with U.S. dollars. If you stay at a hotel in California, or go to a Red Wings hockey game in Detroit, you are "importing" (using) U.S. hotel or entertainment services which must be paid for with U.S. dollars. To get U.S. dollars, you must exchange some of your Canadian dollars. Similarly, a Canadian investor who wants to buy U.S. assets—bonds, stocks, businesses, or real estate—must pay in U.S. dollars, which she buys using Canadian money. When you convert Canadian dollars into U.S. dollars, you are supplying Canadian dollars and demanding U.S. dollars at the same time.

Law of Supply for Canadian Dollars

The law of supply states that as the price of a product/service rises, quantity supplied increases. The exchange rate is the price of the Canadian dollar. So the **law of supply for Canadian dollars** states that as the exchange rate rises, the quantity supplied of Canadian dollars increases.

Figure 6.4 illustrates the relation between the exchange rate and the quantity supplied of Canadian dollars in the foreign exchange market. For simplicity, the numbers are made up, but the pattern is representative of what the actual relationship looks like.

Figure 6.4	Demand for Canadian Dollars in Foreign Exchange Market
Price of 1 Canadian Dollar (US$ per C$)	**Quantity Supplied (billions of Canadian dollars per month)**
US$0.60	30
US$0.70	40
US$0.80	50
US$0.90	60
US$1.00	70
US$1.10	80

As you scan down the two columns, notice that as the price of the Canadian dollar—the exchange rate—rises (appreciates), the quantity supplied of Canadian dollars increases. The exchange rate and the quantity supplied move together because of the import effect.

Import Effect

When the exchange rate is low, for example, US$0.60 per Canadian dollar, the dress that costs $60 in the United States costs $100 in Canada. But if the exchange rate appreciates to US$1.00 per Canadian dollar, the same US$60 dress falls in price to only $60 Canadian. When the exchange rate rises (appreciates), U.S. products/services become less expensive for Canadians, so Canadians will buy more of them. But in order to buy more U.S. products/services with U.S. dollars, Canadians must increase the quantity supplied of Canadian dollars. A rise in the exchange rate increases the quantity supplied of Canadian dollars in the foreign exchange market.

The Prices of the Canadian Dollar: Foreign Exchange Rates

The exchange rate of the Canadian dollar is determined by the interaction of demand and supply in the foreign exchange market. The three columns in Figure 6.5 combine the previous numbers for the quantity demanded of Canadian dollars with the numbers for the quantity supplied.

Figure 6.5 Foreign Exchange Market for Canadian Dollars		
Price of 1 Canadian Dollar (US$ per C$)	**Quantity Supplied (billions of Canadian dollars per month)**	**Quantity Supplied (billions of Canadian dollars per month)**
US$0.60	90	30
US$0.70	80	40
US$0.80	70	50
US$0.90	60	60
US$1.00	50	70
US$1.10	40	80

Look down the numbers in columns one and two together of Figure 6.5. Note that as the price of the Canadian dollar (the exchange rate) rises, the quantity demanded decreases. This is the law of demand for Canadian dollars. As the Canadian dollar appreciates, Canadian exports become more expensive. Non-Canadians buy fewer Canadian exports, so the quantity demanded for Canadian dollars decreases.

Look down the numbers in columns one and three together. Note that as the price the of Canadian dollar rises, the quantity supplied increases. This is the law of supply of Canadian dollars. As the Canadian dollar appreciates, imports become cheaper. Canadians buy more imports, so the quantity supplied of Canadian dollars (which is also a demand for U.S. dollars) increases.

Market-Clearing Exchange Rate   The equilibrium, or market-clearing, exchange rate occurs where the quantity demanded and quantity supplied of Canadian dollars balance. In our example, that exchange rate is US$0.90. When a Canadian dollar sells for US$0.90, the quantity demanded of Canadian dollars (60 billion) equals the quantity supplied of Canadian dollars (60 billion). After the exchange of the quantity demanded and the quantity supplied of dollars, there are no leftover demands or supplies—no shortages or surpluses. The market has been cleared of all buyers and sellers.

The best way to understand why prices—in this case the price of the Canadian dollar—settles at the market-clearing exchange rate of US$0.90 is to look at what happens in the foreign exchange market when prices have not settled—as we did for interest rates in Chapter 5.

At the equilibrium, or market-clearing, exchange rate, quantity demanded and quantity supplied of Canadian dollars are equal. There is a balance of forces and no tendency for change.

Excess Demand for Canadian Dollars

What happens if the exchange rate is US$0.60 per Canadian dollar? Look at the first row of Figure 6.5. At an exchange rate of US$0.60, the quantity demanded of Canadian dollars is $90 billion. But the quantity of Canadian dollars supplied is only $30 billion. There is excess demand—the quantity demanded exceeds the quantity supplied of Canadian dollars. There is a shortage of Canadian dollars in the foreign exchange market.

As in any market with a shortage, competition between buyers (demanders) for the scarce Canadian dollars causes the price of a Canadian dollar—the exchange rate—to rise. As long as the exchange rate is below US$0.90, there will continue to be excess demand. Only when the exchange rate rises to US$0.90 is equilibrium established—the excess demand for Canadian dollars disappears and the market clears.

Excess Supply of Canadian Dollars

What happens if the exchange rate is US$1.10 per Canadian dollar? Look at the last row of Figure 6.5. At an exchange rate of US$1.10, the quantity demanded of Canadian dollars is $40 billion. But the quantity of Canadian dollars supplied is $80 billion. There is excess supply—the quantity supplied exceeds the quantity demanded of Canadian dollars. There is a surplus of Canadian dollars in the foreign exchange market.

As in any market with a surplus, competition between sellers (suppliers) to find customers for the Canadian dollars they can't get rid of causes the price of a Canadian dollar—the exchange rate—to fall. As long as the exchange rate is above US$0.90, there will continue to be excess supply. Only when the exchange rate falls to US$0.90 is equilibrium established—the excess supply of Canadian dollars disappears and the market clears.

A Multitude of Exchange Rates

In the foreign exchange market, the demand for one currency is the supply of another currency. In our example, the demand and supply for Canadian dollars is the same as the supply and demand for U.S. dollars. The demand for Canadian dollars comes from people supplying U.S. dollars. The supply of Canadian dollars comes from people demanding U.S. dollars. Because of these connections between markets for Canadian and U.S. dollars, and between markets for all other currencies, exchange rates can be expressed in many currencies.

Reciprocal Exchange Rates

So far, we have described the exchange rate—the price of a Canadian dollar—only in terms of the number of U.S. dollars it takes to buy a Canadian dollar. We can also describe a related exchange rate—the price of a U.S. dollar—in terms of the number of Canadian dollars it takes to buy a U.S. dollar. Related exchange rates are mirror images of each other.

To calculate a related exchange rate, take the reciprocal of the other exchange rate. If the price of a Canadian dollar is US$0.90, then the price of a U.S. dollar is $1 \div 0.90 = 1.11$. It takes C$1.11 to buy one U.S. dollar. This is simply another way of saying it takes US$0.90 to buy one Canadian dollar. The media in Canada usually report the exchange rate for the Canadian dollar in terms of the number of U.S. dollars it takes to buy a Canadian dollar (US$0.90). That is the exchange rate we will emphasize. But the media in the U.S. usually report the exchange rate for the U.S. dollar in terms of the number of Canadian dollars it takes to buy a U.S. dollar (C$1.11). Those two exchange rates are the same—they are mirror images of each other.

Because of these connections, when the Canadian dollar appreciates against the U.S. dollar (for example, the exchange rate of the Canadian dollar rises from US$0.60 to US$0.90), the mirror image is that the U.S. dollar depreciates against the Canadian dollar (the exchange rate of the U.S. dollar falls from C$1.67 to C$1.11).

Just as the demand for one currency is the supply of another currency, the appreciation of one currency is the depreciation of another.

When the Canadian dollar appreciates against the U.S. dollar, the U.S. dollar depreciates against the Canadian dollar, and vice versa.

Multiple Currencies and Exchange Rates The exchange rate of the Canadian dollar in terms of U.S. dollars is, by far, the exchange rate you will see and hear most about in the media. But there are exchange rates between the Canadian dollar and every other currency in the world, like the yen or euro. And for each of these other exchange rates, there is a reciprocal—the price of the U.S. dollar, yen, or euro in terms of Canadian dollars.

The exchange rates between every pair of currencies, and their reciprocals, are often presented in a table like the one in Figure 6.6. This table contains exchange rates between the Canadian dollar, U.S. dollar, euro, and Japanese yen. Reading down any column, you see the currency at the top expressed in terms of other currencies. The first column, for example, shows the exchange rates for the Canadian dollar in terms of U.S. dollars (US$0.9297), euros (0.6298 euros), and Japanese yen (84.67 yen).

Figure 6.6	Foreign Exchange Cross Rates*			
	Canadian dollar	U.S. dollar	Euro	Japanese yen
Canadian dollar	———	1.0756	1.5878	0.011810
U.S. dollar	0.9297	———	1.4762	0.010980
Euro	0.6298	0.6774	———	0.007438
Japanese yen	84.67	91.08	134.45	———

*As of 28 November 2009.

Reading across any row, you see the reciprocal exchange rates—the exchange rate for each currency in terms of the currency at the left. The first row, for example, shows the exchange rate for each currency in terms of Canadian dollars. One U.S. dollar costs 1.0756 Canadian dollars, 1 euro costs 1.5878 Canadian dollars, and 1 yen costs 0.11810 Canadian dollars.

The dashes (–) in the table are there because the exchange rate for any currency in terms of itself is always one. Because no one wants to buy a Canadian dollar with Canadian dollars on the foreign exchange market, or to buy a U.S. dollar with a U.S. dollar, these number ones are omitted to make the table easier to read.

What all of these connected currencies share is that their exchange rates are determined by the forces of demand and supply in the foreign exchange market. In the next section, we will examine what happens to exchange rates when demand and supply change.

Refresh

6.1

www.myeconlab.com

1. Explain why the title of the section, "How much does that dollar cost?" is not silly at all.

2. When the Canadian dollar was worth $0.63 U.S., what was the reciprocal exchange rate? If you wanted to buy a US$100 bag in the United States, how much would it cost you in Canadian dollars?

3. When you cross the border to shop in the United States, explain how you participate in the foreign exchange market.

6.2 Dancing With Dollars: Fluctuating Exchange Rates

Identify and explain five forces causing exchange rate fluctuations.

Canadian cross-border shoppers dance to the beat of exchange rate fluctuations—buying more when the rate rises and less when the exchange rate falls. Exchange rate fluctuations set the pace for the Canadian consumers' purchases of imports. But what causes the exchange rate—the price of the Canadian dollar—to rise or fall in the first place? Why does the value of the Canadian dollar dance around so much on the foreign exchange market?

Exchange rates are like fantastic, connected dance partners who move quickly and effortlessly together. When one dance partner glides forward, the other glides backward. When demand for Canadian dollars increases, the supply of Canadian dollars decreases. For all currencies, changes in demand also cause changes in supply. The demand for Canadian dollars is also the supply of U.S. dollars, and the supply of Canadian dollars is the demand for U.S. dollars.

FOR YOUR INFORMATION

These changes in demand and supply that cause the price of the Canadian dollar to fluctuate are similar to the microeconomic changes in demand and supply in Appendix D.2. For an increase in demand, market-clearing price rises. For a decrease in supply, market-clearing price rises.

Because of the connections between demand and supply for different currencies, an increase in demand for Canadian dollars is usually accompanied by a decrease in supply of Canadian dollars, so the exchange rate rises.

Forces Changing Demand and Supply   There are five economic forces that cause coordinated changes in demand and supply and explain why exchange rates fluctuate:

- interest rate differentials.
- inflation rate differentials.
- Canadian real GDP changes.
- changes in R.O.W. demands for Canadian exports and R.O.W. prices.
- changes in expectations.

We will continue to use the example of exchanges with the U.S. dollar, but these explanations apply to exchange rates between all currencies.

Interest Rate Differentials

In the interconnected foreign exchange market, money flows almost instantly to where the return on investment, or the interest rate, is highest. Whether investors are buying bonds, stocks, businesses, or real estate, they search out the highest return on their investment they can find. If they can earn five percent on an investment in Canada, they will not settle for a three percent return in the United States. The difference between the two interest rates is called the **interest rate differential**. When interest rates rise in Canada relative to other countries, there is a rise in the Canadian interest rate differential.

A rise in the Canadian interest rate differential makes Canadian assets more attractive to investors. The investors need Canadian dollars to buy those assets, thus increasing the demand for Canadian dollars in the foreign exchange market. Because Canadian investors, like other investors, will now invest more in Canada, they decrease their demand for U.S. dollars, which decreases the supply of Canadian dollars. The increase in demand and decrease in supply of Canadian dollars both work to raise the price of the Canadian dollar. The Canadian dollar appreciates relative to the U.S. dollar and other currencies. Thus a rise in the Canadian interest rate differential causes a rise in the exchange rate as well.

A fall in the Canadian interest rate differential works in the opposite direction. The demand for Canadian dollars decreases, the supply of Canadian dollars increases, and the value of the Canadian dollar falls. The Canadian dollar depreciates relative to the U.S. dollar and other currencies. Thus a fall in the Canadian interest rate differential causes a fall in the exchange rate as well.

interest rate differential: difference in interest rates between countries

Rise in Canadian interest rate differential causes Canadian dollar to appreciate (increases demand and decreases supply of Canadian dollars).

◀ Think of interest rate fluctuations like the distance that dance partners cover on the floor. Do they cover more distance (more fluctuations) when their steps are coordinated or uncoordinated?

Inflation Rate Differentials

Prices of products/services also affect the exchange rate through imports and exports. The **inflation rate differential** is the difference in inflation rates between countries. When the inflation rate rises in Canada relative to inflation rates in the rest of the world, there is a rise in the Canadian inflation rate differential.

When the inflation rate in Canada is higher than inflation rates in other countries, Canadian exports become more expensive for buyers in the rest of the world. The R.O.W. then buys fewer Canadian exports and therefore demands fewer Canadian dollars. As the prices of Canadian products/services rise, imports from the R.O.W. become relatively less expensive for Canadians. Canadians buy more of those cheaper imported products/services and need more U.S. dollars. The increased Canadian demand for U.S. dollars is equivalent to an increased supply of Canadian dollars. The decrease in demand and increase in supply both work to lower the price of the Canadian dollar. The Canadian dollar depreciates relative to the U.S. dollar and other currencies.

Rise in Canadian inflation rate differential causes Canadian dollar to depreciate (decreases demand and increases supply of Canadian dollars).

A rising inflation rate differential also reduces the attractiveness of Canadian assets. Inflation makes real returns (the real interest rate) on investments in Canada lower and therefore less attractive to investors in R.O.W. and in Canada. The demand for Canadian dollars decreases, the supply of Canadian dollars increases, and the price of the Canadian dollar falls.

Real interest rate = nominal interest rate − inflation rate

Thus a rise in the Canadian inflation rate differential—working through import and export prices and real interest rates—causes a fall in the exchange rate.

Canadian Real GDP Changes

Changes in Canadian real GDP affect imports and investors but with opposing effects on exchange rates.

Increased Canadian real GDP has two opposite effects on value of Canadian dollar: increased imports cause slight depreciation; increased investor confidence causes strong appreciation. Net effect is Canadian dollar appreciates.

Increasing Real GDP in Canada — Imports When real GDP increases in Canada, so does aggregate income. With increased real income, Canadian consumers and businesses buy more of most products/services, including more imports. In order to buy a greater quantity of imports, the consumers' demand for U.S. dollars increases. This also increases the supply of Canadian dollars in the foreign exchange market. But this increased supply of Canadian dollars is not accompanied by a decreased demand for Canadian dollars. It's like one of the dancers taking a solo. The effect is still to lower the price of the Canadian dollar, although not as forcefully as when there are coordinated changes in demand and supply.

Increasing Real GDP in Canada — Investors   On the other hand, an increase in real GDP in Canada is economic growth. Investors interpret economic growth as evidence that the Canadian economy will be strong, with profits to be made from Canadian assets. Investors react to increasing real GDP like they do to a rise in the Canadian interest rate differential. Canadian assets become more attractive to investors, which increases the demand for Canadian dollars in the foreign exchange market to buy those assets. The evidence of higher Canadian profits also means that Canadian investors are now more likely to invest in Canada, decreasing their demand for U.S. dollars. This decreases the supply of Canadian dollars in the foreign exchange market. These are two coordinated dance partners moving smoothly together. The increase in demand and decrease in supply of Canadian dollars both work to raise the price of the Canadian dollar — the exchange rate.

Of these two opposite effects — the import effect lowering the price of the Canadian dollar and the growth effect raising the price — the growth effect usually dominates. So when Canadian real GDP increases, the Canadian dollar appreciates relative to the U.S. dollar and other currencies. The next time the media report new data showing strong growth in Canadian real GDP, watch what happens to the exchange rate of the Canadian dollar. Chances are it will rise.

Decreasing Real GDP in Canada   These opposing forces work in reverse when there is a decrease in real GDP in Canada. Decreasing aggregate income decreases the amount of money Canadian consumers have, which in turn decreases their demand for imports. This in turn decreases their demand for U.S. dollars, which decreases the supply of Canadian dollars in foreign exchange markets. The effect is to slightly raise the price of the Canadian dollar.

But a decrease in Canadian real GDP is evidence of economic contraction. Investors worry about future profits, and Canadian assets become less attractive. Since foreign investors are not buying Canadian assets, the demand for Canadian dollars decreases. At the same time, Canadian investors now find U.S. assets relatively more attractive and so demand more U.S. dollars. This increases the supply of Canadian dollars. The decrease in demand and increase in supply of Canadian dollars both work to lower the price of the Canadian dollar.

The contraction effect usually dominates. So when Canadian real GDP decreases, the Canadian dollar depreciates relative to the U.S. dollar and other currencies. The exchange rate of the Canadian dollar falls.

> *If investors are confident that the Canadian economy will be strong, they will be more likely to buy Canadian assets, pushing up the dollar's value.*
>
> *— Bank of Canada*

Decreased Canadian real GDP has two opposite effects on value of Canadian dollar: decreased imports cause slight appreciation; reduced investor confidence causes strong depreciation. Net effect is Canadian dollar depreciates.

Increased R.O.W. demand for Canadian exports causes slight appreciation of Canadian dollar (increases demand for Canadian dollars).

Rising world prices for Canadian resource exports causes appreciation of Canadian dollar relative to non-resource producing currencies (increases demand for Canadian dollars).

R.O.W. and Canadian Exports

Two forces in the rest of the world have important effects on the value of the Canadian dollar:

- demand for Canadian exports
- world prices for Canadian resource exports.

R.O.W. Demand for Canadian Exports In order to buy a greater quantity of Canadian exports, the R.O.W. buyers need more Canadian dollars. Therefore, as the demand for Canadian exports increases, the demand for Canadian dollars increases. But this is not accompanied by a change in the supply of Canadian dollars. The effect, though, is still to raise the price of the Canadian dollar, although not as forcefully as when there are coordinated changes in demand and supply. The Canadian dollar appreciates slightly relative to the U.S. dollar and other currencies.

World Prices for Canadian Resource Exports Canada is a major exporter of oil, gold, potash, nickel, diamonds, and other resources. Prices for these resources are set in worldwide markets. There are no separate Canadian prices for these products. When the world price of oil, for example, rises, non-Canadians will require more Canadian dollars to buy the now more expensive Canadian oil. Rising world prices for Canadian resource exports increases the demand for Canadian dollars. But this does not trigger a coordinated change in the supply of Canadian dollars. The effect, though, is still to raise the price of the Canadian dollar.

I hope you are feeling at least a little confused by this explanation. After all, in the explanation of inflation rate differentials, when prices of Canadian exports rose, demand for exports *decreased*, decreasing demand for Canadian dollars. With relatively cheaper imports available, the supply of Canadian dollars increased, to demand more U.S. dollars to buy U.S. imports. The Canadian dollar depreciated.

The crucial difference between these explanations is that resource prices are set worldwide, not in Canada alone. The differential inflation rate explanation is based on price *differences*. Canadian exports have different prices from substitute products produced in other countries. When Canadian exports become more expensive, buyers switch to cheaper substitutes elsewhere. But a change in the worldwide price of oil applies to all countries. There is no cheaper oil somewhere else. So buyers, paying higher prices, demand more Canadian dollars to buy Canadian oil. The Canadian dollar appreciates relative to the U.S. dollar.

The same upward pressure on exchange rates applies to all countries that are major exporters of resources. When oil prices rise, the Canadian dollar usually appreciates relative to the U.S. dollar, but not against currencies of other oil-producing countries such as Mexico, Venezuela, or Russia, for example. Their currencies also appreciate relative to the U.S. dollar. So the Canadian dollar will tend to appreciate against the currencies of non-oil-producing countries, but not against currencies of other oil-producing counties.

Changing Expectations

The vast majority of the demand for and supply of foreign currencies, including the Canadian dollar, comes from speculators. The average size of a trade on the foreign exchange market is in millions of dollars. Speculators try to make profits by betting on which direction the value of a currency will go. They hope to buy Canadian dollars when the exchange rate is low (like US$0.63 per Canadian dollar) and sell when the exchange rate is high (like US$0.93). If a speculator bought US$1 million worth of Canadian dollars at a price of US$0.63, and sold at a price of US$0.93, she would make a profit of US$300 000! Many fortunes have been made, and lost, on the foreign exchange market.

Because speculators are the major players on the foreign exchange market, changing expectations by speculators about the future value of the Canadian dollar are the dominant force behind fluctuating exchange rates.

Currency speculators are the most important force determining fluctuations of foreign exchange rates.

Self-Fulfilling Expectations   When speculators expect a rise in the future price of the Canadian dollar, they buy Canadian dollars now in the hope of selling them after the value of the dollar rises. Buy low, sell high. The increase in speculative purchases of Canadian dollars increases the demand for Canadian dollars, which raises the price of the Canadian dollar. The Canadian dollar appreciates relative to the U.S. dollar and other currencies.

As long as enough speculators have the same expectation of a rise in the price of the Canadian dollar, the actions they take—buying/demanding Canadian dollars—immediately raise the price of the Canadian dollar and make the expectation come true.

The same logic applies when most speculators expect a fall in the future price of the Canadian dollar. They sell Canadian dollars now, increasing the supply and immediately lowering the price of the Canadian dollar. The Canadian dollar depreciates relative to the U.S. dollar and other currencies.

MAPS3

Reinforcing Other Exchange Rate Forces   Speculators also reinforce and quicken the effects of the other forces on the price of the Canadian dollar. Changes in interest rate differentials, inflation rate differentials, Canadian real GDP, R.O.W. demand for Canadian exports, and world-wide resource prices normally would take months or years to have an impact on exchange rates. But speculators have learned the same economics lessons about exchange rates that you are learning in this chapter. So, for example, as soon as there is an increase in the Canadian interest rate differential, speculators immediately increase their demand for Canadian dollars, confident that the relative rise in Canadian interest rates will eventually lead to a rise in the price of the Canadian dollar. If enough speculators act in the same way at the same time, their increased demand makes their expectation of a higher Canadian dollar come true instantly.

Speculators' expectations of changes in exchange rates can be self-fulfilling, and also reinforce effects of other forces on the price of the Canadian dollar.

Foreign Exchange Speculators

Think of Figure 6.7 as a checklist that speculators in the foreign exchange market use to judge the forces changing the price of the Canadian dollar.

It's a good study device for reviewing the forces that cause fluctuations in the exchange rate of the Canadian dollar on the foreign exchange market.

Figure 6.7   Forces Changing the Price of the Canadian Dollar

Canadian Dollar Appreciates (exchange rate rises)	Canadian Dollar Depreciates (exchange rate falls)
Canadian interest rates rise relative to other countries	Canadian interest rates fall relative to other countries
Canadian inflation rate falls relative to inflation rates in other countries	Canadian inflation rate rises relative to inflation rates in other countries
Real GDP in Canada increases	Real GDP in Canada decreases
R.O.W. demand for Canadian exports increases	R.O.W. demand for Canadian exports decreases
World prices for Canadian resource exports rise	World prices for Canadian resource exports fall
Expectation that Canadian dollar will appreciate	Expectation that Canadian dollar will depreciate

Refresh

6.2

www.myeconlab.com

1. In your own words, explain interest rate differentials and inflation rate differentials.

2. Explain why a demand for Canadian exports by buyers in the R.O.W. does not increase the supply of Canadian dollars in the foreign exchange market.

3. If you were a speculator on the foreign exchange market, what would be the key piece of information you would use in deciding whether to buy or sell Canadian dollars? Explain your choice.

6.3   How Exchange Rates Affect Your Life: International Transmission Mechanisms

Trace the impact of high and low exchange rates on real GDP and inflation.

international transmission mechanisms: how impacts of exchange rates are transmitted to real GDP and inflation

Once all of the forces in the foreign exchange market determine the price of the Canadian dollar, what impact do those fluctuating, dancing exchange rates have on the Canadian economy in general and on you in particular? Exchange rates, by changing the prices we pay for imports, affect all of us as consumers. An appreciating Canadian dollar encourages shopping choices like trips across the border or buying imports rather than Canadian products/services. But fluctuating exchange rates also affect key macroeconomic outcomes—real GDP, unemployment, and inflation.

The **international transmission mechanisms** describe how foreign exchange rates affect real GDP and the price level; that is, how the impacts of exchange rate fluctuations are transmitted to real GDP and inflation. The key to international transmission mechanisms is the impact of exchange rates on exports and imports.

Figure 6.8 illustrates the international transmission mechanisms from the demand and supply of Canadian dollars (at the top) to real GDP and inflation (at the bottom). Start at the top of Figure 6.8 and work down. The demand for Canadian dollars and the supply of Canadian dollars interact in the foreign exchange market to determine the exchange rate. That is the story we have been telling up until now.

Figure 6.8   Transmission Mechanisms from Foreign Exchange Rates to Real GDP and Inflation

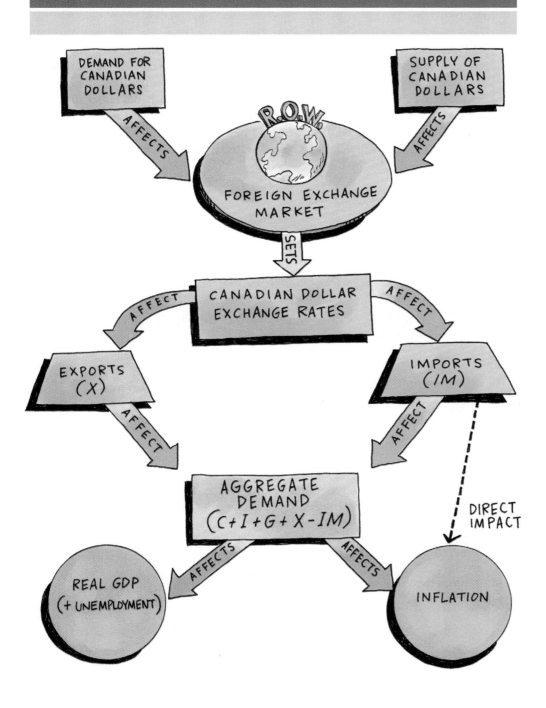

Impact on Net Exports

Now let's consider what happens to exports and imports in Figure 6.8 when the exchange rate of the Canadian dollar appreciates or depreciates.

Appreciating Canadian dollar is a negative aggregate demand shock—decreases net exports; decreasing aggregate demand, decreasing real GDP, increasing unemployment, decreasing inflation.

Appreciating Canadian Dollar Negative Aggregate Demand Shock A higher Canadian dollar makes Canadian exports more expensive for customers in the United States and the rest of the world. When non-Canadians must pay more of their own currencies for Canadian exports, they buy fewer exports. Exports (X) decrease, contributing to a decrease in Canadian aggregate demand. Remember your mantra: aggregate demand equals $C + I + G + X - IM$.

A higher Canadian dollar makes imports from the rest of the world cheaper for Canadian customers. Canadians buy more imports and fewer Canadian products/services. In calculating aggregate demand, imports (IM) are subtracted. So an increase in imports means a decrease in aggregate demand.

Decreases in exports and increases in imports both decrease aggregate demand. An appreciating, stronger Canadian dollar is a negative demand shock causing decreased real GDP, increased unemployment, and deflation (falling average prices). An appreciating Canadian dollar can push the economy into the contraction phase of the business cycle.

High Canadian Dollar Threatens *Twilight* Sequels and Economic Recovery

Breaking Dawn, the fourth film in the blockbuster *Twilight* series, will be filmed in the United States because of the rising value of the Canadian dollar. While earlier *Twilight* movies were filmed in British Columbia, the rising loonie has increased the cost of film services, an important Canadian export.

The softening sales of Canadian exports is of major concern to the Governor of the Bank of Canada, Mark Carney. The October 2009 Monetary Policy Summary notes that while "a recovery in economic activity is . . . under way in Canada, . . . heightened volatility and persistent strength in the Canadian dollar are working to slow growth and subdue inflation pressures."

The stronger Canadian dollar is making exports like film services more expensive, decreasing exports, aggregate demand, and GDP. At the same time, imports are less expensive, which is why the Bank of Canada refers to subdued inflation pressures.

Sources: Bank of Canada Monetary Policy Report Summary, October 2009; "Will Night Set on *Twilight's* B.C. Film Sets?" www.bclocalnews.com/entertainment/70572072.html. Accessed November 20, 2009.

Depreciating Canadian Dollar Positive Aggregate Demand Shock

A lower Canadian dollar makes Canadian exports cheaper for customers in the United States and the rest of the world. When Canadian exports become less expensive, non-Canadians buy more of them. Exports (X) increase, contributing to an increase in aggregate demand. Remember your mantra: aggregate demand equals $C + I + G + X - IM$.

A lower Canadian dollar makes imports from the rest of the world more expensive for Canadian customers. Canadians buy fewer imports and more Canadian products/services. In calculating aggregate demand, imports (IM) are subtracted. So a decrease in imports means an increase in aggregate demand.

Increases in exports and decreases in imports both increase aggregate demand. As explained in Chapter 4, a positive demand shock causes increased real GDP, decreased unemployment, and inflation (rising average prices). A rise in real GDP due to an increase in net exports is sometimes called an *export-led boom*. A depreciating Canadian dollar can push the economy into the expansion phase of the business cycle.

Depreciating Canadian dollar is a positive aggregate demand shock—increases net exports; increasing aggregate demand, increasing real GDP, decreasing unemployment, increasing inflation.

Impact on Inflation

When Canadian exports to the rest of the world rise or fall in price, measured in other currencies, that affects inflation rates in other countries. There is no impact on the Canadian inflation rate.

But when *imports* to Canada fall or rise in price, measured in Canadian dollars, there is a direct impact on the Canadian inflation rate. That impact is represented at the bottom right of Figure 6.8 by the dashed line from imports to inflation.

Appreciating Canadian Dollar Is Deflationary When the exchange rate of the Canadian dollar rises, exports decrease and imports—which fall in price for Canadians—increase. The falling price of imports directly decreases the Canadian inflation rate. A decrease in the inflation rate is deflationary.

This direct decrease in the inflation rate reinforces the indirect impact of decreased net exports on inflation. Decreasing net exports are a negative demand shock, decreasing aggregate demand, decreasing real GDP, increasing unemployment, and decreasing inflation.

Depreciating Canadian Dollar Is Inflationary When the exchange rate of the Canadian dollar falls, exports increase and imports—which rise in price for Canadians—decrease. The inflation rate measures the increase in the average level of all prices, including the prices of imports. This rising price of imports directly increases the Canadian inflation rate.

This direct increase in the inflation rate reinforces the indirect impact of increased net exports on inflation. Increasing net exports are a positive demand shock, increasing aggregate demand, increasing real GDP, decreasing unemployment and increasing inflation.

Appreciating Canadian dollar causes deflation; depreciating Canadian dollar causes inflation.

Exchange Rates and You

You often hear arguments in the media about a "strong" or "weak" Canadian dollar. Since most people think of "strong" as "good" and "weak" as "bad," they conclude that a "strong" Canadian dollar—a higher exchange rate in terms of U.S. dollars—is desirable for Canadians. You now know the truth is not so simple. There are advantages and disadvantages to both a higher and lower exchange rate.

When the Canadian dollar strengthens, or appreciates in value, imports are less expensive and cross-border shopping is better. But an appreciating Canadian dollar acts as a negative demand shock, hurting exporters hardest, decreasing real GDP, increasing unemployment, and decreasing inflation.

When the Canadian dollar weakens, or depreciates in value, imports are more expensive and cross-border shopping is worse for Canadians heading south. But a depreciating Canadian dollar acts as a positive demand shock, helping exporters, increasing real GDP, decreasing unemployment and increasing inflation.

There are advantages and disadvantages to both higher and lower exchange rates.

Refresh 6.3

1. In your own words, explain the connection between exchange rates and aggregate demand.

2. When the media refer to a "weak Canadian dollar," explain what they are telling us.

3. Do you support a higher or lower Canadian dollar measured against the U.S. dollar? Explain your choice.

www.myeconlab.com

6.4 Overvalued Compared to What? Purchasing Power Parity and Rate of Return Parity Anchors

Describe how purchasing power parity and rate of return parity provide standards for exchange rates.

There are advantages and disadvantages to the economy from the ups and downs of the Canadian dollar. But there is no single rate that economists consider the "best" value for the Canadian dollar for the performance of the macro economy.

Still, you will often hear economists in the media describe the Canadian dollar, or another country's currency, as "overvalued" or "undervalued." What do these words mean? These descriptions must be based on a point of reference or some standard. They imply that there is some "value" that is just right.

The two standards that economists and speculators use to predict where exchange rates will eventually settle are purchasing power parity and rate of return parity.

Both of these standards depend on the law of one price.

Law of One Price

Once again, speculators play a key role in setting these standards. By buying low and selling high, speculators enforce the **law of one price**, which states that any time there is a difference in the price of a product/service in two markets, the actions of profit-seekers eliminate that difference and establish a single price.

Imagine this scenario: One carat diamonds are selling for US$1000 in South Africa but US$1500 in Canada. If you buy diamonds in South Africa, and sell them in Canada, you make US$500 per diamond. Buy low in South Africa—sell high in Canada. But as more people pursue these profits, demand for diamonds in South Africa increases, driving their price up. The additional supply of diamonds in Canada drives their price down. That US$500 price difference quickly disappears. As long as there is a difference in price, the profit-driven forces of demand and supply will lead to a single price across both markets. The law of one price applies to all markets, including the foreign exchange market.

law of one price: differences in prices of same product/service across markets will be eliminated by actions of profit-seekers

How Much for a Big Mac? Purchasing Power Parity

While the law of one price causes prices to adjust between markets, the principle of purchasing power parity causes exchange rates to adjust between countries. Parity means equality. According to **purchasing power parity (PPP)**, exchange rates adjust so that money has equal real purchasing power in any country.

Let's look at examples where purchasing power parity holds and where it does not.

purchasing power parity (PPP): exchange rates adjust so that money has equal real purchasing power in any country

When Purchasing Power Parity Holds   There are often multiple prices on book covers, such as US$8.00 in the United States, C$10.00 in Canada. The very same book is selling for two different prices. Or is it?

Suppose the price of the Canadian dollar—the exchange rate—in terms of U.S. dollars is US$0.80. If you buy the book in Canada, you pay C$10.00. If instead you cross the border to buy the book in the United States, you have to exchange your Canadian dollars for U.S. dollars. You get US$0.80 for each loonie. C$10.00 gets you US$8.00 (10.00 × 0.80 = 8.00). Your C$10.00 buys exactly the same book in Canada as it does converted into U.S. dollars in the United States. In other words, your Canadian dollars have the same real purchasing power in both countries. Ten dollars Canadian, at this exchange rate, buys the same book in Canada or in the United States.

The reciprocal exchange rate—the price of a U.S. dollar in terms of Canadian dollars—is 1 ÷ 0.80 or C$1.25.

The same parity applies if we start with an American spending US$8.00 for the book. Instead of buying in the United States, he exchanges his U.S. dollars for Canadian dollars, and gets C$10.00 (8.00 × 1.25 = 10.00). His US$8.00 has the same real purchasing power in both countries.

In this example, the exchange rate of C$1.00 = US$0.80 (and the reciprocal rate of US$1.00 = C$1.25) is the purchasing power parity (*PPP*) exchange rate. The *PPP* exchange rate equalizes the purchasing power of money on both sides of the border.

When Purchasing Power Parity Does Not Hold

To see why purchasing power parity provides an anchor for fluctuating exchange rates, look at what happens to book purchases when there are different exchange rates.

Suppose the exchange rate was C$1.00 = US$1.00. One Canadian dollar exchanges for one U.S. dollar. If you buy the book in Canada, you pay C$10.00. If, instead, you cross the border to buy the book in the United States, you exchange your 10 Canadian dollars (the cost of the book in Canada) for 10 U.S. dollars. You buy the book for US$8.00, and have US$2.00 left over to spend on anything else. Your purchasing power is greater in the United States.

These book buyers discovered that the purchasing power of their currency changed when they crossed borders.

The reciprocal exchange rate in this example is one U.S. dollar for one Canadian dollar. Our American can buy the book for US$8.00 in the United States. If, instead, he crossed the border to buy it in Canada, he exchanges his 8 U.S. dollars for 8 Canadian dollars. He doesn't have enough money to buy the book in Canada. His purchasing power is also greater in the United States.

Can you figure out what will happen to demand and supply for the Canadian dollar? Canadians, now wanting to shop in the United States, will increase the supply of Canadian dollars in order to demand more U.S. dollars in the foreign exchange market. Americans will decrease their demand for Canadian dollars. The combined increase in supply and decrease in demand for Canadian dollars forces the price of the Canadian dollar (the exchange rate) down. As long as there is a difference in the purchasing power of money across the border, the exchange rate will continue to fall. The pressure for a falling price of the Canadian dollar ends only when the Canadian dollar depreciates and again exchanges in this example for US$0.80.

The exchange rate of US$1.00 for a Canadian dollar is higher than the purchasing power parity exchange rate of US$0.80. At this exchange rate, the Canadian dollar is *overvalued* relative to the *PPP* rate with the U.S. dollar.

The same story works in reverse if the exchange rate was C$1.00 = US$0.50 (with the reciprocal rate of US$1.00 = C$2.00). If you were to buy the book in the U.S., your C$10 would exchange for US$5. You could not afford to buy the book in the U.S. Your purchasing power is greater in Canada. An American shopper would have the same experience. His purchasing power would be greater in Canada. As Canadians and Americans decreased the supply and increased the demand for Canadian dollars, the Canadian dollar would appreciate. The exchange rate of US$0.50 for a Canadian dollar is lower than the purchasing power parity exchange rate of US$0.80. At the exchange rate of US$0.50, the Canadian dollar is *undervalued* relative to the *PPP* rate with the U.S. dollar.

The purchasing power parity exchange rate serves as an anchor for fluctuations of the exchange rate above or below it. When the actual exchange rate is different from the *PPP* rate, profit-seeking forces are set in motion, which push the actual exchange rate back towards the *PPP* rate.

Profit-seeking forces push the actual exchange rate back towards the PPP rate.

The Hamburger Standard To calculate the purchasing power parity exchange rate between currencies, you must compare more than the price of a single book. Official calculations use a basket of products/services, much like the basket used to calculate the consumer price index. The problem is that the basket of products/services consumed by a typical household differs among counties. The basket in Japan contain much more sushi and the basket in Canada may contain maple syrup! To get around these complications, economists use other methods to calculate *PPP*.

The Economist magazine publishes a simple and fun calculation of *PPP* called the *Big Mac Index. The Economist's* "basket" is simply a McDonald's Big Mac, which has the advantage of being produced and sold in about 120 countries. Using the United States as the country of comparison, the Big Mac *PPP* is the exchange rate that makes hamburgers cost the same in the United States and other countries. For example, suppose a Big Mac costs US$4.00 in the United States, and 2 pounds in Britain. This makes the Big Mac *PPP* rate US$2.00 per British pound. The Big Mac *PPP* rate compares the number of U.S. dollars it takes to buy a Big Mac in the United States with the cost of a Big Mac in other countries.

Comparing actual exchange rates with the Big Mac *PPP* rate indicates whether a currency is undervalued or overvalued relative to the Big Mac *PPP* rate in U.S. dollars. Figure 6.9 contains examples from *The Economist's* calculations in February 2009, when a Big Mac costs US$3.54 in the United States. The Big Mac *PPP* and actual exchange rates (columns three and four) are expressed as the price of each country's currency in terms of U.S. dollars.

The Big Mac Purchasing Power Parity Rate is the exchange rate that equalizes the cost of hamburgers in the U.S. and other countries.

Figure 6.9	Big Mac Purchasing Power Parity Index			
Country	**Price Big Mac in Local Currency**	**Big Mac PPP Rate (US$/local currency)**	**Actual Exchange Rate (US$/local currency)**	**Under (−) or Over (+) Valuation Local Currency against US$**
Canada	C$4.16	0.85 US$/C$	0.81 US$/C$	−5 %
Japan	290 yen	0.012 US$/yen	0.011 US$/yen	−9 %
Euro area	3.42 euros	1.04 US$/euro	1.28 US$/euro	+24 %
Britain	2.29 pounds	1.54 US$/pound	1.45 US$/pound	−7 %
Brazil	8.02 real	0.44 US$/real	0.43 US$/real	−2 %
China	12.5 yuan	0.28 US$/yuan	0.15 US$/yuan	−48 %

Source: "Big Mac Index," *The Economist*, February 4, 2009 and author's calculations.

Look at the row for Canada. If there were a Big Mac *PPP*, the exchange rate of the Canadian dollar in terms of U.S. dollars would be 0.85. The actual exchange rate was 0.81, 4 cents less. The Canadian dollar was undervalued by 5 percent ($0.04 \div 0.85 = 0.05 = 5\%$) relative to the *PPP* rate for the U.S. dollar.

Notice that actual exchange rates are pretty close to Big Mac *PPP* rates for Canada, Japan, Britain, and Brazil. China's actual exchange rate is farthest from Big Mac *PPP* for reasons we will discuss shortly.

Limitations of Purchasing Power Parity Most descriptions of a currency as overvalued or undervalued are referring to purchasing power parity. *PPP* is an estimate of where we would expect exchange rates to settle eventually.

There are limitations to *PPP* as the anchor point for exchange rates. The *PPP* story assumes all products/services are traded easily and without cost across borders. In reality, there are many costs, including transportation and storage. As well, how many consumers cross borders (to the United States, let alone to Japan or China!) to get haircuts or buy books? Most importantly, the *PPP* story assumes demand and supply of dollars on the foreign exchange market are only to buy exports or imports. You now know the vast majority of demand and supply of currencies is for speculation.

Despite these limitations, purchasing power parity is the best available standard for judging where exchange rates are most likely to settle.

The purchasing power parity exchange rate, however, is not necessarily the "best" rate for the Canadian macroeconomic outcomes of full employment, stable prices, and steady economic growth. Because of the tradeoffs of a lower or higher exchange rate, there is no single "best" value for the Canadian dollar. Exchange rates are not like the unemployment rate, where there is one rate—the natural rate of unemployment—that economists consider to be the "best" rate for the performance of the macro economy.

Money Flows Where Interest Rates are Highest: Rate of Return Parity

The law of one price states that price differences across markets will be eliminated by the actions of profit-seekers, buying low and selling high. In the interconnected foreign exchange market, money flows almost instantly to the highest rate of return on investments—no matter what country it's in.

So why are there differences in rates of return across countries? In 2009, for example, the annual rate of return on bonds in Canada was three percent, while the annual rate of return on bonds of comparable risk in Japan was seven percent. Why weren't these difference eliminated by the law of one price? Why didn't investment dollars flow out of Canada (decreasing demand for Canadian bonds, lowering bond prices) and into Japan (increasing demand for Japanese bonds, raising bond prices), raising Canadian interest rates and lowering Japanese interest rates until they were equal?

The answer is *exchange rate expectations*. For Canadian investors to earn seven percent in Japan, they must first convert Canadian dollars to Japanese yen to buy the Japanese bond. When they sell the Japanese bond at the end of the year, they must then convert the yen back into Canadian dollars. The difference between the three percent return in Canada and the seven percent return in Japan reflects the expected depreciation of the yen against the Canadian dollar (four percent). If these expectations come true, the Canadian investor earns seven percent measured in yen, but then loses four percent when converting yen back into dollars. The net rate of return is three percent, the same rate available in Canada.

Rates of return on investments are equal across countries when expected depreciation/appreciation of exchange rates are accounted for. This is called **rate of return parity** or interest rate parity.

So the law of one price does apply to rates of return across countries. Instead of prices adjusting, exchange rates adjust, equalizing net rates of return.

Would You Like Your Exchange Rate Floating or Fixed?

The exchange rate for the Canadian dollar is called a **floating exchange rate**, determined by demand and supply in the foreign exchange market. Most countries today have floating exchange rates that adjust, or float, with changes in demand or supply.

This was not always so. From the end of World War II to the early 1970s, most countries, including Canada, had **fixed exchange rates**, determined by governments or central banks.

Of the countries listed in Figure 6.9, China is the only one that currently fixes its exchange rate. This fixed rate is the reason why there is a such a large difference between the Big Mac *PPP* rate and the actual exchange rate for China. According to Figure 6.9, the Chinese yuan is significantly *undervalued* relative to the U.S. dollar. This lower exchange rate is a directed policy of the Chinese government. As we have seen, lower or depreciating exchange rates make a country's exports cheaper for customers in the rest of the world. This purposefully undervalued yuan is one reason behind China's strong sales of exports.

There are complex economic and political considerations, beyond the scope of this book, that affect exchange rates, whether they are floating or fixed. But exchange rates are important because of their effect on the key macroeconomic outcomes of real GDP, unemployment, and inflation.

floating exchange rate: determined by demand and supply in foreign exchange market

fixed exchange rate: determined by government or central bank

Refresh 6.4

1. In your own words, explain purchasing power parity and rate of return parity.

2. Explain what this statement might mean: "The Canadian dollar is overvalued compared to the U.S. dollar."

3. Explain the mistake you might make investing in another country if you did not understand the principle of rate of return parity.

www.myeconlab.com

Trading Dollars for Dollars?

Exchange Rates with the Rest of the World

CHAPTER SUMMARY

**6.1 SHUFFLING OFF TO BUFFALO:
DEMAND AND SUPPLY OF CANADIAN DOLLARS**

The demand for products/services and assets from other countries, which must be paid for in local currencies, are behind demand and supply on the foreign exchange market, determining exchange rates.

- **Exchange rate**—price at which one currency exchanges for another currency.
  - Exchange rate is price of 1 Canadian dollar. Exchange rate of C$1.00 = US$0.95 means it takes 95 cents U.S. to buy 1 Canadian dollar.
- **Foreign exchange market**—worldwide market where all countries' currencies are bought and sold in exchange for each other.
- Exchange rates fluctuate (go up and down) constantly.
  - **Currency depreciation**—
    fall in exchange rate of one currency for another.
  - **Currency appreciation**—
    rise in exchange rate of one currency for another.
  - Exchange rates determined by demand and supply in foreign exchange market.
- Non-Canadians' demand for Canadian dollars is demand for Canadian exports, assets, and for speculating on the future value of the Canadian dollar.
- **Law of demand for Canadian dollars**—if exchange rate rises, quantity demanded of Canadian dollars decreases.
  - Higher value of Canadian dollar makes Canadian exports and assets more expensive for non-Canadians, who buy less of them. With fewer sales to non-Canadians, quantity demanded of Canadian dollars decreases.

- Canadians' supply of Canadian dollars is demand for foreign currency to buy imports and assets from rest of the world, and for speculating on future value of Canadian dollar.
- The demand for one currency is the supply of another currency.
- **Law of supply for Canadian dollars**—if exchange rate rises, quantity supplied of Canadian dollars increases.
  - Higher value of Canadian dollar makes R.O.W. imports and assets less expensive for Canadians, who buy more of them. To buy more R.O.W. products/services, Canadians buy more foreign currency, so quantity supplied of Canadian dollars increases.
- At equilibrium, or market-clearing, exchange rate, quantity demanded and quantity supplied of Canadian dollars are equal. Balance of forces, no tendency for change.
  - With excess demand (shortages) for Canadian dollars, competition among buyers causes exchange rate to rise.
  - With excess supply (surpluses) of Canadian dollars, competition among sellers causes exchange rate to fall.
- When Americans demand Canadian dollars, they supply U.S. dollars in exchange. When Canadians demand U.S. dollars, they supply Canadian dollars in exchange.
  - To find reciprocal exchange rate, divide number 1 by other exchange rate.
    If C$1.00 = US$0.90, reciprocal exchange rate is
    US$1.00 = 1 ÷ 0.90 = C$1.11.
  - When Canadian dollar appreciates against U.S. dollar, U.S. dollar depreciates against Canadian dollar, and vice versa.

6.2 DANCING WITH DOLLARS: FLUCTUATING EXCHANGE RATES

Exchange rate fluctuations are caused by changes in interest rate differentials, inflation rate differentials, Canadian real GDP, R.O.W. demand for Canadian exports and world prices, and expectations by speculators.

- **Interest rate differential**—difference in interest rates between countries.
  - Rise in Canadian interest rate differential causes Canadian dollar to appreciate (increases demand and decreases supply of Canadian dollars).
- **Inflation rate differential**—difference in inflation rates between countries.
  - Rise in Canadian inflation rate differential causes Canadian dollar to depreciate (decreases demand and increases supply of Canadian dollars).
- Increased Canadian real GDP has two opposite effects on value of Canadian dollar:
  - Increased imports cause slight depreciation.
  - Increased investor confidence causes strong appreciation.
  - Net effect is Canadian dollar appreciates.
- Increased R.O.W. demand for Canadian exports causes slight appreciation of Canadian dollar (increases demand for Canadian dollars).
- Rising world prices for Canadian resource exports causes appreciation of Canadian dollar relative to currencies of non-resource-producing countries (increases demand for Canadian dollars).

- Currency speculators are the most important force determining fluctuations of foreign exchange rates.
  - Expectations of rise in future price of Canadian dollar causes self-fulfilling appreciation of Canadian dollar (increases demand for Canadian dollars).
  - Speculators reinforce and quicken effects of other forces on the price of the Canadian dollar.
- Figure 6.7, Forces Changing Price of Canadian Dollar, is good review aid.

6.3 HOW EXCHANGE RATES AFFECT YOUR LIFE: INTERNATIONAL TRANSMISSION MECHANISMS

Exchange rates affect real GPD and inflation through international transmission mechanisms affecting net exports, aggregate demand and the price level.

- **International transmission mechanisms**— how impacts of exchange rates are transmitted to real GDP and inflation.
- Appreciating Canadian dollar is a negative aggregate demand shock.
  - Decreases net exports (decreases exports and increases imports); decreasing aggregate demand, decreasing real GDP, increasing unemployment.
  - Decreases inflation.
- Depreciating Canadian dollar is a positive aggregate demand shock.
  - Increases net exports (increases exports and decreases imports); increasing aggregate demand, increasing real GDP, decreasing unemployment.
  - Increases inflation.
- Changing exchange rate for Canadian dollar affects price of imports measured in Canadian dollars and inflation rate.
  - Appreciating Canadian dollar causes deflation.
  - Depreciating Canadian dollar causes inflation.
- Advantages and disadvantages to both higher, lower, exchange rates.
  - Appreciating Canadian dollar makes imports less expensive, but is negative demand shock, hurting exporters, decreasing real GDP, increasing unemployment, and decreasing inflation.
  - Depreciating Canadian dollar makes imports more expensive, but is positive demand shock, helping exporters, increasing real GDP, decreasing unemployment, and increasing inflation.

6.4 OVERVALUED COMPARED TO WHAT? PURCHASING POWER PARITY AND RATE OF RETURN ANCHORS

The law of one price, purchasing power parity, and rate of return parity are the best available standards for predicting where exchange rates eventually settle, despite their limitations.

- All standards for predicting where exchange rates settle are based on **law of one price**—differences in prices of same product/service across markets will be eliminated by actions of profit-seekers.

- **Purchasing power parity (PPP)**—exchange rates adjust so that money has equal real purchasing power in any country.
  - When *PPP* holds, C$10.00 buys exactly same products in Canada—and when converted into U.S. dollars at *PPP* exchange rate—in U.S.
  - When *PPP* does not hold, profit-seeking forces push actual exchange rate back towards *PPP* rate.
  - *PPP* does not account for trading limitations and major role of speculators in influencing exchange rates.
- **Rate of return parity (interest rate parity)**—rates of return on investments are equal across countries, accounting for expected depreciation/appreciation of exchange rates.
  - Because of law of one price, differences across countries in rates of return due to exchange rate expectations.
  - For example: rate of return in Japan = rate of return in Canada − expected depreciation of yen against the Canadian dollar.
- Different systems for determining exchange rates.
  - **Floating exchange rate**—determined by demand and supply in foreign exchange market.
  - **Fixed exchange rate**—determined by government or central bank.

TRUE/FALSE

Circle the correct answer.

You are sitting in the chalet of a ski resort reading this chapter when a famous U.S. Olympic snowboarder sits down beside you and says:

Sweet textbook, dude. I'm reading the same one. I'm studying the exchange rates chapter while training for the upcoming Olympic Games. But, when I was practising a 360-degree backflip on the half-pipe, my textbook fell out of my backpack and the answers got wet and are unreadable. I'd be stoked if you told me if the answers are true or false.

Use this scenario to answer questions 1–15.

6.1 DEMAND AND SUPPLY OF CANADIAN DOLLARS

1. When U.S. Olympians pay for Canadian exports using U.S. dollars, they supply U.S. dollars and demand Canadian dollars.   **True**   **False**

2. The Canadian exchange rate expressed in U.S. dollars is the price at which Canadian dollars exchange for U.S. dollars.   **True**   **False**

3. An exchange rate of US$1.00 = C$0.95 means it takes 95 cents U.S. to buy 1 Canadian dollar.

True **False**

4. The market-clearing exchange rate is always C$1.00 = US$1.00.

True **False**

5. The U.S. dollar buys more products/services in Canada if the value of the Canadian dollar increases from 95 cents U.S. to one U.S. dollar.

True **False**

6. On January 5, 2010, US$1.00 = C$1.04, 1.00 euro = C$1.50. If individuals from these countries were to convert their currency for Canadian dollars that day, the individual selling U.S. dollars would get the most Canadian dollars.

True **False**

6.2 FLUCTUATING EXCHANGE RATES

7. The Canadian dollar depreciates against the U.S. dollar if Canada's inflation rate is rising more than the inflation rate in the United States.

True **False**

8. The Canadian dollar depreciates against the U.S. dollar if Canada's interest rate is rising more than the interest rate in the United States.

True **False**

9. The Canadian dollar appreciates against the U.S. dollar if world prices for Canadian resource exports increase and if R.O.W. demand for Canadian products/services increases.

True **False**

6.3 INTERNATIONAL TRANSMISSION MECHANISMS

10. A strong Canadian dollar is good for all Canadians.

True **False**

11. According to the article in Economics Out There (page 228), a rising Canadian dollar is more terrifying to U.S. film producers than dealing with a cast of blood-thirsty vampires because a rising Canadian dollar increases the cost of Canadian film services.

True **False**

12. A depreciating Canadian dollar increases inflation in Canada.

True **False**

6.4 PURCHASING POWER PARTIY AND RATE OF RETURN PARITY

13. When purchasing power parity holds, US$5.00 buys different quantities of the same products in the United States and Canada.

True **False**

14. If the purchasing power parity exchange rate is C$1.00 = US$0.95, then Americans could pay for a $100 hotel room in Québec City with either 95 U.S. dollars or 100 Canadian dollars.

True   False

15. Rate of return parity holds when the rates of return on Canadian and U.S. investments are equal across the two countries, accounting for expected changes in exchange rates.

True   False

MULTIPLE CHOICE

Circle the correct answer.

6.1 DEMAND AND SUPPLY OF CANADIAN DOLLARS

1. An exchange rate of C$1.00 = US$0.90 means
  A) 1 Canadian dollar is worth 90 cents U.S.
  B) 1 U.S. dollar is worth 111 cents Canadian.
  C) the price of one Canadian dollar is 90 cents U.S.
  D) all of the above.

2. If C$1.00 = US$0.95, the price of one U.S. dollar is
  A) C$0.95.
  B) C$1.05.
  C) US$0.95.
  D) US$1.05.

3. If the exchange rate for the Canadian dollar falls, the quantity
  A) demanded of Canadian dollars decreases.
  B) demanded of Canadian dollars increases.
  C) supplied of Canadian dollars increases.
  D) supplied of U.S. dollars decreases.

4. If more Americans visit Canada and demand Canadian dollars,
  A) the Canadian exchange rate rises.
  B) the Canadian dollar appreciates against the U.S. dollar.
  C) the U.S. dollar depreciates against the Canadian dollar.
  D) all of the above.

5. The Canadian dollar appreciated relative to the U.S. dollar between May 2009 and October 2009. The value of the Canadian dollar remained constant relative to the European euro over this period. This implies that the U.S. dollar
  A) remained constant relative to the Canadian dollar.
  B) appreciated relative to the Canadian dollar.
  C) appreciated relative to the European euro.
  D) depreciated relative to the European euro.

6. The Canadian dollar depreciates if
  A) the Canadian interest rate differential increases.
  B) the Canadian inflation rate differential increases.
  C) world prices for Canadian resource exports increase.
  D) speculators expect a rise in the future price of the Canadian dollar.

7. The impact of increased Canadian real GDP on the Canadian dollar exchange rate is to
  A) increase imports, which causes slight depreciation.
  B) increase investor confidence, which causes strong appreciation.
  C) cause a net appreciation the Canadian dollar.
  D) all of the above.

8. If the Bank of Canada informs speculators that it will not let the value of the Canadian dollar rise any more, then
  A) speculators will react by buying more Canadian dollars.
  B) the demand for Canadian dollars decreases.
  C) the demand for Canadian dollars increases.
  D) the Canadian exchange rate appreciates.

6.3 INTERNATIONAL TRANSMISSION MECHANISMS

9. Changes in exchange rates affect real GDP and inflation through
  A) car transmission mechanisms.
  B) international transmission mechanisms.
  C) purchasing power parity.
  D) interest rate parity.

10. A falling exchange rate for the Canadian dollar
  A) decreases inflation in Canada.
  B) decreases exports.
  C) increases real GDP in Canada.
  D) all of the above.

6.4 PURCHASING POWER PARITY AND RATE OF RETURN PARITY

11. Suppose C$1.00 = US$1.00 and C$1.00 = 0.67 euro. Purchasing power parity holds when the same McDonald's burger, fries, and drink combo sells for
  A) C$10, US$10 and 10 euros.
  B) C$10, US$10 and 6.70 euros.
  C) C$10, US$10 and 15 euros.
  D) C$10, US$20 and 10 euros.

12. Purchasing power parity
    A) is the best available standard for judging exchange rates.
    B) does not account for trading limitations.
    C) does not account for the role of speculators in influencing exchange rates.
    D) all of the above.

13. A floating exchange rate
    A) means the exchange rate will never fall down.
    B) is determined by demand and supply in the foreign exchange market.
    C) was abandoned by most countries by the early 1970s.
    D) all of the above.

14. Due to the law of one price, if the rate of return in Canada is higher than the rate of return in India, then the difference must be due to
    A) interest rates.
    B) interest rate expectations.
    C) exchange rates.
    D) exchange rate expectations.

15. In 2009, the rate of return on bonds in Canada was three percent, while the rate of return on bonds of comparable risk in Japan was seven percent. If the Japanese investor buys a Canadian bond, then she expects the Japanese yen to
    A) appreciate against the Canadian dollar by four percent.
    B) depreciate against the Canadian dollar by four percent.
    C) appreciate against the Canadian dollar by three percent.
    D) depreciate against the Canadian dollar by three percent.

SHORT ANSWER

Write a short answer to each question. Your answer may be in point form.

1. Suppose you are making travel plans for spring break on expedia.ca. You find an all-inclusive vacation package in Cancun (Mexico) for a reasonable price (expressed in Canadian dollars), so you Facebook your friends and tell them about it. Ten days later, when your friends finally agree, the price (expressed in Canadian dollars) jumps by over $100 dollars. You complain to the Mexican company selling the vacation package, but they tell you that their price (in Mexican pesos) hasn't changed. Describe what may have happened.

2. Consider the foreign exchange market for Canadian dollars shown in Figure 6.5.
    A) What is the equilibrium exchange rate?
    B) What is the equilibrium exchange rate expressed in terms of one U.S. dollar?
    C) If the exchange rate is $1.00CA = $1.00US, describe how the exchange rate moves to the market-clearing exchange rate.

3. In 1991, the Canadian dollar was worth 87 cents U.S. By January 2002, the Canadian dollar was worth only 62 cents U.S. The Canadian dollar depreciated because the U.S. economy was growing faster than Canada's during that period and because of a lack of confidence by investors that the Canadian dollar would appreciate. Explain how these factors could play a role in causing the Canadian dollar to depreciate.

4. The Canadian dollar rose between 2002 and 2007 from 62 cents U.S. to above US$1.00.

   A) Was it better to cross the Canada–U.S. border and shop in the U.S. in 2002 or 2007?

   B) The main forces behind the appreciation of the Canadian dollar were rising R.O.W. demand for Canadian exports and rising world prices for Canadian resource exports. Explain how these factors cause the Canadian dollar to appreciate.

   C) For the rest of the world, was it better to buy Canadian dollars in 2002 or 2007?

5. The Canadian dollar ranged from 90 to 94 cents U.S between July 2009 to early October 2009, and then appreciated rapidly, to 96 cents U.S. in mid-October 2009.

   A) The Bank of Canada hinted at taking action to reduce the value of the Canadian dollar. What would be the effects on the economic recovery (in terms of real GDP) if the Canadian dollar continued to rise in value?

   B) Would exporters be happy to hear that the bank of Canada was considering action to weaken the dollar? Why?

6. Suppose that Canada is expected to have rapid inflation relative to the U.S. in 2011.

   A) How does the rise in the inflation rate differential affect the demand for Canadian dollars?

   B) How does the rise in the inflation rate differential affect the supply of Canadian dollars?

   C) How does the rise in the inflation rate differential affect the Canadian exchange rate?

7. Economists often argue that the Canadian dollar tends to appreciate during booms and depreciate during busts, moderating recessions and inflationary periods.

   A) How could a depreciating currency help a country overcome a recession?

   B) How could an appreciating currency help a country through an inflationary period?

8. According to the Economics Out There on page 228, a high Canadian dollar threatens economic recovery and *Twilight* movie sequels.

   A) Why does a higher Canadian dollar threaten economic recovery?

   B) Why does a higher Canadian dollar reduce inflation?

   C) Why does a higher Canadian dollar threaten *Twilight* sequels?

9. Suppose a Wii system sells for $100 in Canada and $95 in the U.S.

   A) If Wiis are the only product traded between the countries, what is the *PPP* exchange rate?

   B) If the exchange rate is C$1.00 = US$0.90, where is your purchasing power greater?

   C) Does an exchange rate of C$1.00 = US$0.90 imply that the Canadian dollar is overvalued or undervalued?

   D) If the exchange rate is C$1.00 = US$0.90, what will happen to the exchange rate over time (according to the purchasing power parity principle)?

10. Suppose you are shopping in Miami, Florida during spring break and trying to decide how many U.S. dollars you need to save for the C$10 cab ride home from the Canadian airport.

    A) How much money is C$10 in U.S. dollars if the exchange rate is C$1.00 = US$0.90?

    B) If the Canadian dollar appreciates before you arrive at the Canadian airport, how will this affect the amount of U.S. dollars you need for the cab ride home from the Canadian airport?

    C) According to *The Economist's* Big Mac Index on page 233, the Canadian dollar is undervalued relative to the *PPP* rate with the U.S. dollar. Would this put pressure on the Canadian exchange rate to appreciate or depreciate? Explain your answer.

---

myeconlab Visit the MyEconLab website at **www.myeconlab.com**. This online homework and tutorial system puts you in control of your own learning with study and practice tools.

Steering Blindly?

Monetary Policy and the Bank of Canada

7.1 Identify the objectives of monetary policy.

7.2 Explain how the Bank of Canada uses open market operations to change target interest rates.

7.3 Trace the impacts of interest rate changes on aggregate demand, inflation, real GDP, and unemployment.

7.4 Explain why monetary transmission mechanisms can be blocked, and how quantitative easing can overcome a balance sheet recession.

7.5 Explain how inflation rate targeting by an independent central bank anchors expectations, helps market economies function, and gets agreement between "Yes" and "No" camps.

IMAGINE DRIVING DOWN a winding mountain road, the kind that makes you wish you owned a beautiful sports car. You have to brake and accelerate through every curve, with rocks on one side and a sheer drop on the other. With the right car, the drive could be exhilarating.

Now imagine that every time you hit the gas pedal or the brakes, there is a 30-second delay before your car responds. You need to anticipate every bend far in advance. It wouldn't take long before you plunged off the road.

That is the challenge facing the Bank of Canada. In this chapter you will learn how the Bank of Canada uses monetary policy to steer the economy towards full employment, stable prices, and steady economic growth. It changes interest rates and the money supply to try and keep the economy on the road to potential GDP with stable prices. But when interest rates change, it takes 18 to 24 months before the full impact on the economy takes effect!

Because it is difficult to get the timing of monetary policy just right, you might expect many suggestions and disagreements from back-seat drivers about the best way to steer the economy. But interestingly, there is much agreement among hands-off and hands-on economists about the Bank of Canada's driving.

The Governor of the Bank of Canada is not elected. Still, as a citizen you should understand how policy choices made by the Bank affect your standard of living, your prospects for finding a job, and the cost of living. The wrong policy choices can send the economy over a cliff into cycles of bust and boom. And knowing how the Bank of Canada is likely to act will help you make smart financial choices.

7.1 What Do Central Banks Do? Bank of Canada's Objectives and Targets

Identify the objectives of monetary policy.

Canada's economy is not run on the barter system. In our monetary-based economy, supply doesn't necessarily create its own demand. Business cycles, like the Great Depression, occur when there are mismatches between aggregate supply and aggregate demand. In an attempt to end economic suffering and private bank failures, Parliament created the Bank of Canada. According to the 1935 *Bank of Canada Act*:

> it is desirable to establish a central bank in Canada to regulate credit and currency in the best interests of the economic life of the nation, to control and protect the external value of the national monetary unit and to mitigate by its influence fluctuations in the general level of production, trade, prices and employment, so far as may be possible within the scope of monetary action, and generally to promote the economic and financial welfare of Canada.

The Bank of Canada's mandate is to control the quantity of money and interest rates to avoid inflation, business cycles, and unemployment. Notice also the reference to "control and protect" the value of the Canadian dollar. The financial sector, interest rates, and exchange rates are all intertwined, as we have seen in Chapters 5 and 6. Those connections are also important for understanding how the Bank of Canada does its job.

The Governor of the Bank of Canada—the driver at the wheel—currently is Mark Carney. His seven-year term as Governor began in February 2008.

> *The goal of Canadian monetary policy is to contribute to solid economic performance and rising living standards for all Canadians by keeping inflation low and stable.*
>
> —Bank of Canada
> 1999 Annual Report

FOR YOUR INFORMATION

Mark Carney was born in Fort Smith, Northwest Territories. He was an economics major at Harvard University as an undergraduate, and received a PhD from Oxford University. Carney worked for 13 years with Goldman Sachs Investment Bank in London, Tokyo, New York, and Toronto before joining the Bank of Canada as a Deputy Governor in 2003.

▲ Shown here just after it opened for business in March 1935, the Bank of Canada was established by an Act of Parliament.

◀ Mark Carney, the Governor of the Bank of Canada arrives in Ottawa to meet with the Minister of Finance. The Governor is responsible for setting monetary policy in Canada.

The Bank of Canada's Job

Chapter 5 identified four roles the Bank of Canada plays in the Canadian economy: issuing currency, acting as banker to banks, acting as a banker to government, and conducting monetary policy. In this chapter, we will focus on the Bank of Canada's responsibility for *monetary policy*—changing the supply of money and interest rates to achieve steady growth, full employment, and price stability. **Price stability** means the inflation rate is low enough that it does not significantly affect people's economic decisions.

Since 1991, the Government of Canada and the Bank of Canada have also agreed to two specific objectives for monetary policy:

- To contain the annual rate of inflation between one percent and three percent, as measured by increases in the consumer price index (CPI). This is called the **inflation-control target**.
- To use monetary policy to achieve the two percent midpoint of that range.

While the Bank of Canada aims for a two percent inflation rate target as measured by the CPI, the Bank also pays close attention to the core CPI (see Chapter 3) which excludes products/services with the most volatile prices from the CPI calculation. The core inflation rate—which the Bank of Canada calls its *operational guide*—provides a better measure of the long-run, underlying trend of inflation.

Notice that these more specific objectives focus entirely on the inflation rate, and do not mention steady growth in living standards, full employment, or the value of the Canadian dollar. As the original Philips Curve demonstrates, there can be tradeoffs between inflation and unemployment, so lower inflation may mean higher unemployment. This is a source of controversy about inflation-control targeting which we will return to later.

No matter what objectives the Bank of Canada chooses to focus on, interest rates are its most important monetary policy tool for achieving them.

monetary policy: changing the supply of money and interest rates to achieve steady growth, full employment, and stable prices

price stability: inflation is low enough that it does not significantly affect people's economic decisions

inflation-control target: range of inflation rates set as a target by a central bank as a monetary policy objective

Refresh

7.1

1. In your own words, explain what monetary policy is and what the Bank of Canada uses it for.

2. In what ways can inflation affect people's economic decisions?

3. Of the Bank of Canada's multiple policy objectives, which one seems most important to you personally? Explain why.

www.myeconlab.com

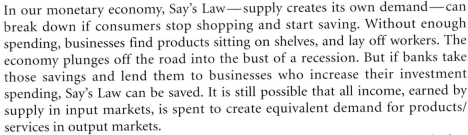

7.2 Target Shooting: Open Market Operations

Explain how the Bank of Canada uses open market operations to change target interest rates.

MAPS3

The interest rate plays a starring role for maintaining Say's Law in a monetary economy. Adjustments in the interest rate—the price of money—can help the economy stay on the road of steady growth in living standards, full employment, and stable prices.

Interest Rate As a Driving Force

In our monetary economy, Say's Law—supply creates its own demand—can break down if consumers stop shopping and start saving. Without enough spending, businesses find products sitting on shelves, and lay off workers. The economy plunges off the road into the bust of a recession. But if banks take those savings and lend them to businesses who increase their investment spending, Say's Law can be saved. It is still possible that all income, earned by supply in input markets, is spent to create equivalent demand for products/services in output markets.

Banks, supervised by the Bank of Canada, are a key driver determining whether or not market economies adjust quickly to maintain steady growth in living standards, full employment, and stable prices.

Interest rates affect what we, as consumers, homeowners, and business-people, can afford to borrow and buy. When interest rates are lower, we can afford to borrow more and spend more, and we save less. When interest rates are higher, we can't afford to borrow, so we spend less and save more. If savings flowing into the banking system cause interest rates to fall, encouraging businesses and consumers to borrow and spend more, then the match between aggregate supply and aggregate demand is restored. The right interest rate can keep the economy on the road towards potential GDP.

Interest rates are determined in money and bond markets *and by central banks*. Bond markets determine long-run interest rates, such as rates for 25-year mortgages and 10- to 30-year government bonds. Central banks can influence short-run interest rates.

In aiming for its two percent target rate of inflation, the Bank of Canada focuses on the **overnight rate**—the interest rate that chartered banks charge each other for one-day loans. That's about as short-run as it gets! The overnight rate then determines all interest rates that banks charge their customers. The overnight rate directly affects rates on lines of credit, rates for consumer and car loans, and rates for variable mortgages.

"I DON'T UNDERSTAND HOW HIGH INTEREST RATES AND THE NATIONAL DEFICIT AFFECT MY ALLOWANCE."

Source: www.CartoonStock.com

▲ This cartoon is showing that when people have to pay high interest rates, they have less to spend—even on their kid's allowance—reducing aggregate demand.

overnight rate:
interest rate banks
charge each other for
one day loans. Main
monetary policy tool.

Every Picture Tells a Story:
Bank of Canada Homepage

To see how the Bank of Canada influences short-run interest rates, go to its excellent website—www. bankofcanada.ca. Figure 7.1 is a December 2009 screen shot from the website. You can see the importance of the inflation-control target and the overnight rate. These key indicators always appear on the Bank of Canada homepage.

At the top is the inflation-control target range of +1 to +3 percent, with the highlighted midpoint target of +2 percent. The most recent inflation rate (from October 2009) was 0.1 percent, showing in the box below the target range.

Next down the page is the Bank of Canada's operational guide—the core CPI—also with a target range of +1 to +3 percent. The most recent core inflation rate was +1.8 percent, right in the middle of the target range.

The Bank of Canada's target for the overnight rate was 0.25 percent. This is the interest rate we are about to examine.

The link to Credit conditions (+ view site) contains detailed information about consumer and business borrowing, and measures of the supply of money, M1 and M2, presented in Chapter 5.

Finally, at the bottom is the current exchange rate for the Canadian dollar in terms of U.S. dollars. Putting the exchange rate on the Bank of Canada home page reflects the important connection between interest rates (which the Bank of Canada helps determine) and exchange rates (which the Bank of Canada does not try to determine). But in setting interest rates, the Bank of Canada is keenly aware of their impact on the value of the Canadian dollar, which in turn affects net exports, real GDP, employment, and inflation.

The next section explains how the Bank of Canada goes about changing interest rates in the economy to match its target rate. Understanding exchange rates—which you explored in Chapter 6—is key to understanding monetary policy.

Moving Targets:
Open Market Operations

The Bank of Canada's specific objective is to keep inflation at the target rate of two percent per year. The Bank also wants full employment and steady growth in real GDP and living standards. This complete set of objectives amounts to driving the Canadian economy on the road to potential GDP at the ideal speed, avoiding the booms and busts of business cycles on either side of the road. The Bank of Canada steers the economy through its monetary policy. It has many tools it can use. The main tool is changing the target for the overnight rate, which in turn changes most other interest rates. Changes in interest rates affect the economy like stepping on the gas or hitting the brakes.

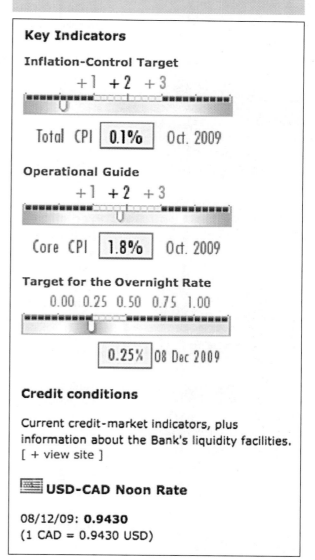

Figure 7.1   Bank of Canada Homepage

Key Indicators

Inflation-Control Target

+1   +2   +3

Total CPI | 0.1% | Oct. 2009

Operational Guide

+1   +2   +3

Core CPI | 1.8% | Oct. 2009

Target for the Overnight Rate

0.00 0.25 0.50 0.75 1.00

| 0.25% | 08 Dec 2009

Credit conditions

Current credit-market indicators, plus information about the Bank's liquidity facilities. [+ view site]

USD-CAD Noon Rate

08/12/09: **0.9430**
(1 CAD = 0.9430 USD)

You can check the current rates at www.bankofcanada.ca.

MAPS3

Accelerating with Lower Interest Rates

When the economy slows down, inflation falls below the target, real GDP falls below potential GDP, and unemployment increases. This is a recessionary gap. To get the economy back up to speed, the Bank of Canada steps on the gas by lowering interest rates. Lower interest rates increase borrowing and spending, decrease savings, and cause the value of Canadian dollar to fall, increasing net exports. Aggregate demand increases and the economy speeds up. The inflation rate rises, real GDP increases, and unemployment decreases.

Braking with Higher Interest Rates

When the economy is speeding too fast, inflation rises above the target, real GDP rises above potential GDP, and unemployment decreases. This is an inflationary gap. To slow the economy down, the Bank of Canada steps on the brakes by raising interest rates. Higher interest rates decrease borrowing and spending, increase savings, and cause the value of Canadian dollar to rise, decreasing net exports. Aggregate demand decreases and the economy slows down. The inflation rate falls, the growth in real GDP decreases, and unemployment increases.

Predicting the Future With Aggregate Supply & Aggregate Demand

The Bank of Canada's steering job for monetary policy sounds relatively simple, until you remember that it can't wait to see if the economy is actually slowing down or speeding up before acting. The impact on the economy of lower or higher interest rates takes up to 24 months to occur. The Bank of Canada has to predict the impact of a change in interest rates on the economy, and especially on the inflation rate, two years in the future!

There is no crystal ball foretelling the future, so the Bank hires economists to form expectations about what they think will happen to the economy. The economists use the tools of aggregate supply and aggregate demand (Chapter 4) to make predictions that the Bank of Canada uses to decide whether to raise, lower, or hold interest rates steady.

Moving Targets Eight Dates a Year

In using monetary policy based on predictions to steer the economy, the Bank of Canada is committed to eight fixed dates each year when it announces whether or not it will change the target for the overnight rate, and, with it, other interest rates.

The Bank of Canada changes the target rate through **open market operations**—buying or selling Government of Canada bonds and Treasury bills (a Treasury bill is just a short-term government bond) on the bond market. The bond market is open to the public—any individual or bank can buy bonds or sell bonds that they hold.

The money market and the bond market are interconnected (see Chapter 5), so the story of open market operations can be told from either perspective.

Changing the Money Supply to Change Interest Rates

This is the money supply perspective story. The money supply—M1—consists of currency in circulation and demand deposits. The Bank of Canada controls the supply of currency. It changes the money supply using open market operations to influence the quantity of demand deposits—which make up 90 percent of the money supply that chartered banks choose to create.

Buying Bonds to Increase the Money Supply

When the Bank of Canada wants to lower interest rates to accelerate the economy, it buys bonds which increases the money supply.

When the Bank of Canada buys a bond from you or from a chartered bank, it effectively pays with cash. That cash deposit increases bank reserves. As we saw in Chapter 5, banks make profits by loaning out excess reserves. With new reserves, the chartered banks make new loans (and matching demand deposits) that people can spend. This increase in demand deposits is an increase in the money supply.

To see the impact on interest rates, let's return to the example from Chapter 5. Figure 7.2 (same as Figure 5.6) shows the initial demand and supply for money, before the Bank of Canada's open market operation.

To lower interest rates and accelerate the economy, the Bank of Canada buys bonds which increases the money supply.

Figure 7.2	Initial Demand and Supply in the Money Market	
Price (interest rate)	Quantity Money Demanded (billions of dollars)	Quantity Money Supplied (billions of dollars)
2%	100	80
4%	90	80
6%	**80**	**80**
8%	70	80
10%	60	80

The market-clearing, or equilibrium, interest rate is six percent, the rate where the quantity of money demanded ($80 billion) equals the quantity of money supplied ($80 billion).

When the Bank of Canada buys bonds and pays with cash, chartered bank reserves increase. Suppose the chartered banks then create $10 billion in new loans, with matching demand deposits. With the increase in demand deposits, the supply of money (M1) increases from $80 billion to $90 billion. The unchanged demand and the new supply of money in the money market are shown in Figure 7.3.

Figure 7.3	Demand and Supply in the Money Market After Bank of Canada Buys Bonds	
Price (interest rate)	Quantity Money Demanded (billions of dollars)	Quantity Money Supplied (billions of dollars)
2%	100	90
4%	**90**	**90**
6%	80	90
8%	70	90
10%	60	90

The market-clearing, or equilibrium, interest rate falls to four percent—the new rate where the quantity of money demanded ($90 billion) equals the quantity of money supplied ($90 billion).

Remember, the interest rate is the price of money. Since the Bank of Canada's open market operation has increased the supply of money, we would expect the price of money—the interest rate—to fall.

You will see the term "basis points" in media stories about changing interest rates. A basis point is one-hundredth of one percent. A fall in interest rates from 6% to 4% is a fall of 200 basis points.

Selling Bonds to Decrease the Money Supply

The same story works in reverse when the Bank of Canada wants to raise interest rates to slow the economy down. It sells bonds to decrease the money supply.

Look back to Figure 7.2. When the Bank of Canada sells a bond, it must be paid. As a result, cash reserves leave the chartered banking system and go to the Bank of Canada. With fewer reserves, chartered banks reduce the quantity of loans (and matching demand deposits) that they make. Suppose the chartered banks reduce loans, with matching demand deposits, by $10 billion. This decrease in demand deposits is a decrease in the money supply from $80 billion to $70 billion (not shown on Figure 7.2).

With unchanged demand for money and a decrease in the money supply to $70 billion, the new market-clearing, or equilibrium, interest rate rises to eight percent, the new rate where the quantity of money demanded ($70 billion) equals the quantity of money supplied ($70 billion).

Changing Bond Prices to Change Interest Rates

Here is the bond market perspective on the story. When the Bank of Canada uses open market operations to buy or sell bonds, it becomes a major player in the bond market. When the Bank of Canada buys bonds, there is a big increase in the demand for bonds. When the Bank of Canada sells bonds, there is a big increase in the supply of bonds.

Buying Bonds Increases the Price of Bonds

When the Bank of Canada buys large quantities of bonds on the bond market, the increase in the demand for bonds causes the price of bonds to rise. Bond prices and interest rates are inversely related. (To recall why, review Section 5.3.) A rise in the price of bonds decreases the interest rate on bonds. By buying bonds, the Banks of Canada drives the interest rate down. In the example in Figures 7.2 and 7.3, the interest rate falls from six percent to four percent.

Selling Bonds Decreases the Price of Bonds

When the Bank of Canada sells large quantities of bonds on the bond market, there is an increase in the supply of bonds. This causes the price of bonds to fall. Bond prices and interest rates are inversely related. A fall in the price of bonds increases the interest rate on bonds. By selling bonds, the Banks of Canada drives the interest rate up. In the selling bonds example above, based on Figure 7.2, the interest rate rises from six percent to eight percent.

Interest Rates Move Together (Mostly)

The Bank of Canada conducts open market operations, buying or selling bonds, to change the overnight rate. Most other interest rates change at the same time.

The overnight rate only affects banks. But the **prime rate**, the interest rate that banks charge to their best, lowest-risk corporate borrowers, equals the overnight rate plus 2 percent. In December 2009, when the overnight loans rate was 0.25 percent, the prime lending rate was 2.25 percent.

Other short-run interest rates for consumer loans, variable rate mortgages, savings accounts, and short-term bonds also change with the overnight rate.

To raise interest rates and slow down the economy, the Bank of Canada sells bonds which decrease the money supply.

When Bank of Canada buys bonds, the increased demand for bonds raises bond prices and lowers interest rates.

When Bank of Canada sells bonds, the increased supply of bonds lowers bond prices and raises interest rates.

prime rate: interest rate on loans to lowest-risk corporate borrowers

Figure 7.4 shows the values for four interest rates in Canada between 1979 and 2009. The overnight rate, the prime rate, and the rate on three-month government Treasury bills (the most common short-term bond) all move up and down together.

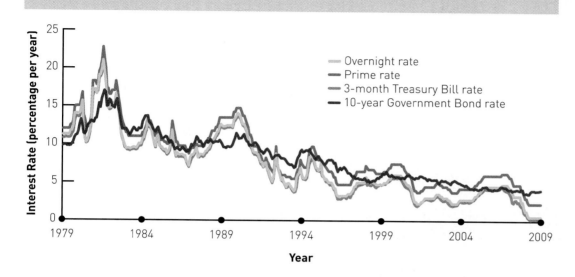

Figure 7.4 Short-Run and Long-Run Interest Rates in Canada, 1979–2009

The interest rate in Figure 7.4 for long-run 10-year government bonds (in red) is different. Long-run interest rates, for government and corporate bonds of 10–30 years, tend to be higher than short-run rates because longer-run bonds are riskier. The longer the time to pay back the loan, the more that can go wrong. Investors require a greater reward for forgoing liquidity for so long. Long-run interest rates also do not fluctuate as much as short-run interest rates, because expectations about the long run are not as volatile as short-run expectations. Long-run rates are set in the bond market.

Now that you understand how the Bank of Canada uses monetary policy to change interest rates, let's look in more detail at how interest rates can help maintain Say's Law and affect the key macroeconomic outcomes of inflation, real GDP, and unemployment.

Refresh

7.2

1. Describe the relationship between the overnight rate, the prime rate, and other interest rates.

2. In your own words, tell the bond market story of how the Bank of Canada uses open market operations to lower or raise interest rates. Point form is fine.

3. How might the overnight rate affect your decision to buy a house now or to wait?

www.myeconlab.com

7.3 Does Money Make the (Real) World Go Around? Transmission Mechanisms

Trace the impacts of interest rate changes on aggregate demand, inflation, real GDP, and unemployment.

When you step on the gas while driving a car, power from the engine travels through the transmission to turn the wheels to make the car go faster. When the Bank of Canada wants to accelerate the economy, it uses open market operations to lower interest rates. The effects of lower interest rates travel through increased spending to increase aggregate demand.

While cars have different gas and brake pedals, the brake for monetary policy is just the accelerator in reverse. To slow the economy down, the Bank of Canada uses open market operations to raise interest rates. The effects of higher interest rates travel through decreased spending to decrease aggregate demand.

In this section, we will examine the details of how monetary policy works.

Turning the Wheels of Aggregate Demand

The effects of monetary policy work through *aggregate demand* to speed up or slow down the economy.

C + I + G + X − IM = Y

OMMMM MM

OMMMMMMM

This economist is using his own special mantra to gain peace. It's the mantra you should also learn by heart.

Do you remember your mantra from Chapters 2 and 4? Planned spending on aggregate demand equals $C + I + G + X - IM$. Aggregate demand is the sum of planned consumer spending (C), business investment spending (I), government spending on products/services (G) and net exports ($X - IM$). To see exactly where interest rates affect aggregate demand, let's return to Figure 2.15, which is reproduced here as Figure 7.5.

The paths in Figure 7.5 are like a winding mountain road, full of turns and twists, tracing the flows of income through inputs markets (on the right) and spending through output markets (in the middle). There are two main paths for transmitting the effects of interest rates to aggregate demand.

Domestic Effects of Interest Rates   The domestic path, within Canada, is highlighted in red. It starts with the banking system, where short-run interest rates are set by the Bank of Canada. Interest rates affect business borrowing (at the bottom) and consumer borrowing (at the top), and then business investment spending (I) and consumer spending (C) (see Chapter 5).

International Effects of Interest Rates   The international path, from the rest of the world (R.O.W), is highlighted in blue. It also starts with the banking system, where short-run interest rates are set by the Bank of Canada. Interest rates affect the value of the Canadian dollar, which is not shown on this diagram. As explained in Chapter 6, changes in the exchange rate affect the prices that the rest of the world pays for Canadian exports (X) and the prices that Canadians pay for imports (IM).

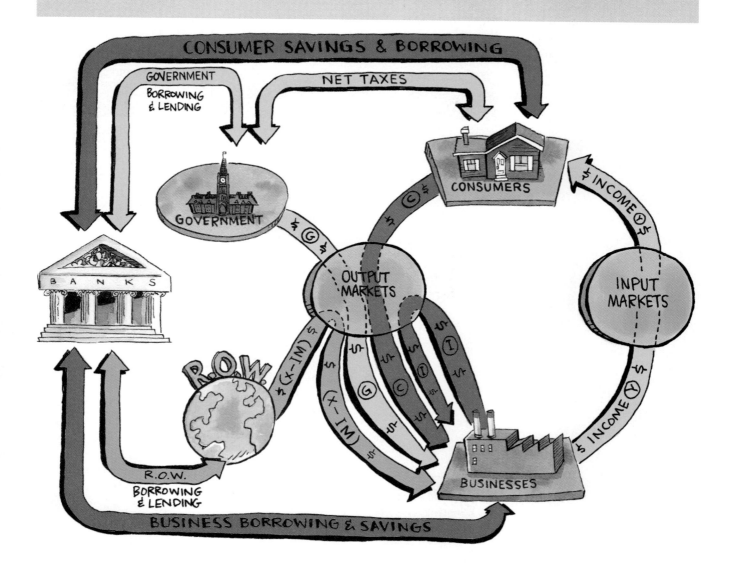

Looking Inside the Transmissions   Figure 7.5 is missing many of the details from both the domestic and international transmission of the effects of interest rates. Fortunately, we have already developed, in Chapters 5 and 6, more detailed diagrams of the missing links in the transmission mechanisms. Let's return to those diagrams to complete the explanation of how the effects of monetary policy are transmitted to the wheels of aggregate demand.

Domestic Monetary Transmission Mechanism: Borrowing and Spending

The details of the domestic monetary transmission mechanism are shown in Figure 7.6, which is Figure 5.7 with the Bank of Canada added at the top.

Figure 7.6 Bank of Canada and Domestic Monetary Transmission Mechanism

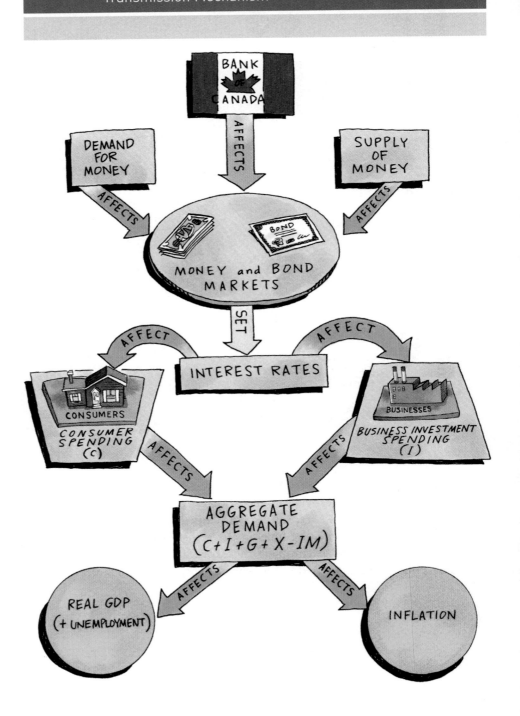

By using open market operations to intervene in the money and bond markets, the Bank of Canada steers short-run interest rates to match its target rate.

Lower interest rates reduce the cost of interest-sensitive purchases that require loans (houses, cars, major appliances), so consumers spend more (C). Business investment spending (I) is heavily financed by borrowing and therefore very interest sensitive. Lower interest rates make investment spending cheaper, so businesses spend more on new factories and equipment.

Lower Interest Rates Are a Positive Aggregate Demand Shock

The domestic effect of lower interest rates is to increase aggregate demand and accelerate the economy. Remember your mantra: aggregate demand equals $C + I + G + X - IM$. Increases in C and I both increase aggregate demand. A positive demand shock causes increased real GDP, decreased unemployment, and rising inflation (Chapter 4).

Lower interest rates are a positive aggregate demand shock, increasing consumption (C) and business investment spending (I).

Higher Interest Rates Are a Negative Aggregate Demand Shock

Higher interest rates increase the cost of borrowing, decrease C and I, and decrease aggregate demand. Higher interest rates are a negative demand shock and cause decreased real GDP, increased unemployment, and decreasing inflation or deflation (Chapter 4).

We still have to add the effects of the international transmission mechanism to these domestic effects to get the net effect of monetary policy.

Higher interest rates are a negative aggregate demand shock, decreasing consumption (C) and business investment spending (I).

International Transmission Mechanism: Exchange Rate Effects

The foreign exchange market, where the value of the Canadian dollar is determined, is not on Figures 7.5 or 7.6. When the Bank of Canada uses open market operations to change short-run interest rates, the Canadian interest rate differential with the rest of the world changes. An decrease in interest rates lowers the Canadian interest rate differential. This causes the Canadian dollar to depreciate on the foreign exchange market. An increase in interest rates raises the Canadian interest rate differential, causing the Canadian dollar to appreciate on the foreign exchange market.

The value of the Canadian dollar, in turn, affects how expensive exports are for the R.O.W., and how expensive imports are for Canadians. For example, if the Bank of Canada lowers the target interest rate, the Canadian dollar depreciates in value.

A lower Canadian dollar makes Canadian exports cheaper for customers in the rest of the world. When Canadian exports become less expensive, non-Canadians buy more of them. A lower Canadian dollar makes imports from the rest of the world more expensive for Canadian customers. Canadians then buy fewer imports and more Canadian products/services.

The details of the international transmission mechanism are shown on the next page in Figure 7.7, which is Figure 6.8 with the Bank of Canada added at the top.

MAPS 2

Figure 7.7   Bank of Canada and International Transmission Mechanism

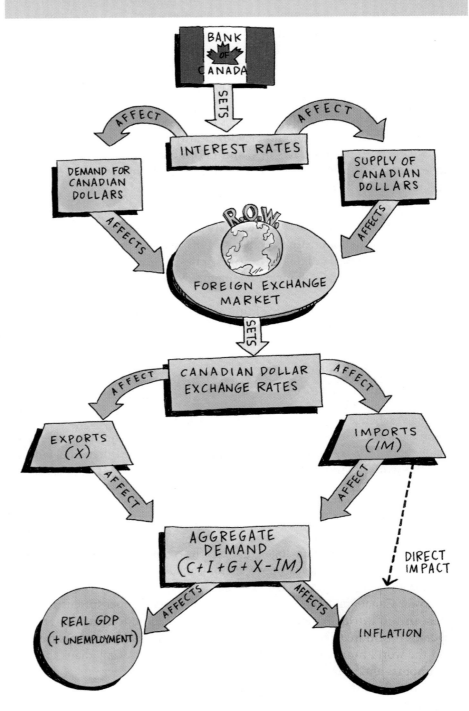

Depreciating Canadian Dollar Positive Aggregate Demand Shock

The international effect of lower interest rates, just like the domestic effect, is to increase aggregate demand and accelerate the economy. Both the increase in exports (X) and the decrease in imports (IM) contribute to an increase in aggregate demand. Remember your mantra: aggregate demand equals $C + I + G + X − IM$. This increase in net exports ($X − IM$) is a positive aggregate demand shock, causing increased real GDP, decreased unemployment, and rising inflation.

Depreciating Canadian dollar is a positive aggregate demand shock, increasing net exports ($X − IM$).

Appreciating Canadian Dollar Negative Aggregate Demand Shock

Higher interest rates cause the Canadian interest rate differential to increase, leading to an appreciation of the Canadian dollar on the foreign exchange market. The higher exchange rate makes exports (X) more expensive for the R.O.W. and imports (IM) cheaper for Canadians. Net exports ($X - IM$) decrease, decreasing aggregate demand. The appreciating Canadian dollar is a negative demand shock causing decreased real GDP, increased unemployment, and decreasing inflation or deflation.

Appreciating Canadian dollar is a negative aggregate demand shock, decreasing net exports (X – IM).

All Together Now: Reinforcing Transmission Mechanisms

Since both the domestic and international transmission mechanisms work in the same direction, they reinforce each other.

Open market operations by the Bank of Canada to lower interest rates increase aggregate demand. This is an appropriate monetary policy for an economy that is predicted to be in a recessionary gap 18 to 24 months from now. If the predicted inflation rate is below the Bank of Canada's target inflation rate of two percent, and real GDP is predicted to be below potential GDP with cyclical unemployment, then lower interest rates will help steer the economy towards potential GDP, full employment, and stable prices.

Open market operations by the Bank of Canada to raise interest rates decrease aggregate demand. This is an appropriate monetary policy for an economy that is predicted to be in an inflationary gap 18–24 months from now. If the predicted inflation rate is above the Bank of Canada's target inflation rate of two percent, and real GDP is predicted to be above potential GDP with an unemployment rate below the natural rate of unemployment, then higher interest rates will help steer the economy towards potential GDP, full employment, and stable prices.

Figure 7.8 is a good study device summarizing the combined effects of monetary policy from domestic and international transmission mechanisms.

> *The time lags inherent in the transmission mechanism make it difficult to conduct monetary policy. In particular, these long time lags mean that central banks must be forward-looking in their policy decisions.*
>
> *—Bank of Canada*

Figure 7.8 Transmission Effects of Monetary Policy

	Monetary Policy	
	Lower Interest Rates	**Raise Interest Rates**
Policy to Correct Output Gaps	Recessionary Gap	Inflationary Gap
Impact on Economy		
Business Investment (*I*) & Consumption (*C*)	Increase	Decrease
Exchange Rate	Depreciates	Appreciates
Net Exports (*X − IM*)	Increase	Decrease
Aggregate Demand	Increases	Decreases
Unemployment	Decreases	Increases
Inflation	Increases	Decreases

Not a Popularity Contest   When the Bank of Canada gets its predictions right, it can use monetary policy to keep the economy moving steadily on the road to potential GDP, and meet its policy objectives of price stability, growth in living standards, and full employment.

Monetary policy is not always politically popular. Consumers and businesses are usually pleased when the Bank of Canada lowers interest rates to fight a recession. But when economic growth picks up speed, with more jobs, more profits, and more income, the Bank of Canada raises interest rates—raising the cost of mortgages, car loans, and business borrowing. People complain, especially because they can't see any inflation in the present. But the Bank of Canada is concerned that 18 to 24 months in the future, continuing growth will cause inflation to rise beyond the target range. One central banker describes his job as "taking away the punch bowl just when the party is getting started." Not a popular move. But successful monetary policy is about moderation—accelerating the economy when it is slowing, and braking when the economy is speeding up.

Successful monetary policy requires that consumers and businesses respond to changing interest rates with changing spending patterns, and that chartered banks adjust loans when reserves change. As we will see in the next section, these macroeconomic players don't always cooperate, and monetary policy can break down, as it did during the Great Recession.

Refresh 7.3

www.myeconlab.com

1. In point form, show how a Bank of Canada open market operation selling bonds affects interest rates, domestic aggregate demand, real GDP, unemployment, and inflation.

2. What is the connection between the value of the Canadian dollar (the exchange rate) and monetary policy's impact on the Canadian economy?

3. Who benefits when the Bank of Canada lowers interest rates? Who benefits when interest rates rise? Explain which policy you would expect to be more politically popular.

7.4 Transmission Breakdowns: Balance Sheet Recessions and Monetary Policy

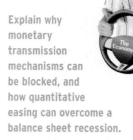

Explain why monetary transmission mechanisms can be blocked, and how quantitative easing can overcome a balance sheet recession.

When the U.S. real estate bubble burst in 2008, the value of mortgage-backed securities plummeted. Investors and banks holding now almost worthless assets were forced to sell other assets to meet their debts. Panicked selling led to bank failures, business bankruptcies, and plunging stock market values. Real GDP started falling, and unemployment soon rose to over 10 percent in the United States and in Canada. The Great Recession had begun.

Recessions are often triggered by a decrease in business investment spending, falling net exports, or rising interest rates. Not the Great Recession. The recession of 2008–2009 is also referred to as a *balance sheet recession*—a contraction caused by the collapse of asset prices. A balance sheet—for businesses, banks, or individuals—shows assets on one side (what you own or earn) and debts or liabilities on the other side (what you owe or spend). When the value of the assets you own falls, you need to cut back on what you spend or owe to restore balance. This proved to be a problem for monetary policy.

Central banks around the world, including the U.S. Federal Reserve and the Bank of Canada, responded to the Great Recession as you would expect from reading this chapter. With a recessionary gap opening, they used open market operations to buy bonds and lower the target interest rate, hoping generally lower interest rates would stimulate borrowing, spending, and aggregate demand.

When the Bank of Canada changes its interest rate target, it almost always does so slowly and incrementally, 25 basis points (0.25 percent) at time, and only eight dates a year. Bankers have a justifiable reputation for being conservative in all ways—wearing conservative dark blue suits and taking conservative, moderate actions. Slow and steady, the bankers say, wins the race and keeps the economics car running smoothly and safely.

In a balance sheet recession, individuals and businesses focus effort on paying down debt and are reluctant to borrow or spend. Even when monetary policy lowers interest rates, the economy remains in recession.

Stepping On the Gas?

The Great Recession prompted the Bank of Canada to dramatically change its driving habits. The threatened collapse of the banking system was so serious, and fears of repeating the Great Depression of the 1930s were so real, that central bankers threw caution to the wind and stepped on the accelerator as hard as they could.

From a target overnight rate of 4.0 percent at the start of 2008, the Bank of Canada began aggressively cutting interest rates. There were unusually large 50 basis point cuts in March 2008, April 2008, and October 2008, lowering the overnight rate to 2.5 percent. Just two weeks later in October (breaking the eight-dates-a-year tradition) the Bank of Canada cut another 25 basis points, followed by an unprecedented 75 basis-point cut in December 2008, bringing the overnight rate down to 1.5 percent. These actions were the equivalent of a conservative banker wearing a pink polka dot suit!

In the first four months of 2009 the Bank of Canada cut another 125 basis points, dropping the overnight rate almost to zero—to 0.25 percent. The Bank of Canada predicted that the overnight rate would stay at 0.25 percent until at least mid-2010.

Go to the Bank of Canada's website bankofcanada.ca and see what the overnight rate is today.

Almost Free Money The corresponding prime rate—the lowest rate charged to businesses or consumers—beginning in April 2009 was 2.25 percent. The prime rate, set 200 basis points above the overnight rate, is a nominal interest rate—it is not adjusted for inflation. The realized real interest rate (see Section 3.3) adjusts the nominal interest rate to remove the effects of inflation.

$$\text{Real interest rate} = \text{nominal interest rate} - \text{inflation rate}$$

With a nominal prime interest rate of 2.25 percent and an inflation rate of about 2 percent, that meant for the last half of 2009 the real interest rate was 0.25 percent, close to zero.

$$\text{Real interest rate} = 2.25 \text{ percent} - 2 \text{ percent}$$

$$\text{Real interest rate} = 0.25 \text{ percent}$$

The real rate of interest—what you have to give up in purchasing power to "buy" money—is more important than the nominal rate of interest for making smart saving and investing decisions. Since the interest rate is the price of money, borrowing money was almost free in the last half of 2009!

Despite almost free money, consumer and business borrowing and spending did not increase as the Bank of Canada had hoped. The Bank of Canada stepped hard on the gas, but the power was not transmitted to the wheels of aggregate demand. What accounts for this transmission breakdown?

Paying Down Debt Instead of Spending: Consumers and Businesses

2009 was a bad year for balance sheets and economies around the world, including Canada's.

Consumers Many consumers were unemployed in 2009, and those lucky enough to be working were worried about losing their jobs. Plunging stock market and asset prices wiped out a large fraction of the value of people's assets—savings, pensions, and retirement accounts. Even though you could borrow money and spend it for almost nothing, there were few takers.

Pessimistic *expectations* about the future were more important than lower interest rates for determining consumers' spending and saving choices. Instead of responding to lower interest rates by saving less and borrowing and spending more, as the Bank of Canada had hoped, consumers did just the opposite. Households cut back on their spending and starting paying off their debts (reducing liabilities) and saving more (increasing assets).

Businesses Businesses reacted similarly. Business investment decisions depend on the cost of borrowing, but also on expectations about future profitability. In the depths of the Great Recession, pessimistic expectations again triumphed over cheaper money. With less valuable assets on their balance sheets, business investment spending decreased with lower interest rates, rather than increasing as the Bank of Canada had hoped.

Money as a Store of Value   Both consumers and businesses used money as a store of value during the Great Recession. With fundamental uncertainty about the future and pessimistic expectations, consumers, businesses, and investors chose the safety of money over both business investment spending and investing in bonds. As Keynes said (Chapter 5), "our desire to hold money is a barometer of our distrust of . . . the future . . . . The possession of money lulls our disquietude." Money provides a way not to spend, blocking the transmission mechanism. The loanable funds market, where businesses borrow to finance investment spending, failed to match spending to savings. With pessimistic expectations, consumers and businesses poured their assets into money, blocking the domestic transmission mechanism.

Government was the only macroeconomic player who spent a lot during the Great Recession. We will discuss government spending in Chapter 8.

Piling Up Reserves Instead of Lending: Banks

The Bank of Canada's monetary policy—buying bonds from individuals and banks—pumped lots of cash into chartered banks' reserves. In the pursuit of profits, banks would normally use the new reserves to make more loans, create more demand deposits, and increase the money supply.

But banks too were suffering from falling asset prices, desperately trying to repair their balance sheets by increasing assets. Banks held on to new cash reserves to protect against the growing number of borrowers who were going bankrupt and defaulting on—not paying back—their loans. Chartered banks did not increase their lending as the Bank of Canada had hoped. They kept the extra cash reserves as assets. Banks opted for prudence over profits. Pessimistic expectations about loan repayments and economic conditions triumphed over potential profits from new loans.

Banks in Canada and the U.S. were hesitant to lend money, except to the most creditworthy customers. In the U.S., banks refused to renew mortgages, even for homeowners who had never missed a mortgage payment and had perfect credit histories.

Ironically, in the U.S. housing boom that led up to the 2008–2009 recession, banks chose profits over prudence, lending money even to those who were not credit-worthy (sub-prime mortgages). Those loose lending practices helped create the housing bubble that triggered the Great Recession. After the bubble burst, banks chose prudence over profits, and the restrictive lending practices, which limited spending, made the recession deeper and longer lasting. The banking system contributed to the cycle of boom and bust.

Flooding the System with Money: Quantitative Easing and the Quantity Theory of Money

When the usual monetary policy tools of open market operations did not restore spending during the Great Recession, central banks did not give up. The U.S Federal Reserve Bank (the "Fed"), headed by Chairman Ben Bernanke (*Time Magazine's* 2009 Person of the Year—see Economics Out There page 268), implemented an additional, more controversial policy tool.

> *It is this flight into cash that makes interest-rate policy such an uncertain agent of recovery . . . . That is why Keynes did not think that cutting the central bank's interest rate would necessarily—and certainly not quickly—[stimulate spending]. This was his main argument for the use of government [spending] to fight a depression.*
>
> *–Robert Skidelsky*

quantitative easing: central bank tool of flooding financial system with money by buying risky bonds, mortgages, and assets from banks. These liabilities on bank balance sheets are replaced with cash assets, enabling banks to make new loans.

Quantitative Easing

Bernanke decided to use a more powerful tool from his monetary policy toolbox—quantitative easing. **Quantitative easing** floods the financial system with money by having the central bank buy risky bonds, mortgages, and assets directly from banks. By eliminating these liabilities on bank balance sheets and replacing them with cash assets, banks are in a better position to make new loans. Quantitative easing succeeded in stabilizing the banking system and had some success increasing lending. But this tool carries risks of inflation further on down the road.

Quantitative easing is similar to open market operations where the central bank buys bonds and pays with cash that increases bank reserves. The difference here is that the central bank is not buying government bonds on the open market, but many kinds of riskier, private commercial assets directly from banks. This increases cash reserves in the banking system, allowing banks to increase loans, demand deposits, and the quantity of money. This is the same result as open market bond purchases. But the central bank assumes more risk than with government bond purchases.

When coming to the aid of banks with troubled balance sheets, central banks around the world, including the U.S. Federal Reserve and the Bank of Canada, play the role of *lender of last resort* (see Section 5.2 and For Your Information).

FOR YOUR INFORMATION

The Bank of Canada's policy as lender of last resort states: "In conditions of severe and unusual stress on the financial system . . . the Bank has authority to provide liquidity through outright purchases of securities issued by any Canadian or foreign entities, including non-financial firms."

The Bank of Canada can use quantitative easing and other means to provide cash (liquidity) to chartered banks to help avoid runs on banks and other difficulties in order "to avoid damaging the interests of unsecured creditors" (innocent depositors like you or me).

ECONOMICS Out There

Obama Pressures Banks to Lend

In December 2009, U.S. President Obama called in the heads of the biggest U.S. banks to pressure them to lend more to small businesses and homeowners. The banks, including American Express, Bank of America, Capital One, Citigroup, JPMorgan Chase, Morgan Stanley, and Wells Fargo, received government money to rebuild their businesses and Obama asked for an "extraordinary" commitment to "help rebuild our economy."

In a TV interview the day before that meeting, Obama said "I did not run for office to be helping out a bunch of fat cat bankers on Wall Street." He did not repeat that line to the bankers.

The bankers point out that their ability to lend has been reduced by the government's insistence that they "hold more assets to shore up their balance sheets and protect themselves from further mortgage and loan defaults by businesses and consumers."

Sources: "Obama tells Banks to boost lending," CBC News, December 14, 2009. Helene Cooper and Eric Dash, "Obama Presses Biggest Banks to Lend More," *The New York Times*, December 15, 2009.

Inflation Risks   The quantity theory of money (you can review it in Section 3.4) is the key to understanding the inflation risks from the policies of quantitative easing or open market operations.

The quantity theory of money states that an increase in the quantity of money causes an equal percentage increase in the inflation rate. The quantity theory is represented as

$$M \times V = P \times Q$$

where M is the quantity of money, V is the velocity of money, P is the price level as measured by the consumer price index, and Q is real GDP.

If (and these are big ifs) velocity (V) is constant and real GDP (Q) is constant at potential GDP, then any increase in the money supply (M) causes an equal percentage increase in the inflation rate (P). Or looking at it from the other direction—if there is an increase in the inflation rate, there must be an accompanying increase in the quantity of money.

Simply put, the quantity theory of money says, "printing money causes inflation." When central banks buy bonds in open market operations and pay with cash, it is similar to printing money. Chartered banks get additional reserves, and can create new demand deposits—part of M1—which are money (without the printed bills). Quantitative easing injects the same kind of cash reserves into the banking system, increasing the money supply.

If (I said *if* would be an important word) the economy were at potential GDP instead of in a deep recession, then these monetary policies would be inflationary. But when real GDP is below potential GDP, increases in the money supply can lower interest rates and stimulate borrowing and spending. Then some of the increase in the money supply on the left side of the equal sign gets applied on the right side of the equal sign to increases in real GDP (Q) rather than increases in the price level (P). Monetary policy can help real GDP grow.

The tricky part is what happens when the economy approaches potential GDP. At that point, any additional money in the banking system would be inflationary. Central banks know that there will come a time when they have to step on the brake ("take away the punch bowl just when the party is getting started"), selling previously purchased bonds and assets.

When chartered banks buy back those bonds and assets from the central bank with cash, reserves leave the banking system and go to the central bank. The decrease in reserves decreases the money supply and raises interest rates, slowing the economy and reducing the risk of inflation. The timing of the monetary "brake" is crucial. If the central bank steps on the brake too soon, it risks halting the recovery. If it waits too long, it risks inflation. Paul Masson, a professor at University of Toronto and former advisor at the Bank of Canada says. "I am not confident, given the lags in monetary policy, that they can exactly get it right."

The risk of getting it wrong can be seen in Zimbabwe (Chapter 1, page 17). There, the central bank printed money recklessly on behalf of the government to finance government spending, and the result was hyperinflation.

Inflation is always and everywhere a monetary phenomenon.

–Milton Friedman
1976 Nobel Prize in Economics

ECONOMICS Out There

Ben Bernanke is *Time Magazine*'s 2009 Person of the Year

Ben Bernanke's leadership as the Chairmen of the U.S. Federal Reserve Bank is widely credited with saving the world from depression. That accomplishment earned him *Time Magazine's* 2009 Award as Person of the Year (Barack Obama won the 2008 award).

In an interview, Bernanke said, "We came very, very close to a depression ... The markets were in anaphylactic shock. I'm not happy with where we are, but it's a lot better than where we could be."

Many central banks followed Bernanke's lead in implementing the innovative policy tool of quantitative easing. Mervyn King, the Governor of the Bank of England, described the policy this way: "People always talk about central banks taking away the punch bowl, but when demand was falling so rapidly, Ben had to put the punch bowl on the table and say, Let's party!'"

Bernanke, an economics professor at Princeton University, had studied the monetary policy blunders of the Great Depression, and "was determined not be the Fed Chairman who presided over Depression 2.0."

The story that captivated Bernanke as a child was about a town with many shoe factories that closed during the Depression, leaving the community so poor that its children went barefoot. "I kept asking, Why didn't they just open the factories and make the kids shoes?'" he recalls.

Bernanke has devoted his career to questions like that: the same question that is posed in the title to Chapter 1 of this book.

Source: http://www.time.com/time/specials/packages/article/0,28804,1946375_1947251_1947520,00.html

Driving with an Unpredictable Transmission: Timing is Everything

Balance sheet recessions cause transmission problems for monetary policy, making it harder to steer the economy towards recovery.

Even when all is going well, the timing of monetary policy—when to step on the accelerator or the brake—is difficult because central banks have to predict the impact up to two years in advance.

But when macroeconomic players resist borrowing, spending, and lending, and instead choose the security of money and savings, monetary policy becomes even more challenging. Balance sheet recessions cause transmission problems for monetary policy, making it harder to steer the economy towards recovery.

Facing falling asset values on their balances sheets, consumers, businesses, and banks make individually smart choices to resist borrowing, spending, and lending. But those individual smart choices do not add up to smart choices for the economy as a whole.

Refresh 7.4

1. How might consumers, businesses, and banks block the monetary transmission mechanism?

2. Why might quantitative easing lead to inflation?

3. In a balance sheet recession, do the individual smart choices made by consumers, businesses, and banks add up to smart choices for the economy as a whole? Explain.

www.myeconlab.com

7.5 Who's Driving? Anchoring Inflation Expectations

The Governor of the Bank of Canada has more power to influence economic outcomes than almost any other Canadian. In a democracy like Canada's, it is unusual for an unelected official to hold that kind of power. The relationship between the Bank of Canada and our elected Parliament contains a classic Canadian compromise between government authority to act and accountability to voters. And speaking of compromises, the hands-off and hands-on camps largely agree on the need for a central bank to prevent runaway inflation expectations and to help markets operate well.

Explain how inflation rate targeting by an independent central bank anchors expectations, helps market economies function, and gets agreement between "Yes" and "No" camps.

Is the Bank or the Government of Canada Driving?

The Bank of Canada has an inflation control target range of 1 to 3 percent. This specific policy objective is set through agreement between the Government of Canada and the Bank of Canada. But the Bank of Canada *alone* sets the monetary policy for achieving that target. The Minister of Finance—for the government—and the Governor of the Bank of Canada jointly decide on the destination of Canada's economic car, but the Governor gets to drive.

If the government and the Governor cannot agree on the policy objectives, the government can legally direct the Bank to accept the government's directions, forcing the Governor to resign. Investors and markets like predictability, so governments are reluctant to quarrel publicly with a Governor of the Bank of Canada. The only Governor forced to resign (see For Your Information) was James Coyne in 1961.

A disagreement over monetary policy would cause stock market values to fall and investors to lose confidence in the stability of the financial system. "Who is in charge?" they would ask. This gives the Bank of Canada considerable independence, even though it is ultimately accountable to Parliament: a classic Canadian compromise between authority to act and accountability to the voters.

Independence Matters The independence of our central bank has important advantages. The hyperinflation in Zimbabwe, like hyperinflations that have occurred elsewhere in the world, is usually a result of the government controlling the central bank and ordering it to print money to finance government spending. That kind of government influence cannot happen in Canada. A more subtle form of government influence might be to have the central bank reduce interest rates and promote economic expansion right before an election. Economic growth and full employment usually help the political party currently in power.

The independence of the Bank of Canada rules out government influences that can lead to monetary policy decisions that are clearly not in the best interests of the country as a whole.

The Bank of Canada has considerable independence, even though it is ultimately accountable to Parliament.

Inflation-Unemployment Tradeoffs and Expectations

Inflation rate targeting is now the only specific objective agreed to by the Government of Canada and the Bank of Canada. These days, when the Bank of Canada mentions the broader objectives in the 1935 *Bank of Canada Act* like "solid economic performance" and "rising living standards," it states that those objectives will be achieved by "keeping inflation low and stable."

There is no longer much controversy over this single-minded focus on inflation targeting, even though the original Philips Curve suggests lower inflation is often tied to higher unemployment.

Central banks in other countries do not have this single focus on inflation. For example, the U.S. *Federal Reserve Act* lists the Fed's (the U.S. central bank) specific objectives as "maximum employment, stable prices, and moderate long-term interest rates."

But by focusing only on inflation-rate targeting since 1991, the Bank of Canada has succeeded not only in keeping inflation within the target range, but in promoting rising living standards and movement towards full employment. It is important to understand the reasons behind the Bank's success. One is that the target has anchored expectations about inflation—everyone knows what to expect. The other is that the target improves the predictability of prices, making smart choices easier for all macroeconomic players.

Speeding is Easier than Braking, So Anchor Expectations The original Philips Curve tradeoff between inflation and unemployment works as long as people's expectations of inflation do not change. Using monetary policy to lower interest rates and accelerate aggregate demand, a central bank can steer towards lower unemployment and higher inflation. But once higher inflation occurs, the gas pedal can get stuck to the floor because of changing expectations—runaway inflation.

If people begin expecting inflation, it creates a self-fulfilling prophecy. Consider this scenario: You are expecting the inflation rate next year to be four percent, and your employment contract is up for renewal. How much of a raise will you ask for?

If you are like most people, you will be thinking, "The cost of living next year will be four percent higher. Unless I get at least a four percent raise, my income won't keep pace with the rising cost of living. My standard of living will go down. I'd better ask for at least a four percent raise."

Once expectations of inflation begin, many people start thinking the same way. Businesses, expecting higher prices for inputs, set output prices higher to protect their profits. Banks, expecting inflation, will increase nominal interest rates on loans to protect the real rate of interest they will receive. When workers, businesses, and banks expect inflation, they reasonably try and protect themselves by pushing up wages, prices of output, and interest rates. This creates self-fulfilling expectations—by reacting to the expectation of inflation we may help cause it.

A reminder from Section 3.5 —the original Phillips Curve is a graph showing an inverse relation between unemployment and inflation.

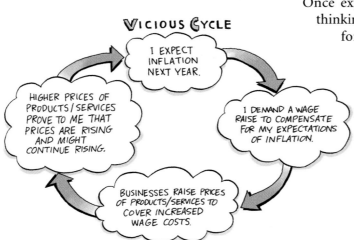

VICIOUS CYCLE

I EXPECT INFLATION NEXT YEAR.

I DEMAND A WAGE RAISE TO COMPENSATE FOR MY EXPECTATIONS OF INFLATION.

BUSINESSES RAISE PRICES OF PRODUCTS/SERVICES TO COVER INCREASED WAGE COSTS.

HIGHER PRICES OF PRODUCTS/SERVICES PROVE TO ME THAT PRICES ARE RISING AND MIGHT CONTINUE RISING.

Once inflation takes hold, expectations of higher inflation rates keep rising, creating a vicious cycle that, if not broken, runs the risk of spiraling out of control. The gas pedal can get stuck to the floor. OPEC sharply increased oil prices in the 1970s. When central banks allowed the quantity of money to increase (see For Your Information at right), inflation took hold, as the quantity theory of money predicts. This led to rising expectations of continued inflation. So, oil prices went up in the 1970s—the quantity of money increased and inflation started—people expected inflation to continue going up—which led to higher inflation in the 1980s.

Once inflation expectations rose and central banks allowed the quantity of money to increase, higher rates of inflation were associated with higher levels of unemployment. The simple tradeoff between higher inflation and lower unemployment that the original Phillips Curve showed for the 1950s and early 1960s no longer existed. Look back at Figure 3.12 on p. 111.

Breaking (and braking) inflation expectations is slow and painful. Once inflation expectations take hold, people and businesses are reluctant to settle for raises that are lower than the expected inflation rate. It takes a long period of recession, with unemployment and depressed businesses sales, before everyone begins accepting more slowly rising wages and prices.

That's what happened in the 1980s. In order to break inflation expectations, a former Governor of the Bank of Canada, Gerald Bouey, and former Federal Reserve Chairman, Paul Volcker, decreased the money supply and raised interest rates dramatically. The prime lending rate in Canada peaked at over 19 percent in 1981. The result was a severe recession. Figure 7.9 shows that this succeeded in bringing down actual inflation (as the quantity theory of money predicts), and expectations of inflation also fell. Notice also that since inflation targeting by the Bank of Canada began in 1991, inflation has stayed within the target range of 1 to 3 percent.

Changing inflation expectations, combined with increases in the money supply, eliminated the original Phillips Curve's simple tradeoff between higher inflation and lower unemployment.

Figure 7.9   Inflation Rates and Targets in Canada, 1960–2009

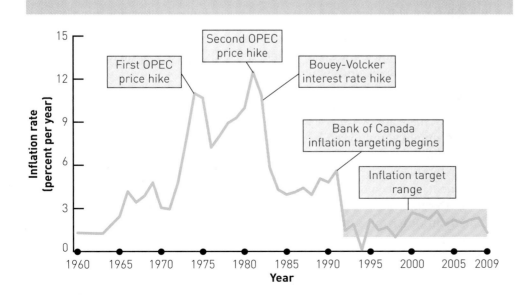

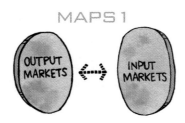

MAPS 1

Inflation expectations go up quickly and easily, but come down slowly and painfully.

Unpredictable prices create risk, discourage business investment, and interfere with price signals important for smart choices in a market economy.

Inflation expectations go up quickly and easily, but come down slowly and painfully. Squashing inflation expectations takes an extended period of high unemployment and economic hardship for consumers and businesses. For this reason, most economists and policymakers now agree that it is important to keep inflation rates low, stable, and predictable. An inflation target range accomplishes this by anchoring inflation expectations.

High Inflation is Unpredictable, Causing Not-Smart Choices High inflation is usually volatile. At higher inflation rates, the speed of price rises becomes erratic and unpredictable.

Unpredictable prices are a serious problem for businesses. Producing for output markets takes time. Business must first buy inputs, produce their products, and then transport them to output markets for sale. All of these steps, connecting input markets and output markets, take time.

Businesses must make commitments today for products/services that will only come to market in the future. If your business is not sure of a steady supply of inputs at predictable prices, your costs are unpredictable and your profits unstable. If prices and the inflation rate are changing unpredictably, it is hard to set your own output price, and to know what demand will be like if your customers are paying more for all other products/services.

With unpredictable inflation, when your business observes rising market prices, you don't know if those prices reflect increased demand for your output (a good thing) or just general inflation (not so good). It is hard to make smart business decisions. Unpredictability creates risk, and risk discourages business investment in future production. Uncertainty interferes with the normal movement of prices—signals for smart choices—in a market economy.

The costs of uncertainty associated with high and unpredictable inflation are important reasons to keep inflation rates low, stable, and predictable.

Hands-Off and Hands-On Agree! Markets Need a Central Bank

It has been a while since I asked the fundamental macroeconomic question:

> If left alone by government, do the price mechanisms of market economies adjust quickly to maintain steady growth in living standards, full employment, and stable prices?

> More simply, if left alone, do markets quickly self-adjust?

Normally, there are two answers. The Yes" camp says markets quickly self-adjust, so government should keep hands-off. The "No" camp says markets can fail to adjust, and therefore there is a hands-on role for government. But, when it comes to the proper role for the Bank of Canada, there are many more agreements between the two camps than disagreements.

Both camps agree on the need for a government-like player like the Bank of Canada in order for a market economy to function properly. Both camps see three of the four roles of the Bank of Canada—issuing currency, acting as banker to banks, and acting as a banker to government—largely as the role of government in setting the rules of the road (see Appendix D.1).

To reap the benefits of a monetary, as opposed to barter, economy, we must have a banking system with a central bank that controls the rules of the road. Those rules include defining and protecting property rights and enforcing contracts between buyers and sellers.

Banks around the world are regulated through rules because they face a tradeoff between profits and prudence. Without regulation, more banks could be tempted to take risks in pursuit of higher and faster profits that might lead to the failure of the bank. When banks fail, not only do bank owners lose money they have invested in the bank, but innocent, trusting depositors, who were not involved in the risky loan decisions, also lose their money. The Bank of Canada, in helping to protect the prudence of the banking system, is protecting the property rights of investors and depositors.

One of the lessons of the Great Recession has been the need for more government oversight of the financial system, with clearer rules of the road and protection for innocent depositors. While chartered banks are already regulated, many other major financial institutions, for example, the investment banks which created sub-prime mortgage-backed securities, are not.

The Bank of Canada also protects the value of money by keeping inflation low and stable, allowing all markets, not just financial markets, to operate smoothly. Predictable prices mean all macroeconomic players—consumers, businesses, the rest of the world, and government—can make smart choices in whatever markets they trade.

On the fourth role of the Bank of Canada—conducting monetary policy—there are some disagreements between the two camps, but there is also a growing consensus around inflation target rules as a compromise.

Hands-Off: Rules for Monetary Policy

The "Yes—markets quickly self-adjust" believers in Say's Law favour a hands-off role for government. They believe that government failure is more likely than market failure. Therefore, they support an independent central bank to keep monetary policy out of the hands of government politicians including Finance ministers. Furthermore, to keep the independent central bank as hands-off as possible, the "Yes" camp supports fixed rules for monetary policy, like targets, that leave no discretion to central bankers.

Besides believing that markets will quickly adjust to any external shocks, the "Yes" camp points to the delays of up to two years before monetary policy has an impact. Those delays increase the odds that policymakers will get the timing wrong and do more harm than good with discretionary monetary policy. Suppose the central bank, expecting a recession, steps on the gas by lowering interest rates. But what if the economy is expanding by the time the economic car finally speeds up? The expansionary policy will steer the car off the cliff into an inflationary boom that eventually turns into a bust. Better, the "Yes" camp says, to leave the driving to the flexibility of markets.

"Yes" camp favours hands-off rules for monetary policy.

Finally, the "Yes" camp believes that the strongest argument for a hands-off monetary policy is the need to anchor inflationary expectations. Without target rules, politicians may be tempted to allow a higher rate of inflation in pursuit of lower unemployment. This would cause the macroeconomic players to lose confidence in a stable and predictable inflation rate. Once inflation starts rising, the gas pedal can get stuck to the floor because of changing expectations, leading to runaway inflation. It takes a long period of recession, with unemployment and depressed businesses sales, before consumers and businesses begin accepting slower rising wages and prices.

Hands-On: Discretion for Monetary Policy

The "No—markets fail to quickly adjust" followers of Keynes favour a hands-on role for government. They believe that market failure is more likely than government failure. Therefore, they are more willing to give government the discretion to set and conduct monetary policy to counter internally generated business cycles.

The "No" camp points to the uncertainty of transmission breakdowns in monetary policy—that a fixed rule for stepping on the interest rate gas or brake will not always produce the same response in the economic car. Therefore, there needs to be an active driver ready to take the wheel and steer.

Finally, the "No" camp points to the short-run tradeoff between inflation and unemployment, arguing that sometimes the cost of keeping inflation low may have too high an opportunity cost—high unemployment, lost production, and economic suffering. Democratically elected politicians, the "No" camp says, should be the ones to decide on that tradeoff.

"No" camp favours hands-on government discretion for monetary policy.

Shake Hands

Despite these disagreements over monetary policy, there is a growing consensus among economists and politicians that the inflation control targeting of the Bank of Canada is an effective compromise between the hands-off emphasis on rules and the hands-on emphasis on government discretion.

First, the government and the Bank of Canada *jointly* set the inflation control target, while the largely independent Bank of Canada *alone* conducts the monetary policy for achieving that target. This compromise combines accountability to voters (favoured by the hands-on camp) with minimum role for government politicians in conducting monetary policy (favoured by the hands-off camp).

Second, the inflation control target is a fixed rule (favoured by the hands-off camp), but has the effect of stabilizing business cycles (favoured by the hands-on camp).

With an inflation control target, the Bank of Canada automatically takes policy action to counter an inflationary boom (by raising interest rates to step on the brakes) or a recessionary bust (by lowering interest rates to step on the accelerator).

Hands-On   Hands-Off

Both camps recognize that business cycles occur, while disagreeing on whether the causes are external (hands-off) or internal (hands-on) to market economies. So both see a role for monetary policy adjustments in avoiding cycles of boom and bust and keeping the economy on the road to steady growth in living standards, full employment, and stable prices.

Third, both camps agree that the short-run tradeoff between inflation and unemployment can be ruined by inflationary expectations. Some hands-on followers of Keynes would like to lower unemployment in the short run at the expense of higher inflation. But most of the "No" camp now sees that the short-run benefits of lower unemployment are not enough to outweigh the long-run costs of unleashing inflation expectations—costs that can include a long, painful period of recession and high unemployment down the road. Both camps agree on the value of an inflation control target in anchoring inflation expectations.

These unusual agreements about the useful roles of the Bank of Canada, between those advocating a hands-off and a hands-on role for government, disappear in the next chapter on fiscal policy.

Both "Yes" and "No" camps largely agree that inflation control targets are an effective compromise between hands-off emphasis on rules and hands-on emphasis on government discretion.

Refresh

7.5

1. What is the relationship between the Bank of Canada and the Government of Canada?

2. Explain why the Bank of Canada's focus on the inflation target has benefits beyond price stability.

3. Look back at Figure 3.12 (Phillips Curve in Canada, 1946–2009) on page 111. Explain why the points from 1973 to 1983 don't fit the original Phillips Curve.

www.myeconlab.com

Steering Blindly?

Monetary Policy and the Bank of Canada

CHAPTER SUMMARY

7.1 WHAT DO CENTRAL BANKS DO?
BANK OF CANADA'S OBJECTIVES AND TARGETS

The Bank of Canada changes the money supply and interest rates, aiming for an inflation control target that will achieve steady growth, full employment, and stable prices.

- Bank of Canada is responsible for **monetary policy**—changing the supply of money and interest rates to achieve steady growth, full employment, and price stability.

  - **Price stability** means inflation rate is low enough to not significantly affects peoples' decisions.

- **Inflation-control target**—range of inflation rates set as a target by central bank as a monetary policy objective.

  - Bank of Canada's target is annual inflation rate of one to three percent measured by CPI.

  - Monetary policy aims for two percent midpoint of that range.

  - Bank of Canada uses core CPI as operational guide about underlying inflation trends.

The Bank of Canada uses open market operations to change interest rates. Buying bonds increases the money supply and raises bond prices, lowering interest rates. Selling bonds decreases the money supply and lowers bond prices, raising interest rates.

- Interest rates are determined in money and bond markets and central banks can influence short-run interest rates.
  - Bank of Canada's main policy tool is the **overnight rate**— interest rate banks charge each other for one day loans.
  - Overnight rate then determines all other interest rates.
- Lower interest rates mean more borrowing and spending, less savings. Higher interest rates mean less borrowing and spending, more savings.
  - In recessionary gap, Bank of Canada lowers interest rates to increase aggregate demand and accelerate the economy.
  - In inflationary gap, Bank of Canada raises interest rates to decrease aggregate demand and slow down the economy.
- Bank of Canada changes target interest rate through **open market operations** —buying or selling government bonds on bond market.
  - Money market and bond market are interconnected, so open market operations can be explained from either perspective.
- From money market perspective, Bank of Canada changes money supply using open market operations to influence quantity of demand deposits (part of M1).
  - To lower interest rates and accelerate economy, Bank of Canada buys bonds, increasing bank reserves, demand deposits, and money supply.
  - To raise interest rates and slow down economy, Bank of Canada sells bonds to decrease bank reserves, demand deposits, and money supply.
- A basis point is one-hundredth of one percent. 1% = 100 basis points.
- From bond market perspective, Bank of Canada changes money supply using open market operations to influence bond prices and therefore interest rates.
  - When Bank of Canada buys bonds, increased demand for bonds raises bond prices and lowers interest rates.
  - When Bank of Canada sells bonds, increased supply of bonds lowers bond prices and raises interest rates.
- When Bank of Canada changes the overnight rate, most other interest rates change in same direction.
  - **Prime rate**—interest rate on loans to lowest risk corporate borrowers.

7.3 DOES MONEY MAKE THE (REAL) WORLD GO AROUND? TRANSMISSION MECHANISMS

Monetary policy affects aggregate demand through reinforcing domestic and international transmission mechanisms connecting interest rates, exchange rates, and spending.

- Open market operations and interest rates affect aggregate demand $(C + I + G + X - IM)$ through
  - Domestic transmission mechanism.
  - International transmission mechanism.
- Domestic transmission mechanism
  - Lower interest rates are positive aggregate demand shock, increasing consumption (C) and business investment spending (I).
  - Higher interest rates are negative aggregate demand shock, decreasing consumption (C) and business investment spending (I).
- International transmission mechanism works through impact of interest rates on exchange rate.
  - Lower interest rate causes depreciating Canadian dollar; positive demand shock increasing net exports $(X - IM)$, increasing inflation.
  - Higher interest rate causes appreciating Canadian dollar; negative demand shock decreasing net exports $(X - IM)$, decreasing inflation.
- Domestic and international transmission mechanisms reinforce each other—use monetary policy to
  - Correct recessionary gap with lower interest rates—aggregate demand increases, unemployment decreases, inflation increases
  - Correct inflationary gap with higher interest rates—aggregate demand decreases, unemployment increases, inflation decreases.
- Monetary policy is about moderation—accelerating when economy is slowing, braking when economy is speeding up.
  - Monetary policy to brake the economy by raising interest rates is often politically unpopular.

7.4 TRANSMISSION BREAKDOWNS: BALANCE SHEET RECESSIONS AND MONETARY POLICY

In a balance sheet recession, individuals and businesses focus effort on paying down debt and are reluctant to borrow or spend. Even when monetary policy lowers interest rates, the economy remains in recession.

- Recessions often triggered by decreasing business investment spending, falling net exports, or rising interest rates.
  - Great Recession (2008–2009) instead triggered by falling asset prices.

- A balance sheet shows assets on one side (what you own or earn) and debts or liabilities on the other side (what you owe or spend).
  - Great Recession was a balance sheet recession—falling asset prices lead individuals and businesses to cut spending, save, and pay down debt.
  - Transmission breakdowns for monetary policy as low interest rates did not increase spending and aggregate demand.
- Transmission breakdowns caused by
  - Consumers—saving more, paying off debts, spending less.
  - Businesses—pessimistic expectations decreasing business investment spending even with lower interest rates.
  - Money as a store of value—giving individuals and businesses a way not to spend.
  - Banks—holding on to cash reserves rather than making new loans, creating demand deposits, and increasing the money supply.
- To counteract transmission breakdowns, central banks used **quantitative easing**—flooding financial system with money by buying risky bonds, mortgages, and assets from banks. These liabilities on bank balance sheets are replaced with cash assets, enabling banks to make new loans.
- Risk of flooding financial system with money is inflation.
  - Quantity theory of money predicts increasing money supply when economy approaches potential GDP will cause inflation.
  - Central banks have a difficult timing problem of applying monetary "brake" of higher interest rates before inflation starts, but not too soon to stop economic recovery.
- Balance sheet recessions cause transmission problems for monetary policy, making it harder to steer economy towards recovery.

**7.5 WHO'S DRIVING?
ANCHORING INFLATION EXPECTATIONS**

Inflation rate targeting by an independent central bank anchors inflation expectations, helps price signals work and combines a hands-off emphasis on rules and hands-on emphasis on government discretion.

- Inflation-control target set jointly by Government of Canada and Bank of Canada.
  - Bank of Canada alone responsible for monetary policy to achieve target.
  - Bank of Canada has considerable independence, but ultimately responsible to Parliament.
- Bank of Canada focused only on inflation rate targeting since 1991.
  - Inflation has stayed within target range.
  - Steered economy towards rising living standards, full employment.
- Advantages of inflation rate targeting
  - Anchoring expectations about inflation.
  - Improving predictability of prices.

- Original Phillips Curve tradeoff between inflation and unemployment works when expectations of inflation do not change.
  - Once inflation arises, changing expectations can be self-fulfilling—by reacting to expectation of inflation we may cause it.
  - Changing inflation expectations, combined with increases in money supply, eliminated original Phillips Curve's tradeoff between higher inflation and lower unemployment.
  - Inflation expectations go up quickly and easily, but come down slowly and painfully.
- Unpredictable prices—due to inflation—create risk, discourage business investment, and interfere with price signals for smart choices.
- "Yes" and "No" camps agree markets need a government-like central bank.
  - Banks regulated because of tradeoff between profits and prudence.
  - Some disagreements between two camps on monetary policy.
- "Yes" camp favours hands-off rules for monetary policy, likes targets, leaving no discretion for central bankers and no opportunity for politicians to influence monetary policy.
  - Believes government failure more likely than market failure.
- "No" camp favours hands-on government discretion for monetary policy to correct transmission breakdown, allowing democratically elected politicians to set policy.
  - Believes market failure more likely than government failure.
- Both "Yes" and "No" camps largely agree that inflation control targets are effective compromise between hands-off emphasis on rules and hands-on emphasis on government discretion.

TRUE/FALSE

Circle the correct answer.

You accidentally schedule a driving lesson for the night before your test on monetary policy. Fortunately, your driving instructor, Lindsay, has an economics degree and offers to quiz you on monetary policy during the lesson. She says:

Steering the economy through monetary policy is similar to steering a car through a winding mountain road. If you can recognize a true or false statement on monetary policy as well as you steer this car, you will do great on your test tomorrow. Tell me if the following statements are true or false.

Use this scenario to answer questions 1–15.

7.1 BANK OF CANADA'S JOB

1. The Prime Minister is the driver at the wheel for Canadian monetary policy.　　**True　　False**

2. The Bank of Canada uses monetary policy to steer the economy towards stable prices, steady economic growth, and full employment.　　**True　　False**

7.2 OPEN MARKET OPERATIONS

3. The Bank of Canada's tool for steering the economy is the inflation rate. **True** **False**

4. The Bank of Canada tries to keep inflation rates between one percent and three percent in order to steer the economy on the right track. **True** **False**

5. The Bank of Canada's number one objective is to drive the Canadian economy on the road to potential GDP at the ideal speed, avoiding the booms and busts of business cycles on either side of the road. **True** **False**

6. When the economy is slowing down, the Bank of Canada steps on the gas by lowering interest rates. **True** **False**

7. When the economy is speeding too fast, the government pulls the Bank of Canada over and tells it to lower interest rates. **True** **False**

7.3 TRANSMISSION MECHANISMS

8. When the central bank steps on the gas, the effects of lower interest rates travel through the transmission mechanism to increase spending and aggregate demand. **True** **False**

9. While cars have different pedals for the gas and brake, monetary policy has one pedal (interest rates) that can be lowered or raised. **True** **False**

10. It is politically popular when the Bank of Canada puts on the brakes by raising interest rates. **True** **False**

7.4 TRANSMISSION BREAKDOWNS

11. The timing of the monetary "brake" is crucial. If the central bank steps on the brake too soon, it risks halting the recovery. If it waits too long, it risks inflation. **True** **False**

12. Balance sheet recessions cause transmission problems for monetary policy, making it harder to steer the economy towards recovery. **True** **False**

7.5 ANCHORING INFLATION EXPECTATIONS

13. The Minister of Finance for the government and the Governor of the Bank of Canada jointly decide on the destination of Canada's economic car, but the Governor gets to drive. **True** **False**

14. Inflation expectations are like driving cars uphill—they go up slowly and painfully, but come down quickly and easily.

True**False**

15. The "Yes" camp says to leave the driving to the government.

True**False**

MULTIPLE CHOICE

Circle the correct answer.

7.1 BANK OF CANADA'S JOB

1. The price stability goal of the Bank of Canada is to keep the

A) unemployment rate low at any cost.

B) inflation rate low at any cost.

C) inflation rate low enough so that it does not significantly affect decisions.

D) inflation rate at zero so that it does not significantly affect decisions.

2. The Bank of Canada's inflation-control target is the

A) CPI.

B) core CPI.

C) CPI, with core CPI as an operational guide.

D) core CPI, with CPI as an operational guide.

7.2 OPEN MARKET OPERATIONS

3. The CPI inflation rate was 0.1 percent in October 2009 and 1.3 percent in December 2009. The CPI inflation rate was

A) in the target range in both October and December.

B) below the target range in both October and December.

C) in the target range in October but not December.

D) in the target range in December but not October.

4. Many central bank governors failed to anticipate how bad the Great Recession would be, and wish they had responded sooner. Ben Bernanke said, "I'm not one of those people who look at this as some kind of video game . . . This is all very real to me." Suppose monetary policy were as simple as pressing a button on a video game. The button that should have been pushed sooner would have

A) increased the inflation rate.

B) raised the overnight interest rate.

C) lowered the overnight interest rate.

D) turned off the video game.

5. Vanessa has a bad credit rating. When she goes to the bank for a loan, the interest rate the bank will offer her is
   A) the target rate.
   B) the prime rate.
   C) between the target rate and the prime rate.
   D) above the prime rate.

6. When the Bank of Canada buys bonds, the
   A) increased demand for bonds raises bond prices and interest rates.
   B) increased demand for bonds raises bond prices and lowers interest rates.
   C) increased supply of bonds lowers bond prices and raises interest rates.
   D) decreased supply of bonds lowers bond prices and lowers interest rates.

7.3 TRANSMISSION MECHANISMS

7. Which statement describes the impact of expansionary monetary policy?
   A) Selling bonds decreases the money supply, raising interest rates, decreasing aggregate demand.
   B) Selling bonds decreases the money supply, lowering interest rates, increasing aggregate demand.
   C) Buying bonds raises the price of bonds, lowering interest rates, increasing aggregate demand.
   D) Buying bonds raises the price of bonds, lowering interest rates, decreasing aggregate demand.

8. The Bank of Canada should increase interest rates today if
   A) the economy is currently in an inflationary gap.
   B) the economy is currently in a recessionary gap.
   C) it expects a recessionary gap 18–24 months into the future.
   D) it expects an inflationary gap 18–24 months into the future.

9. During a recessionary gap, the Bank of Canada should
   A) drink out of the punch bowl.
   B) take away the punch bowl.
   C) add punch to the punch bowl.
   D) catch demons swimming in the punch bowl.

10. An expansionary monetary policy will
   A) lower interest rates and cause the exchange rate to depreciate.
   B) lower interest rates and cause the exchange rate to appreciate.
   C) raise interest rates and cause the exchange rate to depreciate.
   D) raise interest rates and cause the exchange rate to appreciate.

11. If real GDP is less than potential GDP, an increase in the quantity of money will lead to a(n)

    A) increase in both real GDP and the price level.

    B) increase in real GDP and a decrease the price level.

    C) increase in real GDP and no change in the price level.

    D) decrease in both real GDP and the price level.

12. Which statement best describes the Bank of Canada's policy dress code before and during the Great Recession?

    A) "Pink polka dot suits" before and during the Great Recession.

    B) "Conservative blue ties" before and during the Great Recession.

    C) "Pink polka dot suits" before, "conservative blue ties" during the Great Recession.

    D) "Conservative blue ties" before, "Pink polka dot suits" during the Great Recession.

13. Which statement best describes the banking system's choices before and during the Great Recession?

    A) "Profits over prudence" before and during the Great Recession.

    B) "Profits over prudence" before, "prudence over profits" during the Great Recession.

    C) "Prudence over profits" before, "profits over prudence" during the Great Recession.

    D) "Prudence over profits" before and during the Great Recession.

7.5 ANCHORING INFLATION EXPECTATIONS

14. The "No" camp favours

    A) hands-off rules for monetary policy.

    B) fixed rules that leave no discretion for monetary policy.

    C) a role for government in setting monetary policy, but not in conducting monetary policy.

    D) all of the above.

15. Canada has

    A) an inflation-control target jointly decided by Government and Bank of Canada.

    B) a central bank that independently achieves its target.

    C) no government discretion for achieving target.

    D) all of the above.

SHORT ANSWER

Write a short answer to each question. Your answer may be in point form.

1. While Canada, Britain, Australia, the European Union, and other countries target inflation rates, the U.S. Federal Reserve targets both the inflation rate and the unemployment rate.

   A) Has the Bank of Canada been successful since 1991 in pursuing stable inflation as a goal while at the same time promoting higher living standards?

   B) The U.S. Federal Reserve (the U.S. central bank) has "maximum employment, stable prices, and moderate long-term interest rates" as objectives. Critics of the U.S. system say that it is not easy for consumers and businesses to have a clear understanding of the central bank's goals. How can pursuing only stable inflation as a goal lead to better choices by consumers and businesses?

   C) Based on the monetary policy objectives in Canada and the U.S., which country is more like the "Yes" camp?

2. In December 2009, Canada's CPI inflation rate was 1.3 percent and the core inflation rate was 1.5 percent.

   A) Was inflation in the target range in December 2009?

   B) Was inflation below or above the midpoint target range in December 2009?

   C) The core rate of inflation and CPI inflation were expected to increase gradually, returning to two percent in the third quarter of 2011. Why do you think the Bank of Canada kept the overnight rate unchanged in December 2009?

3. Suppose that your boss, Michael Scott from the popular TV show *The Office*, hands you the latest Bank of Canada Monetary Policy Report announcing an increase in the overnight target rate. He asks you the following questions.

   A) Will the increase in the overnight target rate increase interest rates? If so, how?

   B) Will higher interest rates lead to lower spending and higher unemployment? If so, how?

   C) Will higher interest rates affect the value of the Canadian dollar and spending? If so, how?

4. Suppose that your boss, Michael Scott from the popular TV show *The Office*, makes the following (angry) announcement after learning how a higher overnight interest rate will impact spending and real GDP. He says, "The Bank of Canada is restricting growth in the economy, supposedly to fight inflation, even though the CPI has not yet increased. Consumers and businesses are now going to have to pay more when they take out loans."

   A) Why would consumers and businesses complain about monetary policies used to reduce inflationary pressures?

   B) What could you say to Michael to calm him down? (Hint: explain why the Bank of Canada fights demons that are not yet present.)

5. Ben Bernanke, Chairman of the U.S. Federal Reserve, studied the monetary policy mistakes of the Great Depression and was determined not to let "Depression 2.0" happen. In the Great Depression of the 1930s, the central bank obsessed over inflation and responded by raising interest rates, instead of lowering interest rates and expanding the money supply to boost the economy. If Bernanke had the opportunity to ask John Maynard Keynes to comment on the central bank's response during the Great Depression, what do you expect Keynes would say?

6. In November 2009, CPI inflation in England was at the Bank of England's inflation target of two percent. By December 2009, inflation increased to three percent, the biggest monthly increase in over a decade. Meanwhile, unemployment was high and real GDP was below potential GDP, and both were starting to show signs of improvement.

   A) Mervyn King, the Governor of the Bank of England, is the one who described his job as "taking away the punch bowl just when the party is getting started." Explain how his statement applies to monetary policy in this situation.

   B) Would economists from the "Yes" camp argue that the governor of the central bank should take away the punch bowl?

   C) Explain why the costs of uncertainty associated with high and unpredictable inflation are important reasons to keep inflation rates low, stable and predictable.

7. The Great Recession of 2008–2009 is often referred to as a balance sheet recession.

   A) What is a balance sheet recession?

   B) Did the Bank of Canada respond to the Great Recession as a reader of this textbook would expect them to? [Hint: what is supposed to be the effect of almost free money?]

   C) Why is a balance sheet recession a problem for monetary policy?

8. According to *Time Magazine*, the story of the year 2009 was a weak U.S. economy that could have been much weaker if it wasn't for Ben Bernanke. The magazine named Bernanke the Person of the Year for 2009.

   A) The magazine article states that he just happens to be the most powerful nerd on the planet. Why is the top-ranked individual at a central bank considered to be so powerful?

   B) Bernanke used a powerful tool from his monetary policy toolbox— quantitative easing. What is quantitative easing?

   C) How is quantitative easing similar to, and different from, open market operations?

9. Economic growth in Canada was positive towards the end of 2009, but the economy was still below potential GDP.

   A) If the Bank of Canada wanted to use expansionary monetary policy to help real GDP grow at this time, would monetary policy be inflationary? Why or why not?

   B) While many advanced economies were still declining in the fourth quarter of 2009, China's real GDP was growing by about 10 percent and showing signs that the economy was at potential real GDP. Would expansionary monetary policy at the end of 2009 be inflationary in China? Why or why not?

10. The current inflation-control target agreement between the Bank of Canada and the federal government expires at the end of 2011. Suppose that economists make the following two statements regarding their views on potential future changes. Identify the camp of economists ("Yes" camp or "No" camp) that they are likely from.

   A) "With unemployment rates expected to remain above the natural rate of unemployment by the end of 2011, the Bank of Canada should target both inflation and unemployment, as is done in the U.S."

   B) "The Bank of Canada should widen the inflation target range from the existing range of 1–3 percent to 1–4 percent."

(X) myeconlab Visit the MyEconLab website at **www.myeconlab.com**. This online homework and tutorial system puts you in control of your own learning with study and practice tools.

Chapter 8

Spending
Others' Money

Fiscal Policy, Deficits, and National Debt

LEARNING OBJECTIVES

8.1 Use the concepts of injections and leakages to explain the multiplied impact of aggregate demand fiscal policies.

8.2 Identify three aggregate supply policies for growth, and compare the "Yes" and "No" camps on incentive effects and supply-side policies.

8.3 Differentiate cyclical from structural deficits and surpluses, and explain the connections between automatic stabilizers and business cycles.

8.4 Explain the difference between deficits and debts, and identify five arguments about the national debt.

8.5 Distinguish between normative, positive, economic, and political arguments about fiscal policy.

NO ONE LIKES BEING IN DEBT. When governments—federal, provincial, or municipal—spend more than they take in collecting taxes, their budgets are not balanced. They run deficits. Debt starts piling up. Many citizens disapprove, saying, "Get your financial house in order! Avoid debt. Don't spend more than you've got." But is going into debt always a bad choice?

Most individual consumers and businesses regularly make smart choices that involve going into debt. People taking on a mortgage or a car lease are going into debt. Businesses regularly issue bonds to borrow money (go into debt) for building new factories. If debt is sometimes smart for individuals and businesses, can it sometimes be smart for governments?

When spending collapsed during the Great Recession, the only macroeconomic player who kept spending steadily was government. They financed this spending by going into debt. Was this financially irresponsible, or did government spending and debt save the market economy from depression?

In this chapter, you will learn about government spending, its multiplied impact on the economy, and the differences between deficits and debts. The Canadian government had a budget deficit of $6 billion in 2009. That means it had to borrow that much money in that year to do what it wanted to do. As well, by 2009, the government already had a debt of over $500 billion dollars. Is that a cause for alarm, or for celebration of smart choices? Most importantly, you will learn how to analyze the heated mix of economics and politics fuelling most debates about government spending and debt from politicians seeking your votes.

Should the government leave the economy alone, or step in to try to remedy market failures? Hands-off or hands-on? This chapter will help you make up your own mind about the role that government should play in a market economy.

8.1 Spenders of Last Resort: Aggregate Demand Policies for Stabilizing Business Cycles

Use the concepts of injections and leakages to explain the multiplied impact of aggregate demand fiscal policies.

Monetary policy is about money. But what is fiscal policy? *Fiscal* comes from the Latin word *fisc*—the public treasury of Rome. In the time of the Roman Empire, the emperor controlled the public treasury—the *fisc*. Today, governments control the public treasury and fiscal policy is about the changes governments make regarding their purchases, transfers, and taxes in attempting to achieve the key macroeconomic outcomes of steady growth, full employment, and stable prices.

The effects of fiscal policy work through aggregate demand, speeding up or slowing down an economy facing recessionary or inflationary gaps.

Aggregate demand is the sum of planned consumer spending (C), business investment spending (I), government spending on products/services (G), and net exports ($X - IM$).

$$\text{Aggregate Demand} = C + I + G + X - IM$$

To see exactly where fiscal policy affects aggregate demand, let's return yet again to Figure 2.15, which is reproduced here as Figure 8.1.

Fiscal policy is changes in government purchases, taxes, and transfers to achieve macroeconomic outcomes of steady growth, full employment, and stable prices.

Figure 8.1   Enlarged GDP Circular Flow of Income and Spending with Banking System ($)

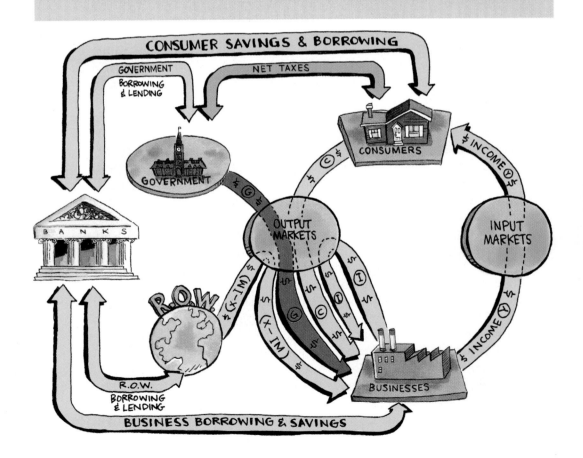

Virtuous and Vicious Circles: Multiplier Effects

In the enlarged GDP circular flow of Figure 8.1, there are two main paths for transmitting the effects of fiscal policy to aggregate demand—government purchases and net taxes.

Government Purchases as Injections   The government purchases path is highlighted in red. When the government builds highways or hires the services of accounting firms, these are purchases of products/services in output markets.

Government purchases are an example of what economists call injections into the circular flow. An **injection** is spending in the circular flow that does not start with consumers—government purchases (*G*), business investment spending (*I*), and exports (*X*) are injections.

Compare Figure 8.1 with previous Figure 2.13, reproduced here as Figure 8.2. Government purchases (*G*), business investment spending (*I*) and exports (*X*), are all new injections of spending into Figure 8.2's simple GDP circular flow. This will be important for understanding the impact of fiscal policy.

injection: spending in the circular flow that does not start with consumers; G, I, and X

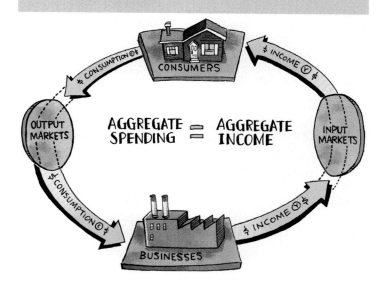

Figure 8.2   Simple GDP Circular Flow of Income and Spending

Net Taxes as Leakages   The net taxes path of fiscal policy is highlighted in Figure 8.1 in blue. Net taxes is a combination of taxes paid by consumers to government and transfer payments (Employment Assistance, Canada Pension) consumers receive from government. Because taxes are greater than transfers (people pay government more than they get), the flow of net taxes is from consumers to government.

Net taxes are an example of what economists call leakages from the circular flow. A **leakage** is spending that leaks out of (leaves) the circular flow, through taxes, savings, and imports.

leakage: spending that leaks out of the circular flow through taxes, savings, and imports

Round and Round the Circle   Injections and leakages, flowing into and out of the circular flow, are key to understanding the multiplied impact of fiscal policy on aggregate demand and GDP. Let's start with government purchases—an injection—and look at what happens in Figure 8.1.

Suppose the government spends $10 million to purchase a new bridge: *G* goes up by $10 million. That means GDP, which equals *C* + *I* + *G* + *X* − *IM*, goes up by the $10 million injection in this first round of spending. Here is the surprise—the full impact is *more than* $10 million. To see how, follow the circle.

The Vancouver 2010 Winter Olympics were predicted to have a huge multiplier effect for the B.C. economy. The impact of the increased tourism, new buildings, and improved infrastructure are estimated to add $6 to $10 billion in new spending in the province before 2015. It is because of such multiplier effects that cities willingly pay millions of dollars for the rights to host the Games.

multiplier effect: spending injection has multiplied impact on real GDP

The initial impact is that the bridge-building business (businesses are at the bottom of the circle) gets $10 million. Following the circle up to the right, that means incomes of everyone working for the business—workers, owners, suppliers—goes up by $10 million. What do people do with that additional income? The government takes some of the income as taxes—a leakage out of the circular flow (the net taxes flow from consumers to government at the top). People save some—another leakage out of the circular flow (the consumer saving and borrowing flow at the very top). People spend the remaining income in output markets on products/services. Some of that new spending is on imports—the final leakage (the net export flow between businesses and R.O.W.). But even after all of those leakages, there will be some new spending on Canadian products/services.

Suppose Canadian businesses receive $5 million in this second round of spending. The story, and the flow around the circle, repeats. There will again be leakages in taxes, savings, and imports, but again, there will be new spending on Canadian products/services. In the third round of spending, businesses will receive, for example, $2.5 million. The circles of spending and income, while continuing, get smaller and smaller, eventually fading away.

The impact of the initial $10 million injection of government spending is multiplied by going around the circular flow. Economists call this the **multiplier effect**—a spending injection has a multiplied impact on real GDP.

The multiplier effect also works in reverse. A reduction in government spending will have a multiplied impact reducing real GDP.

Tax and Transfer Multipliers   There is a similar multiplier effect from changes in taxes or government transfers. A tax cut or an increase in transfer payments reduces leakages. This leaves consumers with more money to spend. The new spending will have a multiplied effect increasing GDP.

In reverse, an increase in taxes or decrease in transfers is an increase in leakages, leaving consumers with less money to spend. The reduced spending will have a multiplied effect, decreasing real GDP.

How Big Are Multiplier Effects?   Changes in government spending on products/services or in net taxes affect aggregate demand and have multiplied effects on real GDP. How big are the effects of these fiscal policy tools that governments can use? Estimates vary, but many place the size of the multiplier effect for government spending around two. A $10 million injection of new spending increases GDP by about $20 million after all of the rounds of spending have finished.

The multiplier effect for tax and transfer changes is not this big. For example, when consumers get a $10 million tax cut, they don't spend the full $10 million on Canadian products/services. They save some of the $10 million and spend some on imports. Because the initial round of new consumer spending will be less than $10 million, the multiplier impact is less than for government spending.

FOR YOUR INFORMATION

The size of multiplier effects varies depending on circumstances. If the economy is close to potential GDP, multiplier effects are smaller — the increased spending drives up prices instead of increasing real GDP.

If the government spending is financed by borrowing, which raises interest rates, business investment spending may decrease, reducing the net effect of the multiplier. This is called crowding out, and is discussed on page 315.

Leakages and the Multiplier Effect   The size of the multiplier effect depends on leakages out of the circular flow of income and spending. The more leakages there are—taxes, saving, imports—the less money gets spent on Canadian products/services in each round of spending. More leakages mean a smaller multiplier effect; fewer leakages mean a larger multiplier effect.

Other Injections: Multiplier Effects and Business Cycles

Multiplier effects don't flow just from government. Any change in injections, from business investment spending or exports, also affects aggregate demand and therefore has a multiplied impact on GDP. Many Canadian business cycles, both recessions and expansions, have been triggered by changes in investment spending or exports.

Business Investment Spending   Business investment spending is the most volatile component of aggregate demand—it fluctuates up and down with changes in interest rates and expectations of future profits. Investment spending (*I*) fluctuates far more than consumption spending (*C*). Consumers, even pessimistic and unemployed consumers, have to spend money to eat and to have a place to live. But businesses can easily postpone spending on new factories or additional machinery. When business investment spending decreases, aggregate demand decreases and there is a multiplied effect on GDP. A collapse in investment spending between 1929 and 1933 was an important cause of the Great Depression. Investment spending dropped almost 80 percent, from $1.4 billion to $0.3 billion. The reverse is also true. Expansions are often triggered by increases in business investment spending that increase aggregate demand with a multiplied impact on GDP.

Export-Led Busts and Booms   Canada is a trading nation. Thirty-six percent of GDP comes from export sales, and eighty percent of our exports are sold to the United States. When the Great Recession started in the United States, it spread to Canada through plunging U.S. demand for Canadian exports, especially automobiles. See Economics Out There (page 294) for the multiplied impact of that fall in injections. You may be surprised by who was affected. In reverse, growing demands from the rest of the world for Canadian exports—especially commodities like oil and other resources—have triggered many expansions. When economic growth is driven by the multiplied effects of increasing exports, it is called *export-led growth*.

Canada exports products ranging from oil and lumber to wheat and gold, but Canada also exports art and entertainment. In 2006, for example, there was over $3 billion in Canadian cultural exports including such TV hit shows *Flashpoint*, *The Border*, *Little Mosque on the Prairie*, *Corner Gas*, and *Degrassi: The Next Generation*. Cirque de Soleil, a modern circus combining circus acts and street-type entertainment, seen here performing in England in 2007, was founded in Quebec in 1984 and currently has over twenty travelling shows performing around the world.

Size of multiplier effects depends on leakages out of the circular flow. More leakages = smaller multiplier, Fewer leakages = larger multiplier.

Any change in injections— G, I or X—affects aggregate demand and has a multiplied impact on GDP.

ECONOMICS *Out There*

The Human Impact of Multiplier Effects

The world's largest manufacturer of glass containers, Owens-Illinois, Inc., permanently shut down its plant in Toronto, putting 400 people out of work. But the employees are not the only victims.

The plant did business with box and machine makers, with electrical contractors and truckers. The employees spent their incomes in local restaurants, on vacations, gifts, homes, and cars.

As part of the multiplier effects of the initial shutdown in spending by Owens-Illinois, a nearby machinist lost his job, a restaurant lost a weekly diner, and a travel agent lost a yearly booking. Jean's Flower Shop lost $150 when the laid-off workers bought one funeral bouquet together instead of each buying one. The struggles of the flower shop hurt Steve's Delivery's six employees, who cut back their spending.

"It's like a chain reaction," says Jorge Gonzalez, a former forklift operator at the Owens-Illinois plant. That's the multiplier effect.

Source: Daniel Dale and Brett Popplewell,"The Ripple Effect of 400 Layoffs," *Toronto Star*, April 12, 2009, pp. A8–9.

Filling the Gaps:
Fiscal Policy and Aggregate Demand

Multiplier effects enhance the effectiveness of fiscal policy as a tool for influencing aggregate demand to counter business cycles.

Fiscal policies to increase government spending, cut taxes, or increase transfers are positive aggregate demand shocks for countering a recessionary gap.

Recessionary Gaps   When the economy is in a recessionary gap, real GDP is less than potential GDP, and the unemployment rate is above the natural rate. Inflation is falling or stable—not a concern. In this situation, governments can increase spending, cut taxes, or increase transfers to increase aggregate demand. These positive aggregate demand shocks accelerate the economy, causing increased real GDP, decreased unemployment, and rising inflation.

That is what governments in Canada did when facing the Great Recession in 2009. Consumers were spending less and saving more. Businesses facing poor sales and banks, unwillingness to lend money, led to cut backs in production and investment spending. Exports to the U.S and the rest of the world had fallen. Governments became the "spenders of last resort," spending when other macroeconomic players were not. Governments used both increased spending and tax cuts in their fiscal policy to fight the recession.

Inflationary Gaps   When the economy is in an inflationary gap, real GDP is above potential GDP, and the unemployment rate is below the natural rate. Unemployment is not a problem, There are shortages of workers and rising wages, not shortages of jobs. Inflation is the major concern. In this situation, governments can decrease spending, raise taxes, or decrease transfers to decrease aggregate demand. These negative aggregate demand shocks slow the economy down, causing decreased real GDP, increased unemployment, and falling inflation.

Fiscal policies to decrease government spending, raise taxes, or decrease transfers are negative aggregate demand shocks for countering an inflationary gap.

Hands-Off and Hands-On Choices for Demand-Side Fiscal Policies

Both the "Yes—markets quickly self-adjust" camp and the "No—markets can fail to adjust" camps agree that fiscal policy can affect aggregate demand, GDP, unemployment, and inflation. Fiscal policy can help match aggregate demand and aggregate supply at potential GDP. Despite that agreement, the two camps disagree about the best fiscal policy to use.

Hands-Off   The "Yes" camp believes that government should keep its hands off of the economy whenever possible.

If fiscal policy is necessary to accelerate the economy, the hands-off position favours tax cuts instead of increased government spending. They argue for putting more money in the hands of private individuals and businesses, who should make their own smart choices about how to best spend their money. The "Yes" camp believes that government spending is subject to political influence and is not always spent where it is needed.

If fiscal policy is necessary to slow down the economy, the hands-off position favours reduced government spending instead of tax increases. This keeps money in the hands of private individuals and businesses, and reduces the size of what they believe is unnecessary government spending.

Bank of Canada interest rate changes (monetary policy) have a slower impact on the economy than increased government spending or tax cuts (fiscal policy). But interest rate changes take effect as soon as the Governor of the Bank of Canada announces them. Fiscal policy changes can take months to pass through parliament.

Both monetary and fiscal policy changes have built-in timing problems. Monetary policy has a timing risk because of the long lags between changes in interest rates and the full impact of those changes on the economy. Fiscal policy has a timing risk of long time lags between recognizing the need for action and actual changes in government spending, taxes, or transfers. The delays in getting tax or spending changes (fiscal policy changes) through parliament increase the odds that policymakers will get the timing wrong and do more harm than good. Better, the "Yes" camp says, to let markets quickly self-adjust rather than risk the possibility of political influence and bad timing from fiscal policy.

"Yes" camp favours tax cuts instead of government spending to accelerate the economy, and spending reductions instead of tax increases to slow down the economy.

Hands-On The "No" camp expects markets to fail often, and sees an essential hands-on role for government to correct those failures. All forms of fiscal policy are acceptable, especially when monetary policy is ineffective due to transmission breakdowns (see section 7.4). But among fiscal policy choices, the hands-on position sometimes favours government spending over tax cuts. They argue that government spending is more effective, since consumers and businesses may save money from tax cuts rather than spend it, causing transmission breakdowns.

If fiscal policy is necessary to slow the economy down, the hands-on position favours tax increases over reduced government spending. This, they say, preserves the government's ability to stabilize the economy. And if the tax increases are progressive, taking more from those with higher incomes, their goal of equity can be furthered.

On the choice between private spending and government spending, the hands-on position is more comfortable with government spending. They argue that democratically elected politicians are the right people to be making choices about how to spend taxpayers' money, and want spending plans to pay attention to equity among different groups in Canada, rather than simply looking for the most efficient expenditure of funds.

"No" camp favours government spending instead of tax cuts to accelerate the economy, and tax increases instead of government spending reductions to slow down the economy.

Multipliers at Work Multiplier effects help explain the ups and downs of business cycles, as well as fiscal policies for counteracting those cycles. Fiscal policies, working through aggregate demand, are a tool that can keep the economy on the road to potential GDP, full employment, and stable prices. There are also fiscal policy tools that affect aggregate supply.

Refresh 8.1

1. In your own words, explain the multiplier effect of government or business spending. Include the concepts of injections and leakages in your answer.

2. In terms of fiscal policy choices, which position — hands-off or hands-on — is closest to your beliefs? Explain.

3. If politicians in your area want to spend millions of dollars to build a stadium to bring a professional sports team to your community, what would your reaction be? Why?

www.myeconlab.com

8.2 Building Foundations: Aggregate Supply Policies for Promoting Growth

Fiscal policies for aggregate demand can help counter the bust and boom of business cycles, keeping the economy moving steadily on the road towards potential GDP, full employment, and stable prices. These government spending, tax, and transfer changes attempt to *match aggregate demand and aggregate supply at potential GDP.*

There is one other key macroeconomic outcome—steady growth in living standards—that calls for a different kind of fiscal policy. Economic growth (see Section 2.2) is the expansion of the economy's capacity to produce products/services—an *increase in potential GDP.* Economic growth happens over time when increases in the quantity and quality of inputs—labour, capital, land, and entrepreneurship—expand the circular flow and increase aggregate supply.

Much economic growth results from increases in the quality of inputs, including technological change. These increases in the quality of inputs increase productivity—each person produces more. Living standards rise when potential GDP per person grows. Increases in aggregate supply, rather than adjustments to aggregate demand, produce economic growth.

Investing in the Future: Policies for Economic Growth

When aggregate supply increases, economic growth can raise living standards by increasing potential GDP per person. Fiscal policies that target aggregate supply attempt to achieve three outcomes—stimulate savings and capital investment, encourage research and development, and improve education and training.

Stimulate Savings and Capital Investment   In the loanable funds market, savings finance investment. When savings increase the supply of loanable funds, it is easier for businesses to borrow to finance investment spending to build new factories or install new machinery. Policies to stimulate savings can increase the quantity of capital available and promote economic growth.

Tax incentives are the fiscal policy tool often used to stimulate savings. If you save money in Tax-Free Savings Accounts (TFSAs) or Registered Retirement Savings Plans (RRSPs), you do not have to pay tax on the income you save or on any gains you make from the saved money. According to financial planners, savings in one of these tax-free accounts is one of the smartest choices you can make with your personal finances. Tax incentives for savings help align your smart individual choices with smart choices for the economy as a whole, promoting economic growth.

Identify three aggregate supply policies for growth, and compare the "Yes" and "No" camps on incentive effects and supply-side policies.

Productivity isn't everything, but in the long run it is almost everything. A country's ability to improve its standard of living over time depends almost entirely on its ability to raise output per worker.

–Paul Krugman
2008 Nobel Prize in Economics

Tax incentives can stimulate savings, increase the quantity of capital, and promote economic growth.

Government can also stimulate savings by changing the mix of taxation in the economy. The Government of Canada collects income taxes (taxing what you earn) and consumption taxes (taxing what you spend). The Goods and Services Tax (GST) and the Harmonized Sales Tax (HST) are consumption taxes—you only pay these taxes when you spend money. If the government collected more of its tax revenue from consumption taxes, and less from income taxes, you would have additional incentives to save your income instead of spending it. Again, this would increase savings and promote economic growth.

Encourage Research and Development

Researchers, whether working in universities or corporate research and development (R&D) laboratories, develop new and better ways of making existing products/services, as well as new and better product/services. Most productivity-improving technological change originates with choices to spend time and money on research and development.

The technological knowledge from research and development spending benefits many businesses and individuals beyond those making the new discoveries. Knowledge is an example of what economists call **externalities**— benefits or costs that affect others external to (not directly involved in) a choice or a trade (see Appendix A.5). Knowledge that benefits others is an example of a **positive externality**. Driving a car has a **negative externality**—other people bear the costs of your car's pollution.

Even well-functioning markets produce too few products/services that have positive externalities, and too many products/services that have negative externalities. So markets tend to produce too few research and development services. Even the "Yes—markets quickly self-adjust" camp recognizes externalities as a source of market failure.

Government can use fiscal policy to encourage research and development through targeted government spending and tax incentives. For example, the government funds the National Science and Engineering Research Council (NSERC), which in turn subsidizes basic scientific research in universities. The government also provides tax incentives to businesses for research and development. These fiscal policies increase research and development activities and help align the smart individual choices of businesses and individuals with smart social choices for the economy as a whole, promoting economic growth.

Improve Education and Training

Human capital—the quality of labour inputs—can be increased through education and training. Education, training, and work experience increase a person's earning potential. Businesses are willing to pay higher wages to workers with more human capital because they are more productive.

positive (or negative) externalities: benefits (or costs) that affect others external to a choice or a trade

Government spending and tax incentives encourage research and development activities, whose positive externalities promote economic growth.

Education and training are services with positive externalities, which means markets produce too few of them. When you get a post-secondary education, your individual benefits include higher lifetime earnings (smart choice!). But there are also external benefits to employers (who do not have to spend as much time and money training you), to governments (because you will require less assistance and can better participate in democratic activities) and to the economy as a whole (because your increased productivity increases potential GDP and potential living standards for all).

Government fiscal policies can increase the amount of education and training available. Government can spend to directly provide education, as it does for kindergarten to grade 12, and government can provide subsidies to schools (as it does to colleges and universities) and to students (bursaries and grants). There are also tax incentives to improve education and training. Registered Education Savings Plans (RESPs) in 2009 granted you $200 for every $1000 deposited, as well as eliminating tax on any gains you made from the saved money. Tuition and training fees are also eligible for tax reductions.

Government spending and tax incentives for education and training increase human capital, creating positive externalities promoting economic growth.

Fiscal Policy Can Increase Potential GDP Fiscal spending and taxing policies can encourage increases in the quantity and quality of inputs, increasing aggregate supply and spurring increases in potential GDP per person. There is one other impact of fiscal policy on aggregate supply—incentive effects.

Supply-Siders and Voodoo Economics: Incentive Effects

Suppose your boss lets you decide how many hours to work this week. She asks, "How many hours will you work if I pay you $15 an hour?" After you answer, she asks, "How many hours will you work if I pay you $20 an hour?" If you are like most people, you are willing to work more hours at $20 an hour than at $15 an hour. The higher wage acts as an *incentive* for you to supply a greater quantity of labour. That is the law of supply (Appendix C.3).

A tax cut can provide the same incentive as a wage increase. Your take-home pay, after the government deducts income tax, is always less than what your boss pays you. If the government cuts your income taxes, your take-home pay rises, just as if your boss had given you a raise.

There are supply-side effects to tax cuts. If the government cuts taxes on labour as well as on capital investments, the quantities of labour and capital inputs supplied to markets will increase, and aggregate supply will increase. Through incentive effects, called **supply-side effects**, a tax cut can increase aggregate supply and potential GDP.

All economists believe that tax cuts will have some incentive effects causing a small increase in aggregate supply. The supply-side effects are small because most people already work as many hours as they can, and don't get much choice from their bosses over how long to work. An increase in take-home pay may encourage a few more hours per week, but not much more.

supply-side effects: the incentive effects of taxes on aggregate supply

Supply-Siders Economists and politicians who believe that there are *powerful* supply-side incentive effects to tax cuts are called *supply-siders*. There is no empirical evidence to support the claims of supply-siders that tax cuts have large effects on aggregate supply. Tax cuts certainly have an impact on the economy, but most of that impact is through increased spending and aggregate demand, as we discussed in section 8.1.

Are you wondering why I am explaining an idea that almost all economists reject as an exaggeration? It is important to know about supply-side effects because many politicians are supply-siders. Politicians who favour a hands-off role for government often use supply-sider arguments to support tax cuts.

The false argument that you will hear goes like this: Tax cuts will *increase*, not decrease, government tax revenues. How is that possible? If tax cuts have powerful incentive effects, people will work many more hours and incomes will go up dramatically. Even though a lower tax rate means that the government gets a smaller cut from every dollar people earn, people are earning so many more dollars from longer hours worked that the total amount of taxes collected increases. Government tax revenues increase instead of decrease.

U.S. President Ronald Reagan—a pioneering hands-off supply-sider—implemented tax cuts in the 1980s expecting increases in tax revenues, but they fell. With tax revenues falling far short of government spending, the U.S. government went heavily into debt. During Reagan's presidency, the U.S. national debt (a concept explored in section 8.4) skyrocketed from US $700 billon to US$3 trillion. In Canada, Ontario Premier Mike Harris was also a supply-sider whose tax cuts also caused reduced tax revenues, despite claims that revenues would increase.

Supply-siders believe that tax cuts have powerful incentive effects, and claim that tax cuts will increase, not decrease, government tax revenues.

▶ British former Prime Minister Thatcher and American former President Reagan believed strongly in supply-side economics. Both cut taxes drastically expecting government revenues to increase. But as most economists predicted, revenues fell, and their governments ran huge deficits.

Too Good To Be True What politicians find appealing about supply-sider arguments is the promise of cutting taxes—which voters like—while not having to reduce government services or go into debt. If supply-side effects were that powerful, tax cuts would have no opportunity cost! But you know that every choice has an opportunity cost (Appendix A). Anyone claiming that a choice has no opportunity cost is making a claim that is too good to be true. No matter what politicians and voters would like to believe, it would take magic to make the supply-sider argument true. That's why economists often refer to supply-sider arguments as "voodoo economics."

Hands-Off and Hands-On Choices for Supply-Side Policies

Both the "Yes—markets quickly self-adjust" camp and the "No—markets can fail to adjust" camps agree that fiscal policy can affect aggregate supply and promote economic growth. Both camps support policies to promote economic growth by encouraging savings, capital investment, research and development, and education and training. And both camps believe there are small supply-side incentive effects of fiscal policy, and reject supply-siders claims.

There are two issues that help explain this unusual agreement between the hands-off and hands-on positions—externalities and the time frame for supply-side policies.

Externalities Make a Difference   Markets produce too few products/services that have positive externalities, and too many products/services that have negative externalities. All economists agree that externalities create market failure. When there are external benefits and costs that people don't pay for, prices don't accurately reflect all costs and benefits. Without accurate price signals, markets can't coordinate smart individual choices with smart social choices for the economy as a whole. Adam Smith's invisible hand fails.

Normally, the "Yes" camp favours a hands-off role for government. They believe that *without externalities*, markets, and the invisible hand of competition, channel individual self-interest to promote efficiency, rising living standards, and the social interest. The "Yes" camp recognizes that externalities, and the market failures they cause, are an exception. Therefore, where externalities exist, there is a role for government to play in correcting market failure.

Research, development, education, and training have positive externalities. So even the "Yes" camp admits there is a role for government fiscal policies to increase aggregate supply in these areas.

To Save or To Spend?   All economists agree that fiscal policies to encourage savings and capital investment will eventually increase aggregate supply and potential GDP.

But don't forget your mantra—aggregate demand $= C + I + G + X - IM$. It is the sum of planned consumer spending (C), business investment spending (I), government spending on products/services (G), and net exports ($X - IM$). An increase in savings means a decrease in consumer spending. So it is possible that the additional savings, that eventually increase aggregate supply, will also cause a decrease today in aggregate demand. Every choice has an opportunity cost!

This is where the "Yes" and "No" camps part company. There can be a tradeoff between increased aggregate supply in the future—through business investment spending—and reduced aggregate demand in the present due to lower spending.

> Often the reason that Adam Smith's invisible hand seems invisible is that it's not there.
>
> —Joseph Stiglitz
> 2001 Nobel Prize in Economics

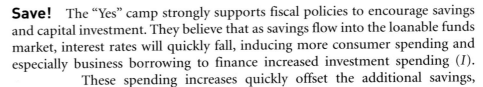

Save! The "Yes" camp strongly supports fiscal policies to encourage savings and capital investment. They believe that as savings flow into the loanable funds market, interest rates will quickly fall, inducing more consumer spending and especially business borrowing to finance increased investment spending (*I*). These spending increases quickly offset the additional savings, restoring aggregate demand to match aggregate supply. While there may be a temporary decrease in aggregate demand, markets quickly adjust. The long-run benefits of increased aggregate supply for economic growth, the "Yes" camp argues, outweigh any short-run mismatches between aggregate demand and aggregate supply.

Spend! The "No" camp is less enthusiastic about government fiscal policies to encourage savings and capital investment. Even though they usually support a hands-on position for the role of government, they worry that businesses, seeing reduced consumer spending, will postpone investment spending. Even if interest rates fall, more pessimistic expectations about future profits will outweigh the reduced costs of borrowing. If business investment decreases, the "No" camp reasons, more savings reduce aggregate demand, causing the economy to contract.

While the "No" camp sees the long-run benefits of increased savings for aggregate supply and economic growth, they are concerned that the short-run decrease in aggregate demand may have recessionary consequences because markets fail to quickly adjust. These short-run adjustment costs might, the "No" camp argues, outweigh the long-run benefits of economic growth. Keynes, the original hands-on economist, quipped that, "In the long run, we are all dead."

Yes and No! Focusing on the long-run effects of increased savings, the two camps do agree that government policies to stimulate saving can promote economic growth. But the camps place difference emphasis on the importance of the long run ("Yes" camp) and the short run ("No" camp).

Refresh

8.2

www.myeconlab.com

1. In your own words, explain how fiscal policy can affect increases in aggregate supply.

2. Why do most economists believe that cutting taxes (supply-side incentive) will not increase tax revenues?

3. What externality do you believe most upsets market equilibrium? Why?

8.3 Are Deficits Always Bad? Government Budget Surpluses and Deficits

If you are working to pay for school and living expenses, you know all about budgets. The word *budget* comes from the Latin word *bulga*, referring to a pouch or wallet and its contents. Today, a budget is a plan of income and spending—money flowing into and out of your wallet.

Governments have budgets too. Governments' incomes come mainly from tax revenues, and governments spend on purchases of products/services and on transfer payments. Fiscal policy—changes in government spending, taxes, and transfers—affects governments' budgets.

The language of budgets applies to individuals, businesses, and governments. But governments are different from individuals and businesses in many important ways.

Differentiate cyclical from structural deficits and surpluses, and explain the connections between automatic stabilizers and business cycles.

Living on $233 Billion a Year: Government Budgets, Revenues, and Spending

Every month you have income coming into your wallet, and spending going out. If your income and spending match, you have a *balanced budget*. If you are like most students, your income is less than your spending, so you have a *deficit*—the amount by which your spending exceeds your income for the month. You have to finance (get money to cover) your deficit by going into *debt*—borrowing from student loans, credit cards, and family. If you are lucky enough to have a month when your income is greater than your expenses, you have a *surplus*—the amount by which your income exceeds your spending for the month. You can use the surplus money to treat yourself (splurge for an extra movie?), to save, or to pay off some of your debts. Government budgets are similar.

Government Revenues Government income is called revenue. It comes from many sources, including personal income taxes, corporate taxes, Employment Insurance premiums paid by workers and employers, GST, and other non-tax areas. Figure 8.3 shows the sources of government revenue. It clearly shows that the income taxes you and I pay make up the bulk (49.8%) of government revenues.

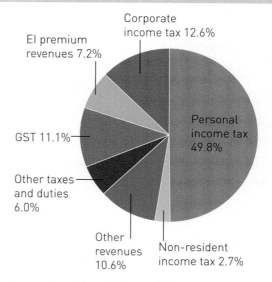

Figure 8.3 Government Revenues for 2008–2009

Corporate income tax 12.6%
EI premium revenues 7.2%
GST 11.1%
Other taxes and duties 6.0%
Other revenues 10.6%
Non-resident income tax 2.7%
Personal income tax 49.8%

Source: *Annual Financial Report of the Government of Canada*, Fiscal Year 2008-2009. Department of Finance.

Government Spending Government spending is on purchases of products/services, transfer payments to businesses and individuals (like Employment Insurance benefits), and interest payments on the national debt (like your interest payments on a credit card balance). Figure 8.4 shows that we are paying 13 percent of our taxes on interest payments (public debt charges) on the accumulated government debt. The largest expenditure is on direct program spending, which includes health care.

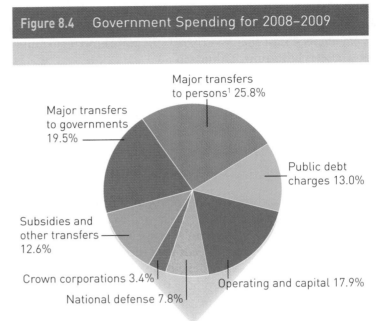

Figure 8.4	Government Spending for 2008–2009

Major transfers to persons[1] 25.8%

Major transfers to governments 19.5%

Public debt charges 13.0%

Subsidies and other transfers 12.6%

Crown corporations 3.4%

National defense 7.8%

Operating and capital 17.9%

Direct program expenses

[1]Includes elderly, EI and children's benefits.
Source: Public Accounts of Canada

*balanced budget:
revenues = spending*

*budget deficit:
revenues < spending*

*budget surplus:
revenues > spending*

Balancing the Budget In comparing revenues and spending, the yearly balance of the government budget, like your monthly budget, has three scenarios.

- **Balanced Budget**—revenues equal spending
- **Budget Deficit**—revenues less than spending
- **Budget Surplus**—revenues greater than spending

Figure 8.5 shows the year-end position of the Government of Canada's budget for selected years between 1987–88 and 2008–09. For each year, there are three numbers—revenues, spending, and the resulting deficit or surplus. Deficits are represented by a negative number, surpluses by a positive number.

Figure 8.5	Government of Canada Budgets, Selected Years, 1987–2009 ($ billions)				
Year	**1987–88**	**1992–93**	**1997–98**	**2007–08**	**2008–09**
Revenues	97.2	124.5	160.9	242.4	233.1
Spending	126.2	163.5	157.9	232.8	238.8
Deficit (−) or Surplus (+)	−29.0	−39.0	+3.0	+9.6	−5.7

Source: Department of Finance, Federal Government Public Accounts. Table 1 Fiscal Transactions. http://www.fin.gc.ca/frt-trf/2009/frt0901-eng.asp.

On the bottom line (pun intended) of the last two columns, notice that the federal budget went from a surplus of $9.6 billion in 2007–08 to a deficit of $5.7 billion in 2008–09. The deficit for 2009–10 is estimated to be much larger, about $54 billion. The move from a budget surplus, to a deficit, to a larger deficit happened as the Canadian economy went into the Great Recession. The connection between increasing deficits and economic recession is not accidental.

Automatic Weapons for Stabilizing Business Cycles

The fiscal policy tools we have described to this point require the government to make explicit decisions to act. To correct a recessionary gap, parliament can decide to cut taxes or increase spending. To correct an inflationary gap, parliament can decide to raise taxes or decrease spending. But there are other fiscal policy tools that work automatically with changes in the business cycle. No government decisions are necessary.

Automatic Stabilizers   Existing taxes and transfer programs are also fiscal policy tools for fighting business cycles. When a negative demand shock causes the economy to contract, real GDP decreases. Government tax revenues automatically fall, returning some money to the other macroeconomic players to spend. Canada's income tax system allows you to use losses in the current year to reduce taxable income in the three previous years. Those taxpayers then receive rebate cheques on taxes previously paid. Transfer payments, in programs like Employment Insurance, automatically increase, supporting consumer spending (*C*) and aggregate demand. These tax and transfer adjustments that automatically occur during business cycles are called **automatic stabilizers**. They counteract changes to real GDP without requiring explicit government decisions. Automatic stabilizers counteract business cycles, and steer the economy back towards potential GDP.

automatic stabilizers: tax and transfer adjustments that counteract changes to real GDP without explicit government decisions

Automatic stabilizers work in both directions. When a positive demand shock causes the economy to expand beyond potential GDP, tax revenues increase and transfer payments decrease. The resulting decrease in aggregate demand pushes the economy back down towards potential GDP.

Automatic stabilizers work like the thermostat in your house, counteracting the weather outside. When it's colder outside, the heat goes on. When it's warmer, the heat goes off. The net result is the temperature inside your house stays stable, despite the fluctuating temperatures outside.

▲

This woman is adjusting the thermostat to keep the temperature inside where she wants it to be. In this way, the temperature inside will automatically be controlled for her comfort regardless of the external weather conditions. Automatic stabilizers work like a thermostat, keeping the economy closer to potential GDP regardless of external shocks.

Since automatic stabilizers were introduced after the Great Depression, business cycles in Canada have been less frequent, and contractions have been less severe.

cyclical deficits and surpluses: created only as a result of automatic stabilizers counteracting business cycles

Government attempts to balance the budget during recessions decrease aggregate demand and make recessions even worse.

Smoothing Business Cycles   Many of these automatic stabilizers did not exist during the Great Depression. Income taxes and transfer programs like Employment Insurance, welfare payments, Canada Pension Plan, and health care were introduced after the Great Depression. Because of automatic stabilizers, business cycles in Canada have been less frequent, and the contractions have been less severe. Automatic stabilizers have done their job, helping to "steady" the key macroeconomic outcome of steady growth.

But every choice, including the choice to introduce automatic stabilizers, has an opportunity cost. Since 2007–2008, the growing government budget deficits and accumulated debt accompanying the Great Recession reflect that opportunity cost.

Automatic Deficits and Surpluses   Automatic stabilizers create automatic deficits and surpluses. Suppose the economy starts at potential GDP and the government budget is balanced. A negative aggregate demand shock pushes the economy into a recession. As automatic stabilizers start working, tax revenues fall and spending on transfer payments increases. A budget deficit is automatically created as the stabilizers do their job.

Alternatively, start again at potential GDP with a balanced government budget. Suppose a positive aggregate demand shock pushes the economy into an expansion. As automatic stabilizers start to work, tax revenues rise and spending on transfer payments decreases. A budget surplus is automatically created.

The deficits and surpluses created only as a result of automatic stabilizers counteracting the business cycle are called **cyclical deficits** and **cyclical surpluses**.

When Balanced Budgets Can Be Bad   Once automatic stabilizers are in place, balancing the budget can be dangerous for an economy. Most individuals try to balance their budgets, and believe that governments should do the same. But look what happens if governments always follow this advice.

If a negative aggregate demand shock pushes the economy into a recession, automatic stabilizers start to work and create a cyclical deficit. If the government tries to balance the budget, it has to either increase revenues or decrease spending. Increasing revenues means raising taxes on consumers or businesses, which will decrease consumer spending (C) or business investment spending (I). Decreasing government spending means reducing government purchases of products/services (G) or reducing transfer payments, which in turn will decrease consumer spending (C).

Remember your mantra—aggregate demand $= C + I + G + X - IM$. The government's attempt to balance the budget during a recession will decrease aggregate demand (decreasing C, I, and G), *making the recession even worse*.

Before Keynes introduced his views on macroeconomics, governments followed the advice to act like financially responsible individuals and balance their budgets. Even without many automatic stabilizers in place, governments raised taxes and decreased spending. These fiscal policies, while well-intentioned, helped make the Great Depression worse.

In 2009, facing the Great Recession, governments around the world followed Keynes's advice, cutting taxes and increasing spending. Deficits in Canada and most countries increased dramatically, as governments acted as "spenders of last resort." Economists from both the "Yes" and "No" camps give credit to this deficit-financed government spending for helping to prevent the recurrence of another Great Depression.

Why Spend Other People's Money?   Budget surpluses can also be a problem. If a positive aggregate demand shock pushes the economy into an expansion, automatic stabilizers start to work and create a cyclical surplus. While you or I are happy with a personal budget surplus, the government surplus is money coming from taxpayers' pockets. Why should the government collect taxes it doesn't need?

If the government accepts this advice, and tries to balance the budget, it has to either decrease revenues or increase spending. Decreasing revenues means cutting taxes on consumers or businesses (which the "Yes, hands-off" camp might support), which will increase consumer spending (C) and business investment spending (I). Increasing government spending (which the "No, hands-on" camp might support), means increasing government purchases of products/services (G) or increasing transfer payments, which in turn will increase consumer spending (C).

The problem is that government attempts to reduce the surplus to balance the budget during an expansion will increase aggregate demand (increasing C, I, and G), *accelerating the expansion beyond potential GDP and increasing the risk of inflation.*

> *Government attempts to balance the budget during expansions increase aggregate demand and increase the risk of inflation.*

Deficits and Surpluses: Cyclical versus Structural

Balanced budgets can be bad fiscal policy, but not always. When the advice for individuals to balance budgets is *always* applied by government to the aggregate economy, the results are destabilizing—worsening both recessions and inflationary expansions. This is an example of the fallacy of composition— what is true for one individual (micro) is not necessarily true for the economy as a whole (macro).

That does not mean that economists favour unlimited government deficits or surpluses. There are other deficits, different from cyclical deficits, that do seriously concern economists. What most economist favour (Section 8.5 examines serious difference between camps about the role of government in the economy) is a policy for government to balance the budget over the business cycle.

Good Balanced Budgets Over the Business Cycle What does it mean to balance the budget over the business cycle? The complete phases of a business cycle (Section 2.3) include an expansion and a contraction. A "good" balanced budget will have a surplus during the expansion and a deficit during the contraction. If the positive amount of the surplus equals the negative amount of the deficit, then the budget is balanced over the business cycle. The money in the government's wallet will be the same at the end of the cycle as it was at the beginning.

This fiscal policy allows for the benefits of automatic stabilizers, while keeping government from spending more or less than it collects in taxes. In this sense, the government can live within its means, like a financially responsible individual, and still help steer the economy.

With a balanced budget over the business cycle, surpluses during expansions offset deficits during contractions.

Deficit Will Linger Half Decade, Watchdog Warns

The Parliamentary Budget Officer (PBO) predicts that "Canadians should expect at least half a decade of federal government deficits," due to the government's "massive stimulus package to tackle the economic downturn."

The projected deficits are $54 billion for 2009–2010 and $43 billion for 2010–2011, declining to $19 billion by 2013–2014. These deficits are not just cyclical deficits due to the Great Recession. They include structural deficits—even if the economy returned to potential GDP by 2013–2014, there would still be a deficit of $19 billion.

To return to a balanced budget at full employment, the government will have to cut spending dramatically or raise taxes. Finance Minister Jim Flaherty—a self-proclaimed hands-off politician who despises deficits—claims his government will never raise taxes. But most economists believe he will be forced to, or risk running continual deficits.

The PBO notes, however, that these deficits "are significantly smaller than those of the 1980s and early 1990s and are also small relative to the size of the economy." Even with five years of deficits adding to the national debt, the national debt as a percentage of GDP will only grow from 29 percent in 2008–2009 to 33.8 percent in 2013–2014.

Source: Steven Chase, "Deficits Will Linger Half Decade, Watchdog Warns," *The Globe and Mail*, January 14, 2009. "Economic and Fiscal Assessment Update," Office of the Parliamentary Budget Officer, Ottawa, November 2, 2009.

Structural Deficits (and Surpluses) at Potential GDP

The deficits (and surpluses) that most concern economists are not cyclical but structural. A **structural deficit** occurs when governments spend more than their revenues *even while the economy is at potential GDP and growing steadily*. Structural deficits are not caused by business cycles. They are built into the structure of government taxes, transfers, and spending programs.

A **structural surplus** occurs when there is a government budget surplus even while the economy is at potential GDP and growing steadily.

There are problems both with structural deficits and structural surpluses. Structural deficits are ongoing. Even when the economy is at full employment, the government has to borrow money. There are no offsetting surpluses. As deficits accumulate, the government must go deeper into debt. The Government of Canada had continuous structural deficits for 20 years between 1975 and 1995. Total deficits (cyclical deficits plus structural deficits) from 1982 to 1995 ranged from roughly $28 billion to $39 billion *every year*. As a result, Canada's accumulated debt increased, from about $34 billion in 1975–1976 to $554 billion in 1995–1996. Think about the interest payments on a debt of $554 billion borrowed dollars! And every Canadian has to help pay for it through taxes!

Structural surpluses also accumulate over time, raising the question of why government keeps collecting taxpayers' money that it is not spending. From 2006 until the Great Recession, Canada's Conservative government had deliberately small structural surpluses. The explicit purpose of those structural surpluses was to start paying down the accumulated debt from past deficits.

But we are getting ahead of the story. To fully understand these issues, we have to examine Canada's national debt—and that's next.

structural deficits and surpluses: budget deficits and surpluses occurring at potential GDP

Refresh
8.3

1. In your own words, explain automatic stabilizers as they apply to the economy. In your explanation, include the terms "surplus" and "deficit."

2. What do economists mean when they use the phrase, "balance the budget over the business cycle?"

3. How might a structural governmental deficit directly affect you?

www.myeconlab.com

8.4 We Owe How Much?! From Deficits to the National Debt

Explain the difference between deficits and debts, and identify five arguments about the national debt.

Your Finances

Month	Deficit	Debt
Jan.	$ 500	$ 500
Feb.	$1000	$1500

What is the difference between a deficit and a debt—two common but often confused words?

Suppose you start the year with no debt. You don't owe anyone money, and you have a zero balance on your credit card. In January, you earn $2000, but spend $2500. You have a deficit of $500 for January—the amount by which your income for the month (money flowing into your wallet) is less than your spending (money flowing out of your wallet). You put the $500 on your credit card, so now you have a debt of $500.

February is an expensive month. You earn $2000 but spend $3000. Your deficit for the month is $1000, and you pay for it by putting another $1000 on your credit card. At the end of February your credit card balance—your debt—is now $1500, the sum of your accumulated deficits.

Deficits and debts have different time dimensions. Deficits (and surpluses) are a *flow*, while debt is a *stock* (see Chapter 2).

▶ Credit and debit cards make shopping and spending very easy. Problems start when you cannot pay enough back at the end of the month to even cover the interest charges. Then deficit spending can become crippling debt.

FOR YOUR INFORMATION

Government budgets run from April 1 to March 31—called the government's fiscal year—rather than the calendar year of January 1 to December 31. Many businesses also use a fiscal year that is different from the calendar year for tax purposes.

The government presents its budget in February for the fiscal year beginning shortly on April 1.

Deficits Are a Flow A *flow* is an amount per unit of time. Your income is a flow. To say your income is $2000 makes no sense, unless we know if it is $2000 a week, $2000 a month, or $2000 a year. The number is meaningful only when there is a time dimension specified. Deficits (and surpluses) are flows. They must be measured for a specified time dimension. In the example above, you had *monthly* deficits for January ($500) and February ($1000). For government, deficits and surpluses are usually measured *annually*—per year.

Debt Is a Stock Debt is a *stock*—a fixed amount at a moment in time. In our example, your debt on February 28 was $1500, the total amount you owed at that moment in time. Canada's national debt on March 31, 2009 was $463.7 billion dollars—the amount the nation owed at that moment in time.

Counting to $500 Billion and Beyond: Measuring the National Debt

The **national debt** (also called the **public debt**) is the sum of past government budget deficits minus the sum of past budget surpluses. The national debt goes back to the creation of Canada. In 1867, the national debt was $76 million, measured in 1867 prices. The national debt in 2009 was $463.7 billion, measured in 2009 prices. The national debt in any year is measured in the nominal prices of that year.

Because prices change from year to year, and the economy is changing, it is difficult to compare the national debt from year to year. The most meaningful measure of the national debt is the national debt as a percentage of GDP. This ratio eliminates complications of price changes and economic growth. Figure 8.6 shows Canada's national debt as a percentage of GDP between 1926 and 2009.

national debt (public debt): total amount owed by government = (sum of past deficits) − (sum of past surpluses)

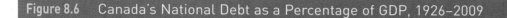

Figure 8.6   Canada's National Debt as a Percentage of GDP, 1926–2009

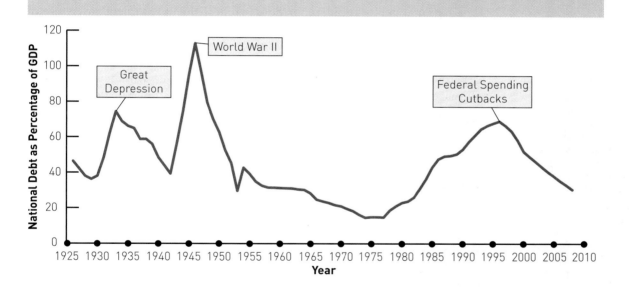

The first two major spikes in the ratio of national debt to GDP were due to the Great Depression (when tax revenues fell and government spending increased) and World War II (due to government spending on the war effort). The big spike from the late 1970s until the mid-1990s was different. This increase was due to a long string of peacetime budget deficits, which kept adding to the accumulated national debt. Then, starting in 1996, the federal government cut spending dramatically, especially transfer payments to provincial governments. From 1997 to 2008, annual budget surpluses reduced both the amount of the national debt and the ratio of the national debt to GDP.

The 2009 ratio of national debt to GDP for Canada was 28.2 percent. This was much lower than the 2009 ratio for the United States (58.2 percent), the UK (62.1 percent), France (67.0 percent), Germany (70.3 percent), Italy (112.8 percent) or Japan (104.6 percent).

What's In a Number?   There are many numbers to consider when examining the national debt. Government debt as a percentage of GDP (28.2 percent), where Canada currently does well relative to other countries, is one number. That number is also much lower than Canada's ratio during the Great Depression (83 percent) or World War II (113 percent).

The amount of the national debt is another number. The national debt reached a peak of $562.9 billion in 1997. It was $463.7 billion in 2009, and projected to be $554 billion in 2010.

You will often see calculations of the national debt as a dollar amount per Canadian. That number is the national debt divided by the population. For 2009 that number was $13,690 per person. In effect you and I and every other person in Canada "owed" $13,690. If I had that balance owing on my credit card, I would be worried! Should we, as citizens, be concerned about these numbers for the national debt? What do the numbers mean?

Bad Debt or Good Debt?
Myths and Problems About the National Debt

Is the national debt a problem, or does it reflect the government's wise use of fiscal policy to help correct past problems of business cycles? There are many arguments about the national debt. Some are based on false assumptions and can be rejected as myths. But there remain reasonable differences between the "Yes" and "No" camps, and among politicians, about whether or not the national debt is a problem, and, if it is a problem, what should be done about it.

Let's examine five of the most common arguments criticizing the national debt to discover if they are based on myths and should be ignored, or are genuine problems and must be considered.

1. Will Canada Go Bankrupt?   If you or I don't repay our debts—pay off that credit card balance—we may go bankrupt, our credit rating will suffer, and it will be difficult to borrow money in the future. Is Canada at risk of bankruptcy and a negative credit rating because since 1867 the country has never paid off the national debt?

This argument is largely a myth. The Government of Canada never has to pay back the national debt—it can simply refinance it. Here's why.

The argument that Canada must pay back the national debt is based on the idea that what is true for an individual must be true for the government. If an 80-year-old man walks into the bank with a small down payment and asks for a 25-year mortgage, the banker will laugh and say no. There is not much chance of the man being alive long enough to repay the loan.

While the man is mortal and will at some point die, the Government of Canada is effectively immortal. Politicians running the federal government come and go, but the country of Canada, its government, and the institutions of parliament remain. They have remained intact since Confederation and are expected to continue to do so.

The Government of Canada never has to pay back the national debt—it can simply refinance it.

The national debt is financed, in large part, by government bonds that have a 30 year maturity. Every year, some of those bonds come due and must be repaid. The Government of Canada repays them by issuing a new set of 30-year bonds and uses that newly borrowed money to pay off the old bonds. This is called refinancing the debt. Old debt is paid off with new debt. The only significant cost is the interest that must continue to be paid—a problem we will examine shortly. With refinancing, the national debt can stay in place without repayment indefinitely—as long as the bondholders trust the Canadian government will make good on all bonds and interest payments that come due. That trust can disappear for countries that borrow too much, with expensive consequences. See For Your Information about Argentina's bankruptcy.

2. Burden for Future Generations

By borrowing money today, is the Government of Canada imposing a burden on future generations who must either repay the debt or at least pay the interest? We have seen that the argument that the debt must be repaid is a myth, but what about the burden of interest payments?

There is undoubtedly interest to be paid. A key question is, who receives the interest payments? About 80 percent of the national debt is held by Canadians. That means the interest payments are mainly going to Canadians. So most interest payments are more of a redistribution of money than a burden on taxpayers. The taxes collected from all Canadians go, in part, to pay interest received by Canadian government bondholders. If more of the Canadian government bonds were to be held by non-Canadians, this argument would become more important. As it stands now, though, the interest payments on the national debt are not a serious problem for future generations.

3. Debt Is Always Bad

"Governments should live within their means, like responsible individuals, and not go into debt." This argument is based on a myth, because most individual consumers and businesses regularly make smart choices that involve going into debt. People taking on a mortgage or a car lease are going into debt. Businesses regularly issue bonds and go into debt to build new factories. Debt is a smart choice if the expected future profits or benefits from spending the borrowed money are greater than the interest costs on the loan.

For government, debt can be a smart choice if the positive impact on the economy of the spending financed by debt is greater than the interest cost. If the debt is used to finance investment in infrastructure—such as roads, bridges, public transit, education, or communications networks—that improve productivity, lower costs, and provide positive externalities to the economy, most economists would see it as a smart choice. And these improvements will mostly benefit future generations. But if the debt is used simply to finance consumption, spent by politicians trying to win votes before an election, most economists would see that as a problem.

What about debt-financed government spending to prevent a recession? The "Yes" camp, favouring a hands-off role for government, might disapprove, while the "No" camp would approve of such hands-on government spending. So while government debt could be a problem, it may also be a smart choice. See Economics Out There (page 315) for one unusual "Yes" camp argument against government debt.

4. Interest Payments Create Self-Perpetuating Debt With a balance on your credit card, you have to make a minimum payment every month. If you don't pay at least the interest owing on your debt, then you have to borrow more to pay the interest, which increases your debt. The balance on your credit card grows. The next month you have to pay interest on this larger balance. It is easy to get caught in this vicious cycle. You may never get out of debt.

Figure 8.7 shows an example of a person paying $50 each month on her credit card balance. Her original balance was $5000. The credit card company charges 2 percent interest per month. After four payments, she has paid $200 but now owes $5202—she is deeper in debt in month four that she was in month one.

Figure 8.7   Self-Perpetuating Debt on a Credit Card

Month	Balance	Payment	Balance after Payment	Interest	Month End Balance
1	$5000	$50	$5000 − $50 = $4950	$4950 × 2% = $99	$4950 + $99 = $5049
2	$5049	$50	$5049 − $50 = $4999	$4999 × 2% = $99.98	$4999 + $99.98 = $5098.98
3	$5098.98	$50	$5098.98 − $50 = $5048.98	$5048.98 × 2% = $100.98	$5048.98 + $100.98 = $5149.96
4	$5149.96	$50	$5149.96 − $50 = $5099.96	$5099.96 × 2% = $102	$5099.96 + $102 = $5202

The Government of Canada faced a similar situation between the mid-1970s and mid-1990s. Persistent yearly deficits increased the national debt, which increased interest payments. Larger interest payments lead to larger yearly deficits. At the end of 1996, interest payments on the national debt had reached $42.4 billion for the year—too high to be sustained.

The opportunity cost of spending that much money on interest alone was extraordinary. To put that number in perspective, interest payments on the national debt in 1996 took 36 cents of every dollar the government collected in revenues. That left only 64 cents of every tax dollar to spend on all government programs. The $42.4 billion interest bill was more money than the government spent that year on all transfers to Canadians including Employment Insurance, Canada Pension Plan, Old Age Security, and national defense *combined*. That interest bill on the national debt represented 30 percent of all government spending. In 1996, the government, recognizing the national debt as a problem, began paying it down. By 2009, public debt charges had fallen to 13 percent of all government spending (see Figure 8.4, page 304).

Canada had persistent yearly deficits between mid-1970s and mid-1990s. The deficits increased the national debt, which increased interest payments, increasing yearly deficits. This vicious cycle was only broken in 1996.

Why Bother?

Robert Barro—a prominent hands-off economist at Harvard University—argues that any government spending financed by going into debt will have no impact on the economy, so why bother?

He argues that consumers, with rational expectations, will expect higher taxes in the future to pay for the interest on the debt. So to save for future taxes, consumers cut back spending now and offset any government spending. The result is government debt without any impact on economy.

The argument—called Ricardian equivalence—was first suggested almost 200 years ago by David

Ricardo, an English economist and member of parliament. Government "stimulus spending is doomed to failure because taxpayers tend to save their stimulus dollars rather than spend them."

Source: Heather Schoffield, "The Ricardian Equivalence Makes a Comeback," *The Globe and Mail*, Report on Business, July 6, 2009.

5. Crowding Out and Crowding In When governments finance the national debt by selling bonds, they increase the supply of bonds, drive down bond prices, and raise interest rates. Those higher interest rates make it more expensive for consumers and businesses to borrow. The reduction in business investment spending caused by debt-financed higher interest rates is called **crowding out**. High government borrowing raises interest rates, which in turn reduces some private investment.

On the other hand, if debt-financed government fiscal policy succeeds in increasing real GDP and expanding economic growth, the improvement in business *expectations* of profitability may increase private investment. This positive impact of debt-financed fiscal policy on expectations and business investment spending is called **crowding in**.

Myth or Truth? Some, but not all, of the arguments about the national debt are based on myths. How do such myths survive? The answer has to do with the explosive mix of economics and politics that fuels most debates about government deficits and debts and the proper hands-off or hands-on role for government in a market economy. And that is our final topic in this chapter.

crowding out:
tendency for government debt-financed fiscal policy to decrease private investment spending by raising interest rates

crowding in:
tendency for government debt-financed fiscal policy to increase private investment spending by improving expectations

Refresh

8.4

1. In your own words, explain the difference between deficits and debt. In your answer, use the terms *flow* and *stock*.

2. Which of the following macroeconomic outcomes are flows and which are stocks: real GDP, unemployment rate, inflation rate, money supply? Explain.

3. Which one of the arguments about the problems of the national debt seems most convincing to you? Why?

www.myeconlab.com

Distinguish between normative, positive, economic, and political arguments about fiscal policy.

Politicians take different positions on fiscal policy, deficits, debt, and whether government should play a hands-off or hands-on role in the economy. Their arguments though, often mix economics with politics, and confuse personal value judgments with statements of fact. One, discussed below, compares deficits to potato chips! How can you, as a citizen, analyze those arguments to make your own informed choice about the role of government in a market economy?

Economists, as well as politicians, disagree on the proper role of government in managing our economy. There is no single right answer. But fiscal policy has a powerful impact on the key macroeconomic outcomes of steady growth, full employment, and stable prices. Your vote—whether for a hands-off or a hands-on politician—influences the direction of future economic policy in Canada, and therefore your own future well being.

Politics

Governments around the world play very different roles in their respective countries. Those different roles are rooted in different political philosophies. Let's look at one set of differences—between the United States and Canada.

The United States was created through a revolution against government interference. Their founding political principles emphasized "life, liberty, and the pursuit of happiness." The focus was on the individual's right to pursue her own destiny, free from government restrictions. The United States has hands-off origins.

Canada, created by an act of government, has founding political principles that stress "peace, order, and good government." Canada, as a civil society, stresses government's responsibility to promote and protect the public good. Canada has hands-on origins.

Today, citizens in both countries are attracted to both hands-off and hands-on approaches for government.

Hands-off words often used with government: intervene, interfere, mistake. Hands-on words often used with government are: act, participate, responsibility.

Loaded Words   The words that are used in arguments about the proper role for government in a society often reveal the speaker's point of view.

For those supporting a hands-off role, the word *government* is often paired with words like *intervene, interfere,* and *mistake.* For example, "the government should not *intervene . . .*," "that is government *interference . . .*," or "it is a *mistake* for government to . . . ." This choice of words shows the speaker believes that the government has no legitimate business in taking action, and if government does act, it usually gets it wrong.

For those supporting a hands-on role, the word *government* is often paired with words like *act, participate,* and *responsibility.* For example, "the government needs to *act* to . . .," "this initiative requires government *participation,*" or "the government has a *responsibility* to . . . ."

Look for these words when listening to a politician's arguments. They are clues to the politician's views on the proper role of government.

Opinions and Facts:
Normative and Positive Statements

There is no right or wrong answer to the question, "What role should government play in our economy?" You might answer, "Government should play a hands-off role" and your sister might answer, "Government should play a hands-on role." The answer depends on your political values, and people have different values or opinions. Economists call these **normative statements**—they involve value judgments or opinions. Normative statements often use the word *should* and cannot be evaluated as true or false by checking the facts.

Positive statements are about what *is*, rather than about what should be. Positive statements *can* be evaluated as true or false by checking the facts. An example of a positive statement is "The Chinese government plays a much larger role in Chinese society than does the Canadian government in Canadian society." We can identify and measure all of the actions taken by the Chinese government and compare them to the actions taken by the Canadian government. If there are more in China, the statement is true. If there are fewer, the statement is false.

In contrast, the statement, "The government in Canada *should* play a larger role like the government in China" is a normative statement—an opinion. Notice the word *should*?

When you hear claims from politicians, or economists, identify if the statement is normative or positive. If it is a normative statement, you can agree or disagree. If it is a positive statement, look for the facts behind the claim to evaluate if it is true or false.

normative statements: about what you believe should be; involve value judgments

positive statements: about what is: can be evaluated as true or false by checking the facts

Economics

Economists also make both normative and positive statements, and it is important to distinguish between them. Economists pride themselves on their positive statements, so let's start with those.

Positive Statements   Here are some examples of positive statements in this chapter:

- Tax incentives stimulate savings, increase the quantity of capital, and promote economic growth.
- Tax cuts will increase government tax revenues.
- The national debt does not have to be repaid, only refinanced.
- Automatic stabilizers create government budget deficits when the economy goes into a recession.

I am not claiming that any of these statements is actually true or false. But you can evaluate a positive statement as true or false by checking the facts. Some of the statements are true, and some are false. Most economists evaluate the claim by supply-siders that "tax cuts will increase government tax revenues" as false because the facts show that when taxes were cut, revenues decreased, not increased. But the claim is still a positive statement—*capable* of being evaluated as true or false by checking the facts.

Normative Statements   Here are examples of normative statements from this chapter. Since they are opinion-based, you have to make up your own mind whether you agree or not.

- Governments should use tax incentives to encourage savings and promote economic growth.
- Governments should increase spending to counteract recessions.
- Governments should pay down the national debt.
- Government should balance the budget over the business cycle.

Let's look at the different possible responses to these normative statements. Tax incentives encourage savings, but the "Yes" and "No" camps disagree about tradeoffs. As savings increase, there is a cost in the present of reduced aggregate demand, but benefits in the future of increased economic growth.

On government spending to counteract recessions, the "Yes" and "No" camps disagree on whether spending or tax cuts are better policy. Even if the camps could agree on the need to counteract recessions with government policy (they don't!), the choice between tax cuts (less government) and spending (more government) depends on hands-off versus hands-on views on the proper role of government.

Paying down the national debt will reduce future interest payments on the debt. But every policy has an opportunity cost. The money could instead be spent on improving infrastructure in the present, which would promote growth in the future. There are no right or wrong choices here, only tradeoffs.

While most economists agree that governments should balance the budget over the business cycle, when politicians go to act on that advice, there may be problems, as you will see in the next section.

Mixing It Up: Politics and Economics

Arguments from politicians about fiscal policy, deficits, and debt often combine politics and economics, creating additional problems in evaluating what you hear. There are two main mix ups.

Will Politicians Follow Economists' Advice?   "Bet you can't eat just one," was an advertising slogan for potato chips. Most economists see the value in government deficits during economic contractions as long as they are offset by government surpluses during expansions, yielding a balanced budget over the business cycle. But there is a potato chip argument—combining politics and economics—against running *any* deficits.

Politicians, not economists, legislate government tax, transfer, and spending programs. Government spending increases and tax cuts can make economic sense in a contraction, but it is hard for politicians to stop spending and raise taxes—both politically unpopular—when the contraction ends. Deficits are too politically tasty to trust politicians to stop at just one. This is an argument that the Premier of Saskatchewan, Brad Wall, made about his fellow politicians. So policy advice that makes economic sense—balance the budget over the business cycle—might be reasonably rejected because it doesn't make political sense.

Are You Hearing a Political or Economic Argument? You will hear politicians argue against the national debt, claiming that governments must act like responsible individuals and never go into debt, or that Canada will go bankrupt when we have to pay back the debt. These sound like economic arguments about debt. But you have seen that some parallels between individuals and governments are false. Responsible individuals and businesses regularly go into debt, and the national debt does not have to be paid back, only refinanced. So these statements are really political, hands-off arguments against a larger role for government, disguised as an economic argument about the national debt.

You can agree or disagree with the arguments based on your own beliefs. But analyze the arguments to separate the political from the economic.

I OWE 500 BILLION DOLLARS!

Hands-Off or Hands-On? You Decide

Arguments over fiscal policy are often the main event for fights between the "Yes, markets quickly self-adjust" camp so hands-off, and the "No, markets fail to adjust" camp so hands-on. Disagreement over taxes versus government spending, and over deficits, surpluses, and the national debt are often heated. But the arguments often mix politics and economics in misleading ways. Sort out the economic arguments from the political arguments so that you can make informed choices as a citizen about hands-off and hands-on roles for government fiscal policy and your own future.

Sort out economic arguments from political arguments so that you can make informed choices as a citizen about hands-off and hands-on roles for government fiscal policy and your own future.

Refresh 8.5

1. Choose two words each that you would use to best describe the hands-on and hands-off approaches to government.

2. In your own words, describe the difference between a normative and positive statement.

3. On fiscal policy, what position would you vote for, hands-off or hands-on? Explain why.

Spending *Others'* Money

Fiscal Policy, Deficits, and National Debt

I OWE 500 BILLION DOLLARS!

CHAPTER SUMMARY

8.1 SPENDERS OF LAST RESORT: AGGREGATE DEMAND POLICIES FOR STABILIZING BUSINESS CYCLES

Fiscal policies—changes in government spending, taxes, and transfers—act as aggregate demand shocks, have multiplied impact on real GDP, and can counter output gaps. "Yes" and "No" camps favour different combinations of fiscal policies.

- *Fiscal policy*—changes in government purchases, taxes, and transfers to achieve macroeconomic outcomes of steady growth, full employment, and stable prices.
- Circular flow transmits effects of fiscal policy.
    - **Injection**—spending in circular flow that does not start with consumers: G (government spending), I (business investment spending), X (exports).
    - **Leakage**—spending that leaks out of circular flow through taxes, savings, and imports.
- **Multiplier effect**—spending injection has multiplied impact on real GDP.
- Multiplied impact increasing real GDP from
    - Increased government spending.
    - Tax cut.
    - Increase in transfers.
- Multiplied impact decreasing real GDP from
    - Decreased government spending.
    - Tax increase.
    - Decrease in transfers.

- Size of multiplier effects depends on leakages out of circular flow.
  - Multiplier effect for tax and transfer changes not as big as for government spending.
  - More leakages = smaller multiplier.
  - Fewer leakages = larger multiplier.
- Any change in injections—*G*, *I*, *X*—affects aggregate demand and has multiplied impact on GDP.
- Fiscal policies to
  - Increase government spending, cut taxes, increase transfers are positive aggregate demand shocks to counter recessionary gaps.
  - Decrease government spending, raise taxes, decrease transfers are negative aggregate demand shocks to counter inflationary gaps.
- "Yes" camp favours tax cuts instead of government spending to accelerate economy; spending reductions instead of tax increases to slow down economy.
- "No" camp favours government spending instead of tax cuts to accelerate economy; tax increases instead of government spending reductions to slow down economy.

8.2 BUILDING FOUNDATIONS: AGGREGATE SUPPLY POLICIES FOR PROMOTING GROWTH

Fiscal policies targeting aggregate supply—tax incentives, support for R&D, education, training—promote economic growth. "Yes" and "No" camps both support government supply-side fiscal policies, but differ in emphasis on long-run ("Yes") or short-run ("No") effects.

- Tax incentives can stimulate savings, increase quantity of capital, promote economic growth.
- **Positive (or negative) externalities**—benefits (or costs) that affect others external to a choice or a trade.
- Government spending and tax incentives for
  - Research and development activities: create positive externalities promoting economic growth.
  - Education and training that increase human capital: create positive externalities promoting economic growth.
- Fiscal spending and tax policies can increase quantity and quality of inputs, increasing aggregate supply and potential GDP per person.
- **Supply-side effects**—the incentive effects of taxes on aggregate supply.
- *Supply-siders* believe tax cuts have powerful incentive effects and will increase, not decrease, government tax revenues.
  - Evidence shows these beliefs are false. Tax cuts reduce revenue.
  - Supply-sider arguments appeal to politicians who promise tax cuts—which voters like—without having to reduce government services or go into debt.
  - Economists often refer to supply-sider arguments as "voodoo economics."

- Because of externalities, "Yes" and "No" camps both support government supply-side fiscal policies to promote growth.
- Fiscal policies that encourage savings, capital investment, and future economic growth can also decrease aggregate demand in the present.
  - "Yes" camp believes long-run benefits of increased aggregate supply outweigh short-run mismatches between reduced aggregate demand and aggregate supply.
  - "No" camp concerned that short-run decreases in aggregate demand cause recession; costs of slowly adjusting markets outweigh long-run benefits of economic growth.

8.3 ARE DEFICITS ALWAYS BAD?
GOVERNMENT BUDGET SURPLUSES AND DEFICITS

Automatic stabilizers create cyclical budget deficits and surpluses while keeping the economy close to potential GDP. Structural deficits and surpluses at potential GDP are more problematic.

- Government budget scenarios:
  - **Balanced budget** — revenues = spending
  - **Budget deficit** — revenues < spending
  - **Budget surplus** — revenues > spending
- **Automatic stabilizers**—tax and transfer adjustments that counteract changes to real GDP without explicit government decisions.
  - During contractions, tax revenues fall and transfer payments increase, supporting spending and aggregate demand, but causing automatic budget deficit.
  - During expansions, tax revenues rise and transfer payments decrease, reducing spending and aggregate demand, but causing automatic budget surplus.
- Automatic stabilizers work like thermostat, keeping economy close to potential GDP regardless of shocks to aggregate demand or supply.
  - Since automatic stabilizers were introduced after Great Depression, business cycles in Canada have been less frequent, contractions less severe.
- **Cyclical deficits and surpluses**—created only as a result of automatic stabilizers counteracting business cycles.
- With automatic stabilizers, government attempts to balance the budget during:
  - Recessions decrease aggregate demand, make recessions worse.
  - Expansions increase aggregate demand, increase risk of inflation.
- With a balanced budget over the business cycles, cyclical surpluses during expansions offset cyclical deficits during contractions.
- Economists most concerned with **structural deficits and surpluses**— budget deficits and surpluses occurring at potential GDP.

Deficits are a flow while debt is a stock. Of five common arguments about national debt, some are myths, some potential problems.

- Deficits and debt have different time dimensions.
  - Deficits and surpluses are *flows*—amounts per unit of time—usually measured per year.
  - Debt is a *stock*—fixed amount at moment in time.
- **National debt (public debt)**—total amount owed by government = (sum of past deficits) − (sum of past surpluses)
  - Canada's national debt in 2009 was $463.7 billion.
  - Canada's 2009 ratio of national debt to GDP was about 28%, compared to United States (58%), United Kingdom (62%), Germany (70%).
- Five common arguments about whether national debt is a problem, or reflects wise government use of fiscal policy to correct past problems of business cycles, are
- 1) Will Canada go bankrupt?
  - Largely a myth.
  - Government of Canada never has to pay back national debt—can simply refinance it.
  - Governments that do not pay debts find it difficult and expensive to borrow on international bond market.
- 2) Burden for future generations.
  - Depends on who receives interest payments on national debt—Canadians or non-Canadians.
  - Canadians currently receive 80% of interest on national debt, so interest payments more redistribution of money than burden.
- 3) Debt is always bad.
  - Myth—consumers with mortgages, car leases, businesses issuing bonds to build factories, make smart choices to go into debt.
  - Government debt can be smart choice if positive impact on economy of spending financed by debt is greater than interest cost.
  - Government debt can be not-smart choice if spending financed by debt for consumption only.
  - "Yes" camp opposes, "No" camp supports, debt-financed government spending to prevent recession.
- 4) Interest payments create self-perpetuating debt.
  - Potential problem of national debt.
  - Canada had yearly deficits between mid-1970s and mid-1990s, which increased national debt and increased interest payments, thereby increasing yearly deficits. Vicious cycle broken in 1996.

- 5) Crowding out and crowding in.
  - Potential problem and benefit of national debt.
  - **Crowding out**—tendency for government debt-financed fiscal policy to decrease private investment spending by raising interest rates.
  - **Crowding in**—tendency for government debt-financed fiscal policy to increase private investment spending by improving expectations.

8.5 ARE DEFICITS LIKE POTATO CHIPS?
HANDS-OFF OR HANDS-ON ROLE FOR GOVERNMENT?

Sort out economic arguments from political arguments so that you can make informed choices as a citizen about hands-off and hands-on roles for government fiscal policy and your own future.

- Political philosophies differ among countries.
  - United States—created through revolution against government interference—has hands-off origins.
  - Canada—created by act of government—has hands-on origins.
  - Citizens today in both countries attracted to both hands-off and hands-on approaches for government.
- Words used in arguments about proper role for government often reveal speaker's point of view.
  - Hands-off words used with *government: intervene, interfere, mistake.*
  - Hands-on words used with *government: act, participate, responsibility.*
- **Normative statements**—about what you believe should be; involve value judgments.
- **Positive statements**—about what is; can be evaluated as true or false by checking facts.
- Identify claims by politicians and economists as normative or positive.
  - If normative, you can agree or disagree.
  - If positive, look for facts to evaluate as true or false.
- Arguments from politicians about fiscal policy, deficits, and debt often mix up politics and economics.
  - Policy advice that makes economic sense—balance the budget over the business cycle—might be rejected because doesn't make political sense; hard for politicians to stop spending and raise taxes when contractions end.
  - Political hands-off arguments against larger role for government often disguised as arguments against national debt.
- Sort out economic arguments from political arguments so you can make informed choices as a citizen about hands-off and hands-on roles for government fiscal policy and your own future.

TRUE/FALSE

Circle the correct answer.

Suppose that after watching the Youtube video "Fear the Boom and Bust: A Hayek vs. Keynes Rap Anthem" (http://econstories.tv/home.html) a few of your classmates are inspired to start a musical group called the "Yo camp". They chose the name "Yo camp" because some group members favour the "Yes" camp of economists and some favour the "No" camp. The songwriter asks you to check if the lyrics of the song on fiscal policy are accurate, because you are the best economics student in the class.

Use this scenario to answer questions 1–15. Five of the questions include lyrics based on popular rap songs—see if you can identify which ones!

8.1 DEMAND POLICIES FOR STABILIZATION

1. If instead of spending money
   you watch a TV show,
   You cause a leakage
   which exits the circular flow.   **True   False**

2. In my 'hood we believe in
   the economist camp spelled N-O!
   This camp favours tax cuts
   when the economy is slow.   **True   False**

3. In recessions, economists like
   fiscal policies increasing real GDP!
   But all economists favour
   tax increases to slow the economy.   **True   False**

4. The multiplier effect drives higher
   the economy's health.
   Government purchases have the largest impact
   on the economy's wealth.   **True   False**

8.2 SUPPLY POLICIES FOR GROWTH

5. If governments reduced
   the amount of taxes that you and I pay,
   They'd make more money
   because we'd work more hours per day.   **True   False**

6. Go Shorty, it's your birthday,
   yeah you can find me at the club,
   I ain't into "voodoo economics"
   so only supply-siders can come give me a hug. **True   False**

7. As Keynes once said,
   in the long run we're all dead,
   Which suggests don't spend
   and save your money instead.   **True   False**

8. Government spending and tax incentives encourage R&D,
The R&D knowledge that benefits others is a positive externality.

True **False**

9. I like big tax cuts
and I cannot lie,
But it raises the deficit,
which you can't deny.

True **False**

10. When a contracting economy gets
that shrinking feeling,
It automatically gets
government spending healing.

True **False**

11. Automatic stabilizers work like
a thermostat for the economy.
They drop spending when the economy's hot;
they drop GDP when it's hot.

True **False**

12. As anyone from
the "Yes" or "No" camp should know,
Debt is always bad,
deficits are a stock and debt is a flow.

True **False**

13. If you asked economists
David Ricardo and Robert Barro,
They'd agree that to finance spending,
governments should borrow.

True **False**

14. I'm not into making a positive statement,
so here's what they call a normative statement:
If you invest your savings in an RRSP,
in the long run it's better for you and me.

True **False**

15. When the economy grows older,
it will be stronger.
They call Canada's founding origins freedom,
just like the United States.

True **False**

MULTIPLE CHOICE

Circle the correct answer.

8.1 DEMAND POLICIES FOR STABILIZATION

1. Fiscal policy is changes in
   A) government purchases.
   B) taxes.
   C) transfers.
   D) all of the above.

2. Which one of the following statements about multipliers is *false*?
   A) Changes in injections affect aggregate demand with a multiplied impact on GDP.
   B) With more leakages you get a bigger multiplier.
   C) The multiplier effect for tax changes is smaller than for government purchases.
   D) The multiplier effect for transfer changes is smaller than for government purchases.

3. Leakages are spending that leaks out of the circular flow through
   A) taxes.
   B) savings.
   C) imports.
   D) all of the above.

8.2 SUPPLY POLICIES FOR GROWTH

4. Which one of the following fiscal policies is *least* likely to increase aggregate supply and potential GDP?
   A) Tax incentives for saving accounts.
   B) Tax incentives for research and development.
   C) Tax incentives for education and training.
   D) Fiscal policies for aggregate demand.

5. If government spending on post-secondary education reduces tuition fees for students, this will
   A) increase the quality of labour inputs.
   B) decrease the quality of labour inputs.
   C) increase the quantity of labour inputs.
   D) decrease the quantity of labour inputs.

6. Supply-siders believe people will respond to a lower income tax rate by
   A) stopping work so they stop paying taxes.
   B) working fewer hours and paying less total taxes.
   C) working more hours and paying the same total taxes.
   D) working more hours and paying more total taxes.

7. Fiscal policies that encourage savings and capital investment can
   A) decrease both aggregate supply and aggregate demand.
   B) decrease aggregate supply and increase aggregate demand.
   C) increase aggregate supply and decrease aggregate demand.
   D) increase both aggregate supply and aggregate demand.

8.3 BUDGET SURPLUSES AND DEFICITS

8. If a country with $50 billion in debt then had revenues of $5 billion and spending of $4 billion, debt at the end of the year will be
   A) $49 billion.
   B) $50 billion.
   C) $51 billion.
   D) $54 billion.

9. The deficits or surpluses that most concern economists are
   A) structural surpluses.
   B) structural deficits.
   C) cyclical surpluses.
   D) cyclical deficits.

10. During an expansion,
   A) both tax revenues and government spending decrease.
   B) tax revenues fall and government spending increases.
   C) tax revenues rise and government spending decreases.
   D) both tax revenues and government spending increase.

8.4 NATIONAL DEBT

11. Which one of the following is a genuine problem with the national debt?
   A) Debt is always bad.
   B) The national debt is a burden for future generations.
   C) Interest payments on the national debt can create self-perpetuating debt.
   D) Canada will go bankrupt because of debt.

12. Crowding out is the tendency for government debt-financed fiscal policy to decrease private investment spending by
   A) raising interest rates.
   B) lowering interest rates.
   C) improving expectations.
   D) reducing expectations.

13. The founding political principles of
    A) Canada have hands-on origins; U.S. have hands-on origins.
    B) Canada have hands-off origins; U.S. have hands-off origins.
    C) Canada have hands-on origins; U.S. have hands-off origins.
    D) Canada have hands-off origins; U.S. have hands-on origins.

14. Most economists agree that the government budget should
    A) always be in deficit.
    B) always be in surplus.
    C) always be in balance.
    D) balance over the business cycle.

15. Which one of the following statements is normative?
    A) Tax incentives stimulate savings, increase the quantity of capital, and promote economic growth.
    B) Tax cuts will increase government tax revenues.
    C) Governments should pay down the national debt.
    D) The national debt does not have to be repaid, only refinanced.

SHORT ANSWER

Write a short answer to each question. Your answer may be in point form.

1. Suppose that during Spring Break you visit your friend's hometown, where a major car manufacturer recently shut down its operations.
    A) Explain how the multiplier effect of a business shutting down works its way through the economy. (Hint: consider Economics Out There on "The Human Impact of Multiplier Effects" on page 294.)
    B) If you and your friend spend the week going out and spending lots of money on food, drinks, and entertainment, explain how the multiplier effect works to turn that spending into a larger impact on GDP.

2. Look at the revenue and spending amounts in Figure 8.5 for selected years between 1987–1988 and 2008–2009.
    A) In which years was there a deficit?
    B) As the Canadian economy went into the Great Recession, how did the budget balance change?
    C) Based on the budget balance in 2008–2009, would the level of debt decrease or increase over the year?

3. Suppose that students on your campus are organizing a protest against high tuition fees, and they ask you for your perspective as an economist.
    A) Describe how students benefit from education.
    B) Describe how society benefits from your higher education.

4. Suppose that the government is considering two ways to return to a balanced budget—raising taxes and reducing spending.

   A) If a government reduces spending on products/services by $20 million, how much will GDP decrease? Hint: assume the typical size of the multiplier mentioned in the chapter.

   B) If a politician says he will never raise taxes even when the economy is strong, does this imply that he is a hands-off or a hands-on economist? Explain your answer.

   C) A government can raise taxes either by raising consumption taxes or by raising income taxes. How might higher consumption taxes change your incentives to save and spend?

5. Suppose a politician in your community is worried about high deficits and a high debt-to-GDP ratio. During her speech, she mentions the Parliamentary Budget Officer's projected deficits of $54 billion for 2009–2010, $43 billion for 2010–2011, and $19 billion by 2013–2014. She also mentions that with five years of deficits adding to the national debt, the national debt as a percentage of GDP will grow from 29 percent in 2008–2009 to 33.8 percent in 2013–2014.

   A) If the economy is expected to return to potential GDP by 2013–2014, are these deficits cyclical? Explain your answer.

   B) Provide evidence that demonstrates Canada's debt-to-GDP ratio is low by comparison to other countries, and by comparison to past ratios in Canada.

   C) The politician then makes the following two statements: "With the aging of the population, there will be a lower percentage of the population working in the future. Therefore, the government should increase its interest payments on the debt now before the debt rises rapidly." Which of the statements is normative, and which of the statements is positive?

6. Suppose that the politician in Question 5 returns to your community but this time with a plan for reducing the debt. She promises to cut taxes, stating that these cuts will create thousands of new jobs and result in higher government revenues.

   A) Do all economists agree that tax cuts increase aggregate supply?

   B) Why do supply-siders believe tax cuts will increase government revenues?

   C) Why do many economists doubt that government revenues increase in response to tax cuts?

   D) Are the incentive effects of lower income taxes likely to be greater in an inflationary gap or a recessionary gap? Explain why.

7. During the recession of 2008–2009, some argued that governments should live within their means, like responsible individuals, and not go into debt.

   A) Under what conditions is going into debt a smart choice for government?

   B) Do all economists agree that governments should be willing to go into a deficit to help counter the decrease in aggregate demand during recessions? Explain your answer.

8. Consider the economic and political reasons why governments go into debt.

   A) How can the federal and provincial governments of Canada finance debt in ways that individuals cannot?

   B) Explain why deficits are too politically tasty to trust politicians to stop at just one.

9. Suppose you are at the shopping mall and debating whether to spend $200 on a new pair of jeans or to invest that $200 in a savings account. You decide to base your decision on what is best for the economy. In this scenario,

   A) What is the tradeoff between savings and spending?

   B) Explain what someone from the "Yes" camp of economists would tell you to do.

   C) Explain what Keynes would tell you to do.

10. For the normative statement "Governments should increase spending to counteract recessions," compare the opinions of the "Yes" camp and "No" camp of economists.

---

myeconlab Visit the MyEconLab website at **www.myeconlab.com.** This online homework and tutorial system puts you in control of your own learning with study and practice tools.

Chapter 9

Are Sweatshops All Bad?

Globalization and Trade Policy

LEARNING OBJECTIVES

9.1 Describe how comparative advantage, specialization, and trade can improve living standards.

9.2 Explain how competition creates winners, losers, and opponents to trade and analyze three forms of protectionism.

9.3 Explain globalization, its pace, and how to evaluate if sweatshop workers are better off with international trade.

9.4 Evaluate the hands-off and hands-on arguments about the role for government in the globalization debate.

GLOBALIZATION IS CHANGING the world, but people do not agree whether the changes are for better or for worse. Controversies over the virtues and evils of trade go back centuries. Today, communication technology and transportation improvements have lowered the costs of international trade and sped up the process of globalization. Your technical support phone call may be answered by someone in Bangalore, India, and a steelworker in Hamilton, Ontario, may have lost a job to a factory worker in Shanghai, China.

Economists and free-trade supporters argue that specialization and trade are key to raising living standards. Supporters point to once struggling countries like Japan, South Korea, Taiwan — and now China and India — whose standards of living continue to rise with international trade. Critics point to sweatshops in third-world countries as one serious negative outcome of globalized trade. Other critics see globalization as just another way that developed countries in the West are using weaker countries as a source of cheap labour and raw materials.

In this chapter, you will learn about comparative advantage — the concept behind all pro-trade arguments — and how it applies not just to international trade, but also to your personal smart choices about jobs and "trading" in local markets for your everyday needs. You will also explore some of the arguments against globalization, including those of the Nobel Prize–winning economist Joseph Stiglitz.

The controversies over trade and globalization return us to the question of the role for government in the global economy. There are new issues about whether government should help those threatened from international competition through direct protection, or with a social safety net, or not at all. What we return to is the need for you — as a citizen of Canada and the world — to make up your own mind on these issues.

9.1 Why Don't You Cook Breakfast? Gains from Trade

Describe how comparative advantage, specialization, and trade can improve living standards.

What did you have for breakfast today? Did you have cereal and orange juice at home, or did you buy coffee and a bagel at Tim Hortons on the way to school? Either way, you made a choice—to make breakfast for yourself, or to buy it from a business. This is the most basic choice you and everyone else makes in trying to do the best you can: do you produce the products and services you want, or do you earn money at a job and use it to trade for products and services made by others?

In today's Canadian economy, most of us earn money by specializing in a particular occupation. We use that money to buy what we want. This specialization and trade has replaced the self-sufficiency of people living in Canada two hundred years ago. Back then, most aboriginal peoples and pioneers made for themselves most of what they needed—hunting and growing their own food, making clothes from animal hides, and building shelters from wood.

Voluntary Trade   What was it that led us away from self-sufficiency to specialization and trade? The simple economic answer is that specialization and trade make us better off. Our standard of living based on specialization and trade, in terms of material products and services, is much higher than it was in the past.

Trade is a key to our prosperity. Why? First of all, trade is voluntary. In a voluntary trade, each person feels that what she gets is of greater value than what she gives up. If there weren't mutual benefits, that is, if each person didn't feel she would be better off, the trade wouldn't happen. It's simple self-interest at work.

If You Trade, Should Canada?

Countries face the same basic choice as individuals. Should Canada try to be self-sufficient, producing everything Canadians want, or should Canada specialize in producing some products/services and trade for the rest? Economists from Adam Smith to today argue that the gains from trade make both individuals and countries better off.

Specialization and trade is widespread in Canada and other countries. Figure 9.1 shows the importance of international trade—trade between countries—for the GDP of selected countries in 2006. Remember your mantra: $GDP = C + I + G + X - IM$. Each green bar represents exports (X) as a percentage of GDP for that county. Each red bar represents imports (IM) as a percentage of GDP.

> "
> *What is prudence in the conduct of every family can scarce be folly in that of a great kingdom. If a foreign country can supply us with a commodity cheaper than we ourselves can make it, better buy it of them with some part of the produce of our own industry, employed in a way in which we have some advantage.*
> "
>
> –Adam Smith
> The Wealth of Nations, 1776

Canada Is a Trading Nation   If you look at Canada in Figure 9.1, exports are 36 percent of GDP. More than one out of every three dollars earned by Canadians comes from the sale of exports to the rest of the world. Imports, which do not contribute to Canadian GDP but do contribute to GDP in the rest of the world, are 34 percent of Canadian GDP. Notice how much more important international trade is to the Candian economy than it is to the U.S. or Japanese economies. Even though the United States and Japan sell a much greater volume of exports than Canada, their domestic economies are much larger. So exports as a percentage of GDP are smaller for the United States and Japan than for Canada. Canada is a trading nation, and our standard of living depends significantly on international trade.

Furthermore, 80 percent of our international trade is with one country—the United States. Much is at stake in our trade relations with the United States because a significant portion of Canadian GDP depends on trade with the United States. And because U.S. GDP is ten times bigger than Canada's, Canada's trade with the United States is much more important to us than the United States' trade with Canada is to them.

Since trade is voluntary, both Canada and the United States must believe they are better off as a result of international trade. How does that happen—where do the mutually beneficial gains from trade come from?

Figure 9.1   The Importance of International Trade:
Exports and Imports as Percentage of GDP, Selected Countries, 2006

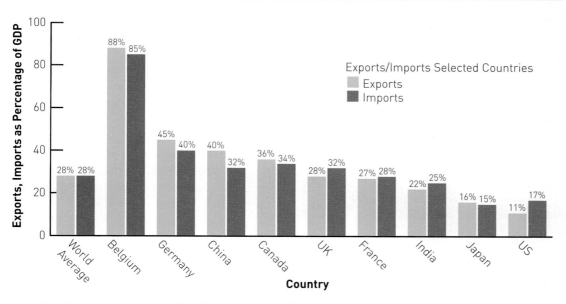

Source: World Development Indicators, http://data.worldbank.org/indicator

Jacqueline produces all of her own wood and bread. Would she be better off if she traded some of her wood for bread?

Bake or Chop?

Opportunity cost is the key to the mutual benefits from trade. To illustrate, let's take a simple, imaginary example of two early Canadians who are each self-sufficient in producing food and shelter. While this example is simple, it contains the basic argument behind every pro-trade position you will ever hear supporting "free trade" or globalization.

Jacqueline grows her own wheat to make bread and chops her own wood for firewood and shelter. If she spends an entire month producing only bread, she can bake 50 loaves. Alternatively, if she spends all of her time chopping wood, she can produce 100 cords (a cord is a measure of cut wood).

Since Jacqueline is self-sufficient, she can consume only what she produces herself, so she must divide her time between baking some bread and chopping some wood. Figure 9.2 shows different combinations of the bread and wood she can produce during the month, depending on how she divides up her time. From these alternative production possibilities, Jacqueline chooses to bake 20 loaves of bread and chop 60 cords of wood.

Samantha, who lives a day's journey away from Jacqueline, also makes her own bread and chops her own wood for firewood and shelter. Samantha is older and weaker than Jacqueline, so if Samantha spends an entire month producing only bread, she can bake 40 loves. Alternatively, if she spends all of her time chopping wood, she can produce a mere 20 cords.

Since Samantha is also self-sufficient, she can consume only what she produces herself. She divides her time and bakes some bread and chops some wood. Figure 9.3 shows different monthly combinations of bread and wood she can produce depending on how she divides up her time. From these alternative production possibilities, Samantha chooses to bake 20 loaves of bread and chop 10 cords of wood.

Figure 9.2	Jacqueline's Monthly Production Possibilities
Bread (loaves)	Wood (cords)
50	0
40	20
30	40
20	60
10	80
0	100

Figure 9.3	Samantha's Monthly Production Possibilities
Bread (loaves)	Wood (cords)
40	0
30	5
20	10
10	15
0	20

Deal or No Deal? Opportunity Cost Rules

How could trade make both Jacqueline and Samantha better off? It doesn't look promising, especially for Jacqueline. She is a better bread maker than Samantha (50 versus 40 loaves baked per month) and a better wood chopper (100 cords versus 20 cords chopped per month). An economist would describe Jacqueline as having an **absolute advantage**—the ability to produce a product/service at a lower absolute cost than another producer—over Samantha in both bread production and wood production. That is, Jacqueline is more productive as a bread maker and as a wood chopper. Her time costs for baking or chopping are lower than Samantha's. If we were to measure dollar costs (which I have left out to keep the example as simple as possible), absolute advantage would mean Jacqueline could produce both bread and wood at lower absolute dollar costs than Samantha could.

If you are not keen on history, then in place of Jacqueline and Samantha, think of China and Canada. If China can produce everything at lower cost than Canada, can there be mutually beneficial gains from trade for both countries? What's in it for China? Won't all Canadians end up unemployed?

absolute advantage: ability to produce a product at lower absolute cost than another producer

Comparative Advantage But mutually beneficial gains from trade do not depend on absolute advantage. They depend on **comparative advantage**—the ability to produce a product/service at a lower opportunity cost than another producer. To figure out comparative advantage, we need to calculate opportunity costs for Jacqueline and Samantha (or for China and Canada).

Jacqueline's choice in Figure 9.2 is between producing 50 loaves of bread or 100 cords of wood. If she chooses to bake 50 loaves of bread, her opportunity cost is 100 cords of wood. If she instead chooses to chop 100 cords of wood, her opportunity cost is 50 loaves of bread. Opportunity cost is the value of the choice not taken.

To compare opportunity costs, it is easier if we measure them per unit of the good chosen. There is a simple, useful formula for opportunity cost:

comparative advantage: ability to produce a product at lower opportunity cost than another producer

$$\text{Opportunity cost} = \frac{\text{Give Up}}{\text{Get}}$$

So Jacqueline's opportunity cost of producing more bread is

$$\frac{\text{Opportunity cost of additional bread}}{} = \frac{100 \text{ cords of wood}}{50 \text{ loaves of bread}} = \frac{2 \text{ cords of wood}}{1 \text{ loaf of bread}}$$

To get each additional loaf of bread, Jacqueline must give up 2 cords of wood.

What is Jacqueline's opportunity cost of producing more wood?

$$\frac{\text{Opportunity cost of additional wood}}{} = \frac{50 \text{ loaves of bread}}{100 \text{ cords of wood}} = \frac{1/2 \text{ loaf of bread}}{1 \text{ cord of wood}}$$

To get each additional cord of wood, Jacqueline must give up half a loaf of bread.

Opportunity Cost and Comparative Advantage If you calculate opportunity costs for Samantha you will find that her opportunity cost of getting an additional loaf of bread is giving up half a cord of wood, and her opportunity cost of getting an additional cord of wood is giving up 2 loaves of bread.

These opportunity cost calculations are summarized in Figure 9.4. Since comparative advantage is defined as lowest opportunity cost (not lowest absolute cost), you can see that Samantha has a comparative advantage in bread-making (give up half a cord of wood versus Jacqueline's 2 cords of wood), while Jacqueline has a comparative advantage in wood-chopping (give up half a loaf of bread versus Samantha's 2 loaves of bread).

Figure 9.4	Opportunity Costs for Jacqueline and Samantha	
	Opportunity Cost of One Additional	
	Loaf of Bread	**Cord of Wood**
Jacqueline	Give up 2 wood (cords)	Give up ½ bread (loaves)
Samantha	Give up ½ wood (cords)	Give up 2 bread (loaves)
Comparative Advantage	**Samantha has comparative advantage (lower opportunity cost) in bread-making**	**Jacqueline has comparative advantage (lower opportunity cost) in wood-chopping**

Smart Deals

Here's the payoff to these calculations. Instead of each pioneer being self-sufficient, and producing everything she needs, look what happens if the pioneers specialize in producing what each is best at, and then trading.

According to comparative advantage, Jacqueline should specialize only in chopping wood, and Samantha should specialize only in baking bread. In this scenario, Jacqueline will produce 100 cords of wood and no bread, and Samantha will produce 40 loaves of bread and no wood.

They then make the day-long journey and agree on a trade of 20 cords of wood for 20 loaves of bread. Jacqueline, the specialized woodchopper, is "exporting" wood and "importing" bread. Samantha, the specialized baker, is "exporting" bread and "importing" wood.

The ratio at which they exchange wood for bread—one cord of wood trades for one loaf of bread in this example—is called the **terms of trade**. In general, the terms of trade are the quantity of exports required to pay for one unit of imports.

After specializing and trading, here are the outcomes:

- Jacqueline ends up with 20 loaves of bread (0 produced plus 20 imported) and 80 cords of wood (100 produced minus 20 exported).
- Samantha ends up with 20 loaves of bread (40 produced minus 20 exported) and 20 cords of wood (0 produced plus 20 imported).

terms of trade: quantity of exports required to pay for one unit of imports

Gains from Trade   Check it out. *After trading, Jacqueline and Samantha are both better off than when each was self-sufficient.* Before trading, for all her strength, the best Jacqueline could produce with 20 loaves of bread was 60 cords of wood. After trading she has the same 20 loaves of bread and more wood — 80 cords. Before trading, the best Samantha could produce with 20 loaves of bread was just 10 cords of wood. After trading she has the same 20 loaves of bread and more wood — 20 cords.

These gains from trade improve both Jacqueline's and Samantha's standards of living. With more wood they can each stay warmer or build better houses. What is remarkable is that these *gains from trade happen without anyone working harder, or without any improvement in technology or new resources.* Both are better off because each has made a smart decision to specialize and trade, rather than each trying to produce everything themselves. Both can have toast for breakfast (bread roasted over a fire), even though each produced only part of what was necessary to make that breakfast.

There are gains for both Jacqueline and Samantha, even though Jacqueline can produce more of both bread and wood than can Samantha. Despite Jacqueline's absolute advantage in producing everything at lower cost, there are still differences in opportunity costs, or comparative advantage. *Comparative advantage is the key to mutually beneficial gains from trade.* The trade can be between individuals, or between countries. That is why China trades with Canada, even though China can produce most things more cheaply than we can in Canada. Trade allows us to work smarter and live better.

Voluntary trade is not a zero-sum game, where one person's gain is the other's loss. Both traders gain. Mutually beneficial gains from trade are caused by differences in comparative advantage. Absolute advantage is not important.

Terms of Trade   For a trade to have mutual benefits, the terms of trade must be somewhere between each trader's opportunity costs. Jacqueline's own opportunity cost of producing a loaf of bread is two cords of wood. Jacqueline is importing bread, "paying" only one cord of wood for each loaf of bread, so for her the imported bread is a bargain. Samantha's own opportunity cost of producing a cord of wood is two loaves of bread. Samantha is importing wood, "paying" only one loaf of bread for each cord of wood, so for her the imported wood is a bargain. Both traders gain.

In this simple example, the gains from trade are split evenly between the traders — the ratio of 1 to 1 (1 loaf for 1 cord) is halfway between the ratios of 2 to 1 and 1 to 2.

Gains from trade are not always split evenly. Different terms of trade would split the gains differently, with more of the gains going to Jacqueline and less to Samantha, or vice versa. But for the trade to occur voluntarily, the terms of trade must be somewhere between the opportunity costs that each trader (or country) faces locally. Exactly where the terms of trade settle in international markets can mean one country gains more than the other. This is one source of controversy we will soon examine. But as long as trade happens voluntarily, both countries still get some gain.

For a trade to have mutual benefits, terms of trade must be between each trader's local opportunity costs.

Technology and Competition   Gains from trade are a big part of rising living standards, even without anyone working harder, or any improvement in technology or any new resources. But competition and technological advances also contribute to rising living standards. Those forces create more gains and winners from trade, but also create losers. The losers from new competition and new technologies are major players in the story of why not everyone welcomes international trade.

Refresh

9.1

www.myeconlab.com

1. Explain the difference between absolute advantage and comparative advantage.

2. How is the concept of personal gain reflected in voluntary trade?

3. The best auto mechanic in town (who charges $120 per hour) is also a better typist than her office manager (who earns $20 per hour). Should the mechanic do her own typing? [Hint: The best alternative employment for the office manager is another office job that also pays $20 per hour.]

9.2 What's So Wonderful About Free Trade? Protectionism and Trade

Explain how competition creates winners, losers, and opponents to trade and analyze three forms of protectionism.

If voluntary trade brings mutual benefits, why do so many people and politicians oppose "free trade?" Arguments to "buy Canadian," or to "protect Canadian businesses and jobs" by taxing or excluding inexpensive imports are arguments against free trade. Complaints against the "outsourcing of Canadian jobs to non-Canadians," or calls for government to compensate domestic producers "harmed by foreign competition" are calls for government to take a hands-on role in international trade. Economists usually come down on the side of free trade. What do they see differently from the critics of free trade?

Creative Destruction on a Global Scale

In addition to mutually beneficial gains, freer trade increases competition. This creates opponents to freer trade.

The completion of the Canadian Pacific Railway in 1885 connected previously separate markets in Halifax, Montreal, Toronto, Winnipeg, the prairies, and Vancouver. This trans-Canada railway brought lower transportation costs, which allowed farmers and businesses anywhere in Canada to sell across the county, opening up new possibilities for specialization and trade. Many more Jacquelines and Samanthas could now easily specialize and gain the advantages of trading in a large national market.

But newly connected markets also brought new competition. Grain farmers in Quebec faced competition from prairie farmers who could produce wheat more cheaply. Even with the added transportation costs, grain from Saskatchewan was cheaper in Montreal than Quebec-grown grain. Textile businesses in Winnipeg faced new competition from lower-cost, higher-volume factories in Toronto. Increased trade and specialization increased competition in every market across Canada.

Free trade, one of the greatest blessings which a government can confer on a people, is in almost every country unpopular.

—Thomas Macaulay
British MP, 1824

Creative Destruction   Connections to new markets bring connections to new competitors. A local producer may have been a big fish in her small, local pond. But increased trade has her now swimming in much bigger ponds with much bigger fish. Some fish, and some businesses, don't survive.

Businesses compete in markets by figuring out new ways to beat their rivals. Businesses do this through cutting costs, developing new technologies of production, inventing new products, exploiting economies of large-scale production, or finding new or cheaper sources for raw materials and resources.

Over time, these competitive innovations, which result from the endless quest for profits, make businesses and labour more productive and improve living standards and product choices for consumers. This is Schumpeter's process of *creative destruction*, described in Section 2.2. Adam Smith's invisible hand channels the restless energy of profit-seeking self-interest into the public good of rising living standards. That is the positive, creative part of creative destruction.

These gains from specialization, trade, competition, and innovation also have a down side—destruction of less productive, higher-cost, and less popular products and businesses. Nineteenth century Québec wheat farmers and Manitoba textile companies went out of business in the face of new, more productive Canadian competition. Many twenty-first century auto workers in Ontario lost their jobs to robotic assembly lines in South Korea. These failed businesses and lost jobs are the opportunity costs of the gains from trade.

The jobs lost through trade, competition, and innovation come under the Chapter 3 definition of *structural unemployment*—unemployment due to technological change or international competition that makes workers' skills obsolete in Canada.

On the whole, consumers and businesses in Canada benefit from specialization, trade, and increased competition. Productivity and overall living standards improve. That is why we are so much better off than Canadians 200 years ago. But trade creates winners and losers. The losers pay a high price for the changes brought on by increased specialization and trade.

Winners and Losers from International Trade

When new international markets open up through trade—connecting Canada to other countries—who wins and who loses within Canada? The main winners are Canadian consumers and exporters. The main losers are businesses and workers in import-competing industries.

Winners   Consumers gain from lower prices and greater product variety that result from new imports. If imports sell successfully in Canada, there is a comparative advantage to the country selling to Canadians.

Canadian businesses that export gain from access to new markets and new customers. If Canadian exports sell successfully in the rest of the world, there is a comparative advantage to those Canadian businesses. Export businesses have more sales, more profits, and will hire more workers. Workers in exporting businesses gain from more jobs and higher wages.

Losers   Canadian businesses that cannot successfully compete with the new imports lose. These domestic businesses face stiffer competition and lower prices, as businesses in the rest of the world have a comparative advantage in selling to Canadian customers. Workers in import-competing businesses also lose, as their jobs disappear and wages fall with shrinking sales in Canada.

In the process of creative destruction, gains from specialization, trade, competition, and innovation destroy less productive, higher-cost, and less popular products and businesses.

Structural unemployment is due to technological change or international competition that makes workers' skills obsolete in Canada.

Winners from international trade include Canadian consumers (lower prices, greater product variety), Canadian exporters (increased sales and greater profits), and Canadian workers in exporting industries (more jobs, higher wages).

Losers from international trade include Canadian business in import-competing industries (decreased sales, lower prices and profits) and Canadian workers in import-competing industries (fewer jobs and lower wages).

Worldwide international exports of products/services was 22 times higher in 2000 than in 1950. About 40 percent of these products/services are delivered via containers on large ships like the one shown here.

tariff:
tax applied to imports

No Competition In My Backyard! Protectionism

Those who lose from international trade, facing threats to their businesses and jobs, turn for help to elected politicians—the government. Workers and businesses in Canadian import-competing industries look for protection from the bigger fish that appear when Canadian markets get connected to international markets. Government protection of their economic livelihood takes three main forms: tariffs, import quotas, and domestic subsidies.

Tariffs   A **tariff** is a tax applied to a product/service imported into a country. The Canadian business importing the product must pay the tariff to the Canadian government. That tariff is a business cost, which is passed on to consumers, increasing the price of the product.

Tariffs are attractive to governments everywhere for three reasons. First, tariffs raise revenues for the government to spend. Second, tariffs win votes and campaign donations for politicians from businesses and workers in import-competing industries. Third, because tariffs are a tax on non-Canadians who don't vote, there is little political damage from raising tariffs. While tariffs raise the price paid by Canadian consumers for the taxed imports, the tariff is not identified at the cash register. Consumers and voters usually do not blame the government for the higher import prices.

Figure 9.5 shows the history of tariffs in Canada since Confederation in 1867. The vertical axis measures the average tariff rate as a percentage of the value of imports.

Figure 9.5   Canadian Tariffs, 1867–2009

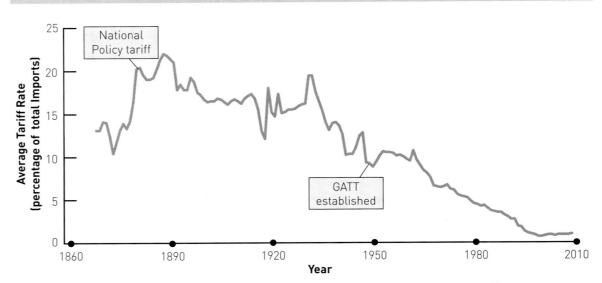

Source: *Historical Statistics of Canada*, 2nd ed., Series G485; Statistics Canada, Table 380-0034, series v499996, Table 380-0017, series v646958.

Tariffs increased significantly after Confederation, and stayed relatively high until the 1930s. In 1947, the international General Agreement on Tariffs and Trade (GATT) began an ongoing process of reducing tariffs in member countries around the world. GATT evolved into the World Trade Organization (WTO). Today, most tariffs in Canada have disappeared.

Where tariffs still apply, they protect domestic producers competing with imports. Because consumers must pay a higher price—including the tariff—for the imported products, competing domestic producers win from higher prices and profits. Canadian consumers lose from higher prices.

◀ About 150 countries, including Canada, belong to the World Trade Organization (WTO)—www.wto.org—which describes itself as "the only international organization dealing with the global rules of trade between nations." Its main function is to ensure that trade flows as smoothly, predictably, and freely as possible. These protesters strongly disagree with the decisions the WTO is making. They believe the WTO should not interfere with a country's internal politics.

Import Quotas While tariffs raise the *price* of imports, quotas limit the *quantity* of products/services that can be imported into Canada during a year. For example, Canada imposes **import quotas** on meat, eggs, dairy products, and steel.

With reduced supply and restricted competition, Canadian producers who compete with these imports win from higher prices. Higher prices for the product means the quantity sold in Canada is less than with freer trade. But the quantity sold by Canadian producers increases. With quotas, Canadian import-competing industries gain. There are higher prices and profits for the businesses and more jobs and higher wages for workers. Canadian consumers again lose from higher prices.

import quota:
limit on quantity of a product/service that can be imported

Domestic Subsidies The most common and controversial form of protectionism today is **subsidies to domestic producers**. A subsidy is a government payment to domestic producers of products/services that are threatened by international competition. Many governments, especially in Europe and the United States, provide subsidies for agricultural products like cotton and grain. Canada makes heavy use of subsidies to protect the dairy industry. Again, the businesses and workers being subsidized are winners while consumers lose by paying higher prices.

subsidies to domestic producers:
government payment to domestic producers of product/service

The Politics of Trade Policy

Why do governments often respond to domestic producers' requests for protection from international competition? The answer is not obvious, since the higher prices and reduced variety of products hurt far more Canadians—especially consumers—than the small number of businesses and workers helped in import-competing industries. But the unequal distribution of the gains and losses creates political pressures for government to help those who lose from international trade.

Domestic Trade Politics   A large number of consumers would gain from freer international trade, but the gain for each consumer is small. Each of us, as consumers, would benefit from slightly lower prices of imported products/services. The slightly higher prices caused by protectionism are not easily noticed. Even if consumers did realize they were paying, for example, five percent more for a product because of tariffs, quotas, or subsidies, most would not feel strongly enough to pressure politicians.

The impact for the small number of businesses and workers who would lose from freer international trade is very large. Many such businesses and workers in import-competing industries stand to lose their lifetime investments and their jobs. Facing such great losses, those affected have strong incentives to exert as much political pressure as possible through voting, political action, and campaign contributions. Their goal is to capture the support of politicians to legislate tariffs, quotas, or subsidies.

Because the domestic losers from international trade have far more at stake than the winners, political pressure from those who lose can result in government protection from the increased competition and creative destruction of international trade. That protection will leave Canadians as a whole worse off—without the gains of rising living standards from increased competition and creative destruction. Those in the "Yes" camp, believing that markets are best left alone by government, point to protectionism as an argument for a government hands-off policy. They argue that protectionist policies are a government failure that is a bigger problem than market failure.

Competition from any new market, even within Canada, can threaten existing industries. There has even been pressure on provincial governments to provide protection against Canadian businesses and workers in other provinces. Many provinces had laws requiring government purchases to come only from businesses within the province, and for government jobs to go only to provincial residents.

In 1994, the Canadian provinces signed the Agreement on Internal Trade to prevent provinces from erecting new trade barriers and to reduce existing ones. Nonetheless, some Canadian businesses claim that trade between provinces is still more difficult than trade between Canada and the United States!

> The number of consumers who gain from free trade is large, but the gain for each consumer is small. The number of businesses and workers in import-competing industries who lose from free trade is small, but the loss for each is large. The unequal distribution of gains and losses produces political pressure for protectionism to help the losers.

International Trade Politics The unequal distribution of gains and losses also affects international trade politics between counties. Through decades of negotiations between developed and developing countries, the WTO has been trying to reduce protectionist policies and promote freer international trade. Such trade could potentially benefit far more people than it harms. But the sticking point is political pressure in many countries from import-competing industries to protect themselves from competition.

Developed countries—especially the United States and some countries in Europe—want freer access to markets in developing countries of Africa, Asia, and South America for the products and services they export. The list includes pharmaceuticals, intellectual property (patents on drugs that cannot be undersold by cheaper generic drugs), copyright on movies and music (not allowing pirated DVDs), and patents on inventions and technology so they cannot simply be copied. But the United States and some countries in Europe are unwilling to remove domestic protectionist measures—especially domestic subsidies—from their agricultural and textile industries. The developing countries, which produce cotton, grains, and textiles, want access to those protected markets. Canada, while generally supportive of freer trade, is unwilling to remove subsidies to Canadian producers of dairy products, poultry, eggs, and wheat.

The political influence in many countries of the affected, protected industries is recognized as the barrier in these international trade negotiations.

Even though freer trade could potentially benefit more people than it harms, political pressure from import-competing industries in many countries is a barrier in international trade negotiations.

Arguments for Protectionism?

The politics of protectionism helps us understand why there are opponents to freer trade. There are two common arguments for protectionism that sound believable, but that fail to incorporate comparative advantage. There are also some valid, but limited, arguments for protectionism. Let's examine them.

Saving Canadian Jobs One argument states that tariffs, quotas, and subsidies can save jobs in Canadian import-competing industries. But freer trade creates jobs in Canadian export industries. Imports also create jobs in Canada for those businesses that sell and service the imports.

While eliminating tariffs, quotas, and subsidies will cost jobs in Canadian import-competing industries, freer trade creates more jobs than are lost.

Freer trade costs jobs in Canadian import-competing industries, but creates more jobs than are lost.

Necessary to Compete with Cheap Foreign Labour When Canada entered into the North American Free Trade Agreement (NAFTA) in 1994, many tariffs and quotas were eliminated among Canada, the United States, and Mexico. Many people predicted a "giant sucking sound" from jobs draining out of Canada and the United States into Mexico, because wages for labour were so much lower there. That did not happen.

Low-skill, low-wage jobs requiring little education did move to Mexico. But the evidence suggests that the total number of jobs in Canada has increased because of greater exports to expanded North American markets. The mistake in this argument about competing with cheap foreign labour is the focus on absolute cost and absolute advantage, instead of comparative advantage. While Mexico has a comparative advantage for some products, Canada has a comparative advantage for others. Mexico too has benefited from the mutual gains from trade.

Protecting national security and cultural identity are valid, limited arguments for protectionism.

Valid, Limited Protectionism Arguments Freer trade leads to increased specialization and reliance on other countries to supply products/services. While there are gains from trade, there are also risks from that reliance.

Canada would not want to rely entirely on a another country for strategic products like military equipment, energy, and other essentials. In the event of a war, what if your only suppliers of strategic products turned out to be enemies? To avoid that risk, governments may protect strategic domestic industries.

Another non-economic risk of freer trade is the threat to a country's cultural identity. Canada's reliance on U.S. trade brings with it exposure to the culture of a county that is ten times as large. In the name of protecting Canada's cultural identity, the government restricts imported content of radio and television programs, restricts broadcast licences to domestic providers, and subsidizes the production of Canadian culture in the form of domestic books, movies, music, and other media.

Trade Wars: Powerful Argument Against Protectionism

Supporters of tariffs, quotas, and subsidies rarely mention one of the most important arguments against protectionism—the risk of retaliation by other countries. Protectionist policy can trigger a trade war.

That is what happened during the Great Depression. In an attempt to protect U.S. jobs and businesses, the U.S. government introduced the Smoot-Hawley tariff. Other countries quickly retaliated with their own tariffs, and international trade collapsed, contributing to the length and severity of the Great Depression.

This is an example of the fallacy of composition at work. One country may temporarily make itself better off through tariffs, but when all countries do the same, then all end up worse off.

While the mutually beneficial gains from trade are real, so are the political pressures of protectionism. Those political pressures appear clearly in debates about globalization.

▶

In response to the Great Recession, in 2009 the U.S. introduced laws requiring state and local governments to buy products/services only from U.S. producers, even if the costs were higher than from Canadian producers. Canada protested, and worked out a trade deal where Canadian producers could compete for U.S. government contracts, and U.S. producers could compete for Canadian government contracts.

Refresh 9.2

1. Identify the winners and losers from international trade.

2. Explain the process of creative destruction. In your answer, include how this process is both positive and negative.

3. Present a counterargument to those who demand government protection for their industry from cheaper imports.

9.3 Globalization and Its Discontents: Is Free Trade the Problem?

Explain globalization, its pace, and how to evaluate if sweatshop workers are better off with international trade.

There are other opponents of expanded international trade beyond businesses and workers in import-competing industries. Some social activists, human rights organizations, and anti-market groups worry about what they see as the harmful consequences of international trade. At a student demonstration against free trade, one passionate activist asked the crowd,

> "Who made your T-shirt? . . . Was it a child in Vietnam? Or a young girl from India earning 18 cents per hour? . . . Did you know that she lives 12 to a room? . . . That she is forced to work 90 hours each week, without overtime pay? . . . That she lives not only in poverty, but also in filth and sickness, all in the name of Nike's profits?"

Anti-globalization critics view uncontrolled international trade as the cause of many undesirable problems in developing countries: low wages, poverty, poor working conditions, farmers who can no longer make a living, high-priced drugs from Western pharmaceutical companies, environmental damage, and local governments undermined by bureaucrats from international organizations. These critics view the competition from expanded international trade as a "race to the bottom" that will result in low wages, low standards for working conditions, greater pollution, and lower taxes (especially on corporations) in every country, both developing and developed.

Many anti-globalization protestors target two international organizations—the World Bank and the International Monetary Fund (IMF).

The World Bank and International Monetary Fund

At the end of World War II, the same 1947 international conference that created GATT also created the World Bank and the IMF. These international organizations—currently with 186 member nations—were created as the world struggled to recover from the devastation of war. Their mission was to support countries' economic growth and development through trade.

The World Bank is not a traditional bank. Its name is an abbreviation for two related institutions—the International Bank for Reconstruction and Development (IBRD) and the International Development Agency (IDA). Currently, the World Bank describes its mission as "inclusive and sustainable globalization." The IRBD focuses on reducing poverty in middle-income countries, while the IDA focuses on the world's poorest countries. The World Bank does act like a bank in loaning money at low interest or no interest to countries for economic development projects.

The IMF describes its mission as fostering global monetary cooperation, securing financial stability, facilitating international trade, promoting high employment and sustainable economic growth, and reducing poverty.

You are probably wondering why anti-globalization protestors target these organizations, whose missions do not seem to match the criticisms. The story behind the protests comes from the policies that the World Bank and IMF use to achieve their missions.

Hands-Off Policies for Developing Countries

Economists and policymakers at the World Bank and the IMF believe that free trade policies based on comparative advantage are best for helping developing countries achieve rising standards of living. Specialization, trade, competition, and connected international markets will, they argue, create a tide of wealth that will eventually lift all countries up. These free trade policies come directly from the "Yes" camp's answer to the fundamental macroeconomic question:

> If left alone by government, do the price mechanisms of market economies adjust quickly to maintain steady growth in living standards, full employment and stable prices?

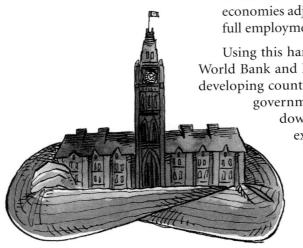

Using this hands-off view of the role of government, policymakers at the World Bank and IMF set "free market" conditions on loans and assistance to developing countries, especially during the 1990s. Those conditions required governments to enforce contracts and property rights—cracking down on pirated software, DVDs, and low-cost copies of expensive pharmaceutical drugs. Other hands-off conditions included removing regulations from labour markets, eliminating protectionist tariffs and quotas to allow imports from developed countries, lowering taxes on businesses to encourage private investment, and privatizing state-run industries—returning those industries to private businesses. Economists usually support freer trade and a prominent role for markets. But these hands-off views were especially strong during the 1990s. That decade saw the collapse of state communism in East Germany and the USSR, and the failure of their notoriously inefficient state-run industries. There was also rampant corruption among many governments of developing countries. Hands-on policies could not succeed if governments could not be trusted to spend loan money on the projects and people who needed it most. There was much evidence supporting a hands-off position. Government failure seemed a bigger problem than market failure.

Joseph Stiglitz Changes the Debate

Economists often dismiss protestors opposing free trade and free markets as misguided do-gooders who simply do not understand the concept of comparative advantage. But the globalization debate changed when a prominent economist added his voice to those of the protesters.

Joseph Stiglitz, a professor at Columbia University, served on the Council of Economic Advisors under U.S. President Bill Clinton. In 1997, Stiglitz became chief economist at the World Bank. He left the World Bank after three years, and was awarded the Nobel Prize in Economics in 2001. As an insider at the World Bank, and winner of the most prestigious prize an economist can get, Stiglitz's criticisms counted. He published an influential, bestselling book in 2002 which provides the title of this section—*Globalization and Its Discontents*.

Joseph Stiglitz, a Nobel Prize–winning economist, was the chief economist at the World Bank from 1997 to 2000. His arguments against a strictly hands-off position for world monetary institutions gave stronger support for the anti-globalization critics.

Stiglitz's criticisms of the strongly hands-off policies of the World Bank and the IMF, and the responses from other pro-trade economists (see Economics Out There, below) helped to reconcile the apparent contradiction between pro-trade arguments that gains for trade are the key to rising living standards, and the anti-globalization accusations that global trade causes harm in so many ways.

In order to understand the debate triggered by World Bank and IMF policies, protestors, and Stiglitz's book, it is helpful to first establish some facts about globalization.

Globalization and Its Discontents

Controversy over globalization and the roles of the World Trade Organization (WTO), World Bank, and International Monetary Fund (IMF) made a dramatic public appearance with raging street battles and huge demonstrations at the 1999 meeting of the WTO in Seattle, Washington. Conflict erupted at most major meetings of these organizations over the next few years.

The Economist magazine published an important "Survey on Globalization" in September 2001, in anticipation of the scheduled joint annual meeting of the World Bank and IMF. That meeting was cancelled in the wake of the September 11 attacks in the United States.

Stiglitz's book appeared in 2002 with much publicity, and prompted many responses. Two of the more notable responses were *In Defense of Globalization* (2004), by Jagdish Bhagwati, another Columbia University professor and columnist for *The New York Times* and *The Wall Street Journal* and *Why Globalization Works* (2004) by Martin Wolf, a former senior economist at the World Bank and associate editor of the *Financial Times* in London.

Naomi Klein, a Canadian activist and columnist for *The Nation* and the *Guardian* published *The Shock Doctrine: The Rise of Disaster Capitalism* in 2007, continuing the controversy. Klein argues that America's "free market" policies have come to dominate the world through the exploitation of disaster-shocked people and countries.

What Is Globalization?

Controversy swirls around the consequences of globalization—is globalization a force for good or for evil? Does globalization bring rising living standards or a descent into poverty? Before trying to reconcile pro- and anti-globalization arguments in the next section, let's start with a simple definition. **Economic globalization** is the integration of economic activities across borders, and through markets. When markets in one country are connected to markets in other countries, economic activities are connected, or integrated. The technical support for your computer may come from a business in India. The potash used by factories in the Czech Republic to make glass may come from Saskatchewan. The T-shirt you wear may be made from cotton grown in Texas but woven into cloth in Shanghai.

economic globalization: integration of economic activities, across borders, through markets

Why Is Globalization Happening?

The underlying motivation for the spread of integrated economic activity across borders is the same as it was for Jacqueline and Samantha. Voluntary trade is motivated by self-interest, profits from innovation, and mutually beneficial gains. Connections to bigger ponds in international markets provide new opportunities for gains, but also new competitors and new threats of creative destruction. There are winners and losers from globalization, just as there are winners and losers from trade within a country.

Self-interest is always present as a motive for expanded trade. The pace of globalization is speeding up due to falling costs for both transportation and communications technologies. It is quickly becoming cheaper and easier to connect markets among countries, in the same way that the railroad reduced the cost of connecting markets across Canada.

Globalization is speeding up due to falling transportation and communication costs and the elimination of government barriers to trade.

Globalization is also speeding up from the elimination of government barriers to trade. Free trade agreements between countries, decreasing tariffs, quotas, and domestic subsidies combined with efforts of the WTO, World Bank, and IMF to reduce protectionist policies impeding trade speed globalization.

Globalization itself—the integration of economic activities, across borders, through markets—is neither good nor bad. But the consequences of globalization for different groups can be good or bad.

Sweatshops versus Farms

The new markets and opportunities that arise from globalization may not look good to us, even though the participants see them as a vast improvement in their lives. When we hear of the low pay and working conditions in some sweatshops, our first thoughts—like those of the activist quoted at the start—may be that these workers are being exploited in the interest of corporate profits.

But that does not explain why millions of young Chinese women voluntarily choose low-wage factory jobs over life on the farm in rural China. One woman, Liang Ying, who fled to the Shenzhen factory zone in southern China, felt almost anything was better than life on the family rubber farm:

> "Every morning, from 4 a.m. to 7 a.m. you have to cut through the bark of 400 rubber trees in total darkness. It has to be done before daybreak, otherwise the sunshine will evaporate the rubber juice. If you were me, what would you prefer, the factory or the farm?"

People in the West may regard low-paying jobs at Nike as exploitation, but for many people in the developing world, working in a factory is a far better option than staying down on the farm and growing rice.

—Joseph Stiglitz
2001 Nobel Prize in Economics

www.amazon.ca/Globalization-Its-Discontents-Joseph-Stiglitz/dp/0393324397

In evaluating sweatshop jobs always ask a key question about opportunity cost. Are workers lives better, or worse, compared to a situation without globalization, trade, and the factory jobs that follow? This is the same question behind the Jacqueline and Samantha example—are they better off with specialization and trade, or better off being self-sufficient? Behind the law of supply (Appendix C.1) is the basic idea that to hire labour (or any other input), businesses must pay at least the value of the best alternative use of the worker's time.

When workers voluntarily choose the sweatshop over the farm, it is because, from their perspective, factory jobs make them better off. What looks like poverty to us, and is poverty by Western standards, is a rising standard of living for the workers by their standards.

Economists ask the opportunity cost question about sweatshops—are workers lives better or worse compared to a situation without globalization, trade, and the factory jobs that follow?

Sweatshops Throughout History

The story of workers migrating from farms to factory jobs is not new. In the original English cotton factories of the late 1700s, people with few opportunities moved from farms to the original sweatshops in cities. While the working conditions and pay were abysmal, they were better than the alternative.

The same pattern repeated in the U.S. cotton industry in New Hampshire and Massachusetts in the 1800s, where many French Canadians worked. The pattern continued in the Japanese textile industry in the 1920s and in Korea and Taiwan in the 1970s and 1980s. In all of these countries, standards of living and working conditions improved over time. Some of those improvements came from governments playing a hands-on role, and some happened when the government took a hands-off position.

As globalization connected the original British textile industry to new markets and new competitors, less competitive textile industries in older countries declined. Creative destruction created winners and losers. But since overall standards of living have continued to rise in the countries whose textile industries ultimately lost out to new competitors—first England, then the United States, Japan, South Korea, and Taiwan—new and better-paying jobs were created in other export industries where the countries held a comparative advantage.

FOR YOUR INFORMATION

The term *sweatshop* comes from England in the 1800s where the middleman who directed others in garment-making was called a *sweater*. Merchants purchased garments from the middleman, who subcontracted the work to women and children who were paid by the piece for clothing they produced. The workplaces created for this sweating system were called sweatshops. Sweatshops now refer to any factory or workshop where manual workers are employed at low wages for long hours and under poor conditions.

Winners and Losers From Globalization

Globalization continues this pattern today. While specialization and trade can bring mutually beneficial gains to countries, there are individual groups within a country who win and who lose.

Jamaica, for example, reduced trade barriers to milk imports in 1992. Local dairy farmers were losers, having to compete with cheaper imports of milk powder. Jamaican milk production dropped significantly. But poor children, who could get imported milk more cheaply, were winners.

With a better understanding of what globalization is, can we reconcile the apparent contradiction between pro-trade arguments (that gains for trade are the key to rising living standards), and the anti-globalization accusations that global trade causes harm in so many ways? That is our final topic.

Refresh 9.3

1. In your own words, define economic globalization. Provide one example where globalization has affected you.

2. Identify the forces that speed up globalization, and the forces that slow it down.

3. What argument would you make to counter the claim that all sweatshop workers are exploited by big business?

www.myeconlab.com

Hands-Off or Hands-On Again? Governments and Global Markets

Evaluate the hands-off and hands-on arguments about the role for government in the globalization debate.

Is globalization a force for good or for evil? Does globalization bring rising living standards or a descent into poverty? The answers to these questions lead back to the fundamental macroeconomic question. But this time, the context is not within a country, but across connected countries. Should governments be hands-off or hands-on in the global economy?

Hands-On for Stiglitz

One of Stiglitz's valuable contributions to the globalization debate is to make explicit the importance of the hands-off versus hands-on question.

Although a great believer in markets, Stiglitz's own position is hands-on, favouring an "important, if limited, role for government to play." He contrasts his hands-on position with the free-market, free-trade policies supported by the World Bank and the IMF in the 1990s—the hands-off position criticized by anti-globalization protestors.

"The IMF's policies . . . based on the . . . presumption that markets, by themselves, lead to efficient outcomes, failed to allow for desirable government interventions in the market, measures which can guide economic growth and make everyone better off. What was at issue . . . is . . . conceptions of the role of the government . . ."*

Social Safety Nets The hands-on position believes government has a responsibility to maintain a social safety net to support the economic welfare of citizens left behind by trade and markets—especially labour markets which determine incomes. Specialization, trade, and creative destruction—whether within a country or between countries—inevitably create winners and losers. In Canada, there are many government programs to assist those who lose from expanded trade. There are Employment Insurance benefits for the unemployed, job retraining programs, social assistance payments, and health care benefits that do not depend upon a person having a job.

Most poor, developing countries lack a social safety net, so the competitive forces of creative destruction can lead to poverty and misery as jobs disappear in import-competing industries. Social safety net programs cost money that governments in poor countries may not have. But even if those governments wanted to create such programs, the strong hands-off policies prescribed by the World Bank and the IMF in the 1990s restricted their ability to operate or finance—through higher taxes—such safety net programs. The strong hands-off policies for labour markets also discouraged government regulation of working conditions. Bureaucrats and policymakers at the World Bank and IMF, rather than local governments, influenced decisions about local social programs.

*www.amazon.ca/Globalization-Its-Discontents-Joseph-Stiglitz/dp/0393324397

Opening the Door to Trouble   Stiglitz's book appeared to validate many concerns of anti-globalization critics. But his hands-on policy choice, like any choice, has an opportunity cost. And the opportunity cost of allowing the government to act hands-on brings us to the arguments presented by the hands-off position.

Hands-Off for *The Economist* Magazine

Once governments take a hands-on role in helping people and industries who lose from the creative destruction of market competition, the door is open for special interest groups to ask for government help in protecting them from such competition in the first place.

Buried in Wool   The protectionism that exists today in global trade is not new. In England in the 1600s—before the rise of the cotton textile industry—virtually all clothes were made of wool from domestic sheep. The British East India Company connected to new markets in India, and began importing hand-spun calico cotton into England. The new fabric was cheap, light, washable, colourful, and was an instant hit with consumers. Of course, local wool sales suffered, and the wool industry persuaded parliament to pass protectionist measures. All students and professors at the universities were required by law to wear only wool garments, and corpses could only be buried wrapped in wool.

A law was passed in 1701 banning all imports of calico cotton entirely (a quota of zero!). The wool industry thought it had won, but the innovative profit-seeking forces of creative destruction led English entrepreneurs to set up industrial cotton factories in England that eventually crushed the sales and political influence of the wool industry.

In hindsight, such protectionist measures look ridiculous. But the motivation for protectionism is exactly the same today as it was then.

Whose Side Are They On?   *The Economist* magazine has been reporting from England on global economic stories, including stories on the cotton industry, since 1843. *The Economist* supports free markets and globalization, and generally opposes government "interference" in economic or social activity.

As part of the debate over globalization, *The Economist* published the following editorial. What is striking is the support it seems to give to the anti-globalization critics.

> Rich countries' trade rules, especially in farming and textiles, still discriminate powerfully against poor countries. Rich countries' subsidies encourage wasteful use of energy and natural resources, and harm the environment. . . . rich countries' protection of intellectual property discriminates unfairly against the developing world. And without a doubt, rich countries' approach to financial regulation offers implicit subsidies to their banks and encourages reckless lending; it results, time and again, in financial crises in rich and poor countries alike.
>
> All these policies owe much to the fact that corporate interests exercise undue influence over government policy. [Critics] are right to deplore this. But undue influence is hardly new in democratic politics; it has not been created by globalisation forcing governments to bow down. . . . If allowed to, all governments are happy to seek political advantage by granting preferences.

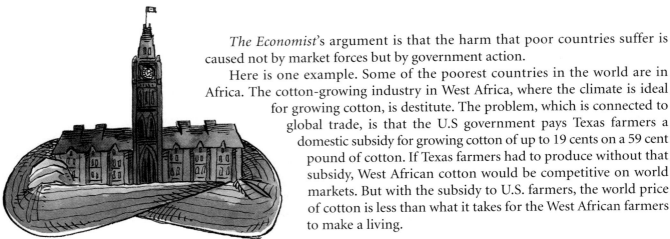

The Economist's argument is that the harm that poor countries suffer is caused not by market forces but by government action.

Here is one example. Some of the poorest countries in the world are in Africa. The cotton-growing industry in West Africa, where the climate is ideal for growing cotton, is destitute. The problem, which is connected to global trade, is that the U.S government pays Texas farmers a domestic subsidy for growing cotton of up to 19 cents on a 59 cent pound of cotton. If Texas farmers had to produce without that subsidy, West African cotton would be competitive on world markets. But with the subsidy to U.S. farmers, the world price of cotton is less than what it takes for the West African farmers to make a living.

Practice What You Preach   Some of the opposition to the free trade policies of the World Bank, IMF, and WTO stem from what from anti-globalization critics and governments of poor countries perceive as the hypocrisy of Western trade proposals. In recent WTO negotiations, richer Western countries pushed for reduced tariffs, quotas, and subsidies on products they exported, but continued to protect their own industries—especially agriculture and textiles—where import competition from poorer developing countries might threaten their domestic industries. This was noted by The Economist in the editorial above.

To be fair, poorer developing countries did the same during the negotiations. They pushed for expanded access to Western markets for products they export, while still trying to protect their domestic industries from Western import competition.

Power struggles over tariffs and subsidies between rich and poor countries affect the terms of trade and how the gains are divided.

Terms of Trade   This is a power struggle between governments of rich and poor countries, which explains the impasse of the current WTO negotiations. The terms of trade—quantity of exports required to pay for one unit of imports—are largely determined by prices in international markets. The power struggle over tariffs and subsidies, though, strongly influences the terms of trade.

Stiglitz argues that an earlier, 1995 round of WTO negotiations yielded an agreement that *lowered* the prices some of the poorest countries in the world received for their exports relative to what they paid for their imports. The result was that some of the poorest countries were actually made *worse off* as a result of this agreement.

Shake Hands?

Specialization and trade—whether within a country or across the globe—inevitably create winners and losers. The competitive forces of creative destruction will generally cause rising standards of living, but can also cause poverty and misery as jobs disappear in import-competing industries. Both the hands-on and hands-off positions recognize these unfortunate outcomes as the side effects of specialization, trade, and economic growth.

Limited Role for Government? Stiglitz's hands-on position sees an important, but limited, role for government. Government should, he argues, maintain a social safety net to support the economic welfare of citizens left behind by trade and markets—especially labour markets that determine incomes.

The hands-off position sees many of the unfortunate outcomes resulting not from trade, but from government interference in markets. Tariffs, quotas, and domestic subsidies—responses to political pressure from industries and workers harmed by competing imports—can distort the terms of trade and put industries and workers in the poorest countries at a disadvantage.

Markets Failure or Government Failure? As a citizen of Canada and the world, you must decide which policies you will support around globalization and trade. There are no right or easy choices, only trade-offs.

If you think it is important for government to help those who lose from expanded trade in import-competing industries—in Canada or abroad—you run the risk that the government will also succumb to political pressure and implement protectionist policies that slow both the expansion of trade and economic growth. If you support this hands-on position, you are betting that market failure is worse than government failure. The failure of markets to produce rising standards of living, full employment, and stable prices is more likely and costly than government failing by succumbing to political pressure from special interests for market protection.

If you think the markets are best left alone to produce economic growth that will eventually benefit all, you run the risk that those who lose from expanded trade in import-competing industries will end up in poverty and misery. If you support this hands-off position, you are betting that government failure is worse than market failure. The failure of government, that comes from implementing protectionist policies that are not in society's best interests, is more likely and costly than markets failing in the form of falling living standards for those in import-competing industries.

Figure 9.6 summarizes the trade-offs for the hands-off and hands-on positions on government's role in trade policy.

Figure 9.6	Government and Global Markets: Hands-Off or Hands-On?	
	Camp	
	Yes — Left Alone, Markets Quickly Self-Adjust: Hands-Off	No — Left Alone, Markets Fail to Adjust: Hands-On
Role of government	None	Limited to maintaining social safety net supporting those left behind by trade and markets
Risk of chosen role for Government	Losers in import-competing businesses get no assistance in adjusting	Government succumbs to political pressure for protectionism
Which failure is worse?	Believe government failure is worse that market failure	Believe market failure is worse than government failure

Travels of a T-Shirt   Pietra Rivoli, a business school professor at Georgetown University, witnessed the student demonstration against free trade reported on page 347. In response, she decided to travel the world, following the globally integrated production path of a T-shirt. She bought the T-shirt in Florida. It was made from Texas cotton and manufactured in China. She was trying to determine whether the accusations of the student activist about the harmful effects of globalization were justified.

In the conclusion of the book that she wrote about her travels (see Economics Out There, below) she asked what she should say to the student activist demonstrating against free trade who was

"so concerned about the evils of the race to the bottom, so concerned about where and how her T-shirt was produced? I would tell her to appreciate what markets and trade had accomplished for all of the sisters in time who have been liberated by life in a sweatshop, and that she should be careful about dooming anyone to life on the farm. I would tell her that the poor suffer more from exclusion from politics than from the perils of the market, and that if she has activist energy left over it should be focused on including people in politics rather than shielding them from markets."

Hands-On   Hands-Off

Rivoli's travels led her to the conclusion that the harmful outcomes we witness from globalized trade have less to do with market forces, and more to do with governments protecting domestic industries and workers. Those tariffs, quotas, and domestic subsidies, she argues, force prices below subsistence levels for producers in poorer countries. The resulting adverse terms of trade and poverty, she maintains, are due to government protectionist policies.

Her advice, to anyone who agrees with her argument, is to become politically involved to protect the interests of foreign workers, but not by opposing free trade. Instead, she suggests opposing protectionist policies while supporting safety net policies. It is a combination of hands-off and hands-on.

Travels of a T-Shirt in the Global Economy
Many of the stories about textiles in this chapter can be found in the easy-to-read and fascinating book by Pietra Rivoli, *The Travels of a T-Shirt in the Global Economy: An Economist Examines the Markets, Power, and Politics of World Trade* (2009).

Your Hand at the Ballot Box   The globalization debate includes many points of view. You have read arguments by the World Bank and IMF, *The Economist*, and Professors Stiglitz and Rivoli. It is possible that the suggestion of Professor Rivoli combining hands-off and hands-on policies is achievable—if government failure is less likely than market failure. It is also possible that her suggestion will make things worse—if the government failure she fears is more likely than market failure.

Governments respond to political pressure. If you care about globalization, you will have to decide on your own stand when voting for elected politicians—the people who set policy.

1. In point form, summarize either the hands-on or hands-off arguments on global trade.

2. Present a case for either the hands-on or hands-off argument for increasing global trade.

3. How would you answer the fundamental macroeconomic question, "If left alone by government, do price mechanisms of market economies adjust quickly to maintain steady growth in living standards, full employment, and stable prices?" Explain your response in macroeconomic terms.

www.myeconlab.com

Are Sweatshops All Bad?

Globalization and Trade Policy

CHAPTER SUMMARY

9.1 WHY DON'T YOU COOK BREAKFAST?
GAINS FROM TRADE

Opportunity cost and comparative advantage are key to understanding why specializing and trading makes us all better off.

- With voluntary trade, each person (or country) feels that what they get is of greater value than what they give up.

- Canada is a trading nation—36 percent of Canadian GDP is from sale of exports to the rest of the world.

- **Absolute advantage**—ability to produce a product/service at a lower absolute cost than another producer.

- **Comparative advantage**—ability to produce a product/service at a lower opportunity cost than another producer.

- Opportunity cost $= \dfrac{\text{Give up}}{\text{Get}}$

- Comparative advantage is key to mutually beneficial gains from trade. Trade makes individuals (or countries) better off when each specializes in product/service where each has comparative advantage (lower opportunity cost) and then trades for other product/service.

- Even if one individual (or country) has *absolute* advantage in producing everything at lower cost, differences in *comparative* advantage allow mutually beneficial gains from specializing and trading.

- **Terms of trade**—quantity of exports required to pay for one unit of imports.
  - For mutual benefits, terms of trade must be between each trader's local opportunity costs.
  - Different terms of trade will split the gains differently.

Freer trade creates winners and losers from the competitive process of creative destruction. Concentrated losses in import-competing industries create political pressure for protectionism despite overall gains.

- Freer trade increases competition, creating opponents to freer trade.
  - Connections to new markets brings new competitors.
- In the process of *creative destruction*, gains from specialization, trade, competition, and innovation destroy less productive, higher-cost, and less popular products and businesses.
  - Gains are increased productivity and higher living standards for consumers and businesses on the whole.
  - Job losses in form of *structural unemployment*—technological change or international competition make workers' skills obsolete in Canada.
- Trade opening up new international markets creates winners and losers in Canada.
  - Winners—Canadian consumers (lower prices, greater product variety), Canadian exporters (increased sales, greater profits), Canadian workers in exporting industries (more jobs, higher wages).
  - Losers—Canadian businesses in import-competing industries (decreased sales, lower prices, profits), Canadian workers in import-competing industries (fewer jobs, lower wages).
- Government responses to protect losers from freer trade—tariffs, import quotas, domestic subsidies. Businesses and workers in import-competing industries win from protection. Canadian consumers lose from higher prices.
  - **Tariff**—tax applied to imports, raising price of product to consumers.
  - **Import quota**—limit on quantity of a product/service that can be imported.
  - **Subsidies to domestic producers**—government payment to domestic producers of products/services.
- Unequal distribution of gains and losses produces political pressure for protectionism to help the losers.
  - Number of consumers who gain from free trade is large, but gain for each consumer is small.
  - Number of businesses and worker in import-competing industries who lose from free trade is small, but loss for each is large.
- Protectionism leaves Canadians as a whole worse off.
  - "Yes" camp sees protectionist policies as government failure that is a bigger problem than market failure.
- Even though freer trade could potentially benefit more people than it harms, political pressure from import-competing industries in countries is a barrier in international trade negotiations.
- Freer trade costs jobs in Canadian import-competing industries, but creates more jobs than are lost.

- With North American Free Trade Agreement (NAFTA), low-skill, low-wage jobs lost in Canada, but total jobs in Canada increased.
- Protecting national security and cultural identity are valid, limited arguments for protectionism.
- Protectionism creates risk of retaliation, triggering trade war that can collapse international trade, making all countries worse off.

9.3 GLOBALIZATION AND ITS DISCONTENTS: IS FREE TRADE THE PROBLEM?

While anti-globalization critics view sweatshops as the outcome of globalization and free-market policies, economists ask whether workers are better off or worse off with international trade.

- Anti-globalization groups view international trade as causing problems in developing countries and target two international organizations:
  - World Bank.
  - International Monetary Fund (IMF).
- Economists and policymakers at World Bank and IMF, especially during 1990s, attached "free market" hands-off conditions to assistance to developing countries.
  - Joseph Stiglitz, former chief economist at World Bank, criticized hands-off policies.
- **Economic globalization**—integration of economic activities, across borders, through markets.
  - Globalization speeding up due to falling transportation and communication costs, elimination of government barriers to trade.
- Sweatshops—historical consequence of globalization going back 200 years—provide low-wage jobs, often under poor working conditions.
  - Anti-globalization critics view sweatshops as exploitation for corporate profits.
  - Economists ask the opportunity cost question—are workers lives better off, or worse off, compared to a situation without globalization, trade, and the factory jobs that follow?

9.4 HANDS-OFF OR HANDS-ON AGAIN? GOVERNMENTS AND GLOBAL MARKETS

On the role of government in global markets, hands-off position views government failure as worse than market failure; hands-on position views market failure as worse than government failure.

- In contrast to hand-off policies of World Bank and IMF, Stiglitz and hands-on economists support limited role for government.
  - Maintain social safety net to support those left behind by trade and markets.

- *The Economist* magazine and hands-off economists worry that opening the door to government will result in protectionist policies.
  - Argue that poor countries suffer from globalization caused by government protectionist policies, not from market forces.
- In trade negotiations at World Trade Organization (WTO),
  - Developed countries want reduced tariffs, quotas, subsidies on products they export, but continued protection of their own industries—agriculture, textiles—where import competition from developing countries might threaten their domestic industries.
  - Developing countries want expanded access to Western markets for products they export, but continued protection of their domestic industries from Western import competition.
  - Power struggles over tariffs and subsidies between rich and poor countries affects terms of trade—how gains are divided.
- As a citizen of Canada and the world, you can take a position on globalization.
  - "Yes" camp takes government hands-off position—markets best left alone to produce economic growth that eventually benefits all; risk is losers in import-competing industries get no assistance in adjusting; believe government failure worse than market failure.
  - "No" camp takes government hands on position—government should help losers from expanded trade in import-competing industries; risk is government succumbs to political pressure for protectionism; believe market failure worse than government failure.

TRUE/FALSE

Circle the correct answer.

You and your friend Ursula have been studying together for the macro exam that's coming up soon. You are invited to stay for dinner. At the table, her great-grandfather, who is close to 100 years old, suddenly announces, "The trouble with the world today is young people buy too many things from other countries—that's the problem! When I was young, if I needed something, I made it myself." You and Ursula roll your eyes. You both know that's not true, so you suggest a game of true or false. You invite the other dinner guests to discuss the following statements on globalization and trade. What answers should they give?

Use this scenario to answer questions 1–15.

9.1 GAINS FROM TRADE

1. The concepts of comparative advantage, specialization, and trade are consistent with Ursula's great-grandfather's belief in self-sufficiency.   **True**   **False**

2. Voluntary trade implies that self–interest is at work.	**True**	**False**
3. Canadian exports are a smaller percentage of Canada's GDP than exports are for U.S. GDP.	**True**	**False**
4. Ursula and her great-grandfather will be willing to trade apples for oranges if their terms of trade are between each trader's local opportunity costs.	**True**	**False**
5. The variety of foods such as tuna, coffee, tea, and the many different fruits being served for dinner at Ursula's home are examples of the gains from trade and specialization.	**True**	**False**

9.2 PROTECTIONISM AND TRADE

6. Ursula's great-grandfather, like most consumers, is an economic winner when new international trade markets open up for Canada.	**True**	**False**
7. Ursula's great-grandfather was a technician in a factory that made vacuum-tube radios in the 1950s. When new technology emerged, his company changed over to produce transistor-type radios. This is a positive outcome of creative destruction.	**True**	**False**
8. Tariffs raise the price of imports into Canada, raise money for the government, and allow older, less competitive businesses to keep operating. Tariffs therefore are completely beneficial for a country.	**True**	**False**
9. Political pressure for protectionism occurs because freer trade results in big losses for some businesses and workers, and small gains for each consumer.	**True**	**False**
10. Many economists agree with Ursula's great-grandfather's idea of "making it ourselves" when it comes to products/services that protect our national security.	**True**	**False**

9.3 GLOBALIZATION AND SWEATSHOPS

11. Most hands-off and hands-on policymakers agree on the need for freer trade. They disagree on how it is implemented.	**True**	**False**
12. Globalization forces workers in developing countries to choose lower-paying jobs in sweatshops over higher-paying farm jobs.	**True**	**False**

9.4 GOVERNMENTS AND GLOBAL MARKETS

13. Being invited for a "free" dinner at Ursula's house is an example of a government social safety net.   **True**   **False**

14. Rivoli, in her book *Travels of a T-Shirt*, argues that globalization can improve the economic lives of most people if countries develop social safety nets and oppose protectionist policies.   **True**   **False**

15. Your vote can influence how Canada responds to globalization and international trade.   **True**   **False**

MULTIPLE CHOICE

Circle the correct answer.

9.1 GAINS FROM TRADE

1. An easy way to calculate opportunity cost is to use the formula

   A) $\dfrac{\text{Give up}}{\text{Get}}$

   B) $\dfrac{\text{Get}}{\text{Give up}}$

   C) Give up − Get

   D) Get − Give up

2. Voluntary trade improves our standard of living by moving us from self-sufficiency to

   A) making our own breakfast.

   B) calculating the opportunity costs for any change.

   C) specializing and trading.

   D) transferring mutual benefits.

3. Having absolute advantage in producing a product/service means having

   A) higher absolute costs than your competitor.

   B) lower opportunity costs than your competitor.

   C) lower absolute costs than your competitor.

   D) higher opportunity costs than your competitor.

4. Having a comparative advantage in the production of any product/service means having

   A) greater absolute costs than your competitor.

   B) lower opportunity costs than your competitor.

   C) lower absolute costs than your competitor.

   D) greater opportunity costs than your competitor.

5. Mutually beneficial gains from trade come from
   A) absolute advantage.
   B) comparative advantage.
   C) self-sufficiency.
   D) the United States.

6. All of the following are forms of protectionism *except*
   A) tariffs.
   B) terms of trade.
   C) import quotas.
   D) domestic subsidies.

7. For a voluntary trade to have mutual benefits, the terms of trade must
   A) be between each trader's local opportunity costs.
   B) be greater than each trader's local opportunity costs.
   C) be less than each trader's local opportunity costs.
   D) divide the gains equally.

8. Jobs lost through competition and innovation are part of
   A) creative trading.
   B) cyclical employment.
   C) frictional unemployment.
   D) structural unemployment.

9. Creative destruction, in the end,
   A) ruins most economies.
   B) creates more jobs than it destroys.
   C) makes it much harder to import products/services.
   D) eliminates gains from trade.

10. Creative destruction occurs when
    A) one country establishes absolute advantage over its trading partners.
    B) the United States stops trading with Canada.
    C) businesses and workers agree on a new profit structure.
    D) new technologies or greater international competition arise.

11. When new international markets open up for Canadian businesses, usually
    A) everybody wins.
    B) nobody wins.
    C) consumers win.
    D) consumers lose.

9.3 GLOBALIZATION AND SWEATSHOPS

12. Economic globalization is the integration of
- **A)** banks, businesses, and labour.
- **B)** economic activities in developed countries.
- **C)** markets in developing nations.
- **D)** economic activities through markets across borders.

13. When economists evaluate sweatshops, they ask the question, "Are sweatshop
- **A)** workers' wages too low?"
- **B)** workers exploited for corporate profits?"
- **C)** workers' lives better than a situation without the sweatshop jobs?"
- **D)** workers' lives better than the lives of workers in the developed world?"

9.4 GOVERNMENTS AND GLOBAL MARKETS

14. In the debate surrounding globalization, the hands-on camp believes
- **A)** government should provide social safety nets.
- **B)** government failure is worse than market failure.
- **C)** businesses should provide social safety nets.
- **D)** sweatshops should all be shut down.

15. The forces that encourage creative destruction also generally cause
- **A)** rising standards of living.
- **B)** some job loss.
- **C)** some job creation.
- **D)** all of the above.

SHORT ANSWER

Write a short answer to each question. Your answer may be in point form.

1. Suppose you and your roommate alternate doing housework (cooking and cleaning) and joint economics assignments each week (one week you do both activities, and in the next week he does both activities). You are better than your roommate at both activities. In one hour, you can either finish the joint assignment or complete all of the housework. In one hour, he can either do one-half of the joint assignment or complete three-quarters of the housework.

- **A)** In which activities do you have an absolute advantage? A comparative advantage?

- **B)** Suppose you offer your roommate a deal so that each of you specializes in one activity. In which activity should you specialize? Why?

2. Consider this scenario. Your friend offers you a ticket to the Leafs/Senators hockey game on Saturday night. He'll give you the ticket free if you pick up all other expenses. You usually work Saturday nights, so if you take the offer you will have to take the night off work. Explain what costs you would include in deciding whether the "free" ticket was worth taking. That is, what are the opportunity costs of your friend's gift?

3. Use the formula in Section 9.1 for discovering opportunity cost to calculate the opportunity cost for each loaf of additional bread for Jacqueline if she could produce:

A) 150 cords of wood or 75 loaves of bread in one month.

B) 50 cords of wood or 100 loaves of bread.

C) 300 cords of wood or 100 loaves of bread.

4. Consider Jacqueline and Samantha from section 9.1, who specialize and trade to become better off. Suppose that Jack, a new person in town, is deciding between specialization (in either bread or wood) and being self-sufficient. Jack's production possibilities are illustrated in the following chart:

Jack's Production Possibilities (monthly)	
Bread (loaves)	Wood (cords)
70	0
60	15
50	30
40	45
30	60
20	75
10	90
0	105

If Jack chooses to be self-sufficient, he prefers spending his time making 20 loaves of bread and 75 cords of wood.

Who has the comparative advantage between

A) Jack and Jacqueline?

B) Jack and Samantha?

5. Suppose Jack makes the announcement that he will go into partnership with either Jacqueline or Samantha depending upon who makes him the best offer, that is, the offer that leaves him better off after trading. Assume that 20 loaves of bread can be traded for 20 cords of wood. With whom will Jack go into partnership?

6. According to the Economics Out There on page 356, sweatshops are not all bad. Explain this position taking the concepts of *terms of trade* and *opportunity cost* into account.

7. List five examples of globalization that have a direct or indirect impact on you.

8. Your friend's family business—making parts for electronic communication devices—faces new international competition from a factory in China that can make the same parts cheaper. Your friend wants you to sign a petition demanding that the government put a tariff on the Chinese parts coming to Canada. This, they say in their petition, will make the Chinese product more expensive than theirs and allow them to continue with business as usual. Using the concept of creative destruction, explain to your friend why you won't sign the petition.

9. A federal election has been called. You know that government policy has a great effect on your life and your future prospects. Consider the following three scenarios. Imagine that you are living in these locations. At an all-candidates meeting for each scenario, you ask each candidate, "Do you believe in a government hands-off or a hands-on approach?" What answer in each case would get your vote?

A) You fish in a small fishing village on the east coast where the entire economy depends upon catching, processing, and selling fish products. Your livelihood is based on getting the best price for your fish.

B) You are a high-tech engineer working in a big city. Your company gets its market share by being innovative. It boasts that it's always first to the market with new communication devices. The company depends upon new ideas and new markets to keep growing.

C) You are a student at a community college earning a degree in sales and marketing. Your future depends upon Canada's continued growth nationally and internationally. You want to see more job opportunities open up so you will have a fulfilling career after graduation.

10. The fundamental macroeconomic question is:

If left alone by government, do the price mechanisms of market economies adjust quickly to maintain steady growth in living standards, full employment, and stable prices?

Restate this question in your own words.

Summing Up

You and I have finished our last trip around the enlarged GDP circular flow. But this diagram will continue to be your best guide to making smart choices for the rest of your life.

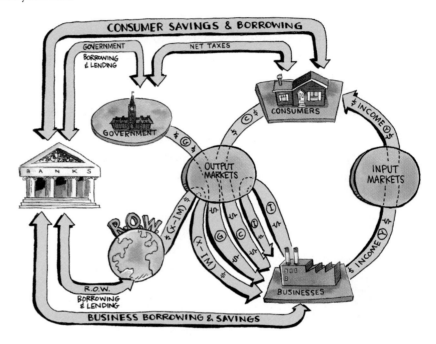

We looked at the five macroeconomic players—consumers, businesses, government, the Bank of Canada and the banking system, and the rest of the world (R.O.W.)—whose combined choices create the macroeconomic outcomes we live with.

To understand how the economy as a whole works, and how well it is performing, focus on specific, targeted aspects of the economy. The three MAPS point to the connections you should focus on.

MAPS 1

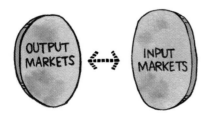

Focus on the connections between input markets and output markets for both demand and supply sides.

MAPS 2

Focus on the connections between Canada and the rest of the world.

MAPS 3

Focus on the connection between money/banks/expectations and the input and output markets of the circular flow.

The MAcroeconomics Positioning System (MAPS) helps you see clearly through the macroeconomics forest, through media reports on the economy, and through the debates on the best economic policies for Canada and the rest of the world. By focusing on these "connections" you will be able to determine the success or breakdown of macroeconomic performance.

These MAPS help you make up your own mind about the fundamental macroeconomic question:

If left alone by government, do the price mechanisms of market economies adjust quickly to maintain steady growth in living standards, full employment, and stable prices?

When the economy performs well, as Say's Law and the "Yes" camp predict, these connections work well in coordinating individuals' choices and supporting economic growth. Government should keep its hands-off.

When the economy falters, as Keynes and the "No" camp predict it will without government policy assistance, these connections break down and stall economic growth. Smart choices for you do not turn into smart choices for all. Government must be hands-on.

While there is no single right answer to the fundamental macroeconomic question, I hope you have developed a strategy you can use to form your own answer. Remember, economists and politicians disagree about the answer, do not fit entirely into one camp or the other, and shift camps as economic conditions change. Most likely, your position will be some combination of the "Yes" and "No" positions, depending on the particular economic issue or policy.

My aim, through this look at macroeconomics, was to help you better understand the world around you, make smarter choices for personal success, and make smarter choices as a citizen.

The only way for me to know how close I've come to achieving the goal of helping you choose wisely is to hear from you. Let me know what works for you in this book—and, more importantly, what doesn't. You can write to me at **avicohen@yorku.ca**. In future editions I will acknowledge by name all students who help improve *Economics for Life: Smart Choices for All?*

Professor Avi J. Cohen
Department of Economics
York University

Glossary

A

absolute advantage: ability to produce a product/service at lower absolute cost than another producer (p. 337, p. 414)

aggregate quantity demanded: quantity of real GDP macroeconomic players plan to demand at different average price levels (p. 136)

aggregate quantity supplied: quantity of real GDP macroeconomic players plan to supply at different average price levels (p. 129)

automatic stabilizers: tax and transfer adjustments that counteract changes to real GDP without explicit government decisions (p. 305)

B

balanced budget: revenues = spending (p. 304)

bank run: many depositors withdraw cash all at once (p. 185)

bond: financial asset where borrower promises to repay the original value at a specific future date, and to make fixed regular interest payments (p. 174)

budget deficit: revenues < spending (p. 304)

budget surplus: revenues > spending (p. 304)

business cycles: ups and downs of overall economic activity, measured as fluctuations of real GDP around potential GDP (p. 10, p. 56)

C

central bank: government institution responsible for supervising commercial banks and financial institutions and for regulating the supply of money (p. 182)

changes in aggregate demand: aggregate demand will change with changes in expectations, interest rates, government policy, GDP in R.O.W., and exchange rates (p. 140)

comparative advantage: ability to produce a product/ service at lower opportunity cost than another producer (p. 337, p. 415)

complements: products/services used together to satisfy the same want (p. 445)

Consumer Price Index (CPI): measure of average prices of fixed shopping basket of products and services (p. 95)

contraction: period during which real GDP decreases (p. 57)

core inflation rate: inflation rate excluding volatile categories (p. 98)

cost-push inflation: rising average prices caused by decreases in supply (p. 111)

creative destruction: competitive business innovations generate profits for winners, improving living standards for all, but destroy less productive or less desirable products and production methods (p. 54)

crowding in: tendency for government debt-financed fiscal policy to increase private investment spending by improving expectations (p. 315)

crowding out: tendency for government debt-financed fiscal policy to decrease private investment spending by raising interest rates (p. 315)

currency: government-issued paper bills and coins (p. 181)

currency appreciation: rise in exchange rate of one currency for another (p. 213)

currency depreciation: fall in exchange rate of one currency for another (p. 213)

cyclical deficits and surpluses: created only as a result of automatic stabilizers counteracting business cycles (p. 306)

cyclical unemployment: due to fluctuations in economic activity over the business cycle (p. 92)

D

decrease in demand: decrease in consumers' willingness and ability to pay (p. 444)

deflation: persistent fall in average prices and rise in the value of money (p. 101)

demand: consumers' willingness and ability to pay for a particular product/service (p. 435)

demand deposits: balances in bank accounts that depositors can withdraw on demand by using a debit card or writing a cheque (p. 181)

demand-pull inflation: rising average prices caused by increases in demand (p. 109)

demand shocks: factors other than average prices changing aggregate demand (p. 140)

discouraged workers: want to work but have given up actively searching for jobs (p. 89)

disposable income: aggregate income minus net taxes (p. 65)

E

economic globalization: integration of economic activities across borders and through markets (p. 350)

economic growth: expansion of economy's capacity to produce products/services; increase in potential GDP per person (p. 46)

economic growth rate: annual percentage change in real GDP per person (p. 50)

economics: how individuals, businesses, and governments make the best possible choices to get what they want, and how those choices interact in markets (p. 409)

elastic demand: large response in quantity demanded when price rises (p. 450)

elastic supply: large response in quantity supplied when price rises (p. 480)

elasticity (or price elasticity of demand): measures by how much quantity demanded responds to a change in price (p. 449)

elasticity of supply: measures by how much quantity supplied responds to a change in price (p. 480)

equilibrium price: the price that balances forces of competition and cooperation so that there is no tendency for change (p. 501)

excess demand (or shortage): quantity demanded exceeds quantity supplied (p. 497)

excess supply (or surplus): quantity supplied exceeds quantity demanded (p. 498)

exchange rate: price at which one currency exchanges for another currency (p. 212)

expansion: period during which real GDP increases (p. 57)

F

fallacy of composition: what is true for one is not true for all; whole is greater than the sum of the parts (p. 6)

fiscal policy: changes in government purchases and taxes/transfers to achieve macroeconomic outcomes of steady growth, full employment, and stable prices (p. 20)

fixed exchange rate: determined by government or central bank (p. 235)

floating exchange rate: determined by demand and supply in foreign exchange market (p. 235)

flow: amount per unit of time (p. 41)

foreign exchange market: worldwide market where all countries' currencies are bought and sold in exchange for each other (p. 212)

fractional-reserve banking: banks hold only a fraction of deposits as reserves (p. 185)

frictional unemployment: due to normal labour turnover and job search; healthy part of changing economy (p. 91)

full employment: there is only frictional, structural, and seasonal unemployment (p. 92)

G

globalization (economic): integration of economic activities, across borders, through markets (p. 350)

government failure: government policy fails to serve the public interest (p. 13)

gross domestic product (GDP): value of all final products and services produced annually in Canada (p. 16)

H

human capital: increased earning potential from work experience, on-the-job training, and education (p. 47)

I

implicit costs: opportunity costs of investing your own money or time (p. 422)

import quota: limit on quantity of a product/service that can be imported (p. 343)

incentives: rewards and penalties for choices (p. 412)

increase in aggregate supply: increase in economy's capacity to produce real GDP caused by increases in quantity or quality of inputs (p. 130)

increase in demand: increase in consumers' willingness and ability to pay (p. 444)

increase in supply: increase in businesses' willingness to produce (p. 475)

inelastic demand: small response in quantity demanded when price rises (p. 450)

inelastic supply: small response in quantity supplied when price rises (p. 480)

inferior goods: products/services you buy less of when your income increases (p. 445)

inflation: rising average prices and falling value of money (p. 17)

inflation-control target: range of inflation rates set as a target by a central bank as a monetary policy objective (p. 249)

inflation rate: annual percentage change in the consumer price index (p. 96)

inflation rate differential: difference in inflation rates between countries (p. 222)

inflationary gap: real GDP above potential GDP (p. 57)

injection: spending in the circular flow that does not start with consumers; G, I, and X (p. 291)

interest rate: price of holding money: what you give up by not holding bonds (p. 177)

interest rate differential: difference in interest rates between countries (p. 221)

interest rate parity (rate of return parity): rates of return on investments are equal across countries, accounting for expected depreciation/appreciation of exchange rates (p. 234)

international transmission mechanisms: how the impacts of exchange rates are transmitted to real GDP and inflation (p. 226)

investment spending: business purchases of new factories and equipment (p. 19)

L

labour force: employed + unemployed (p. 87)

labour force participation rate: percentage of working-age population in the labour force (employed or unemployed) (p. 87)

law of aggregate demand: as average level of prices rises, aggregate quantity demanded decreases (p. 136)

law of aggregate supply: as average level of prices rises, aggregate quantity supplied increases (p. 129)

law of demand: if the price of a product/service rises, quantity demanded decreases (p. 440)

law of demand for Canadian dollars: if the exchange rate rises, quantity demanded of Canadian dollars decreases (p. 214)

law of one price: differences in prices of same product/service across markets will be eliminated by actions of profit-seekers (p. 231)

law of supply: if the price of a product/service rises, quantity supplied increases (p. 473)

law of supply for Canadian dollars: if the exchange rate rises, quantity supplied of Canadian dollars increases (p. 216)

leakage: spending that leaks out of the circular flow through taxes, savings, and imports (p. 291)

lender of last resort: central bank's role of making loans to banks to preserve the stability of the financial system (p. 183)

liquidity: ease with which assets can be converted into the economy's medium of exchange (p. 174)

M

macroeconomics: analyzes performance of the whole Canadian economy and global economy; the combined outcomes of all individual microeconomic choices (p. 5, p. 420)

marginal benefits: additional benefits from the next choice, and changes with circumstances (p. 422, p. 436)

marginal cost: additional opportunity cost of increasing quantity supplied, and changes with circumstances (p. 464)

marginal opportunity costs: additional opportunity costs from the next choice (p. 422, p. 470)

market: the interactions of buyers and sellers (p. 494)

market-clearing price: the price when quantity demanded equals quantity supplied (p. 500)

market demand: sum of demands of all individuals willing and able to buy a particular product/service (p. 440)

market for loanable funds: banks coordinate the supply of loanable funds (savings) with the demand for loanable funds (borrowing); the interest rate is the price of loanable funds (p. 144)

market supply: sum of supplies of all businesses willing to produce a particular product /service (p. 472)

microeconomics: analyzes choices that individuals in households, individual businesses, and governments make, and how those choices interact in markets (p. 6, p. 420)

monetary policy: Bank of Canada changes interest rates and the supply of money to achieve macroeconomic outcomes of steady growth, full employment, and stable prices (p. 20)

monetary transmission mechanism: how the impact of money is transmitted to real GDP (p. 194)

money: anything acceptable as a means of paying for products/services (p. 172)

multiplier effect: spending injection has multiplied impact on real GDP (p. 292)

N

national debt (public debt): total amount owed by government = (sum of past deficits) − (sum of past surpluses) (p. 311)

natural rate of unemployment: unemployment rate at full employment, when there is only frictional, structural, and seasonal unemployment (p. 93)

negative (or positive) externalities: costs (or benefits) that affect others external to a choice or a trade (p. 298, p. 423)

net taxes: taxes minus transfer payments (p. 65)

nominal GDP: value at current prices of all final products/services produced annually in a country (p. 40)

nominal interest rate: observed interest rate; equal to number of dollars received per year in interest as percentage of number of dollars saved (p. 99)

normal goods: products/services you buy more of when your income increases (p. 445)

normative statements: about what you believe should be; involve value judgments (p. 317)

O

open market operations: buying or selling government bonds on the bond market by the Bank of Canada (p. 252)

opportunity cost: cost of best alternative given up (p. 411)

output gap: real GDP minus potential GDP (p. 58)

overnight rate: interest rate banks charge each other for one day loans; main monetary policy tool (p. 250)

P

paradox of thrift: attempts to increase savings cause aggregate savings to decrease because of falling employment and incomes (p. 7)

Phillips Curve: graph showing inverse relation between unemployment and inflation (p. 108)

positive (or negative) externalities: benefits (or costs) that affect others external to a choice or a trade (p. 298, p. 423)

positive statements: about what is; can be evaluated as true or false by checking the facts (p. 317)

potential GDP: real GDP when all inputs—labour, capital, land/resources, and entrepreneurial ability—are fully employed (p. 45)

potential GDP per person: potential GDP divided by population (p. 45)

preferences: your wants and their intensities (p. 434)

price elasticity of demand (or elasticity): measures by how much quantity demanded responds to a change in price (p. 449)

price stability: inflation is low enough that it does not significantly affect people's economic decisions (p. 249)

prime rate: interest rate on loans to lowest-risk corporate borrowers (p. 254)

productivity: measured as quantity of real GDP produced by an hour of labour (p. 53)

property rights: legally enforceable guarantees of ownership of physical, financial, and intellectual property (p. 495)

public debt (national debt): total amount owed by government = (sum of past deficits) − (sum of past surpluses) (p. 311)

purchasing power parity (PPP): exchange rates adjust so that money has equal real purchasing power in any country (p. 231)

Q

quantitative easing: central bank tool of flooding financial system with money by buying risky bonds, mortgages, and assets from banks; these liabilities on bank balance sheets are replaced with cash assets, enabling banks to make new loans (p. 266)

quantity demanded: amount you actually plan to buy at a given price (p. 439)

quantity supplied: quantity you actually plan to supply at a given price (p. 467)

quantity theory of money: increase in the quantity of money causes an equal percentage increase in the inflation rate (p. 106)

R

rate of return parity (interest rate parity): rates of return on investments are equal across countries, accounting for expected depreciation/appreciation of exchange rates (p. 234)

real GDP: value at constant prices of all final products/services produced annually in a country (p. 43)

real GDP per person: real GDP divided by population (p. 44)

real interest rate: nominal interest rate adjusted for effects of inflation (p. 99)

recession: two or more successive quarters of contraction of real GDP (p. 57)

recessionary gap: real GDP below potential GDP (p. 57)

Rule of 70: number of years it takes for initial amount of savings to double is roughly 70 divided by annual percentage growth rate (p. 52)

S

Say's Law: supply creates its own demand (p. 10)

scarcity: the problem that arises because we all have limited money, time, and energy (p. 410)

seasonal unemployment: due to seasonal changes in weather (p. 92)

shortage (or excess demand): quantity demanded exceeds quantity supplied (p. 497)

stagflation: simultaneous recession (higher unemployment) and inflation (higher average prices) (p. 111)

stock: fixed amount at a moment in time (p. 49)

structural deficits and surpluses: budget deficits and surpluses occurring at potential GDP (p. 309)

structural unemployment: due to technological change or international competition that makes workers' skills obsolete in Canada (p. 91)

subsidies to domestic producers: government payment to domestic producers of products/services (p. 343)

substitutes: products/services used in place of each other to satisfy the same want (p. 444)

sunk costs: past expenses that cannot be recovered (p. 466)

supply: businesses' willingness to produce a particular product/service because price covers all opportunity costs (p. 467)

supply shocks: events directly affecting businesses' costs, prices, and supply (p. 111)

supply-side effects: the incentive effects of taxes on aggregate supply (p. 299)

surplus (or excess supply): quantity supplied exceeds quantity demanded (p. 498)

T

tariff: tax applied to imports (p. 342)

technological change: improvements in the quality of capital (p. 47)

terms of trade: quantity of exports required to pay for one unit of imports (p. 338)

total revenue: all money a business receives from sales, equal to price per unit (P) multiplied by quantity sold (Q) (p. 452)

U

unemployed: not employed and actively seeking work (p. 17)

unemployment rate: percentage of people in labour force who are unemployed (p. 87)

V

value added: value output minus value intermediate products/services bought from other businesses (p. 59)

velocity of money (V): number of times a unit of money changes hands during a year (p. 105)

Answers to the Study Guide Questions

CHAPTER 1

TRUE/FALSE

1. True
2. True
3. False. Superstars at microeconomics may not be superstars at macroeconomics.
4. False. This is an example of fallacy of composition, because a collection of individual superstars may not function as a superstar team. (They may argue a lot and not be able to work effectively together.)
5. True
6. True
7. False. The Lazy Far Right Party prefers a hands-off approach because it believes markets quickly self-adjust to produce desirable outcomes.
8. False. If fewer products/services per person are available to satisfy alien wants, then the standard of living enjoyed by aliens is likely declining.
9. False. More workers looking for work, but unable to find work, is bad news.
10. True
11. True
12. False. To purchase Canadian exports, they simply need to convert their money into Canadian dollars.
13. False. The Central Bank can supervise the banking system and financial markets.
14. False. Employers can choose from large pool of job applicants.
15. False. You would want to know all of MAPS1, MAPS2, and MAPS3 to get a complete understanding of the performance of their economy, and the impact on your investment.

MULTIPLE CHOICE

1. **b)** both had a stock market crash
2. **d)** all of the above
3. **b)** unemployment.
4. **c)** supply creates its own demand.
5. **d)** markets will quickly-self adjust if left alone by government.
6. **b)** Conservative Party of Canada.
7. **d)** all of the above.
8. **b)** an ex-student who has graduated and is looking for work.
9. **a)** average price level in the economy.
10. **b)** investment spending.
11. **d)** all of the above.
12. **c)** Bank of Canada.
13. **d)** all of the above.
14. **a)** the chance of finding a job decreases.
15. **a)** connection between households and consumers.

SHORT ANSWER

1. **a)** Microeconomics looks at the trees; macroeconomics looks at the forest. Microeconomics looks at the smart choices of individual consumers and businesses while macroeconomics looks at the combined market outcomes of all those individual choices.
   b) According to Adam Smith's invisible hand, price signals in markets create incentives so that while each individual acts only in his self-interest (a microeconomic focus), the unintended consequence is the production of all of the products and services we want (a healthy forest).
2. **a)** If an indiviudal producer increases output, and prices do not change much, her income from sales will rise. If every producer increases output at the same time, then each individual's income may fall, since a large increase in supply may cause the market price to fall so much that all producers end up with less income than before. The fall in price may have a greater effect than the increase in output.
   b) If an individual consumer saves more, his savings increase. According to the Paradox of Thrift, if all consumers attempt to increase savings, savings can decrease because businesses react to lower consumer spending by laying off workers or reducing their work hours, which in turn reduces their income available to save.
3. **a)** Housing prices were inflating because of rising demand from homeowners, real estate investors, mortgage lenders, and financial institutions. People began to expect that prices would continue to rise, and that demand caused housing prices to rise.
   b) When rising prices are based on expectations, not on economic fundamentals, a change in expectations can quickly burst a bubble. Once investors started expecting prices to fall, they sold their investments to avoid losses from falling prices.

That selling caused housing prices to fall, leading more people to expect prices to fall, leading to more selling, and a rapid collapse in prices. When housing prices began to fall, the bubble burst.

4. **a)** Like a domino-effect, a decline in one economy (in this case the U.S. economy) can lead to a decline in the Canadian economy. The U.S. buys Canadian exports. When the U.S. reduces purchases of Canadian exports, that affects the Canadian economy.

   b) Reduced demand and/or lower prices for a country's exports will reduce their income levels.

5. **a)** With decreased demand for products/services, businesses experience falling prices of output. Between lower quantities and lower prices, businesses will want to have fewer workers.

   b) Taxes take money from you and give it to the government. With government transfers, the government gives you money instead of taking it away.

   c) Fiscal policy

6. **a)** Fiscal policy

   b) Monetary policy

7. **a)** Keynesians would post a support message because they believe that a hands-on approach is required to achieve steady growth in living standards, full employment and stable prices.

   b) Canadians should support stimulus packages in other countries because we partly rely on their purchases of our exports— MAPS 2.

8. **a)** Higher GDP, lower unemployment, stable prices

   b) Higher GDP, higher living standards and stable prices

9. **a)** Hands-off

   b) Hands-off

   c) Hands-on

   d) Hands-on

   e) Hands-on

   f) Hands-on

10. **a)** Yes, price and wage stickiness imply that the economy may fail to quickly self-adjust. Fiscal policy by the government could therefore lead to a better macroeconomic outcome than a hands-off approach. Government policies are needed because the "long run" may be very long… and in the long run, "we are all dead" as Keynes said.

    b) Union leaders would oppose pay cuts; employers would be worried about negative employee reactions and the impact on worker morale and productivity.

    c) A business might employ more workers if its wage costs were lower, but it does not follow that the same is true for all businesses together, since lower wages might reduce income and spending, which could reduce employment.

CHAPTER 2

TRUE/FALSE

1. False. The increase in nominal GDP could have been due to inflation.
2. False. The increase in real GDP was accompanied by population growth, so that real GDP per person is not 18 times higher.
3. True.
4. False. According to Figure 2.3, nominal GDP rose faster than real GDP ever since the 1960s.
5. True.
6. False. The invention of the cell phone, a technological change, increased the quality of capital.
7. False. When farmers increase the productivity of their land by using fertilizers, the real source of increased output is not better quality land, but better farming techniques using fertilizer as a capital input.
8. True.
9. False. The expansion reached a peak (not trough) in 1990.
10. True.
11. False. No contribution to GDP because there was no new production or value added in 2008.
12. False. GDP would be unaffected. Consumption would increase but net exports would decrease by that same amount since he is purchasing an import.
13. True.
14. False. GDP per person is the best measure of material standards of living, but doesn't account for many other factors affecting well-being.
15. False. Real GDP per person is an imperfect measure of well-being: factors such as crime, pollution, and freedom in a country are not included.

MULTIPLE CHOICE

1. **c)** produced in a country, including gross-looking products and services
2. **a)** 1935 and quantities in 1935
3. **b)** real GDP remains unchanged
4. **d)** all of the above
5. **b)** 2.5%
6. **c)** higher stock market prices
7. **c)** productivity
8. **c)** growth is negative for two quarters in a row
9. **d)** positive for an inflationary gap
10. **d)** all of the above
11. **d)** all of the above
12. **d)** you lose your job because your employer replaces you with a paper shuffler machine that costs $200.
13. **c)** decreases by $50 000
14. **d)** all of the above
15. **b)** $0 and GDP increases by $400

SHORT ANSWER

1. **a)** Consumption (iPod purchase), investment (new tattoo piercing gun), government purchase (scientific research), export (wine to Japan), import (electronics from Japan).
   b) Consumption (chain-smoking), investment (building a factory in a small community that results in traffic pollution), government purchase (weapons of mass destruction), export (opium), import (guns).
2. **a)** It will start with an incline (the "roaring twenties").
   b) 9 seconds after it starts (in the Great Depression that began in 1929).
   c) 60 seconds after it starts (in 1980).
   d) 4 (one representing 1929, one representing 1980, one representing 1990, and one representing 2008).
   e) 9 seconds in (the Great Depression).
   f) 30–50 seconds, since Figure 2.7 shows that the highest average annual growth rate occurred between 1950 and 1970.
   g) Probably not. He or she will enjoy the 80th to 87th second (representing 2000–2007), but it will then sharply decline with 3 seconds left (representing the Great Recession in 2008).
   h) Verify with the figures and illustrations provided in this chapter.
3. **a)** The missing value for Paradise Island (Government spending) is 10. The value for Lost Island (Net Exports spending) is −1.
   b) Consumption is the largest component of GDP on Paradise Island.
   c) Imports, since net exports (which is exports minus imports) is negative.
4. **a)** $16 million = value of pop in 2010 prices + value of popcorn in 2010 prices = $(5 \times \$2) + (6 \times \$1)$
   b) $50 million = value of pop in 2011 prices + value of popcorn in 2011 prices = $(10 \times \$3) + (10 \times \$2)$
   c) $16 million = value of pop in 2010 prices + value of popcorn in 2010 prices = $(5 \times \$2) + (6 \times \$1)$
   d) $30 million = value of pop in 2010 prices + value of popcorn in 2010 prices = $(10 \times \$2) + (10 \times \$1)$
   e) Real GDP per person in 2010 = $16 million ÷ 1 million people = $16 per person. Real GDP per person in 2011 = $30 million ÷ 1 million people = $30 per person.
   f) X = (real GDP per person in 2011 − real GDP per person in 2010) ÷ real GDP per person in 2010 × 100 = $(\$30 − \$16) ÷ \$16 × 100 = 87\%$.
5. **a)** **i)** The farmer's value added is $3 = $3 (output) − $0 (intermediate products).
   ii) The brewer's value added is $3 = $6 (output) − $3 (intermediate products).
   iii) The Beer Store's value added is $4 = $10 (output) − $6 (intermediate products).
   b) GDP = Value added = $10 = $3 + $3 + $4

   c) GDP in this simple example is what Barry pays to the Beer Store every week = $10.
   d) When we add the value of input's incomes we get aggregate income $10 = wages + profits + rent = ($1 + $2 + $3) + ($1 + $1) + $2. Therefore, yes, Say's Law holds true in this example.
6. **a)** Canada's economic growth ranked first in 2005, ranked second in 2006, and ranked third in 2007.
   b) All countries are expected to have negative growth in 2009, and all countries are expected to have positive growth in 2010 except the United Kingdom.
   c) Less than 8 years since 70/9% growth rate = 7.8 years.
7. **a)** In the fourth quarter of 2008, since GDP then fell in two consecutive quarters (the fourth quarter of 2008 and the first quarter of 2009).
   b) Consumption is highest (for any year).
   c) Government spending.
   d) Imports, which declined by $100,000 million (or $100 billion).
   e) Net exports increased since over this period since exports declined by less than imports declined.
   f) No, disposable income decreased over this period.
   g) Real disposable income would have increased only if prices declined at a faster rate than the rate at which disposable income declined.
8. **a)** High employment and high hours of work will result in more labour quantity and therefore more output (GDP).
   b) One less day of work will translate into lower output (GDP), unless employees who get time off work harder (more productive) when they get back on the job.
   c) If labour quantity decreases or starts to increase at a much slower rate than before, this will reduce the amount of products and services produced.
   d) Productivity is measured as output per hours worked. So if output decreases and hours worked increases, productivity must decline.
   e) When entrepreneurs come up with improvements in management techniques, corporate organizations, or worker/management relations that improve productivity, this increases potential GDP.
9. **a)** Obesity rates increased, household debt increased, the gap between the rich and the poor increased, greenhouse gas emissions increased.
   b) Open ended, it depends on what values ("weights") you place on these things.
   c) Yes.
10. **a)** When consumption is weighted more, the IEWB (red line) is closer to real GDP per person (black line) than when all components of the IEWB are weighted equally (blue line).
    b) United States has the highest score if 100% weight on consumption. Norway has the highest score if you 10% weight on consumption and 30% each for the others.
    c) Answer depends on choice.

CHAPTER 3

TRUE/FALSE

1. True.
2. False. Unemployed last month but not in the labour force this month because he gave up searching.
3. True.
4. False. Number of employed stayed the same and number of unemployed decreased. Therefore, the unemployment rate decreased. Last month it was 50% = unemployed ÷ labour force × 100 = 2 ÷ (2 + 2) × 100. This month it was 33% = 1 ÷ (1 + 2) × 100.
5. True.
6. True.
7. False. B.J. is cyclically unemployed. If there is cyclical unemployment, an economy cannot be at full employment.
8. False. The economy was at full employment last month because there was no cyclical unemployment (A.J. and B.J. are employed, C.J. and V.J. are structurally unemployed, and D.J. is not in the labour force).
9. False. Stagflation, not stagnation, if prices are rising and output is decreasing.
10. False. It would overestimate A.J.'s true cost of living increase since A.J. does not consume the products/ services that were rising in price and therefore does not experience an increase in his cost of living.
11. False. Real interest rate is zero since it is calculated as the nominal interest rate minus the inflation rate.
12. True.
13. False. Velocity = 2 because $M \times V = 100$, and $M = 50$.
14. True.
15. False. With cost-push inflation, inflation and unemployment change in the same direction.

MULTIPLE CHOICE

1. **b)** Miguel is frictionally unemployed since he starts a job soon.
2. **d)** working or searching for work, Salma is part of labour force.
3. **b)** (20 million ÷ 25 million) × 100 = 80 percent.
4. **d)** there is lower labour force participation.
5. **d)** those seeking work moved to Alberta
6. **c)** unemployed would increase.
7. **b)** frictional unemployment.
8. **b)** unemployment above the natural rate means cyclical unemployment.
9. **a)** (126 − 120) ÷ 120 × 100 = 5 percent, which is above the Bank of Canada's target range of one to three percent for inflation.
10. **d)** all of the above
11. **d)** all of the above
12. **b)** this is the definition of velocity.
13. **b)** velocity and real GDP.
14. **b)** stagflation is a combination of high unemployment and high inflation.
15. **b)** OPEC oil price shocks occurred in the 1970s.

SHORT ANSWER

1. **a)** Unemployed.
   b) Employed.
   c) Employed until laid off, then frictionally unemployed until she found her new job, then employed again.
   d) Unemployed.
   e) Not in the labour force.
2. **a)** (8 ÷ 100) × 100 = 8 percent
   b) (7 ÷ 100) × 100 = 7 percent
   c) (7 ÷ 99) × 100 = 7.07 percent
3. **a)** The number of unemployed and the unemployment rate generally rise when the economy is in the recession phase of a business cycle.
   b) The cost of not working is lost income and production. Fewer people working implies that fewer products/services are available in output markets to meet everyone's needs.
   c) If the decline in the unemployment rate is because people stop looking for work because they can't find any, then this means that economic conditions are getting worse.
4. **a)** The switch from full-time jobs to part-time jobs does not impact the size of the employed population since part-time jobs are a form of employment. However, the proportion of the labour force that is underutilized would increase if these individuals wish to remain employed full time.
   b) Structural unemployment.
   c) Cyclical unemployment.
   d) They were close to the natural rate of unemployment if there was no cyclical unemployment.
5. **a)** Only cyclical unemployment should be reduced to zero.
   b) Some forms of unemployment are unhealthier. Seasonal unemployment is natural and difficult to discourage. Some frictional unemployment is good because you want individuals to take the time to find the jobs where they would be most productive. Structural unemployment is an unfortunate result of a process that is healthy for the economy (creative destruction). Cyclical unemployment is the unhealthiest because it results in widespread reductions in output and employment.
   c) Searching for a new job after a job separation is like searching for a new girlfriend/boyfriend after a break-up. You could rebound from your previous relationship by settling for the first new girlfriend/ boyfriend that comes along. However, those who wait for the right match might end up being happier in the long run. Similarly, waiting for the right job after a job separation may lead to greater happiness in the long run.

d) Structural—provide job training so that the unemployed can obtain the skills that are in demand. Frictional—provide information on job opportunities so that the unemployed can find jobs faster. Seasonal—help unemployed individuals find non-seasonal employment. Cyclical—invest in construction projects during a recession to stimulate job creation.

e) Cyclical unemployment is reduced when the economy improves. Structural unemployment is reduced when workers retrain.

6. a) Anya faced an inflation rate of 10 percent since the grocery prices she faces increased by 10 percent. However, the inflation rate in the economy may be much different, since it is based on a (weighted) average of the prices for 600 products and services.

b) Ignoring that the basket of products has changed will lead to an overestimate of the increase in her cost of living, since the quality of living improves with better products.

c) Anya's grocery purchasing power decreased because her income rose more slowly than the inflation rate.

d) Inflation reduces the purchasing power of any savings you have. After inflation, her savings buys less than before. Her realized real interest rate on her savings (nominal interest rate − inflation rate) will be zero, since the nominal interest rate (10 percent) is equal to the inflation rate. Her $110 dollars at the end of the year buys the same quantity of groceries as her $100 bought last year.

7. a) Consumers now have incomes of $3000 to spend.

b) Prices will rise as each consumer offers more money in an attempt to get products/services, until the percentage rise in prices matches the percentage rise in the quantity of money.

c) The quantity of money and the inflation rate, will have increased by 200 percent = (2000 ÷ 1000) × 100.

d) Demand-pull inflation.

8. a) When member countries of OPEC reduced the supply of oil, oil prices rose. Businesses raised prices to cover their costs (higher energy costs resulted from the oil price increase). Consumers responded to the higher prices by buying fewer products/services, which resulted in unemployment. Therefore, unemployment increased while inflation increased. The Phillips curve predicts that when inflation increases, unemployment decreases.

b) Cost-push inflation since it was the decrease in supply caused by increasing costs that triggered the inflation.

c) Yes, since the target range for inflation is between one and three percent.

d) The trend between 2002 and 2007 is consistent with the Phillips Curve if in years when the unemployment rate was high, the inflation rate was low and if in years when the unemployment was low, the inflation rate was high.

9. a) Yes, stable inflation enables Alvero to raise the nominal wage offer, and that would make the job look more attractive to employees who haven't accounted for inflation.

b) If businesses pay their workers higher wages, they may need to cover costs by raising output prices. Even just the expectation of inflation can cause inflation ("self-fulfilling" expectations)—if businesses increase wages and output prices in expectation of higher prices by competitors, then this can cause inflation.

c) It takes time to hire new workers and to buy new equipment. Unpredictability of input costs and output prices creates risk, and risk discourages business investment in future production.

d) As long as the observed (nominal) wage stays the same or increases, workers and labour unions will likely tolerate a reduction in real wages (although it reduces their purchasing power). Therefore, Alvero can more easily reduce wages if inflation is occurring.

10. a) Yes, but just barely. Prices increased by 0.1 percent.

b) The inflation rate fell in four provinces: Prince Edward Island, Nova Scotia, New Brunswick, and Alberta.

c) The CPI would have risen by more if it excluded the decline in energy prices. Therefore, the core rate of inflation, which excludes energy and other volatile prices, would be higher than the CPI.

CHAPTER 4
TRUE/FALSE

1. False. Economic growth occurs if there is an increase in the quantity or quality of inputs. An increase in the CPI—the average level of prices—leads to an increase in aggregate quantity supplied, but no change in the quantity or quality of inputs. Economic growth is an increase in aggregate supply, not an increase in aggregate quantity supplied.

2. True.

3. False. The rest of the world does not supply any part of Canadian GDP. The impact on Canada of more R.O.W. skates may be a decrease in demand for Canadian hockey skates.

4. False. An increase in input costs such as energy prices is a negative supply shock, which decreases aggregate supply.

5. False. A decrease in aggregate supply requires a decrease in the quantity or quality of inputs. This is a decrease in aggregate quantity supplied, that is, a decrease in choices about how many hours to work from unchanged, existing labour inputs.

6. True.

7. True.

8. False. Government transfer payments are not part of direct spending on products/services; transfer payments increase aggregate demand by increasing planned consumer spending (*C*).

9. False. When the Canadian dollar rises in value, our exports become more expensive and the U.S. demands fewer of them.
10. False. The "No" camp believes that a mismatch can occur (aggregate demand for real GDP < aggregate supply of real GDP) and markets can fail to adjust quickly.
11. True.
12. False. The "Yes" camp believes that the government can make things worse; they can be part of the problem not the solution.
13. True.
14. False. "Yes" (hands-off) camp believes this, not "No" (hands-on) camp.
15. False. The "Yes" (hands-off) camp believes potential GDP is restored quickly because additional savings will cause interest rates to fall and investment spending to increase.

MULTIPLE CHOICE

1. **a)** business supply plans to increase inputs increase aggregate supply.
2. **a)** aggregate supply of real GDP increases if productivity increases or input prices decrease.
3. **d)** more schooling increases the quality of inputs, which increases aggregate supply.
4. **c)** $17 000 = $20 000 − $6000 + $3000.
5. **b)** investment spending is the most volatile, unpredictable component, and is postponeable.
6. **a)** if China buys more Canadian oil, Canadian exports and aggregate demand both increase.
7. **b)** higher taxes or reduced government transfers decrease aggregate demand.
8. **c)** more disposable income increases planned consumption spending and aggregate demand.
9. **d)** demand shocks cause unemployment and inflation to move in opposite directions.
10. **b)** negative supply shocks cause stagflation.
11. **c)** business investment spending based on borrowed funds can save Say's Law.
12. **d)** all agree on shocks and equilibrium, but not on the role of government.
13. **d)** wages are sticky because workers and employers resist wage reductions, and contracts cannot be changed easily.
14. **b)** other answers describe "No" camp.
15. **a)** Dunder's announcement resembles the Keynesian view of sticky wages.

SHORT ANSWER

1. **a)** In equilibrium, the aggregate demand for online services equals the aggregate supply of online services. In equilibrium, no one is kicking himself or herself, because at the equilibrium price, everyone who wants a service has one and everyone who offers a service has a user.

b) Suppliers may be kicking themselves because they have too many services offered. There would then be unsold services (aggregate demand less than aggregate supply). Or suppliers may be kicking themselves because they realize they could have offered more services. They did not offer enough services to satisfy unexpected consumer demand (aggregate supply less than aggregate demand).

c) A negative demand shock, since planned spending decreases.

2. **a)** Success in business depends on anticipating the market because you can get rich if you produce products/ services that consumers want at the time consumers want them, or if you correctly anticipate where stock prices or real estate values are going.

b) Businesses have to anticipate what consumers will be demanding when the product/service finally gets to market, just as hockey players without the puck (demanders) have to anticipate where the puck will be.

3. **a)** "No" camp. Recessions and expansions—the world of Keynes's business cycles—are the result of mismatches between aggregate supply and aggregate demand.

b) "Yes" camp. According to the "Yes" camp, investment spending choices are logical calculations, which resemble Spock's style of making decisions.

c) "No" camp. Price mechanisms in markets function like an economic thermostat—if the weather outside gets hotter or colder, a thermostat automatically adjusts the air conditioning or heat to maintain the indoor temperature right where it should be. The "No" camp believes price mechanisms adjust slowly to aggregate supply and demand shocks.

d) "Yes" camp, since they believe that government is part of the problem, not part of the solution.

e) "No" camp, since the bed was put into "saltwater," which is associated with followers of Keynes.

4. **a)** If fewer individuals are available to work, a decrease in inputs causes a negative supply shock (just like an oil price hike).

b) If planned consumer spending decreases, this will also be a negative demand shock.

c) Labour market—unemployment eventually causes wage rate to fall, increasing hiring of labour until full employment is restored. Output markets— initially higher prices fall due to surpluses and falling wage costs, increasing sales of products/ services until back to level of potential GDP. International trade market—eventually falling Canadian prices increase net exports, increasing Canadian real GDP and decreasing unemployment. Loanable funds market—additional savings cause interest rates to fall, increasing investment spending, increasing Canadian real GDP, and decreasing unemployment.

5. **a)** When the price level increases, businesses see the prices of their output increasing while the prices of their inputs remain unchanged. It is a smart decision for each business then to increase output, and so aggregate quantity supplied increases.

   b) The macroeconomic law of aggregate supply.

   c) If there is a positive supply shock (e.g. input costs decrease), Monique's willingness to supply increases because at any unchanged price, a business can earn more for each product/service produced. If the positive supply shock affects all businesses, this causes an increase in aggregate supply.

6. **a)** Savings seems to threaten Say's Law, since all income earned in input markets is not spent demanding products/services in output markets.

   b) If banks loan out savings to businesses who use it for investment spending, that offsets consumer savings, restoring equality between aggregate income and aggregate spending.

   c) Banks coordinate the supply of loanable funds (savings) with the demand for loanable funds (borrowing). The interest rate is the price of loanable funds.

   d) When interest rates decrease, borrowing to finance investment projects becomes cheaper and more investment projects become profitable, and consumers are able to borrow more and spend more. In both cases, aggregate demand increases. The increased investment spending also increases quantity and quality of inputs, so potential GDP and real GDP per person increase over time.

   e) Say's Law can only be rescued if businesses invest the saved money.

7. **a)** When consumers are pessimistic about their economic future—expecting that they may be laid off or have their work hours reduced—they may reduce spending. Therefore, consumer pessimism would have reduced aggregate demand in late 2008 and early 2009. When consumers become more optimistic about their economic future—expecting more or better-paying jobs to be available—they may increase spending, therefore leading to increased aggregate demand.

   b) When investors become more optimistic about future economic conditions, investment spending increases and aggregate demand increases.

   c) If entrepreneurs and businesses anticipate increased demand, they will increase aggregate supply by increasing their inputs by investing in new technology or hiring new workers.

8. **a)** Falling oil prices is a positive supply shock because it reduces costs. A falling value of the Canadian dollar is a positive demand shock because Canadian exports become cheaper to the rest of the world, increasing exports and aggregate demand.

   b) Rising oil prices is a negative supply shock that causes stagflation—rising average prices, decreased real GDP, and increased unemployment. A rising value of the Canadian dollar is a negative demand shock that causes a recessionary gap—falling average prices, decreased real GDP, and increased unemployment.

9. **a)** Animal spirit-types because people jumped on the bandwagon of investing money in the real estate market without solid facts.

   b) The "No" camp, since the "Yes" camp believes people are logical-thinking, perfect calculators of profits and losses.

   c) The "No" camp, since the "No" camp believes decisions are based on animal spirits—a gut-level instinct to act.

10. **a)** Open ended. If real GDP steadily increased after June 2009 (due to positive shocks), the economy followed a "V" shape. If real GDP increased but then declined before rising again, the economy followed a "W" shape.

    b) The supply shock chosen should match one of the examples in Figure 4.2. The demand shock chosen should match one of the examples in Figure 4.4.

CHAPTER 5
TRUE/FALSE

1. True.
2. False. Since money pays no interest but bonds pay interest, sometimes it is smarter to want to hold less money and more bonds.
3. False. An increase in interest rates increases the opportunity cost of holding money, decreasing the quantity demanded of money.
4. True.
5. False. Even though the value of money does not change with interest rates, its purchasing power is threatened by inflation.
6. False. This just shifts money from one component of M1 (demand deposits) to another (currency).
7. False. Currency is a small fraction of the money supply (six percent of M2).
8. True.
9. False. The quantity demanded of money depends on the interest rate.
10. False. M1 will decrease but since chequing and saving accounts are both part of M2 there is no change in M2.
11. False. Bonds are riskier because changes in the interest rate change the market price of the bond. Inflation reduces the purchasing power of both money and bonds.
12. True.
13. False. When interest rates are high, the opportunity cost of holding money is high, so people will use money to buy more bonds.

14. True.
15. False. The "Yes" camp believes external supply shocks, not money, are the main source of business cycles.

MULTIPLE CHOICE

1. **a)** money provides liquidity and you give up interest earned on bonds.
2. **c)** economists agree on the functions of money except store of value.
3. **d)** the problem is finding a seller who has what you want and who wants what you are selling.
4. **d)** all commodity monies.
5. **d)** debit card transfers your deposit money to seller.
6. **c)** money in a chequing account counts for M1 and M2; a savings account counts for M2 only.
7. **d)** coins and paper money (currency) are fiat money and both count for M1 and M2.
8. **a)** loans are riskiest and earn banks the highest interest rates. Treasury bills are low risk and low interest rate.
9. **b)** the Northern Rock Bank had a bank run in 2007.
10. **a)** the Bank of Canada does not make currency; the Royal Mint does.
11. **d)** interest rates and market price of bonds move in opposite directions; rises in market price creates unexpected profit (buy low, sell high).
12. **b)** causes people to sell bonds to get money, lowering bond prices and raising interest rates.
13. **d)** all of the above.
14. **a)** money can directly affect inflation through quantity theory of money; indirect effect on GDP and unemployment.
15. **d)** monetary transmission mechanism includes interest rates and aggregate demand.

SHORT ANSWER

1. **a)** Money is anything acceptable as a medium of exchange.
   b) Mint chocolate may serve as a means of exchange and unit of account, but is not a good store of value since it eventually goes bad. It may not be accepted as a means of exchange since it would be easily counterfeited (so sellers would not trust its value).
   c) The Governor of New France issued paper money printed on playing cards.
   d) Cigarettes can serve as an adequate means of exchange and unit of account (can divide cartons into packs and packs into individual cigarettes), but are not a good store of value since they eventually go bad, can crumble, or go up in smoke.
2. **a)** Johnny Cash's wealth is more liquid since cash is the most liquid form of wealth.
   b) The interest rate is the price of money—what you give up by holding cash. When the interest rate falls, the quantity of money demanded increases for both James and Johnny.

3. **a)** Opportunity cost of holding money increases when interest rates rise.
   b) M1 decreases and M2, which includes M1, also decreases. Bonds are not part of M1 or M2.
   c) Yes, CIBC thought the interest rate was at the market-clearing interest rate because they did not expect interest rates to change. The market-clearing, or equilibrium, interest rate balances quantity demanded and quantity supplied. There is no tendency for change.
   d) It is better to sell the bonds over those next six to eight months, since the market price of the bonds will fall when interest rates rise.
4. **a)** Your demand for money will increase because when income increases, you buy more products/services, which means you need to use more money to make those purchases.
   b) Probably more of both forms of money. More fiat money (currency) for smaller daily transactions, and more demand deposits for the larger purchases you can now afford.
   c) Demand for money will increase because more money is needed to finance a greater value of purchases.
   d) Inflation increases the demand for money because in order to maintain the same level of purchases (or alternatively, the purchasing power) when money is worth less, more money is needed.
5. **a)** Banks face a tradeoff between profits and prudence. A smaller fraction of reserves and higher risk loans may get the bank more profits, but at the cost of giving up safety and risking customers' deposits and trust.
   b) When a bank loans you money for a car or mortgage on a house, the bank owns the car or the house, as collateral, until you pay off the loan. If you default on the loan, the bank can sell the property to recover the value of the loan. Banks also charge higher interest payments on loans that they consider to be riskier.
   c) Without regulation, more banks may take greater risks in pursuit of profits that could lead to the failure of the bank, which would cause bank owners and trusting depositors to lose their money.
   d) With fractional-reserve banking, there is risk of a bank run—many depositors withdrawing cash at the same time. The bank may not have enough cash reserves to pay all depositors.
   e) First, most bank customers rarely demand cash. Second, in the rare event that customers withdraw more demand deposits or currency than the bank has available, chartered banks can borrow from each other and from the Bank of Canada (the lender of last resort) to meet their customers' demands and maintain trust.
6. **a)** Fewer products/services can be purchased if access to money is not readily acceptable. Cash can be sent to friends, family, customers, and suppliers quickly and easily.

b) Mobile money is deposit money, since it can be withdrawn quickly without penalty.

c) Can't be stolen or damaged in a fire or flood.

7. a) Set up a really safe place (indestructible) to store people's money and loan out their money to others. As a lender, you earn interest on the loan. So just by offering to hold onto money and then lending you earn profits.

b) IOUs—paper convertible into money.

c) In case depositors want to withdraw their money, it is important to keep some reserves.

d) The risk of a bank run—many depositors withdraw cash at the same time—increases because depositors are more concerned with bank failure if expectations are pessimistic.

8. a) The opportunity cost is the forgone interest.

b) As followers of Keynes would predict, households are holding cash to avoid risk and to have the benefits of liquidity. By holding cash, households are betting that earning no interest will be better than losing their savings with higher-interest but risky investments.

c) Currency and deposits are part of M1 and M2, but treasury bills are not deposits and are not part of either M1 or M2.

9. a) If interest rates are above the market-clearing rate, there is excess supply of money; people buy bonds to get rid of money; increased demand for bonds causes bond prices to rise and interest rates to fall; lower interest rates reduce the cost of consumer and business borrowing; spending increases (positive aggregate demand shock); real GDP increases.

b) If interest rates are below the market-clearing rate, there is excess demand for money; people sell bonds to get money; reduced demand for bonds causes bond prices to fall and interest rates to rise; higher interest rate increase the cost of consumer and business borrowing; spending decreases (negative aggregate demand shock); real GDP decreases.

10. a) Economists agree that money solves the problem of the double coincidence of wants, causes inflation, and changes in the demand and supply of money can indirectly affect key macroeconomic outcomes through the monetary transmission mechanism.

b) According to followers of Keynes and the "No" camp, money gives people a way not to spend. Worried consumers and businesses may not put their savings into the loanable funds markets, and businesses may postpone investment spending. Therefore, holding money can block the transmission mechanism so the loanable funds market does not match spending to savings.

c) Say and the "Yes" camp argue the opposite. Money allows savings to flow easily through the loanable funds market to facilitate business borrowing for investment spending. The economy quickly ends up with a match of aggregate supply and aggregate demand.

CHAPTER 6

TRUE/FALSE

1. True.
2. True.
3. False. It means it takes 95 cents Canadian to buy 1 American dollar.
4. False. The market-clearing exchange rate occurs when the quantity demanded and quantity supplied of Canadian dollars are equal. That rate fluctuates with changes in demand and supply of Canadian dollars.
5. False. The U.S. dollar buys fewer products/services if it depreciates against the Canadian dollar.
6. False. The individual selling euros would get the most Canadian dollars because each euro is worth $1.50CA and each American dollar is worth $1.04CA.
7. True.
8. False. A rise in the Canadian interest rate differential causes the Canadian dollar to appreciate because it increases demand and decreases supply of Canadian dollars.
9. True.
10. False. A higher exchange rate for the Canadian dollar has advantages (imports are less expensive and cross-border shopping is better) and disadvantages (fewer exports and lower real GDP).
11. True.
12. True.
13. False. When purchasing power parity holds, $5.00US buys exactly the same quantity of a product in both the U.S. and Canada.
14. True.
15. True.

MULTIPLE CHOICE

1. **d)** all of the above.
2. **b)** the reciprocal exchange rate of C$1 = US$0.95 is US$1 = C$1.05.
3. **b)** price and quantity demanded of a currency move in opposite directions, and price and quantity supplied move in the same direction.
4. **d)** all of the above.
5. **d)** if the US dollar depreciates against the Canadian dollar and the Canadian dollar remains constant against the European dollar, then the US dollar must have depreciated against the European dollar.
6. **b)** rise in Canadian inflation rate differential causes Canadian dollar to depreciate (decreases demand and increase supply of Canadian dollars).
7. **d)** increased real GDP increases imports and investor confidence, resulting in a net appreciation of the dollar.
8. **b)** expectations of a fall in future price of Canadian dollar causes self-fulfilling depreciation of Canadian dollar (decreases demand for Canadian dollars).
9. **b)** exchange rates affect real GPD and inflation through international transmission mechanisms.

10. **c)** depreciating Canadian dollar is a positive aggregate demand shock: increases net exports and real GDP.
11. **c)** purchasing power parity holds when C$10 has the same purchasing power when converted into US dollars (US$10) and European euros (15 euros).
12. **d)** all of the above.
13. **b)** floating exchange rates are determined by the foreign exchange market and became more popular after the 1970s.
14. **d)** difference across countries in rates of return are due to differences in exchange rate expectations.
15. **b)** Japanese investor earns three percent measured in Canadian dollars, but then gains four percent when converting Canadian dollars back into yen if her expectation that the yen depreciates against the dollar by four percent comes true.

SHORT ANSWER PROBLEMS

1. The value of the Canadian dollar depreciated against the Mexican peso. Your Canadian dollars buy fewer Mexican pesos than they did when you looked at the prices 10 days ago, therefore making foreign products/services more expensive.
2. **a)** C$1 = US$0.90.
   b) US$1 = C$1.11.
   c) At an exchange rate of US$1.00, there is an excess supply (quantity supplied exceeds quantity demanded) of Canadian dollars in the foreign exchange market. With an excess supply of Canadian dollars, competition among sellers causes the exchange rate to fall until it reaches the market-clearing rate.
3. Investors interpret lower real GDP growth as evidence that there are lower profits to be made from Canadian assets. Expectations of a fall in the future price of the Canadian dollar causes a self-fulfilling depreciation of the Canadian dollar (decreases demand for Canadian dollars).
4. **a)** It was better to shop in the U.S. in 2007 since a higher Canadian dollar can purchase more U.S. products and services.
   b) Increased R.O.W. demand for Canadian exports causes slight appreciation of the Canadian dollar (increases demand for Canadian dollars). Rising world prices for Canadian resource exports causes appreciation of Canadian dollar relative to currencies of non-resource producing countries (increases demand for Canadian dollars).
   c) It was better to buy Canadian dollars in 2002 (and to sell Canadian dollars in 2007), since it is more profitable to buy the Canadian dollar when it is low and sell when it is high.
5. **a)** A higher Canadian dollar reduces exports and Canadian real GDP, slowing economic recovery.
   b) Yes. Exporters prefer a lower Canadian dollar, which makes the prices of Canadian exports more internationally competitive to R.O.W.

6. **a)** If the Canadian dollar is expected to lose more value than the U.S. dollar, this decreases the demand for Canadian dollars relative to U.S. dollars.
   b) If the Canadian dollar is expected to lose more value than the U.S. dollar, traders increase the supply of Canadian dollars now—selling Canadian dollars to buy U.S. dollars.
   c) A rise in Canadian inflation rate differential causes Canadian dollar to depreciate since it decreases demand and increases supply of Canadian dollars.
7. **a)** A depreciating currency increases exports, aggregate demand, and real GDP.
   b) An appreciating currency reduces the price of imports, directly decreasing the inflation rate. Exports also decrease, decreasing aggregate demand, real GDP, and inflation and increasing unemployment.
8. **a)** A higher Canadian dollar makes exports like film services more expensive, decreasing exports, aggregate demand, and GDP.
   b) Inflation decreases because a higher Canadian dollar reduces the price of imports (the inflation rate measures the increase in the average level of all prices, including imports), which is what the Bank of Canada refers to as "subdued" (or quiet) inflationary pressures.
   c) A higher Canadian dollar threatens *Twilight* sequels because the cost of filming services in Canada rises relative to the cost of filming services in the United States.
9. **a)** C$1 = US$0.95.
   b) Your purchasing power is greatest in Canada. If you go to the U.S. and exchange C$100 for US$90, you do not have enough money to buy the Wii since it is US$95. If you exchange the $90US for C$100, you can buy the Wii in Canada for C$100 and have US$5 to spend on something else.
   c) The exchange rate of $0.90US for a Canadian dollar is lower than the purchasing power parity exchange rate of US$0.95. At this exchange rate, the Canadian dollar is undervalued relative to the *PPP* rate with the US dollar.
   d) According to the *PPP* principle, the Canadian exchange rate will rise in order to equalize the purchasing power in both countries. Americans will increase their demand for Canadian dollars, which will lead to an increase in the Canadian exchange rate.
10. **a)** US$9.
    b) If the value of the Canadian dollar rises relative to the US dollar, then the US$9 will no longer be enough for the C$10 cab ride.
    c) Profit-seeking forces push the actual exchange rate back towards the *PPP* rate. So, if the Canadian dollar is undervalued, then it is below the *PPP* exchange rate, and there would be pressure for the exchange rate to appreciate.

CHAPTER 7

TRUE/FALSE

1. False. The Governor of the Bank of Canada is the driver at the wheel.
2. True.
3. False. The Bank of Canada steers the economy by changing the target for the overnight interest rate.
4. True.
5. False. Full employment and stable growth in real GDP and living standards are objectives, but the number one objective is to keep the inflation rate between 1% and 3%.
6. True.
7. False. When the economy is speeding too fast, the Bank of Canada steps on the brakes by raising interest rates.
8. True.
9. True.
10. False. It is politically unpopular when the Bank of Canada raises interest rates because this reduces GDP and income in the economy.
11. True.
12. True.
13. True.
14. False. Inflation expectations go up easily but come down painfully.
15. False. The "Yes" camp says to leave the driving to the flexibility of markets (not government).

MULTIPLE CHOICE

1. c) the goal of price stability is to keep the inflation rate low enough so that it does not significantly affect decisions.
2. c) the Bank of Canada's inflation-control target is the CPI, with core CPI as an operational guide.
3. d) the CPI inflation rate was in the target range of between 1% and 3% in December but not October.
4. c) lowering the overnight interest rate sooner may have increased spending.
5. d) the interest rate given to high-risk borrowers is above the prime rate.
6. b) when the Bank of Canada buys bonds, the increased demand for bonds raises bond prices and lowers interest rates.
7. c) when the Bank of Canada buys bonds, the increased money supply lowers interest rates, which increases aggregate demand.
8. d) the Bank of Canada raises interest rates if it expects an inflationary gap 18–24 months into the future.
9. c) the Bank of Canada should add punch to the bowl (lower interest rates) if the economy is in a recessionary gap.
10. a) expansionary monetary policy is a lowering of interest rates, which causes the value of the Canadian dollar to decrease.
11. a) if real GDP is less than potential GDP, an increase in the quantity of money will lead to an increase in both real GDP and the price level.
12. d) the Bank of Canada was conservative before the Great Recession, but not conservative during the Great Recession.
13. b) the banks chose profits over prudence before the Great Recession, and prudence over profits during the Great Recession.
14. c) the "No" camp favours a limited role for government in monetary policy.
15. d) all of the above.

SHORT ANSWER PROBLEMS

1. a) By focusing only on inflation-rate targeting since 1991, the Bank of Canada has succeeded not only in keeping inflation within the target range every year since 1991, but also in promoting rising living standards and movement towards full employment.
   b) Pursuing only stable inflation as a goal anchors expectations about inflation (everyone knows what to expect) and improves the predictability of prices (making smart choices easier for all macroeconomic players).
   c) Canada is more like the "Yes" camp because, with a single objective for monetary policy, there is less discretion for the government and the central bank.

2. a) Yes, it was between 1% and 3%.
   b) Inflation was below the midpoint target range, which is 2%.
   c) Inflation was anticipated to be at the midpoint target of 2% in the third quarter of 2011, which is 18–24 months later. The time lags in the transmission mechanism mean that central banks must be forward-looking in their policy decisions. If inflation is currently in the target range and is soon expected to be at the midpoint target, then there is no need to change the overnight rate.

3. a) Yes. The Bank of Canada raises the target interest rate by selling government bonds on the bond market. When the Bank of Canada sells a bond to you or to a chartered bank, the Bank of Canada must be paid. As a result, cash reserves leave the chartered banking system and go to the Bank of Canada. With fewer reserves, chartered banks reduce the quantity of loans that they make, which decreases the money supply. A decrease in money supply increases the price of money (interest rates).
   b) Higher interest rates increase borrowing costs for consumers and businesses, therefore reducing borrowing, spending, and aggregate demand. The inflation rate falls, the growth in real GDP decreases, and unemployment increases.
   c) Yes. Higher interest rates increase the Canadian interest rate differential, causing the Canadian

dollar to appreciate on the foreign exchange market. A higher dollar reduces net exports and aggregate demand. It makes Canadian exports more expensive for customers in the rest of the world (exports fall) and makes it less expensive for Canadians to buy foreign products/services (imports rise).

4. **a)** Consumers and businesses are usually unhappy when the Bank of Canada raises interest rates to fight inflation because it raises the cost of mortgages, car loans, and business borrowing. People complain, especially when they don't see any inflation in the present.

   b) The Bank of Canada is concerned that 18–24 months in the future, continuing growth will cause inflation to rise beyond the target range.

5. The "No" camp points to the short-run tradeoff between inflation and unemployment, arguing that sometimes the cost of keeping inflation low may have too high an opportunity cost—high unemployment, lost production, and economic suffering. Therefore, Keynes would argue that the central bank should have been more worried about high unemployment.

6. **a)** With the economy starting to show signs of improvement, the party was just getting started. However, with inflation above the target, the Governor's job is to increase the overnight rate. Taking away the punch bowl is similar to raising interest rates because higher interest rates reduce spending and increase unemployment (through the transmission mechanism).

   b) Yes, because taking away the punch bowl (raising interest rates) will anchor inflation expectations and the "Yes" camp supports fixed targets for monetary policy that leave no discretion to central bankers.

   c) Unpredictability creates risk and risk discourages business investment in future production. Uncertainty interferes with prices signals for smart choices because businesses don't know if rising prices reflect increased demand for their output or just general inflation.

7. **a)** A balance sheet recession is a contraction in real GDP caused by the collapse of asset prices. When the value of the assets you own falls, you need to cut back on what you spend or owe to restore balance.

   b) Yes. The Bank of Canada responded to the Great Recession as you would expect from reading this chapter. With a recessionary gap opening, they lowered the target interest rate, hoping generally lower interest rates would stimulate borrowing, spending, and aggregate demand. The target overnight rate decreased from 4.0 percent (at the start of 2008) until it almost reached zero (0.25 percent).

   c) Facing falling asset values on their balance sheets, consumers, businesses, and banks make individually smart choices to resist borrowing, spending, and

lending (in order to pay off debts while interest rates are low). However, these individually smart choices do not add up to smart choices for the economy as a whole, since unemployment continues to rise and living standards continue to fall.

8. **a)** The top-ranked individual at a central bank (which is called a Governor in Canada and a Chairman in the U.S.) drives the economy through monetary policy.

   b) Quantitative easing floods the financial system with money by having the central bank buy risky bonds, mortgages, and assets directly from banks. By eliminating these liabilities on bank balance sheets and replacing them with cash assets, banks are in a better position to make new loans.

   c) Quantitative easing is similar to open market operations—the central bank buys bonds and pays with cash that increases bank reserves, demand deposits, and quantity of money. The difference is that the central bank is not buying government bonds on the open market—it buys many kinds of riskier assets directly from banks.

9. **a)** According to the quantity theory of money, when real GDP is below potential GDP, some of the increase in the money supply gets applied to increases in real GDP and some gets applied to increases in the price level. Expansionary monetary policy is less likely to be inflationary when the economy is below potential GDP.

   b) If the economy were at potential GDP, then expansionary monetary policies would be inflationary (more money causes inflation).

10. **a)** "No" camp, because these is more choice for government policy.

    b) "No" camp. Allowing for higher inflation means allowing for lower unemployment in the short run, and more choice for government policy.

CHAPTER 8

TRUE/FALSE

1. True.
2. False. "No" camp favours government spending instead of tax cuts to accelerate the economy.
3. False. "Yes" camp favours spending reductions to slow down the economy. "No" camp favours tax increases to slow down the economy.
4. True.
5. False. Empirical evidence shows tax revenues fall with cuts in the tax rate.
6. False. Those who disagree with supply-sider arguments often refer to it as "voodoo economics." Supply-siders would not want your hug.
7. False. Keynes, the original hands-on economist, believes that the short-run adjustment costs of savings might outweigh the long-run benefits for economic growth.

8. True.
9. True.
10. True.
11. False. Automatic stabilizers drop transfers when the economy's hot and increase taxes when it's not. (With a stronger economy, incomes are higher, so individuals and businesses overall pay more taxes.)
12. False. Debt is a stock and sometimes a smart choice. Deficits are a flow.
13. False. Ricardo and Barro would agree that government spending financed by borrowing (going into debt) will have no impact on the economy.
14. True.
15. False. Canada's founding principles are peace, order, and good government. The U.S.'s founding principles are life, liberty, and the pursuit of happiness.

MULTIPLE CHOICE

1. **d)** all affect aggregate demand.
2. **b)** the size of the multiplier effect depends on leakages out of the circular flow. The fewer the leakages, the larger the multiplier.
3. **d)** all are income not spent on Canadian GDP.
4. **d)** fiscal policies attempt to match aggregate demand and aggregate supply at potential GDP.
5. **a)** more students will go to school and get educated, increasing the quality of labour inputs.
6. **d)** supply-siders claim total tax revenues increase as a result of tax rate cuts.
7. **c)** there can be a tradeoff between increased aggregate supply in the future—through business investment spending financed by more savings—and reduced aggregate demand in the present due to lower spending.
8. **a)** if revenue is $1 billion greater than spending, this will reduce debt by $1 billion (from $50 billion to $49 billion).
9. **b)** structural deficits are the greatest concern because debt rises and so do interest payments.
10. **c)** increase in real GDP increases tax revenues. Decrease in unemployment leads to decrease in transfer payments.
11. **c)** true when interest payments cause budget deficits which, in turn, increase the national debt and interest payment..
12. **a)** if government sells bonds to finance debt, increased supply of bonds drives down bonds prices and raises interest rates, making it more expensive for businesses to borrow.
13. **c)** Canada was created by an act of British government; U.S. was created through revolution against government.
14. **d)** most economists agree that governments should run deficits in recessions and run surpluses during expansions, balancing over the business cycle.
15. **c)** use of the word "should" indicates a value judgement.

SHORT ANSWER PROBLEMS

1. **a)** If a business shuts down, not only will those who worked for the business lose their jobs, but also those who depended on that business for sales may also lose their jobs. If the laid-off workers spend less on products/services, this also affects the output and incomes of other businesses.
   b) Spending triggers a multiplier process—e.g., the owners and workers at the restaurants, clothing stores, bars, or night club will spend part of the extra income generated from your purchases. This spending induces second-round increases in consumption spending, leading to a final change in real GDP that it is larger than the value of the amount of money you and your friend spent.
2. **a)** There was a deficit in 1987–88, 1992–93, and 2008–09.
   b) The budget went from a surplus in fiscal year 2007–08 of $9.6 billion to a deficit in fiscal year 2008–09 of $5.7 billion.
   c) A deficit causes debt to rise.
3. **a)** When you get a post-secondary education, your individual benefits include higher lifetime earnings.
   b) Employers benefit because they do not have to spend as much time and money training you. Governments benefit because you will require less assistance and can better participate in democratic activities. The economy as a whole benefits because your increased productivity increases potential GDP and potential living standards for all.
4. **a)** Estimates vary, but many place the size of the multiplier effect for government spending around 2. A $20-million reduction in spending on products/services reduces GDP by about $40 million after all of the rounds of spending have finished.
   b) The "Yes" camp (hands-off) favours spending reductions instead of tax increases to slow down the economy, because this reduces the size of government.
   c) If the government collected more of its tax revenue from consumption taxes (taxing what you spend), and less from income taxes (taxing what you earn), you would have additional incentive to save your income instead of spending it.
5. **a)** These deficits include structural deficits, since even if the economy returned to potential GDP by 2013–14 there would still be a deficit of $19 billion.
   b) Canada's 2009 ratio of national debt to GDP was 28.2 percent. This was much lower than the 2009 ratio for the United States (58.2 percent), the UK (62.1 percent), France (67.0 percent), Germany (70.3 percent), Italy (112.8 percent) or Japan (104.6 percent). The debt-to-GDP ratio is also much lower than Canada's ratio during the Great Depression (83 percent) or World War II (113 percent).
   c) The first statement is positive because it can be evaluated by checking the facts. The second statement is normative because it is a value judgement.

6. a) Yes, all economists believe that tax cuts will have some incentive effects causing a small increase in aggregate supply.

b) If tax cuts have powerful incentive effects, people will work many more hours and incomes will go up dramatically. Even though a lower tax rate means that the government gets a smaller cut from every dollar people earn, people are earning so many more dollars from longer hours worked that the total amount of taxes collected increases. Government tax revenues increase instead of decrease.

c) There is no empirical evidence to support the claims of supply-siders that tax cuts have large effects on aggregate supply. The supply-side effects are likely small because most people already work as many hours as they can, and don't get much choice from their bosses over how long to work. An increase in take-home pay may encourage a few more hours per week, but not much more.

d) In a recessionary gap, jobs are harder to find and harder to keep, so individuals will have even less choice from their bosses over how many more hours to work, resulting in smaller incentive effects.

7. a) For government, debt can be a smart choice if the positive impact on the economy of the spending financed by debt is greater than the interest cost. If the spending improves productivity, lowers costs, and provides positive externalities to the economy, most economists would see it as a smart choice.

b) Economists from both the "Yes" and "No" camps give credit to this deficit-financed government spending for helping to prevent the recurrence of another Great Depression. Robert Barro—a prominent hands-off economist at Harvard University—argues that any government spending financed by going into debt will have no impact on the economy, so why bother?

8. a) The government never has to pay back the national debt—it can live' long enough to pay debts (government bonds that reach maturity) using money borrowed by issuing new bonds (old debt is paid off with new debt).

b) Since the national debt does not have to be paid back, only refinanced, until many years later, it is hard for politicians to stop spending or raise taxes because both fiscal policies are politically unpopular.

9. a) There can be a tradeoff because additional savings that eventually increase aggregate supply also cause a decrease today in aggregate demand.

b) To save. The "Yes" camp argues that the long-run benefits of increased aggregate supply for economic growth outweigh any short-run mismatches between aggregate demand and aggregate supply.

c) To spend. Keynes and the "No" camp worry that businesses, seeing reduced consumer spending, will postpone investment spending, reducing aggregate demand, causing the economy to contract. They believe markets fail to quickly adjust, so short-run

adjustment costs might outweigh the long-run benefits of economic growth. In other words, in the long run, we are all dead, so forget about the long-run benefits of saving and spend the $200 today!

10. Economist camps disagree on whether spending or tax cuts are better policy to accelerate the economy. Even if the camps could agree on the need to counteract recessions with government policy (they don't!), the choice between tax cuts (less government) and spending (more government) depends on hands-off versus hands-on views on the proper role of government.

CHAPTER 9
TRUE/FALSE

1. False. Comparative advantage, specialization, and trade reduce self-sufficiency.
2. True.
3. False. Exports as a percentage of GDP are 36 percent for Canada and 28 percent for the U.S..
4. True.
5. True.
6. True.
7. True.
8. False. Tariffs, like all protectionist policies, hurt consumers by making imports more expensive. Tariffs protect some businesses that are non-competitive.
9. True.
10. True
11. True.
12. False. Workers make smart economic choices by selecting the job that provides the best benefits. Sweatshop jobs pay more than farm jobs.
13. False. Social safety nets are government programs to assist citizens through difficult economic moments in their lives. Employment Insurance is an example of a Canadian social safety net.
14. True.
15. True.

MULTIPLE CHOICE

1. **a)** $\frac{\text{give up}}{\text{get}}$
2. **c)** specializing and trading move us away from self-sufficiency and create more wealth for all.
3. **c)** you are able to produce all products/services at a lower cost than the competitors.
4. **b)** you are able to produce at a lower dollar cost than the competition.
5. **b)** specializing in the product/service where you have a competitive advantage makes trading mutually beneficial.
6. **b)** terms of trade describe the ratio at which traded products exchange.
7. **a)** participants must do better with trade than they could do locally.

8. **d)** structural unemployment is caused by jobs becoming obsolete due to new technologies or international competition.

9. **b)** jobs gained through new businesses and higher productivity outweigh the jobs lost in less competitive businesses.

10. **d)** new technology or increased international competition pressures old businesses to change or close.

11. **c)** businesses and workers in import-competing industries lose, but consumers gain from better, less expensive products/services.

12. **d)** markets become more connected and interdependent.

13. **c)** economists ask the opportunity cost question, "Are workers lives better off, or worse off, compared to a situation without globalization, trade, and the factory jobs that follow?"

14. **a)** hands-on camp believes in a limited role for government to protect workers who lose from trade.

15. **d)** jobs are gained through new technologies and international competition but lost when out-dated businesses close.

SHORT ANSWER PROBLEMS

1. **a)** You have an absolute advantage in both housework and assignments, because you can do more of each in an hour than can your roommate. To find comparative advantage, compare your opportunity costs (give up ÷ get) with your roommate's. Your opportunity cost of getting 1 additional hour of housework done is 1 hour of assignments foregone. Your opportunity cost of getting 1 additional hour of assignments done is 1 hour of housework foregone.

   Your roommate's opportunity cost of getting 1 additional hour of housework done is 0.67 hour of assignments foregone. Your roommate's opportunity cost of getting 1 additional hour of assignments done is 1.5 hours of housework foregone.

   So you have a comparative advantage (lower opportunity cost) in assignments and your roommate has a comparative advantage in housework.

   b) You should specialize in doing the economics assignments and your roommate should specialize in housework.

2. Include all money costs (gas, parking, food and beverages at the game, etc.) and opportunity costs (earnings given up).

3. **a)** $150 \div 75 = 2$.
   b) $50 \div 100 = \frac{1}{2}$.
   c) $300 \div 100 = 3$.

4. **a)** The opportunity cost of Jack spending all his time making bread (expressed per unit of what he gets) is $\frac{105}{70} = \frac{3}{2}$ cords of wood.
   The opportunity cost of Jack spending all his time cutting wood (expressed per unit of what he gets) is $\frac{70}{105} = \frac{2}{3}$ loaf of bread.
   The opportunity cost of Jacqueline spending all her time making bread (expressed per unit of what she gets) is $\frac{100}{50} = 2$ cords of wood.
   The opportunity cost of Jacqueline spending all her time cutting wood (expressed per unit of what she gets) is $\frac{50}{100} = \frac{1}{2}$ loaf of bread.
   Therefore, Jack has a comparative advantage in making bread and Jacqueline has a comparative advantage in chopping wood.

   b) The opportunity cost of Jack spending all his time making bread (expressed per unit of what he gets) is $\frac{105}{70} = \frac{3}{2}$ cords of wood.
   The opportunity cost of Jack spending all his time cutting wood (expressed per unit of what he gets) is $\frac{70}{105} = \frac{2}{3}$ loaf of bread.
   The opportunity cost of Samantha spending all her time making bread (expressed per unit of what she gets) is $\frac{20}{40} = \frac{1}{2}$ cord of wood.
   The opportunity cost of Samantha spending all her time cutting wood (expressed per unit of what she gets) is $\frac{40}{20} = 2$ loaves of bread.
   Therefore, Jack has a comparative advantage in chopping wood and Samantha has a comparative advantage in making bread.

Opportunity Costs for Jack and Jacqueline		
	Opportunity Cost of 1 Additional . . .	
	Loaf of Bread	**Cord of Wood**
Jack	Give up $\frac{105}{70} = \frac{3}{2}$ wood (cords)	Give up $\frac{70}{105} = \frac{2}{3}$ bread (loaves)
Jacqueline	Give up $\frac{100}{50} = 2$ wood (cords)	Give up $\frac{50}{100} = \frac{1}{2}$ bread (loaves)

Opportunity Costs for Jack and Samantha		
	Opportunity Cost of 1 Additional . . .	
	Loaf of Bread	**Cord of Wood**
Jack	Give up $\frac{105}{70} = \frac{3}{2}$ wood (cords)	Give up $\frac{70}{105} = \frac{2}{3}$ bread (loaves)
Samantha	Give up $\frac{20}{40} = \frac{1}{2}$ wood (cords)	Give up $\frac{40}{20} = 2$ bread (loaves)

5. Before trade, Jack gets 20 loaves of bread and 75 cords of wood. If Jack trades with Jacqueline, he specializes in making bread because this is the activity he has a comparative advantage in. After trading with Jacqueline, Jack ends up with 50 loaves of bread (the 70 he produced minus the 20 he traded away) and 20 cords of wood (the 0 he produced plus the 20 he traded for). This is worse than his allocation when being self-sufficient, which could have been 50 loaves of bread and 30 cords of wood (that is, he produces the same number of loaves of bread but 10 fewer cords of wood by trading with Jacqueline, compared to being self-sufficient).

If Jack trades with Samantha he specializes in cutting wood because this is the activity he has a comparative advantage in. After trading with Samantha, Jack ends up with 20 loaves of bread (the 0 he produced plus the 20 he traded for) and 85 cords of wood (the 105 he produced minus the 20 he traded away). This is better than his allocation when being self-sufficient, which is 20 loaves of bread and 75 cords of wood (that is, he produces the same amount of loaves of bread but gets 10 additional cords of wood by trading with Samantha, compared to being self-sufficient).
To summarize:

Jack's Consumption Possibilities				
	Before Trade (2 possibilities shown)		After Trading with Jacqueline	After Trading with Samantha
Loaves of bread	20	50	50	20
Cords of wood	75	30	20	85

Therefore, Jack will prefer to go into partnership with Samantha.

6. The workers trade their time and way of life for the higher wages they receive by choosing the sweatshop over the farm. The factories get inexpensive labour. Both parties feel they are getting more than they give up. The terms of trade appear fair to both the workers and the factory owners.

7. Here are some examples you may have included in your list.
- More and different types of foods available all year round.
- Cheaper prices for many imported products such as computers and TVs.
- Faster innovation in many products such as iPods and cell phones.
- Wider and more inexpensive choices for manufactured goods such as cars and clothes.
- Greater competition in a variety of services such as entertainment and travel, reducing costs and increasing availability.
- Probably more and better job opportunities for you after you graduate.

8. You explain the following to your friend.
- By allowing the Chinese competition all consumers will benefit by getting lower prices.
- Your friend's business could benefit by finding ways to be more efficient and productive and reducing their costs.
- If Canada puts on a tariff, China could retaliate and put tariffs on Canadian exports entering China, which would hurt many Canadian businesses.
- Protectionist policies usually end up hurting more Canadians than they help.

9. a) Hands-on: you would want the government to control the importation of fish products to lessen your competition.
b) Hands-off: you would want access to as much international information and as many markets as possible.
c) Hands-off: you will want to have access to as many opportunities both nationally and internationally as possible.

10. Your answer may be like this one:
Should the government take a hands-off or hands-on approach to changes in the market place to insure a stable environment for as many people and businesses as possible, or should it take a hands-off position and trust that the market will adjust quickly enough to overcome any problems created by global forces.
Whatever your answer, it should contain the following ideas.
- "Left alone by government" means a hands-off position.
- Hands-off means government does not interfere with the marketplace.
- Government involvement means a hands-on position.
- Hands-on means that government will put policies in place that affect the market.
- Some examples of government involvement are protectionist policies and Employment Insurance.

Introduction to Appendices

If you have not previously studied microeconomics, you should read the four appendices **before** starting *Economics for Life: Smart Choices for All?*

   The four appendices come from *Economics for Life: Smart Choices for You*—the microeconomics companion textbook. Microeconomics looks at smart choices of individual consumers and individual businesses, while macroeconomics looks at the combined market outcomes of all those individual choices.

   These microeconomic chapters present the core concepts that you can use regularly to make smart choices in your life as a consumer, as a business person, and as an informed citizen. The Three Keys shown are at the heart of making smart choices and are at the heart of these chapters. You can always spot them by the key icon in the margin.

   The Three Keys are like a map, helping you choose a direction to take at decision points—forks in the road. When you come to a fork in the road—a decision point, the three keys will help you focus on the information that is most useful to your making a smart choice.

   Once you understand the Three Keys, you will have the necessary foundation for studying macroeconomics, which asks the question, "When all the smart choices of individuals are combined, is the result the best outcome for the economy as a whole?"

Three Keys to Smart Choices

Appendix **A**

What's in Economics for You?

Scarcity, Opportunity Cost, and Trade

LEARNING OBJECTIVES

After reading this appendix, you should be able to:

A.1 Explain scarcity and describe why you must make smart choices among your wants.

A.2 Define and describe opportunity cost.

A.3 Describe how comparative advantage, specialization, and trade make us all better off.

A.4 Explain how markets connect us all using the circular flow of economic life.

A.5 Illustrate and explain the Three Keys to Smart Choices.

WHAT DO YOU WANT OUT OF LIFE? Riches? Fame?
Love? Adventure? A successful career? To make the world a better place?
To live a life that respects the environment? To express your creativity?
Happiness? Children? A long and healthy life? All of the above?

Economics will help you get what you want out of life. Many people
believe economics is just about money and business. But the real
definition of **economics** is how individuals, businesses, and governments
make the best possible choices to get what they want, and how those
choices interact in markets.

The title of this book comes from a quote by Nobel Prize-winning
author George Bernard Shaw: "Economy is the art of making the most
of life." Economics is partly about getting the most for your money, but
it is also about making smart choices generally. I wrote this book
because I believe that if you learn a little economics, it will help you
make the most of your life, whatever you are after. That same knowledge will also help you better understand the world around you and
the choices you face as a citizen.

You don't need to be trained as an economist to lead a productive and
satisfying life. But if you can learn *to think like an economist*, you can
get more out of whatever life you choose to lead, and the world will be
better for it.

economics:
how individuals,
businesses, and
governments make the
best possible choices to
get what they want,
and how those choices
interact in markets

A.1 Are You Getting Enough? Scarcity and Choice

Explain scarcity and describe why you must make smart choices among your wants.

Can you afford to buy everything you want? If not, every dollar you spend involves a choice. If you buy the Nintendo Wii, you might not be able to afford your English textbook. If you treat your friends to a movie, you might have to work an extra shift at your job or give up your weekend camping trip.

It would be great to have enough money to buy everything you want, but it would not eliminate the need to make smart choices. Imagine winning the biggest lottery in the world. You can buy whatever you want for yourself, your family, and your friends. But you still have only 80-some years on this planet (if you are lucky and healthy), only 24 hours in a day, and a limited amount of energy. Do you want to spend the week boarding in Whistler or surfing in Australia? Do you want to spend time raising your kids or exploring the world? Will you go to that third party on New Year's Eve or give in to sleep? Do you want to spend money on yourself, or set up a charitable foundation to help others? Bill Gates, one of the richest people on Earth, has chosen to set up the Bill and Melinda Gates Foundation. With billions of dollars in assets, the Foundation still receives more requests for worthy causes than it has dollars. How does it choose which requests to fund?

Economists call this inability to satisfy all of our wants the problem of **scarcity**. Scarcity arises from our limited money, time, and energy. All mortals, even billionaires, face the problem of scarcity. We all have to make choices about what we will get and what we will give up. Businesses with limited capital have to choose between spending more on research or on marketing. Governments have to make similar choices in facing the problem of scarcity. Spending more on colleges and universities leaves less to spend on health care. Or if governments tried to spend more on all social programs, the higher taxes to pay for them would mean less take-home pay for all of us.

Because none of us — individuals, businesses, governments — can ever satisfy all of our wants, smart choices are essential to making the most of our lives.

scarcity:
the problem that arises
because we all have
limited money, time,
and energy

Refresh

A.1

1. Define scarcity.

2. What does the definition of economics have to do with scarcity?

3. Social activists argue that materialism is one of the biggest problems with society: If we all wanted less, instead of always wanting more, there would be plenty to go around for everyone. What do you think of this argument?

www.myeconlab.com

A.2 Give It Up for Opportunity Cost! Opportunity Cost

Scarcity means you have to choose, and if you want the most out of what limited money and time you have, you need to make smart choices. A choice is like a fork in the road. You have to compare the alternatives and then pick one. You make a smart choice by weighing benefits and costs.

Define and describe opportunity cost.

Choose to Snooze?

What are you going to do with the next hour? Since you are reading this, you must be considering studying as one choice. If you were out far too late last night, sleep might be your alternative choice. If those are your top choices, let's compare benefits of the two paths from the fork. For studying, the benefits are higher marks on your next test, learning something, and (if I have done my job well) perhaps enjoying reading this appendix. For sleep, the benefits are being more alert, more productive, less grumpy, and (if I have done my job poorly) avoiding the pain of reading this appendix.

If you choose the studying path, what is *the cost of your decision*? It is the hour of sleep you give up (with the benefits of rest). And if you choose sleep, the cost is the studying you give up (leading to lower marks).

In weighing the benefits and costs of any decision, we compare what we get from each fork with what we give up from the other. For any choice (what we get), its true cost is what we have to give up to get it. The true cost of any choice is what economists call **opportunity cost**: the cost of the best alternative given up.

opportunity cost: cost of best alternative given up

Opportunity Cost Beats Money Cost

For smart decisions, it turns out that opportunity cost is more important than money cost. Suppose you win a free trip for one to Bermuda that has to be taken the first week in December. What is the money cost of the trip? (This is not a trick question.) Zero — it's free.

But imagine you have a business client in Saskatoon who can meet to sign a million-dollar contract *only* during the first week in December. What is the opportunity cost of your "free" trip to Bermuda? $1 million. A smart decision to take or not take the trip depends on opportunity cost, not money cost.

Or what if you have an out-of-town boyfriend, and the only time you can get together is during the first week in December? What is the opportunity cost of taking your "free" trip for one? Besides losing out on the benefits of time together, you may be kissing that relationship goodbye.

All choices are forks in the road, and the cost of any path taken is the value of the path you must give up. Because of scarcity, every choice involves a trade-off — to get something, you have to give up something else. *To make a smart choice, the value of what you get must be greater than the value of what you give up.* The benefits of a smart choice must outweigh the opportunity cost.

> **FOR YOUR INFORMATION**
>
> If there were an official slogan for the concept of opportunity cost, it would be, "There is no such thing as a free lunch." The usual meaning of the slogan is that there are strings attached to any gift: the giver will expect something in return. The economist's take on the slogan is that every choice involves a trade-off: To get anything, including lunch, you must always give up something else. What you give up may be money or time, but every choice has an opportunity cost.

Scarcity means every choice involves a trade-off.

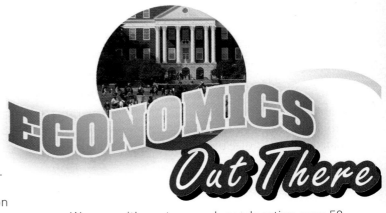

ECONOMICS Out There

Where Have All the Men Gone?

Women make up 60 percent of the undergraduate college and university population. Why do women so outnumber men? There have been many explanations, from women's liberation to schools' rewarding girls' more obedient behaviour and punishing boys' ADD (attention deficit disorder). There is also a simple economic explanation based on opportunity cost.

- Think of going or not going to college or university as a fork in the road.
- Weigh the costs and benefits of each choice. Everyone pays the same tuition and fees, but the benefits given up with each choice are different for women and men.
- More women than men go to college and university because the cost of *not* going is higher for women — men's alternative is higher-paying blue-collar jobs. Women's alternative tends to be lower-paying clerical or retail jobs.

Women with post-secondary education earn 50 to 80 percent more a year than women with only a high-school diploma. Men with the same post-secondary education earn only 25 to 30 percent more a year than men with only a high-school diploma. The *gap in pay* between high-school and post-secondary women is larger than the same gap for men.

Because of the differences in opportunity cost — women who don't go to college or university *give up* a bigger income gain than men do — the rate of return for a college diploma or university degree is 9 percent for women, and only around 6 percent for men. Incentives matter, and people are responding to the incentives. For women, it pays more to get a post-secondary education.

---

incentives: rewards and penalties for choices

If you read the preface, you might recognize that this section is about the Three Keys to Smart Choices, which re-appear in Section A.5.

Refresh A.2

Incentives Work Since smart choices compare costs and benefits, obviously your decision will change with changes in costs or benefits. We all respond to **incentives** — rewards and penalties for choices. You are more likely to choose a fork with a reward, and avoid a fork with a penalty. A change in incentives causes a change in choices. If your Saskatoon business deal was worth only $100 instead of one million dollars, you might take the trip to Bermuda. If you had been out really late last night, you would be more likely to sleep than to study. If you had a test tomorrow instead of next week, you would be more likely to study than to sleep.

To make the most out of life and make smart decisions, you always need to be asking the question, "What is the opportunity cost of my choice, and do the benefits outweigh the opportunity cost?"

1. What is the opportunity cost of any choice?

2. What is the biggest difference between the money cost of attending college and the opportunity cost?

3. This weekend, your top choices are going camping with your friends or working extra hours at your part-time job. What facts (think rewards and penalties), if they changed, would influence your decision?

www.myeconlab.com

A.3 Why Don't You Cook Breakfast? Gains from Trade

Define and describe opportunity cost.

What did you have for breakfast today? Did you have cereal and orange juice at home, or did you buy coffee and a bagel at Tim Hortons on the way to school? Either way, you made a choice — to make breakfast for yourself, or to buy it from a business. This is the most basic choice you and everyone else makes in trying to do the best you can: Do you produce yourself the products/services you want, or do you earn money at a job and then buy (or trade money for) products/services made by others?

These days, that basic choice sounds absurd. We all work (or hope to) at jobs, earning money by specializing in a particular profession or occupation. We use that money to buy what we want. Even a "homemade" breakfast uses cereal and juice bought at a supermarket. But if you go back only a few hundred years in Canadian history, most aboriginal peoples and pioneers were largely self-sufficient, making for themselves most of what they needed — hunting and growing their own food, making clothes from animal hides, and building shelters from wood.

Voluntary Trade   What happened to lead us all away from self-sufficiency toward specializing and trading? The historical answer to that question is complex, but the simple economic answer is that specializing and trading makes us better off, so of course people made that basic choice. It's simple self-interest at work.

Our standard of living, in terms of material products/services, is much higher than it was hundreds of years ago in Canada. The irony is that *as individuals* we are hopeless at supporting ourselves compared to our ancestors. Yet *collectively* our standard of living is vastly superior.

Trade is the key to our prosperity. Trade makes all of us better off. Why? Trade is voluntary. Any time two people make a voluntary trade, each person must feel that what they get is of greater value than what they give up. If there weren't mutual benefits, the trade wouldn't happen.

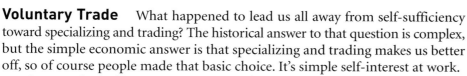

When you "trade" money for coffee at Tim's, that is a voluntary exchange. If you thought you would be better off keeping the money instead of the coffee, you wouldn't pay. If Tim's weren't better off with your money instead of the coffee, it wouldn't sell.

Bake or Chop?

It turns out that opportunity cost is the key to the mutual benefits from trade. To illustrate, let's take a simple imaginary example of two early Canadians who are each self-sufficient in producing food and shelter.

Jacqueline grows her own wheat to make bread, and chops wood for fire and shelter. If she spends an entire month producing only bread, she can make 50 loaves. Alternatively, if she spends all her time chopping wood, she can produce 100 cords. Her monthly choice of how to spend her time looks like this:

Since Jacqueline is self-sufficient, that means she can consume only what she produces herself, so she must divide her time and produce some bread and some wood. Figure A.1 shows different combinations of bread and wood she can produce, depending on how she divides up her time during the month. From these production possibilities, Jacqueline chooses to produce 20 loaves of bread and 60 cords of wood.

Figure A.1   Jacqueline's Production Possibilities (monthly)

Bread (loaves)	Wood (cords)
50	0
40	20
30	40
20	60
10	80
0	100

Samantha, who lives a day's journey away from Jacqueline, also grows her own wheat to make bread, and chops wood for fire and shelter. Samantha is older and weaker than Jacqueline, so if Samantha spends an entire month producing only bread, she can make 40 loaves. Alternatively, if she spends all her time chopping wood, she can produce only 20 cords.

Since Samantha is also self-sufficient, and can consume only what she produces herself, she divides her time and produces some bread and some wood. Figure A.2 shows different monthly combinations of bread and wood she can produce, depending on how she divides up her time. From these production possibilities, Samantha chooses to produce 20 loaves of bread and 10 cords of wood.

Figure A.2   Samantha's Production Possibilities (monthly)

Bread (loaves)	Wood (cords)
40	0
30	5
20	10
10	15
0	20

Deal or No Deal? Do the Numbers

absolute advantage: ability to produce a product at lower absolute cost than another producer

How could trade make both Jacqueline and Samantha better off? It doesn't look promising, especially for Jacqueline. She is a better bread maker than Samantha (50 loaves versus 40 loaves) *and* a better wood chopper (100 cords versus 20 cords). An economist would describe Jacqueline as having an **absolute advantage** — the ability to produce a product/service at a *lower absolute cost* than another producer — over Samantha in both bread production and wood production. That is, Jacqueline is more productive as a bread maker and as a wood chopper. If we were to measure dollar costs (which I have left out to keep the example as simple as possible), absolute advantage would mean Jacqueline could produce both bread and wood at lower absolute dollar costs than could Samantha.

If you are not keen on history, then in place of Jacqueline and Samantha, think China and Canada. If China can produce everything at lower cost than Canada, can there be mutually beneficial gains from trade for both countries? What's in it for China? Won't all Canadians end up unemployed?

Comparative Advantage But mutually beneficial gains from trade do not depend on absolute advantage. They depend on what economists call **comparative advantage** — the ability to produce a product/service at a *lower opportunity cost* than another producer. To figure out comparative advantage, we need to calculate *opportunity costs* for Jacqueline and Samantha.

Jacqueline's choice in Figure A.1 is between producing 50 loaves of bread or 100 cords of wood. If she chooses to bake 50 loaves of bread, the opportunity cost is 100 cords of wood. If she instead chooses to chop 100 cords of wood, the opportunity cost is 50 loaves of bread. Opportunity cost is the value of the fork in the road *not taken*.

To compare opportunity costs, it is easier if we measure them per unit of the product chosen. There is a simple, useful formula for opportunity cost:

$$\text{Opportunity cost} = \frac{\text{Give Up}}{\text{Get}}$$

So Jacqueline's opportunity cost of producing more bread is

$$\begin{array}{c}\text{Opportunity cost of} \\ \text{additional bread}\end{array} = \frac{100 \text{ cords of wood}}{50 \text{ loaves of bread}} = \frac{2 \text{ cords of wood}}{1 \text{ loaf of bread}}$$

To get each additional loaf of bread, Jacqueline must give up 2 cords of wood.

What is Jacqueline's opportunity cost of producing more wood?

$$\begin{array}{c}\text{Opportunity cost of} \\ \text{additional wood}\end{array} = \frac{50 \text{ loaves of bread}}{100 \text{ cords of wood}} = \frac{\frac{1}{2} \text{ loaf of bread}}{1 \text{ cord of wood}}$$

To get each additional cord of wood, Jacqueline must give up $\frac{1}{2}$ loaf of bread.

If you calculate opportunity costs for Samantha you will find that her opportunity cost of getting an additional loaf of bread is giving up $\frac{1}{2}$ cord of wood, and her opportunity cost of getting an additional cord of wood is giving up 2 loaves of bread.

These opportunity cost calculations are summarized in Figure A.3. Since comparative advantage is defined as lowest opportunity cost (not lowest absolute cost), you can see that Samantha has a comparative advantage in bread-making (give up $\frac{1}{2}$ cord of wood versus 2 cords of wood), while Jacqueline has a comparative advantage in wood-chopping (give up $\frac{1}{2}$ loaf of bread versus 2 loaves of bread).

comparative advantage: ability to produce a product/service at lower opportunity cost than another producer

Opportunity cost of any choice is value of the fork in the road not taken.

Figure A.3 Opportunity Costs for Jacqueline and Samantha

| | Opportunity Cost of 1 Additional | |
	Loaf of Bread	Cord of Wood
Jacqueline	Gives up 2 cords of wood	Gives up 1/2 loaf of bread
Samantha	Gives up 1/2 cord of wood	Gives up 2 loaves of bread
Comparative Advantage	Samantha has comparative advantage (lower opportunity cost) in bread-making	Jacqueline has comparative advantage (lower opportunity cost) in wood-chopping

Smart Deals

Here's the payoff to these calculations. Instead of each pioneer being self-sufficient, and producing everything she needs, look what happens if the pioneers specialize in producing what each is best at, and then trade.

According to comparative advantage, Jacqueline should specialize in only chopping wood, and Samantha should specialize in only making bread. If so, Jacqueline will produce 100 cords of wood and no bread, and Samantha will produce 40 loaves of bread and no wood. If they then make the day-long journey and trade 20 cords of wood for 20 loaves of bread:

- Jacqueline ends up with 20 loaves of bread (0 produced plus 20 traded for) and 80 cords of wood (100 produced minus 20 traded away);
- Samantha ends up with 20 loaves of bread (40 produced minus 20 traded away) and 20 cords of wood (0 produced plus 20 traded for).

Check it out. *After trading, Jacqueline and Samantha are both better off than when they were each self-sufficient.* Before trade, the best Jacqueline could produce with 20 loaves of bread was 60 cords of wood, for all her strength, while after trade she has the same amount of bread and more wood. Before trade, the best Samantha could produce with 20 loaves of bread was just 10 cords of wood, while after trade she has the same amount of bread and more wood.

What is remarkable is that these *gains from trade,* which improve both Jacqueline's and Samantha's standard of living (with more wood they can stay warmer or build better houses), *happen without anyone working harder, or without any improvement in technology or new resources.* Both are better off because they have made smart decisions to specialize and trade, rather than each trying to produce only what each will consume. Both can have toast for breakfast (bread roasted over a fire), even though each produced only part of what was necessary to make the breakfast.

Notice also that there are gains for both Jacqueline and Samantha, even though Jacqueline can produce more bread and wood than Samantha can. Despite Jacqueline's absolute advantage in producing everything at lower cost, there are still differences in opportunity costs, or comparative advantage. *Comparative advantage is the key to mutually beneficial gains from trade.* The trade can be between individuals, or between countries. That is why China trades with Canada, even though China can produce most things more cheaply than we can in Canada. There are still differences in comparative advantage based on opportunity costs. Trade allows us all to work smarter.

So the next time you buy breakfast, don't feel guilty about spending the money when you could have cooked it yourself — feel smart about specializing and trading to make yourself better off!

Voluntary trade is not a zero-sum game, where one person's gain is the other's loss. Both traders gain. Mutually beneficial gains from trade are caused by differences in comparative advantage. Absolute advantage is not important.

Refresh A.3

1. Explain the difference between absolute advantage and comparative advantage.

2. If you spend the next hour working at Sears, you will earn $10. If you instead spend the next hour studying economics, your next test score will improve by 5 marks. Calculate the opportunity cost of studying in terms of dollars given up per mark. Calculate the opportunity cost of working in terms of marks given up per dollar.

3. The best auto mechanic in town (who charges $120/hour) is also a better typist than her office manager (who earns $20/hour). Should the mechanic do her own typing? (*Hint:* The best alternative employment for the office manager is another office job that also pays $20/hour.)

A.4 Choosing Your Way: The Circular Flow of Economic Life

Canada is a very large country, the second largest in the world in terms of geographical area. Have you ever had the urge to follow in the footsteps of our ancestors and explore the land — perhaps a trip to the northernmost tip of the Northwest Territories, or a cross-country trip from Newfoundland to British Columbia? No? Why not think about it?

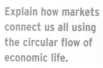

Explain how markets connect us all using the circular flow of economic life.

Why Maps (and Economists) Are Useful

How do you start planning your trip? The satellite photo of Canada below, while amazing to look at, is not very useful. It contains too much information and too little information. How can that be? The photo captures every aspect of Canada that can be seen from space — lakes, rivers, mountains, and forests. But the photo doesn't reveal smaller details that are important for your trip — most importantly, roads, railways, or ferry services.

A hybrid (combined) map version of the same photo shows you the auto route (on the next page) along the Trans-Canada Highway (you've decided it's too cold to go up north). Why is the hybrid map so much more useful than the satellite photo? Because it focuses your attention on the information that is most relevant for your task, and leaves all other information in the background.

Learning to think like an economist allows you to look at life like the hybrid map. The key "roads" to making smart choices start to stand out, and making difficult decisions and understanding the complex world around you don't seem to be such daunting tasks.

There are an almost infinite number of choices we could look at, so to keep things manageable, let's limit ourselves to the opening definition of economics: Economics is about how individuals, businesses, and governments make the best possible choices to get what they want, and about how those choices interact in markets. (We will look at markets more closely in Appendix D, but for the moment, think of a market as the interaction of buyers and sellers.)

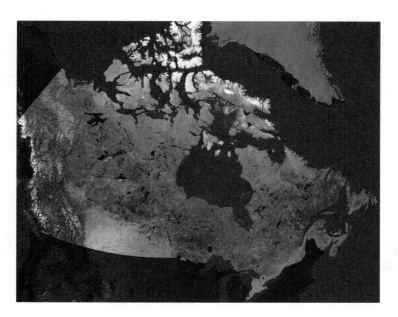

Satellite photo of Canada — not useful for trip planning.

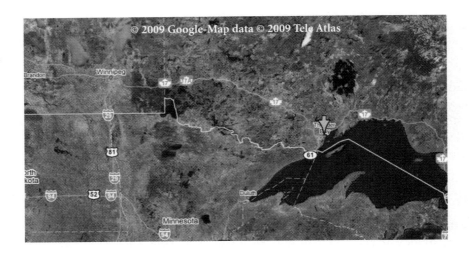

Hybrid map of part of Canada along the Trans-Canada Highway — useful for trip planning.

Another good definition of economics was made in 1890 by Alfred Marshall, the first-ever professor of economics, who created economics as a separate subject at the University of Cambridge. Marshall said: "Economics is the study of mankind in the ordinary business of life."

Going in Circles to Find the Way

Even limiting ourselves to these definitions of economics, the choices are still overwhelming. Imagine 35 million people spread out over 10 million square kilometres, engaged in the "ordinary business of life," earning a living, specializing in producing products/services, selling, and buying. Instead of trying to capture every detail of every action and choice (like the satellite photo), Figure A.4 shows a hybrid map version of the same economic activity.

Figure A.4	Circular Flow of Economic Life

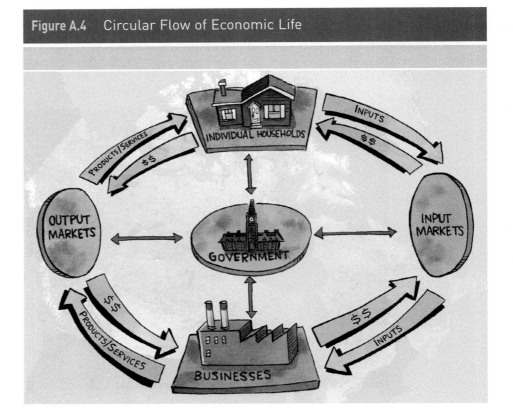

Figure A.4, which economists call the "circular flow of economic life," shows you the simplest big picture of how an economist thinks about economic choices. All the complexity of the Canadian economy is reduced to three sets of players: households, businesses, and governments. Individuals in households ultimately own all of the inputs of an economy — labour (the ability to work), natural resources, capital equipment, and entrepreneurial ability. Even the assets of the largest corporations, such as Inco, Ford, or Research In Motion, are ultimately owned by individual shareholders. Households and businesses interact in two sets of markets — input markets (where businesses buy the inputs they need to produce products/services), and output markets (where businesses sell their products/services). Governments (in the middle) set the rules of the game and can choose to interact, or not, in almost any aspect of the economy.

Follow the Flow Clockwise   Follow the circle, starting at the top. Individuals in households sell or rent to businesses the labour, resources, capital, and entrepreneurial abilities they own. This is the outer blue flow on the right-hand side of the circle, from top to bottom. In exchange, businesses pay wages and other money rewards to households. This is the inner green flow on the right-hand side of the circle, from bottom to top. These exchanges, or trades, happen in input markets, where households are the sellers and businesses are the buyers. When Mr. Sub hires you to work in a Mr. Sub store, that interaction happens in an input market—the job market.

Businesses then use those inputs to produce products/services, which they sell to households. This is the outer blue flow on the left-hand side of the circle, from bottom to top. In exchange, households use the money they have earned in input markets to pay businesses for these purchases. This is the inner green flow on the left-hand side of the circle, from top to bottom. These exchanges, or trades, happen in output markets, where households are the buyers and businesses are the sellers. These are markets where you buy your breakfast from a store or supermarket, your cars from Ford or Toyota, your piercings from a neighbourhood piercing parlour, and so on.

At the end of the trip around the circle, households have the products/services they need to live, and businesses end up with the money. That sets the stage for the next trip around the circle, where businesses again buy inputs from individuals in households, and the flow goes on.

So there you have it—a hybrid map to begin your economics road trip toward understanding and making smart choices.

It's All Greek to Me: Microeconomics or Macroeconomics?

"One size fits all" does *not* apply to maps. The hybrid map of Canada with the highlighted Trans-Canada Highway may be fine for planning the big picture of your trip, but when you are trying to get to a hostel in downtown Winnipeg from the Trans-Canada, a detailed city map is far more useful. Depending on the task, economists also use different kinds of "maps."

The economic way of thinking, while always concerned with smart choices and their interactions in markets, can be applied on different scales to understand *microeconomics* and *macroeconomics*.

Microeconomics

Microeconomics "Micro" comes from the Greek word *mikros,* meaning "little" or "small." A microscope lets us see little details of an object. A micro-manager supervises every tiny detail of an employee's work (ever had a boss like that?). A detailed city map has a micro scale. **Microeconomics** analyzes the choices made by individuals in households, individual businesses, and governments, and how those choices interact in markets.

Microeconomic choices for individuals include whether to go to college or to get a job, whether to be self-sufficient or to specialize and trade, whether to take out a bank loan or to run up a credit card balance, and whether to get married or to stay single. (Yes, there is even a microeconomic analysis comparing the costs and benefits of marriage!)

Microeconomic choices for businesses include what product/service to produce, how much to spend on research and development of new products, which technology to use, which marketing strategy to use, and whether to outsource manufacturing to China versus producing in Canada.

Microeconomic choices for governments focus on *individual industries.* For example, should the government step in and regulate the emerging voice-over-IP phone industry (services such as Skype and Vonage), or let competition determine the winners and losers? How would a carbon tax affect car sales?

microeconomics: analyzes choices that individuals in households, individual businesses, and governments make, and how those choices interact in markets

Macroeconomics

Macroeconomics When we step back from individual details and look at the big picture, we are taking a "macro" view. Macro comes from the Greek word *makros,* meaning "large." The macrocosm is the cosmos, or the whole of a complex structure. A macrobiotic diet consists of whole, pure foods based on Taoist principles of the overall balance of yin and yang. **Macroeconomics** analyzes the performance of the whole Canadian economy and the global economy, the combined outcomes of all individual microeconomic choices. In the circular flow in Figure A.4, instead of focusing on the individual exchanges in markets macroeconomics focuses on the *whole* circle, the *combined outcomes* of all of the individual interactions in markets.

Macroeconomics focuses on overall outcomes of market interactions, including Canadian unemployment, inflation rates, government deficits and surpluses, interest rates set by the Bank of Canada, the value of the Canadian dollar, and international trade. Macroeconomics also examines the policy choices governments make that affect the whole economy — for example, whether to play an active economic role by spending and taxing (more likely for New Democrats) or to leave the economy alone (more likely for Progressive Conservatives), whether to raise or lower taxes, whether to raise or lower interest rates, and whether to defend the value of the Canadian dollar or let it be determined by economic forces. Since government macroeconomic policy choices will affect your personal economic fortunes, as a citizen you have a personal incentive to learn some macroeconomics so you can make more informed choices when voting for politicians.

macroeconomics: analyzes performance of the whole Canadian economy and global economy—the combined outcomes of all individual microeconomic choices

Looking at the Trees or the Forest? The difference between micro and macro views is reflected in the titles of this book *(Economics for Life: Smart Choices for You)* and its companion book *(Economics for Life: Smart Choices for All)*. This book, with the subtitle *Smart Choices for You,* is about microeconomics — individual choices. The companion book, with the subtitle *Smart Choices for All,* is about macroeconomics — the combined market outcomes of all choices. Micro looks at the individual trees, while macro looks at the forest.

Refresh

A.4

www.myeconlab.com

1. Who are the three sets of players in the circular flow of economic life?

2. When you find a job through Workopolis.com or Monster.ca, what kind of market are you participating in? Is the answer different for the business that hires you?

3. Find one story in today's news that you think is about microeconomics, and one that is about macroeconomics. What is the difference between microeconomics and macroeconomics in terms of these stories?

A.5 The Three-Key Map to Smart Choices: Weigh Marginal Benefits and Costs

Good road maps make travel easier. Figure A.5 shows a second, more detailed hybrid economic "map" to help guide all of your microeconomic choices toward being smart choices. This "map" consists of three keys to consider when standing at any fork in the road, when making any choice. While these three keys don't look like a traditional map (no pictures, colours, roads, or lines), they serve the same function as do maps — focusing your attention on the information that is most useful for making a smart choice, and leaving all other information in the background.

For each key, pay special attention to the red words and italicized words in the explanations on the following page.

Illustrate and explain the Three Keys to Smart Choices.

Figure A.5 Three Keys to Smart Choices

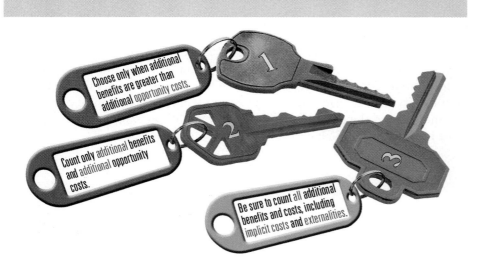

1. Choose only when additional benefits are greater than additional opportunity costs.

2. Count only additional benefits and additional opportunity costs.

3. Be sure to count all additional benefits and costs, including implicit costs and externalities.

Key 1: Opportunity Costs Rule

To make a smart choice, when you weigh benefits against costs, additional benefits must be greater than additional *opportunity costs*. When counting costs, people who make dumb decisions usually count only money costs, rather than opportunity costs. Remember the "free" trip to Bermuda? The money cost was zero, but the opportunity cost was the $1-million deal you would have given up. Or think about your decision to go to college. For that fork in the road, the additional benefits include the higher lifetime income you will earn from your education. The additional costs are the money spent on tuition and books (these money costs are also opportunity costs, as you could have spent the same money to buy other things), as well as the income you give up by not working full time. The additional benefits must be greater than all additional opportunity costs (and the data show that they are — so congratulations on a smart choice!).

Key 2: Look Forward Only to Additional Benefits and Additional Opportunity Costs

If you are deciding whether or not to study for the next hour, the tuition you paid for this course is irrelevant. You can't get it back, whether you choose to study or not. When standing at a fork in the road, don't look back, only look forward. The previous decisions you made or money you spent are history and can't be undone. The past is the same no matter which fork you choose now, so it shouldn't influence your choice.

Your choices should weigh the *additional* benefit from the next hour of studying against the *additional* cost (giving up sleep, or perhaps working an extra hour at your part-time job). It's not the total benefit of all hours spent studying or the average benefit of an hour of studying that matters, only the *additional* benefit. Economists use the word "marginal" instead of "additional," so you can also read Key 2 as "Count only **marginal benefits** — additional benefits from your next choice — and **marginal opportunity costs** — additional opportunity costs from your next choice." Appendix B will explain marginal benefits, and Appendix C will explain marginal costs. Thinking like an economist means thinking at the margin.

marginal benefits: additional benefits from the next choice

marginal opportunity costs: additional opportunity costs from the next choice

Key 3: Implicit Costs and Externalities Count, Too

If you invest $1000 in your own business, and expect to get $1100 in a year, is that a smart choice? You don't know until you compare the best alternative use of your money. If the best your bank pays is $1050 in a year, invest in your business. But if the bank is paying 20 percent interest, paying $1200 in a year, your business is not a smart choice. Economists use the term **implicit costs** to describe the opportunity costs of investing your own money or time. These implicit costs will not show up on the books your accountant would prepare. But smart choices must incorporate implicit costs.

implicit costs: opportunity costs of investing your own money or time

Negative Externalities

Driving a car is expensive. Think of the gas bill alone for driving clear across Canada! But your costs also include car payments, insurance, repairs, licence fees, tolls, and parking. What's more, as expensive as those costs are, they don't cover the total cost of driving a car. Your car also emits pollution, but you don't pay for the costs of damage to the environment from acid rain, or for the increased medical costs to treat patients suffering from asthma and other pollution-related illnesses. Economists call these costs that you create, but don't pay directly, **negative externalities**. They are costs that affect others who are external to a choice or trade. But from a social point of view, external costs should be included in making smart decisions.

negative (or positive) externalities: costs (or benefits) that affect others external to a choice or a trade

Positive Externalities

There are also **positive externalities**, benefits that affect others who are external to a choice or trade. If you plant a beautiful garden in your front lawn, you certainly benefit, but so do all of your neighbours who take in the colours and fragrances. Again, from a social point of view, positive externalities should be included in making smart decisions, but they are not.

Market economies like ours in Canada tend to produce too many products/services that have negative externalities, and too few products/services that have positive externalities. Government policy can play an important role in adjusting for external costs and benefits to result in smart decisions for society.

Moving On

Now that you have your economic maps to guide you, let's get on with the journey. You will use the Three Keys to make smart decisions time and again. Don't worry if they seem a bit sketchy for now. Each time we use them, we will fill in some of the pieces that might seem to be missing.

The "maps" in Figures A.4 and A.5 will help you learn to think like an economist, which in turn will help you get more out of whatever life you choose to lead, as well as help you make better decisions as a citizen.

Refresh
A.5

1. Can you combine the Three Keys into a single sentence that begins with "Choose only when . . . " and that uses all the economist's terms explained under Steps 2 and 3? That sentence is the key to this entire course.

2. Your employer pays you $1 for every kilometre you drive your own car on company business, or allows you to use a company car at no expense. In deciding whether to drive your own car or use the company car, which of the following costs are relevant to your decision: Purchase price of your car? Yearly licence fee? Insurance premiums? Depreciation? Gasoline costs? Explain your answer.

3. Highway 407 ETR in Toronto is a toll road that uses transponders to keep track of how many kilometres you drive, and then sends a monthly bill. Highway 401 runs parallel to Highway 407 and is free. Why do drivers voluntarily pay the tolls? (Use opportunity cost in your answer.) Suppose the government could estimate the cost per kilometre of the pollution damage from your driving, and send you a similar monthly bill. How would that additional cost affect your decision to drive?

What's in Economics for You?

Scarcity, Opportunity Cost, and Trade

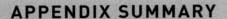

APPENDIX SUMMARY

A.1 ARE YOU GETTING ENOUGH?
SCARCITY AND CHOICE

Because you can never satisfy all of your wants, making the most out of your life requires smart choices about what to go after, and what to give up.

- **Economics** is how individuals, businesses, and governments make the best possible choices to get what they want, and how those choices interact in markets.
- Problem of **scarcity** arises because of limited money, time, and energy.

A.2 GIVE IT UP FOR OPPORTUNITY COST!
OPPORTUNITY COST

Opportunity cost is the single most important concept both in economics and for making smart choices in life.

- Because of scarcity, every choice involves a trade-off — you have to give up something to get something else.
- The true cost of any choice is the **opportunity cost** — cost of best alternative given up.
- For a smart choice, the value of what you get must be greater than value of what you give up.
- **Incentives** — rewards and penalties for choices.
- You are more likely to choose actions with rewards (positive incentives), and avoid actions with penalties (negative incentives).

A.3 WHY DON'T YOU COOK BREAKFAST?
GAINS FROM TRADE

Opportunity cost and comparative advantage are key to understanding why specializing and trading make us all better off.

- With *voluntary* trade, each person feels that what they get is of greater value than what they give up.

- **Absolute advantage** — ability to produce a product/service at a lower absolute cost than another producer.
- **Comparative advantage** — ability to produce a product/service at a lower opportunity cost than another producer.
- Opportunity cost $= \dfrac{\text{Give Up}}{\text{Get}}$
- Comparative advantage is key to mutually beneficial gains from trade. Trade makes individuals better off when each specializes in the product/service where they have a comparative advantage (lower opportunity cost) and then trades for the other product/service.
- Even if one individual has an *absolute* advantage in producing everything at lower cost, as long as there are differences in *comparative* advantage, there are mutually beneficial gains from specializing and trading.

A.4 CHOOSING YOUR WAY:
THE CIRCULAR FLOW OF ECONOMIC LIFE

The circular-flow diagram of economic life is a map showing how markets connect us all. It illustrates how smart choices by households, businesses, and governments interact in markets.

- All the complexity of the Canadian economy can be reduced to three sets of players — households, businesses, and governments.
  - In input markets, households are sellers and businesses are buyers.
  - In output markets, households are buyers and businesses are sellers.
  - Governments set rules of the game and can choose to interact in any aspect of the economy.
- **Microeconomics** analyzes choices that individuals in households, individual businesses, and governments make, and how those choices interact in markets.
- **Macroeconomics** analyzes performance of the whole Canadian economy and global economy, the combined outcomes of all individual microeconomic choices.

A.5 THE THREE-KEY MAP TO SMART CHOICES:
WEIGH MARGINAL BENEFITS AND COSTS

The three-key plan summarizes the core of microeconomics. It provides the basis for smart choices in all areas of your life.

- Three Keys to Smart Choices:
  1. Choose only when additional benefits are greater than additional *opportunity costs.*
  2. Count only *additional* benefits and *additional* opportunity costs.
  3. Be sure to count *all* additional benefits and costs, including *implicit costs* and *externalities.*
- Marginal = "additional."
- **Marginal benefits** — additional benefits from next choice.
- **Marginal opportunity costs** — additional opportunity costs from next choice.
- **Implicit costs** — opportunity costs of investing your own money or time.
- **Negative** (or **positive**) **externalities** — costs (or benefits) that affect others external to a choice or a trade.

TRUE/FALSE

Circle the correct answer.

A.1 SCARCITY AND CHOICE

1. Economics is about how individuals, businesses, and governments make the best possible choices to get what they want, and how those choices interact in markets.   True   False

2. People who win the lottery don't have to make smart choices.   True   False

A.2 OPPORTUNITY COST

3. Opportunity cost is equal to money cost.   True   False

4. In 2007 the Government of Canada announced a $1000 Apprenticeship Incentive Grant to cover the costs of tuition, travel, and tools for apprentices in the sealing trades. This will eliminate the opportunity cost of being an apprentice for those who receive the cash grant.   True   False

5. According to "Economics Out There" on p. 6, men have a larger incentive to get a post-secondary education because *not* getting a post-secondary education results in a relatively worse outcome compared to women.   True   False

A.3 GAINS FROM TRADE

6. Traditionally, women have specialized in unpaid work at home and men have specialized in paid work outside the house. One possible explanation for this could be that men held a comparative advantage in performing housework (for example, cooking, cleaning, and child care).   True   False

7. The theories of comparative advantage, specialization, and trade in this appendix are consistent with the belief that "opposites attract."   True   False

8. Sheryl and Darrel are trying to decide who should stay at home to take care of their newborn child and who should continue to work full-time outside the house. Sheryl makes $30 an hour and Darrel earns $26 an hour. If both are equally effective (or "productive") at taking care of the child, then based on *opportunity costs* Sheryl should stay at home to take care of their newborn.   True   False

9. The proportion of families with both parents working outside the home and sharing child care responsibilities has risen in recent decades. This indicates that specialization and the traditional division of gender roles are becoming much less common in Canada.   True   False

10. Government programs that make child care more affordable, such as Quebec's $7-a-day child-care program, would likely increase the proportion of parents who work outside the home.   **True**   **False**

A.4 THE CIRCULAR FLOW OF ECONOMIC LIFE

11. The labour market — where employers demand labour and employees supply labour — is an output market.   **True**   **False**

12. In input markets, households are sellers and businesses are buyers; in output markets, households are buyers and businesses are sellers.   **True**   **False**

13. Decisions to go to college or take out a loan are macroeconomic choices.   **True**   **False**

A.5 WEIGH MARGINAL BENEFITS AND COSTS

14. Implicit costs are the opportunity costs of investing your own money or time.   **True**   **False**

15. Negative externalities are benefits that affect others external to a choice or a trade.   **True**   **False**

MULTIPLE CHOICE

Circle the correct answer.

A.1 SCARCITY AND CHOICE

1. You can't get everything you want because you are limited by
   A) time.
   B) money.
   C) energy.
   D) all of the above.

2. Scarcity is
   A) not a challenge for governments.
   B) not a challenge for celebrities.
   C) not a challenge for people who win the lottery.
   D) a challenge for everyone.

3. Economics does not focus on
   A) individuals / households.
   B) animals.
   C) businesses.
   D) government.

4. Opportunity cost includes

   A) time you give up.

   B) energy you spend.

   C) money you spend.

   D) all of the above.

5. In deciding whether to study or sleep for the next hour, your decision should consider all of the following *except*

   A) how much tuition you paid.

   B) how tired you are.

   C) how productive you will be in that hour.

   D) how much value you place on sleeping in that hour.

6. From 1991 to 2001, the proportion of 25- to 29-year-old women with university degrees rose from 21 percent to 34 percent, while the proportion of 25- to 29-year-old men with degrees rose from 16 percent to 21 percent. There is a similar trend for college diplomas. More woman than men are getting post-secondary education because

   A) the gap in pay between post-secondary and high-school graduates is higher for women than it is for men.

   B) the cost of not going to post-secondary education is higher for women.

   C) the opportunity cost of going to post-secondary education is lower for women.

   D) all of the above.

7. According to the table, all of the following statements are true *except*

Median Annual Earnings	Men	Women
College diploma	$51 000	$43 000
High-school diploma	$37 000	$32 000

   A) people with college diplomas earn more than people with high-school diplomas.

   B) men with high-school diplomas earn more than women with high-school diplomas.

   C) men with college diplomas earn more than women with college diplomas.

   D) women with high-school diplomas earn more than men with high-school diplomas.

8. If the resource-rich sector of Alberta's economy starts to slow down,

   A) opportunity costs of upgrading to a college diploma will increase.

   B) opportunity costs of upgrading to a college diploma will decrease.

   C) incentives to drop out of college will increase.

   D) all of the above.

9. Mutually beneficial gains from trade come from
  A) absolute advantage.
  B) comparative advantage.
  C) self-sufficiency.
  D) China.

10. The easiest way to calculate opportunity cost is
  A) $\dfrac{\text{give up}}{\text{get}}$
  B) $\dfrac{\text{get}}{\text{give up}}$
  C) give up – get
  D) get – give up

A.4 THE CIRCULAR FLOW OF ECONOMIC LIFE

11. Which of the following is *not* a microeconomic choice for businesses?
  A) What interest rates to set
  B) What products/services to supply
  C) What quantity of output to produce
  D) How many workers to hire

12. Which of the following is *not* a microeconomic choice for governments?
  A) Increasing tuition rates
  B) Taxing automobile emissions
  C) Increasing the exchange rate of the Canadian dollar
  D) Increasing the number of taxi licences

13. In the circular-flow diagram,
  A) households ultimately own all the inputs of an economy.
  B) governments set the rules of the game.
  C) businesses are sellers and households are buyers in output markets.
  D) all of the above.

A.5 WEIGH MARGINAL BENEFITS AND COSTS

14. All of the following should be considered when making smart choices, *except*
  A) external costs and benefits.
  B) past costs and benefits.
  C) implicit costs.
  D) additional costs and additional benefits.

15. For any activity, failure to consider
  A) past costs will result in too much of that activity.
  B) past benefits will result in too little of that activity.
  C) external costs will result in too much of that activity.
  D) external benefits will result in too much of that activity.

SHORT ANSWER

Write a short answer to each question. Your answer may be in point form.

1. You're trying to decide whether to go camping with your friends or spend a quiet weekend at home with your significant other. What incentives (think rewards and penalties), if changed, may influence your decision?

2. Olga chooses to live at home rather than move into residence during her first year of college. She often brags about the fact that she saves a lot of money by living at home. Provide some examples of what Olga may have given up by choosing to live at home.

3. Suppose the government was worried about the decline of young men in post-secondary education. What incentives might encourage more men to pursue further education?

4. Your friend has an extra ticket to the Calgary Flames–Ottawa Senators game on a Saturday night. He says he will give you the ticket for free if you pay for all other expenses. You usually work Saturday nights, so if you go you will have to take the night off work. Explain what costs you would include in deciding whether or not to go to the "free" game.

5. Seat belts save lives. Suppose that a city doubles the penalty for being caught driving without a seat belt in attempt to increase seat belt use among drivers.
   A) Explain how this policy will influence driver behaviour.
   B) Now suppose the city evaluates the policy and finds that the number of fatalities actually *increased* after the policy was introduced. Can you think of a reason why this may have occurred?

6. Consider Jacqueline and Samantha from Section A.3, who specialize and trade to become better off. Suppose that Jack, a new person in town, is deciding between specializing (in either bread or wood) and being self-sufficient. Jack's production possibilities are illustrated below:

Jack's Production Possibilities (monthly)	
Bread (loaves)	**Wood (cords)**
70	0
60	15
50	30
40	45
30	60
20	75
10	90
0	105

If Jack chooses to be self-sufficient, he prefers spending his month making 20 loaves of bread and cutting 75 cords of wood.

Determine who has the comparative advantage between

A) Jack and Jacqueline

B) Jack and Samantha

7. Suppose Jack tells Jacqueline and Samantha that he will form a partnership with the woman who makes him best off after trade. Assuming that 20 cords of wood can be traded for 20 loaves of bread, with whom would Jack prefer to go into a partnership?

8. Back in the old days, professors and students could smoke in the classrooms. Today, smoking indoors in public places is illegal.

A) Provide an example of an "external cost" that indoor smokers fail to consider when deciding to light up inside the classroom.

B) Do you think that those who smoked indoors considered the "external cost" in their decision to smoke? Why or why not?

C) Another way to discourage smoking is to tax the activity. If people respond to incentives, how would we expect smokers to adjust their behaviour in response to an increase in a cigarette tax?

9. Mrs. and Mr. Singh are encouraging both their son and daughter to get a full-time job right after completing high school. According to what you learned from "Economics Out There" on p. 6, which child should they encourage *less* to go to work?

10. From a social point of view, external costs should be included in making smart decisions, but sometimes they are not. In each of the following examples, determine whether the market economy (in the absence of government policy) would result in too few or too many products/services being produced. Then describe one policy or program that the government has in place to force individuals to consider these costs or benefits when they make decisions.

A) Pollution levels

B) Smoking levels

C) Education levels

myeconlab Visit the MyEconLab website at **www.myeconlab.com**. This online homework and tutorial system puts you in control of your own learning with study and practice tools.

Making Smart Choices

The Law of Demand

LEARNING OBJECTIVES

After reading this appendix, you should be able to:

B.1 Describe what determines your willingness to pay for a product/service.

B.2 Identify why smart choices depend on marginal benefit, not total benefit, and explain what changes marginal benefit.

B.3 Describe the relationship between price and quantity demanded, and identify the role of substitutes.

B.4 Explain the difference between a change in quantity demanded and a change in demand, and distinguish five factors that change demand.

B.5 Define elasticity of demand and explain how it determines business pricing strategies.

BELIEVE IT OR NOT, economics is not really about money. It is about how individuals, businesses, and governments make the best possible choices to get what they want. Smart choices help you achieve happiness and success for yourself and others, help businesses make profits, and help governments spend your tax dollars wisely to make Canada a better place.

Of course, not all choices are smart or wise choices, and the Three Keys to Smart Choices from Appendix A are the keys to distinguishing smart from not-smart. The three keys are discussed more fully in this appendix.

This appendix focuses on choices you make every day as a consumer, and on the implications of those choices for how businesses price what they sell you. Economists use the term *demand* to summarize all of the influences on consumer choice.

B.1 Put Your Money Where Your Mouth Is: Weighing Benefits, Costs, and Substitutes

Describe what determines your willingness to pay for a product/ service.

You've just finished an intense workout at the gym and desperately want something to drink. You usually bring along your favourite Gatorade (which costs $3 a bottle), but today you forgot it. The snack bar has bottled water and juice, but no Gatorade. Your buddy, who is always trying to make a buck, says, "I have a bottle of what you want — how much will you pay for it?"

Besides wondering if this guy is really a buddy, what do you think about to determine how much you are willing to pay him? Obviously, how thirsty you are and how refreshed you expect to feel from the drink matter a lot. But just because you badly want Gatorade does not mean you will pay, say, $10 for the bottle.

What are your alternatives? You could buy a water or juice for $2, but they don't have the electrolytes for your muscles that Gatorade does. You could drink water from the faucet in the locker room for free. You could head home and drink the bottle you forgot, or head to a store to buy your Gatorade for $3.

You decide you so want the Gatorade *now* that you are willing to make an offer. You know your entrepreneurial buddy won't take less than the $3 he paid for the bottle, so you are willing to pay $4. You make the purchase, quench your thirst — and then ditch the buddy.

We all make hundreds of choices a day that are similar — what to eat, what to wear, what to buy, whether to spend time studying, working, working out, or partying, whom to vote for. . . . All these choices are based (consciously or unconsciously) on a comparison of expected benefits and costs. This is Key 1 of the Three Keys to Smart Choices from Appendix A: Choose only when additional benefits are greater than additional *opportunity costs*.

Choosing a substitute depends on what you will pay, what substitutes are available, and what they cost. Can you think of anything you use in life that doesn't have a substitute?

How Badly Do You Want It? The first part of the comparison requires you to have a sense of the expected benefits from choosing this product, service, experience, or use of your time. The expected benefit question is, "How badly do you want it?" What satisfaction do you expect to get from this choice? The want and the satisfaction might be quite logical — I want a warm coat so I won't freeze during the winter in Calgary; I want water because I am thirsty. I want to spend the evening studying because I have a test tomorrow. Or your desire for the latest, thinnest cell phone may be based on more emotional reasons — wanting to look cool, or to impress others, or just because, well, you want it. Businesses spend money on advertising, in part, to convince you to want their product. Economists describe all of your wants — and how intense each want is — as your **preferences**.

preferences: your wants and their intensities

What Will You Give Up? For the second part of the comparison, the cost question is, "How much are you willing to give up for it?" I purposely chose the words "give up" when you might have expected me to say, "How much are you willing to pay for it?" There's a reason for this choice, just as there are reasons for all of your choices. Many things we want — Gatorade or cell phones — we have to pay for with money. But with many other things we want, what we have to give up is our time or our effort. Spending the evening studying means not partying with friends or working at your part-time job. Cost always means opportunity cost — what you are willing to give up.

What determines *how much* you are willing to give up? Certainly, how badly you want it plays a role. But just as important is what your alternative choices are. There are substitutes for everything — water for Gatorade, a yoga class for a gym workout, long underwear or a move to Florida for winter coats. Substitutes need not be exactly the same product/service. Substitutes just have to basically satisfy the same want. For any choice you want to make, what you are willing to pay or give up depends on what substitutes are available, and what they cost.

The final factor determining how much you are willing to give up is how much you can afford. Are you able to pay the price of the product/service you want? Can you afford to take the time to party all evening when you have a test tomorrow?

The list of things we want is endless. But the choices we actually make reflect our willingness — and ability — to give up something in exchange. Economists use the term **demand** to describe consumers' willingness and ability to pay for a particular product/service (not just what consumers want). You must put your money (or time) where your mouth is in order to demand a product/service. And those demands, or choices, are smart choices only when expected benefits are greater than opportunity costs.

What you are willing to give up depends on available substitutes and their cost.

What you can "afford" is not just about money, it is also about time. You have limited dollars and limited time.

demand: consumers' willingness and ability to pay for a particular product/service

Refresh

B.1

1. What is the difference between wants and demands?

2. How many songs or albums by your favourite musician or group have you bought? How many have you copied or downloaded? What determined your choice between buying and downloading?

3. You have just started at a college that is a 30-minute drive from home or a 90-minute transit ride. How would you make a smart choice between taking the transit or buying a car? What are the important issues on the benefits comparison? On the cost comparison?

B.2 Living On the Edge: Smart Choices Are Marginal Choices

You make a smart choice only when expected benefits are greater than opportunity costs. But the benefits or satisfaction you expect to get depend on the circumstances.

Marginal Benefits Change with Circumstances

To see how benefits change with circumstances, let's return to the Gatorade example. Suppose you remembered to bring a bottle to the gym, and gulped it all after your workout. If your greedy buddy then asked you how much you were willing to pay for another bottle, chances are it would be much less than the $4 you were willing to pay when you had few convenient Gatorade alternatives. The *additional* benefit you will get from his second bottle is less than the benefit you got from your thirst-quenching first bottle. So your willingness to pay is less for the second bottle.

What if you have a test tomorrow, and you have to choose between spending the evening studying or going to a party with a friend? If you have been studying like mad for days already, the *additional* benefit of a few more hours might not help much, so you choose to party. But if you have been busy working at your job all week and haven't cracked a book, the *additional* benefit of studying will be large, and you give up the party time.

In both cases, the *additional* benefit you expect, and your willingness to pay (either in money or giving up party time you value), depends on the circumstances. The economist's term for *additional* benefit is **marginal benefit**. Marginal means "on or at the edge," just like the margins of these textbook pages are at the edges of the pages.

Key 2 of the Three Keys to Smart Choices says that when you compare expected benefits and costs, count only *additional* benefits and *additional* costs, or marginal benefits and marginal costs. Here we are explaining marginal benefits; in Appendix C we will explain marginal costs.

A smart decision to study (or not) does not depend on the total value of all hours spent studying, or the average value of an hour spent studying, but only on the *marginal* value of the additional time spent studying (compared with the additional cost of giving up those hours).

What if you choose to spend the evening studying, and your friend gets angry and shouts, "Is your stupid economics course more important than I am?!" At the margin, the answer is yes. Your choice to study tonight doesn't necessarily mean that, overall, you value the course more than the friend (well, depending on the friend, you might). What your choice means is that tonight, at the margin, you value the next few hours spent studying more than you value spending the next few hours with your friend.

marginal benefit: additional benefit from a choice, and changes with circumstances

The difference between total growth and marginal growth is the difference between "How tall are you?" and "How much have you grown?" Did your family mark your height on every birthday?

But margins, and circumstances, change. Your choice would be different if you had another week before the test, or if you hadn't seen your friend for months. The value you place on an activity or thing depends on the margin, and *that* additional value is marginal benefit.

Your friend's angry accusation comes from the common mistake (not smart) of looking at choices as all or nothing — friend versus economics. That's not the (smart) choice you made at the margin — the marginal benefit of the time spent studying tonight was greater than the value, or marginal benefit, of the same time spent with your friend.

Making smart choices means living life on the edge.

ECONOMICS Out There

Coke's Automatic Price Gouging

In the late 1990s, Coca-Cola Co. was working on technology to automatically raise prices in soft-drink vending machines on hot days. Critics — calling the plan "shameful" and a "cynical ploy" to exploit consumers "when they are most susceptible to price gouging" — suggested Coca-Cola should abandon the plan. The company claimed it was fair that the price should rise with demand, and that the machines simply automate that process. Unconvinced, critics warned that the plan would only alienate customers, with the reminder that "archrival Pepsi is out there, and you can hardly tell the difference."

- The public reaction to these variable-price vending machines was so negative that Coca-Cola never introduced them.

- However, the strategy is based on the correct observation that willingness to pay changes with circumstances — the principle of marginal benefit.

- The strategy failed not because the economics were wrong, but because the idea of paying different prices for the same product seemed so unfair — "price gouging." (There are examples where consumers accept businesses charging different consumers different prices for the same product — cellphone minutes cost providers the same, whether daytime, evening, or weekend. Why are prices different? *Hint:* Consumer willingness to pay.)

- Notice the line about Pepsi — substitutes are always available, which limits willingness to pay for any product, regardless of the marginal benefit.

Source: "Coke's Automatic Price Gouging," *San Francisco Chronicle*, October 29, 1999, p. A22.

The Diamond/Water Paradox

The distinction between looking at choices at the margin (smart) instead of as "all or nothing" or total-value choices helps make sense of the diamond/water paradox you may have heard about. What's more valuable in providing benefit or satisfaction — diamonds or water? One answer is water. Water is essential for survival, while diamonds are an unnecessary frill. But then why do diamonds cost far more than water?

You can solve the paradox by distinguishing marginal value from total value. You would die without any water, so you would be willing to pay everything you can for the first drink. But when water is abundant and cheap, and you are not dying of thirst, what would you be willing to pay, at the margin, for your next drink today? Not much. Marginal benefit is low, even though the total benefit of all water consumed (including the first, life-saving drink) is high.

Diamonds won't keep you alive, but they are relatively scarce, and desirable for that very reason. What would you pay for what is likely your first diamond? A lot. Marginal benefit is high. But because diamonds are scarce, there aren't many out there (compared to drinks of water), so total benefit is low. But willingness to pay depends on marginal benefit, not total benefit, so people are generally willing to pay more for a diamond (high marginal benefit) than for a glass of water (low marginal benefit).

Marginal benefit, as we will see in Appendix D, is important not only for making smart choices, but also for explaining how prices are determined in the real world.

Willingness to pay, a key part of demand, depends on marginal benefit, not total benefit. If you think about total benefit you will get confused in Section B.3. Think marginal!

Refresh B.2

1. What is marginal benefit, and on what does it depend?

2. Why are you willing to pay more for a diamond than a glass of water even though water is essential for survival and diamonds are an unnecessary luxury?

3. You and your entrepreneurial buddy have a concession stand on the beach. It is a hot, sunny, crowded day, and you are selling a few $5 collapsible umbrellas as sun parasols. The skies suddenly darken, rain begins to pour, and your buddy quickly switches the umbrella price sign to $10. Will you sell more or fewer umbrellas? Explain your thinking, including your analysis of the customer's decision.

www.myeconlab.com

B.3 When the Price Isn't Right: The Law of Demand

After weeks of boring bus rides to school and overhearing too many other riders' personal cell phone conversations, you finally decide to buy an iPod. You research the alternatives and decide to buy the low-capacity Nano. You would have loved a bigger hard drive or an iPhone, but decided you couldn't afford those.

Describe the relationship between price and quantity demanded, and identify the role of substitutes.

Quantity Demanded

Let's presume you made a smart choice, so the additional benefit of this iPod (listening pleasure and blocking out the world) is greater than the additional cost (the $150 price tag). You are willing and able to pay $150. Sold! An economist would say that, at the price of $150, your *quantity demanded* of iPod Nanos is 1.

Quantity demanded, as we will see, is not the same as *demand.* **Quantity demanded** is the amount you actually plan to buy at a given price, taking into account everything that affects your willingness and ability to pay.

We saw in the previous section that when circumstances change the additional benefit, your choice may change. The second bottle of Gatorade wasn't worth as much as the first, and the value of an iPod would change if you were driving to school in a car with a radio instead of riding the bus. But our focus here is not on benefits. Our focus is on *what happens to your buying decision when the additional cost (what you pay) changes.*

Changing Prices Change Quantity Demanded   What if this iPod model were priced at $175 instead of $150? How might that change your decision to buy? You might want an iPod so badly that you would be willing to pay $175, judging that the additional benefit is still greater than the $175 cost. (That means that at $150, you felt you were getting a bargain!) But since you are a smart shopper and have limited income, you would still be thinking carefully about alternatives. There are substitutes for everything. For music and sound-blocking there are other (cheaper) MP3 players, used iPods, music downloaded to your cell phone, radios, or your older sister's ancient Discman. The extra $25 cost might be enough to change your choice from an iPod Nano to one of these substitutes. And if the price were $225, you, along with many more consumers out there, would definitely change your smart choice away from an iPod Nano to a substitute. At a price of $225, your quantity demanded is zero.

What if Nanos went on sale for $75 instead of $150? Given your willingness and ability to pay, this is such a bargain that you decide to buy two — one for you, and one as a gift for your boy/girlfriend. At a price of $75, your quantity demanded is two.

quantity demanded: amount you actually plan to buy at a given price

If we put your combinations of prices (willingness to pay) and quantities demanded into a table, it looks like Figure B.1.

Figure B.1 Your Demand for the iPod Nano	
Price (willing to pay)	**Quantity Demanded**
$ 75	2
$150	1
$225	0

As your eye goes down the two columns, notice that as the price rises, the quantity demanded decreases. In general, when prices rise, consumers look for substitutes. When something becomes more expensive, people economize on its use.

Water or Brooms?   Households in the City of Toronto used to pay a flat monthly rate for water that didn't change with the quantity of water used. So the *additional* cost of using more water was zero. With "free" marginal water, many residents would "sweep" their sidewalks and driveways with a hose. But when water became metered, so that users paid for each additional cubic metre, many gave up this practice and started sweeping with a broom. (Only economics teaches you that water and brooms are substitutes!) Other reactions to higher water prices included putting bricks in toilet tanks to save water, placing flow regulators on showers, taking showers instead of baths, and planting groundcover that consumes less water than grass. With a higher price for water, the quantity demanded decreased.

The Law of Demand

The market for any product or service consists of millions of potential customers, each trying to make a smart choice about what to buy. **Market demand** is the sum of the demands of all individuals willing and able to buy a particular product/service.

Whether it is the market for iPods, water, or anything else, substitutes exist, so that consumers buy a smaller quantity at higher prices, and a larger quantity at lower prices. This inverse relationship (when one goes up, the other goes down) between price and quantity demanded is so universal that economists call it (somewhat grandiosely) the **law of demand**: If the price of a product/service rises, the quantity demanded of the product/service decreases. The law of demand works as long as other factors besides price do not change. The next section will explore what happens when other factors do change. Will the law of demand then fail? Stay tuned.

When the price of a product rises, consumers switch to cheaper substitutes. The quantity demanded of the original product, at the now higher price, decreases.

market demand: sum of demands of all individuals willing and able to buy a particular product/service

law of demand: if the price of a product/service rises, quantity demanded decreases

Market Demand for Water   Figure B.2 illustrates the inverse relationship between price and quantity demanded for the market demand for water.

Figure B.2	Market Demand for Water
Price **(per cubic metre)**	**Quantity Demanded** **(000's of cubic metres/month)**
$1.00	5
$1.50	4
$2.00	3
$2.50	2
$3.00	1

The law of demand is yet another way of saying that when something becomes more expensive, people economize on its use. This law helps explain many decisions beyond shopping decisions. Mother Teresa's charity wanted to open a shelter for the homeless in New York City. When city bureaucrats insisted on expensive but unnecessary renovations to the building, the charity abandoned the project. Mother Teresa didn't abandon her commitment to the poor. When the cost of helping the poor in New York went up, she decided that, at the margin, her efforts would do more good elsewhere. For her charity, a shelter elsewhere was a substitute for a New York shelter.

Because there are substitutes for everything, higher prices create incentives for smart consumers to reduce their purchases of more expensive products/services and look for alternatives.

A change to a new behaviour can often be encouraged by an increase in the cost of an old behaviour. How much would a litre of gas have to cost before you switched to a bicycle?

Refresh B.3

1. What is the law of demand?

2. You own a car and work at a job that is not accessible by public transit. If the price of gasoline goes up dramatically, does the law of demand apply to you? Explain the choices you might make in response to this increase in price.

3. You have plans to go to a concert tonight, but your mother, who is helping you pay for school, says that it's very important to her that you instead come to Grandma's birthday party. Explain how your decision to celebrate with Grandma illustrates the law of demand in terms of your concert plans.

www.myeconlab.com

B.4 Moving the Margins: What Can Change Demand?

Explain the difference between a change in quantity demanded and a change in demand, and distinguish between five factors that change demand.

The price of gasoline in Halifax rose from $0.99 per litre to $1.36 per litre between 2006 and 2008. But the quantity of gasoline motorists bought actually *increased*. Does that disprove the "law of demand"?

If nothing else changed except the price of gasoline, the answer would be yes — and I'd have to quit this job as an economist and do something more socially useful, like being a trash collector.

But I, and other economists, have enough confidence in the law of demand that if we observe a rise in price leading to an *increase* in purchases, we take it as a signal that something else must have changed at the same time.

Economists use the concept of *demand* to summarize all the influences on consumer choice. Your demand for any product/service reflects your willingness and ability to pay. In the examples of Gatorade, iPods, and water, we have seen that your willingness to pay depends on things like your preferences, what substitutes are available, and marginal benefit. Your ability to pay depends on your income.

As long as all these factors (and a few more) do not change, the law of demand holds true: If the price of a product/service rises, the quantity demanded decreases.

But when change happens, economists distinguish between two kinds of change:

- If the price of a product/service changes, that affects *quantity demanded*.
- If anything else changes, that affects *demand*.

Quantity demanded is a much more limited term than *demand*. Only a change in price changes quantity demanded. A change in any other influence on consumer choice changes demand. This may sound like semantic hair-splitting — quantity demanded versus demand — but it is important for avoiding not-smart thinking.

Why Bother Distinguishing Between Quantity Demanded and Demand?

Suppose you observe a witch placing a curse on some poor young man, who dies a month later. The apparent conclusion is that the curse was fatal. But if the witch had been secretly poisoning his food with arsenic all along, what was the real cause of death? Something else changed that was really behind the observed result.

What if a gasoline supplier decides to raise his prices to increase his sales, based on the observed result that when gasoline prices rose, motorists bought more gasoline. What do you think would happen? Would this be a smart choice?

We live in a complicated world, where everything depends on everything else. There are obvious connections between events like a lottery windfall increasing your spending, or high CD prices increasing music downloads. But non-economic events like the weather can affect coffee prices, and a whiff of a terrorist threat can sink airline stock prices. So when you observe a change in the economy like increased gasoline purchases, how do you decide what caused it when so many interdependent things can change at the same time? (Was the young man's death caused by curse, arsenic, or natural causes?)

In the real world, everything is related to everything else, making it difficult to distinguish an event's actual causes from apparent causes. Scientists use controlled laboratory experiments to keep all interrelated factors unchanged. Economists can't conduct controlled experiments. Instead, we use distinctions like change in quantity demanded versus change in demand to mentally mimic controlled experiments.

Controlled Experiments Scientists deal with this interdependence problem by performing controlled experiments in a laboratory. The law of gravity claims that, all other factors unchanged, objects fall at the same rate regardless of their weight. So if we drop a bowling ball and a feather from a tall building, and find the bowling ball hits the ground first, does that disprove the law of gravity? No, because we are not controlling for air resistance, which changes the path of the feather more than the bowling ball. To accurately test the law of gravity, we must perform the same experiment in a laboratory vacuum, so that we eliminate, or control for, the influence of air resistance as an "other factor." We need to keep all other factors unchanged.

Economists, and citizens like you, have it much tougher than scientists. We can't pause everything in the world except for the factors we are interested in. Instead, we have to use economics to make sense of the changes. The distinction between a change in quantity demanded and a change in demand is the economist's way of trying to mentally mimic a controlled experiment.

The law of demand is the simplest of all the interdependent relationships. *If nothing else changes,* a rise in the price of gasoline will cause a decrease in the quantity demanded of gasoline.

Let's look at the more complicated parts (like air resistance for the law of gravity) — all the important "other things" that can cause a change in demand.

Five Ways to Change Demand

Only a change in the price of a product/service itself changes *quantity demanded* of that product/service. But there are five important other factors that can change market demand — the willingness and ability to pay for a product/service. They are:

- Preferences
- Prices of related products
- Income
- Expected future prices
- Number of consumers

Preferences There are many reasons why businesses advertise, but ultimately they are trying to get you to want their product, to persuade you that you need what they sell. Remember that economists use the term "preferences" to describe your wants and their intensities — so, for an economist, advertising is about increasing your preferences for a product/service.

Most car commercials are not about information but about showing you a fabulous, fun driving experience that the manufacturer wants you to believe will be yours only if you buy its car.

All businesses want to increase your preferences, because if they succeed in increasing the intensity of your want or desire for their product you will be willing to pay more for it. If Apple were to run a successful ad campaign that makes you and many other consumers feel you can't live (and be cool) without an iPod, what would happen to your willingness and ability to pay, according to our earlier example? Look at Figure B.3 on the next page.

Price (before advertising)	Price (after advertising)	Quantity Demanded
$ 75	$100	2
$150	$200	1
$225	$300	0

Before advertising, you were willing and able to pay $150 for one iPod (row 2), while after you are now willing to pay $200. Before you were willing to buy two iPods at a price of $75 each (row 1), while after you will pay $100 each and buy two.

Your ability to pay has not changed in this example, it's just that you are willing to give up more of your unchanged income because the intensity of your wants has increased. Advertising has succeeded in moving the margin, increasing both the marginal benefit you expect to get from the iPod and your willingness to pay. Economists call any increase in consumers' willingness and ability to pay an **increase in demand**. Consumers will now be willing to pay a higher price for the same quantity of a product.

Changes in preferences can also cause a decrease in demand. What if a Health Canada study shows conclusively that regular listening to an iPod causes serious hearing loss and causes mushrooms to grow out of your ears? If you and other consumers believe the study, consumers' willingness and ability to pay decreases, which results in a **decrease in demand** for iPods. Consumers will now be willing to pay only a lower price for the same quantity of a product.

When the Rolling Stones played their only 2006 Canadian concert in Moncton, New Brunswick, what happened to the demand for hotel rooms in Moncton? The large number of fans attending the concert increased the willingness to pay and *increased the demand* for hotel rooms. On the other hand, think of demand by tourists for hotel rooms in Toronto before and after the 2003 SARS epidemic. The fear of infectious disease decreased tourists' preferences for Toronto hotel bookings. With decreased willingness to pay, there was a decrease in demand for Toronto hotel rooms.

Any change in preferences causes a change in demand. An increase in preferences causes an increase in demand. A decrease in preferences causes a decrease in demand.

Prices of Related Products

Many products/services you choose to buy are related. Changes in price of a different, related product/service will affect your demand for the original product/service. There are two main types of related products: substitutes and complements.

Substitutes are products/services that can be used in place of each other to satisfy the same want. Examples of substitutes are iPods and other MP3 players for listening to music, or water and Gatorade for quenching thirst.

increase in demand: increase in consumers' willingness and ability to pay

decrease in demand: decrease in consumers' willingness and ability to pay

A change in preferences causes a change in demand, not a change in quantity demanded.

substitutes: products/services used in place of each other to satisfy the same want

What happens to your demand for iPods when the price of other MP3 players falls drastically? You are not willing to pay as much for an iPod, as your smart choice now involves a much cheaper alternative. A fall in the price of a substitute causes a decrease in demand for the related product.

If the price of water skyrockets because of a drought, your willingness to pay for Gatorade increases. A rise in the price of a substitute causes an increased demand for the related product.

Complements are products/services that tend to be used together to satisfy the same want. iTunes and iPods are complementary products, as are hot dogs and hot dog buns, or cars and gasoline.

If song prices at the iTunes Store drop from 99 cents to 49 cents, that makes owning an iPod more attractive, and will increase your willingness to pay for an iPod. A fall in the price of a complement causes an increased demand for the related product because the cost of using both products together has decreased.

When gasoline prices rose significantly in 2008, gas-guzzling 8-cylinder SUVs became much more expensive to operate. The rise in gas prices caused a decrease in the demand for 8-cylinder SUVs. A rise in the price of a complement causes a decreased demand for the related product because the cost of using both products together has increased.

Income   If you now had a million dollars, that would have a large impact on your demand for products/services. Demand reflects your willingness and ability to pay. With more money, or more income, you are more able (and still willing) to pay for things and not worry about it. But not always.

Take your demand for iPods from Figure B.3, before any advertising (columns 1 and 3). If your income increased, the impact on your willingness and ability to pay would be similar to the impact of an increase in preferences (column 2). At each quantity, you are still willing and now *able to pay more*, so the increase in income causes an increase in demand. The intensity of your wants doesn't change with a change in income, but what you have to *give up in other products/services* falls. With more income, you can spend more on an iPod and still have lots of extra cash to buy other things. Higher income lowers your real opportunity cost of spending. There is more "get" and less "give up."

If unfortunately your income falls, so does your ability to pay, and your demand for iPods would decrease.

Economists call products like iPods **normal goods** — products/services that you buy more of when your income increases. For a normal good, an increase in income causes an increase in demand, and a decrease in income causes a decrease in demand.

But not all products are normal goods. Can you think of products/services you buy now as a poor student that you will buy *less of* when your income goes up? If you have been living on Kraft Dinner, you may never want to eat it again once you can afford real food. And what about those endless bus rides? If you could afford a car, what would happen to your demand for public transit?

Economists call these products/services, where an increase in income causes a *decrease* in demand, **inferior goods** — products/services that you buy less of when your income increases. Similarly, a decrease in income causes an increase in demand for inferior goods.

complements: products/services used together to satisfy the same want

normal goods: products/services you buy more of when your income increases

inferior goods: products/services you buy less of when your income increases

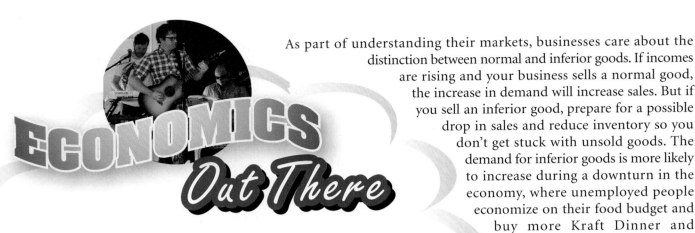

As part of understanding their markets, businesses care about the distinction between normal and inferior goods. If incomes are rising and your business sells a normal good, the increase in demand will increase sales. But if you sell an inferior good, prepare for a possible drop in sales and reduce inventory so you don't get stuck with unsold goods. The demand for inferior goods is more likely to increase during a downturn in the economy, where unemployed people economize on their food budget and buy more Kraft Dinner and Hamburger Helper.

Expected Future Prices

Smart choices depend not only on prices and incomes today, but also on our expectation of future prices. Consumers choose between substitutes, and one of many possible substitutions is a purchase tomorrow for a purchase today. We do this all the time with gasoline. If it's the weekend and you decide to wait until mid-week to buy gas because you expect the price to fall, that decreases your demand for gasoline today. Likewise, if you are expecting prices to rise, you fill up now, increasing your demand for gasoline today. Notice that your decision is not determined by the current price (that would be a quantity demanded decision), but only by whether you expect the current price (whatever it may be) to fall or rise in the future.

An expected future price fall causes a decrease in demand today. An expected future price rise causes an increase in demand today.

A fall in expected future price causes a decrease in demand today (bargain in future). A rise in expected future price causes an increase in demand today (bargain today).

Number of Consumers So far, for all the factors that change demand, the explanations are the same for a single individual as they are for the group of all consumers whose combined willingness and ability to pay make up market demand. For any quantity demanded, we examine how a change in each factor affects the price the consumer is willing and able to pay. Each such change in demand changes marginal benefit and moves the margin. For the fifth factor, the number of consumers, the explanation makes more sense if we reverse the story. Start with any price, and examine how a change in consumer numbers affects quantity demanded. For each price, if the number of consumers increases, we need to add together all the quantities demanded by all consumers at that price.

Let's take our earlier table of the market demand for water, and add a third column showing the quantity demanded after many new households move into the city and start using water. Take a look at Figure B.4.

Figure B.4　Market Demand for Water with More Households

Price (cubic metre)	Quantity Demanded (000's of cubic metres/month)	Quantity Demanded with More Households (000's of cubic metres/month)
$1.00	5	10
$1.50	4	8
$2.00	3	6
$2.50	2	4
$3.00	1	2

Not surprisingly with additional households (last column), at any price (first column) the quantity demanded is greater than it was originally (middle column). The increased number of consumers causes an increase in demand, just as an increase in preferences or an increase in income (for normal goods) causes an increase in demand. A decrease in the number of consumers causes a decrease in demand, just as a decrease in the price of a substitute product/service or a decrease in expected future prices causes a decrease in demand.

Any increase (or decrease) in demand can be described in alternative ways. For the four previous factors, the description for an increase in demand is:

- At any given quantity demanded, consumers are willing and able to pay a higher price.

For the number of consumers, the description for an increase in demand is:

- At any given price, consumers plan to buy a larger quantity.

For an increase in demand, these two alternative descriptions of the connection between price and quantity demanded are summarized in Figure B.5. Depending on the economic event you are trying to make sense of, sometimes you will use one description, and sometimes the other.

Increased number of consumers causes an increase in demand. Decreased number of consumers causes a decrease in demand.

Figure B.5　Relating Price and Quantity Demanded for an Increase in Demand

Given quantity demanded	⟷	Higher price
Higher quantity demanded	⟷	Given price

Saving the Law of Demand

You have learned to distinguish between a change in quantity demanded (caused by a change in the price of the product) and a change in demand (caused by changes in preferences, prices of related products, income, expected future prices, and/or number of consumers). Can we now explain why, when gasoline prices increased from $0.99 per litre to $1.36 per litre between 2006 and 2008, the quantity of gasoline motorists bought actually increased? Can we save the law of demand?

According to the law of demand, if the price of a product rises, the quantity demanded of the product decreases (as long as other factors besides price do not change). The rise in gas prices alone would have caused a decrease in quantity demanded, *but other things also changed.*

While a complete explanation is more complex (involving supply factors from Appendix C as well as demand), a major change was the increased number of drivers and cars on the road. This increase in the number of consumers increased demand for gasoline. The impact of the increase in demand outweighed the impact of the decrease in quantity demanded.

To conclusively explain whether the witch's curse or the arsenic killed the poor young man, you need a controlled experiment. And without the economist's equivalent of a controlled experiment — the mental distinction between quantity demanded and demand — you never would have been able to explain what happened in the gasoline market.

Figure B.6 is a good study device for reviewing the difference between the law of demand (focused on quantity demanded) and the factors that change demand.

Figure B.6	Law of Demand and Changes in Demand
The Law of Demand	
The quantity demanded of a product/service	
Decreases if:	*Increases if:*
■ price of the product/service rises	■ price of the product/service falls
Changes in Demand	
The demand for a product/service	
Decreases if:	*Increases if:*
■ preferences decrease	■ preferences increase
■ price of a substitute falls	■ price of a substitute rises
■ price of a complement rises	■ price of a complement falls
■ income decreases (normal good)	■ income increases (normal good)
■ income increases (inferior good)	■ income decreases (inferior good)
■ expected future price falls	■ expected future price rises
■ number of customers decreases	■ number of customers increases

Refresh
B.4

1. Explain the difference between a change in quantity demanded and a change in demand. Distinguish the five factors that can change demand.

2. Roses sell for about $40 a bouquet most of the year, and worldwide sales are 6 million bouquets per month. Every February, the price of roses doubles to $80 a bouquet, but the quantity of roses demanded and sold also increases, to 24 million bouquets per month. The cost of producing roses doesn't change throughout the year. Can you explain what else is going on that saves the law of demand?

3. There are some "status goods," like Rolex watches, that people want to own *because* they are expensive. In contradiction to the law of demand, if Rolex watches were less expensive, few "status seeking" consumers would demand them. Is there any way to reconcile these products/services with the law of demand? You might think about what it is that consumers are buying — watches or status? And how does the existence of cheap "knock-off" imitations of Rolex watches fit with the law of demand?

B.5 Just How Badly Do You Want It? Price Elasticity of Demand and Total Revenue

Don't you love a good sale — 50 percent off, 70 percent off? Most consumers do. No matter how much you are willing and able to pay for a product/service, it's always a treat to pay less, which leaves you with cash to buy more of anything you want.

But do *businesses* love a good sale? Profit-seeking businesses would rather charge higher prices for what they sell. But to get consumers to buy, businesses must pick price points that match the market's (all consumers') willingness and ability to pay. Higher prices might not always be best for business. Why do businesses have 70-percent-off sales, voluntarily lowering prices and bringing in less per unit?

I'm sure you have heard the answer to this question: "They'll make it up on volume!" Lower prices mean lower profit margins per unit, but a greater quantity sold.

How do businesses decide whether they will be better off selling to consumers at a higher price or a lower price?

We know from the law of demand that (all other things unchanged) a rise in price causes a decrease in quantity demanded, and a fall in price (sale's on!) causes an increase in quantity demanded (more volume). A smart business pricing decision depends on by how much quantity demanded changes when price changes. What changes more, the price or the quantity? This responsiveness of quantity demanded to a change in price is related to just how badly consumers want the product/service.

◄

Sales are good for consumers, but are they always bad for businesses?

The tool that businesses use every day to measure consumer responsiveness and make pricing decisions is what economists call the **price elasticity of demand** (say *that* three times quickly for a tongue twister). This section will help you make sense of that tool, which businesses mercifully abbreviate to elasticity. **Elasticity** measures by how much quantity demanded responds to a change in price.

elasticity (or price elasticity of demand): measures by how much quantity demanded responds to a change in price

Measuring Your Responsiveness

Whenever you see the word "elasticity," think "responsiveness."

Elasticity is all about responsiveness. When you pull on an elastic, by how much does it stretch or respond? When the price of a product changes, price elasticity of demand measures by how much quantity demanded responds.

If you have diabetes, you have a high willingness to pay for insulin. What happens to the quantity of insulin demanded when the price rises? Not much decrease. If the price rises enough, quantity demanded may decrease slightly as diabetics who are poorest perhaps try to get by with a little less per dose. But for the market demand for insulin, there is very little response of quantity demanded to a rise in price. Economists describe the demand for insulin as **inelastic**: There is a small response (or "give") in the quantity demanded when price rises.

inelastic: for inelastic demand, small response in quantity demanded when price rises

What about the market demand for yellow tennis balls? If the price of yellow tennis balls rises, what happens? Most players consider green or orange tennis balls to be identical substitutes, and aren't willing to pay a premium for yellow. Players switch to non-yellow balls, so the quantity demanded of yellow tennis balls decreases drastically. There is a large response of quantity demanded to a rise in price. The demand for yellow tennis balls is called **elastic**: there is a large response in the quantity demanded when price rises.

elastic: for elastic demand, large response in quantity demanded when price rises

Businesses use a simple formula to calculate elasticity.

$$\text{Price elasticity of demand} = \frac{\text{Percentage change in quantity demanded}}{\text{Percentage change in price}}$$

The formula assumes that all of the other five factors that can affect demand are unchanged, so this is a controlled measurement of just the relationship (in the law of demand) between quantity demanded and price.

Let's substitute some numbers into the formula for our examples.

For insulin, if a 10-percent rise in price causes a 2-percent decrease in quantity demanded, the calculation is

Demand is inelastic when the calculation of $\frac{(\% \text{ change in quantity})}{(\% \text{ change in price})}$ gives a value less than 1.

$$\text{Price elasticity of demand for insulin} = \frac{2 \text{ percent}}{10 \text{ percent}} = 0.2$$

Because the percentage change in quantity in the numerator (2) is less than the percentage change in price in the denominator (10), the value for elasticity is less than 1. Any elasticity value less than 1 is considered to be inelastic.

(If you are thinking that my math isn't quite right, good for you! Technically, the correct answer would be − 0.2. However, even an economist will ignore the negative sign in calculating price elasticity of demand. You will be pleased to know that economists don't like negative numbers any more than you do.)

For yellow tennis balls, if a 10-percent rise in price causes a 50-percent decrease in quantity demanded, the calculation is

Demand is elastic when the calculation of $\frac{(\% \text{ change in quantity})}{(\% \text{ change in price})}$ gives a value greater than 1.

$$\text{Price elasticity of demand for yellow tennis balls} = \frac{50 \text{ percent}}{10 \text{ percent}} = 5$$

Because the percentage change in quantity in the numerator (50) is greater than the percentage change in price in the denominator (10), the value for elasticity is greater than 1. Any elasticity value greater than 1 is elastic. So when the value for elasticity is less than 1, demand is inelastic. Are you wondering what demand is called when elasticity is exactly equal to 1? No, I didn't think so. But for the sake of completeness, here's your answer: When elasticity equals 1, demand is "unit elastic." The percentage change in quantity equals the percentage change in price.

One other way to think about the different values for elasticity is willingness to shop elsewhere if you don't get a low price.

If the price rises for products/services with:

- *inelastic demands,* consumers have a low willingness to shop elsewhere.
- *elastic demands,* consumers have a high willingness to shop elsewhere.

Why Are You (Un)Responsive? Factors Determining Elasticity

Three main factors influence price elasticity of demand, or "willingness to shop elsewhere if you don't get a low price": the availability of substitutes, time to adjust, and proportion of income spent on a product/service. Let's look at each.

Available Substitutes   The law of demand says that when something becomes more expensive, people economize on its use and look for substitutes. The more substitutes there are, the easier it is to switch away from a product/service whose price rises, and the more elastic is demand. Yellow tennis balls have excellent substitutes, so the demand for tennis balls is elastic. Insulin has almost no substitutes, so the demand for insulin is inelastic.

The more, and better, substitutes available, the greater elasticity of demand.

Time to Adjust to Price Rise   When prices rise, it often takes time to adjust and to find substitutes. If gasoline prices rise and you have to drive to work, you can't do much initially to decrease your quantity of gasoline demanded — you can cut back on pleasure driving and errands. With more time, you could arrange a car pool, and with much more time, you might buy a more fuel-efficient car or move closer to work. Time allows consumers to find substitutes. The longer the time to adjust to a price rise, the more elastic demand becomes.

The longer time to adjust to a price rise, the more elastic demand becomes.

Proportion of Income Spent on a Product/Service   Suppose the price of salt doubles from $1 per kilo to $2 per kilo. By how much will you reduce your quantity demanded of salt? Not much. What if the price of a car doubles from $20 000 to $40 000? The quantity demanded of cars will collapse. The key difference between the examples is in the proportion of income spent on the product. We spend a tiny fraction of our income on salt, so a big price rise doesn't increase our total expenditure much. But buying a car is often the largest purchase you will make, other than buying a house: A big price rise makes it unaffordable. The greater the proportion of income spent on a product, the greater the elasticity of demand.

The greater the proportion of income spent on a product, the greater elasticity of demand.

When Are Price Cuts Smart Business? Elasticity and Total Revenue

If you hold a 70-percent-off sale, consumers will be happy, but will your business be better off? Whether a business will be better off from raising prices or cutting prices depends on the elasticity of demand for its product/service.

"Better off," in this appendix, means the business will have higher total revenue. **Total revenue** is all of the money received from sales, and is equal to the price per unit (P) multiplied by the quantity sold (Q).

$$\text{Total revenue} = P \times Q$$

A wonderfully simple relationship exists between elasticity and total revenue. When a business cuts prices,

- if demand for its product/service is *elastic,* the percentage increase in quantity is greater than the percentage decrease in price, so *total revenue* ($P \times Q$) *increases.*
- if demand for its product/service is *inelastic,* the percentage increase in quantity is less than the percentage decrease in price, so *total revenue* ($P \times Q$) *decreases.*

Figure B.7 summarizes the relationship between elasticity and total revenue for a price cut.

Figure B.7	Elasticity and Total Revenue	
When Demand Is:		**Price Cut Causes:**
Elastic (> 1)	% change in Q > % change in P	Increased total revenue
Inelastic (< 1)	% change in Q < % change in P	Decreased total revenue

For the sake of completeness, when demand is unit elastic (= 1), the percentage increase in quantity equals the percentage decrease in price, so total revenue remains the same.

Price Cuts Are Smart When Facing Elastic Demand   So a price cut is a smart decision when your business faces elastic demand. You receive a lower price on each unit sold, but you do make it up on volume! The percentage increase in quantity outweighs the percentage decrease in price, so total revenue increases.

If you are selling yellow tennis balls, consumers' demand for your product is elastic, which means that if they don't get a low price, they are very willing and able to shop elsewhere because good substitutes are available. When you cut the price of yellow tennis balls even a little, you attract all of the bargain-hunters who are currently using green or orange tennis balls. Your total revenue increases because the large increase in quantity outweighs the small cut in price.

total revenue: all money a business receives from sales, equal to price per unit (P) multiplied by quantity sold (Q)

Price cuts are the smart choice facing elastic demand, and increase total revenue.

Price Rises Are Smart When Facing Inelastic Demand   The smart decision when your business faces inelastic demand is to raise prices. You receive a higher price on each unit sold, and while you lose some sales, the percentage increase in price is greater than the percentage decrease in quantity, so total revenue increases.

If you are selling insulin, consumers' demand is inelastic, which means that they will not easily shop elsewhere because there are no good substitutes. When you raise the price of insulin, you don't lose many customers. Your total revenue increases because the increase in price outweighs the small decrease in quantity.

Smart Pricing Decisions Depend on Elasticity of Demand   Price elasticity of demand is important for any business pricing decision, even the price you get in haggling with a car dealer. Most consumers hate haggling over price because the dealer has better information about costs and knows how low he is willing to go on price. Your best strategy as a buyer is to try to convince the dealer that you will walk out if you don't get a low price, that you don't like this particular car that much and are considering alternative models from other manufacturers, or that you are not very wealthy. In other words, *you want the dealer to believe that your demand is elastic,* that you are willing to shop elsewhere if you don't get a low price because good substitutes are available. If you convince the dealer, then his best pricing decision is to offer you a very low price, because he believes that if he doesn't he will lose the sale entirely.

On the other hand, if the dealer thinks that you are not likely to walk out, that you love this particular car much more than any alternatives, or that you are wealthy and not price conscious, he takes these as signals that your demand is inelastic. His best pricing decision, because he believes this is a pretty sure sale, is to try to convince you to take expensive options that will actually increase the price above the sticker price.

All businesses have to live by the law of demand — a rise in price causes a decrease in quantity demanded. Smart businesses choose their price points depending on how much consumers' quantity demanded responds to a change in price — in other words, on price elasticity of demand.

Refresh B.5

1. Explain the relationship between price and quantity demanded for inelastic demand and for elastic demand.

2. If a jewellery store cuts its prices by 20 percent, and finds that its quantity sold increases by 40 percent, calculate its price elasticity of demand. Is it elastic or inelastic?

3. Concession stands at movie theatres charge high prices for popcorn, drinks, and other refreshments. This pricing strategy increases total revenue. What does that imply about the price elasticity of demand for refreshments in movie theatres? What theatre policy helps make this demand elastic or inelastic?

www.myeconlab.com

Making *Smart* *Choices*

The Law of Demand

APPENDIX SUMMARY

B.1 PUT YOUR MONEY WHERE YOUR MOUTH IS: WEIGHING BENEFITS, COSTS, AND SUBSTITUTES

Your willingness to buy a product/service depends on your ability to pay, comparative benefits and costs, and the availability of substitutes.

- **Preferences** — your wants and their intensities.
- **Demand** — consumers' willingness and ability to pay for a particular product/service.
- For any choice, what you are willing to pay or give up depends on the cost and availability of substitutes.

B.2 LIVING ON THE EDGE: SMART CHOICES ARE MARGINAL CHOICES

Key 2 for smart choices states, "Count only additional benefits and additional costs." Additional benefit means marginal benefit — not total benefit — and marginal benefit changes with circumstances.

- **Marginal benefit** — additional benefit from a choice, and changes with circumstances.
- Marginal benefit explains the diamond/water paradox. Why do diamonds cost more than water, when water is far more valuable for survival? Willingness to pay depends on marginal benefit, not total benefit. Because water is abundant, marginal benefit is low. Because diamonds are scarce, marginal benefit is high.

B.3 WHEN THE PRICE ISN'T RIGHT: THE LAW OF DEMAND

If the price of a product/service rises, the quantity demanded decreases. Consumers economize on products/services that become more expensive by switching to substitutes.

- **Quantity demanded** — amount you actually plan to buy at a given price.
- **Market demand** — sum of demands of all individuals willing and able to buy a particular product/service.

- **Law of demand** — if the price of a product/service rises, quantity demanded decreases.

B.4 MOVING THE MARGINS: WHAT CAN CHANGE DEMAND?

Quantity demanded is changed only by a change in price. Demand is changed by all other influences on consumer choice.

- Demand is a catch-all term summarizing all possible influences on consumers' willingness and ability to pay for a particular product/service.
  - **Increase in demand** — increase in consumers' willingness and ability to pay.
  - **Decrease in demand** — decrease in consumers' willingness and ability to pay.
- Demand changes with changes in preferences, prices of related goods, income, expected future price, and number of consumers. For example, demand increases with:
  - increase in preferences.
  - rise in price of a **substitute** — products/services used in place of each other to satisfy the same want.
  - fall in price of a **complement** — products/services used together to satisfy the same want.
  - increase in income for **normal goods** — products/services you buy more of when your income increases.
  - decrease in income for **inferior goods** — products/services you buy less of when your income increases.
  - rise in expected future prices.
  - increase in number of consumers.

B.5 JUST HOW BADLY DO YOU WANT IT? PRICE ELASTICITY OF DEMAND AND TOTAL REVENUE

Elasticity measures how responsive quantity demanded is to a change in price, and determines business pricing strategies to earn maximum total revenue. To earn maximum total revenue, businesses cut prices when demand is elastic and raise prices when demand is inelastic.

- The tool that businesses use to measure consumer responsiveness when making pricing decisions is **elasticity** (or **price elasticity of demand**), which measures by how much quantity demanded responds to a change in price.
- The formula is:

$$\text{Price elasticity of demand} = \frac{\text{Percentage change in quantity demanded}}{\text{Percentage change in price}}$$

- **Inelastic** — For inelastic demand, small response in quantity demanded when price rises.
  - Example: Demand for insulin by a diabetic.
  - Value for formula is less than one.
  - Low willingness to shop elsewhere.

- **Elastic** — For elastic demand, large response in quantity demanded when price rises.
  - Example: Demand for yellow tennis balls.
  - Value for formula is greater than one.
  - High willingness to shop elsewhere.
- The price elasticity of demand of a product/service is influenced by:
  - substitutes — more substitute goods mean more elastic demand.
  - time to adjust — longer time to adjust means more elastic demand.
  - proportion of income spent on a product/service — greater proportion of income spent means more elastic demand.
- **Total revenue** — (all money a business receives from sales) = price per unit (P) multiplied by quantity sold (Q).
  - Price rises are the smart choice facing inelastic demand, and increase total revenue.
  - Price cuts are the smart choice facing elastic demand, and increase total revenue.

TRUE/FALSE

Circle the correct answer.

B.1 WEIGHING BENEFITS, COSTS, AND SUBSTITUTES

1. Demand is the same as wants.   **True**   **False**

2. Your willingness to pay for a product depends on what substitutes are available, and what they cost.   **True**   **False**

B.2 SMART CHOICES ARE MARGINAL CHOICES

3. Marginal cost is the same as additional cost.   **True**   **False**

4. The flat fee charged at an all-you-can-eat restaurant should not influence how much food you eat once you are seated.   **True**   **False**

5. Marginal benefit is always equal to average benefit.   **True**   **False**

B.3 THE LAW OF DEMAND

6. Quantity demanded is the same as demand.   **True**   **False**

7. If the price of a product/service changes, that affects quantity demanded.   **True**   **False**

B.4 WHAT CAN CHANGE DEMAND?

8. If your willingness to pay decreases, there will be a decrease in demand.   **True**   **False**

9. If your ability to pay decreases, there will be an increase in demand. **True False**

10. Throughout the month of December, the quantity of video game consoles purchased often increases even as the price rises. This violates the law of demand. **True False**

B.5 PRICE ELASTICITY OF DEMAND AND TOTAL REVENUE

11. When customers react quickly to a price change, this product has high elasticity of demand. **True False**

12. Any elasticity value less than 1 is considered to be inelastic. **True False**

13. The fewer substitutes available, the greater the elasticity of demand. **True False**

14. When negotiating a price on an expensive purchase, you want the dealer to believe that your demand is elastic — that is, that you are willing to shop elsewhere if you don't get a low price because good substitutes are available. **True False**

15. Total revenue ($P \times Q$) decreases when a business lowers the price of an inelastic good. **True False**

MULTIPLE CHOICE

Circle the correct answer.

B.1 WEIGHING BENEFITS, COSTS, AND SUBSTITUTES

1. Economists describe the list of your wants and their intensities as
   A) demand.
   B) supply.
   C) benefit.
   D) preferences.

2. Costs are
   A) worth money.
   B) whatever we are willing to give up.
   C) the answer to the question "What do we want?"
   D) whatever we are willing to get.

3. All-you-can-eat buffet restaurants charge a fixed fee for eating. With each plate that Anna consumes, she experiences

   A) decreasing marginal costs to eating.

   B) increasing marginal costs to eating.

   C) decreasing marginal benefits to eating.

   D) increasing marginal benefits to eating.

4. Thinking like economists, a dating couple should break up when the

   A) total benefits of dating are greater than the total costs of dating.

   B) total costs of dating are greater than the total benefits of dating.

   C) additional benefits of dating are greater than the additional costs of dating.

   D) additional costs of dating are greater than the additional benefits of dating.

5. Peter would like to have two cars, one for everyday and the other for special occasions. However, he has only $10 000, so he buys only one car. His quantity demanded of cars is

   A) 1.

   B) 2.

   C) 20 000.

   D) 40 000.

B.3 THE LAW OF DEMAND

6. When the price of a product rises,

   A) consumers look for more expensive substitutes.

   B) quantity demanded increases.

   C) consumers look for cheaper substitutes.

   D) consumers use more of the product.

7. If home owners were charged for garbage collection on the basis of the number of garbage bags used, this would result in a(n)

   A) increase in demand.

   B) decrease in demand.

   C) increase in quantity demanded.

   D) decrease in quantity demanded.

8. What of the following is most likely to be an inferior good?

    A) Fast food

    B) Antique furniture

    C) School bags

    D) Textbooks

9. Demand

    A) increases with a rise in price.

    B) is the same as quantity demanded.

    C) changes with income.

    D) decreases with a rise in price.

10. If the price of cars went up, the demand for tires would

    A) increase.

    B) decrease.

    C) stay the same.

    D) depend on the price of tires.

11. Which of the following could cause an increase in demand for a product?

    A) Increase in income

    B) Decrease in income

    C) Increase in the price of a substitute

    D) All of the above

12. If Kraft Dinner is an inferior good, then a rise in the price of Kraft Dinner will cause a(n)

    A) decrease in demand for Kraft Dinner.

    B) increase in demand for Kraft Dinner.

    C) increase in the quantity demanded of Kraft Dinner.

    D) decrease in the quantity demanded of Kraft Dinner.

13. If a business lowers prices, total revenue increases if price elasticity of demand is

    A) less than 1.

    B) greater than 1.

    C) equal to 1.

    D) equal to 0.

14. The fact that butter and margarine are close substitutes makes

    A) demand for butter more elastic.

    B) demand for butter more inelastic.

    C) butter an inferior good.

    D) margarine an inferior good.

15. After visiting a number of restaurants in Paris where fee-for-service toilets are commonplace, a Canadian restaurant owner decides to charge customers a fee for bathroom use. How will bathroom use inside the owner's restaurant most likely change?

    A) Quantity demanded will decrease; total revenue will fall.

    B) Quantity demanded will increase; total revenue will rise.

    C) Quantity demanded will decrease; total revenue will rise.

    D) Quantity demanded will increase; total revenue will fall.

SHORT ANSWER

Write a short answer to each question. Your answer may be in point form.

1. What is a smart choice?

2. If you don't have enough money to buy a product, can you still have a demand for it?

3. Consider the diamond/water paradox — diamonds are very expensive but not required for life, but water, a necessity for life, is relatively inexpensive. What if you are Bill Gates walking through the desert alone with pockets full of diamonds? How will this affect your marginal benefits?

4. Advertising is designed to increase your preference for a product/service. Provide an example of a slogan that has changed or shaped your preferences.

5. Suppose your community council is considering the idea of returning to a flat monthly rate payment scheme for water usage. Explain what will happen to the demand for the following products.

    A) Water

    B) Orange juice

    C) Soap

    D) Rubber ducky bath toys

6. Identify which factor (preferences, prices of related products/services, income, expected future prices, or the number of consumers) will cause a *change in demand* in the following circumstances:

   A) The impact of building a new apartment on the demand for groceries at the local store

   B) The impact of downloading music on the demand for CDs

   C) The impact on the demand for cars of delaying buying expensive items in anticipation of a future decrease in the GST

7. Young drivers account for more than 35 percent of all drivers involved in fatal accidents, despite representing only 20 percent of all licensed drivers. Often, alcohol is involved. Explain how each of the following policies would affect the demand for alcohol.

   A) Increasing the minimum age for drinking.

   B) Raising the price (through higher taxes) of alcohol.

   C) Using advertising campaigns to discourage alcohol usage.

8. State whether demand for the following products/services is elastic or inelastic.

   A) Pimple medication

   B) Pencils

   C) Clothes

   D) Parasuco jeans

   E) Newspaper

   F) Toilet paper

9. Evidence suggests that babies are a *normal good* for lower income earners and an *inferior good* for higher income earners. Explain what this means by using the definitions of "normal" and "inferior" goods.

10. In the women's clothing market, which is likely to be more inelastic, demand for the latest fashions or demand for clothing in general? Use your answer to explain why when clothing stores have sales they usually exclude the latest arrivals.

Show Me the Money

The Law of Supply

LEARNING OBJECTIVES

After reading this appendix, you should be able to:

C.1 Explain why marginal costs are ultimately opportunity costs.

C.2 Define sunk costs and explain why they do not influence smart, forward-looking decisions.

C.3 Describe the relationship between price and quantity supplied, and identify the roles of higher profits and marginal opportunity costs of production.

C.4 Explain the difference between a change in quantity supplied and a change in supply, and list five factors that change supply.

C.5 Explain elasticity of supply and how it helps businesses avoid disappointed customers.

MONEY IS THE MARKET'S REWARD to individuals or businesses who give up something of value. Your boss rewards you with an hourly wage for supplying labour services. A business producing a top-selling product is rewarded with profits (as long as revenues are greater than costs).

What goes into decisions to sell, or supply, services or products to the market? What price do you need to get to be willing to work? How much money does it take before a business is willing to supply?

This appendix focuses on choices businesses make every day in producing and selling. Economists use the term *supply* to summarize all the influences on business decisions.

Business decisions seem more "objective" than consumer decisions which seem to be based on "subjective" desires and preferences. After all, there is a bottom line in business with prices, costs, and profits. But business supply decisions are not as straightforward or objective as you might think.

C.1 What Does It Really Cost? Costs Are Opportunity Costs

Explain why marginal costs are ultimately opportunity costs.

Supply, like demand, starts with decision makers choosing among alternative opportunities by comparing expected benefits and costs at the margin.

How Much to Work?

It's Sunday night and your boss calls in a panic, begging you to work as many hours as possible next week. You normally work 10 hours a week, but the extra money would come in handy. The timing, however, couldn't be worse. You have two midterms the following week, and your out-of-town boy/girlfriend is coming in next weekend for the only visit you will have in two months. How many hours then are you willing to work?

Of course you will make a smart choice, weighing the additional benefits and costs of working extra hours. The additional, or marginal, benefits are the $10 per hour you earn (plus something for the boss's goodwill). The additional costs are opportunity costs — the alternative uses of the time you have to give up.

You want to attend all your classes, keep time for studying for midterms, and definitely keep the weekend free. You are willing to give up the 10 hours a week you spend playing *World of Warcraft*. When your boss hears you are willing to work only a total of 20 hours, while she is hoping for 60 hours, she instantly replies, "What if I pay you double time for all your hours next week?"

Well, that changes things. At $20 per hour, you will willingly give up your game time, skip a few classes where you are not having a test, but still keep the weekend free. You are up to 35 hours of work, but your boss is totally desperate and asks again, "What if I pay you triple time?"

At that price, you will also cut back on your sleep, reduce your study time, and try to reschedule your weekend visit. (Is the visit worth giving up $500 for a weekend's work?) Your boss relaxes a bit when you promise 55 hours.

Notice that the quantity of work or time that you are willing to supply to your boss increases as the price she pays you rises. In order to get you to divert more of your time from alternative uses, she has to offer you more money (which increases her costs).

For your supply decision, there are always alternative uses of your time, and each use has a different cost to you. Your game time is worth the least to you, the weekend time the most. As the price offered for your time rises, you work more, first giving up the least valuable alternative use of time, and then giving up increasingly valuable time. Your willingness to work changes with circumstances, depending on the price offered and the opportunity cost — the value you place on alternative uses of your time.

The economist's term for the additional opportunity cost associated with alternative uses of your time is **marginal cost** — the additional opportunity cost of increasing the quantity of whatever is being supplied. For you, the opportunity cost, or marginal cost, of an hour of game time is less than the opportunity cost, or marginal cost, of an hour of weekend time. As you shift your time away from alternative uses to work, *the marginal cost of your time increases*. You give up the least valuable time first, and continue giving up increasingly valuable time as the price you are offered rises.

Your willingness to work depends on the price offered and on the opportunity costs of alternative uses of your time.

marginal cost: additional opportunity cost of increasing quantity supplied, and changes with circumstances

Comparing Demand and Supply Decisions There are similarities between the demand decisions from Appendix B and your supply decision. For products or services you are thinking of buying, there are always substitutes available, which is why consumers buy less of a product/service as the price rises — we all switch to cheaper alternatives. Willingness to pay depends on available substitutes and changes with circumstances — the marginal benefit of the first bottle of Gatorade is greater than the marginal benefit of the second bottle. For the hours you are thinking of supplying, there are always alternative uses of your time, with different values to you. Willingness to supply hours depends on those alternatives and changes with circumstances — the opportunity cost of giving up your gaming hours is less than the opportunity cost of giving up your weekend hours. That is one reason why suppliers supply more as the price rises — higher prices are necessary to compensate for the higher opportunity costs of more additional time (or other resources) given up.

There are also two important differences between smart demand choices and smart supply choices. First, for demand, marginal benefit — the maximum you are willing to pay — *decreases as you buy more.* For supply, marginal cost — the minimum you need to be paid — *increases as you supply more.*

Second, the comparison of benefits and costs is reversed. For demand, marginal benefit is your subjective satisfaction, and marginal cost is measured in dollars — the price you must pay. For supply, marginal benefit is measured in dollars — the hourly wage rate you earn — and marginal cost is an opportunity cost, the value of alternative uses of the time that you must give up.

What Do Inputs *Really* Cost?

Any business supply decision involves the same smart choice between marginal benefit and marginal cost as your work decision. The marginal benefit or reward from selling is measured in the dollar price you receive, and all marginal costs are ultimately opportunity costs.

Let's look at a business: Paola's Piercing and Fingernail Parlour (PPF Parlour). To supply her services to the market, Paola, like any businessperson, has to buy inputs (studs, tools, polish), pay rent to her landlord, and pay wages to her employees. What do those hard dollar actual costs have to do with opportunity costs? Which costs are *real* costs?

Take the nickel studs Paola buys today for $1 each from a stud supplier. If the world price of nickel rises because of increasing demand from China for the metal, Paola will have to pay more for her studs. The stud supplier will sell to Paola only as long as she pays as much as the best price he can get from another customer, whether in China or Canada. Paola's stud cost has to cover the opportunity cost of the stud supplier.

The same goes for Paola's rent or the wages she pays to her employees. If Paola's landlord can find another tenant willing to pay more for the shop space, then once Paola's lease is up, she will have to pay that higher amount or the landlord will rent to the other tenant. If Paola's employees, like you, have alternative uses of their time that they value more than what she pays, or if they can get job offers elsewhere at higher wages, Paola will have to match the offers or start advertising for help wanted.

Every buying or selling choice is a fork in the road. Buying — there are substitute products. Selling — there are alternative uses of your time. Opportunity cost of any choice is value of best alternative you give up.

Supply and demand choices reverse the comparison of benefits and costs. Supply — marginal benefit is measured in dollars (wage you earn); marginal cost is opportunity cost of time. Demand — marginal benefit is satisfaction you get; marginal cost is measured in dollars (price you pay).

When businesses purchase an input, marginal cost can be stated in dollars. But marginal costs are ultimately opportunity costs, value of best alternative use of that input.

To hire or purchase inputs, a business must pay a price that matches the best opportunity cost of the input owner. The real cost of any input is determined by the best alternative use of that input. All marginal costs are ultimately opportunity costs. Marginal costs can be stated in dollars, but they are an opportunity cost — the value of the best alternative use of that input.

As we will see in the next section, Paola's smart business supply decision will depend on whether the price she receives for a piercing (marginal benefit) is greater than her marginal opportunity costs.

Refresh C.1

www.myeconlab.com

1. What is the real cost to a business of hiring or purchasing any input?

2. Microsoft released a limited supply of Xbox 360s in 2005 with a list price — or "real" price — of $400. The units immediately started selling on eBay and other online auction websites for far more than $400. What do you think determined the "real" price of an Xbox?

3. If a recession makes it much harder for workers to find better-paying jobs, what might happen to Paola's labour costs?

C.2 Forget It, It's History: Sunk Costs Don't Matter for Future Choices

Define sunk costs and explain why they do not influence smart, forward-looking decisions.

Past expenses are not part of additional opportunity costs and have no influence on smart choices.

sunk costs: past expenses that cannot be recovered

Paola must base her business supply decisions on her real costs, which are ultimately opportunity costs. But some expenses are not part of opportunity costs. This is another aspect of supply decisions that is not as straightforward as you might think.

Past expenses that cannot be reversed are *not* part of opportunity costs. If Paola has signed a year's lease for her rent that she cannot get out of, then her rent becomes irrelevant for her future decisions. How can that be?

Paola's decisions, or your decisions, are always forward looking. A smart decision about which fork in the road to take compares the expected future benefits and expected future costs of each path. When Paola has to decide whether to supply more piercings or fingernails, or to choose between buying new tools or hiring more employees, the rent expense is the same, so its influence cancels out. The past expense of rent paid (or legally contracted for) is the same no matter which fork Paola chooses, so it doesn't influence her decision.

These irreversible costs are called **sunk costs** — past, already-paid expenses that cannot be recovered. In other words, they are history. And history doesn't matter for forward-looking decisions. Sunk costs are the monies that have already been spent and cannot be recovered.

Suppose you have paid your tuition for this semester, and the refund date has passed. Your boss's request for extra hours comes at a time when you are already finding it hard to juggle work and school, and you are considering dropping out.

Your decision to drop out and work full-time (making your boss very happy), versus staying in school, depends on how you evaluate the expected benefits and costs of each fork in your career road. Dropping out and working more means more income right away, while staying in school means less income now but probably more in the future. The tuition you paid is history. You can't get it back no matter which fork you choose, so it is not part of the opportunity costs of either choice.

Refresh C.2

1. Why aren't sunk costs part of the opportunity costs of forward-looking decisions?

2. Suppose you have just paid your bus fare. A friend in a car pulls up and offers you a ride. Explain how you would decide between staying on the bus or taking the ride, and the influence of the paid fare.

3. If you bought a $100 textbook for a course, and then dropped out after the tuition refund date, is that $100 a sunk cost? Explain your answer.

www.myeconlab.com

C.3 More for More Money: The Law of Supply

Demand is not just what you want, but your willingness and ability to pay for a product/service — putting your money where your mouth is. Similarly, the economist's idea of supply is not just offering things for sale. **Supply** is the overall willingness of businesses (or individuals) to produce a particular product/service because the price covers all opportunity costs of production.

Let's look at how an economist would describe your supply decision about how many hours to work at your part-time job. Figure C.1 combines price information — the minimum wage you are willing to accept — and the quantity of work you will supply at each wage.

Describe the relationship between price and quantity supplied, and identify the roles of higher profits and marginal opportunity costs of production.

supply: businesses' willingness to produce a particular product/service because price covers all opportunity costs

Figure C.1	Your Supply of Hours Worked
Price per Hour (minimum willing to accept)	**Quantity Supplied** (hours of work)
$10	10–20
$20	35
$30	55

At a price of $10 per hour, your quantity supplied of work could be anywhere between 10 and 20 hours. At $20 per hour, your quantity supplied of work is 35 hours, and at $30 per hour, your quantity supplied is 55 hours.

Quantity supplied, as we will see, is not the same as supply. **Quantity supplied** is a more limited concept — the quantity you actually plan to supply at a given price, taking into account everything that affects your willingness to supply work hours.

quantity supplied: quantity you actually plan to supply at a given price

As your eye goes down the two columns in Figure C.1, notice that as the price rises, the quantity supplied increases. (What happens to quantity demanded as price rises?) In general, when prices rise, individuals and businesses devote more of their time or resources to producing or supplying — more money stimulates more product/service supplied. The two reasons for this are the quest for profits (higher prices usually mean higher profits) and the need for a higher price to cover higher marginal opportunity costs — your weekend time is worth more to you than your computer game time.

Let's take the economist's idea of supply and apply it to Paola's willingness to supply a particular quantity of piercings at a particular price.

Body Piercings or Nail Sets?

Businesses, like consumers, make smart choices based on economic advantage. Paola's first choice is *what to produce* with her resources — the labour and equipment she has in her shop. She can do body piercing, and she can also paint fingernails. Let's limit her choices to full body piercings and full sets of fingernails to allow the simple, made-up numbers below.

The PPF Parlour has special tools both for piercing and nail painting. There are four people working (including Paola). All four are equally skilled at piercing (the business started with just piercing), but their fingernail skills differ from expert (Paola) to beginner (Parminder). Figure C.2 shows the different combinations of fingernail sets and piercings the PPF Parlour can produce in a day.

Figure C.2	PPF Parlour: Maximum Daily Combination of Fingernails and Piercings Produced	
Combination	**Fingernails (full sets)**	**Piercings (full body)**
A	15	0
B	14	1
C	12	2
D	9	3
E	5	4
F	0	5

At one extreme (combination A) all four workers do fingernails only, so they can produce 15 fingernail sets and no piercings. If Paola starts shifting some of her staff from fingernails to piercings, she can move to combination B (14 fingernail sets and 1 full body piercing). Shifting more staff and equipment out of fingernails and into piercing gives her combination C (12 fingernail sets and 2 piercings), and then combinations D (9 fingernail sets and 3 piercings) and E (5 fingernail sets and 4 piercings). Combination F is the other extreme, where the PPF Parlour produces only piercings — 5 piercings and 0 fingernail sets. As we will see, the pattern of numbers in Figure C.2 has a lot to do with differences in fingernail skills.

What Do Paola's Choices Cost Her?

So far, these numbers don't make much business sense — they are just the numbers of piercings and nail sets that the PPF Parlour can possibly produce. To make sense of the numbers for Paola's business supply decisions, we have to translate them into marginal costs.

Remember that all costs are ultimately opportunity costs. The cost of acquiring or producing products/services is the value of the best alternative opportunity we must give up to get them. To get more body piercings, Paola gives up doing full nail sets. Opportunity cost is what we give up divided by what we get:

$$\text{Opportunity cost} = \frac{\text{Give up}}{\text{Get}}$$

Figure C.3 shows, in the last column, the marginal opportunity costs to Paola of producing more piercings.

Figure C.3	PPF Parlour's Marginal Opportunity Costs		
Combination	Fingernails (full sets)	Piercings (full body)	Marginal Opportunity Cost of Producing More Piercings (fingernail sets given up)
A	15	0	
B	14	1	$\frac{(15-14)}{1} = 1$
C	12	2	$\frac{(14-12)}{1} = 2$
D	9	3	$\frac{(12-9)}{1} = 3$
E	5	4	$\frac{(9-5)}{1} = 4$
F	0	5	$\frac{(5-0)}{1} = 5$

What is the marginal opportunity cost of producing the first full body piercing? To move from 0 to 1 piercing (from combination A to B), Paola must give up 1 fingernail set, because fingernail production drops from 15 to 14 sets as some staff time switches from fingernails to piercing. In exchange, she gets 1 piercing. So substituting into the formula, the marginal opportunity cost of the first piercing is

$$\frac{1 \text{ (fingernail set)}}{1 \text{ (piercing)}} = 1 \text{ (fingernail set per piercing)}$$

To produce a second piercing (moving from combination B to C), Paola must give up 2 fingernail sets (14 − 12 sets). The marginal opportunity cost of the second additional piercing is 2 fingernail sets given up per piercing. The third piercing (moving from combination C to D) has a marginal opportunity cost of 3 fingernail sets given up (12 − 9 sets) per piercing. In moving the last of her staff to piercing, for the fifth full body piercing she gives up 5 fingernail sets (5 − 0 sets). The marginal opportunity cost of the last additional piercing — the fifth — is 5 fingernail sets given up per piercing.

Costs Are Costs Are Costs — It's How You Look at Them

If you are wondering what the difference is between opportunity cost, marginal cost, and marginal opportunity cost — since they seem like the same thing — good for you! You are not confused. *All opportunity costs are marginal costs, and all marginal costs are opportunity costs.*

Opportunity cost and marginal cost are two sides of the same coin. Opportunity cost focuses on the value of the opportunity *given up* when you make a decision. On the flip side, marginal cost focuses on the *additional cost* that the decision produces. Paola must give up 5 fingernail sets in deciding to produce the fifth piercing. So the marginal opportunity cost of the fifth piercing is 5 fingernail sets. **Marginal opportunity cost** is the complete name for any cost relevant to a smart decision.

Figure C.4 illustrates the economic sense of these numbers. Each finger measures the marginal opportunity cost of additional piercings produced (along the horizontal axis) in terms of fingernail sets given up per piercing (shown on the vertical axis).

Figure C.4   Increasing Marginal Opportunity Cost

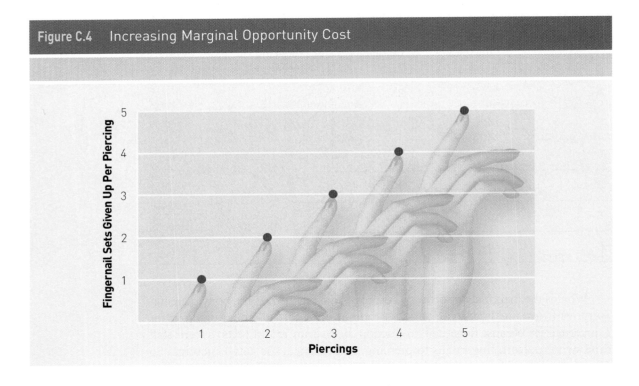

Notice that as Paola produces additional piercings, her marginal opportunity costs increase, from 1 fingernail set given up for the first piercing to 5 fingernail sets given up for the fifth piercing. This is the same pattern we saw in the decision to shift your time away from alternative uses to working more hours — the marginal cost of additional time given up increases as you give up increasingly valuable uses of your time.

Are the reasons for Paola's increasing marginal opportunity costs the same as for your work decision? This is an important question, and the answer is not obvious. Paola's increasing marginal opportunity costs arise because her staff and equipment are not equally good at piercing and painting. Paola is better (more productive) at doing fingernails than is Parminder, and the tools can't be easily switched between tasks — nailpolish brushes and emery boards aren't much help in piercing.

Why Marginal Opportunity Costs Increase These differences in productivity cause increasing marginal opportunity costs. Think about Paola as she decides to reduce her fingernail output and produce the first piercing. Remember that all staff are equally skilled at piercing. Which staff member will she switch first to piercing? As an economizer, she will switch the person who is least productive for fingernails — Parminder. So her given up, or forgone, fingernail production is relatively small (1 set). To increase her piercing output more, she has to then switch staff who are slightly better at doing fingernails, so the opportunity cost is higher (2 fingernail sets). And who is the last person she switches when she moves entirely to piercing? Of course, it is Paola herself — the best nail painter — so the opportunity cost of that fifth piercing is the highest, at 5 fingernail sets given up.

Increasing marginal opportunity costs arise because inputs are not equally productive in all activities. There are always opportunity costs in switching between activities because time spent on piercing can no longer be spent on fingernails. But *increasing* opportunity costs arise because of the differing skill levels of the staff being switched. If all of Paola's staff and equipment were equally good at piercing and fingernail painting, the opportunity costs would always be the same, no matter what combinations of piercings and fingernails she produced. But in the real world, most inputs are not like that; they are different.

The reasons for Paola's increasing marginal opportunity costs are not quite the same as the reasons for your decision to supply more work hours as the price rises, but there is much overlap. For your work decision, increasing marginal opportunity costs arise from differences in the value of alternative uses of your time (from computer games to weekend fun). For Paola's decision to supply additional piercings, increasing marginal opportunity costs arise from differences in employee skill levels and equipment in producing alternative services. What is shared among the reasons is alternative uses (of time or inputs) with increasing opportunity costs.

Show Me the Money: Paying for Opportunity Costs

So far, all of the numbers in this example are measured in full body piercings or fingernail sets. But Paola, as a profit-seeking entrepreneur, will want to make a smart supply decision based on dollar prices. Luckily, there is an easy conversion here from body decorations to dollars. Suppose that fingernail full sets sell for $20. Then the marginal opportunity costs for producing additional piercings appear in Figure C.5.

> *Increasing marginal opportunity costs arise because inputs are not equally productive in all activities.*

> *Where inputs are equally productive in all activities, marginal opportunity costs are constant.*

Figure C.5 PPF Parlour's Supply of Piercings	
Price (marginal opportunity cost or minimum willing to accept per piercing)	**Quantity Supplied** (piercings)
$ 20	1
$ 40	2
$ 60	3
$ 80	4
$100	5

The marginal opportunity cost of producing the first piercing is $20 (the cost of 1 nail set given up); of the second piercing, $40 (2 nail sets given up); all the way up to $100 for the fifth piercing. So if Paola is to be willing to produce 1 piercing, she needs to receive a price of at least $20 to cover the costs of the alternative use of her inputs. To continue to produce more piercings, she needs to receive higher prices to cover her higher marginal opportunity costs. Paola won't produce the fifth piercing unless she receives at least $100 for it, because that is what she would be giving up from the best alternative use of her inputs (5 fingernail sets at $20 each). So the price of a piercing will determine what quantity of piercings Paola will decide to produce. The higher the price, the greater quantity of piercings Paola supplies.

The Law of Supply

Just as you are willing to supply more hours of work only if the price you are paid rises, Paola's business must receive a higher price in order to be willing to supply a greater quantity to the market. She needs the higher price to compensate for her increasing marginal opportunity costs as her production of piercings increases.

As the price offered for your time rises, you work more, first giving up the least valuable alternative use of time, and then giving up increasingly valuable time. Your willingness to work changes with circumstances, depending on the price offered and the cost — the value you place on alternative uses of your time.

As the price offered for piercings rises, Paola switches inputs from producing nail sets to piercings, first giving up the least productive inputs for nail sets, and then giving up increasingly productive inputs for nail sets. Paola's willingness to supply piercings changes with circumstances, depending on the price offered and the cost — the value of lost nail sets from the alternative uses of the inputs.

Usually, many businesses are willing to supply the market for any product/service. Like Paola's, each business tries to make a smart choice about *what* to supply, and *how much* to supply. Whether it is the output markets for piercings or nail sets, the input market for labour, or anything else, businesses and individuals always have alternative uses of their inputs, and will supply a larger quantity only at a higher price.

Market supply is the sum of the supplies of all businesses willing to produce a particular product/service. Suppose there were 100 piercing businesses exactly like Paola's. The market supply of piercings is the sum of the supplies of all piercing businesses, and looks like Figure C.6.

In output markets, the left side of the circular-flow diagram (Figure 1.4, p. 12), businesses are suppliers, and households are demanders. In input markets, the right side of Figure 1.4 — individuals/households are suppliers, and businesses are demanders. On either side, higher prices increase quantity supplied.

market supply: sum of supplies of all businesses willing to produce a particular product/service

Figure C.6	Market Supply of Piercings
Price (marginal opportunity cost or minimum willing to accept per piercing)	**Quantity Supplied** (piercings)
$ 20	100
$ 40	200
$ 60	300
$ 80	400
$100	500

Quantity Willing to Supply and Price Willing to Accept   Recall that the general definition of supply is businesses' overall willingness to supply a product/service because the price covers all opportunity costs of production. Figure C.6 shows, for each price, the particular quantity supplied by all piercing businesses combined.

If we read the numbers from left to right (from price to quantity supplied), the first row of the table tells us that at a price of $20 per piercing, all businesses together are willing to supply the quantity of 100 piercings. As your eye moves down the table and price rises, the quantity supplied also increases, until at a price of $100 per piercing the quantity supplied is 500 piercings.

Another way to read the numbers in Figure C.6 is from right to left (from quantity supplied to price). Starting with the first row again, that reading tells us this: For businesses to be willing to supply 100 piercings, the minimum price they are willing to accept (that covers all opportunity costs of production) is $20 per piercing. To be willing to supply 500 piercings, the minimum price they are willing to accept is $100 per piercing (because of increased opportunity costs).

This positive relationship between price and quantity supplied (both go up together) is so universal that economists call it the **law of supply**: If the price of a product/service rises, the quantity supplied of the product/service increases. Higher prices create incentives for increased production through higher profits and by covering higher marginal opportunity costs of production.

The law of supply works as long as other factors besides price do not change. The next section will explore what happens when other factors do change.

law of supply: if the price of a product/service rises, quantity supplied increases

Refresh
C.3

1. Why does Paola need a higher price to be willing to supply more body piercings?

2. If you could spend the next hour studying economics or working at your part-time job, which pays $10 an hour, what is your personal opportunity cost, in dollars, of studying?

3. Suppose the PPF Parlour was producing only piercings and no fingernail sets. If Paola wanted to start producing some fingernail sets, which staff person would she switch to fingernails first? Who would she switch last? Explain your answers.

www.myeconlab.com

C.4 Changing the Bottom Line: What Can Change Supply?

Explain the difference between a change in quantity supplied and a change in supply, and list five factors that change supply.

The average price of a notebook computer in Canada fell from around $2000 in 2002 to under $1000 in 2007. But the quantity of notebook computers businesses sold *increased*.

Does that contradict the "law of supply"?

If nothing else changed except the price of notebooks, the answer would be yes. Why would notebook producers be willing to supply more notebooks at lower prices? Something is not right. But like evidence that appears to disprove the law of demand, a fall in price that leads to an increase in quantity supplied is a signal that something else must have changed at the same time.

Economists use the term *supply* to summarize all of the influences on business decisions. In the examples of your work decision or Paola's piercings, that willingness to supply depends on things like the value of alternative uses of time or inputs and marginal opportunity costs.

As long as these factors (and some others) do not change, the law of supply holds true: If the price of a product/service rises, the quantity supplied increases.

But when change happens, economists distinguish between two kinds of change:

- If the price of a product/service changes, that affects *quantity supplied*.
- If anything else changes, that affects *supply*.

This distinction is just like the distinction in Appendix B between quantity demanded and demand.

Uncorking the Okanagan

In the Okanagan region of B.C. — an area known in particular for its fruit production — large excavation machines are ripping out apple trees to make way for a new crop: grapes. Local landowners hope the switch will allow them to make more profits from their property by jumping into the province's booming wine industry. Landowner Bryan Hardman says that in the past he has been a price taker, but is setting up his own winery because he "wants to be a price maker, and believes the wine business is the place to do it."

- This anecdote beautifully illustrates the law of supply. Higher prices and profits are creating incentives to increase quantity supplied of grapes and wine.

- It's also an illustration of how all inputs must be paid their opportunity costs. Even though the Okanagan Valley is a world-class area for apple-growing, landowners can make more money switching to grapes — more than covering their opportunity costs — so they do.

- If land is not equally productive for grape-growing, which apple orchards would you expect to be dug up and replanted with grapes first? Which will be replanted last?

Source: Wendy Stueck, in *The Globe and Mail* (Toronto), October 7, 2006.

Only a change in the price of a product/service itself changes *quantity supplied* of that product/service. There are five other important factors that can change market supply — the willingness to produce a product/service. They are:

- Technology
- Prices of inputs
- Prices of related products/services produced
- Expected future prices
- Number of businesses

Technology

Paola is ecstatic because she has just bought a newly invented piercing gun that allows her employees to double the number of piercings they do in a day. This increase in productivity from the new technology reduces her costs. Word spreads quickly, and all of the other piercing parlour owners realize that if they are to stay competitive, they, too, have to adopt the new technology. The result is an increase in market supply, which is shown in Figure C.7.

Figure C.7	Market Supply of Piercings Before and After a Technology Improvement	
Price (marginal opportunity cost or minimum willing to accept per piercing)	**Quantity Supplied** (before technology improvement)	**Quantity Supplied** (after technology improvement)
$ 20	100	200
$ 40	200	400
$ 60	300	600
$ 80	400	800
$100	500	1000

If we read the numbers from left to right, at any price, each business will make more profits given that its costs are lower, and so it will want to supply more piercings. At a price of $20, before the new technology, businesses were willing to supply 100 piercings (column 2). At an unchanged price of $20, with the new technology, businesses are now willing to supply 200 piercings (column 3). Economists call this an **increase in supply** — an increase in the overall willingness of businesses to supply at any price. This can be described in two equivalent ways. At any unchanged price, businesses are now willing to supply a greater quantity because costs are lower and profits are higher. Or, for producing any unchanged quantity, businesses are now willing to accept a lower price because costs are lower.

If we instead read the numbers from right to left, for any quantity supplied, after the new technology lowers costs, the minimum price businesses are willing to accept falls. In Figure C.7, before the new technology, to be willing to supply 200 piercings businesses needed a minimum price of $40 per piercing (row 2). After the new technology, to be willing to supply 200 piercings, businesses now need a price of only $20 per piercing (row 1). The new technology has lowered Paola's and other piercers' marginal opportunity costs, so they can accept a lower price while still covering all costs. Either way, the result is an increase in supply.

increase in supply: increase in businesses' willingness to produce

An improvement in technology causes an increase in supply, not a change in quantity supplied.

Prices of Inputs

Paola and other businesses have to pay a price for inputs that matches the best opportunity cost of the input owner. If those opportunity costs and input prices go down, Paola's costs decrease. At any price for piercings, lower costs mean Paola will earn higher profits, so she will want to supply more. The effect of lower input prices on market supply is the same as a technology improvement. In Figure C.7, the last column of numbers for quantity supplied could also have been caused by lower input prices for studs, lower rent, or lower wages to employees. Lower input prices increase market supply.

In reverse, higher input prices mean higher costs for Paola and, at any price, lower profits. Therefore, market supply will decrease.

Prices of Related Products and Services

The PPF Parlour can produce both piercings and fingernail sets. What happens to Paola's supply of piercings when the price of fingernail sets falls from $20 to $10 per set? Since Paola wants to earn maximum profits, which product will she produce more of, and which less of, when the price of fingernail sets falls? Take a minute to see if you can answer that question before reading on.

When the price of fingernail sets falls, Paola will supply more piercings and fewer fingernail sets. You probably reasoned that when the price of fingernail sets falls, they are less profitable to produce, so Paola will shift more of her resources to producing piercings. You are correct. A fall in the price of fingernail sets causes an *increase in supply of piercings*.

But there is another way to reason out the answer to the question. The lower price of fingernail sets lowers Paola's marginal opportunity cost of producing piercings. The real opportunity cost of producing more piercings is the fingernail sets Paola must give up. When those fingernail sets fall in price, Paola's marginal opportunity cost for producing piercings decreases. So the minimum price Paola needs to receive to be willing to supply any given quantity of piercings falls. In reverse, a rise in the price of fingernail sets causes a *decrease in supply of piercings*.

A change in the price of related products/services produced causes a business to reconsider its most profitable choices. A business will choose to supply more of one product/service when alternative products/services it produces fall in price, and supply less when alternative products/services it produces rise in price.

Expected Future Prices

What happens to the supply of a product/service when the expected future price of the product/service changes? Recall from Appendix B that consumer demand changes if consumers expect lower or higher prices in the future. The same holds true for businesses. If Paola expects falling piercing prices in the future, she will try to supply more now, while the price is relatively high. When future prices are expected to fall, supply increases in the present.

If Paola expects future prices to rise, she may reduce her current supply to the market and increase her supply when prices and profits are higher. When future prices are expected to rise, supply decreases in the present.

Number of Businesses

An increase in the number of businesses increases market supply. Figure C.8 adds a third column to Figure C.6 showing the quantity supplied after the number of businesses doubles.

Figure C.8 Market Supply of Piercings with More Businesses		
Price (marginal opportunity cost or minimum willing to accept per piercing)	Quantity Supplied (100 businesses)	Quantity Supplied (200 businesses)
$ 20	100	200
$ 40	200	400
$ 60	300	600
$ 80	400	800
$100	500	1000

It is no surprise that with the additional businesses (column 3), at any price (column 1) the quantity supplied is greater than originally (column 2). The increased number of businesses causes an increase in supply, just as an improvement in technology or a fall in input prices causes an increase in supply. A decrease in the number of businesses causes a decrease in supply, just as a rise in the price of a related product/service or an increase in expected future prices causes a decrease in supply.

An increased number of businesses causes an increase in supply. A decreased number of businesses causes a decrease in supply.

Why would businesses enter (increase supply) or exit (decrease supply) a market? Typically, if profits are high, new competitors will enter a market, increasing the market supply. If profits are lower than available elsewhere in the economy, competitors will exit from the market, decreasing market supply. Those exiting businesses will search for more profitable uses of their resources.

Summary

Any increase (or decrease) in supply can be described in alternative ways. We have used these alternatives, in reading the tables of numbers from left to right (from price to quantity supplied) or from right to left (from quantity supplied to price). The left-to-right description of an increase in supply is:

- At any given price, businesses are willing to supply a larger quantity.

  The right-to-left description of an increase in supply is:
- At any given quantity supplied, businesses are willing to accept a lower price because their marginal opportunity costs of production are lower.

For an increase in supply, these two alternative descriptions of the connection between price and quantity supplied are summarized in Figure C.9. Depending on the economic event you are trying to make sense of, sometimes you will use one description, and sometimes the other.

Figure C.9 Relating Price and Quantity Supplied for an Increase in Supply		
Given price	⟷	Higher quantity supplied
Lower price	⟷	Given quantity supplied

Saving the Law of Supply

A change in quantity supplied (caused by a change in the price of the product/service itself) differs from a change in supply (caused by changes in technology, prices of inputs, prices of related products/services produced, expected future prices, and/or number of businesses). Can you now explain why, when notebook computer prices fell from $2000 to under $1000, the quantity of notebooks sold actually *increased*? Is the "law of supply" really a law?

If the price of a product/service falls, the quantity supplied decreases, *as long as other factors do not change*. The fall in notebook prices alone would have caused a *decrease* in quantity supplied, not an increase. But other things also changed. While a complete explanation involves demand factors from Appendix B as well as supply, major changes include technological improvements in computer chips and falling prices of inputs. These *increased the supply* of notebook computers. Using the right-to-left reading of an increase in supply in Figure C.9, at any given quantity supplied, businesses were willing to accept a lower price because their marginal opportunity costs of production were lower. The impact of the increase in supply outweighed the impact of lower prices in decreasing quantity supplied.

Figure C.10 is a good study device for reviewing the difference between the law of supply (focused on quantity supplied) and the factors that change supply.

Figure C.10 Law of Supply and Changes in Supply

The Law of Supply

The quantity supplied of a product/service

Decreases if:	Increases if:
■ price of the product/service falls	■ price of the product/service rises

Changes in Supply

The supply for a product/service

Decreases if:	Increases if:
_ _ _ _ _	■ technology improves
■ price of an input rises	■ price of an input falls
■ price of a complement rises	■ price of a complement falls
■ price of a related product/service rises	■ price of a related product/service falls
■ expected future price rises	■ expected future price falls
■ number of businesses decreases	■ number of businesses increases

Refresh C.4

1. Explain the difference between a change in quantity supplied and a change in supply, and distinguish the five factors that can change supply.

2. Suppose you are working at two part-time jobs, babysitting and pizza delivery. After many younger babysitters start offering to work for less, your babysitting clients will now pay only $6 per hour instead of $8 per hour. What will happen to your supply of hours for delivering pizzas? Explain.

3. When the price of nail sets falls, none of Paola's hard dollar costs change. Is there an effect on the quantity of piercings Paola chooses to supply?

C.5 How Far Will You Jump for the Money? Price Elasticity of Supply

Explain elasticity of supply and how it helps businesses avoid disappointed customers.

The Magic Christian, a 1969 movie written in part by Monty Python and starring Peter Sellers and Ringo Starr (of the Beatles), is a satire on greed. A wealthy man with a perverse sense of humour performs bizarre social experiments to see what respectable people will do for money. In a memorable scene, people dive into a pool of excrement because they can keep any of the gold coins they find at the bottom.

What would it take to get you to dive into that pool? In pondering your answer (and please do forgive me for placing this image in your mind's eye), you might also be wondering what on earth this has to do with smart supply decisions.

We know from the law of supply that (all other things unchanged), a rise in price causes an increase in quantity supplied. A smart business supply decision depends on *by how much* you increase quantity supplied when the price rises.

What might you do to earn a dollar? A thousand dollars? A million? What makes the difference?

What price would it take for you to "supply" a dive into the pool? By how much will you increase your work hours in response to your boss's higher wages? What determines by how much Paola increases her quantity supplied of piercings as the price of piercings rises?

The law of supply tells us that price and quantity supplied increase together and decrease together. The last question we will look at is this: What changes more, the price or the quantity? This *responsiveness* of quantity supplied to a change in price is related to greed and the quest for profits, but mostly it has to do with how easy or costly it is to increase production.

Responsiveness Again   I am hoping the word "responsiveness" reminds you of the concept of elasticity from Appendix B. There, the price elasticity of demand measured the responsiveness of the quantity demanded by consumers to a change in price. **Elasticity of supply** measures by how much quantity supplied by businesses responds to a change in price.

Just as was the case for demand, the quantity supplied can be inelastic (unresponsive to a change in price) or elastic (very responsive). Let's look at some examples.

You are standing by the pool in *The Magic Christian,* but simply cannot bring yourself to jump. Even with an astronomical increase in the price — from only, say, a loonie at the bottom to a million gold coins — you stay put. Your "supply" of jumps is totally unresponsive to even a huge increase in price. This is inelastic supply in the extreme.

More realistically, consider an industry like gold mining. When the world price of gold rises, what happens to the quantity of gold supplied? Not much, and certainly not much quickly. Gold is hard to find, and prospecting for new gold fields is very expensive and takes years, even decades. The supply of new gold nuggets is *inelastic,* because quantity supplied is relatively unresponsive to even large rises in price. For **inelastic** supply, there is a small response in quantity supplied when the price rises.

At the other extreme, the supply of snow-shovelling services in most Canadian towns is relatively elastic. If the price offered rises even modestly, there is a willing supply of kids with shovels who don't have many other equally well-paying chances to work. And for anyone with a truck, it's not difficult or expensive to attach a plow and clear driveways in your spare time, before or after your regular job. Even a small rise in price causes a large increase in the quantity supplied of shovelling services, so supply is elastic. For **elastic** supply, there is a large response in quantity supplied when the price rises.

Measuring Business Responsiveness

This is the simple formula for calculating elasticity of supply:

$$\text{Elasticity of supply} = \frac{\text{Percentage change in quantity supplied}}{\text{Percentage change in price}}$$

The formula assumes that all of the other five factors that can affect supply are unchanged, so this is a controlled measurement of just the relationship (in the law of supply) between quantity supplied and price.

If the percentage change in quantity supplied (the numerator) is less than the percentage change in price (the denominator), elasticity of supply is less than 1 and is inelastic. Quantity supplied is relatively unresponsive to a change in price.

If the percentage change in quantity supplied (the numerator) is greater than the percentage change in price (the denominator), elasticity of supply is greater than 1 and is elastic. Quantity supplied is relatively responsive to a change in price.

Calculating Elasticity of Supply   Let's substitute some numbers into the formula, going back to your decision to work more hours for your boss. When she asked, you were willing to work 20 hours at $10/hour. When she then offered you $20/hour (a 100-percent increase), you agreed to supply 15 additional hours, for a total of 35 hours. If we convert the increase in quantity into a percentage (15 additional hours/20 original hours = 75 percent), your elasticity of supply is

$$\text{Elasticity of supply} = \frac{75 \text{ percent}}{100 \text{ percent}} = 0.75$$

That is a relatively inelastic response on your part (and your boss was disappointed!), as a 100-percent increase in pay led you to increase your supply of hours by only 75 percent.

As a comparison, imagine that the same offer of double time had gone to one of your co-workers who was not in school, was working 10 hours a week, and had just received a massive credit card bill. He offers to supply 50 more hours, for a total of 60 hours. His increase in quantity of hours supplied is 500 percent (50 more hours/10 original hours), so his elasticity of supply is

$$\text{Elasticity of supply} = \frac{500 \text{ percent}}{100 \text{ percent}} = 5$$

He has a relatively elastic response (good thing for you that your boss agreed to your triple-time hours first), as a 100-percent increase in pay would lead to a 500-percent increase in his supply of hours.

Gearing Up (Production) Can Be Hard to Do: Factors Determining Elasticity of Supply

What causes supply to be inelastic for some individuals and businesses and elastic for others? Two important causes are the availability of additional inputs and the time it takes to produce the product/service.

If Paola can easily hire more employees and buy more studs, all at the same prices, then her supply of piercings will tend to be elastic. Even a small rise in the price of piercings (in the denominator) will cause her to increase her quantity supplied (in the numerator) because her profits will increase. But if, as she tries to increase her quantity supplied, she faces higher opportunity costs and has to pay more for her inputs, it will take a big rise in the price of piercings (in the denominator) to get her to provide even a small increase in quantity (in the numerator). In that case, her supply is inelastic.

Availability of Input   Availability of inputs also helps explain the difference between supply elasticities for gold mining and snow shovelling. It is difficult to find new inputs for mining (gold deposits), while it is easy to attract new workers to snow shovelling. Easy availability of inputs makes for more elastic supply, while difficulty and costly availability of new inputs makes for more inelastic supply.

Time   To see the importance of time, compare Paola's supply with the supply in the gold-mining industry. When the price of piercings rises, Paola can quickly adjust her quantity supplied. When gold prices rise, it can take years or even decades for the quantity supplied to adjust, because it takes time to discover and exploit new mines. Industries with quick time to production tend to have more elastic supplies, and industries with slow time to production tend to have more inelastic supplies.

Supply is inelastic when the calculation of
$$\frac{(\% \text{ change in quantity supplied})}{(\% \text{ change in price})}$$
gives a value less than 1.

Supply is elastic when the calculation of
$$\frac{(\% \text{ change in quantity supplied})}{(\% \text{ change in price})}$$
gives a value greater than 1.

Elasticity of supply depends on availability of additional inputs and the time production takes.

Why Do We Care About Elasticity of Supply?

Elasticity of supply allows more accurate projections of future outputs and prices, (smart choices) helping businesses avoid disappointed customers.

In 2007, the Alberta housing market was booming. Oil revenues were raising incomes for everyone in the industry and beyond, and new workers were moving into the province to take well-paying jobs. New-home builders were expanding the quantity supplied of housing as fast as they could, but ended up disappointing many customers when they couldn't deliver the quantities or the prices promised. It is never good business to promise more than you can profitably deliver, and understanding elasticity of supply is important for avoiding such broken promises. Shortages and higher wages in the building trades limited the profitable availability of inputs. Housing construction, although not as time-consuming as mining, does take time to adjust to new price conditions. A smart entrepreneur can't change these business conditions, but he or she can use an understanding of elasticity of supply to make more accurate projections of outputs and prices, and avoid disappointed customers.

It is always a smart business decision to pay no more for an input than you have to. Your boss, in her desperate triple-time wage offer to you, might have paid more than she needed to for the extra work hours, compared to your co-worker who had a more elastic supply of labour. Knowing about elasticity of supply enables smart, informed choices, and can only help a business's bottom line.

Refresh C.5

www.myeconlab.com

1. Explain the relationship between price and quantity supplied for inelastic supply and for elastic supply.

2. If your boss offers you a 20-percent raise, and in response you work 10 percent more hours, how would you describe your price elasticity of labour supply?

3. Your business is about to launch an advertising campaign boasting about your current low prices. You are hoping the ads will bring in many more customers. Explain why you need to be concerned about your elasticity of supply.

Show *Me* *the* Money

The Law of Supply

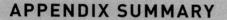

APPENDIX SUMMARY

C.1 WHAT DOES IT REALLY COST? COSTS ARE OPPORTUNITY COSTS

Businesses must pay higher prices to obtain more of an input because opportunity costs change with circumstances. The marginal costs of additional inputs (like labour) are ultimately opportunity costs — the best alternative use of the input.

- **Marginal cost** — additional opportunity cost of increasing quantity supplied, and changes with circumstances
  - For working example, you are supplying time, and marginal cost of your time increases as you increase quantity of hours supplied.
- Differences between smart supply choices and smart demand choices:
  - For supply, marginal cost increases as you supply more.
  - For demand, marginal benefit decreases as you buy more.
  - For supply, marginal benefit is measured in $ (wages you earn); marginal cost is opportunity cost of time.
  - For demand, marginal benefit is satisfaction you get; marginal cost is measured in $ (price you pay).

C.2 FORGET IT, IT'S HISTORY: SUNK COSTS DON'T MATTER FOR FUTURE CHOICES

Sunk costs that cannot be reversed are not part of opportunity costs. Sunk costs do not influence smart, forward-looking decisions.

- **Sunk costs** — past expenses that cannot be recovered.
- Sunk costs are the same no matter which fork in the road you take, so they have no influence on smart choices.

C.3 MORE FOR MORE MONEY: THE LAW OF SUPPLY

If the price of a product/service rises, quantity supplied increases. Businesses increase production when higher prices either create higher profits or cover higher marginal opportunity costs of production.

- **Supply** — businesses' willingness to produce a particular product/service because price covers all opportunity costs.
- **Quantity supplied** — quantity you actually plan to supply at a given price.
- **Marginal opportunity cost** — complete name for any cost relevant to a smart decision.
  - All opportunity costs are marginal costs; all marginal costs are opportunity costs.
- Increasing marginal opportunity costs arise because inputs are not equally productive in all activities.
  - Where inputs are equally productive in all activities, marginal opportunity costs are constant.
- **Market supply** — sum of supplies of all businesses willing to produce a particular product/service.
- **Law of supply** — if the price of a product/service rises, quantity supplied increases.
  - In output markets, businesses are suppliers and households are demanders.
  - In input markets, individuals/households are suppliers and businesses are demanders.
  - For both types of markets, higher prices increase quantity supplied.

C.4 CHANGING THE BOTTOM LINE: WHAT CAN CHANGE SUPPLY?

Quantity supplied is changed only by a change in price.
Supply is changed by all other influences on business decisions.

- Supply is a catch-all term summarizing all possible influences on businesses' willingness to produce a particular product/service.
- Supply changes with changes in technology, prices of inputs, prices of related products/services produced, expected future prices, number of businesses. For example, supply increases with:
  - improvement in technology.
  - fall in price of an input.
  - fall in price of a related product/service.
  - fall in expected future price.
  - increase in number of businesses.
- **Increase in supply** — increase in businesses' willingness to supply. Can be described in two equivalent ways:
  - At any unchanged price, businesses are now willing to supply a greater quantity.
  - For producing any unchanged quantity, businesses are now willing to accept a lower price.

C.5 HOW FAR WILL YOU JUMP FOR THE MONEY? PRICE ELASTICITY OF SUPPLY

Elasticity of supply measures how responsive quantity supplied is to a change in price, and depends on the difficulty, expense, and time involved in increasing production. With elastic supply, businesses can easily and inexpensively increase production; with inelastic supply, it is difficult and expensive to increase production.

- **Elasticity of supply** measures by how much quantity supplied responds to a change in price.

- The formula is:

$$\text{Elasticity of supply} = \frac{\text{Percentage change in quantity supplied}}{\text{Percentage change in price}}$$

- **Inelastic** — For inelastic supply, small response in quantity supplied when price rises.

  – Example: supply of mined gold.

  – Value for formula is less than 1.

- **Elastic** — For elastic supply, large response in quantity supplied when price rises.

  – Example: snow-shovelling services.

  – Value for formula is greater than 1.

- Elasticity of supply of a product/service is influenced by:

  – availability of additional inputs — more available inputs means more elastic supply.

  – time production takes — less time means more elastic supply.

- Elasticity of supply allows more accurate projections of future outputs and prices, helping businesses avoid disappointed customers.

TRUE/FALSE

Circle the correct answer.

C.1 COSTS ARE OPPORTUNITY COSTS

1. When higher-paying jobs are harder to find for workers, a business will have to pay more to hire labour.
   True   **False**

2. Any smart business supply decision involves a choice between a business's marginal benefit (or reward) from supplying (or selling) its product/service and the business's marginal opportunity cost of producing the product/service.
   True   **False**

3. Any smart worker supply decision involves a choice between a worker's marginal benefit (or reward) from supplying (or selling) her work and the worker's marginal opportunity cost of working.
   True   **False**

4. Gordie's marginal opportunity cost of spending an extra hour on Facebook increases if he suddenly has the opportunity to go on a date with his high school crush.

True   **False**

5. Businesses should consider the monthly rent when deciding whether to produce more of a product/service.

True   **False**

6. Sunk costs are part of opportunity costs.

True   **False**

7. Businesses need to receive higher prices to compensate for increasing marginal opportunity costs as output increases.

True   **False**

8. Opportunity cost equals what you get divided by what you give up.

True   **False**

9. As you shift your time *away* from watching TV in order to work more hours, the marginal opportunity cost of working decreases.

True   **False**

10. All opportunity costs are marginal costs, and all marginal costs are opportunity costs.

True   **False**

11. A rise in the price of inputs used by businesses decreases market supply.

True   **False**

12. A rise in the price of a related product/service a business produces increases market supply of the other product/service.

True   **False**

13. Supply is inelastic if a rise in price causes a very responsive change in quantity supplied.

True   **False**

14. The federal government of Canada introduced a Working Income Tax Benefit in its Budget 2007. This policy increases the return from working because it reduces the tax paid on earnings. We know that women's work-supply decision is more "elastic" to wages than men's, so women are more likely to benefit from this policy than are men.

True   **False**

15. If a 10-percent rise in price causes quantity supplied to increase by 40 percent, supply is elastic.

True   **False**

MULTIPLE CHOICE

Circle the correct answer.

C.1 COSTS ARE OPPORTUNITY COSTS

1. Your opportunity cost of watching *American Idol* increases if
   A) it is your favourite TV show.
   B) you have a very expensive television.
   C) you have an exam the next day.
   D) all of the above.

2. The opportunity cost of going to school is highest for someone who
   A) has to give up a job paying $10 an hour.
   B) has to give up a job paying $15 an hour.
   C) loves school.
   D) has to give up a volunteer opportunity.

3. Which statement is *false*?
   A) Marginal costs are opportunity costs.
   B) Opportunity costs are marginal costs.
   C) Sunk costs are marginal costs.
   D) Marginal opportunity costs increase as quantity increases.

C.2 SUNK COSTS DON'T MATTER FOR FUTURE CHOICES

4. Gamblers on slot machines often believe that the more they lose, the greater are their chances of winning on the next turn. However, the chances of winning on any turn are actually random — they do not depend on past turns. Therefore, the money lost on the previous turn is a(n)
   A) total cost.
   B) sunk cost.
   C) smart cost.
   D) opportunity cost.

5. Your friend Larry is deciding whether to break up with his current girlfriend, Lucy. He tells you that his number-one reason for wanting to stay with her is because of his tattoo, which says "I love Lucy." Based on economic thinking, you should advise him to ignore the fact that he has a tattoo because it is a(n)
   A) opportunity cost.
   B) marginal cost.
   C) sunk cost.
   D) total cost.

6. If all workers and equipment are equally productive in all activities, the opportunity cost of increasing output is always

   A) increasing.

   B) decreasing.

   C) the same.

   D) low.

7. The law of supply applies to an individual's decision to work because

   A) as the wage rises, the quantity of hours a worker is willing to supply increases.

   B) as the price workers receive rises, the quantity of hours a worker is willing to supply increases.

   C) workers need to be compensated with higher wages in order to work more hours to cover their increasing marginal opportunity costs.

   D) all of the above.

C.4 WHAT CAN CHANGE SUPPLY?

8. Which factor below does *not* change supply?

   A) Prices of inputs

   B) Expected future prices

   C) Price of the supplied product/service

   D) Number of businesses

9. The supply of a product/service increases with a(n)

   A) improvement in technology producing it.

   B) rise in the price a related product/service produced.

   C) rise in the price of an input.

   D) rise in the future price of the product/service.

10. The market supply of tires decreases if

    A) the price of oil — a major input used to produce tires — rises.

    B) tire-making technology improves.

    C) the expected future price of tires falls.

    D) new tire companies enter the market.

11. The furniture industry has shifted to using particle-board (glued wood chips), rather than real wood, which reduces costs. This

    A) increases supply.

    B) decreases supply.

    C) leaves furniture supply unchanged.

    D) impact on supply depends on demand.

12. The statement "Even after the reward was doubled, nobody volunteered for the mission" illustrates

    A) the law of supply.

    B) elastic supply.

    C) inelastic supply.

    D) inelastic demand.

13. Supply is most likely to be elastic for producing

    A) snow shovels.

    B) gold.

    C) houses.

    D) notebook computers.

14. There would be a high elasticity of supply for a business

    A) in a small town with no available workers.

    B) in a large town with many available workers.

    C) with workers who are lazy and unwilling to work additional hours.

    D) with workers who threaten to quit if their hours are reduced.

15. Since real trees take a very long time to grow, this year's supply of real Christmas trees is

    A) low.

    B) high.

    C) elastic.

    D) inelastic.

SHORT ANSWER

Write a short answer to each question. Your answer may be in point form.

1. Your boss asks you to work 20 additional hours next weekend. If you work those 20 hours, you will not be able to see your significant other. You really value the time you spend with your significant other, and the only time you've gone a weekend without seeing each other was when your friends offered to pay you $300 to spend the weekend with them instead. You agreed because this is the minimum amount you must be compensated for giving up a weekend with your significant other.

    A) Should you agree to work the 20 weekend hours if your boss pays your regular hourly wage rate of $10?

    B) Should you agree to work the 20 weekend hours if your boss pays the overtime rate of $15 per hour for the whole weekend?

2. Employees do not like working long weekdays and on weekends, so employers offer higher wages for the extra time in the form of "overtime pay," which could be up to three times the regular wage. Why is it important for businesses to offer overtime pay?

3. Suppose the government is considering raising income tax rates, which effectively reduces the wage that an individual earns. Research shows that women's decision to work is more sensitive to wage rates than is men's (women's decision to work is more elastic to wage rates). Explain how raising income tax rates will impact men and women differently. Who is less likely to work after the policy is implemented?

4. As wages go up, we work longer hours. Research indicates that some workers, such as medical surgeons, may work *fewer* hours in response to a wage increase. Why might surgeons make this decision? Would this violate the law of supply?

5. Your friend Pablo opens up a tattoo parlour because he thinks body art is a profitable industry. He is trying to forecast how different factors in the industry would affect supply in the market for tattoos. He knows you are taking a course in economics and asks you to verify whether his predictions are true or false.

   A) The entry of new businesses into the (hot) industry will increase supply.

   B) An increase in the minimum wage will increase supply.

   C) A rise in the price of piercings (a related service) will reduce supply of tattoos.

   D) An improvement in tattoo technology will increase supply.

   E) A rise in the price of tattoos will increase supply.

6. Dell tried to compete with Apple's iPod and invested millions of dollars into a factory to produce its own MP3 player. After months of poor sales, Dell started to look into the possibility of abandoning the player (which it eventually did). However, one of the top managers said it would be a mistake to abandon the project after so much money had been spent. What would be your advice?

7. A rise in oil prices causes many other products to become more expensive to produce, especially products with high transportation costs and oil-based plastics. How will the higher oil price affect the supply of these other products?

8. An unexpected fall heat wave makes consumers desperate to buy more air conditioners, but suppliers have none in stock. What factors might affect how quickly suppliers can restock their shelves? What does this have to do with the price elasticity of supply?

9. Rumour has it that Avril Lavigne is giving a concert in her home town of Napanee, Ontario. The first 50 fans get in free! You are 20 minutes away from Napanee and are considering speeding for the rest of the way. Speeding fines on Highway 401 outside Napanee are $110 for driving 120 km/hr, $143 for driving 130 km/hr, and $295 for driving 140 km/hr.

   A) If you are going 120 km/hour, what is the marginal cost if you speed up to 130 km/hour and get caught (assuming you *would* have been caught if you continued going at 120 km/hour)?

   B) If you are going 130 km/hour, what is the marginal cost of speeding up to 140 km/hour and getting caught (assuming you *would* have been caught if you continued at 130 km/hour)?

   C) Compare the marginal cost of speeding up from 120 km/hour to 130 km/hour, with the marginal cost of speeding up from 130 km/hour to 140 km/hour. Why do you think the police have set up the fines this way?

10. List three things you have personally supplied in your life for someone else's consumption (for example, working at a summer job, donating blood, providing friendly advice, and so on). In each case, what were the most important considerations that affected your supply decision?

Coordinating Smart Choices

Demand and Supply

LEARNING OBJECTIVES

After reading this appendix, you should be able to:

D.1 Describe how buyers and sellers compete and cooperate in markets.

D.2 Explain how shortages and surpluses affect prices.

D.3 Identify how market-clearing prices coordinate the smart choices of consumers and businesses.

D.4 Illustrate how changes in demand and supply affect market-clearing prices and quantities.

HAVE YOU EVER organized a big party and felt like it was a miracle everything worked out? There are so many details to look after and responsibilities to coordinate—who's bringing (or buying) the food and drinks, ice, music, toilet paper? Who's going to deal with crashers? Now imagine organizing one day in the life of a small town—or, if your imagination is up to it, in Toronto. Think about the millions of consumers who each make hundreds of decisions about what to eat or which movie to rent. Now think about the thousands of businesses that decide what to produce, where to find inputs, who to hire. Consumers find that, somehow, businesses have produced just about everything they want to buy—for a price. With no one in charge, it seems miraculous. How are all those billions of decisions coordinated so that you (and everyone else) can find the food you want for breakfast and the DVD you want at the video store, let alone places to live, water, jobs, and gas?

If all that doesn't seem enough of a miracle, consider that the coordination problem is a fast-moving target. Japanese food becomes fashionable, condos eclipse houses, new immigrants arrive with different tastes—and yet businesses adjust, and we all continue to find the changing items we are looking for.

Markets and prices are the keys to these apparent miracles. As consumers, we each make smart choices in our own interests. Businesses make smart choices in pursuit of profits. Markets, when they work well, create incentives that coordinate the right products and services being produced in the right quantities and at the right locations to satisfy our wants. This appendix explains how markets form prices, which provide signals and incentives coordinating the smart choices of consumers and businesses.

> *It is not from the benevolence of the butcher, the brewer, or the baker that we expect our dinner, but from their regard to their own interest.*
> *–Adam Smith,*
> *The Wealth of Nations, 1776*

D.1 What's a Market?

market:
the interactions of
buyers and sellers

Rolling Stone magazine named Jimi Hendrix the number-one rock guitarist of all time. Suppose you really want a vinyl copy of his first album, *Are You Experienced*. You can check out the local used album/CD stores, you can prowl garage sales for 60-something-year-olds cleaning out their basement album collections, or you can go online to eBay. These are all markets. A **market** is not a place (physical or virtual) or a thing: it's a process — the interactions between buyers and sellers. Markets exist wherever there is a process of competing bids (from buyers, or demanders) and offers (from sellers, or suppliers). What is common to all the markets above is a negotiation between a buyer and a seller that results in an exchange.

Markets Mix Competition and Cooperation

Markets are an unlikely mix of competition and cooperation. There is competition between buyers trying to get the same product. This is most obvious in auction markets like eBay, where you bid against other buyers and the highest bid wins. But even in a store with fixed prices or at a garage sale, you are competing with other potential buyers on a first-come, first-served basis.

Sellers also compete with each other for customers. Whether offering an album or artichokes, sellers try to get customers to buy from them by offering a lower price, better service, or higher quality than their competitors.

The cooperation in markets that is harder to see is between buyer and seller. Because any purchase or sale is voluntary, an exchange between a buyer and seller happens only when both sides end up better off. If you paid $100 for that rare Jimi Hendrix album, you must have felt that the benefit or satisfaction you would get is worth at least $100 (or you wouldn't have bought it). If the seller accepted $100, she felt that was at least the minimum she wanted to receive to give up the album (or she wouldn't have sold it).

Using the economist's terms for smart choices from Appendices B and C, for you, the buyer, the marginal benefit of the album is at least as great as its price (marginal opportunity cost). For the seller, the price is at least as great as her estimate of marginal opportunity cost (the next best offer for the album). As long as the album — or any other product — sells voluntarily in a market, both sides are better off. Both buyer and seller have made smart choices.

Sure, you would have loved to pay less than $100, and the seller would have preferred to get $200. "Better off" doesn't require the buyer to get the lowest possible price or the seller to get the highest possible price. Both participants in the exchange are better off just as long each one has made a smart choice.

Voluntary exchange is cooperative at heart, and both sides win. Businesses want satisfied customers who will return, and they make money when they supply products/services that consumers want to buy. Consumers are better off when businesses supply products/services that provide satisfaction that is worth (or of greater value than) the price.

The Rules of the Game

For markets to work and voluntary exchanges to happen, some basic rules of the game are necessary. Through laws, government must define and protect property rights and enforce contracts between buyers and sellers. **Property rights** are rules that ensure that when you own something, no one can take it away from you by force. Property can be physical property (land, buildings, cars), financial property (stocks, bonds, savings), and intellectual property (music, books, or software resulting from creative effort, and protected by copyright and patents).

Without property rights, there would be no incentive to produce anything for exchange. Imagine that you operate a car-detailing business and have just finished a beautiful and time-consuming job on a 2009 Honda Acura. The owner of the car comes along, says thanks, and drives away without paying. If no laws protected you against theft, what incentive would you have to continue your business? While this example may sound outrageous, it's not much different from the case of a band that produces an album for sale, only to have it downloaded for free without the band or the record company being paid. Without property rights, most of our time and energy would have to go into protecting our property, rather than producing products/services.

While property rights are a prerequisite for anything to be produced, governments must also enforce agreements between buyers and sellers. For a successful exchange, both buyer and seller must deliver what they agreed to, and there must be some legal "referee" to settle disputes.

Consider the enormous amount of trust involved when you make an online purchase on eBay. The seller trusts you will pay. You trust the product will be delivered. This trust does not happen accidentally.

Part of the reason eBay has been successful is that it has implemented rules that foster the necessary trust. The PayPal system guarantees that payments made by the buyer are received by the seller. And the ability of buyers to give anonymous and public feedback about their experiences with a seller creates enormous incentives for sellers to "produce" happy customers. If these informal rules don't work, the legal system is still the ultimate referee. This enormous trust between complete strangers is the foundation for the billions of voluntary exchanges that happen every day in all markets. Even passionate supporters of "free markets" acknowledge that there is an important role for government in defining and enforcing property rights so that free and voluntary exchanges can happen in markets.

property rights: legally enforceable guarantees of ownership of physical, financial, and intellectual property

Refresh D.1

1. What is a market?

2. You are negotiating with a car dealer over the price of a new car. Explain where competition enters the process and where cooperation enters.

3. The Recording Industry Association of America's (RIAA) mission is "to foster a business and legal climate that supports and promotes our members' . . . intellectual property rights worldwide." Have you ever downloaded music? If so, what arguments do you use to counter RIAA's defence of property rights?

www.myeconlab.com

Explain how shortages and surpluses affect prices.

Why do most stores sell Gatorade for $3 a bottle, and doughnuts for 99 cents? Think back to the smart choices that consumers (Appendix B) and businesses (Appendix C) make: Prices play a central role. Consumers compare prices and marginal benefit *(buy if the marginal benefit is greater than the price)*, while businesses compare prices and marginal opportunity costs *(sell if the price is greater than the marginal opportunity costs)*. Where do these prices come from?

Prices are the outcome of a market process of competing bids and offers. These negotiations between buyers and sellers may be obvious on eBay or at garage sales, but when you buy Gatorade at the corner store or a coffee and bagel at Tim Hortons, the store has set the price and there is no negotiation. The only "process" seems to be the cashier swiping your debit card or making change. For most purchases we make as consumers, the answer to the question "Where do prices come from?" seems to be "Businesses set prices." What gives?

It's true that in a market economy, businesses are free to set any price they choose. But no one can force consumers to buy at any price, and competing businesses may set lower or higher prices. So why do prices settle at particular numbers?

The economist's short answer to these questions about where prices come from is . . . (drum roll) . . . the interaction of demand and supply, in markets with appropriate property rights! But that answer, while true, is pretty useless. We can point to anything that happens in an economy and say, in our best educated voice, "It is all determined by the laws of demand and supply." The longer and more useful answer exposes the hidden interactions between buyers and sellers, and also explains the miracles of markets in providing the products/services we want.

Prices are the outcome of a market process of competing bids (from buyers) and offers (from sellers).

Rules of the Game Necessary for All Games, Not Just Markets

The game of football can be considered a model for how markets have developed. The earliest version, folk football, was played in medieval England—there were few rules, and the ones that were in place came about spontaneously and based on custom. There was "little skill . . . just muscle." The sport continued this way for centuries, until folk football morphed into soccer and rugby, and official rules were adopted. Skill started to matter, and the new forms of football were embraced the world over.

Typical markets grow in the way folk football did—evolving spontaneously, driven by participants, unstructured to the point when rules begin to develop. Only when the rules become formal does a market reach its full potential. "An absolutely free market is like folk football, a free-for-all brawl. A real market is like American football, an ordered brawl."

Like other markets, eBay is not a free-for-all brawl because of the rules and procedures that have evolved to ensure trust and enforce contracts. Instead of competition between two football teams, there is competition between thousands of buyers, and between thousands of sellers. But the rules allow cooperative deals to be struck.

Source: John McMillan, *Reinventing the Bazaar*, Norton, 2002, pp. 12–13.

Prices in Action

Paradoxically, the best way to understand why prices settle at particular numbers is to look at what happens in markets when prices have not settled. Let's begin the story of "Where do prices come from?" by looking at what happens when markets are not working to coordinate smart choices, leaving frustrated consumers and producers.

Since the story has to explain particular numbers, it will be helpful to have … particular numbers! Let's use a simple set of made-up numbers for the market for piercings (recall our example of Paola's Piercing and Fingernail Parlour, introduced in Appendix C).

The best way to understand why prices settle at particular numbers is to look at what happens in markets when prices have not settled.

Figure D.1 Market Demand and Supply for Piercings		
Price	Quantity Demanded	Quantity Supplied
$ 20	1200	200
$ 40	900	400
$ 60	600	600
$ 80	300	800
$100	0	1000

The three columns in Figure D.1 show alternative market prices for piercings (column 1), and, for each price, the quantity of piercings demanded (column 2) and supplied (column 3). If you gaze down columns 1 and 2 together, you see that as the price rises, the quantity demanded decreases. This is the law of demand. As a product becomes more expensive, consumers economize on its use and search for cheaper substitutes. If you gaze down columns 1 and 3 together, you see that as the price rises, the quantity supplied increases. This is the law of supply. Higher prices increase business's willingness to supply, because higher prices mean higher profits and the ability to profitably cover higher marginal opportunity costs. While the particular numbers will be useful, all our stories really need is the general pattern of numbers. Higher prices generally lead to decreased quantity demanded and to increased quantity supplied in almost all markets.

We know from the law of demand that consumers prefer lower prices, and we know from the law of supply that businesses prefer higher prices. How do prices get set in a way that reconciles these opposing goals?

Frustrated Buyers What if the market price of piercings were $40 in parlours all around town? You might think that this relatively low price would make for happy consumers, but the number in Figure D.1 tells another story. Look at row 2, where the price of a piercing is $40. Consumers want to buy 900 piercings, but Paola and her competitors are willing to supply only 400 piercings. While the 400 people who are able to buy a piercing for $40 will be happy, there are 500 frustrated buyers (900 – 400 = 500) who are willing and able to pay $40 but who can't get a parlour to do the piercing. This is a **shortage**, where quantity demanded exceeds quantity supplied. In markets with shortages, or **excess demand**, consumers experience long lineups and out-of-stock items at stores. Businesses experience products flying off the shelves and any inventories quickly dwindling to zero.

shortage or excess demand: quantity demanded exceeds quantity supplied

Shortages encourage competition among buyers. The consumers who most want the piercing will be willing to pay a bit more than $40, rather than being left with nothing. Buyers may bid for the scarce piercings (just like on eBay), driving up the price. Even if buyers don't actively bid up prices (when was the last time you offered to pay extra at Tim Hortons in hopes that they would find one more glazed doughnut for you?), sellers find that they can raise prices and still sell everything they have produced. Either way, shortages create pressure for prices to rise.

Rising prices provide signals and incentives, which are the key to how markets meet our wants. For businesses, higher prices are a signal, like a hand waving persistently in a classroom, saying, "Higher profits over here!" Higher prices and higher profits create an incentive for businesses to produce more and increase their quantity supplied. For consumers, higher prices mean we must revisit our smart choices. As prices go up, some consumers will give up on buying piercings and switch their planned purchases to some cheaper form of body decoration, like henna tattoos or costume jewellery. Quantity demanded decreases with higher prices.

Both adjustments — the increase in quantity supplied, and the decrease in quantity demanded — work to eliminate the shortage.

Frustrated Sellers

Instead of $40, what if the market price of piercings was $80? Look at row 4 of Figure D.1. At the relatively high price of $80, consumers want to buy only 300 piercings, but piercing parlours are eagerly willing to supply 800 piercings. So, all over town, parlours are expecting customers who don't show up, and idle piercers are sitting and reading newspapers. Parlours happily sell 300 piercings at $80, but are frustrated to the tune of 500 unsold piercings (800 − 300 = 500) they were willing to supply at that price. This is a **surplus**, where quantity supplied exceeds quantity demanded. In markets with surpluses, or **excess supply**, businesses experience underemployed resources, unsold products sitting on shelves, or rising inventories in warehouses. Those consumers willing and able to buy at the high price experience their choice of where to buy and sellers who are eager to please.

Surpluses encourage competition among sellers. The businesses that are most efficient or desperate for sales will cut their prices rather than be faced with empty piercing beds or unsold products. Some businesses will hold sales, or offer extras in trying to woo customers (free nail set with any piercing!). As discounts appear, consumers will be less willing to pay the $80 price. Surpluses create pressure for prices to fall.

Falling prices also provide signals and incentives, but in the opposite direction to rising prices. For consumers, falling prices are an incentive to buy more of now less expensive products/services, switching from substitutes whose prices have not changed. And as prices fall, more people can afford to buy. More smart decisions result in buying products/services with lower prices. Quantity demanded increases. For businesses, falling prices are bad news — a warning signal of "lower profits ahead." They will decrease the quantities they are willing to supply, and switch inputs to more profitable opportunities. Paola will move some of her staff from piercing to fingernail painting. Quantity supplied decreases with falling prices.

Both adjustments — the increase in quantity demanded, and the decrease in quantity supplied — work to eliminate the surplus.

Adjusting Prices and Quantities In these stories of shortages and surpluses, price adjustments play the key role. You may be thinking that the prices you observe in most markets don't adjust continuously and, in fact, settle for long times at particular values. Even the question I posed — "Why do prices settle at particular numbers?" — seems inconsistent with the stories about prices rising or falling in reaction to shortages and surpluses. There is a reconciliation, however.

Most businesses have some *market power*, which means they have some control over setting prices. Businesses pick a price point that they expect will make the most profits, taking into account all cooperative and competitive forces. For a mutually beneficial exchange with a cooperating customer, price must be less than the customer's marginal benefit but also must profitably cover the business's marginal opportunity costs. The price point also must be competitive with what other similar businesses charge. Once a business picks a price point, it may turn out to be too low (shortages develop and products sell out quickly) or too high (resulting in surpluses, underemployed resources, and rising inventories). But over time, especially in the face of competition, businesses adjust price points in reaction to market conditions of shortages or surpluses.

Quantity adjustments also play an important role in the stories of how markets react to shortages or surpluses. When your favourite video store finds a popular movie is always out and frustrated customers come to the desk looking for it, the store orders more copies. Shortages lead to incremental increases in quantity supplied. If your local corner store regularly orders one case of Gatorade a week, but finds not all of the bottles are selling, it cuts back to ordering one case every other week. Surpluses lead to incremental decreases in quantity supplied. In response to excess demand or excess supply, businesses adjust quantities continuously, and can do so in small increments to match changing market conditions. When your boss asks you to work an extra shift next week, or your neighbourhood Tim Hortons bakes 10 dozen chocolate doughnuts a day instead of 13 dozen, those are quantity adjustments.

Even when prices don't change, shortages and surpluses also create incentives for frequent quantity adjustments to better coordinate smart choices of businesses and consumers.

What is remarkable about all of these price adjustments (not so frequent) and quantity adjustments (frequent) is that no consumer or business needs to know anything about anyone's personal wants or production capabilities. Prices (and quantities) serve as signals to both consumers and businesses, and all anyone has to do is consider his or her own self-interest. As long as an imbalance exists between quantity demanded and quantity supplied, prices will eventually adjust and send signals for consumers and businesses to change their smart decisions.

With excess demand, as long as prices are higher than marginal opportunity costs, businesses have an incentive to increase quantity supplied because there are profits to be made. And as long as the same prices are higher than consumers' marginal benefit (willingness and ability to pay), consumers have an incentive to search for cheaper substitutes and decrease quantity demanded.

With excess supply, as long as prices are lower than marginal opportunity costs, businesses have an incentive to decrease quantity supplied because they are losing money. And as long as the same prices are lower than consumers' marginal benefit, consumers will buy more of a product that feels like a bargain.

Consumers and businesses take all of these signals, and each make self-interested smart decisions based on the price. As a byproduct of all these individual decisions made by complete strangers, markets provide the products/services we want.

Refresh

D.2

www.myeconlab.com

1. Define a shortage, and explain who competes and what happens to prices.

2. Old Navy decides to price a new line of jeans at $75, which covers all marginal opportunity costs as well as a healthy profit margin. If Old Navy has priced the jeans too high, what signals does the company receive? What actions might Old Navy take next?

3. Most provincial parks charge a fixed price for a camping permit, and allow you to reserve specific campsites well in advance. By the time a summer holiday weekend arrives, all the permits are taken. There is excess demand, and no price adjustment. If you want to reserve your favourite campsite for next year, how do you compete, and who do you compete against?

D.3 When Prices Sit Still: Market-Clearing Prices Balancing Quantity Demanded and Quantity Supplied

Identify how market-clearing prices coordinate the smart choices of consumers and businesses.

So, after reading all these stories of rising prices (from shortages) and falling prices (from surpluses), you may be wondering, "When do prices finally sit still, and settle at particular values?" Indulge me one last time in looking at the numbers in Figure D.1. Look at row 3, where the price of a piercing is $60. At $60, consumers want to buy 600 piercings, and all of the piercing parlours combined want to supply 600 piercings. At last, quantity demanded equals quantity supplied. With no shortages or surpluses, there are no competitive forces pushing prices up or down. Consumers are happy because every person who is willing and able to pay $60 gets a piercing. Businesses are happy because the $60 price profitably covers their marginal opportunity costs for the 600 piercings they are willing to supply.

There are consumers out there who would have demanded a piercing at $20, but think $60 is outrageous. They don't get pierced. But they have made a smart decision: For them, a piercing isn't worth $60, or $60 is more than they can reasonably afford. They make a smart choice to spend their money elsewhere, and thus are not putting pressure on piercing prices. Likewise, there are parlours out there that would have supplied more piercings if the price were $80, but $60 doesn't cover their marginal opportunity costs so they are using their resources to produce something else (nail sets? pedicures?) they can sell at a price that profitably covers marginal opportunity costs.

This price ($60 in our example) that coordinates quantity demanded and quantity supplied is so important that economists have two names for it. (Sort of like how you have at least two names — including nicknames — for people who are important to you.)

Market-clearing price is the first name for the market price that equalizes quantity demanded and quantity supplied. At the market-clearing price, there are no longer any frustrated buyers or sellers. There is a match for every buyer and seller, and all go home happy. Everyone who makes a voluntary exchange of $60 for a piercing (both the consumers buying and the parlours selling) is better off, or they wouldn't have bought and sold.

market-clearing price: the price when quantity demanded equals quantity supplied

The second name for the market price that equalizes quantity demanded and quantity supplied is **equilibrium price**. *Equilibrium* is a term from physics that means a balance of forces (see FYI in the margin). The equilibrium price exactly balances the forces of competition and cooperation to coordinate the smart choices of consumers and businesses. At the equilibrium price, there is no tendency for change (until some new event occurs to disturb the balance, as we will see in the next section) and no incentives for anyone — consumers or businesses — to change their own, self-interested, smart decisions. No one is kicking himself for making a mistaken purchase or missing a better opportunity. Everyone has done the best they can in their exchanges, given the wants and resources they started with.

Why is this particular "price that sits still" so important that it gets two names? It is the culmination of the forces of cooperation and competition that explains the miracle of the market. Ironically, when markets are functioning well and clearing, we don't pay much attention to this miracle. We find what we want for breakfast at Tim Hortons, the DVDs we like are on the shelf at the video store, and we find jobs, gas for our cars, and all the other products/services that satisfy our wants. And businesses find customers for all the products/services they want to profitably supply. Often, it's only when something goes wrong — perhaps a labour dispute or a natural disaster that disrupts supplies — that we realize how conveniently we usually find what we want to buy.

The fact that consumers find that businesses have produced just about everything they want to buy, and with no one in charge, and that billions of decisions get coordinated is due to . . . (drum roll reprise) . . . the interaction of demand and supply, in markets with appropriate property rights! The law of demand is shorthand for the smart choices of consumers. The law of supply is shorthand for the smart choices of businesses. Market-clearing prices (and quantities) result when smart choices are coordinated. The forces of competition (between consumers, and between businesses) are balanced with the forces of cooperation (voluntary, mutually beneficial exchanges between consumers and businesses). The key to this outcome is that price signals in markets create incentives so that while each person acts only in her own self-interest, the unintended consequence is the production of all the products/services we want.

Perhaps the most famous phrase in economics that describes this outcome is Adam Smith's "invisible hand" in his 1776 book, *The Wealth of Nations*:

> When an individual makes choices, "he intends only his own gain, and he is in this . . . led by an invisible hand to promote an end which was no part of his intention. . . . By pursuing his own interest he frequently promotes that of the society more effectually than when he really intends to promote it."

equilibrium price: the price that balances forces of competition and cooperation, so that there is no tendency for change

FOR YOUR INFORMATION
Definition of *equilibrium*: "A condition in which all acting influences are cancelled by others, resulting in a stable, balanced, or unchanging system." Synonym: *balance*.

Price signals in markets create incentives so that while each person acts only in her own self-interest, the unintended consequence is the production of all the products/services we want.

Refresh D.3

1. Name and define the two other names for "prices that sit still."

2. Explain the balance between the forces of competition and cooperation at "prices that sit still." (I can't give away the answer to question 1, can I?)

3. In an attempt to promote the social good of energy conservation, Toronto Hydro introduced the Peaksaver Program. Participating households received a $25 reward for allowing a "peaksaver" switch to be installed on their central air conditioners, which briefly turns off the air conditioner during peak demand times on hot summer days. Do you think the program would work without the $25 reward? How does this illustrate the "invisible hand"?

www.myeconlab.com

Illustrate how changes in demand and supply affect market-clearing prices and quantities.

We live in a fast-paced society where change happens regularly. Food and clothing go in and out of style, technology is constantly changing the way we communicate and how and what we produce, and business may boom in Alberta and bust in New Brunswick. Even if markets succeed in temporarily coordinating the plans of consumers and businesses and settle at market-clearing prices, what about when change happens? Will markets still coordinate the right products/services being produced in the right quantities at the right locations to satisfy our wants when the "right" target keeps moving?

Believe it or not, all the stories about shortages, surpluses, adjusting prices, and quantities actually had very limited change. Yes, prices and quantities changed, and smart decisions changed — but in the background, I was holding constant almost everything else.

All the stories began with the numbers in Figure D.1, which illustrate the law of demand (when price rises, quantity demanded decreases) and the law of supply (when price rises, quantity supplied increases). We could focus carefully on those relationships between price and quantity because we were holding constant all other influences on consumers' choices and on businesses' choices.

Remember the Appendix B distinction between a change in quantity demanded (caused by a change in price) and a change in demand? Five factors can cause a change in demand. Name at least three and win a prize! Answers: changes in preferences, prices of related products, income, expected future prices, and number of consumers. All of those are unchanged in the numbers in Figure D.1. And remember that Chapter 3 distinction between a change in quantity supplied (caused by a change in price) and a change in supply? The five factors that can cause a change in supply (changes in technology, prices of inputs, prices of related products produced, expected future prices, number of businesses) also are all unchanged in Figure D.1.

Don't decide to give up on this appendix because you fear I plan to slog through changes in all 10 factors. To get you to break time faster, I'll combine the explanations into just four groups: what happens to market-clearing prices and quantities when there are increases or decreases in demand, and increases or decreases in supply.

Increases in Demand

When the Japanese food craze hit about 10 years ago, there was an increase in demand for sushi, triggered by a change in preferences. Increased demand drives up the market price, and restaurants responded to that signal of higher profits by increasing the quantity supplied of sushi. Any other factor that increases demand will cause a rise in the market-clearing price and an increase in the quantity supplied.

For an increase in demand, market-clearing price rises, and quantity supplied increases.

Decreases in Demand

With business booming in Alberta from oil revenues in 2007, many people moved from New Brunswick out west. What did this decrease in population do to the real estate market in New Brunswick? There was a decrease in demand, which drove down the market price, and there was a decrease in the quantity supplied of new housing. Any other factor that decreases demand will cause a fall in the market-clearing price and a decrease in the quantity supplied.

For a decrease in demand, market-clearing price falls, and quantity supplied decreases.

Increases in Supply

The relentless improvement in semiconductor technology makes it cheaper to produce computers and causes an increase in the supply of computers. Market price falls as Dell and HP compete for customers by lowering prices to reflect their lower costs of production. Consumers respond to lower prices by increasing their quantity demanded of computers. Any other factor that increases supply will cause a fall in the market-clearing price and an increase in the quantity demanded.

For an increase in supply, market-clearing price falls, and quantity demanded increases.

Decreases in Supply

The business boom in Alberta drove up wages, as businesses competed for scarce workers. The going wage, even in fast-food restaurants, rose from $10 to $15. For restaurants, this rise in inputs prices caused a decrease in supply. Restaurants were then willing to supply meals only at higher prices, and the market price of meals rose. Rising prices caused customers to rethink their smart food choices, and quantity demanded of restaurant meals decreased. Any other factor that decreases supply will cause a rise in the market-clearing price and a decrease in quantity demanded.

For a decrease in supply, market-clearing price rises, and quantity demanded decreases.

Still On Target

Markets are adept at reacting to change. Whether there are shortages, surpluses, or changes in any of the 10 factors affecting demand or supply, markets react quickly because prices create incentives for consumers and businesses to adjust their smart choices. Price signals in markets create incentives so that while each person acts only in her own self-interest, the result (coordinated through Adam Smith's invisible hand of competition) is the miracle of continuous, ever-changing production of the products/services we want.

FOR YOUR INFORMATION

The text gives a relatively simple explanation about what happens to market-clearing prices and quantities. There are more complicated cases where demand increases and supply decreases, and vice versa. Those stories don't have clear outcomes for both prices and quantities — even with our Appendix B mental equivalents of controlled laboratory experiments (distinctions between changes in quantity demanded and changes in demand) — so I am skipping them.

Those kinds of complications are part of the reason why Max Planck, the originator of quantum physics, gave up studying economics because he found it too difficult!

Refresh D.4

1. What happens to the market-clearing price and quantity when demand increases? When demand decreases? When supply increases? When supply decreases?

2. Predicting changes in market-clearing prices and quantities is harder when *both* demand *and* supply change at the same time. You run a halal butcher shop in Ottawa and expect an increase in the number of Muslims in Ottawa. Rents for retail space are also falling all over town. What do you think will happen to the market-clearing price for halal meat? What will happen to the quantity sold?

3. In response to the business boom in Alberta, the city of Edmonton offered $200 per month rent subsidies to low-income families so they could afford to live and work in the city. What impact would this effective *increase in income* have on rents? What do you think was the intention of the subsidies?

www.myeconlab.com

Coordinating *Smart* *Choices*

Demand and Supply

APPENDIX SUMMARY

D.1 WHAT'S A MARKET?

Markets connect competition between buyers, competition between sellers, and cooperation between buyers and sellers. Government guarantees of property rights allow markets to function.

- **Market** — the interactions of buyers and sellers.
- Because any purchase or sale is voluntary, an exchange between a buyer and seller happens only when both sides end up better off.
  - Buyers are better off when businesses supply products/services that provide satisfaction (marginal benefit) that is at least as great as the price paid.
  - Sellers are better off when the price received is at least as great as marginal opportunity costs.
- **Property rights** — legally enforceable guarantees of ownership of physical, financial, and intellectual property.

D.2 WHERE DO PRICES COME FROM? PRICE SIGNALS FROM COMBINING DEMAND AND SUPPLY

When there are shortages, competition between buyers drives prices up. When there are surpluses, competition between sellers drives prices down.

- When the market price turns out to be too low:
  - **shortage,** or **excess demand** — quantity demanded exceeds quantity supplied.
  - shortages create pressure for prices to rise.
  - rising prices provide signals and incentives for businesses to increase quantity supplied and for consumers to decrease quantity demanded, eliminating the shortage.

- When the market price turns out to be too high:

  - **surplus,** or **excess supply** — quantity supplied exceeds quantity demanded.

  - surpluses create pressure for prices to fall.

  - falling prices provide signals and incentives for businesses to decrease quantity supplied and for consumers to increase quantity demanded, eliminating the surplus.

- Even when prices don't change, shortages and surpluses also create incentives for frequent *quantity adjustments* to better coordinate smart choices of businesses and consumers.

D.3 WHEN PRICES SIT STILL: MARKET-CLEARING PRICES
BALANCING QUANTITY DEMANDED AND QUANTITY SUPPLIED

Market-clearing prices coordinate the smart choices of consumers and businesses, balancing quantity demanded and quantity supplied.

- The price that coordinates the smart choices of consumers and businesses has two names:

  - **market-clearing price** — the price when quantity demanded equals quantity supplied

  - **equilibrium price** — the price that balances forces of competition and cooperation, so that there is no tendency for change

- Market-clearing prices balance the forces of competition (between consumers and between businesses) with the forces of cooperation (voluntary, mutually beneficial exchanges between consumers and businesses).

- Price signals in markets create incentives, so that while each person acts only in her own self-interest, the result (coordinated through Adam Smith's invisible hand of competition) is the miracle of continuous, ever-changing production of the products/services we want.

D.4 MOVING TARGETS:
WHAT HAPPENS WHEN DEMAND AND SUPPLY CHANGE?

When demand or supply change, market-clearing prices and quantities change. The price changes cause businesses and consumers to adjust their smart choices. Well-functioning markets supply the changed products and services demanded.

- For a change in demand (caused by changes in preferences, prices of related products, income, expected future prices, number of consumers)

  - an increase in demand causes a rise in market-clearing price, and an increase in quantity supplied.

  - a decrease in demand causes a fall in market-clearing price, and a decrease in quantity supplied.

- For a change in supply (caused by changes in technology, prices of inputs, prices of related products produced, expected future prices, number of businesses)

  - an increase in supply causes a fall in market-clearing price and an increase in quantity demanded.

  - a decrease in supply causes a rise in market-clearing price and a decrease in quantity demanded.

TRUE/FALSE

Circle the correct answer.

Apu Nahasapeemapetilon opens an outdoor iced cappuccino stand on his street in order to sell coffee to neighbours during peak hours of the day. Apu's product is unique enough that it allows him some choice in what price to charge. Use this scenario to answer questions 1 to 9.

D.1 WHAT'S A MARKET?

1. If customers are allowed to steal the iced cappuccinos without paying, this would still be a market.   **True**   **False**

2. The price should cover what it costs to make the iced cappuccinos, but not the cost of Apu's time.   **True**   **False**

D.2 PRICE SIGNALS FROM COMBINING DEMAND AND SUPPLY

3. In order for price and quantity adjustments to occur in this market, Apu needs to be aware of the personal wants of his neighbours.   **True**   **False**

4. If Apu prices above the maximum price that consumers are willing to pay, then he will end up with excess supply.   **True**   **False**

5. If Apu prices below the maximum price that consumers are willing to pay, then he will lose out on potential profits.   **True**   **False**

D.3 MARKET-CLEARING PRICES BALANCING QUANTITY DEMANDED AND QUANTITY SUPPLIED

6. If Apu sets a price that leaves him with no excess demand and no excess supply, he has found the equilibrium price.   **True**   **False**

D.4 WHAT HAPPENS WHEN DEMAND AND SUPPLY CHANGE?

7. An unexpected health warning links iced cappuccino consumption to severe obesity. The following causal chain of events would likely follow in the local coffee market: **True**   **False**

(*Hint:* Assume that Apu's neighbours are not like Homer Simpson and *would* care about the health effects!)

Demand $\downarrow$ → surplus → price $\uparrow$ → quantity supplied $\uparrow$ and quantity demanded $\downarrow$ → equilibrium (surplus disappears)

8. The Simpson family decides to also set up an iced cappuccino stand. The following causal chain of events would likely follow in the local coffee market:

   Supply $\uparrow$ $\rightarrow$ shortage $\rightarrow$ price $\uparrow$ $\rightarrow$ quantity supplied $\uparrow$ and quantity demanded $\downarrow$ $\rightarrow$ equilibrium (shortage disappears)

   True   **False**

9. Apu's wife gives birth to quintuplets, which increases the value of his time. The following causal chain of events would likely follow in the local coffee market:

   Supply $\downarrow$ $\rightarrow$ shortage $\rightarrow$ price $\uparrow$ $\rightarrow$ quantity supplied $\uparrow$ and quantity demanded $\downarrow$ $\rightarrow$ equilibrium (shortage disappears)

   True   **False**

10. Warmer weather appears to be giving cats a chance to mate three times each year instead of the usual two times a year (that is, due to global warming, more cats are on the prowl). The result has been a sharp increase in the cat population. The Humane Society last year had to find homes for roughly 6000 cats, compared with 3000 cats five years ago. Therefore, this is a good time to buy cats from the Humane Society.

   True   **False**

11. Durham University researchers report Scottish grey seals are having more sex thanks to global warming. This is because, as drinking water becomes scarce, the females must travel farther distances and other males are able to seduce them. The market price for seal coat fur will likely increase.

   True   **False**

12. Ontario had a ratio of 27 students for each full-time professor in 2005–06, while other provinces, on average, had a ratio of 18-to-one. Given that enrolment in Ontario universities is expected to continue to increase, it is estimated that Ontario needs 11 000 more professors by the end of the decade. If universities reduced qualification requirements to allow students with college degrees to teach introductory university courses, this action would help reduce the shortage.

   True   **False**

13. In the early 2000s, many Canadians were worried about the "brain drain" (that is, Canada's most talented workers moving to the U.S. for jobs after obtaining a good education in Canada). Recent evidence suggests that the brain drain has been plugged, as more Canadians prefer to stay home and a lot more Americans are coming north. In 2005, almost 11 000 Americans came north, double the number in 2000, and more of them had at least a bachelor's degree. All else being equal, this will put upward pressure on the wages of workers in jobs requiring a bachelor's degree.

True   False

14. Canada Summer Jobs is an initiative by the federal government that provides wage subsidies to help small Canadian companies create career-related summer jobs for students between the ages of 15 and 30. This initiative will likely increase the demand for workers.

True   False

15. Organ donation saves hundreds of lives each year across Ontario, yet there are not enough available donors to meet the demand for organ transplants. In 2007, the Ontario government invested $4 million in a new plan to boost organ donations, which includes funding to reimburse living donors for pre-approved expenses, such as accommodation, meals, travel, and lost income. This new plan will likely lead to an increase in the quantity of organs supplied.

True   False

MULTIPLE CHOICE

Circle the correct answer.

D.1 WHAT'S A MARKET?

1. The place where buyers and sellers meet is called
   A) a store.
   B) an economy.
   C) a party.
   D) a market.

D.2 PRICE SIGNALS FROM COMBINING DEMAND AND SUPPLY

2. If a market is not at the market-clearing price,
   A) prices adjust.
   B) prices send signals for consumers and businesses to change their smart decisions.
   C) quantities adjust.
   D) all of the above.

3. Which of the following is *not* a quantity adjustment?

   A) Tim Hortons asking its workers to work overtime

   B) Blockbuster ordering extra copies of *Harry Potter*

   C) Leon's Furniture Ltd. eliminating sales tax on all patio furniture items

   D) a fish processing plant laying off 10 percent of its workers

D.3 MARKET-CLEARING PRICES BALANCING QUANTITY DEMANDED AND QUANTITY SUPPLIED

4. A price at which there are no shortages and no surpluses is a

   A) maximum price.

   B) minimum price.

   C) affordable price.

   D) market-clearing price.

5. In equilibrium,

   A) the price consumers are willing to pay equals the price suppliers are willing to accept.

   B) consumers would like to buy more at the current price.

   C) producers would like to sell more at the current price.

   D) all of the above.

D.4 WHAT HAPPENS WHEN DEMAND AND SUPPLY CHANGE?

6. If demand increased and supply decreased, this would lead to

   A) higher prices.

   B) lower prices.

   C) chaos.

   D) a shortage in the market.

7. The following will cause a reduction in prices:

   A) demand increases and supply decreases.

   B) demand increases and supply increases.

   C) demand decreases and supply decreases.

   D) demand decreases and supply increases.

8. A surplus can be eliminated by

   A) increasing supply.

   B) decreasing the quantity demanded.

   C) allowing the price to fall.

   D) allowing the quantity bought and sold to fall.

The Canadian Restaurant and Foodservices Association predicts a shortfall of 44 300 food and beverage workers in British Columbia by 2015. Use this information to answer questions 9 to 11.

9. This implies that, in British Columbia,
   A) demand for restaurant food exceeds supply of restaurant food.
   B) supply of restaurant food exceeds demand for restaurant food.
   C) demand is greater than supply for restaurant workers.
   D) supply is greater than demand for restaurant workers.

10. A shortage creates pressure for prices to change. In the British Columbia example, this may be represented through
    A) an increase in the price of labour (workers).
    B) an increase in the wage paid to employees in the restaurant business.
    C) an increase in labour costs for restaurant businesses.
    D) all of the above.

11. If the price offered to workers (that is, the wage) in restaurant businesses in B.C. increases, then
    A) the quantity of work supplied will increase.
    B) the quantity of work demanded will decrease.
    C) more workers will be looking for work.
    D) all of the above.

12. According to the Canadian Restaurant and Foodservices Association, "The labour shortage is the number one issue for restaurant operators in Alberta, who are coping with an estimated shortfall of 11 000 employees in the food-service industry alone." This implies that
    A) there is no demand for food service.
    B) the demand for food service is less than the supply of food service.
    C) the demand for food service is equal to the supply of food service.
    D) the demand for food service is greater than the supply of food service.

13. The Children's Fitness Tax Credit was introduced by the Government of Canada to provide parents with a tax credit (benefit) of up to $500 to register a child under the age of 16 in a program of physical activity. Therefore,
    A) demand for Harry Potter novels may increase.
    B) demand for Harry Potter novels may decrease.
    C) supply of Harry Potter novels may increase.
    D) supply of Harry Potter novels may decrease.

14. Recent research shows that the dramatic rise in obesity in the United States is due more to the overconsumption of unhealthy foods than it is to underactivity. As a result of this finding,

    A) the demand for potato chips is likely to increase.

    B) the demand for GoodLife Fitness gym memberships is likely to increase.

    C) the demand for nutrition-promoting foods will increase.

    D) all of the above.

15. Since 1960, there has been a dramatic increase in the number of working mothers. Based on this information alone, we can predict that the market for child-care services has experienced a(n)

    A) increase in demand.

    B) decrease in demand.

    C) increase in quantity demanded.

    D) decrease in quantity supplied.

SHORT ANSWER

Write a short answer to each question. Your answer may be in point form.

1. The price set in a market is much more than a number. What functions does a price perform for the buyers and sellers? And what is so special about the "market-clearing price"?

2. Apu wants to set the market equilibrium price, so he surveys all three families on his street in order to determine how many cappuccinos per day they are willing to buy at different prices. He gives them four price options. Their answers can be summarized on the following table.

Price per Iced Capuccino	Flanders Family Quantity Demanded	Van Houten Family Quantity Demanded	Simpson Family Quantity Demanded	Market Quantity Demanded
$1	2	5	5	12
$2	1	3	4	8
$3	0	1	3	4
$4	0	0	2	2

Apu also estimates his costs and determines how many iced cappuccinos he is willing to sell. Market demand and Apu's supply are summarized in the following table:

Price per Iced Capuccino	Market Quantity Demanded	Apu's Quantity Supplied
$1	12	7
$2	8	8
$3	4	9
$4	2	10

A) What is the market-clearing price? Explain.

B) If Apu sets the price above $2, will there be a shortage or surplus in the market? Explain.

C) If Apu sets the price above $2, will there be pressure for the price to rise or fall? Explain.

3. Rising housing prices in Alberta have motivated some Albertans to migrate to Saskatchewan. In fact, housing prices in Saskatchewan are at record levels. Using a demand and supply framework, explain why prices in Saskatchewan's housing market are rising.

4. Billions of dollars will be invested in energy-related projects across Alberta over the next 20 years, prompting Albertans to ask where the workers for these projects will come from. In 2007, the Alberta government warned that it is facing a shortfall of 100 000 workers by 2015, with at least 40 000 of those positions in the oil and gas sector. "It's in the whole economy . . . whether it's the Tim Hortons or a new restaurant that can't find people to serve coffee and food because there's not enough people to keep the restaurants or coffee shops open."

A) A union proposal calls for 14.5-percent wage increases over two years, barely above Alberta's nation-leading inflation rate of 6.5 percent. Explain why unions are asking for such high wage increases for their workers.

B) The skilled labour shortage is prompting many companies to look overseas for employees. If companies can hire many temporary foreign workers, how might this affect the wages that workers in Alberta receive?

5. Suppose a natural disaster increases the need for flashlights. Outline the steps the market will go through to communicate this information to not only the makers of flashlights, but also the makers of flashlight-making equipment.

6. High birth rates in the 1950s caused school overcrowding in the 1970s and 1980s, while the 1990s saw some schools closed down in the same neighbourhoods. If education is a product, identify: (a) the consumer, and (b) the supplier. Why do you think the school system keeps experiencing shortages and surpluses?

7. Temporary job placement agencies, such as Ontario Works, make it easier for workers to find jobs and for employers to find workers. Would the presence of a temporary job placement agency (in any given market) result in an increase, decrease, or uncertain change in the wages paid to workers?

8. Due to labour shortages, employers are allowed to hire temporary foreign workers (TFWs) once the employer proves the Canadian labour pool is exhausted. Between 1996 and 2005, the number of TFWs doubled in Canada to 145 871. If the Government of Canada eliminated this program, what would happen to the wages of Canadian workers who were previously competing with TFWs for jobs?

9. Suppose the Nudist Party wins the next federal election because all the clothed citizens forgot to vote. The Nudists pass a law making it illegal to produce clothes. The shift in party power causes a shift in preference away from buying clothes.

   A) The cost of supplying clothes is now very high given that it is illegal to do so. Assuming that the demand for clothes reduces only slightly (in comparison), how would this affect the market price for clothes?

   B) Now suppose that the police don't take the law seriously (where would officers pin their badges?), and put zero effort into enforcement. Assuming that the cost of supplying clothes is no different than it was before the election, how would the market price for clothes be affected?

10. In 2007, the Government of Canada proposed ending work permits for foreign strippers. According to a representative from the Adult Entertainment Association of Canada, "This is one of the professions where there is a worker shortage." Explain how the proposed legislative amendment would impact the price for adult entertainment if it were to be implemented.

myeconlab Visit the MyEconLab website at **www.myeconlab.com**. This online homework and tutorial system puts you in control of your own learning with study and practice tools.

Answers to the APPENDIX
Study Guide Questions

APPENDIX A
TRUE/FALSE

1. True
2. False. Even people who win the lottery can never satisfy all of their wants; they also face trade-offs and have to make smart choices.
3. False. The opportunity cost is the value of what you give up to take that path, action, or activity.
4. False. The grant covers the money cost of getting an apprenticeship but does not cover the opportunity cost — the total value of what the individual gives up by taking an apprenticeship, which includes the money that the individual could have earned in a job that year.
5. False. Women have a larger incentive because the return on post-secondary education — the gap between the incomes of post-secondary graduates and high-school graduates — is higher for women than it is for men.
6. False. If men held a comparative advantage in performing housework then traditional gender roles would be reversed (that is, men would have been the ones doing the housework) because individuals are supposed to specialize in the activity where they hold a comparative advantage.
7. True
8. False. Darrel should stay home because the hourly wage he gives up to stay at home ($26) is less than the wage Sheryl gives up ($30).
9. True
10. True
11. False. The labour market is an input market.
12. True
13. False. They are microeconomic choices.
14. True
15. False. They are the costs that affect others.

MULTIPLE CHOICE

1. **d)** all of the above.
2. **d)** a challenge for everyone.
3. **b)** animals.
4. **d)** all of the above.
5. **a)** how much tuition you paid.
6. **d)** all of the above.
7. **d)** women with high-school diplomas earn more than men with high-school diplomas.
8. **b)** opportunity costs of upgrading to a college diploma will decrease.
9. **b)** comparative advantage.
10. **a)** give up/ get.
11. **a)** what interest rates to set.
12. **c)** Increasing the exchange rate of the Canadian dollar
13. **d)** all of the above.
14. **b)** past costs and benefits.
15. **c)** external costs will result in too much of that activity.

SHORT ANSWER

1. Weather, cost of trip (gas), if your partner tells you the relationship is over if you go, if your partner offers to cook for you or take you out to dinner if you stay.
2. Freedom, some privacy, parties at the residence, readily available study partners.
3. Decreasing tuition costs or guaranteeing minimum pay levels for people with degrees.
4. Include all money costs (gas, parking) and opportunity costs (earnings given up).
5. **a)** The increased penalty represents a rise in the price (or cost) of not wearing a seat belt, which will likely motivate more individuals to wear their seat belt.
   b) Drivers adjust their behaviour and drive more dangerously because they think they are now safe wearing a seat belt.
6. **a)** The opportunity cost of Jack spending all his time making bread (expressed per unit of what he gets) is $\frac{105}{70} = \frac{3}{2}$ cords of wood.

   The opportunity cost of Jack spending all his time cutting wood (expressed per unit of what he gets) is $\frac{70}{105} = \frac{2}{3}$ loaf of bread.

   The opportunity cost of Jacqueline spending all her time making bread (expressed per unit of what she gets) is $\frac{100}{50} = 2$ cords of wood.

   The opportunity cost of Jacqueline spending all her time cutting wood (expressed per unit of what she gets) is $\frac{50}{100} = \frac{1}{2}$ loaf of bread.

Opportunity Costs for Jack and Jacqueline

	Opportunity Cost of 1 Additional . . .	
	Loaf of Bread	**Cord of Wood**
Jack	Give up $\frac{105}{70} = \frac{3}{2}$ wood (cords)	Give up $\frac{70}{105} = \frac{2}{3}$ bread (loaves)
Jacqueline	Give up $\frac{100}{50} = 2$ wood (cords)	Give up $\frac{50}{100} = \frac{1}{2}$ bread (loaves)

Therefore, Jack has a comparative advantage in making bread and Jacqueline has a comparative advantage in chopping wood.

b) The opportunity cost of Jack spending all his time making bread (expressed per unit of what he gets) is $\frac{105}{70} = \frac{3}{2}$ cords of wood.

The opportunity cost of Jack spending all his time cutting wood (expressed per unit of what he gets) is $\frac{70}{105} = \frac{2}{3}$ loaf of bread.

The opportunity cost of Samantha spending all her time making bread (expressed per unit of what she gets) is $\frac{20}{40} = \frac{1}{2}$ cord of wood.

The opportunity cost of Samantha spending all her time cutting wood (expressed per unit of what she gets) is $\frac{40}{20} = 2$ loaves of bread.

Opportunity Costs for Jack and Samantha

	Opportunity Cost of 1 Additional . . .	
	Loaf of Bread	**Cord of Wood**
Jack	Give up $\frac{105}{70} = \frac{3}{2}$ wood (cords)	Give up $\frac{70}{105} = \frac{2}{3}$ bread (loaves)
Samantha	Give up $\frac{20}{40} = \frac{1}{2}$ wood (cords)	Give up $\frac{40}{20} = 2$ bread (loaves)

Therefore, Jack has a comparative advantage in chopping wood and Samantha has a comparative advantage in making bread.

7. Before trade, Jack gets 20 loaves of bread and 75 cords of wood. If Jack trades with Jacqueline, he specializes in making bread because this is the activity he has a comparative advantage in. After trading with Jacqueline, Jack ends up with 50 loaves of bread (the 70 he produced minus the 20 he traded away) and 20 cords of wood (the 0 he produced plus the 20 he traded for). This is worse than his allocation when being self-sufficient, which could have been 50 loaves of bread and 30 cords of wood (that is, he produces the same number of loaves of bread but 10 fewer cords of wood by trading with Jacqueline, compared to being self-sufficient).

If Jack trades with Samantha he specializes in cutting wood because this is the activity he has a comparative advantage in. After trading with Samantha, Jack ends up with 20 loaves of bread (the 0 he produced plus the 20 he traded for) and 85 cords of wood (the 105 he produced minus the 20 he traded away). This is better than his allocation when being self-sufficient, which is 20 loaves of bread and 75 cords of wood (that is, he produces the same amount of loaves of bread but gets 10 additional cords of wood by trading with Samantha, compared to being self-sufficient).

To summarize:

Jack's Consumption Possibilities

	Before Trade (2 possibilities shown)		After Trading with Jacqueline	After Trading with Samantha
Loaves of bread	20	50	50	20
Cords of wood	75	30	20	85

Therefore, Jack will prefer to go into partnership with Samantha.

8. **a**) Smokers often ignore the cost that non-smokers incur from inhaling their cigarettes. If they considered this cost in their decision-making process, then they may have found that the cost exceeded the benefit.

   b) No — if they did, they wouldn't have smoked indoors because the external cost would likely have been high enough to offset personal gains.

   c) Since a tax represents a rise in price to the end user, an increase in the tax on cigarettes should cause smokers to reduce the number of cigarette packs they buy, assuming they are sensitive to changes in the price. However, it is possible that some smokers may be addicted to the point where they cannot reduce their consumption.

9. The parents should be more willing to allow the daughter to pursue post-secondary school instead of work as the difference between college and without-college earnings is greater for women.

10. **a**) Too much pollution; carbon taxes, fines for cars that don't pass emission tests

    b) Too high; cigarette taxes, banning smoking indoors

    c) Too little education; tuition subsidies, loans

APPENDIX B
TRUE/FALSE

1. False. Demand is a stronger word, meaning willing and able to pay.
2. True
3. True
4. True
5. False. Marginal benefit will equal average benefit only in special circumstances. For example, if a basketball player with a shooting percentage of 50 percent successfully makes one out of her next two shots, then the additional points she adds are equal to the amount of points she usually (on average) adds.
6. False. Quantity demanded is a much more limited term than demand. Only a change in price changes quantity demanded. A change in any other influence on consumer choice changes demand.
7. True
8. True
9. False, for normal goods. A decrease in income causes a decrease in demand. But True, for inferior goods.
10. False. As the holidays get nearer, people's willingness and ability to pay for certain products/services increases, for any given price. Therefore, an increase in demand drives the rising prices.
11. True
12. True
13. False. The fewer substitutes there are, the harder it is to switch away from a product whose price rises, and the less responsive and elastic is demand.

14. True
15. True

MULTIPLE CHOICE

1. **d**) preferences.
2. **b**) whatever we are willing to give up.
3. **c**) decreasing marginal benefits to eating.
4. **d**) additional costs of dating are greater than the additional benefits of dating.
5. **a**) 1.
6. **c**) consumers look for cheaper substitutes.
7. **d**) decrease in quantity demanded.
8. **a**) fast food
9. **c**) changes with income.
10. **b**) decrease.
11. **d**) all of the above
12. **d**) decrease in the quantity demanded of Kraft Dinner.
13. **b**) greater than 1.
14. **a**) demand for butter more elastic.
15. **c**) quantity demanded will decrease; total revenue will rise.

SHORT ANSWER

1. For a smart choice when making a decision, consider only additional (marginal) costs and additional (marginal) benefits of the decision. Ignore all sunk costs.
2. No. Demand is a willingness and ability to pay, so when you can't pay, your ability does not exist.
3. Water is scarce in the desert, so its marginal benefit is very high, while having pockets full of diamonds makes their marginal benefit low. In this situation, the price of water may exceed the price of diamonds.
4. Answers will vary but may include such responses as; "There's always Coca-Cola" (you should keep on having colas); "You've always got time for Tim Hortons" (go out of your way but come to the doughnut shop); "Harveys: Have it your way" (have a customized burger every time).
5. **a**) Quantity demanded will increase because price of consuming additional water has fallen to zero.

   b) Demand will decrease because water, a substitute product, is now cheaper.

   c) Demand will increase because water, a complement product, is now cheaper, allowing longer showers.

   d) Demand will increase because these are a complement product.
6. **a**) Number of consumers

   b) Prices of related products/services

   c) Expected future prices
7. (a) and (c) decrease demand. (b) causes a decrease in quantity demanded.

8. **a)** Elastic
   b) Elastic
   c) Inelastic
   d) Elastic
   e) Elastic
   f) Inelastic
9. Lower income earners respond to increases in income by having more children. Higher income earners respond to increases in income by having fewer children.
10. Demand for the latest fashions is more inelastic than demand for clothing in general. Shoppers are willing to pay higher prices for the latest fashions, but will snatch up older fashions if the price is right.

APPENDIX C
TRUE/FALSE

1. False. When workers have fewer alternatives, they may be willing to accept lower wages.
2. True
3. True
4. True
5. False. Monthly rent payments are sunk costs that are not relevant to the decision of how much to produce.
6. False. Sunk costs are not part of opportunity costs.
7. True
8. False. Opportunity cost equals what you give up divided by what you get.
9. False. As you spend more time in any activity (for example, working instead of relaxing), the marginal opportunity cost of doing that activity increases.
10. True
11. True
12. False. Rise in price decreases market supply of the other product/service.
13. False. Supply is elastic when quantity supplied is very responsive to price.
14. True
15. True

MULTIPLE CHOICE

1. c) you have an exam the next day.
2. b) has to give up a job paying $15 an hour.
3. c) sunk costs are marginal costs
4. b) sunk cost.
5. c) sunk cost.
6. c) the same.
7. d) all of the above.
8. c) price of the supplied product/service
9. a) improvement in technology producing it.
10. a) the price of oil — a major input used to produce tires — rises.
11. a) increases supply.

12. c) inelastic supply.
13. a) snow shovels.
14. b) in a large town with many available workers.
15. d) inelastic.

SHORT ANSWER

1. **a)** No — you would receive only $10/hour × 20 hours = $200 for the weekend, which is lower than the value you place on spending time with your significant other on a weekend ($300).
   b) Perhaps — you would receive $15/hour × 20 hours = $300 for the weekend, which is equal to the value you place on spending time with your significant other. You may want to say no if you place additional value on other things that you may have to miss out on by working (for example, watching television, talking on MSN, going on Facebook, and so on). On the other hand, you may want to say yes if these other additional benefits from saying no are lower than some other additional benefits from saying yes (for example, getting on your boss's good side).
2. Employees who spend up to one-third of their life at work — 8 hours out of 24 in a day — value their free time. As employers want workers to put in more hours of work, the workers' free time becomes more scarce and valuable, so the marginal opportunity cost of an additional hour of work is greater.
3. Since women's decision to work is more elastic/sensitive to wage rates, higher income taxes (lower wage rates) will lead to women reducing their hours worked more than it would for men.
4. Some workers (particularly those with high income) will respond to wage increases by working fewer hours because they value additional hours of leisure over additional hours of work at this wage rate (possibly because they are earning so much money). This would violate the law of supply because as the price of labour (the wage) rises the quantity of labour supplied decreases.
5. **a)** True
   b) False. Higher wages — higher input prices — decrease supply.
   c) True
   d) True
   e) False. It will increase quantity supplied, not supply.
6. The money invested in the factory is a sunk cost because it cannot be undone. This cost, however, should not be considered in the decision to abandon the project. The project should be abandoned only if the additional costs of operating the business exceed the additional benefits.
7. Oil is a major input in the production of these products, so higher prices of inputs will cause their supply to decrease.

8. To produce air conditioners and bring them to the market is not easy; it involves long supply chains and the cooperation of many companies on wholesale and retail levels. Therefore, the price elasticity of supply of air conditioners is low (inelastic).

9. a) $33
   b) $152
   c) Fines have been set so that the marginal cost of raising your speed an additional 10 km/hour when you are already going at 130 km/hour is higher than when you are going at 120 km/hour ($152 versus $33). This is done to deter drivers from speeding at really high rates.

10. Open ended

APPENDIX D
TRUE/FALSE

1. False. Transactions would not be voluntary and there would be no incentive to supply the product to consumers.
2. False. Price should cover all opportunity costs.
3. False. Price and quantity adjustments do not require the consumer or business to know anything about anyone's personal wants or production capabilities.
4. True
5. True
6. True
7. False. The surplus would put pressure on the price to fall because if prices increased Apu would sell even less and his surplus would grow larger.
8. False. An increase in supply will cause a surplus rather than a shortage.
9. True
10. True
11. False. The increased supply lowers the price of grey seals, which reduces the cost of producing seal coat fur, which results in a lower price charged to the consumer.
12. True
13. False. More Americans coming to Canada with a bachelor's degree will increase the supply of these workers and create downward pressure on the wages of educated workers.
14. True
15. True

MULTIPLE CHOICE

1. **d)** a market.
2. **d)** all of the above.
3. **c)** Leon's Furniture Ltd eliminating sales tax on all patio furniture items.
4. **d)** market-clearing price.
5. **a)** the price consumers are willing to pay equals the price suppliers are willing to accept.
6. **a)** higher prices.
7. **d)** demand decreases and supply increases.
8. **c)** allowing the price to fall.
9. **c)** demand is greater than supply for restaurant workers.
10. **d)** all of the above.
11. **d)** all of the above.
12. **d)** the demand for food service is greater than the supply of food service.
13. **b)** demand for *Harry Potter* novels may decrease.
14. **c)** the demand for nutrition-promoting foods will increase.
15. **a)** increase in demand.

SHORT ANSWER

1. The market price performs a communication function between buyers and sellers. A rise in price will communicate to suppliers that more must be produced and brought to the market, while a fall in price will communicate to the suppliers that they should produce less. The market-clearing price is the price at which no shortages or surpluses occur and no signals are sent to firms and consumers to change their smart choices.

2. a) $2, since this is the price for which there is no shortage or surplus.
   b) Quantity supplied is greater than quantity demanded, so there will be a surplus.
   c) Apu will end up with excess inventory, which will create pressure for the price to fall.

3. The demand for houses in Saskatchewan have increased because more Albertans are moving to Saskatchewan. This puts an upward pressure on housing prices in Saskatchewan if the supply of housing available remains the same over this time.

4. a) In a shortage, workers are in scarce supply and have a bargaining advantage.
   b) The use of temporary foreign workers reduces the size of the shortage in Canada, which lowers the price (wage) offered to workers.

5. The panic buying of flashlights will raise the price, signaling a profit opportunity of increasing the production of flashlights. The increased production (increased quantity supplied) will need more flashlight parts and equipment, generating additional demand for those inputs. Inputs prices will rise, and the quantity supplied of inputs will increase, and the need for flashlights will be satisfied.

6. Consumers in this case would be parents and children, while the supplier would be the government and its school boards. However, the school system is free and so no price signals are communicated from consumers to suppliers. The needs of consumers and the resources of school boards are not coordinated, which causes shortages and surpluses. The centralized system of communication doesn't work as efficiently and effectively as the market system.

7. The effect on wages is uncertain. Job placement agencies make markets function better, bringing together workers (suppliers) and employers (demanders). As a result, we would expect more workers hired, but there isn't enough information about shortages or surpluses to predict what would happen to wages.

8. It would reduce the available supply of these workers and put an upward pressure on the price (wage) offered to Canadian workers.

9. **a)** Given that the cost of producing or selling clothes is now very high, the supply of clothes to the market will decrease and cause an increase in clothing prices. Although clothing prices will fall slightly because of the comparatively smaller fall in demand for clothes, the overall effect will be to raise prices.

   b) If the cost of supplying clothes is no different than before the election, the slight fall in demand is the only impact on market prices. Therefore, prices of clothes will decrease in this situation.

10. Denying work permits to foreign strippers would increase the shortage of adult entertainment workers. This would put an upward pressure on the price (wage) offered to adult entertainment workers, which increases the cost and raises the price of supplying adult entertainment services.

Index

Barro, Robert, 315
barter exchange, 172, 173, 196
benefits, weighing, 418–419
Bernanke, Ben, 265, 267, 268
Bhagwati, Jagdish, 349
Big Mac Index, 233, 233*f*
Bloc Québécois, 14
Bloomsbury Group, 10
bond markets, 188, 190–191
bonds, 174
    and interest rates, 174, 188–190, 254
    vs. money, 175, 189–190
    and money supply, 253–254, 253*f*
"boom and bust" of business cycles, 57
borrowers, 102
Bouey, Gerald, 271
budget
    balanced budget, 303, 304, 306–307, 307, 308
    budget deficit. *See* budget deficit
    budget surplus. *See* budget surplus
    fiscal year, 310
budget deficit
    automatic deficits, 306
    cyclical deficits, 306
    as flow, 310
    Great Recession, 305
    meaning of, 303, 304
    structural deficit, 309
budget surplus
    automatic deficits, 306
    cyclical surpluses, 306
    described, 304
    problems, 307
    structural surplus, 309
business
    business choices, 19, 66
    competition, 54
    demand choices, 137–138
    in input markets, 8
    interest rates, and cost of business borrowing, 195
    investment spending. *See* investment spending
    as macroeconomic player, 19
    number of, and supply, 461
    in output markets, 9
    paying down debt *vs.* spending, 264–265
    supply choices, 130–131

business cycles, 10, 56
    aggregate demand and aggregate supply, 146–150
    aggregate demand policies, 290–296
    automatic stabilizers, 305–306
    "boom and bust" of, 57
    contraction, 57
    and economic growth rates, 51
    expansion, 57
    export-led busts and booms, 293
    generally, 56
    and government failure, 13
    and herd mentality, 154
    and inflation, 57–58
    market price responses to, 151–156
    and money, 196–199, 199*f*
    most recent complete Canadian business cycle, 56*f*
    and multiplier effects, 293
    origins, 151–156, 157*f*
    output gaps, 57–58
    phases of, 57
    stabilization of, 290–296
    and unemployment, 57–58
business investment spending.
    See investment spending

C

Canada
    inflation in, 97, 97*f*, 271*f*
    Phillips Curve, 109*f*, 111*f*
    as trading nation, 335
    and UN Human Development Index (HDI), 69
    unemployment in, 88, 88*f*
Canada Pension Plan, 5
Canadian dollar
    see also exchange rates
    appreciation, 213
    demand, 214–215
    depreciation, 213
    excess demand for, 218
    exchange rate, 213*f*
    exchange rates, 217–220
    fluctuating exchange rates, 220–226
    forces changing price of, 220–226, 226*f*
    foreign exchange market for, 217, 217*f*
    inflation, impact on, 229
    law of demand for Canadian dollars, 214

    law of supply for Canadian dollars, 216
    net exports, impact on, 228–229
    prices of the Canadian dollar, 217–220
    supply, 215–216
capital, 47
capital investment, 297–298, 301–302
Carney, Mark, 228, 248*f*
cash holdings, 198
Central Africa Republic, 69
central banks, 182
    see also Bank of Canada
    exit strategy, 267
    functions of, 248–249
    Great Recession, responses to, 263–268
    and money, 182–186
    need for, 272–275
chartered banks
    see also banking system
    bank failures, 185
    Bank of Canada, as lender of last resort, 183
    banking tradeoffs, 186
    loans, 185, 186
    money, creation of, 183–186
    probabilities and bank runs, 185
    regulation of, 182
    reserves, 185, 265
    sources and uses of funds, 186*f*
Chase, Steven, 308*n*
choices
    Bank of Canada, 20
    banking system, 20
    business choices, 19, 66
    and circular flow, 65–66
    consumer choices, 19, 65
    costs of, 452–453
    government choices, 20, 66
    marginal benefits, 420
    rest of the world (R.O.W.), 21
    smart choices, keys to, 405–407, 405*f*, 420
Chrysler, 176
CIBC, 182
circular flow
    and aggregate demand, 135–136, 135*f*
    with banking system, 65–66, 65*f*, 135*f*
    and choices, 65–66
    enlargement of, 62–64, 63*f*, 65–66, 65*f*

Credits

Photo Credits

CHAPTER 1

p. 3 WDG Photo/Shutterstock; **p. 4** (middle) Anthony Leung; Shutterstock (TV); David Buffington/Photodisc/Getty Images (house); Creatas/Jupiterimages (woman); **p. 4** (bottom) www.CartoonStock.com; **p. 5** Toronto Star Syndicate, 2003. All rights reserved/CP Images; **p. 6** Leonid Shcheglov/Shutterstock; **p. 7** SuperStock, Inc./Getty Images; **p. 10** Tim Gidal/Hulton Archives/Getty Images; **p. 12** © 2007 Richard Stallman and Inne ten Have; **p. 17** (top) Oscar F. Chuyn/Shutterstock; **p. 17** (bottom) Tsvangirayi Mukwazhi/AP Photo/CP Images; **p. 23** © 2009 Google—Map data © 2009 Tele Atlas

CHAPTER 2

p. 39 Neale Cousland/Shutterstock; **p. 41** Robert Genat/Transtock Inc./Alamy/GetStock.com; **p. 47** iofoto/iStockphoto.com; **p. 48** Todd Korol/Aurora Photos/Corbis; **p. 49** Michael Czosnek/iStockphoto.com; **p. 53** (top) Ted Soqui/Corbis; **p. 53** (bottom left) Associated Press/AP Images; **p. 53** (bottom right) Slobo Mitic/iStockphoto.com; **p. 54** Evening Standard/Hulton Archive/Getty Images; **p. 59** Monkey Business Images/Shutterstock; **p. 67** IS658/Image Source/Alamy; **p. 68** (top) Sean Locke/iStockphoto.com; **p. 68** (bottom) Niko Guido/iStockphoto.com

CHAPTER 3

p. 85 Geoffrey Robinson/Alamy/GetStock.com; **p. 89** Alan Marsh/First Light; **p. 90** www.statcan.gc.ca/start-debut-eng.html; **p. 97** Bank of Canada; www.bankofcanada.ca/en/rates/inflation_calc.html; **p. 100** www.ScienceCartoonsPlus.com; **p. 102** © 2008 Ted Rall. Used by permission of Universal Uclick. All rights reserved; **p. 110** Doug Wilson/Historical/Corbis

CHAPTER 4

p. 127 AP Photo/CP Images; **p. 129** Juergen Bosse/iStockphoto.com; **p. 131** iofoto/Shutterstock; **p. 132** Greg Balfour Evans/Alamy/GetStock.com; **p. 136** PhotoEdit/Alamy/GetStock.com; **p. 138** Adrian Brown/TCPI/CP Images; **p. 139** © 2008 Doug Savage. www.savagechickens.com; **p. 143** Ramsey and Muspratt (portrait); G. C. Harcourt and Prue Kerr, Joan Robinson, © 2009 Palgrave Macmillan.

Reproduced with permission of Palgrave Macmillan (cover design); **p. 152** CBS Photo Archive/Getty Images; **p. 153** (top) Tetra Images/Alamy; **p. 153** (bottom) George A. Akerlof and Robert J. Shiller, Animal Spirits: How Human Psychology Drives the Economy, and Why It Matters for Global Capitalism, © 2009 Princeton University Press. Reproduced with permission.

CHAPTER 5

p. 171 National Currency Collection, Currency Museum, Bank of Canada; **p. 173** Jeff Rotman/Alamy/GetStock.com; **p. 175** Anthony Leung; **pp. 180–181** National Currency Collection, Currency Museum, Bank of Canada; **p. 183** Winnipeg Free Press/Ken Gigliotti/CP Images; **p. 184** Schaefer Elvira/Shutterstock; **p. 185** Anthony Eva/Alamy/GetStock.com; **p. 198** Feng Yu/Shutterstock

CHAPTER 6

p. 211 Paul Maguire/Shutterstock; **p. 212** Karin Hildebrand Lau/Shutterstock; **p. 221** Network Photographer/Alamy/GetStock.com; **p. 228** Samuel Knopfler/Alamy/GetStock.com

CHAPTER 7

p. 247 Evgeny Murtola/Shutterstock; **p. 248** (left) Sean Kilpatrick/CP Images; **p. 248** (right) Bank of Canada Head Office, ca. 1938/Associated Screen News/Bank of Canada Archives PC300.5-62; **p. 250** www.CartoonStock.com; **p. 266** Shutterstock; **p. 268** Mark Wilson/Getty Images

CHAPTER 8

p. 289 Lijuan Guo/Shutterstock; **p. 292** Javier Soriano/AFP/Getty Images; **p. 293** Alamy/GetStock.com; **p. 294** Picsfive/Dreamstime.com/GetStock.com; **p. 300** Tom Hanley/Alamy/GetStock.com; **p. 305** Gina Sanders/Shutterstock; **p. 308** Jean-Francois Rivard/Shutterstock; **p. 310** Marie C. Fields/Shutterstock; **p. 315** INTERFOTO/Alamy/GetStock.com

CHAPTER 9

p. 333 Rob Crandall/SCPhotos/Alamy; **p. 342** Rafael Ramirez Lee/Shutterstock; **p. 343** WorldFoto/Alamy/GetStock.com; **p. 346** Aqua/Shutterstock; **p. 348** Alex Kraus/vario images GmbH & Co.KG/Alamy; **p. 349** WorldFoto/Alamy/GetStock.com; **p. 356** Phil Humnicky/Georgetown University

APPENDIX A

p. 393 Shutterstock (snow), Painet (beach);
p. 395 Dave Whamond; **p. 396** WorldFoto/Alamy;
p. 397 Dave Whamond; **p. 398** (Fig. A.1 & A.2 background) Dave Whamond; **pp. 401–2** (Fig. A.4 background) Elvele Images Ltd/Alamy; **p. 402** © 2009 Google—Map data © 2009 Tele Atlas

APPENDIX B

p. 417 Toby Burrows/Digital Vision/Getty Images;
p. 418 Shutterstock (snow), Painet (beach); **p. 420** Dave Whamond; **p. 421** Oramstock/Alamy; **p. 424, 428** (Fig. B.1 & B.3 background) Daniel Hurst/Editorial/Alamy;
p. 425, 431 (Fig. B.2 & B.4 background) Deniz Ünlüsü/ Shutterstock; **p. 425** © Philip Harvey/Terra/Corbis;
p. 430 Frazer Harrison/Getty Images; **p. 433** Getty Images

APPENDIX C

p. 447 Ben Margot/AP Photo/CP Images; **pp. 452–3** (Fig. C.2 & C.3 background) Digital Vision/Alamy; **p. 454** (Fig. C.4 background) Photodisc; **pp. 455–6, 459, 461** (Fig. C.5, C.6, C.7 & C.8 background) Radius Images/Alamy; **p. 458** Ian Wilson/iStockphoto; **p. 463** Getty Images

APPENDIX D

p. 477 Corbis RF/Alamy; **p. 480** Ben Margot/AP Photo/CP Images; **p. 481** (Fig. 4.1 background) Digital Vision/Alamy

Figure Credits

CHAPTER 2

p. 42, Fig. 2.1 Leacy, F. H., ed. 1983. Historical Statistics of Canada. 2nd ed. Series F32 and F55. Ottawa: Statistics Canada; Statistics Canada CANSIM Table 380-0017, http://cansim2.statcan.gc.ca. Accessed on August 6, 2009;
p. 43, Fig. 2.2 Statistics Canada CANSIM Table 380-0017, http://cansim2.statcan.gc.ca. Accessed on August 6, 2009;
p. 45, Fig. 2.3 Leacy, F. H., ed. 1983. Historical Statistics of Canada. 2nd ed. Series F55. Ottawa: Statistics Canada; Statistics Canada CANSIM Table 380-0017, Table 51-0001, series v466668 and Table 51-0026, series v480567, http:// cansim2.statcan.gc.ca. Accessed on August 6 and 13, 2009; World Economic Outlook, Statistical Appendix, International Monetary Fund, April 2009, www.imf.org/ external/pubs/ft/weo/2009/01/weodata/index.aspx; Parkin, M. and R. Bade. 2006. Economics: Canada in the global environment. 6th ed., **pp. 790–798**. Toronto: Pearson Education Canada; **p. 46**, Fig. 2.4 Leacy, F. H., ed. 1983. Historical Statistics of Canada. 2nd ed. Series F55. Ottawa: Statistics Canada; Statistics Canada CANSIM Table 380-0017, Table 51-0001, series v466668 and Table 51-0026, series v480567, http://cansim2.statcan.gc.ca. Accessed on August 6 and 13, 2009; World Economic Outlook, Statistical Appendix, International Monetary Fund, April 2009, www.imf.org/external/pubs/ft/weo/2009/01/weodata/index .aspx; Parkin, M. and R. Bade. 2006. Economics: Canada in the global environment. 6th ed., **pp. 790–798**. Toronto: Pearson Education Canada; **p. 47**, Fig. 2.5 Leacy, F. H., ed. 1983. Historical Statistics of Canada. 2nd ed. Series D113 and D120. Ottawa: Statistics Canada; Statistics Canada CANSIM Table 282-0087, http://cansim2.statcan.gc.ca. Accessed on August 12, 2009; **p. 50**, Fig. 2.6 Leacy, F. H., ed. 1983. Historical Statistics of Canada. (2nd ed.). Series F55. Ottawa: Statistics Canada; Statistics Canada CANSIM Table 380-0017, Table 51-0001, series v466668 and Table 51-0026, series v480567, http://cansim2.statcan.gc.ca. Accessed on August 6 and 13, 2009; **p. 51**, Fig. 2.7 Maddison, A. 1991. Dynamic forces in capitalist development. Oxford: Oxford University Press; World Bank. 2001. World Development Report 2002: Building institutions for markets. (Report No. 22825). New York: Oxford University Press; World Bank. 2002. World Development Report 2003: Sustainable development in a dynamic world. (Report No. 24705). New York: Oxford University Press; World Bank. 2003. World Development Report 2004: Making services work for poor people. (Report No. 26895). Washington, DC: Author; World Bank. 2004. World Development Report 2005: A better investment climate for everyone. (Report No. 28829). Washington, DC: Author; World Bank. 2005. World Development Report 2006: Equity and Development. (Report No. 32204). Washington, DC: Author; World Bank. 2006. World Development Report 2007: Development and the next generation. (Report No. 35999). Washington, DC: Author; World Bank. 2007. World Development Report 2008: Agriculture for development. (Report No. 41455). Washington, DC: Author; World Bank. 2008. World development report 2009: Reshaping economic geography. (Report No. 43738). Washington, DC: Author;
p. 56, Fig. 2.9 Bank of Canada. www.bank-banque-canada.ca/ en/rates/indinf/product_data_en.html. Accessed September 1, 2009; **p. 80** (Table, Question 6) OECD. 2009. OECD Economic Outlook, Vol. 2009/1, OECD Publishing, http://dx.doi.org/10.1787/eco_outlook-v2009-1-en, table 1, Real GDP, http://dx.doi.org/10.1787/662053280818; **p. 81** (Table, Question 7) Statistics Canada, Canadian Economic Accounts Quarterly Review, catalogue number 13-010-X, June 1, 2009; **p. 83** (Table, Question 10A) Centre for the Study of Living Standards' Index of Economic Well-Being. www.csls.ca/iwb/weights.xls. Values represent the absolute change in the scaled indexes relative to the 1971 base. Consumption-biased means that consumption flows receive a weight of 70% while the three remaining components each receive a weight of 10%.

CHAPTER 3

p. 86, Fig. 3.1 Statistics Canada, The Daily, June 5, 2009, Latest release from the Labour Force Survey; CANSIM Table 282-0087, http://cansim2.statcan.gc.ca. Accessed on August 6, 2009; **p. 88**, Fig. 3.2 Leacy, F.H., ed. 1983.

Historical Statistics of Canada. 2nd ed. Series D124-145. Ottawa: Statistics Canada; Statistics Canada CANSIM Table 282-0002, series v2461224 and Table 282-0087, series v2062815, http://cansim2.statcan.gc.ca. Accessed on August 6 2009; **p. 90** Fig. 3.3 Statistics Canada CANSIM Table 282-0085, http://cansim2.statcan.gc.ca. Accessed on September 10, 2009; **p. 90** Fig. 3.4 Statistics Canada CANSIM Table 282-0087, http://cansim2.statcan.gc.ca. Accessed on September 10, 2009; **p. 96,** Fig. 3.7 Statistics Canada, Consumer Price Index Reference Paper, catalogue no. 62-553 Occasional, Table 1; **p. 97** Fig. 3.8 Statistics Canada CANSIM Table 326-0021, http://cansim2.statcan.gc.ca. Accessed on September 2, 2009; Bank of Canada. Consumer price index, 1995 to present, www.bank-banque-canada.ca/en/cpi.html. Accessed on September 3, 2009; **p. 98** Fig. 3.9 Statistics Canada CANSIM Table 326-0021, Table 326-0002, series v2007198, Table 326-0021, series v41695540 http://cansim2.statcan.gc.ca. Accessed on September 3, 2009; Bank of Canada. Consumer price index, 1995 to present, www.bank-banque-canada.ca/en/cpi.html. Accessed on September 3, 2009; **p. 109** Fig. 3.11 Leacy, F.H., ed. 1983. Historical Statistics of Canada. 2nd ed. Series D135-145. Ottawa: Statistics Canada; Statistics Canada CANSIM Table 326-0021, http://cansim2.statcan.gc.ca. Accessed on September 2, 2009; **p. 111,** Fig. 3.12 Leacy, F.H., ed. 1983. Historical Statistics of Canada. 2nd ed. Series D135-145. Ottawa: Statistics Canada; Statistics Canada CANSIM Table 282-0002, series v2461224, Table 282-0087, series v2062815, Table 326-0021, http://cansim2.statcan.gc.ca. Accessed on September 2, 2009; **p. 125** (Table, Question 10) Statistics Canada, Release from the Consumer Price Index, July 18, 2009, http://www.statcan.gc.ca/subjects-sujets/cpi-ipc/cpi-ipc-eng.htm

CHAPTER 5

p. 182, Fig. 5.3 Bank of Canada via Statistics Canada CANSIM Table 176-0020, http://cansim2.statcan.gc.ca. Accessed on February 12, 2010; **p. 186,** Fig. 5.4 Bank of Canada via Statistics Canada CANSIM Table 176-0011, http://cansim2.statcan.gc.ca. Accessed on February 12, 2010

CHAPTER 6

p. 213, Fig. 6.1 Bank of Canada via Statistics Canada CANSIM Table 176-0064, http://cansim2.statcan.gc.ca. Accessed on February 12, 2010; **p. 233,** Fig. 6.9 © The Economist Newspaper Limited, London, February 4, 2009 Chapter 7; **p. 251,** Fig. 7.1 www.bankofcanada.ca/en/index.html **p. 255,** Fig. 7.4 Bank of Canada via Statistics Canada CANSIM Table 176-0043, http://cansim2.statcan.gc.ca. Accessed on February 13, 2010; **p. 271,** Fig. 7.9 Statistics Canada CANSIM Table 326-0021, http://cansim2.statcan.gc.ca. Accessed on September 2, 2009; Bank of Canada. Consumer price index, 1995 to present, www.bank-banque-canada.ca/en/cpi.html. Accessed on September 3, 2009

CHAPTER 8

p. 303, Fig. 8.3 Annual Financial Report of the Government of Canada, Fiscal Year 2008-2009. Cat. No. F1-25/2009E-PDF. Ottawa: Department of Finance. Reproduced with the permission of the Minister of Public Works and Government Services, 2010; **p. 304**, Fig. 8.4 Annual Financial Report of the Government of Canada, Fiscal Year 2008-2009. Cat. No. F1-25/2009E-PDF. Ottawa: Department of Finance. Reproduced with the permission of the Minister of Public Works and Government Services, 2010; **p. 304**, Fig. 8.5 Department of Finance, Federal Government Public Accounts, Table 1, Fiscal Transactions. http://www.fin.gc.ca/frt-trf/2009/frt0901-eng.asp. Reproduced with the permission of the Minister of Public Works and Government Services, 2010; **p. 311**, Fig. 8.6 Statistics Canada CANSIM series d11473, v151548 and v646937, http://cansim2.statcan.gc.ca. Accessed on August 6, 2009 and February 16, 2010; Urquhart, M.C. 1993. Gross National Product, Canada, 1870–1926: The Derivation of the Estimates. Kingston and Montreal: McGill-Queen's University Press

CHAPTER 9

p. 335, Fig. 9.1 The World Bank: World Development Indicators; http://data.worldbank.org/indicator; **p. 342**, Fig. 9.5 Leacy, F. H., ed. 1983. Historical Statistics of Canada. 2nd ed. Series G485. Ottawa: Statistics Canada; Statistics Canada CANSIM Table Table 380-0034, series v499996 and Table 380-0017, http://cansim2.statcan.gc.ca. Accessed on August 6, 2009

Literary Credits

CHAPTER 1

p. 11 Keynes, John Maynard. 1923. A Tract on Monetary Reform. London: Palgrave Macmillan. Reprinted with permission of Palgrave Macmillan; **p. 25** Keynes, John Maynard. The Collected Writings of John Maynard Keynes, Volume XII. Edited by Sir Austin Robinson and D.E. Moggridge. London: Palgrave Macmillan, 1983. Reprinted with permission of Palgrave Macmillan

CHAPTER 4

p. 137 and 154 Keynes, John Maynard. 1936. The General Theory of Employment, Interest and Money, pp. 149–150. London: Palgrave MacMillan. Reprinted with permission of Palgrave Macmillan

CHAPTER 5

p. 174 Keynes, John Maynard. 1937. The General Theory of Employment. The Quarterly Journal of Economics 51 (2): 215–216. Cambridge, MA: The MIT Press; **p. 176** Keynes,

John Maynard. 1936. *The General Theory of Employment, Interest and Money*. London: Palgrave MacMillan. Reprinted with permission of Palgrave Macmillan

CHAPTER 6

p. 223 www.bankofcanada.ca/en/backgrounders/bg-e1.html

CHAPTER 7

p. 265 "The Remedist," Robert Skidelsky, NY Times Magazine, December 12, 2008

CHAPTER 8

p. 297 Krugman, Paul. 1994. *The Age of Diminished Expectations*. 2nd ed. Cambridge, MA: The MIT Press; **p. 301** Stiglitz, Joseph. 2010. *Homoeconomicus: The Impact of the Economic Crisis on Economic Theory*. Atlanta, GA: American Economics Association Annual Meeting; **p. 313** (FYI) Settling Up. October 29, 2009. The Economist; Argentina's debt negotiations. October 29, 2009. The Economist; Argentina in $1bn loan default. December 13, 2002. London: BBC News World Edition. http://news.bbc.co.uk/2/hi/business/2573183.stm; **p. 319** Wall, Brad. February 16, 2010. Saskatoon: Greater Saskatoon Chamber of Commerce luncheon address

CHAPTER 9

p. 347 Rivoli, Pietra. 2009. *The Travels of a T-Shirt in the Global Economy*, p. vii. 2nd ed. Hoboken: John Wiley & Sons, Inc.; **p. 350** From GLOBALIZATION AND ITS DISCONTENTS by Joseph E. Stiglitz. Copyright © 2002 by Joseph E. Stiglitz. Used with permission of W.W. Norton & Company, Inc.; **p. 352** From GLOBALIZATION AND ITS DISCONTENTS by Joseph E. Stiglitz. Copyright © 2002 by Joseph E. Stiglitz. Used with permission of W.W. Norton & Company, Inc.; **p. 353** © The Economist Newspaper Limited, London, A Different Manifesto, September 27, 2001; **p. 356** Rivoli, Pietra. 2009. *The Travels of a T-Shirt in the Global Economy*, p. vii. 2nd ed. Hoboken: John Wiley & Sons, Inc.

APPENDIX B

p. 430 IF I HAD $1000000 Words and Music by STEVEN PAGE and ED ROBERTSON © 1994 WB MUSIC CORP. and TREAT BAKER MUSIC. All Rights Administered by WB MUSIC CORP. All Rights Reserved. Used by Permission of ALFRED PUBLISHING CO., INC.